I0762231

MACK

FACE TO FACE

An Artist's Life

ROBERT FLECK

in collaboration with Sophia Sotke

HIRMER

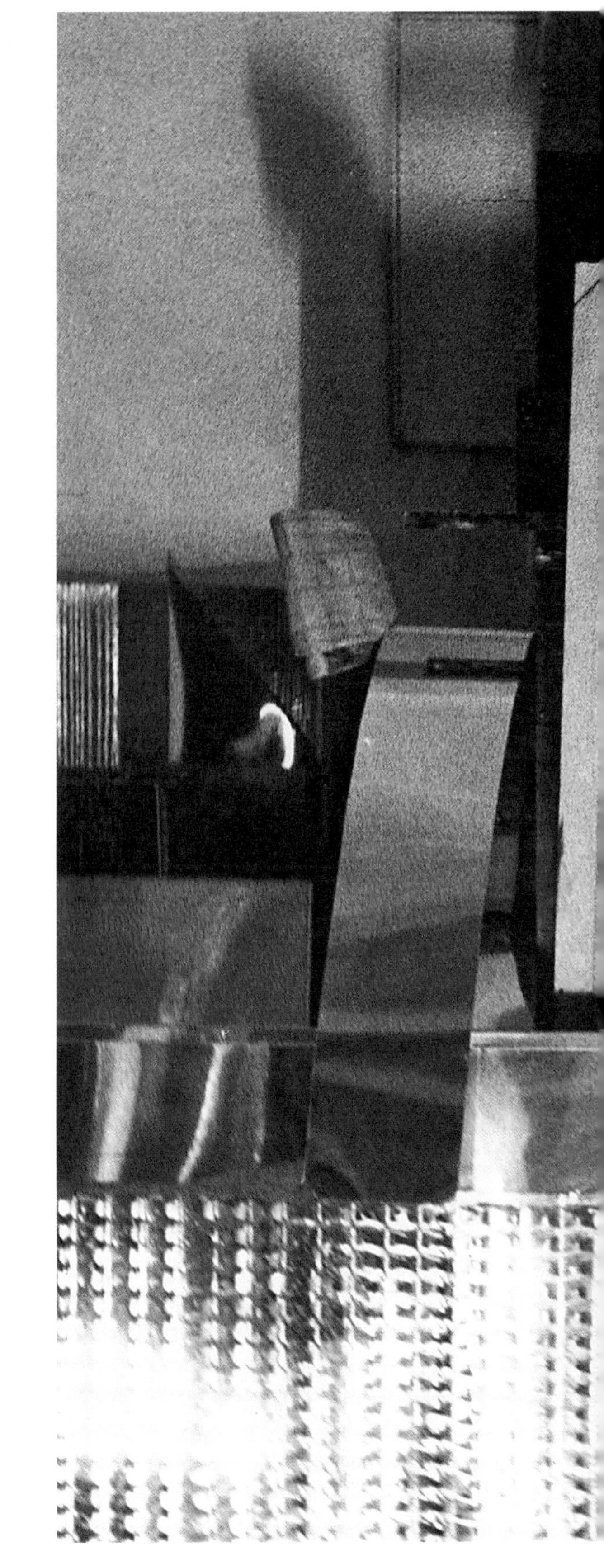

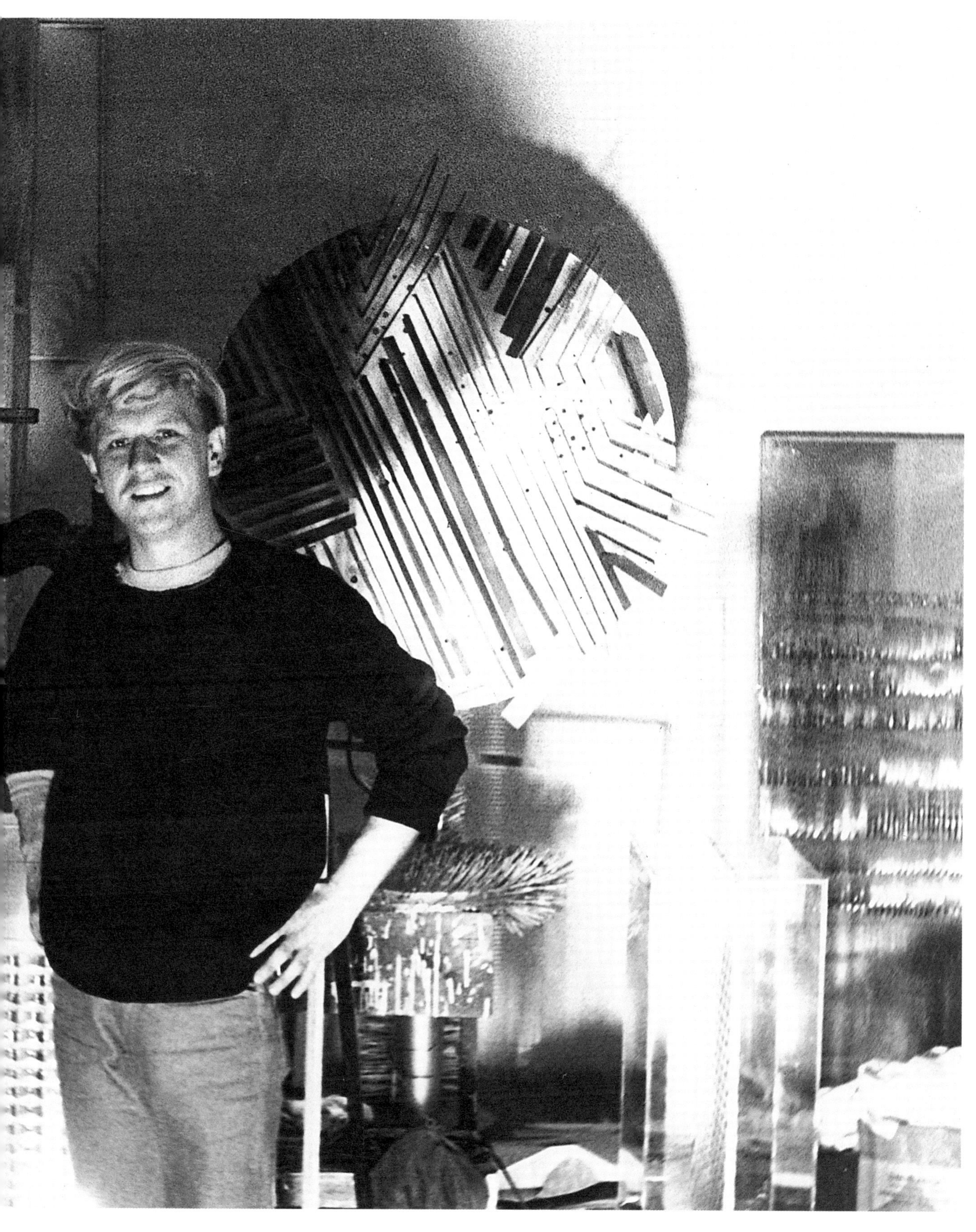

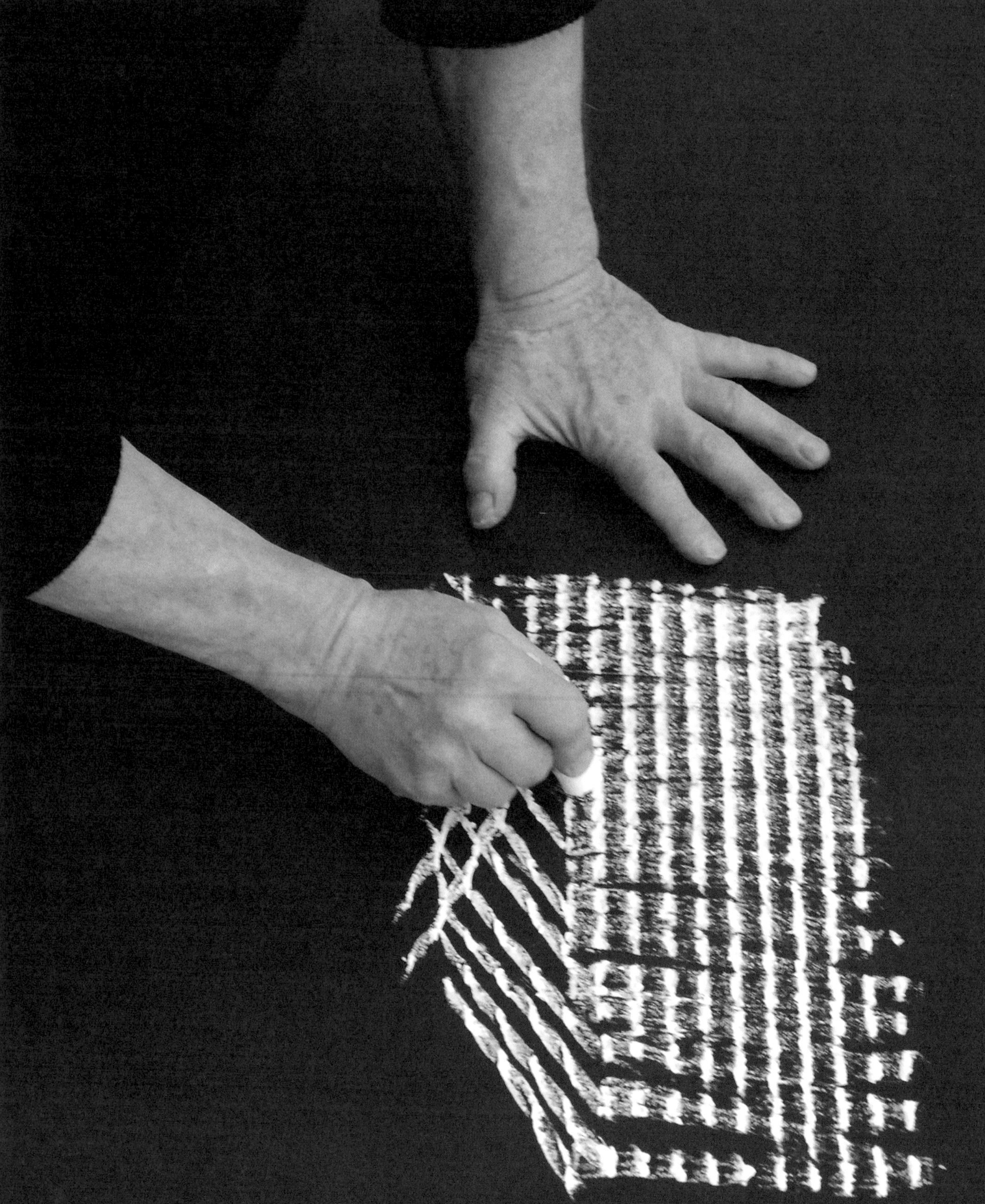

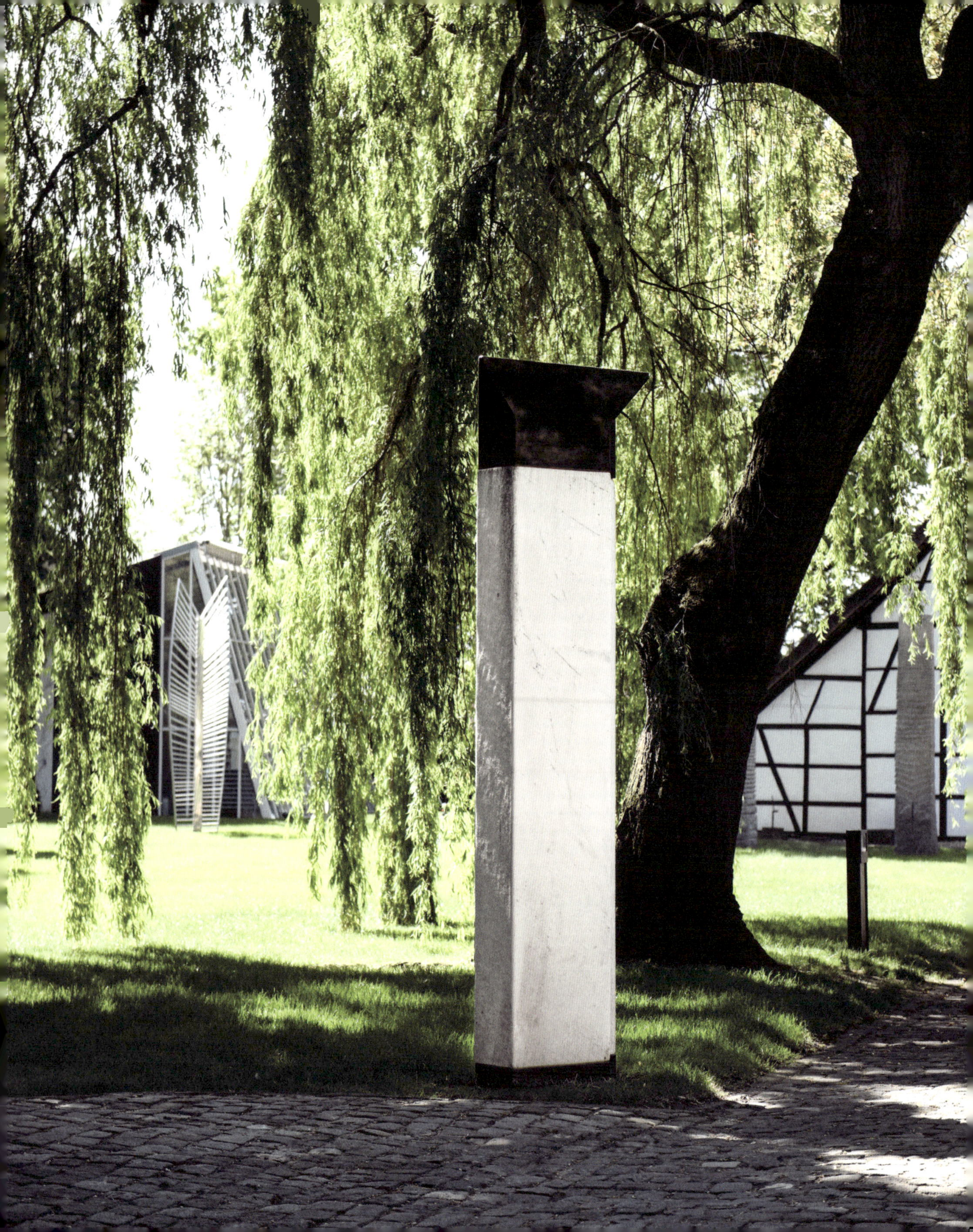

A VISIT

Entrance area of
the Huppertzhof in
Mönchengladbach
2020

A visit with Heinz Mack at the Huppertzhof, where his studio, residence, workshop, and a small building used as an office are located (fig. p. 13). The Huppertzhof is in the part of Mönchengladbach closest to Düsseldorf. The date is 22 September 2023. The meeting came about because the day before a group of patrons of the Kunsthaus Zürich had been given a tour of the Düsseldorf Academy of Art, where Heinz Mack studied from 1950 to 1953. Today he is an honorary member of the academy. Along with Joseph Beuys, Nam June Paik, and Gerhard Richter, Heinz Mack is one of the artists who, from the 1960s to the present day, have given this institution a worldwide reputation. While Beuys died in 1986 and Paik twenty years later, Mack and Richter, who is a year younger, are still in the studio every day. At the Huppertzhof, we meet regularly with Mack for conversations that form the basis of this book. Since 2020, they have taken place on Fridays, when things are a little more relaxed than on the preceeding weekdays, when the studio is caught up in the hustle and bustle of the international art business.

We are a team of four people today, as we usually are when we meet with the artist. Antonia Lehmann-Tolkmitt, an expert on ZERO and Mack, co-authored the comprehensive monograph on the artist published in 2019. Sophia Sotke, an art history graduate from the University of Düsseldorf, joined Mack's studio in 2013. She is intimately familiar with the artist's oeuvre, details of which are available digitally in a comprehensive database in the studio, and completed her doctorate at the University of Cologne in 2020 on Mack's *Sahara Project* (1959–97). Florentine Bücker, a painting student at the Düsseldorf Academy of Art, joined the team in 2023. One day she asked if there was a project she could get involved in, because she was in fact quite bored at the academy, where she had dreamed of studying as a teenager. She is now transcribing the audio recordings of our conversations with the artist, from which the quotations in the side columns of this book are taken.

Entering the Huppertzhof is always a change of scenery. Leaving behind a mundane industrial and commercial park and equally faceless residential buildings, you find yourself in a magical sculpture park hidden from public view. On a well-kept, unevenly laid out green area with two ponds, about two dozen large sculptures are arranged in an irregular pattern, all of them vertical except for two cubes. They are made of various materials, including sandstone, marble, mirrors, reflective polished aluminium, steel, granite, and glass. Sometimes they combine several materials. The constellation in which the sculptures are placed is intuitive, visually conceived, without any apparent concept. But how little of this is coincidental can be seen when the narrow mirror stele – on the left-hand side of the park, in front of the artist's glass studio, between four granite steles, about seven metres high – reflects the surrounding sculptures in irregular succession as you pass by, thus dissolving the space, which you nevertheless perceive with your eyes at the same time. One begins to sense what this artist is concerned with: light and its reflection, space and its perpetual transformation by light, but also what was called 'material veracity' in the modern sculpture of the twentieth century and has been abandoned in postmodern sculpture since around 1980. Every material has its own intrinsic characteristics and its own weight, and in terms of material veracity, the sculpture must respect and make this visible. This artist is obviously able to do this perfectly. Marble is heavier than sandstone and has to be treated differently. Steel is different from glass, not to mention aluminium and mirror surfaces. The aluminium and mirror sculptures create immaterial and virtual appearances, while the marble and stone sculptures do not hide their weight of 1.5 to 7 tonnes, but they do not seem heavy because of the dissolution of the surface through irregular groove structures, where the light is refracted. When Tony Cragg, a fellow sculptor from Wuppertal who has also received great international recognition, entered this sculptural biotope for the first time a few years ago, he exclaimed: 'Who still makes stone sculptures anymore?' In 2021, however, Cragg organised an exhibition of the 'stone sculptor' Mack at his Waldfrieden Sculpture Park in Wuppertal, which has become a milestone (see pp. 234–236).

But we are not here to study this ensemble. We have been here so many times that we know it by heart. And yet the contrast between the banality of the outside world and the subtle, poetic, and visually well-considered placement of these sculptures between the three thatched farmhouses of the Huppertzhof shows, time and again, what an artist can achieve who has pursued his vision for decades without having to work on the side, and who has been able to make a living from his art, with his works influencing society with newly invented visual experiences, sense perceptions, and worldviews.

The artist is waiting for us in the glass studio. This is a building whose function only becomes apparent once you are inside (fig. p. 22). It allows maximum light, unlike most artists' studios. The light can be dimmed by motorised curtains that Mack can lower at any time when he is working. The artist usually stands in full light when painting. He designed this studio himself, with its huge glass surface. Together with a second studio in Ibiza, it is his central place of work (fig. p. 21). Here, at the edge of the window, experimental forms for sculptural works can be seen in direct sunlight, to be observed until they are eventually realised. But it is mainly here that Mack has painted since 1991, when, with the *Chromatic Constellations*, painting once again began to play a leading role in his oeuvre, after his early paintings and the *ZERO* works (1956–68). If you walk around here, as unobtrusively as possible, you will see an extraordinary collection of CDs: the whole range of classical, modern, and contemporary 'serious' music – a collection that could easily belong to a musicologist. Heinz Mack listens to the recordings while he paints his *Chromatic Constellations* or determines the structural constellations that define his sculptures, which he can only

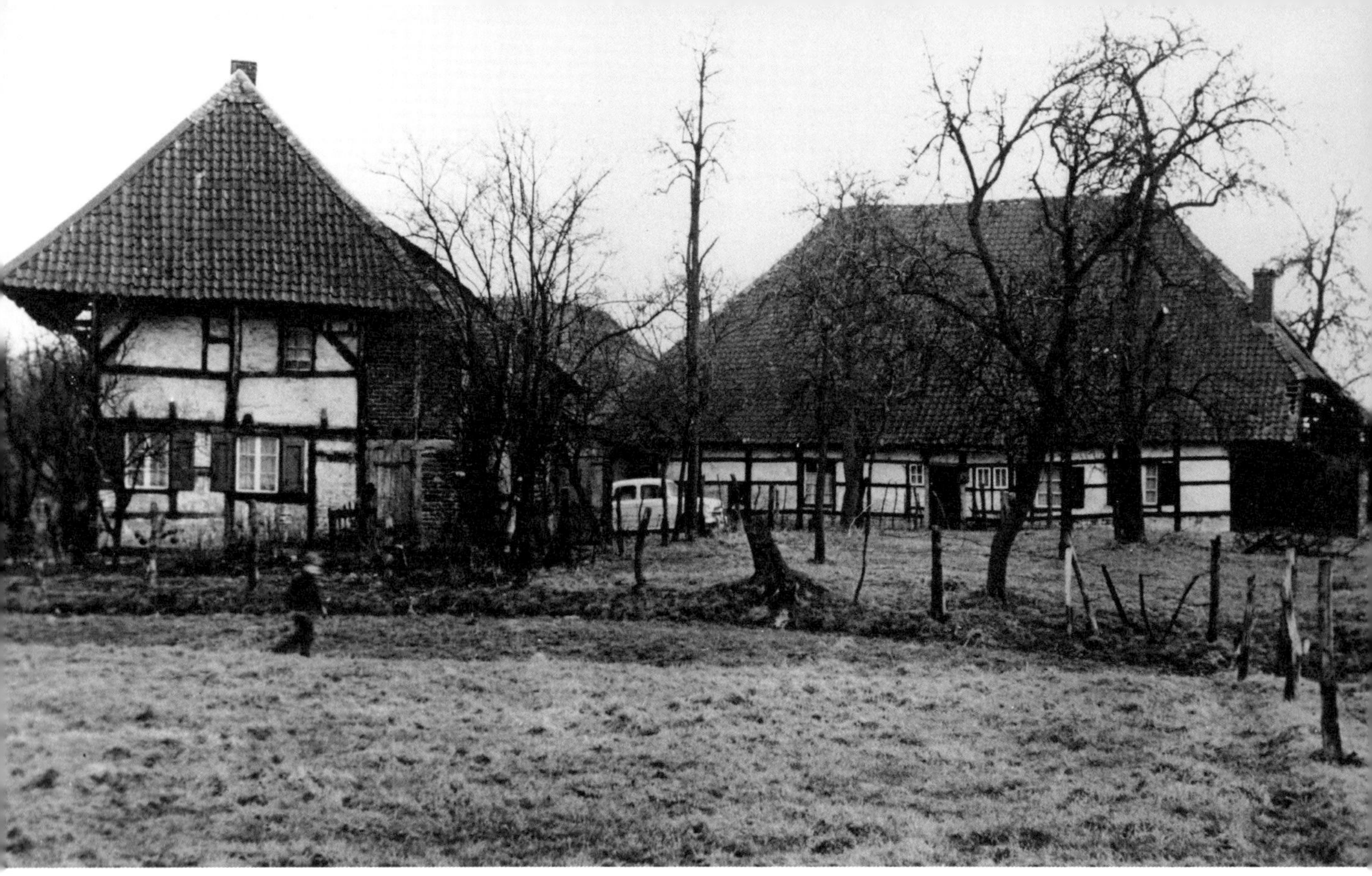

The Huppertzhof in
Mönchengladbach
early 1960s

The Huppertzhof in
Mönchengladbach
today

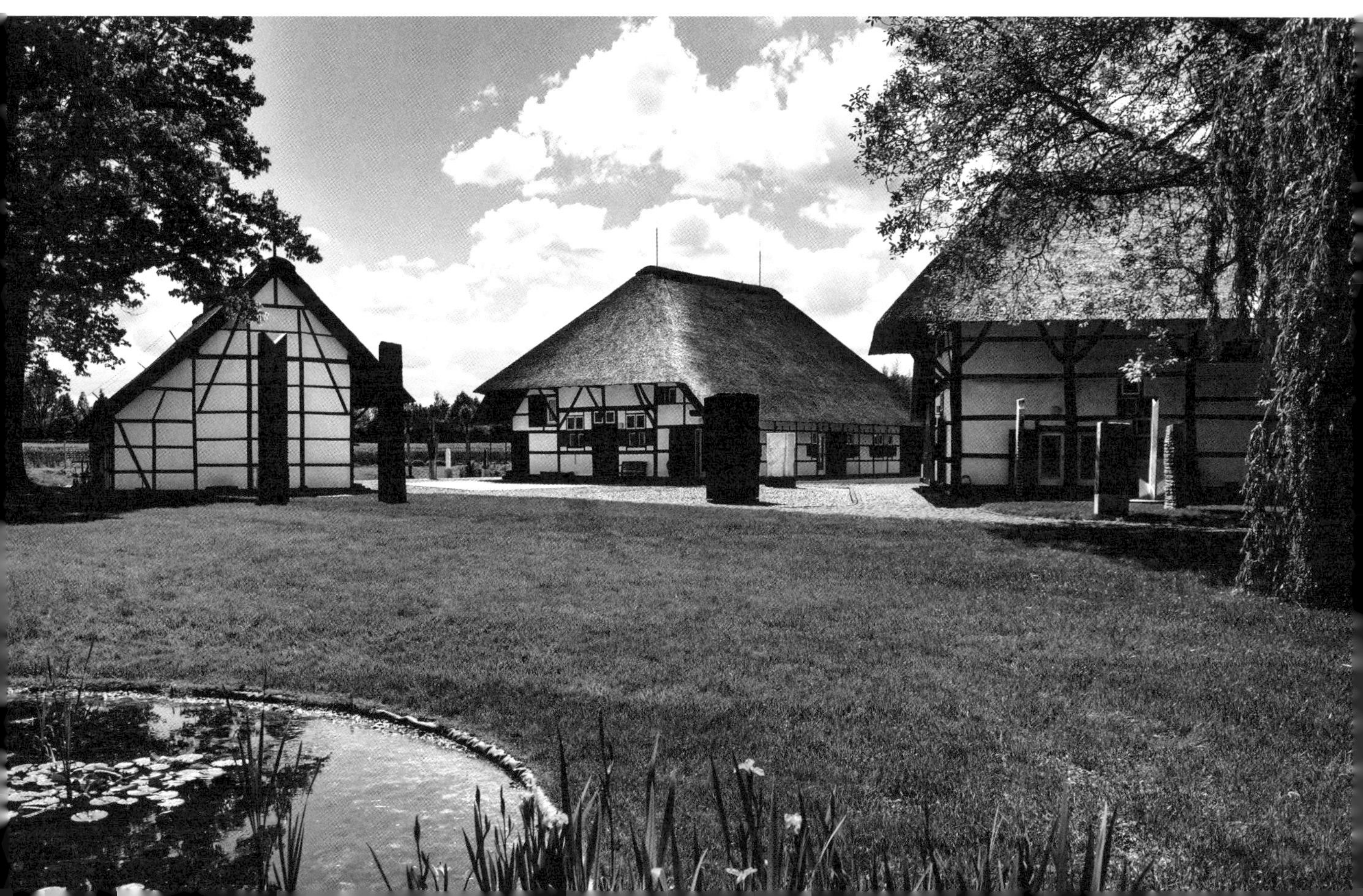

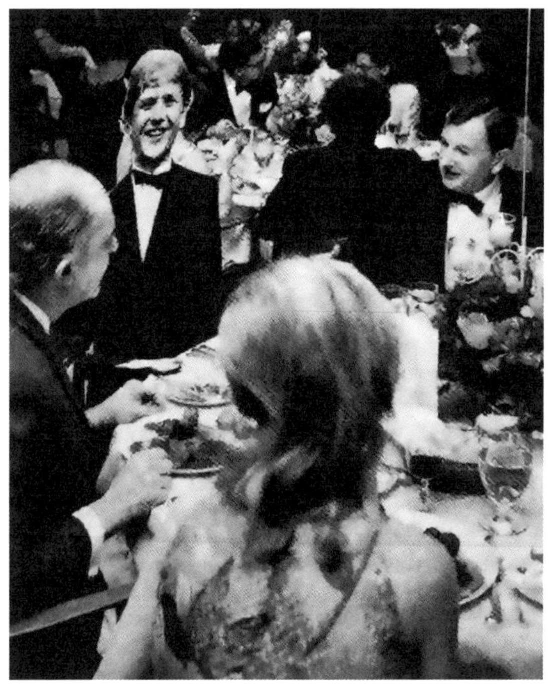

In 1969 Heinz Mack accepts an invitation from David Rockefeller and jokingly sends a life-size photograph of himself in a dinner jacket mounted on cardboard to him in New York. It is folded so that it can sit at the table with the other guests and listen to the conversations.

to a limited extent execute himself due to the nature of the materials, though he is always present when they are realised. The glass studio also contains an extraordinary array of the finest oil pastels, all used, and acrylics. Everything is immediately at hand when Mack – always alone – is in the studio. For many years, his life has been organised so that he goes to the studio every day, even Saturdays and Sundays. Trips to Ibiza, where his other studio is located, or public appearances at his own exhibitions and other events are the exception. The artist does not know the meaning of the word 'holiday'. This reveals his peculiar relationship with time. Heinz Mack is extremely punctual when he has an appointment. But he has refused to wear a wristwatch since his youth. When he was a secondary school art teacher in the 1950s and early 1960s, this peculiarity sometimes betrayed him and made him late for his own classes, especially when he had driven through at night from Paris after a meeting with Jean Tinguely and Yves Klein. But now, as so often, he is right on time in the glass studio to receive the four of us. Ute Mack comes out of her office in the little house of the Huppertzhof and says: 'It's nice to see you all. My husband has prepared something in the studio. I don't know what it is. I'll see you all at lunch.'

Heinz Mack is not very tall; he is well built and the most pleasant and at the same time most challenging person to talk to. He shows us a very large painting in progress in the studio with the continuous glass front. Our first thought is: What, at your age you're climbing such a high ladder? On previous visits he had always insisted that he had never done any sport. But once he showed us the self-imposed routine of exercises he does every day. None of us could have kept up with him. So he was now working on a painting almost on the scale of Henri Matisse's stained-glass windows (1947–51) in the Chapelle du Rosaire in Vence: a multi-coloured *Collage* measuring three by six metres. And this at the age of ninety-two.

Half a year earlier, after his exhibition at the Osthaus Museum Hagen, where some of these very recent works were shown, we had discussed the fact that the paintings had become radical since the lockdowns of the COVID-19 pandemic, because they show seemingly 'impossible' adjacencies of colours. We immediately started talking about how to develop this further. But Heinz Mack is not an artist who works with certainties and concepts. Instead, he always tries to do things in a new way.

»

Three years after I moved back to Düsseldorf from New York in 1966, I received a very personal invitation to dinner from David Rockefeller, whom I had visited twice with Marisol. I was touched. I had a photograph taken of myself at a scale of 1:1, that is, 1.72 metres tall, wearing the dark suit I had worn in eighth grade, and which had been with me for more than two decades. At the time it was taken, I still had a lot of blonde hair on my head and my whole face was beaming. This photo was printed on paper – a large photo was quite a feat in those days. I glued it to a piece of cardboard and folded it several times so that it would fit into a large envelope. At the dinner, David Rockefeller actually sat with my double in a chair next to him, and a photo of it even appeared in *Time Magazine*. New York is still important to me.

« (JUNE 2023)

»

In my painting, the eye is invited to constantly move back and forth across the picture plane. But in central perspective, from the Renaissance onwards, the gaze is practically fixed. There are paintings by Bruegel or Bosch in which thousands of small images are built into the picture. But on the whole, paintings from the Renaissance to Picasso are centralised compositions. The space is captured from one direction, which gives it a certain stability. In my work, the eye moves back and forth endlessly. Sure, you can take in the painting at a glance: 'There are several colours.' But then it starts, the movement of the eye back and forth. The painting is like an instrument. Someone looks at it and looks away again. Someone says: 'How many colours are there?' – 'Yes, I didn't really see them.' It takes quite some time.

(APRIL 2023) «

Heinz Mack has a degree in philosophy and keeps abreast of developments in the field by reading authors such as Max Bense and Gernot and Hartmut Böhme. He reads the *Frankfurter Allgemeine Zeitung* every morning and the *Jüdische Allgemeine* once a week, something of a duty for a German after the Holocaust. You can't fool him about philosophical questions. He also often tells us who is working at the highest level in art criticism. He entrusted the catalogue raisonné of his sculptures from 2003 to 2020 to Beat Wyss, one of the most unconventional thinkers on art.[1] Above all, however, any conversation with Mack in front of one of his paintings immediately takes on a philosophical tone. Not as a contrived observation, but as a question: 'What do you have to say about this picture, this attempt?'

»

In 1940, Matisse also found himself in a situation where he was uncertain because there was a risk, because it was not clear how things were going to develop. But then he said that all the important discoveries in painting would not have happened without this risk. So, I asked myself: What has happened in my own life? In which years did something happen to me that could be called risky, because I made a decision on my own that was full of risk? Basically, my life as an artist is structured and built on that.

(OCTOBER 2023) «

But this time the conversation revolves around the question: What is this new book about? The artist sees it as a kind of legacy. In the monograph *Heinz Mack: A 21st Century Artist*, Antonia Lehmann-Tolkmitt and I tried to summarise the unique position of Mack's oeuvre in theoretical and thematic terms. The artist is very pleased with the book, which was published in 2019. It has been well received. Peter Weibel, a world-renowned artist and theoretician and director of the ZKM | Center for Art and Media Karlsruhe for a quarter of a century, reacted enthusiastically at the time and subsequently initiated the major Mack exhibition at the ZKM, which took place from September 2023 to April 2024 as Weibel's last exhibition. But the question arose: Aren't there other, completely different aspects? Can we dig deeper? Can we ask Heinz Mack more questions?

The artist responded on two levels. He made available to us what might be called his private archive. This consists of five bulging Leitz ring binders in which he has been collecting notes, sketches, and ideas for decades, either in a deliberately disorganised way or in an intuitive order. Even his wife Ute Mack, who runs the Mack Studio, and their daughter Valeria Mack, as well as Sophia Sotke and Bettina Weiand, the second art historian in the studio, have never seen this material. The material from the ZERO period from 1957–58 to 1966 is stored and made available for research at the ZERO foundation in Düsseldorf, which Heinz Mack co-founded and to which he donated a substantial amount of archival

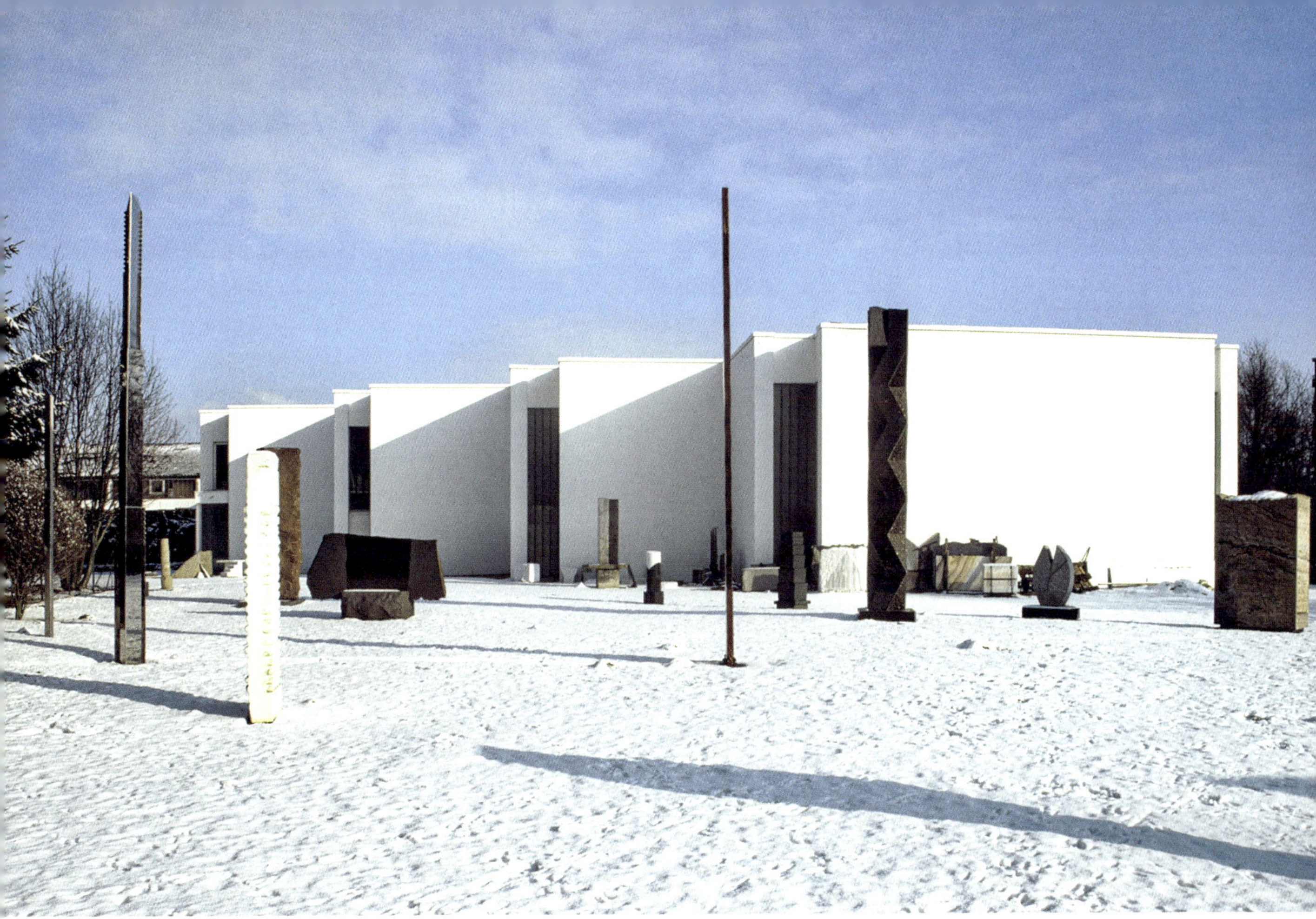

Heinz Mack's large tripartite studio with sculpture park in Mönchengladbach
1990s

»

Later, when I took on the ZERO period, I asked myself: 'Have you lost your mind? You're dealing with things that actually have nothing to do with you at all.' But it's a subject that cannot be denied because, after all, I'm a contemporary witness, and there are hardly any of us left.

(JANUARY 2023) «

»

If we design the book so that quotations from me appear in the side column, the reader will have the feeling that Heinz Mack is personally showing them what he has done or experienced.

(DECEMBER 2023) «

»

There are phenomena that have not been sufficiently explored in art history. When the Germans occupied southern France, they searched for Jews there. It was the same everywhere. Large transports left Nice for Auschwitz. During this time, Matisse's companion was suspected and constantly interrogated. His daughter was also arrested and imprisoned. You have to bear that in mind. During this time, Matisse painted pictures of flowers. I understand that very well. It's not comparable, but I've been in the situation several times where people have said, 'What are you doing, Mack, at a time when everything is going haywire in the world?' I've said this is my way of protesting against a world that has lost its bearings, that's ugly and horrible and evil. That I do things that are the opposite

material. Personal archive holdings from earlier and later years were lost in a fire in September 1984, which destroyed the thatched roof and upper floor of one of the Huppertzhof buildings. But what remained in five Leitz ring binders is considerable. One sees, unfiltered, how the artist thinks, how he creates groups of works, how he reflects, how he relates to things in the world and how he writes theoretical formulations about his own work in order to reflect on it and also to reassure himself.

The role of drawings and construction drawings for the sculptural work is also revealed, as is the cyclical nature of his entire oeuvre, in which a dozen ideas, references, and motifs that have sustained it for seventy years (pp. 183–210) recur. It is quite rare for an artist to be so open about his work, his heart, the beginnings of his ideas and his indignations. Much of this has been included in this book, also in the form of facsimiles.

Heinz Mack also mentioned that when it comes to monographs on individual artists, he has a favourite, namely *Henri Matisse: A Novel* (1971), written by Louis Aragon, one of the most outstanding novelists and poets of twentieth-century France, who, together with André Breton and Philippe Soupault, founded Surrealism. The book is the result of an unusual encounter: in the autumn of 1940, after the French defeat at the hands of Nazi Germany, Aragon, a member of the Resistance, went into hiding in Nice and from there visited Matisse, whom he had admired since his student days. They discussed the foundations of Matisse's artistic thinking. The artist asked Aragon to write about him, and the result was a pamphlet published under a pseudonym and distributed clandestinely by the French Resistance: *Matisse ou la Grandeur* appeared in late 1941 as a samizdat publication. Aragon later revisited his texts on Matisse, including this first one. At the time, the artist had sent Aragon comments on this text in the form of letters and drawings, which can be found in the side column of the original edition of *Henri Matisse: A Novel*, creating a unique dialogue between the author and the artist. This side column is quite wide and seems to be autonomous in relation to the main text, while at the same time being in dialogue with it. We have adopted this principle in the present book. The side column contains statements by Heinz Mack from the conversations held for this book since 2020, as well as older quotations from the artist, each in free association with the main text.

What Heinz Mack also appreciates about *Henri Matisse: A Novel* is that it is a 'spectral' book, as the artist himself says: 'Aragon's book has a spectral quality. This book, for which we are having our conversations, should also have that, because my work is spectral.'[2] Aragon began compiling the texts he had written on Matisse in 1970, after the death of his wife Elsa Triolet, a central author of Russian Constructivism, which in turn is fundamental for Mack. An associative rather than chronological sequence of chapters aims to multiply the points of view. This also lent itself to a cyclical progression of the work, as is characteristic of Mack's oeuvre.

of that. That's what I meant, that Matisse was protesting in his own way by saying, 'I'm not going to let this get to me.' There's a wonderful picture of a bowl that was done when the Wehrmacht was at Matisse's door, an incredibly beautiful picture, so simple, as if a child had painted it.

« (DECEMBER 2023)

As with all our meetings with the artist, lunch is served in the main building of the Huppertzhof from around 12:30 pm. Ute and Valeria Mack manage the work, exhibitions, books, storage, sales, the catalogue raisonné, and a thousand other things throughout the day. The main building, like the whole of the sculpture-strewn grounds, has a charm that is breathtaking. Situated at the eastern end of Mönchengladbach, the Huppertzhof is the oldest farm for miles around (fig. p. 12). It was not money, but commitment that brought the artist to such a property. In the second half of the 1960s, Mönchengladbach's city councillor for cultural affairs, Busso Diekamp, asked the gallerist Alfred Schmela, a major figure in the West German art world since 1957, if he knew of an artist who was looking for a lot of space and who would also repair the building, the Huppertzhof. Schmela replied that Mack had returned from New York, was going through a divorce and living in Düsseldorf. He was looking for a place like this. A successful artistic career is very often linked to property issues. Those who can afford a flat and a studio, or who have a long-term, rent-controlled, and non-cancellable lease, are out of the danger zone. When Heinz Mack moved into the main Huppertzhof building in 1967, it was a wreck. Homeless people lived in an outbuilding that now houses the administration of Mack's oeuvre. He told them that he was a freelance artist and just as poor as they were, and that he thought they could understand each other. Over the years, he rented the two farm buildings belonging to the estate from the owner, the city of Mönchengladbach, built the glass studio, and turned the grounds into a biotope that is also the largest sculpture park in the region. It is not open to the public, but it is a reserve in more ways than one.

»

We don't have a title for this [now completed] book yet. But I would like the working concept to be 'cosmos'. However, this word is far too grandiloquent, so I would reject it as a title. But there is something in this concept: namely that my work is not a one-way street. Rather, I am in a state of traffic chaos, with dozens of intersecting streets. Anyone who has been to Los Angeles will understand what I mean by this tangle of streets. I'm in this spaghetti salad with my work, and that has to be expressed somewhere in this book.

« (DECEMBER 2023)

Heinz and Ute Mack usually only walk through the beautiful living room in the main building because they are so busy every day – unless there are important guests with whom they can talk in peace in this ensemble. Two of Heinz Mack's *Chromatic Constellations* hang opposite each other. The two paintings are the same size, almost square, and fill the walls. They hang here as if on trial. The *Chromatic Constellations* created since 2020 have a striking feature: they are constructed from disharmonies of adjacent and distant colours (fig. pp. 276–277), no longer from harmonious colour relationships as before (fig. p. 198). Such daring is often found in the late work of an artist, where leaps occur – it is a risk-taking gesture without safeguards, which sometimes, as in the famous examples of Paul Cézanne and Paul Gauguin around 1900, directly influenced the younger art of their time. Since 2020, basically since the beginning of the pandemic, Heinz Mack has painted more than a dozen works that have added a new dimension to his oeuvre. With the *Chromatic Constellations*, he has been playing through Johann Wolfgang von Goethe's colour wheel in an abstract way since 1991, transforming it into a polychrome painting that dialectically undermines the idea of ZERO. At the same time, Mack has been reversing the process in his paintings since 2020 by allowing a disruptive contrast between colour fields to take effect, destabilising the painting, sustaining it on the canvas and saving it in a dynamic equilibrium. We have not yet finished learning about this artist.

» I come back to the subject of utopia. Wieland Schmied wrote about my work in his book *Utopie und Wirklichkeit* (Utopia and Reality)[3]: 'With Heinz Mack, utopia has failed, but at a very high level.'[4] I like that very much.

(OCTOBER 2023) «

We leave the Huppertzhof at around 2:30 pm. But first Mack invites us to the music room on the upper floor, where there is a first-class stereo system and a concert grand piano that is always in tune. Every day at this time, the artist plays it for a quarter to half an hour. Even if you don't know it, you can tell straight away that he was originally meant and wanted to be a pianist. On this day, he plays modern Spanish music from the inter-war period, completely focused on himself, with a rhythmic complexity that is almost impossible for us listeners to follow. He plays from memory, with the same 120 per cent commitment as in his sculptural work. One gets the impression that this is not relaxation, but work, necessary work. *Il fait ses gammes*, one would say in French, loosely translated: he is practising a way of dealing with rhythms, structures, and pitches that also serves him in his painting, which he will continue later in the afternoon and on the following days in the glass studio. His playing is on a concert level and creates a magical atmosphere. Suddenly, unexpectedly, he closes the keyboard cover with determination and says: 'That's enough.' He must now take his midday nap – another part of his daily routine – before returning to the glass studio until sunset.

In the afternoon sun, the sculptural ensemble of the Huppertzhof is ideally illuminated. There are several large fields to the south-west, as no buildings are allowed to interfere with the flight path of Mönchengladbach's sports airport. As a result, the light enters this field of sculptures unhindered, refracting unspectacularly but constantly. Stepping out of this biotope onto the busy street provides the opposite of the shock of our arrival, thrown back into our contemporary world, on the edge of a commercial park, which is after these impressions of an almost incomprehensible banality.

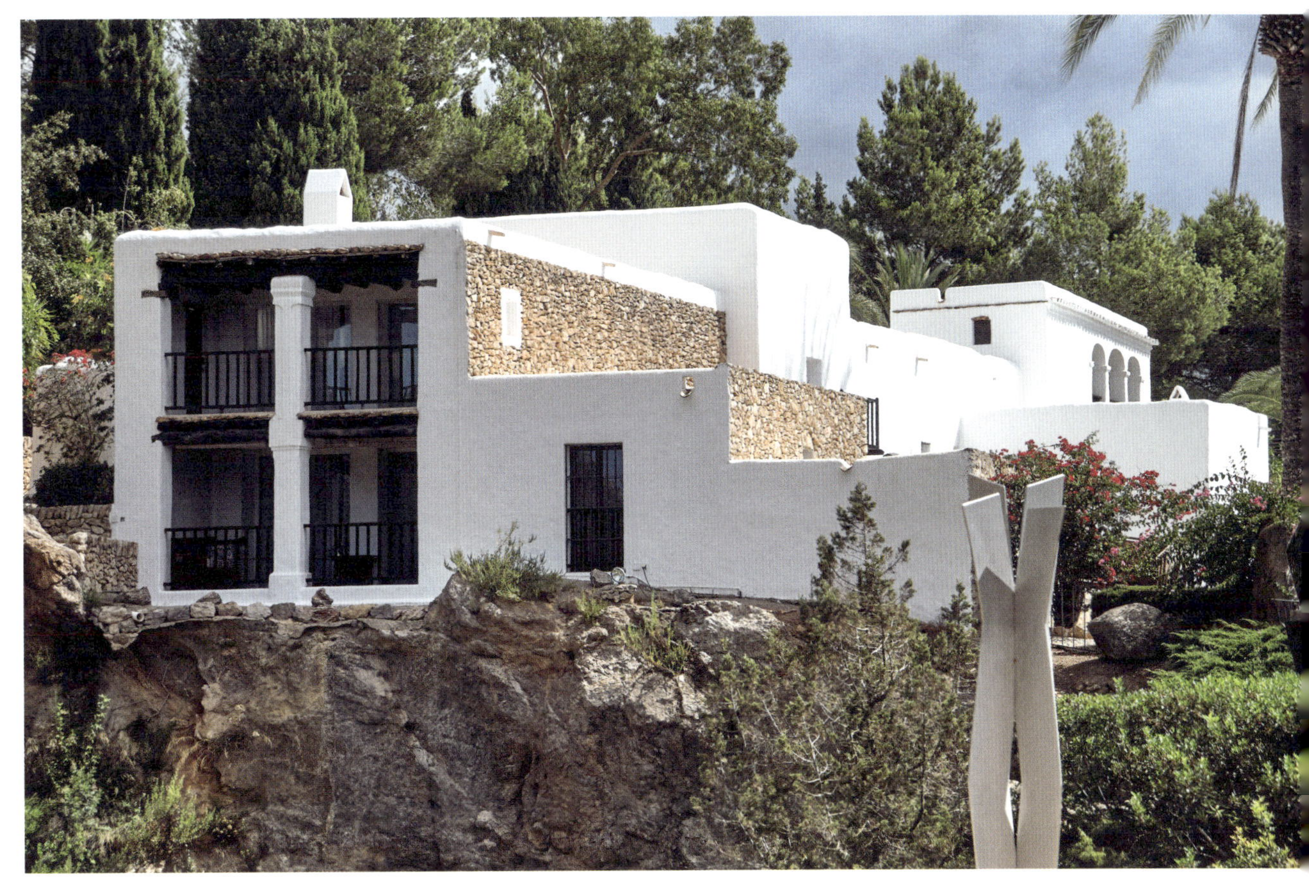

View of the artist's studio at
the finca Can Micali, Ibiza
2009

Heinz Mack in his glazed
studio at the Huppertzhof,
Mönchengladbach
2016

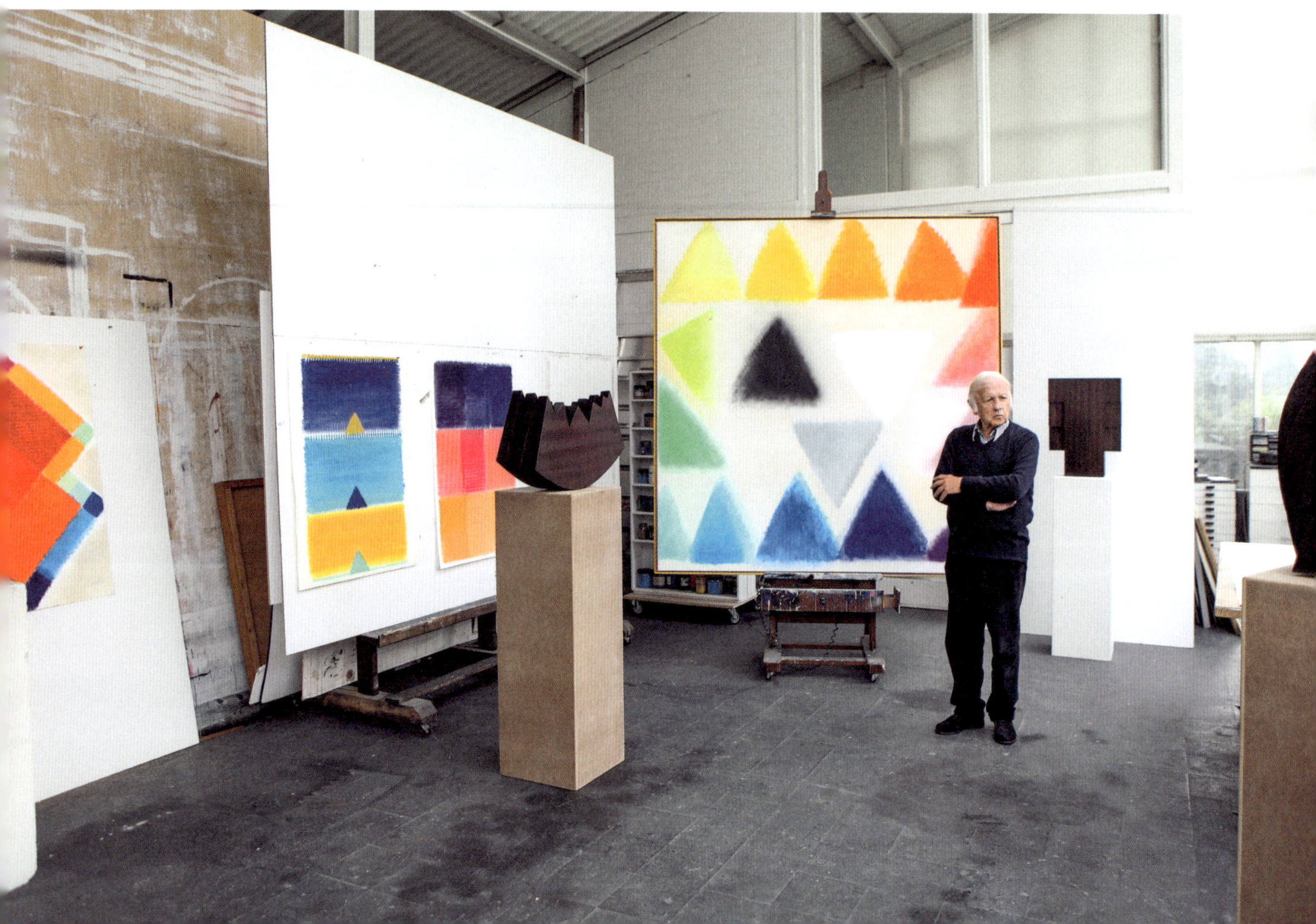

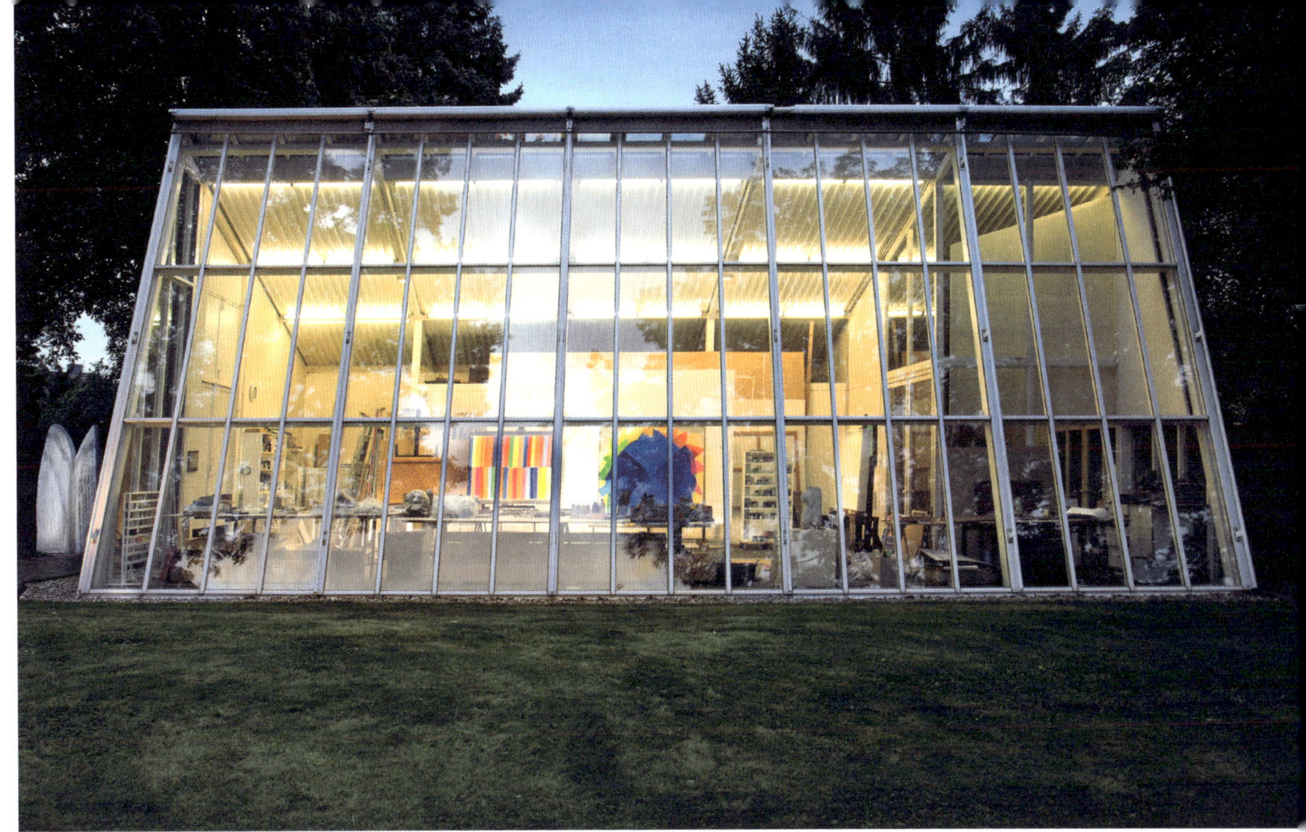

View into the artist's glazed studio at the Huppertzhof, Mönchengladbach
2015

III.50 h.mach

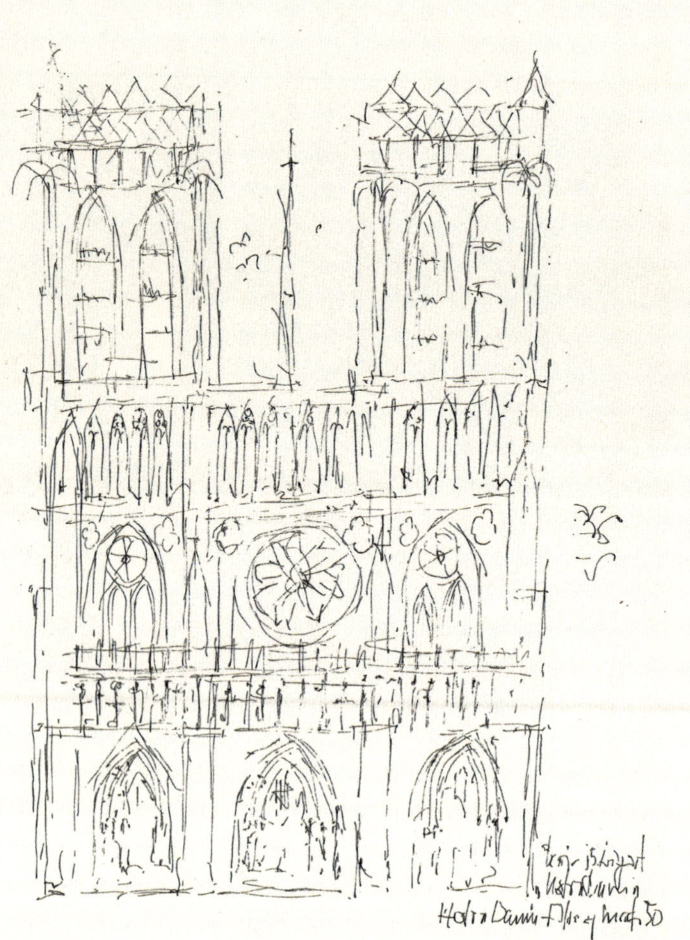

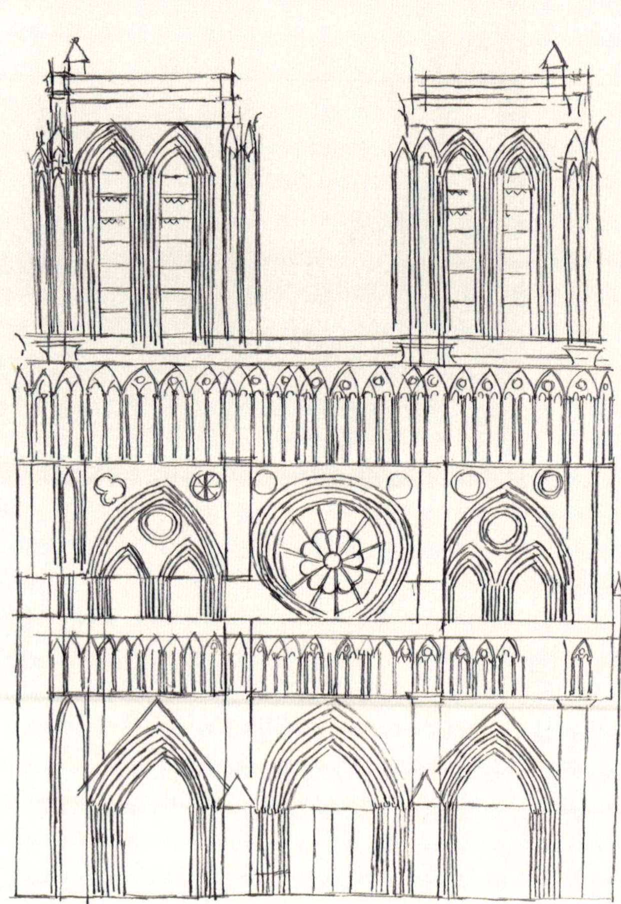

PARIS
1950

Notre Dame de Paris
1950

'Until then, I had only seen ruins.'[5] In August 1950, Heinz Mack was standing in Paris. Stepping out of the Gare du Nord, he was struck by the verticality and beauty of a city that had not been destroyed. The Second World War had ended just five years earlier. The cities of the Rhineland were still landscapes of ruins (fig. p. 27). At that time, professors and students were still removing the rubble from the bombed-out building of the Düsseldorf Academy of Art. They were carrying out the reconstruction work themselves. By contrast, the historic centre of Paris was miraculously spared from Allied and German bombing raids, not least thanks to the popular uprising that liberated the city in August 1944.

»

I was enrolled at the Düsseldorf Academy of Art and had completed my first semester. Suddenly I was called into the director's office. He gave a real lecture, even though it was just the two of us. He had heard that I had talent. His remarks culminated in the statement: 'Heinz Mack, never become sharp, because sharp tips break off easily.' My only thought was: 'A...hole'. His secretary told me that I would get fifty marks as a stipend and that I could do whatever I wanted with it. The only thing I wanted to know was how to get to Paris. At that time, it was by train.

(DECEMBER 2022) «

In 1950, travelling to France as a German student was still very complicated. You needed a visa and accommodation. The administrative office of the 'Catholic German Student Organisation, Secretariat of the Foreign Office – Liaison Office to Pax Romana' in Bonn, the provisional capital of the Federal Republic of Germany, founded in 1949, authorised Heinz Mack's stay from 10 to 30 August 1950. The permit was written in a tone that is incomprehensibly authoritarian to today's ears. It was still written in administrative Nazi German. On the back, Heinz Mack noted: 'I don't know yet if this is the address! / Host in Paris: / Centre d'Echanges Internationaux 33 / Boulevard de Courcelles in Paris VIIIe / important'.[6] The original document continues: 'Klaus is leaving on 16/8/50 / please give him the new shoes.'[7]

Boulevard de Courcelles runs along Parc Monceau, about an hour's walk from the Gare du Nord. Mack was thus underway in one of the most impressive and affluent districts of Paris, built between 1880 and 1900. All the streets lead to the Arc de Triomphe. It was in this part of the city that Marcel Proust began writing *À la recherche du temps perdu* (In Search of Lost Time) in 1906. This route alone must have been a wonder to the nineteen-year-old.

At that time, Franco-German relations did not yet exist in their present form. From 1940 to 1944–45, Germany had been the occupying power in France. Now France was one of the four occupying powers in Germany. In 1947, resistance fighters and former concentration camp inmates had set up a 'Committee for Exchange with the New Germany' in Paris, with the young political scientist Alfred Grosser on its board. But this remained marginal. In May 1950, the German-born French Foreign Minister Robert Schuman presented a plan that would later become the basis for European unification. However, it was not until 1952 that the European Coal and Steel Community was created as the first organ of reconciliation between Germany and France.

Heinz Mack's stay in Paris took place at a time when the future relations between the two countries were not yet foreseeable. At the same time, the post-war years

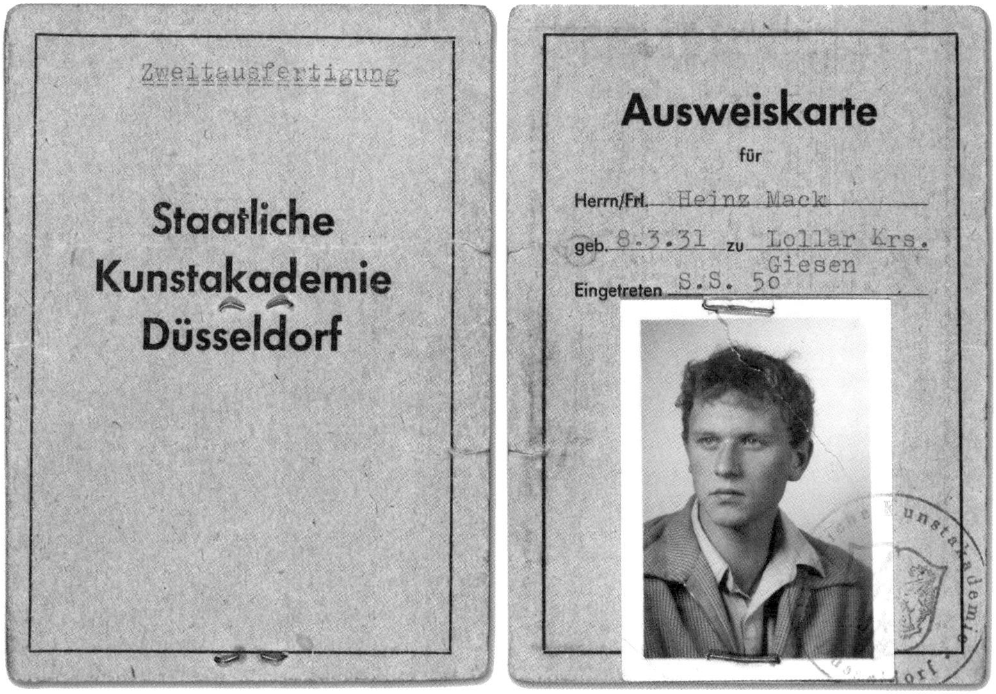

Zweitausfertigung

Staatliche
Kunstakademie
Düsseldorf

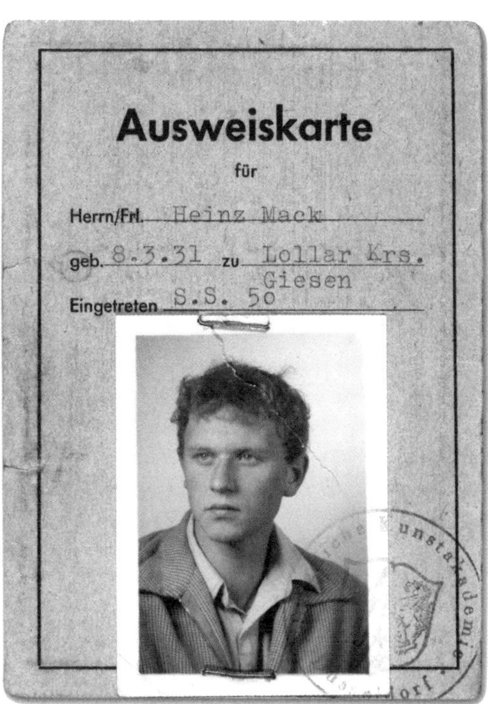

Ausweiskarte
für
Herrn/Frl. Heinz Mack
geb. 8.3.31 zu Lollar Krs. Giesen
Eingetreten S.S. 50

Heinz Mack's student card, State Academy of Art, Düsseldorf
1950

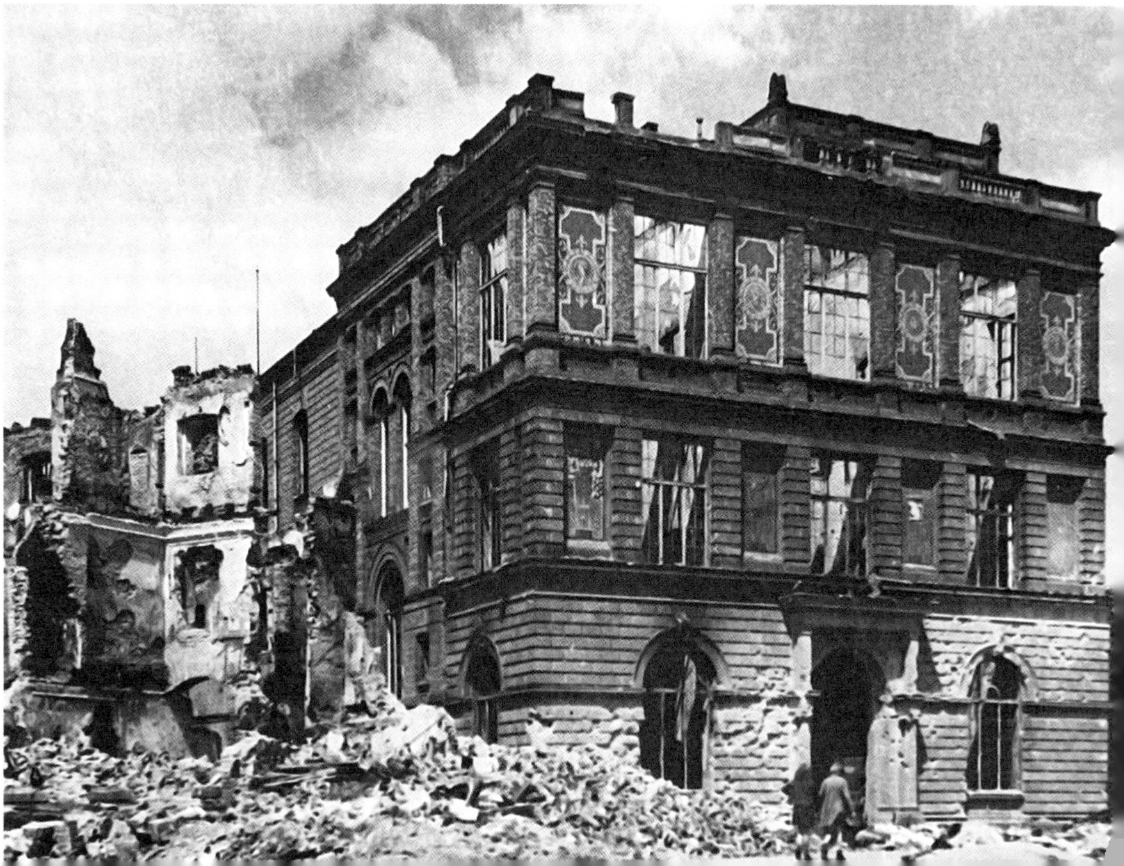

The Düsseldorf Academy of Art in ruins
1946

in Paris had produced a first-rate artistic, philosophical, and literary flowering. During the four years of occupation, all free activity had to take place underground. After the self-liberation of Paris in August 1944, there was a creative awakening on a rare scale, characterised by the keywords existentialism (Jean-Paul Sartre, Albert Camus), feminism (Simone de Beauvoir), structuralism (Claude Lévi-Strauss), phenomenology (Maurice Merleau-Ponty), Surrealism (André Breton, Louis Aragon), the new historiography (the Annales school), the beginnings of the Nouveau Roman in literature and the Nouvelle Vague in film, and the triumph of free abstract painting in the Art Informel and Tachism movements. This was aided by the fact that France's museum, gallery, publishing, and university landscape had survived the Occupation largely unscathed. It was a far cry from the cultural destruction left behind by the Nazi regime in Germany. At the same time, new players were arriving from the Resistance and from emigration in North and South America.

Heinz Mack lived in an international student residence. Internationality was the second important experience of his stay in Paris. Exchanges with people from other countries had been largely forbidden in Nazi Germany. In contrast, British, US-American, Latin American and Western European students lived on Boulevard de Courcelles. In this situation, it was an advantage that Heinz Mack, despite his sporadic attendance at school during the war, already spoke quite good English from his temporary enrolment at a modern-language secondary school.

» This is the second oldest photo of me that I have, taken in 1950 in Paris at Café de Flore, the existentialist café that still exists today (fig. p. 29). I was nineteen years old. I had found some discarded newspapers somewhere and made myself a paper jacket. Shortly afterwards, it completely disintegrated in the rain. An Anglo-Saxon student in the dormitory, probably from a better background, a medical student, said: 'Now we'll buy you a new jacket.' The next day, after a nice visit to the museum, I painted a watercolour for him. That was my gift in return for the jacket. I wore it the next time I went to Café de Flore.

(DECEMBER 2022) «

'I was a lone traveller back then,' he says today.[8] The city was practically car-free. You could almost dream of that impression today. 1950 was a key year for post-war art in Paris. Jean Dubuffet pushed through his idea of Art Brut and the dissolution of panel painting, while a gallery exhibition for the first time juxtaposed the radical positions of the Parisian painting scene – Dubuffet, Hans Hartung, Pierre Soulages, and Wols – with the emerging New York School around Willem de Kooning, Arshile Gorky, and Jackson Pollock.[9] Heinz Mack was unaware of this during his first stay. Galleries were still small shops, and the art business was based on word of mouth.

Nevertheless, he also went to Saint-Germain-des-Prés and Café de Flore, the centre of intellectual life at the time. Simone de Beauvoir and Jean-Paul Sartre, the two philosophical authorities of the post-war period, were regulars there. Sartre had become the most highly regarded philosopher of the post-war period thanks to the concept of existentialism and his book *L'Être et le néant* (Being and Nothingness), published in 1943. The book had already been translated into German in 1948, and Heinz Mack worked through it a few years later while studying philosophy in Cologne, adopting

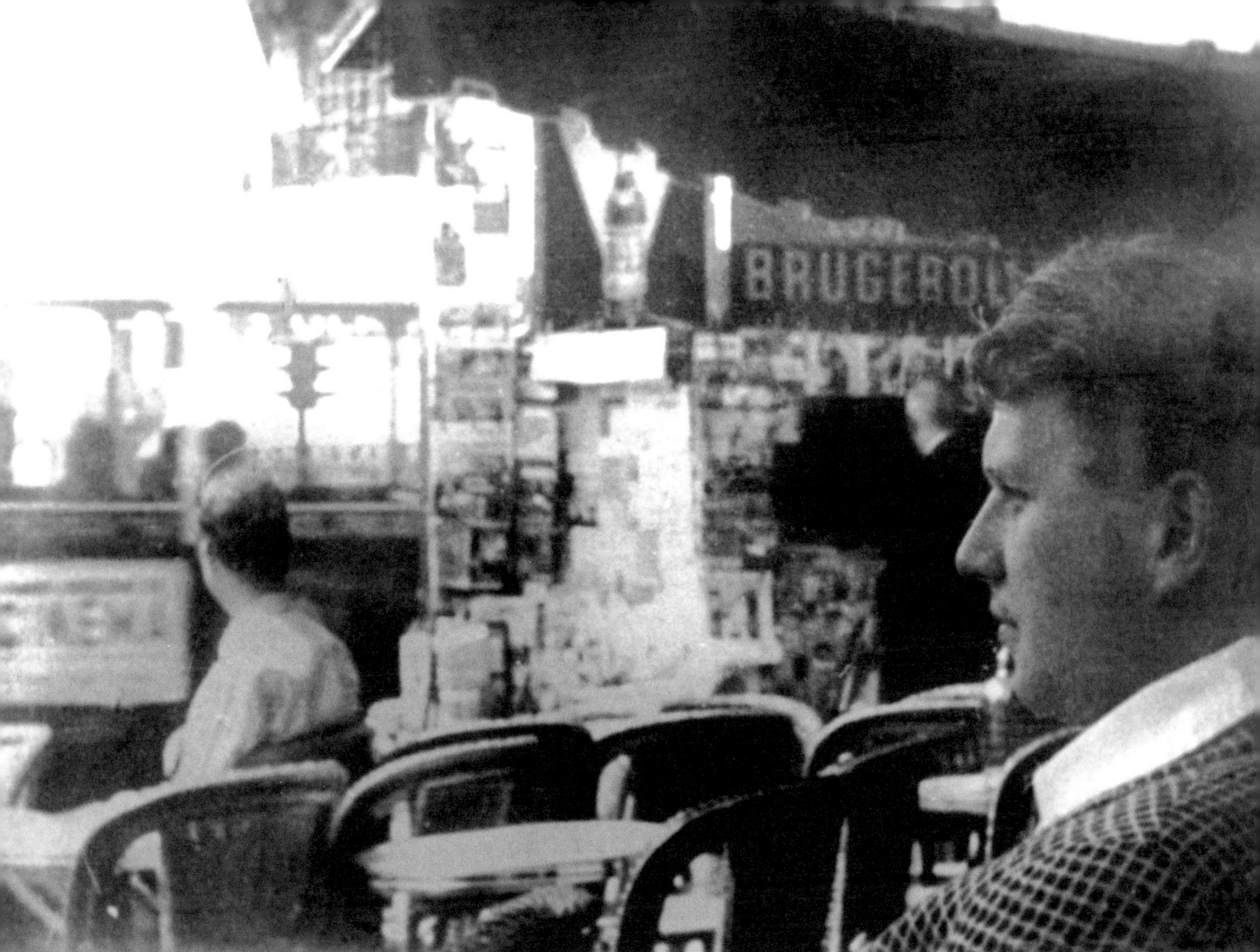

Heinz Mack at Café
de Flore, Boulevard
Saint-Germain, Paris
1950

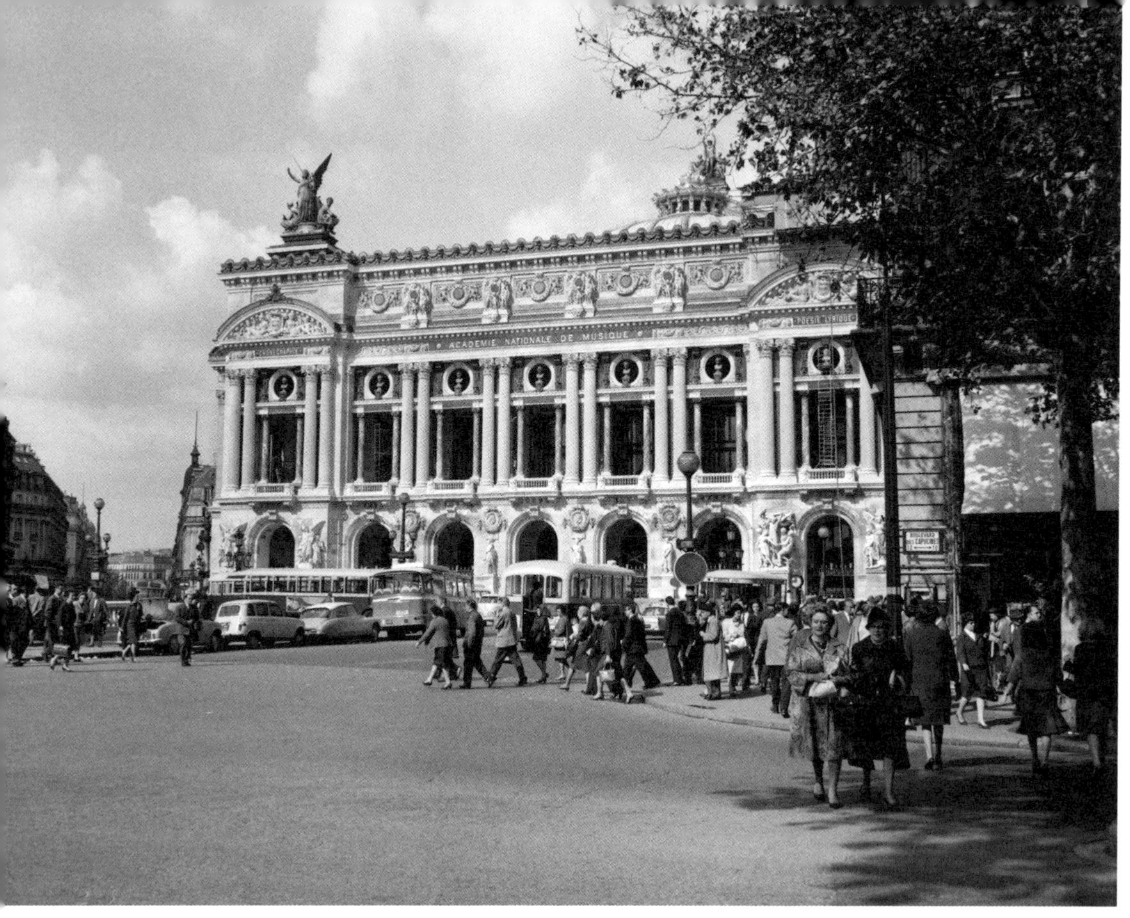

The Opéra Garnier, Paris
1950s

much of Sartre's concept of commitment for his own artistic attitude, in which everything is presented with an existential unconditionality to this day. The way in which Sartre dealt with the concepts of metaphor, time, ornament, and beauty in his book from the Resistance period also remains an important reference today. During a visit to the Huppertzhof, Heinz Mack showed us the complete works of Sartre in the German edition published by Rowohlt in his private library. He had been introduced to the *genius loci* in 1950. Here we are miles away from the intellectual roots generally attributed to the future co-founder of ZERO.[10]

» I was never really interested in Surrealism. But I was very impressed by Breton's book, *Nadja*. «

(JANUARY 2023)

Surrealism also experienced its second great heyday around 1950. Some of its main protagonists returned from exile in the United States, including the ethnologist Claude Lévi-Strauss, who in those years was adapting Russian linguistic structuralism to the whole of the social sciences, to which Mack's work contains profound references: It was from the concept of 'structure' that he and Otto Piene invented ZERO in 1957–58.[11] Like Lévi-Strauss, André Breton, the leader of Surrealism, had returned from New York. Heinz Mack came into contact with this world after his visit to Paris through his affinity with Joan Miró in his early paintings. He never adopted the methodology of Surrealist painting, namely the treatment of the unconscious and the fantastic.[12] However, his work from the ZERO years to the present day has much to do with the Surrealist principles of unrestricted experimentation and automatism. Mack reinvented both in the ZERO works from 1957–58 onwards. However, this was not based on dream work, but on the concept of sequence and freely evolving structure. In this respect, his visit to Paris in 1950 laid the foundations for his later work.

When the artist also emphasises that he was impressed by Breton's 1928 novel *Nadja* – it was first published in German in 1960 – he is not only referring to the way in which the author's automatistically described wanderings through the streets of Paris are interrupted by suggestive photography in a collage-like manner.[13] *Nadja* is also a grandiose description of how the Surrealist group of the 1920s built up an effective network of like-minded artistic personalities who, convinced that they formed an artistic avant-garde,[14] conquered the artistic and real worlds together. The ZERO movement with Heinz Mack, Otto Piene, and Günther Uecker realised this model independently and just as effectively from 1958–60 onwards. Heinz Mack's interest in the poets Paul Éluard and Louis Aragon are other lasting 'souvenirs' of Surrealism.[15]

Museums were not visited by the masses as they are today. One was usually alone in a museum hall. In the Petit Palais, the municipal art museum in Paris, Mack discovered paintings by Joan Miró, the Spanish Surrealist, then fifty-seven years old and living again in Paris. They showed him a possible path to follow. He bought a postcard of a painting by Miró. In those years of paper shortages, postcards were a new medium for visualising art, affordable and, above all, the first multi-coloured reproductions of paintings.

In the Petit Palais, Heinz Mack also stood, more transfixed than ever, in front of *Nature morte aux oranges* (Still Life with Oranges), which Henri Matisse had painted in Tangier in 1912 (fig. p. 33). The museum guard was concerned about the perseverance with which this very blond young German remained in front of the Matisse painting. At the age of eighty, Henri Matisse was still in the midst of his creative process. It was during this period, partly due to illness, that he produced his now legendary cut-outs, which had an immense influence on younger generations of artists as an early transgression of panel painting by a leading old master of modernism. They were so innovative that Matisse's son Pierre, one of the leading art dealers in New York at the time, refused to exhibit them. Only a young German art dealer, Heinz Berggruen, showed them in his small gallery in the Saint-Germain-des-Prés district, two streets away from Café de Flore.

» I went to the Petit Palais to look at Matisse's *Still Life with Oranges*, and then again the next day. I looked at it for so long that a guard came up to me and wanted to know why I was standing in front of it for so long.

(DECEMBER 2022) «

In 1950, all this was the present. Matisse died in 1954, Fernand Léger in 1955, and Breton in 1966. Heinz Mack later learned that the painting by Matisse that had made such an impression on him – and which continues to impact the conception of his *Chromatic Constellations* since 1991, which are freely derived from it – belonged to Pablo Picasso, who had bought it from Matisse at an exhibition almost forty years earlier, which in turn had touched Matisse deeply. Picasso had lent the painting to the exhibition at the Petit Palais in 1950. Today, Matisse's painting is in the Musée Picasso in Paris, which houses the works of art that were handed over to the French state from the artist's estate after Picasso's death in 1973 to pay the inheritance tax.

These numerous museum visits to the Petit Palais, Matisse's painting, and Miró as a possible point of reference were key experiences for Heinz Mack. The dimension that lies in his work stems from this, as does the standard he sets himself when he enters the studio. Like Mack's work, Matisse's canvas is open and experimental, and his *Nature morte aux oranges* is an unfinished finished painting in a way that very few succeed in being. Without such an inner standard, Mack cannot imagine making art – or rather, without it, making art is not honest, responsible, and upright for him. This moral impulse plays an important role in his work.

In August 1950, Paris offered a different dimension of art and intellectual activity to that which could be felt in Düsseldorf at the same time. In the years that followed, until around 1964, the city on the Seine remained at the centre of Heinz Mack's interest. He travelled there regularly, at times as often as he could. Looking at

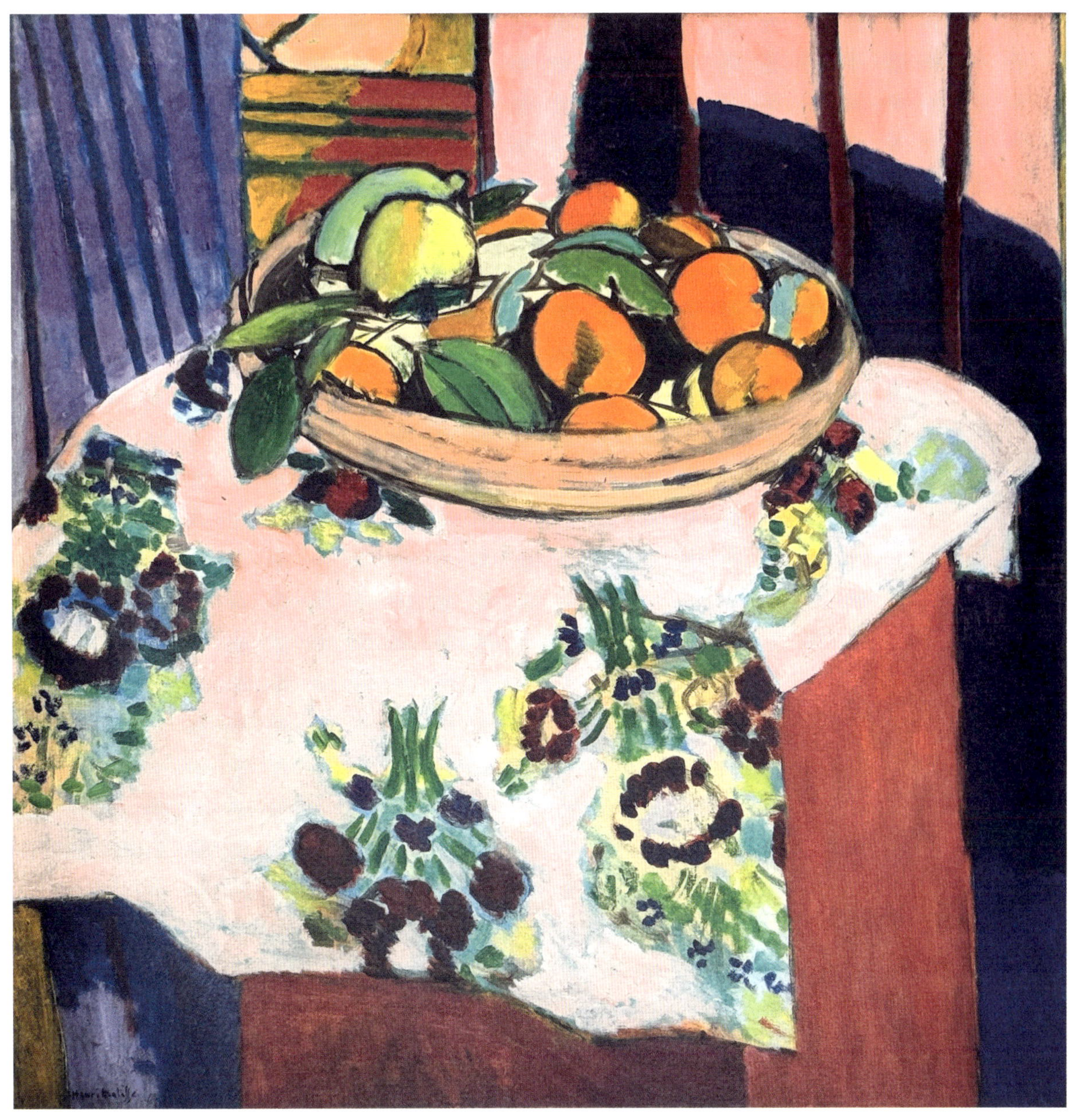

Henri Matisse
Nature morte aux Oranges
(Still Life with Oranges)
1912

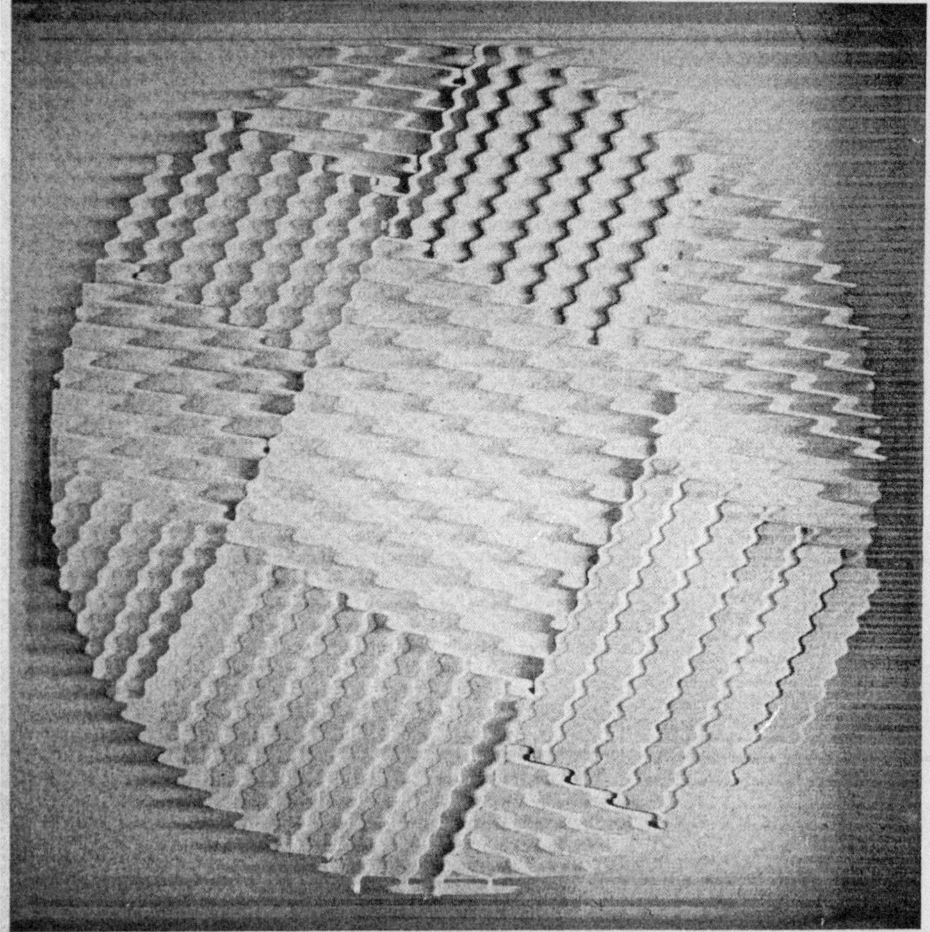

Poster for Heinz Mack's exhibition at the Musée d'art moderne de la Ville de Paris
1973

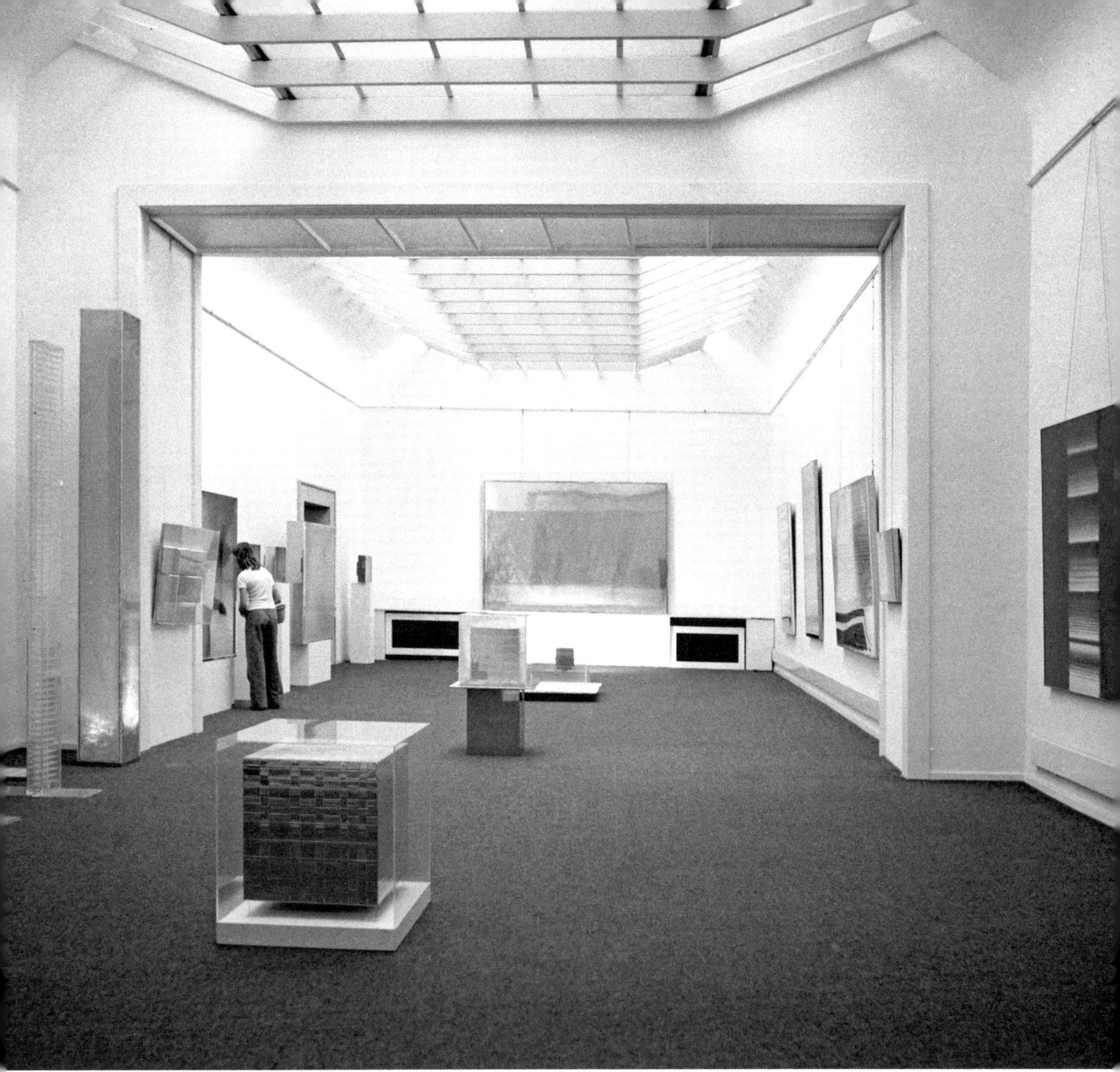

Installation view, Musée
d’art moderne de la
Ville de Paris
1973

»

At that time, around 1950, I was still very much infected by music. I was very impressed by the first opera I ever saw in my life. Somehow, I managed to get a standing-room ticket for the Opéra de Paris, on Place de l'Opéra. It was *Bolivar* by Darius Milhaud, one of the most important composers of the time. None of this would have been possible in Germany at that time. I had standing room right under the ceiling, and yet this opera fascinated me enormously. The set was designed by Fernand Léger, one of the founders of Cubism, who was still alive, just like Matisse, Miró, and Picasso, and worked in Paris. Milhaud's opera was written during the war. Its formal language, with its sequencing, a very structural way of thinking about music, influenced by 'Russian Constructivism' – via Nadia Boulanger, the teacher of the Groupe des Six, to which Milhaud belonged – had nothing to do with German art of the time.

(DECEMBER 2022) «

his solo and group exhibitions in Paris, it becomes clear that his roots in the French metropolis went far beyond the circle around Yves Klein and Jean Tinguely, the counterpart to ZERO in Düsseldorf.[16] In April 1959, he had a one-man show, *Reliefs lumineux et peintures de Mack*, at Galerie Iris Clert, which represented Yves Klein and Jean Tinguely, with the first presentation of his ZERO reliefs. In the autumn of 1960, he took part in the *2ème Festival d'art d'avant-garde*, a legendary event in the revolutionary atmosphere of that year, when the Nouveau Réalisme around Yves Klein emerged as an early response to ZERO and American Pop Art.[17] This was followed in December 1961 by a second solo exhibition on the Seine, this time at Galerie Denise René, one of the most important galleries for new art with a first-rate roster of artists in the fields of optical and kinetic Concrete Art, also of Latin American origin. It was here that an essential link was established with Mack's later work, which was broader than that of the ZERO aesthetic. In 1964, the artist was represented at *Le Salon Comparaisons*, one of the most important annual exhibitions, in the survey show *L'Art jeune contemporain en Allemagne*, and in 1965 at the 4th Paris Biennale, founded in 1959 by André Malraux,[18] who awarded him a prize.[19] In 1973, the Musée d'art moderne de la Ville de Paris showed Mack's work in the first solo exhibition of a living German artist in this museum since 1945 (fig. pp. 34 f.), curated by André Berne-Jouffroy, a curator of the highest calibre. The catalogue offers a different interpretation of the work than on this side of the Rhine.

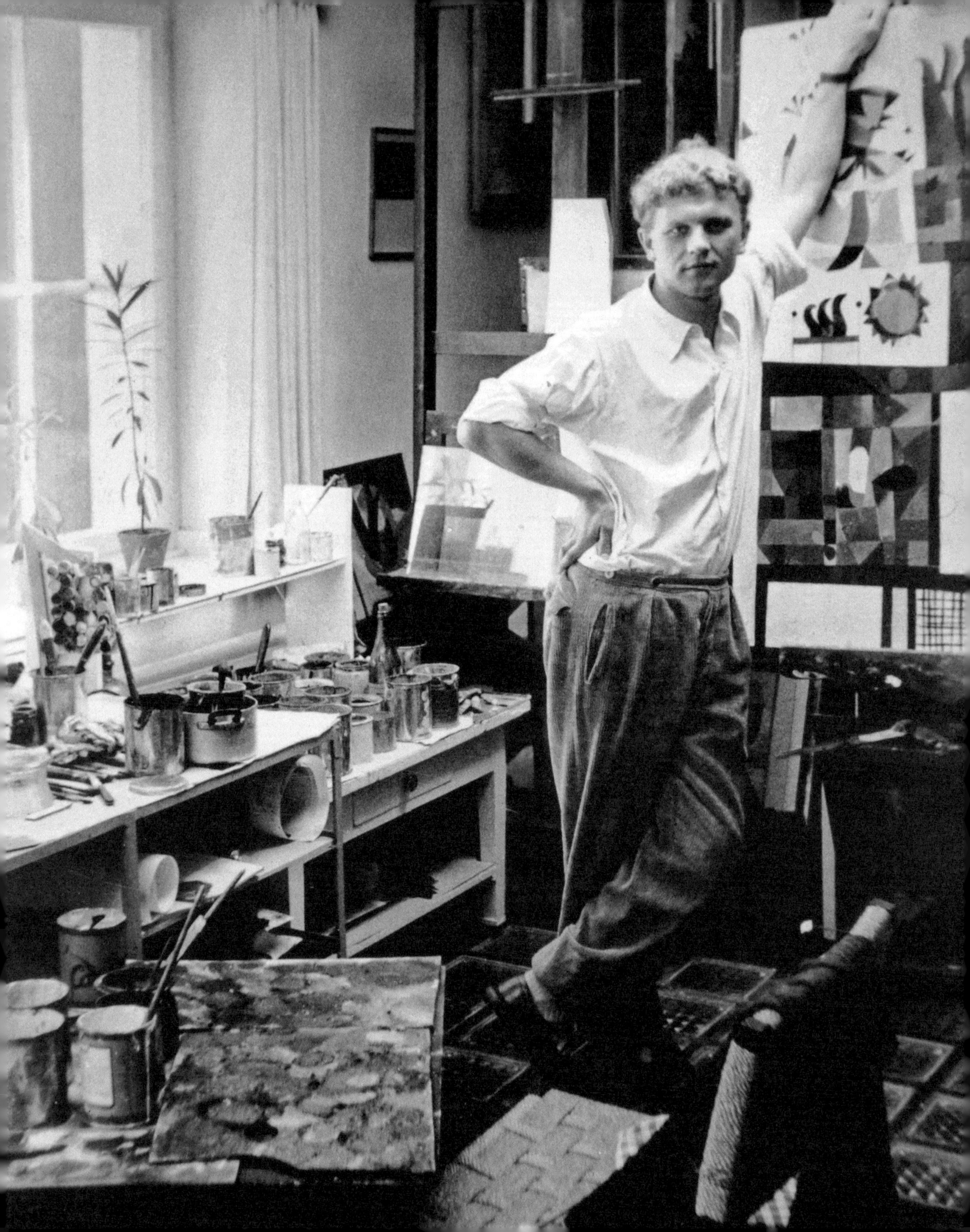

EARLY PAINTINGS

Heinz Mack in his studio
at Herzogstraße 44,
Düsseldorf
c. 1952

During our visit to the Huppertzhof in September 2023, Heinz Mack shows us the paintings he has prepared. As always, he is very solemn and serious, as if a lot depends on it here and now. This is his way, his personality, his character. Like few artists, he has a certain understanding of order and diligence, even of moral duty. At the same time, he smiles at his seriousness and has his own sense of humour, even about himself. You can always tell that he takes great pleasure in making art and working with the material. Today he is more tense than usual. It's obviously about something special.

» My time at university had nothing to do with a normal period of study.
(SEPTEMBER 2023) «

» These are the oldest paintings I still possess (figs. pp. 41, 48). Most of the others have either been given away or lost. I've now done something that was quite laborious: I've cleaned all the old paintings again, put a protective film on them and put mouldings around them. When I did the paintings, a third of the Düsseldorf Academy of Art was still in ruins; the building had partly collapsed (fig. p. 27). I first had to clear away the bricks so that I would have a place to work. I found these old stretcher frames in the boiler room. It was the cheapest material available. I couldn't afford any canvas at all, nettle cloth at best. So I went to a clothes shop in Königsallee, charmed the young salesgirls as best I could and asked: 'Haven't you got any nettle cloth left? I've got some money in my pocket.' It was all very sad. It seemed important to me to preserve these paintings now. They were made between 1950 and 1954. Some of them are not up to par. But I can't deny that I did them.
(SEPTEMBER 2023) «

Only gradually does it become clear that these are early paintings he wants to show us, from his time as a student at the Düsseldorf Academy Art and after. They had previously been stored in a warehouse.

The paintings from his student days show a study of modernism. The surviving works from 1950 to 1954[20] show two strands of development. One is based on the experience of Miró's works during his stay in Paris in 1950 (p. 32) and attempts to find a basis for his own artistic work against this background. Another decisive influence in this line is Paul Klee. The corresponding paintings are small-scale, puzzle-like, in a combination of linear signs, especially arrows, and chessboard-like or freely arranged areas of colour. From today's perspective, this could be seen as a foreshadowing of later works. However, it probably has more to do with a consistent sensibility than a conceptual relationship. The pictorial idea and pictorial thought of the early paintings have no inkling of the independence of structure and rhythm and thus have virtually no connection with the artist's later work. It is striking that these works have nothing to do with other German painting of the 1950s – with the abstraction of Art Informel or Willi Baumeister, or with figurative, expressionist works such as those by Karl Hofer – but rather with the École de Paris and its poetics. There are no more than ten paintings from this period. They are made up of pieces of nettle cloth, packing paper, or wooden surfaces put together in a makeshift manner.

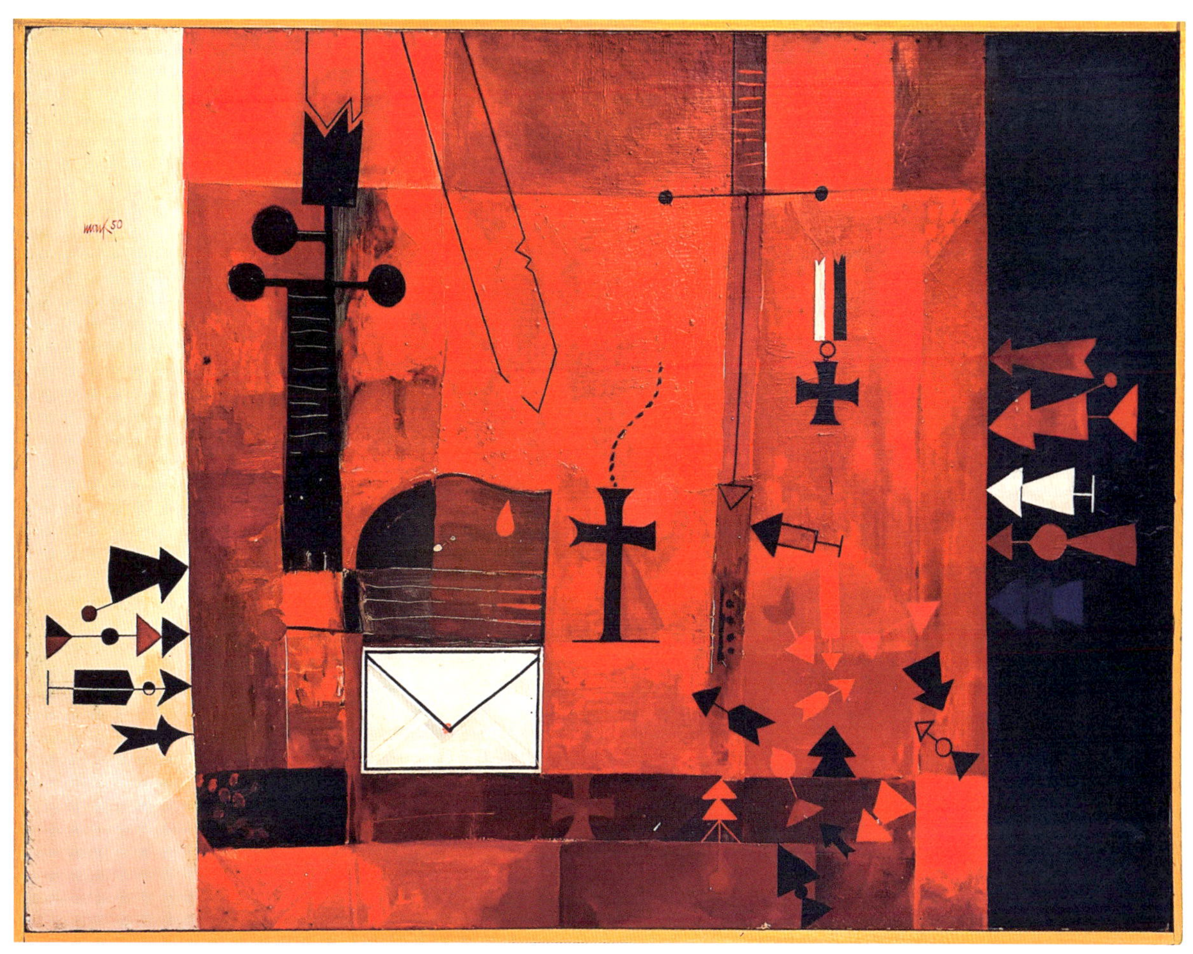

Untitled
1950

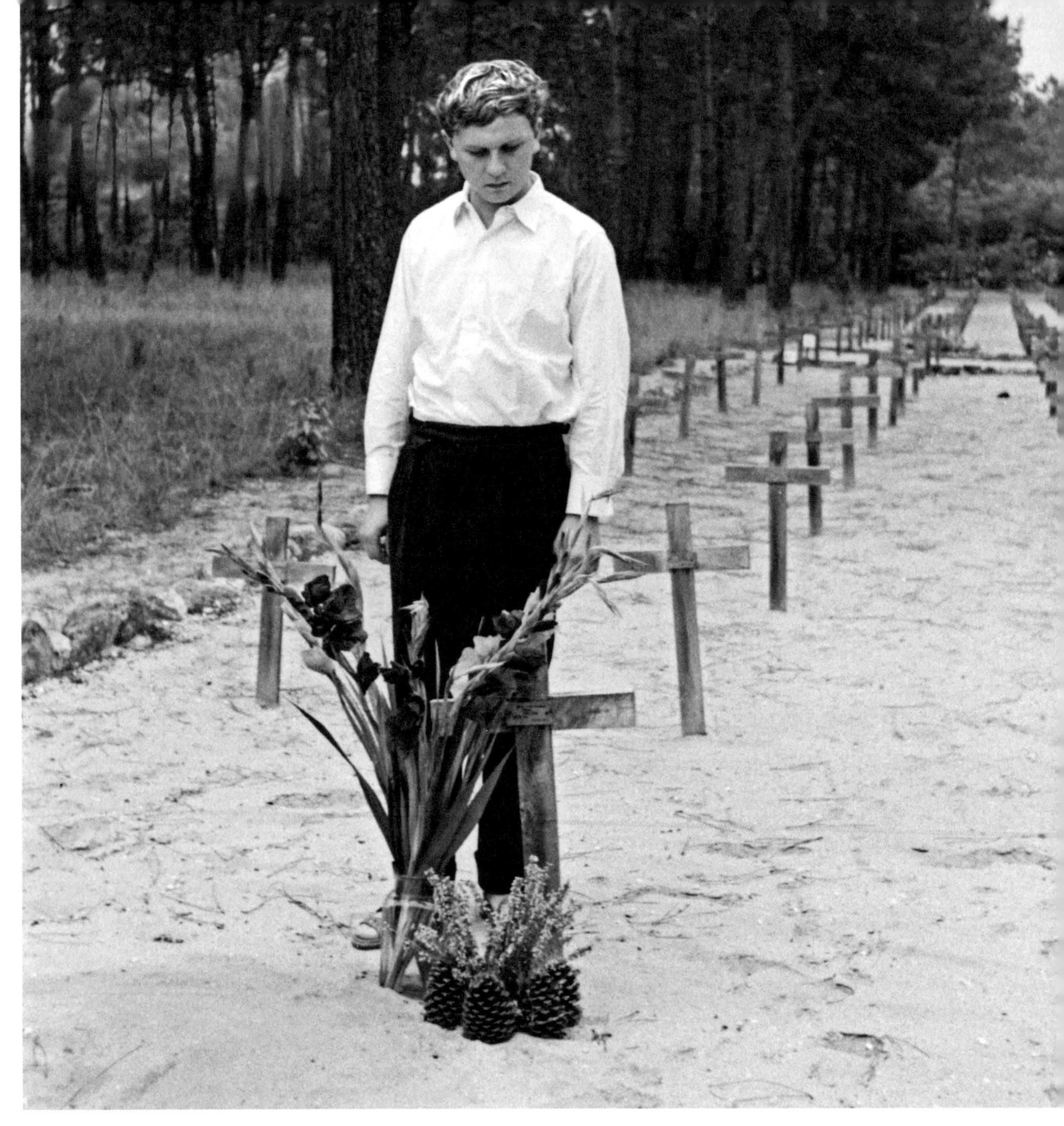

Mack at his father's
grave near Bordeaux
1948

The artist has prepared a painting on an easel. Hardly anyone has ever seen such a 'Mack'. The picture inspired by Miró was painted in 1950 (fig. p. 41). But everything is different from Miró. The ground is monochrome red. Heinz Mack says: 'Because I had no other colour.' Miró's signs can be seen on the surface: arrows, a cross, but also a direct piece of reality with a painted envelope, as in the *papiers collés* by Georges Braque and Pablo Picasso from 1912 onwards. It is a dramatic painting. It refers to the letter notifying the family of the death of Mack's father in a prisoner-of-war camp near Bordeaux. The signs reminiscent of Miró and the monochrome ground nevertheless give the painting an abstract quality.

One should not try to read into this painting any anticipation of his later work. There are radical breaks in between. It is all the more interesting that Heinz Mack retrieved the painting in the late summer of 2023, restored it and inscribed on the reverse: 'Painted in 1950 and cleaned and restored by myself in 2023'. A return to the beginning. For the painting represents such a beginning. Like many beginnings, there is something awkward about it. The borrowings from Picasso and Miró had been transformed into a 'thought-image', a *memento mori*. It is about loss, war, mourning, emptiness.[21]

»

You say that my early work actually has nothing to do with German painting of the 1950s. It's more École de Paris. Yes, I can also say very succinctly, as far as one can say it at all: compared to what my fellow students were doing, it's something completely different. If anything, they were all influenced by German post-war Expressionism. In some cases, I was not taken very seriously.

« (SEPTEMBER 2023)

»

My father didn't come back from the war in 1945. We didn't know whether he was alive or not. My mother, my sister and I had to wait three years before the International Red Cross finally told us that he had died of typhus in a French prisoner-of-war camp near Bordeaux and had been buried there. I was seventeen years old. I went to Bordeaux without my mother's permission, as she was against it at first. I still don't know how I got there. I actually found my father's grave, and someone took a photo with my camera (fig. p. 42). That photo meant a lot to my mother. I painted the picture two years later (fig. p. 41). It's an attempt to come to terms with it. You can see the letter and my father's medals from the First World War. You can see the influence of Miró. It seemed like a viable path. When I spoke enthusiastically about Miró at the academy, nobody knew who he was, not even the professors. I soon gave up on the Miró story.

« (SEPTEMBER 2023)

»

Germany was a graveyard. The older pupils at the secondary school were very successful early on in bartering and on the black market. The headmaster, a former lieutenant commander and officer, still wore his uniform. The German teacher had only one leg. A crutch served as the other. He had been wounded as a tank driver. He drummed

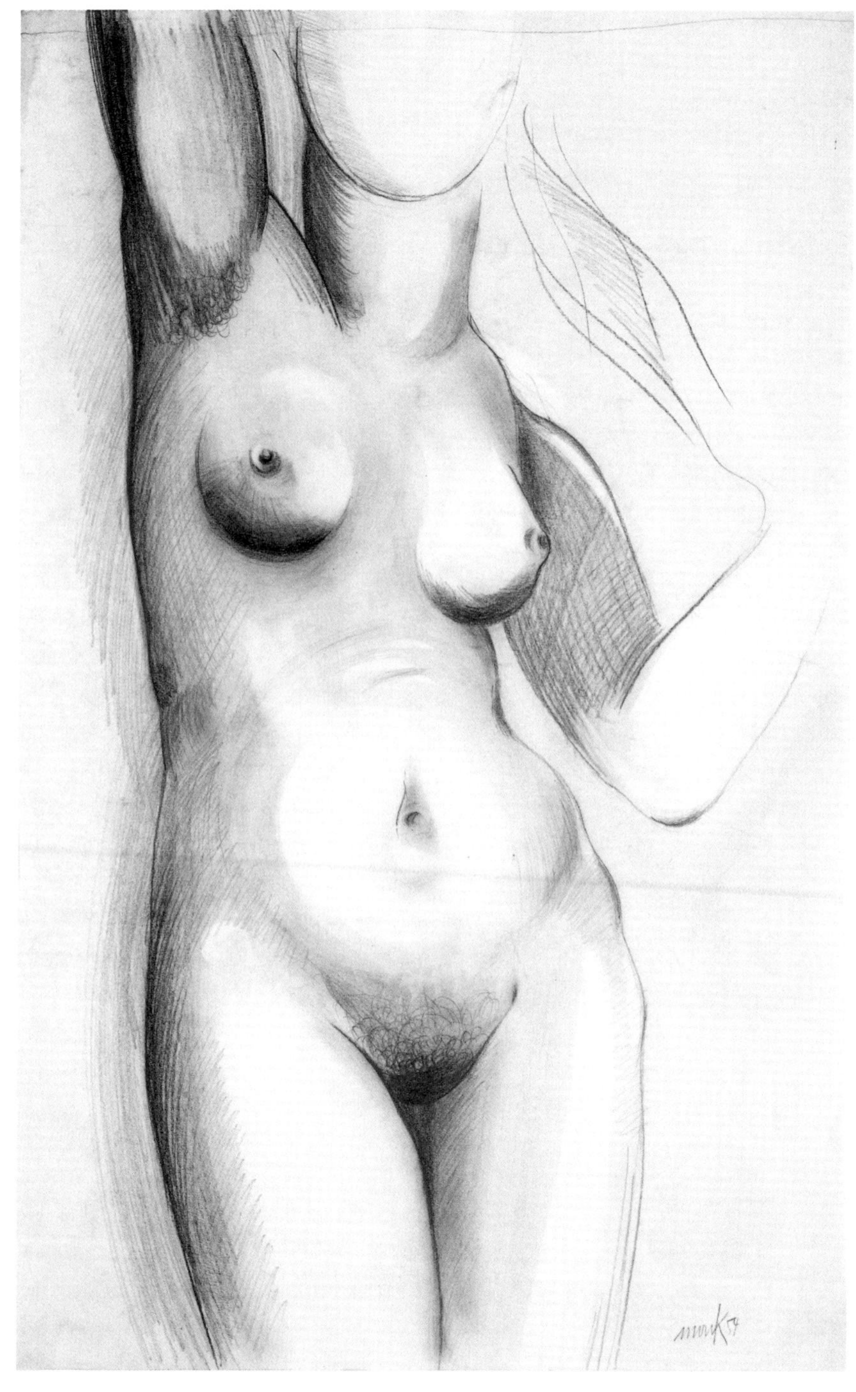

Untitled (Female Nude)
1954

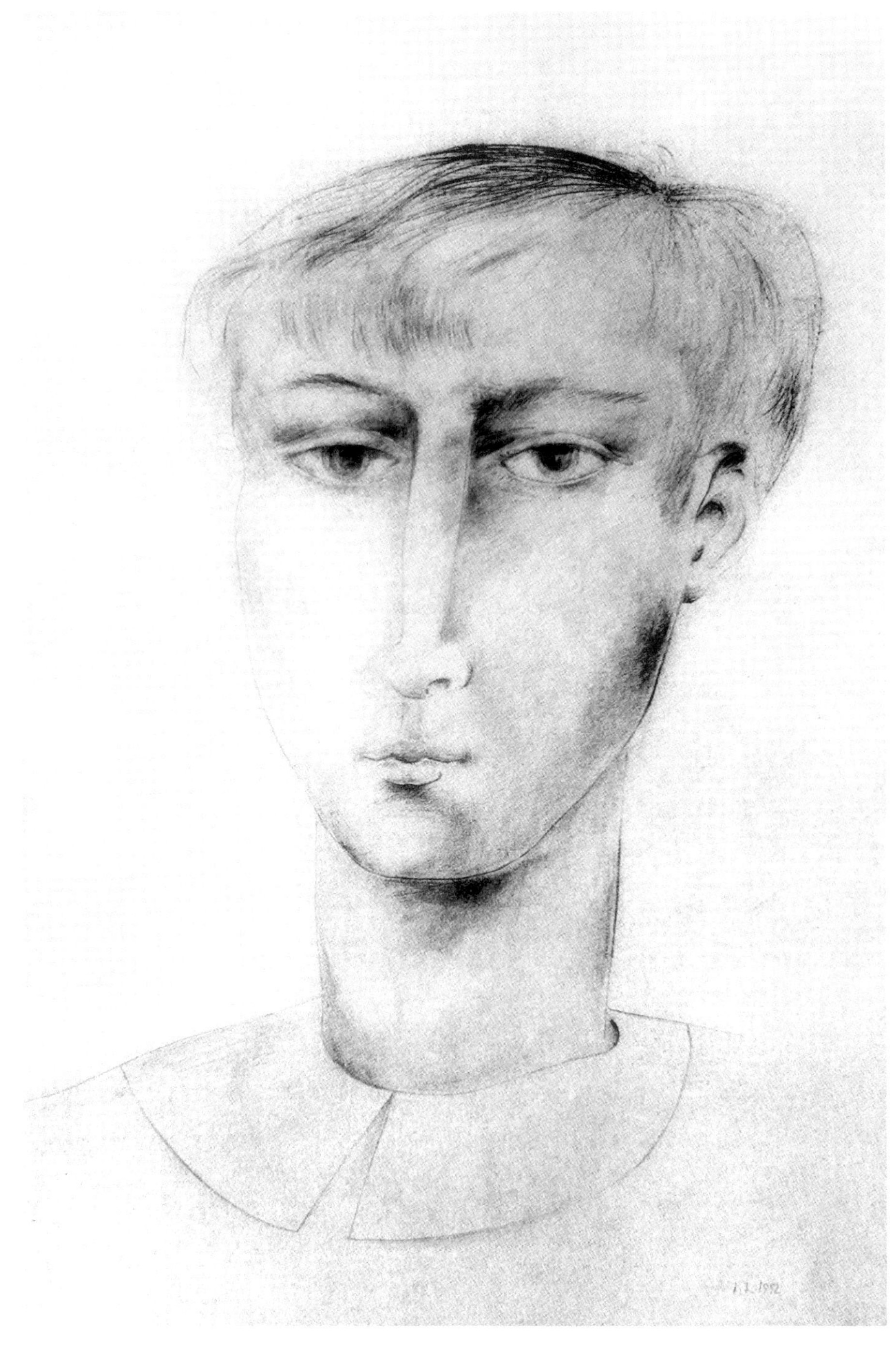

Self-Portrait
1952

into our heads: How do you get out of here mentally? Study Goethe! He went on to teach philosophy at the university in Münster. So we did a lot of philosophical things. Now I'm the last survivor of our class. Even around 1950, the atmosphere was more depressive than positive. Of course there was the upswing, the famous upswing that began at that time. But there was also a great tendency towards melancholy. There were a lot of suicides. My first wife's father also committed suicide, which is sad. He was a very intelligent man. It was a very apathetic atmosphere we lived in at that time.

(SEPTEMBER 2023) «

»

What were the most important decisions? At the age of ten, without my parents' knowledge, I enrolled myself in secondary school. My father was at war, my mother in Krefeld, and my grandmother, with whom I had been evacuated to the countryside in Lollar in Hesse, wasn't interested. In 1949, before I had even finished school in Krefeld, I applied to the Düsseldorf Academy of Art and was accepted a year later, after I had passed my A-levels.[22] I didn't want to be a pianist under any circumstances – but what else was there to consider? And in 1956 I had the feeling that I'd learned a lot and tried a lot, not without success, with a group exhibition at the Kaiser Wilhelm Museum in Krefeld and other things. But the decision was: I want to forget everything, have nothing to do with it anymore. I have to start all over again.

(SEPTEMBER 2023) «

The second strand of development that runs through the painting of these years is different. Here, the nineteen to twenty-three-year-old art student Heinz Mack tried to find a feeling for the large form, for a structure of forms that encompassed the entire surface of the painting. Towards the end of his studies, he produced very interesting paintings such as *Untitled* from 1953 (fig. p. 48). There is a great deal of talent and already a sense of autonomy in the layering of the fields of colour. What is striking, however, is that each painting was a new first attempt and strikingly different from the previous one, with recognisable elements of essential modernist painting from the first half of the twentieth century. They were tried out, so to speak, bit by bit.

Among the early paintings, there is one on a found piece of wood that is surprisingly lyrical, without the internal contrasts that characterise the other paintings from this period. Mack now turns it over and says that it was covered with a varnish that has ruined it over the decades, which is why it cannot be restored: 'I'm going to destroy it.' Otherwise, his work might be misjudged in the future.

The years immediately after the war can be summed up with a few incidents. Heinz Mack kept a flower painting with the inscription 'Winter 1947 Heinz Mack'. In a letter to a school friend, he describes how, after being evacuated during the war to Lollar in Hesse – where he was born in 1931 before growing up in Krefeld – he went back to live with his grandmother and aunt in the countryside because there was not enough to eat in the Rhineland in the immediate post-war years.[23] He remembers that, during a meal that his mother had prepared for his older sister and him, tears suddenly ran down her cheeks. When asked why she was crying, she replied: 'Because I can't still your hunger.' Heinz Mack's sister Lieselotte, whom he considered to be more talented than himself, decided to leave school before her A-levels in order to bring money home. These years left a lasting impression on the artist. The situation continued during his student years.

In the first decade after the war, Heinz Mack developed an indignation that continues to permeate his artistic personality, his 'habitus', to use Pierre Bourdieu's term, to this day. Like very few important artists of his generation, he is marked by a constant, even daily, indignation. How this is expressed in his work, how it may lead to its reinterpretation, remains a question for younger generations of scholars.

»

It says here: 'For my mother', 1954. My mother was a very simple woman. So she had to put up with me becoming an artist. I painted this harbour view of the Mediterranean for her for Christmas. It's a terribly kitschy painting. But I can't throw it away, for my mother's sake.

« (SEPTEMBER 2023)

»

Back then, I didn't have the money to rent my own room. So I was always very happy when I found a bed somewhere with friends or colleagues. Hans Salentin lay on one cot and Walter Cüppers on another. The space between them was just wide enough for me to lie down. Walter Cüppers's wooden leg lay next to me. These are things you never forget. For a while, I lived in the academy without permission. I slept on the platform where the nude model stood during the day.[24] The caretaker liked me and turned a blind eye. One day a visitor from the ministry came and found my socks hanging on a line to dry. I was almost expelled. I also looked for any way I could to earn money. Once I wore an advertisement for Persil detergent. I had to carry a whole advertising pillar and walk through the old town, humiliated by passers-by. I didn't really like that job.

« (SEPTEMBER 2023)

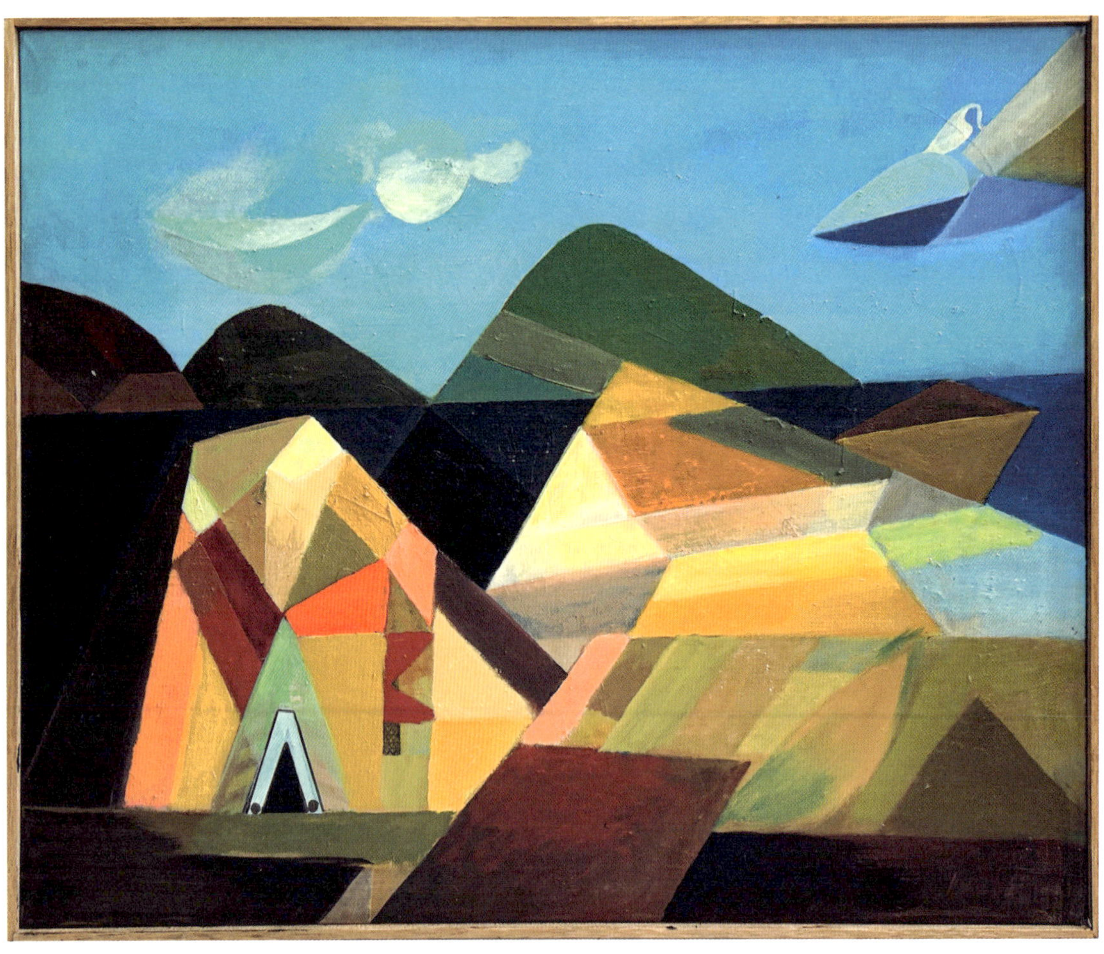

Untitled
1953

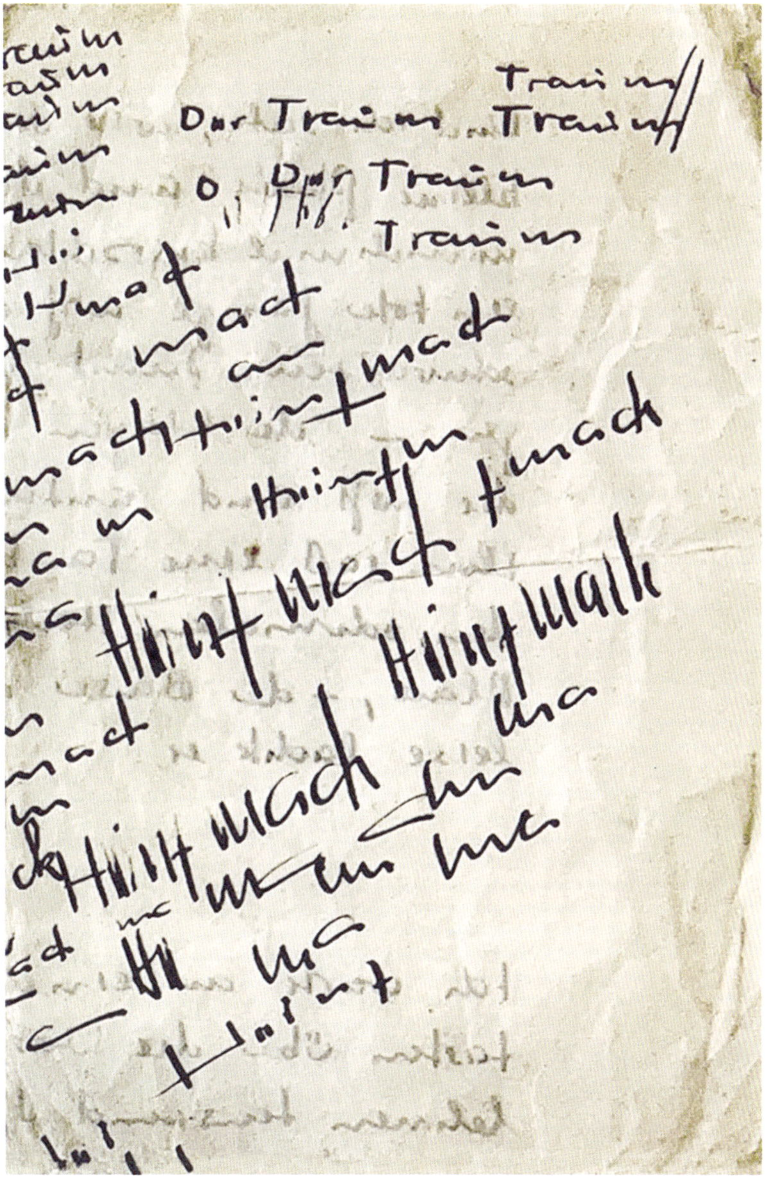

Handwriting experiments on
the way to a signature
c. 1950

Was there a 'zero hour' for post-war art in Germany?[25] This question has been the subject of endless debate in art history and art criticism since 1950. Given the great continuity in personnel and artistic practice, there was no such thing as a 'zero hour' for German post-war art. For Heinz Mack's generation, the real 'zero hour' of German post-war art was the silence of the older generation about what had happened between 1933 and 1945, and their outrage at it.[26] The student Mack reacted to this with a curiosity that is rarely encountered. To this day, it structures his actions. His intellectual goal was to escape the void, to understand what had happened and to gain from it a relationship to the world.

»

In all seriousness, I would like to mention the fact that during my entire time at school, not once, not a single word was said about what the Nazi era was and why the war ended. What was it all about? It was an absolute taboo. Why was Germany now a country occupied by foreign powers who won the war? When I came to the academy, I really wanted to know if they had an answer to what happened during the Nazi era, what happened in art until 1933. None of the teachers said anything about this, not even the man who was responsible for art history. Soon I wanted to know: What kind of people are teaching here? Otto Pankok was the only artist at the academy who was prepared to show the students what he himself was doing during that period. During the Nazi era, he had been a passionate advocate for the Sinti and Roma minority and was against the entire Nazi order.

(SEPTEMBER 2023) «

Heinz Mack's original life plans were centred around music. A music teacher in Giessen recognised his extraordinary talent for the piano at an early age. Mack was trained as a pianist while still at secondary school. After the war, it was initially forbidden to go out after dark. With lessons after school, Mack often returned to Lollar late. Once, while walking home alone in the dark after his piano lesson, a drunken occupying soldier severely injured his left hand with a broken beer bottle. His little finger was almost severed. Due to the circumstances, he received emergency treatment from a vet at the veterinary clinic. A career as a pianist was now out of the question.

»

The first art exhibition in Düsseldorf was held at the Kunstpalast in 1952. It was called – here it comes – *Eisen und Stahl* (Iron and Steel). I took a very close look at it. 'Iron and steel' was, of course, the slogan par excellence for the barbaric German-ness that had begun in the First World War. The catalogue begins with fifty steel barons of the Ruhr region. The whole thing was a shameless self-promotion of the industry, and they sold it as art. I found it unbearable. Among the 550 participants were all artists who had been stars during the Nazi era. So that's already an issue.

(SEPTEMBER 2023) «

The cultural scene in Krefeld was small but of high quality. In the house of the parents of Klaus Jürgen-Fischer, a classmate, there were strange pictures on the wall, including a large-format print of a blue horse motif by Franz Marc. It was the first modernist picture Mack ever saw.[27] Although it was 1948 – the founding of the Federal Republic of Germany was imminent – he was firmly told not to talk about it. With the help of his father, Karl Georg Fischer, Klaus Jürgen-Fischer and Heinz Mack printed a school newspaper: *Der Einfaltspinsel* (The Simpleton). Mack was then summoned to the headmaster's office, as any publication had to be approved by the British military authorities. Mack's justification was that we were now living in a democracy and that pupils should therefore also have the right to express their own opinions. The newspaper still exists in his archive. A second issue was not printed. In 1949, Karl Georg Fischer founded the art book publishing house Agis-Verlag für bildende Kunst in Krefeld, which in 1955 took over *Das Kunstwerk*, for many years the leading art magazine in West Germany. Klaus Jürgen-Fischer, who had studied painting with Mack at the Düsseldorf Art Academy, became editor-in-chief. The two fell out over ZERO in 1958.

»

Even later, in Krefeld, where I lived again from 1947 onwards, there were no official concerts because the concert halls had burned down. That's why house concerts were organised. I had to show off my talent there from time to time. That made an incredible impression on me as a pupil. Because before that I had only been in the village in Lollar. That's a great memory for me. I had piano lessons with a demanding teacher, Prof. Dr Wolf von Brandis, until I graduated from secondary school. But I also realised that practising as a pianist for six hours a day was not my thing. So the injury that prevented such a career ultimately worked in my favour, as painful as it was at the time. As an A-level pupil, I drew a lot and gave sheets to classmates who helped me with my homework.

« (SEPTEMBER 2023)

»

For a long time, German art book publishers rarely published anything about modern art, which had been condemned by the Nazis. Even the 1955 documenta in Kassel showed only artists over sixty. That changed with Expo 58 in Brussels, which showed younger contemporary art, including American art. Some people knew a bit more before that. But not us young artists. Otto Piene and Günther Uecker knew as little as I did.

« (SEPTEMBER 2023)

»

The philosophy professor I chose at the University of Cologne was extremely demanding. His colleagues' lecture theatres were full to bursting. With Bruno Liebrucks, there were only ten of us. He could not be fooled. You had to know Latin. Ancient Greek was also on the syllabus. Before the final exam, he used a typewriter to write a text for me to analyse. The subject had absolutely nothing to do with me. Five minutes before the exam, I said to him. 'We were talking about something completely different.' He rushed off, came back and had written a new text that I could do something with.

(SEPTEMBER 2023) «

To study art education, you had to take a second subject. Mack chose philosophy at the University of Cologne,[28] as did his fellow student and friend Otto Piene. Studying philosophy is demanding. You learn that philosophy is a precise craft in which you have to deal with concepts very meticulously. In Mack's case, the study of philosophy had a profound effect on his artistic work. When Mack deals with the dimensions of light, time, and structure, he knows their philosophical history inside out.[29]

Two philosophical currents that one would not expect at first glance in his later oeuvre have played a significant role since his student days: firstly, phenomenology. Heinz Mack took his state examination in philosophy in 1956 on Nicolai Hartmann, who, as a neo-Kantian in the 1920s, had switched to this twentieth-century philosophical movement initiated by Edmund Husserl and Martin Heidegger, but kept his distance from Heidegger's ideologically ambivalent esotericism.[30] Hartmann had taught in Göttingen until 1950. They were therefore in the immediate present. Mack worked with the published transcripts of his lectures from 1949. From phenomenology, the artist derived intentionality as a principle of cognition, without which the concept of his art would not be possible. The same applies to other principles of phenomenology, such as that appearance is not appearance but truth, while being in the world excludes any dualism, including that of artwork and recipient. Phenomenology is a secret key to Mack's work.

From today's perspective, there is an interesting aspect to this. The young Michel Foucault, like the whole generation of French structuralist and post-structuralist philosophers about five years older than Heinz Mack, was interested in Husserl's phenomenology, which was all the rage in France in the 1950s. In his aborted dissertation project, he describes it as an opportunity for philosophy to escape the traps of psychology.[31] This, too, is a key to Heinz Mack's work, in which the de-psychologisation of art is taken to an extreme, which can serve as an inspiration for many approaches to his work.

Secondly, Heinz Mack was interested in existential philosophy.[32] From this he derived his profoundly serious attitude, according to which art and art-making are only justified if they have a profound existential dimension and are practised accordingly. This excludes, for

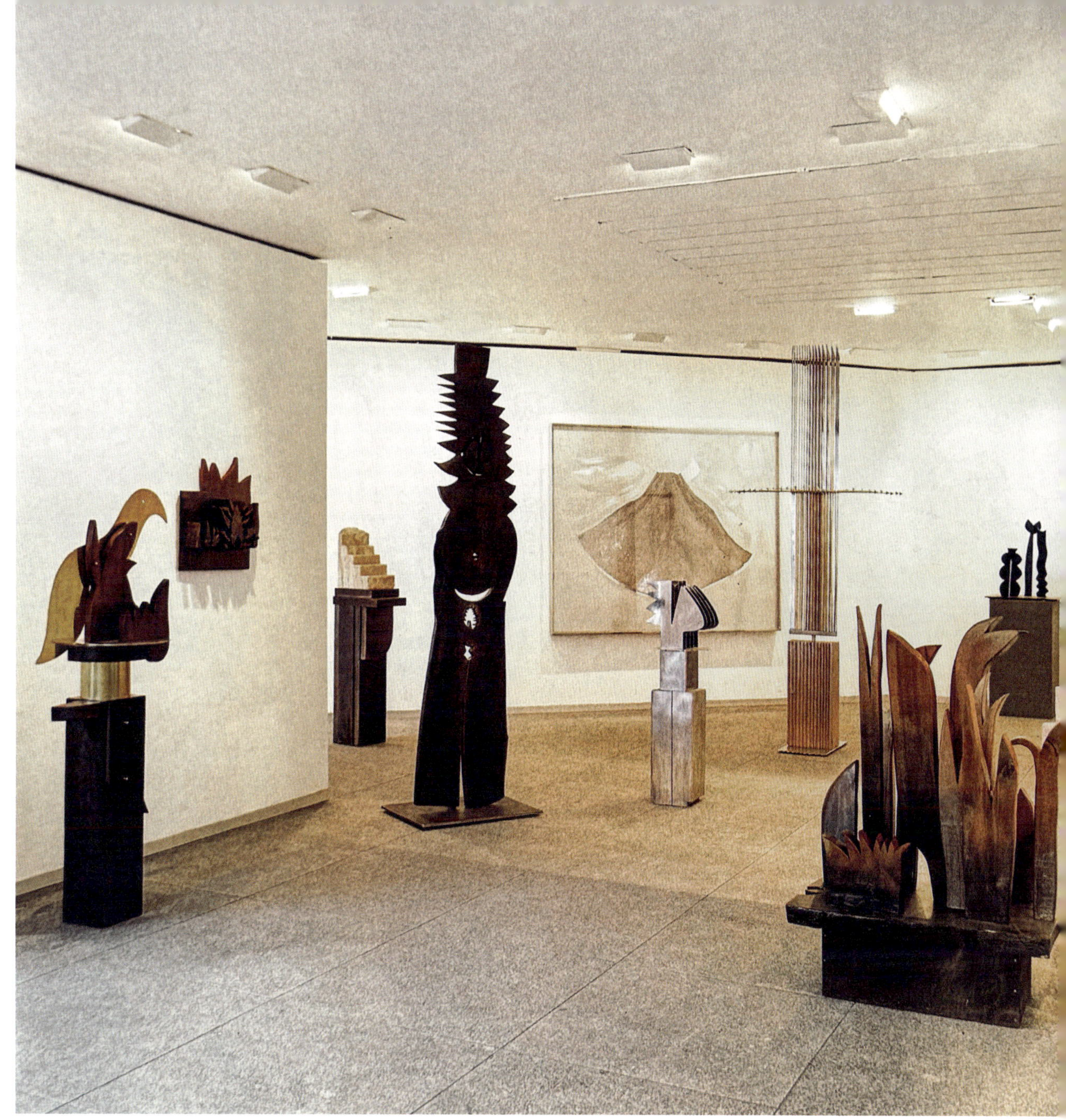

Installation view
Heinz Mack. Unbekannte Skulpturen, 1954–1984,
Galerie Denise René – Hans Mayer, Düsseldorf
1984

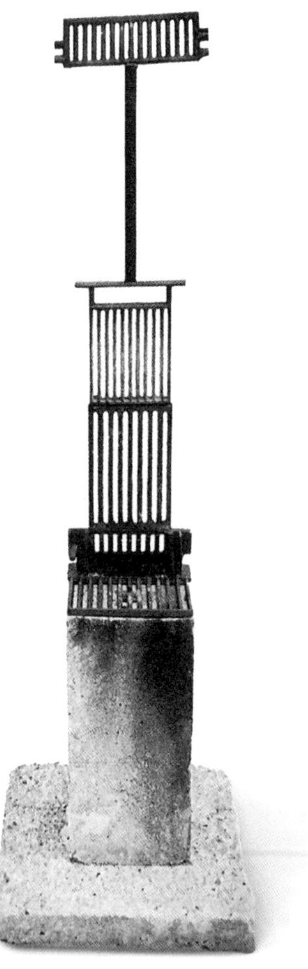

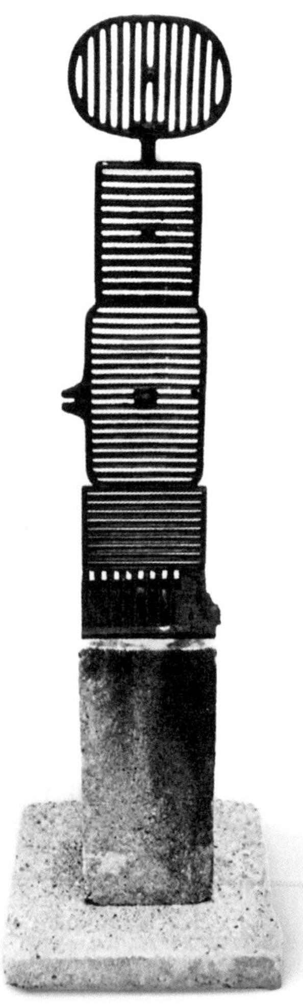

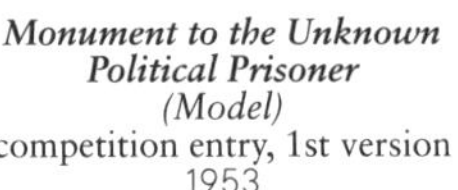

Monument to the Unknown Political Prisoner
(Model)
competition entry, 1st version
1953

Monument to the Unknown Political Prisoner
(Model)
competition entry, 2nd version
1953

example, the use of irony as an artistic medium. At the same time, this attitude has the advantage that it is not necessary to use expressionist means to achieve great intensity of expression, but that pure, non-functional means of expression are more appropriate.

At the Düsseldorf Academy of Art, art history lectures took place in the reconstructed assembly hall. There was no lecture theatre. Only a few books in the library had escaped the Nazi destruction of documents on modern art. They were passed around during the lecture so that the students could look at the black-and-white illustrations.

Heinz Mack read *Problematik der Gegenwartskunst* (The Problem of Contemporary Art) by Wilhelm Worringer early on, published in 1948 as a slim volume without illustrations. The art historian, who had provided German Expressionism with theoretical support in 1908 with *Abstraktion und Einfühlung* (Abstraction and Empathy), thus produced the first competent book on the essential artistic questions of the post-war period alongside Willi Baumeister's *Vom Unbekannten in der Kunst* (The Unknown in Art), published in 1947. This created points of contact between the generations.

The artist from whom Heinz Mack learned most during his studies was the sculptor and graphic artist Ewald Mataré. He had been appointed to Düsseldorf in 1931 thanks to Paul Klee, who was dismissed after the Nazis seized power and reinstated in 1945 (Klee had died in 1940). Mack's sculptural work is still characterised today by the fact that he worked alongside Mataré at his workbench on his own first sculptural experiments, mainly in wood. Mataré allowed his students to work alongside him on an equal footing, as was said at the time, in accordance with the medieval concept of the masons' lodge, which he tried in vain to impose on the entire art academy. Mack's relief-like wooden sculptures – developed from his nature drawings after Johann Wolfgang von

»

The very first book I read by Albert Camus was definitely Sisyphus.[33] It fascinated me because I found a connection with Voltaire's *Candide*. I was interested in everything that had to do with the war, because I wanted to know what had happened there. For example, I read Grimmelshausen's *Simplicissimus*, about the Thirty Years' War. I also studied Sartre's writings on Judaism.[34] And at the same time, as a young man, I saw no leading figure at all. There was Gandhi, Albert Einstein, Albert Schweitzer, also in terms of music, and the then President of the Federal Republic, Theodor Heuss, was a personality who radiated something like humanity.

« (SEPTEMBER 2023)

»

My mother had implored me: 'Please, if you want to be an artist, at least become a teacher so that you can earn money.' But that also led me to Ewald Mataré. I went to him and said: 'I promised my mother that I would become a teacher. But I want to become a sculptor, and actually wanted to study with you.' He said he was not allowed to take students into his class because his colleagues had agreed not to. After he said that, he paused for a long time, and I took that silence to mean: you can be my guest if you need me, if you want to know something from me. I took that opportunity quite often. What I really learned from him was the language of the material, that wood has its own language, and if you don't understand the language of the material, you can't make anything out of it. He was also the first person to point out to me very clearly that monumentality does not depend on centimetres. He once saw me experimenting with one of these wooden sculptures and said: 'Everything you install outdoors has to be conceived twice as large in the studio. The outdoor space embraces the sculpture so much that if the proportions aren't right, it won't stand up to it.'

« (SEPTEMBER 2023)

Obelisk
forecourt of the Saalhausen primary school,
North Rhine-Westphalia
1952

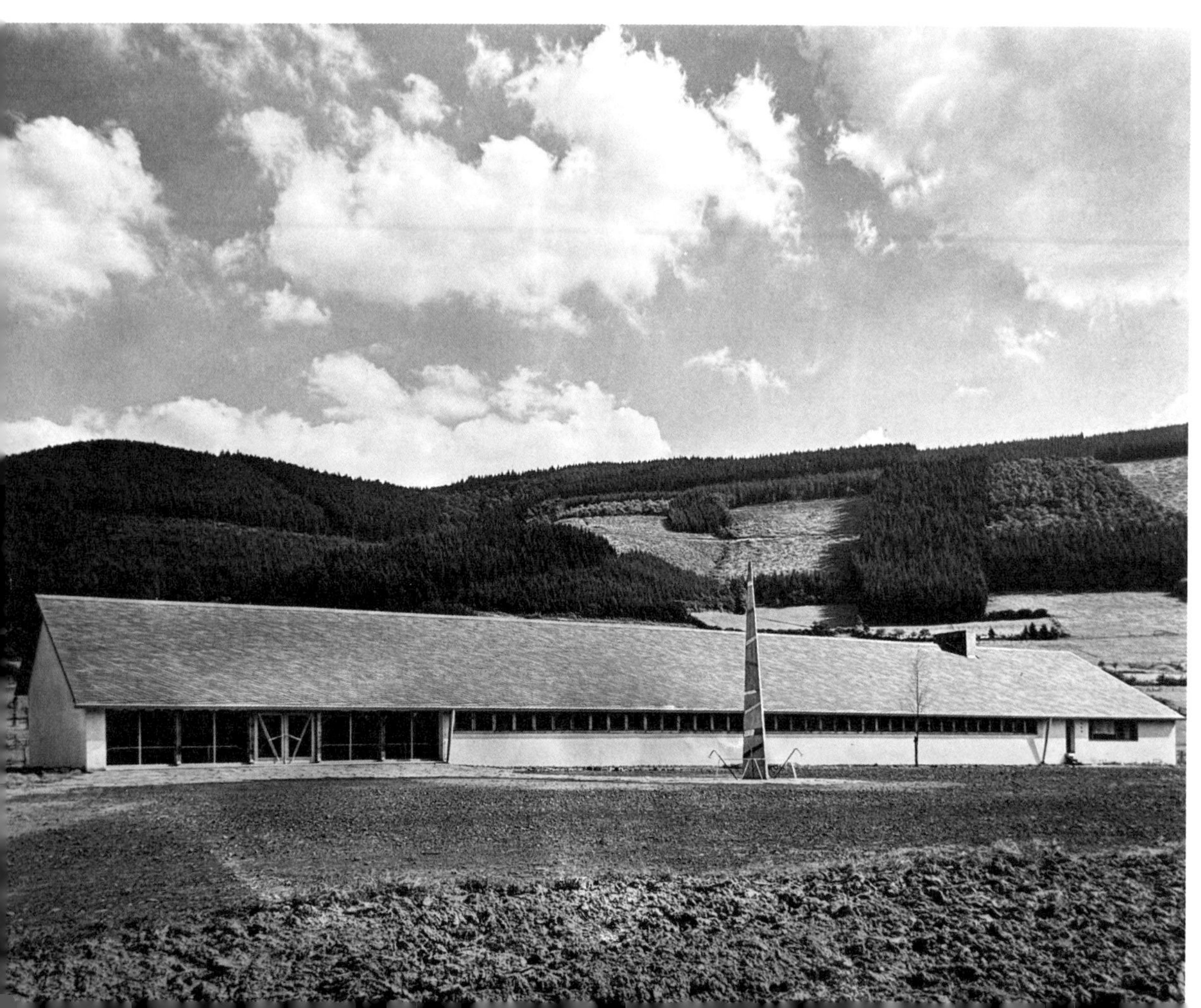

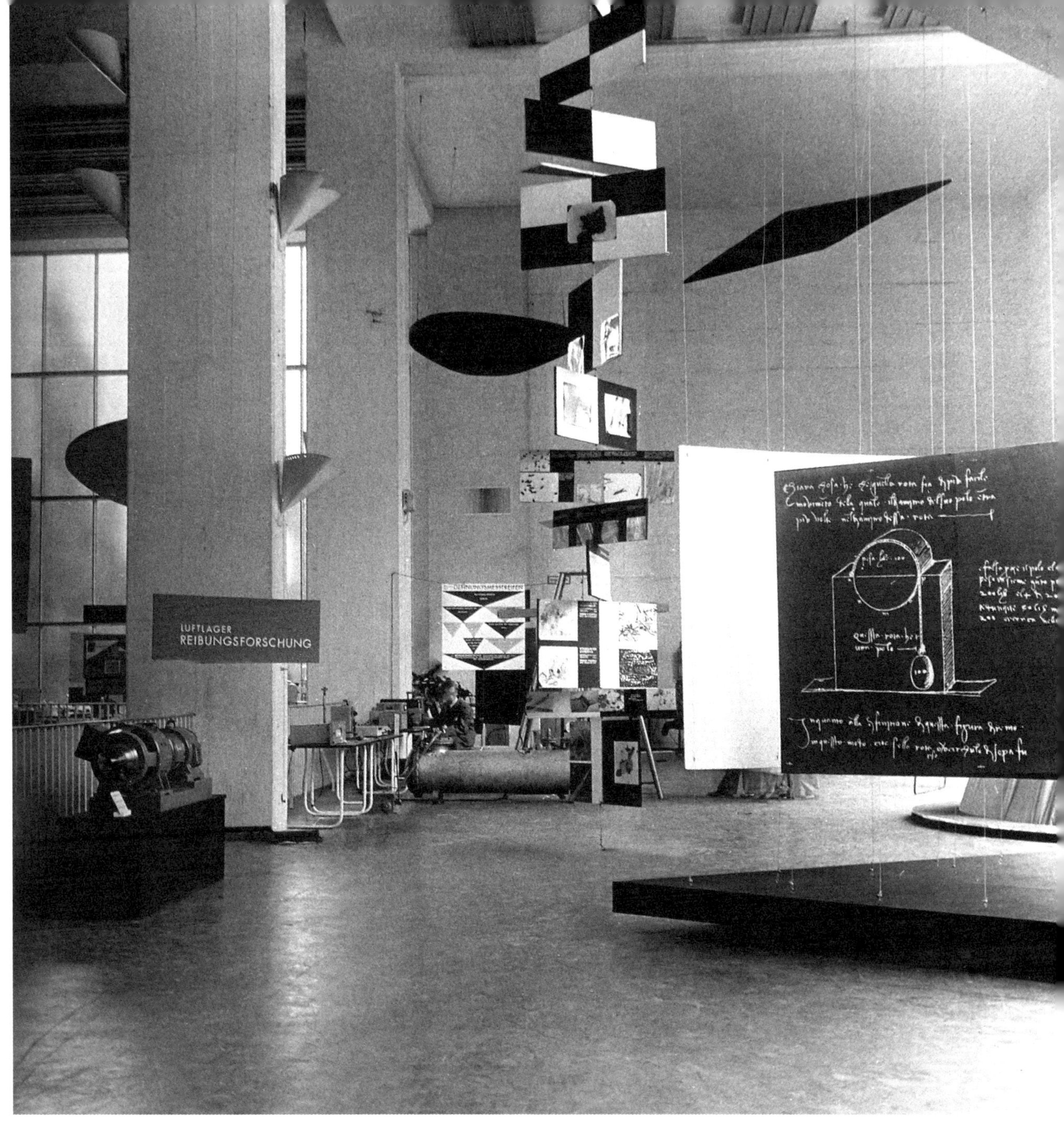

View of the industrial exhibition
Alle sollen besser leben,
Ehrenhof, Düsseldorf
1953

Goethe, pre-structural, naturalistic, and at the same time abstract (fig. p. 53) – are the most enduring element of his early work and have been present in the artist's major museum exhibitions over the last fifteen years. They radiate an inner monumentality, much like Mataré's small sculptures.

» Beuys was ten years older than me. I was the youngest, by the way. I was the youngest in my A-levels, and I was also the youngest at the academy. Now I'm no longer the youngest.
(SEPTEMBER 2023) «

From Mataré, Mack also learned free rhythms and a strong sense of form. On Mataré's advice, he also created large-scale wooden sculptures, often assembled in collage form, one of which stands today in the music room at the Huppertzhof. With the *Obelisk* of 1952 (fig. p. 56), a nine-metre-high, quadrangular stele, which functions as a sundial pointer, accompanied by a drinking fountain and playground, in front of a school building in Saalhausen, the twenty-one-year-old succeeded in making his first convincing statement in a public space. Above all, Mataré taught him how to deal respectfully and dialogically with sculptural materials and their wide range of organic and inorganic elements.

At Mataré's workbench, Mack sometimes worked alongside Joseph Beuys, who was ten years his senior and had served in the Luftwaffe on the Eastern Front during the Second World War. They respected each other until Beuys's untimely death in 1986, although neither artist had much use for the other's approach. They were also far apart ideologically, as evidenced by the fact that Beuys, as head of a sculpture class at the Düsseldorf Academy of Art from 1961 to 1972 and even after, was often dressed in a Nazi Luftwaffe winter coat.

Mack's friendship with Egon Schneider-Esleben, an architecture student of almost the same age, led to an unusual commission in 1953 through the latter's older brother, the already well-known architect Paul Schneider-Esleben. With no previous experience in the field, Heinz Mack and Otto Piene were involved in the design of an industrial fair in Düsseldorf, which offered and propagated designs for the affluent society under the title *Alle sollen besser leben* (Everyone Should Live Better, 1953). The exhibits were presented not on pedestals but on platforms suspended between taut steel cables (fig. p. 57). Mack gave Euclidean forms, which can be developed from straight lines of varying lengths, exciting curves right up to the corners. The seemingly free forms were still reminiscent of the geometry they contained. It was also a critique of the emerging kidney-shaped table aesthetic of the 1950s. Thanks to the steel cables between which they were suspended, the platforms could support great weights. Among the exhibits were the first three American computers to be transported to Germany, each weighing as much as a safe. One of them crashed down in front of the assembled press as it was being lifted onto the platform because the chain broke: a total loss. Nobody was injured. The crane company was at fault, and the students were paid. During the transition from the post-war years to the time of the economic miracle, unimagined opportunities opened up.

All in all, the budding artist was well on his way, especially with his teaching career behind him. In fact, he was one of the best in his graduating class. If there had been an established exhibition and gallery system in the Federal Republic of Germany at that time, as there was in Paris, he would have been integrated there immediately. He would have had exhibitions and lived from the sale of his work. At the same time, he would have been forced to continue his style, which had not yet reached its end, in order to live steadily from the sale of his works. Many artistic talents become interesting but insignificant artists in this way. The institutional misery of art in the post-war period in Germany and the teaching profession, which made Mack financially independent, spared him this. In 1953, together with his fellow student Otto Piene, he joined the newly founded Gruppe 53, which relied on self-organisation in the absence of a professional gallery in Düsseldorf.[36]

»

Looking back, our courage in accepting the commission to design display elements for an industrial trade fair seems to me to have been reckless, as was Paul Schneider-Esleben's courage in passing on such a commission to students. This architect was very interested in modern art, which is quite rare.[35]

« (SEPTEMBER 2023)

»

I spent a whole summer desperately trying to paint in the Tachist style, with the result that I ended up in a really serious artistic crisis.

« IN: MARION AGTHE, 'FRAGEN AN HEINZ MACK', 1993[37]

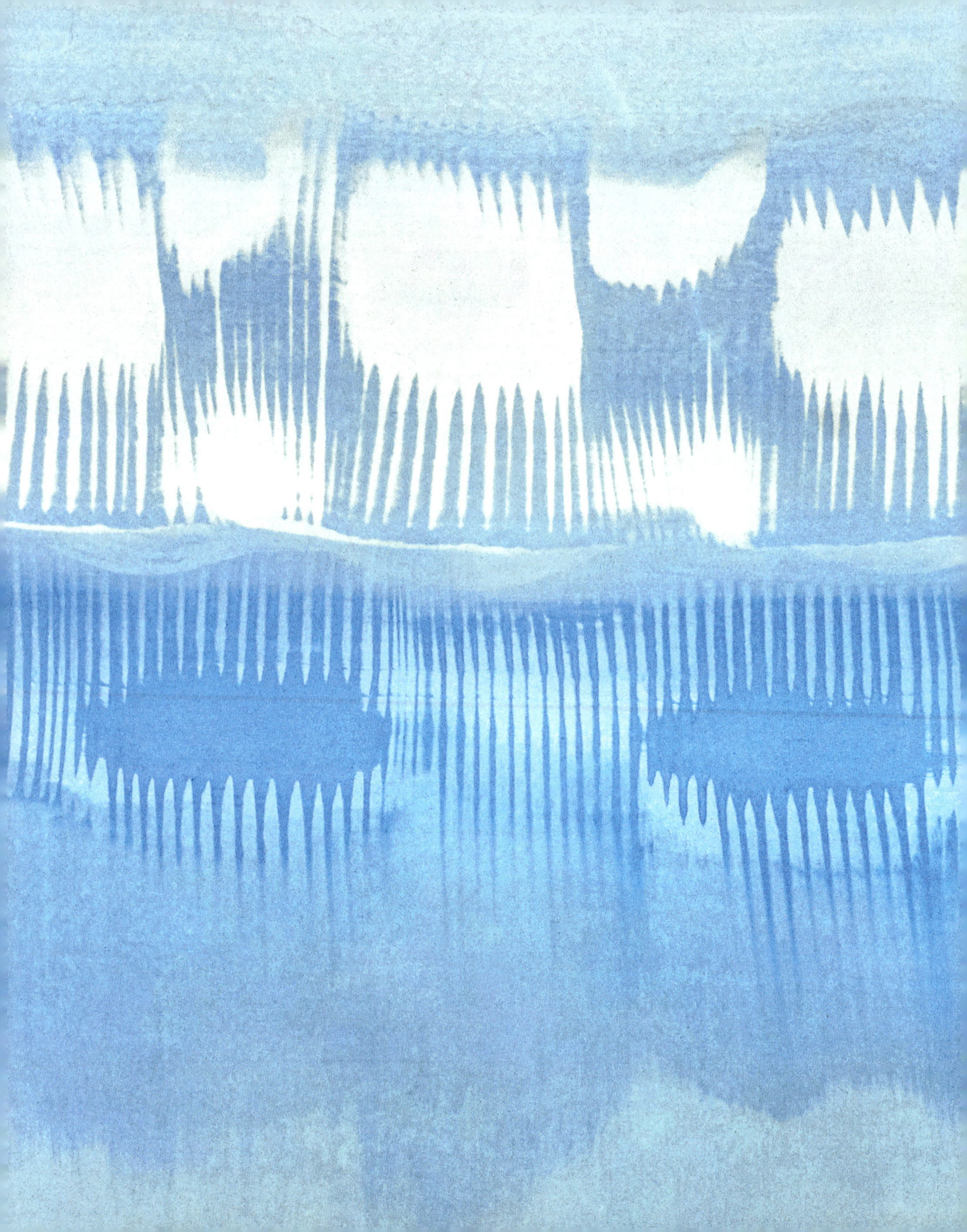

ZERO AND THE BEGINNING OF POSTMODERNISM

The Sky Over Samarkand
(detail)
1963
Premio Marzotto Selezione,
1964

'ZERO! ZERO it shall be called,' exclaimed Heinz Mack or Otto Piene – which of the two is not documented – in March 1958 at an intersection in Düsseldorf, not far from their studios, located next to each other in the same building at Gladbacher Straße 69 (fig. p. 67). The scene was Düsseldorf's Rhine harbour, then still used for trade. The first traffic lights had been installed at intersections. Pedestrians now had to wait for the green light. It was here that one of the two young artists had the quoted epiphany.[38]

Mack and Piene had been students at the Düsseldorf Academy of Art together and were also brothers in spirit for several years. They were both looking for a way out of a personal artistic crisis that was also an objective crisis, namely that of the increasingly exhausted abstract painting of the West German style, which had emerged from the imitation of French Art Informel and Tachism. They practised this kind of painting themselves, but with less and less conviction. As for many artists in the Rhineland, the opening exhibition of Alfred Schmela's gallery in Hunsrückstraße in Düsseldorf's old town in May 1957 was a turning point. It featured monochrome paintings by Yves Klein from Paris.[39] Heinz Mack was instrumental in bringing this show to Düsseldorf.[40] Nevertheless, it was the first exhibition of Yves Klein's work that he saw, and he recognised its impact.

This was the beginning of a new era for art on this side of the Rhine. Klein's *Monochromes* showed that it was possible to work in a completely different way from the gestural abstraction or figurative realism that dominated German post-war art at the time. Alfred Schmela also proved to be an exceptional salesman and organisational talent at this inaugural exhibition. Unlike the gallerists in Paris and Milan, he found buyers for Klein's *Monochromes*,[41] and in the summer of 1957 he placed Klein and his artist friend Jean Tinguely in art projects for the new Musiktheater im Revier in Gelsenkirchen, the largest cultural building in the young Federal Republic of Germany (FRG). It opened in late 1959 with Yves Klein's 270-square-metre wall reliefs – to this day, the largest work of visual art commissioned by the FRG in terms of surface area.

In March 1958, Mack was twenty-seven and Piene almost thirty years old. They were present on the Düsseldorf art scene but had not yet made a name for themselves. The few institutions for contemporary art in the Rhineland were of no help in their search for a new beginning. With the exception of Haus Lange in Krefeld, none of

Dynamic Structure White on Yellow
1963

the museums exhibited works by living artists. The Kunstverein für die Rheinlande und Westfalen in Düsseldorf made a timid attempt to champion post-war abstraction, which was still not accepted by the public. Between 1958 and 1961, neither the Kunstverein nor the Düsseldorf Academy of Art invited Yves Klein to give a lecture or participate in an exhibition, despite his frequent visits to Düsseldorf and the surrounding area. The director of the Kunstverein at the time, Karl-Heinz Hering, later wrote that this was all too new.[42] Artists' alliances such as Gruppe 53, to which Mack and Piene themselves belonged until 1959, and the group Junger Westen in the Ruhr region seemed far too harmless to them. There had to be something else, something more future-oriented, which they thought was somehow possible. But what could it be?

So they had to help themselves. Starting in the spring of 1957, Heinz Mack and Otto Piene repeatedly organised *Evening Exhibitions* in their 'double studio' (fig. p. 66). They took place in Piene's larger space (his things were then temporarily stored in Mack's studio). These *Evening Exhibitions*, each lasting only a few hours, became a sensation. The range of contemporary visual art on offer in West Germany in the years immediately after the war was still small. An *Evening Exhibition* in Mack and Piene's studio could also be a lecture, such as the one given by Max Bense on 10 December 1957 to accompany the presentation of works by Klaus Jürgen-Fischer.[45] Bense, a professor of philosophy from Stuttgart, was alone in West Germany in his embrace of structuralism – in opposition to the mythologising thinking of Martin Heidegger – and in the 1960s he rose to become an international reference in sign theory, along with Roland Barthes and Umberto Eco. In the autumn of 1957, even before defining ZERO's self-image, but during the creation of the first paintings and reliefs now classified as ZERO works, Mack and Piene brought the testimonials and points of reference they were interested in on the way to a new art into their studios with their *Evening Exhibitions*.[46]

The seventh *Evening Exhibition* was held on 24 April 1958. Its title: *Das rote Bild* (The Red Picture). Mack and Piene had invited forty-four artists, both male and female,[47] of different orientations, all

»

Otto Piene and I soon realised that it was wrong to show our work in the context of Gruppe 53.[43] I destroyed my paintings from that period. This went hand in hand with the idea of looking for a completely new beginning and strictly forgetting everything I had learned up to that point. To dare a boundless, completely new beginning – that's what I tried to understand with the help of my musical training as a pianist. Instead of mastering complex tonal structures with ten fingers at the same time, I now only had to strike a single note with one finger. I was looking for a way out, and not just in one direction, but in all directions. I challenged myself not to stand still, but to move. I soon realised that experimentation was essential if the unknown was to come to me. Baumeister's book *The Unknown in Art*[44] was also a key experience for me.

(MAY 2024) «

of whom contributed red pictures.[48] On this occasion, Mack and Piene founded a magazine, for which the word 'ZERO' was chosen as the title. This first issue of *ZERO* is a slim booklet printed on red paper with simple means – technically very basic, but impressive. The word 'ZERO' appears in it and is also printed in capital letters on the invitation card for the exhibition. Later, the orthographic spelling 'Zero' became dominant, also in literature. For some years now, the name of the art movement as a whole has mostly been written in capitals.

The word 'ZERO' immediately stood programmatically for a new beginning: for going back to a zero point in art and always starting anew from there, for a direct approach to light and the other elements (such as fire in Piene's work), for a radically new formal language based on structure, rather than on composition, and for the concrete use of new materials such as aluminium and Plexiglas[49] to open up the future in new types of sculptural works and to (re)construct a utopian content in art. ZERO art still embodies this aspiration today.[50]

From 1957 onwards, Heinz Mack restricted his paintings to black and white values – in other words, light and non-light – in vertically or horizontally arranged parallel lines that are not geometrically modulated. He wrote the text 'The New Dynamic Structure', which appeared in the first issue of *ZERO* and referred not only to his own paintings, but to a new form of painting as a whole.[52] An explicit source of inspiration was Piet Mondrian's three paintings from the *Boogie Woogie* series, made in New York between 1940 and 1944. In accordance with the principle that the formal act 'is stimulated and directed by the sensitivity of the artist's hands',[53] this structural painting is far removed from the geometric abstraction of Constructivism and the interwar and post-war movement around the artists' association Cercle et Carré (Circle and Square). 'Irrespective of the aesthetic aspect, a unified energy arises in a structure when one part passes its functional energy to an adjacent part, and so on, the purpose of which is the continuous energetic exchange of this multitude of parts, so that the energy field emerges as a whole in its totality

»

I impart vibration to a color, i.e., I give the color structure, or I give the color its form. The notion of shaping in the traditional sense is no longer relevant. Overcoming variegation with color itself means that we must give up composition in favor of a simple structure zone, i.e., the simple coming together of all pictorial elements. The only way for the painter to reach unity in a work is by knowing precisely the function of each of its constituents. A totally charmless structural element – only reasonable when equipped with, or representing, a pictorial meaning – replaces the charming detail. [...] To me such an element of structure is, for instance, a certain number of parallel straight lines in a horizontal or vertical arrangement. The pattern of such lines is infinitely variable. The principle involved is the simultaneous and periodic sequence of lines. (These straight lines need not be precise.) Every zone in between two straight lines displays an immensely rich structure of color and form; with regards to the latter, I give accidental creation a real chance, whereas I place the straight lines intentionally. While individual parallel zones gradually transform themselves from zone to zone, at the same time they retain their distinct but mutual character; this is how they begin to vibrate.

« ('THE NEW DYNAMIC STRUCTURE', MAY 1958)[51]

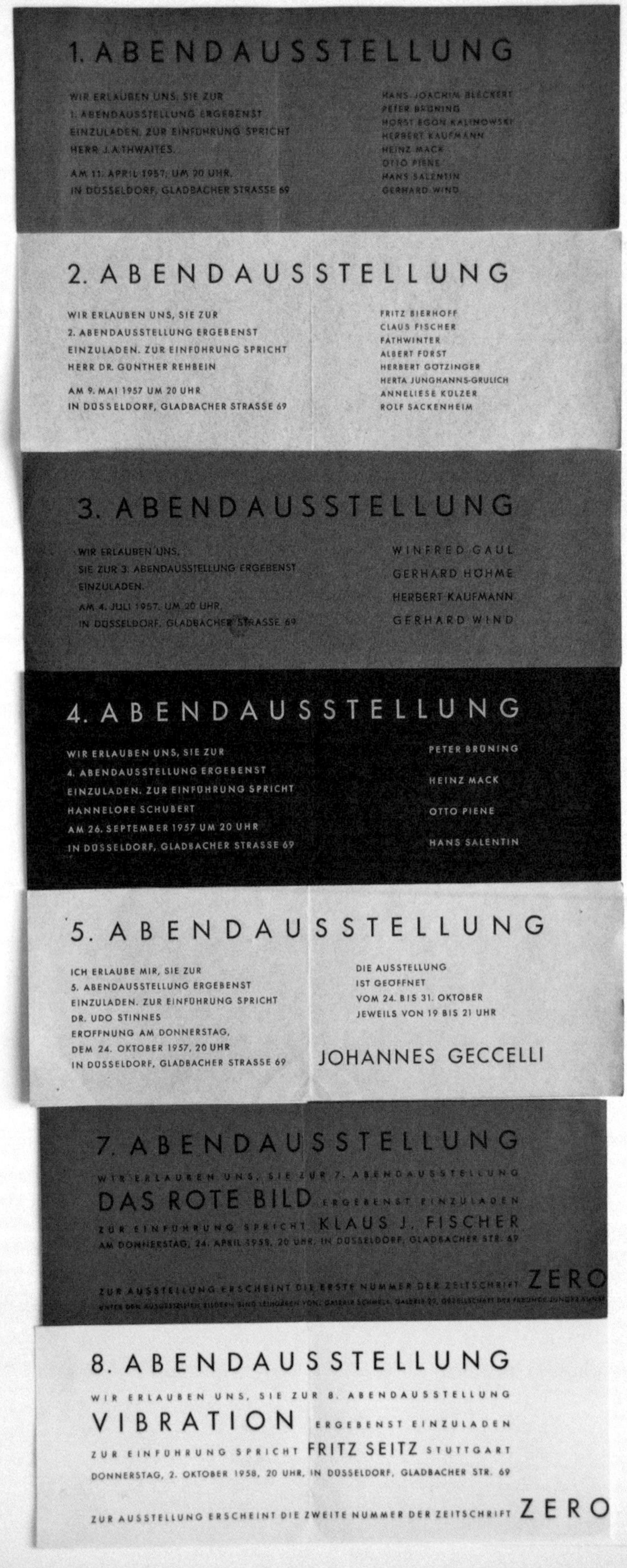

1. ABENDAUSSTELLUNG

WIR ERLAUBEN UNS, SIE ZUR
1. ABENDAUSSTELLUNG ERGEBENST
EINZULADEN. ZUR EINFÜHRUNG SPRICHT
HERR J. A. THWAITES.

AM 11. APRIL 1957, UM 20 UHR,
IN DÜSSELDORF, GLADBACHER STRASSE 69

HANS-JOACHIM BLECKERT
PETER BRÜNING
HORST EGON KALINOWSKI
HERBERT KAUFMANN
HEINZ MACK
OTTO PIENE
HANS SALENTIN
GERHARD WIND

2. ABENDAUSSTELLUNG

WIR ERLAUBEN UNS, SIE ZUR
2. ABENDAUSSTELLUNG ERGEBENST
EINZULADEN. ZUR EINFÜHRUNG SPRICHT
HERR DR. GÜNTHER REHBEIN

AM 9. MAI 1957 UM 20 UHR
IN DÜSSELDORF, GLADBACHER STRASSE 69

FRITZ BIERHOFF
CLAUS FISCHER
FATHWINTER
ALBERT FÜRST
HERBERT GÖTZINGER
HERTA JUNGHANNS-GRULICH
ANNELIESE KÜLZER
ROLF SACKENHEIM

3. ABENDAUSSTELLUNG

WIR ERLAUBEN UNS,
SIE ZUR 3. ABENDAUSSTELLUNG ERGEBENST
EINZULADEN.
AM 4. JULI 1957, UM 20 UHR,
IN DÜSSELDORF, GLADBACHER STRASSE 69

WINFRED GAUL
GERHARD HÖHME
HERBERT KAUFMANN
GERHARD WIND

4. ABENDAUSSTELLUNG

WIR ERLAUBEN UNS, SIE ZUR
4. ABENDAUSSTELLUNG ERGEBENST
EINZULADEN. ZUR EINFÜHRUNG SPRICHT
HANNELORE SCHUBERT
AM 26. SEPTEMBER 1957 UM 20 UHR
IN DÜSSELDORF, GLADBACHER STRASSE 69

PETER BRÜNING
HEINZ MACK
OTTO PIENE
HANS SALENTIN

5. ABENDAUSSTELLUNG

ICH ERLAUBE MIR, SIE ZUR
5. ABENDAUSSTELLUNG ERGEBENST
EINZULADEN. ZUR EINFÜHRUNG SPRICHT
DR. UDO STINNES
ERÖFFNUNG AM DONNERSTAG,
DEM 24. OKTOBER 1957, 20 UHR
IN DÜSSELDORF, GLADBACHER STRASSE 69

DIE AUSSTELLUNG
IST GEÖFFNET
VOM 24. BIS 31. OKTOBER
JEWEILS VON 19 BIS 21 UHR

JOHANNES GECCELLI

7. ABENDAUSSTELLUNG

WIR ERLAUBEN UNS, SIE ZUR 7. ABENDAUSSTELLUNG
DAS ROTE BILD ERGEBENST EINZULADEN
ZUR EINFÜHRUNG SPRICHT KLAUS J. FISCHER
AM DONNERSTAG, 24. APRIL 1958, 20 UHR, IN DÜSSELDORF, GLADBACHER STR. 69

ZUR AUSSTELLUNG ERSCHEINT DIE ERSTE NUMMER DER ZEITSCHRIFT ZERO

8. ABENDAUSSTELLUNG

WIR ERLAUBEN UNS, SIE ZUR 8. ABENDAUSSTELLUNG
VIBRATION ERGEBENST EINZULADEN
ZUR EINFÜHRUNG SPRICHT FRITZ SEITZ STUTTGART
DONNERSTAG, 2. OKTOBER 1958, 20 UHR, IN DÜSSELDORF, GLADBACHER STR. 69

ZUR AUSSTELLUNG ERSCHEINT DIE ZWEITE NUMMER DER ZEITSCHRIFT ZERO

Invitations to seven of the eight *Evening Exhibitions*, held in the Düsseldorf studios of Heinz Mack and Otto Piene from April 1957 to October 1958

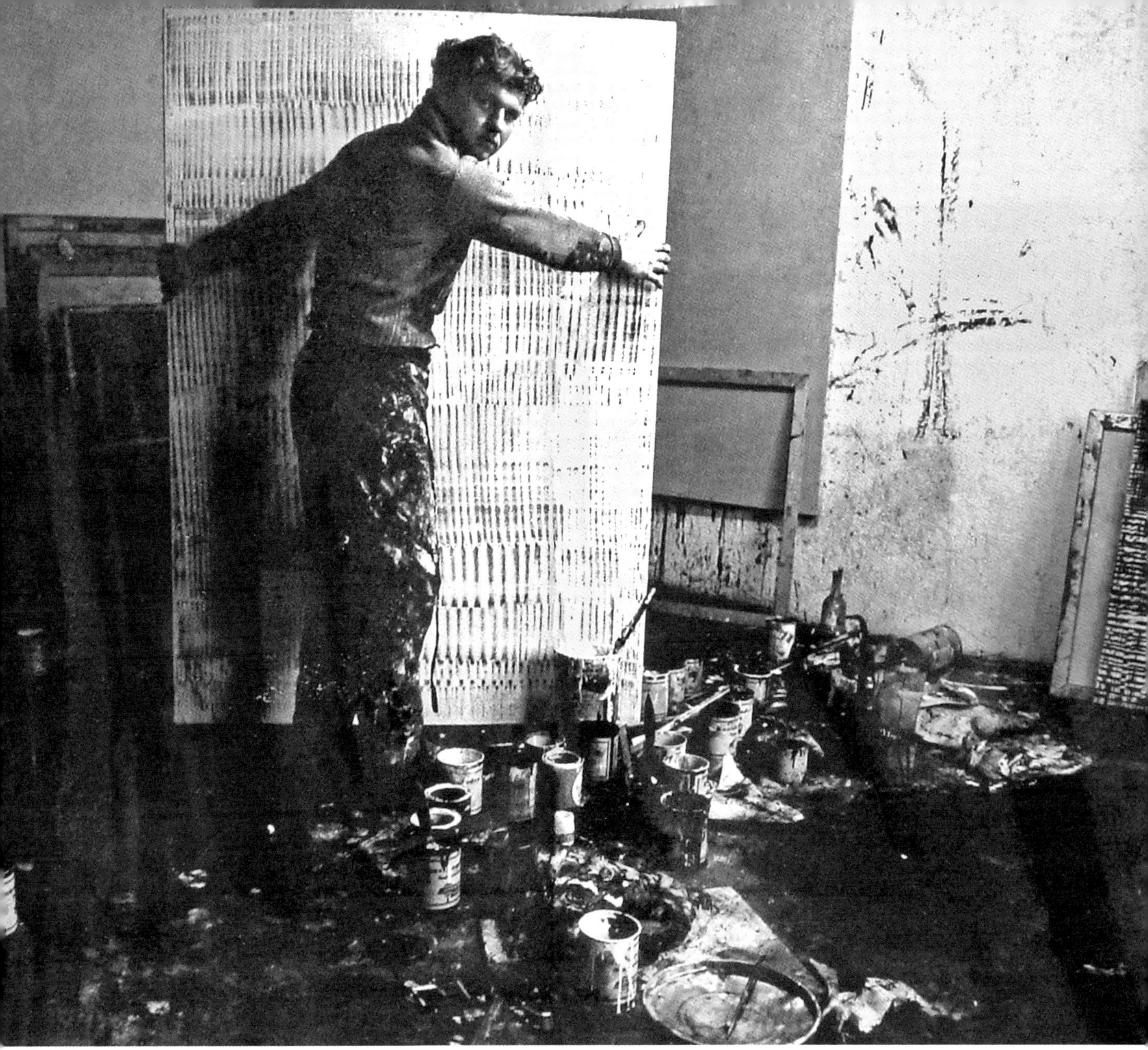

Heinz Mack with a
Dynamic Structure
in his studio at Gladbacher
Straße 69, Düsseldorf,
c. 1958

»

The exclusiveness of a completely nonrepresentational, dynamic pictorial structure – light years away from nature – will become an expression of pure emotion, unveiling a new reality, about whose secret beauty we can only speculate.

('THE NEW DYNAMIC STRUCTURE', MAY 1958)[56] «

and uniformity.'[54] This is the artist's own formula, which has underpinned Mack's oeuvre in all its facets since the attempt to find a new foundation became concrete. Many artistic parameters were redefined: 'Above all, the new structural order of pictorial space will be determined by the space value of colour and its frequency.'[55] The result is a 'virtual vibration'. At the same time, art was characterised by a utopian gesture and aspiration that had last been seen in Constructivism and Surrealism.

Several factors contributed to the fact that the exclamation 'ZERO!' did not fade away without an impact, but on the contrary, triggered a dynamic that continues to this day. The term has the power of a youthful gesture that does not care about conventions and that, with inner necessity, cries out a deep dissatisfaction with the art scene of its time. ZERO also had a direct connection: on 1 February 1958, the United States launched its first space rocket, *Explorer 1*. Unlike *Sputnik 1*, with which the Soviet Union had inaugurated space travel the previous autumn, the launch phase was broadcast live on *the* audio-visual media of the time, radio and television, with a short time delay in the Federal Republic of Germany. This was the first 'countdown' to be seen by the general public. An engineer at Cape Canaveral spoke loud and clear: 'Eight, seven, six, five, four, three, two, one, ZERO!' The word was new and highly topical in the German-speaking world. It stood both for the first rocket launch into space to be broadcast to the public and for a zero point from which the future would begin.[57] The word was also catchy, compact, and memorable in a way that only 'Pop' was in the art scene of the time, which Richard Hamilton transferred from the sphere of advertising into a collage[58] for the exhibition *This is Tomorrow*, organised by artists at the Institute for Contemporary Art in London in 1956, and which, with Pop Art, especially in the United States from 1962 onwards, became the term for an art that adopted pictorial forms from the trivial culture of consumer society and thus revolutionised representational art.[59]

However, the essential prerequisite for ZERO to have an impact and become established lies in the innovative power of the works. Mack's paintings, known today as 'ZERO painting', each consist of a horizontal or vertical sequence of narrow areas in one or at most two colours, with a sequence of flatness and slight elevation that extends across the entire picture surface (fig. p. 63). The ambient light refracts in its own way on the flat and slightly raised areas of the painting. This subtle action of the light from the reflection, which takes place in a low threshold area in front of the canvas plane, is the actual content of this new type of painting.[60]

With a bold gesture that still commands respect today, ZERO threw out most of the parameters of modern and post-war art. The revolution represented by these paintings took place on three levels. It began with a radical reduction in the means of expression and the language of form. The almost picture-filling sequence of minimally raised and flat zones of one or two colours or of black and white (fig. p. 70) reduced the means of expression to the opposition of sign and non-sign, whereby the signs with the very small elevations or the concept of sign itself are almost neutralised. In these paintings, we can still see a beginning, the beginning of a new concept of form that informs the most diverse areas of contemporary art.

On a second level, the elimination of expression took place in Heinz Mack's ZERO painting. Expression, either as the artist's self-expression or as the expression of objective forces or harmonies, represented the basic idea of modern art in the first six decades of the twentieth century.[62] On the monochrome or bichrome canvas surfaces, however, the pictorial event expresses nothing. The material speaks for itself. This also points to a new concept of material in contemporary art, one that pervaded the ZERO movement and somewhat later also became decisive in Nouveau Réalisme and Minimalism.

» I have told you several times that the best text that has ever been written about me in relation to the ZERO period is the text by Dieter Honisch.[61] Absolutely the best text, and one day you should take the time to read it. It's simply a very important text. I would like to see another exhibition that does justice to this text. And that fulfils what is also expressed in this text, that something has happened in art that goes far beyond the normal. «

(MAY 2024)

On a third level, composition was overtaken by structure. Composition, with the harmonious or dissonant distribution of forms on the picture support, had characterised the entire European art tradition since the Renaissance around 1500. In the natural sciences and humanities, its abandonment corresponded to structuralism, which developed from the 1920s onwards and became dominant in the post-war period alongside existential philosophy and phenomenology. At first glance, Mack's concept of 'dynamic structure' appears

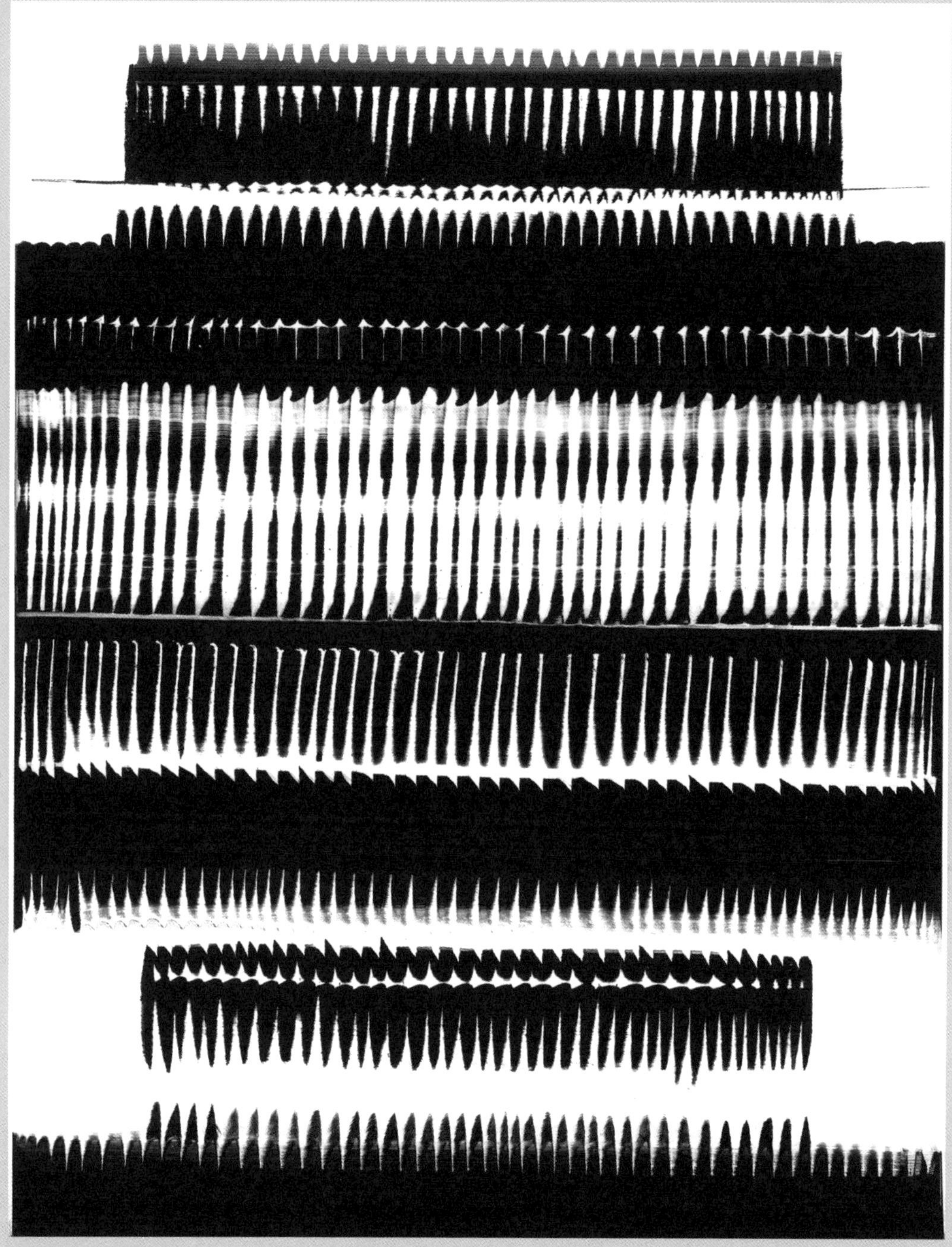

Cardiogram of My Heart, No. 2
1962

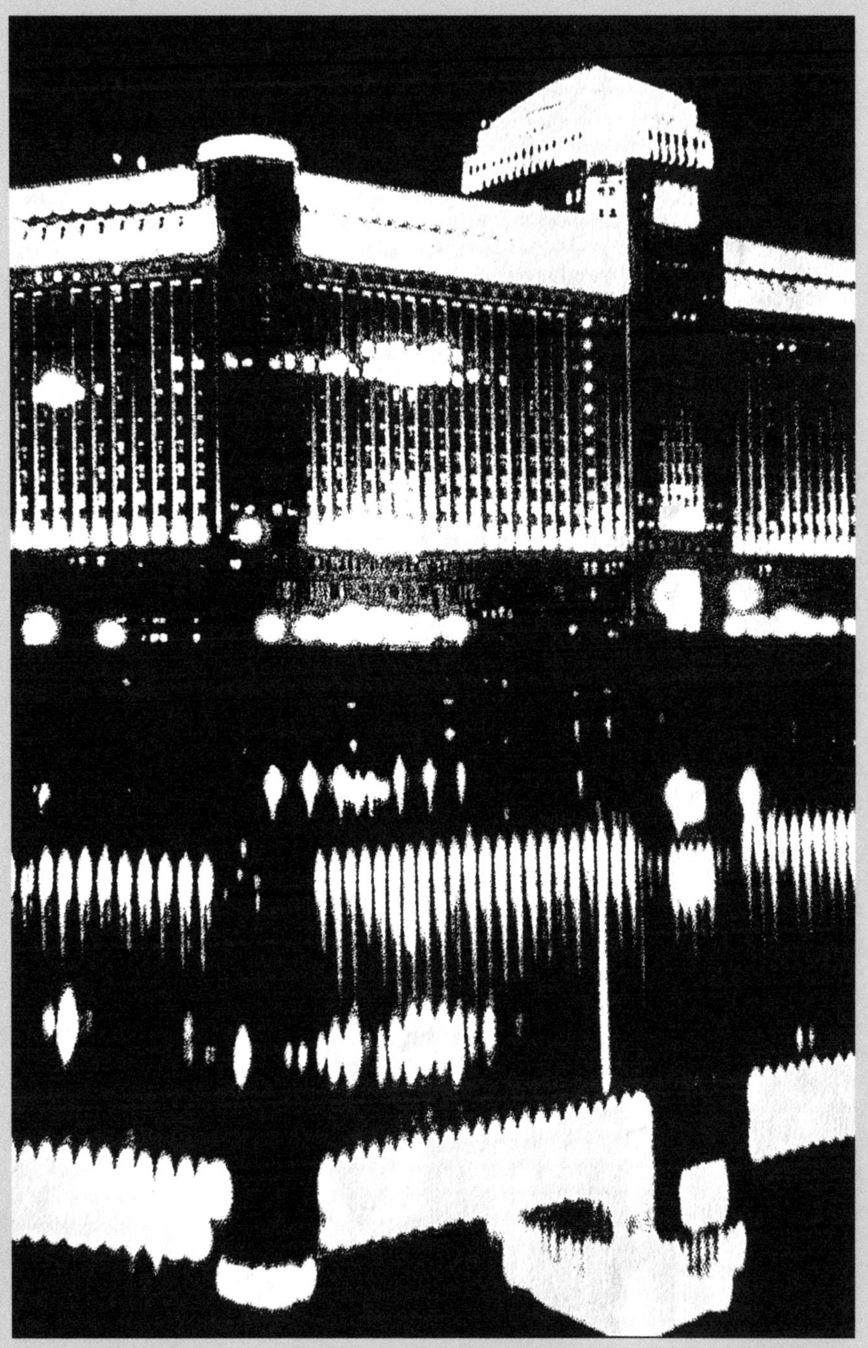

Merchandise Mart, Chicago, 1930s,
the world's largest building at
the time of its opening

to be a contradiction in terms, but it has a parallel in the contemporary structuralist debate. The second generation of structuralists, later called post-structuralists,[63] were particularly interested in the internal dynamics of political, social, and aesthetic structures. In purely artistic terms, the 'new dynamic structure' means that a structuralist image, explicitly introduced as the future of art, must have an internal tension that cannot be calculated in advance, making the artist's intuition more important than ever, even as the traditional form of artistic intention is eliminated.

» There are some structures that are very coarse and others that are very fine. There is an interaction between the overall format and the number of elevations and depressions. That has to result in a field somewhere. And if you were to extend it ad ultimo, you would lose something crucial, namely the energy, the field of tension. When the light falls on it, there are also optical fields of tension somewhere, and this tension would be paralysed if I were to extend it ad ultimo. This tension between the individual elements must be maintained. Otherwise, a certain indifference arises, which is perceived as boredom.

(JANUARY 2024) «

These paintings on canvas, which in themselves already exhibit a relief form, soon developed into actual reliefs, combinations of sculpture and panel painting, which in some respects constitute the pictorial paradigm of Mack's oeuvre. In them we find the sequence of heightening and deepening, of light reflection and its absence, of almost neutralised sign and non-sign from Mack's ZERO painting, with an even more pronounced spatial aura and seizure of space, a central theme of Mack's oeuvre.

The highly experimental creation of the reliefs went hand in hand with the inclusion of new, hitherto non-artistic materials such as aluminium, whose light-reflecting effect far exceeds that of paint, so that in the *Light Reliefs* made of pressed metal foils, light literally became the object, the material, and the content of art (fig. p. 74), no longer merely indirectly represented and alluded to as in painting and sculpture up to that point.

'The abstract painters had painted the world full. All we had left was the sky', said Heinz Mack a few years ago.[64] This refers to the idea of using the elements themselves instead of traditional pictorial means: air, fire (central to Otto Piene's work), earth (sand appears very early in Mack's work, as does the idea of working in the desert), and water. The fifth 'element' is light. In this way, the combination of radical simplicity and complex diversity that characterises ZERO art is created on several levels. It is expressed on the poster for Heinz Mack and Otto Piene's first joint exhibition abroad – at Galerie St. Stephan in Vienna[65] in January 1961 – which listed the following: 'oil paintings light reliefs light dynamos drawings smoke drawings light ballet light graphics' (fig. p. 76). It was around this time that Günther Uecker, also a graduate of the Düsseldorf Academy of Art, joined the founding duo of ZERO. His simple yet complex nail reliefs on a white background introduced another iconic approach to the artistic thinking that came to define the name 'ZERO'.

ZERO can be interpreted as a regression, as a relapse to an outdated technical level of artistic design, as Theodor W. Adorno, the philosopher of the Frankfurt School who was influential at the time, did in his aesthetic theory in relation to all modern art since Cubism and abstraction.[67] ZERO can be accused of a naïve belief in technology and the future of industrial society, a recurring theme in 1960s publications on the art of the time, sometimes with the claim that this was an irresponsible attitude. However, ZERO can also be seen as an initial artistic spark that, with the simplification of starting from point zero in aesthetic endeavour – to make a statement that reflects light, or not – swept aside an infinite number of stale residues of modern art, thus creating space for new approaches of all kinds. The painting was also conceived as an anticipation of the future. What a gesture, one must exclaim approvingly from today's perspective.

The intellectual-historical contexts of early ZERO art remain to be explored, for example in Roland Barthes's seminal text *Le Degré zéro de l'écriture*, published in 1954,[68] in which the French word *zéro* is synonymous with a neutral form of writing. This concept became influential worldwide with the literature of the Nouveau Roman and in the films of the Nouvelle Vague from around 1955, similar to the neo-serial music of Pierre Boulez, Jean Barraqué and Luciano Berio, which was essentially anchored in the Studio for Electronic Music of the West German broadcasting company WDR in Cologne.[69] Here, too, the question was how to overcome outdated compositional principles without a new system like that of Wassily Kandinsky in his late work or Arnold Schönberg with his twelve-tone system, however much these were admired. This intellectual-historical context is fundamental to Mack's interpretation of the ZERO idea.

»

ZERO was soon talked about in the media. We were also very much despised. The press made fun of us. Even a man who later became an important museum director and was a journalist at the time, Karl Ruhrberg,[66] spoke of the 'revolution of the drawing teachers' because I was a drawing teacher. That was the headline of his criticism: 'Revolution of the Drawing Teachers'. That was degrading. On Königsallee in Düsseldorf, people blocked my way so that I couldn't go any further, looked at me and threw a five-mark piece at my feet: 'Go to the hairdresser!' They recognised my face from the newspaper. But we were prepared to do anything to attract attention. All in all, it must have had the effect that young people were doing something that was unusual, that had a certain – I'll put it another way – a certain revolutionary process. So there was a certain revolutionary spirit.

« (DECEMBER 2023)

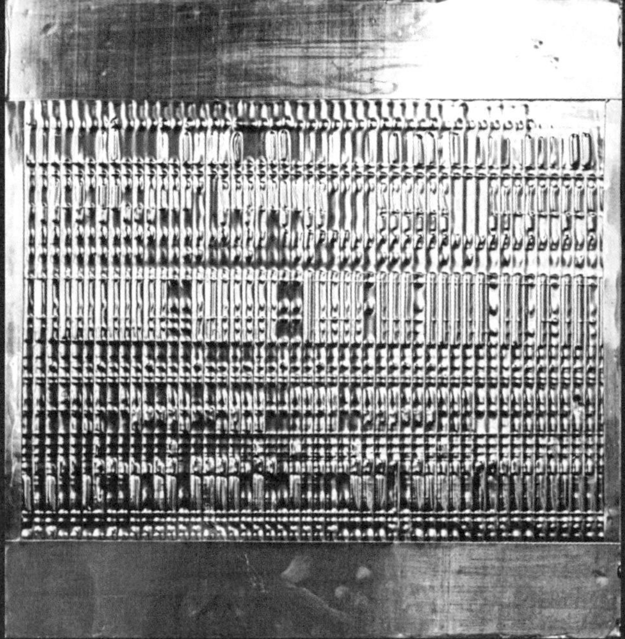

Light Relief
1959/60

Classical Micro-Relief
1959

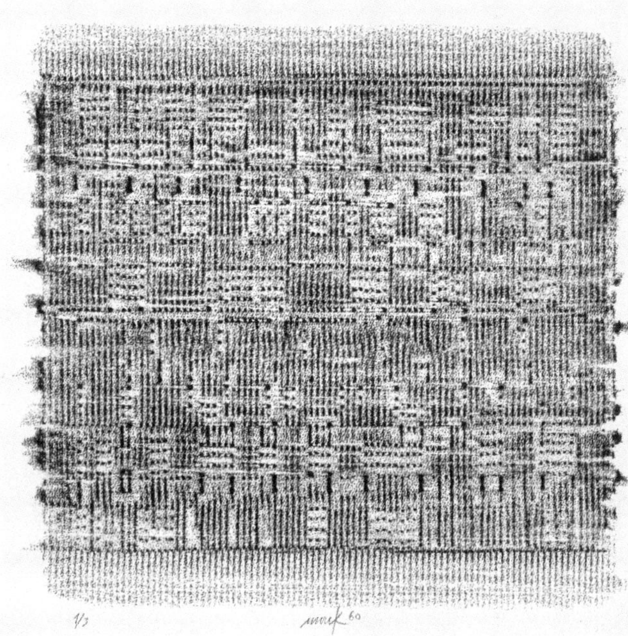

Untitled
1960

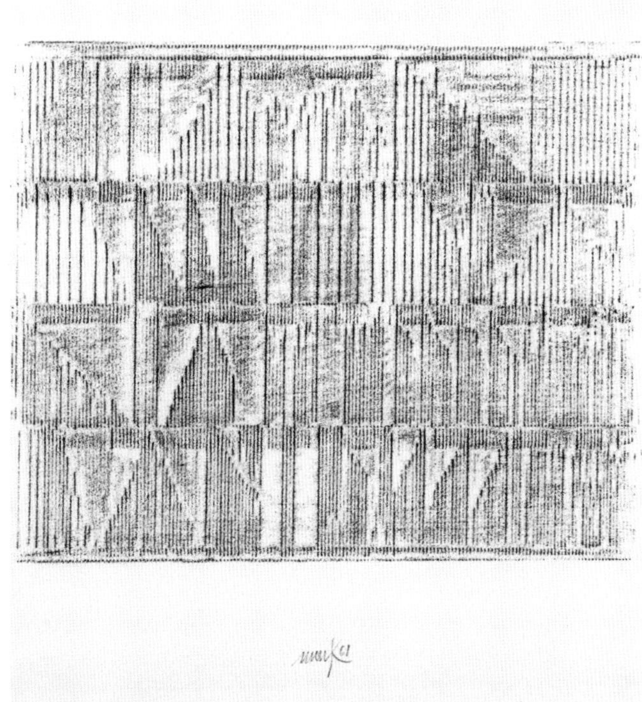

Untitled
1961

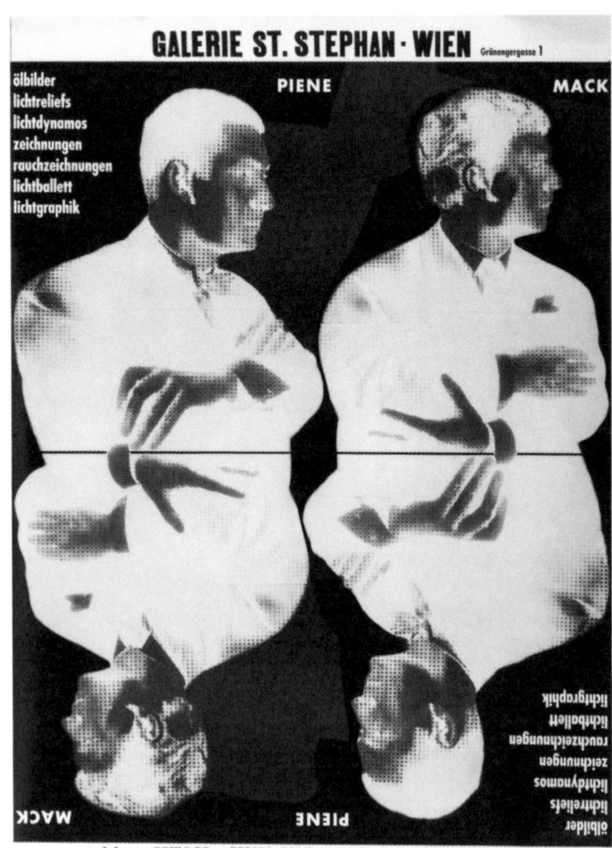

Poster for the exhibition of works by Heinz Mack and Otto Piene, Galerie St. Stephan, Vienna
1961
designed by Heinz Mack

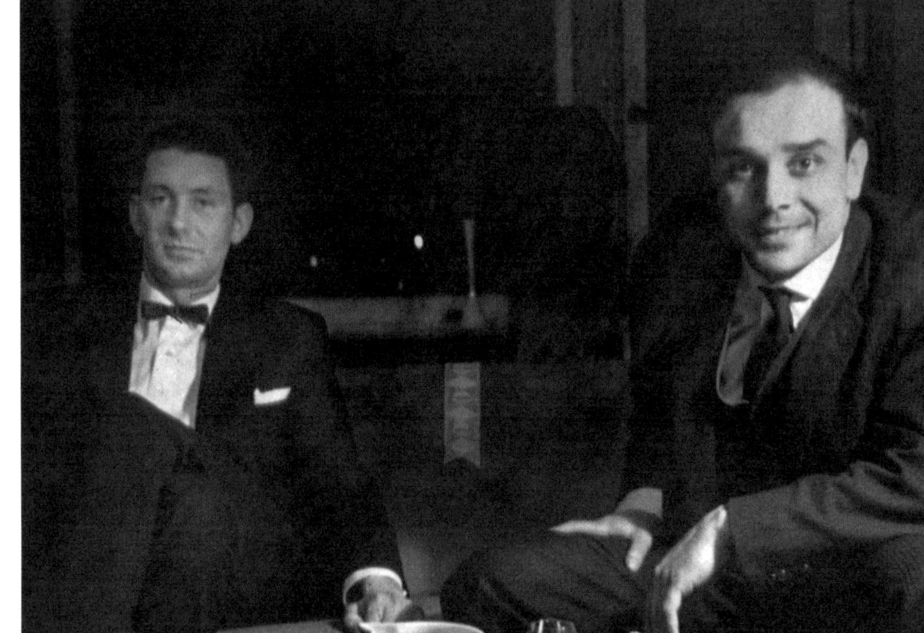

Otto Piene and Yves Klein, photographed by Mack
1958

Mack and Piene interpreted the idea of ZERO differently from the outset. They had been fellow students at the Düsseldorf Academy of Art and, around 1960, were like brothers, inventing something together that could only be presented in this way at such a young age. Nevertheless, there are different ways of dealing with light, which suddenly became a post-expressive medium in its own right. In Piene's work, light, bound in fire, is a metaphysical force, as in German idealism. Mack's concept of light, on the other hand, was already nominalistic in the ZERO years: light is light.[70] It has to do with presence, with reflection, with a new perception, not with hidden forces, things and truths.

»

I always think back to those early days around 1960, when there was a lot of optimism, also in an artistic sense. We were very spirited. We were very youthful, very optimistic. In contrast to a lot of writers who were walking on a tightrope, as if they were on a high mountain, and they weren't looking up to the sky, which would have been interesting, but they were always looking down into the abyss, something like that. That was much more mysterious to them, what was happening in the deep abyss, and they weren't interested in the air above. But we were only interested in the air.

« (OCTOBER 2023)

On 24 October 1960, Yves Klein and the art critic Pierre Restany founded the artists' group Nouveaux Réalistes in Paris, not least to counter the growing pan-European appeal of the Düsseldorf ZERO idea.[71] Otto Piene then argued in favour of countering this Parisian initiative with the term 'Neuer Idealismus' (New Idealism). Mack was resolutely against it, and Uecker did not consider it appropriate either. The dissolution of the Düsseldorf ZERO group in 1966 was thus preordained, as was the later discussion about whether ZERO had ended that very year, which Mack still firmly believes today, while Piene insisted to the end that ZERO, invented in the Rhine harbour in 1958, would live on forever.[72]

Hundreds of works by Mack, Piene, and Uecker were created in just a few years. Today, everything in their oeuvres from this period is legendary. Another question remains: Was ZERO Düsseldorf the first postmodern art movement? Had anyone before this group overturned the entire formal repertoire of twentieth-century classical modernism in such a way? Had any art movement before it so decisively demonstrated that all the narratives of abstraction, continued figuration, Expressionism, Constructivism, Surrealism, and Abstract Expressionism were suddenly no longer relevant, thus opening up a new art space in which everything became possible, which is not least characteristic of today's eclectic art scene?

»

To put it bluntly, we were in a very optimistic mood, and we also had a lot of fun writing poems together, throwing words at each other when we went for a walk, and several ZERO poems came out of that: 'The moon is round, the milk is yellow' and so on. Freely fantasised.

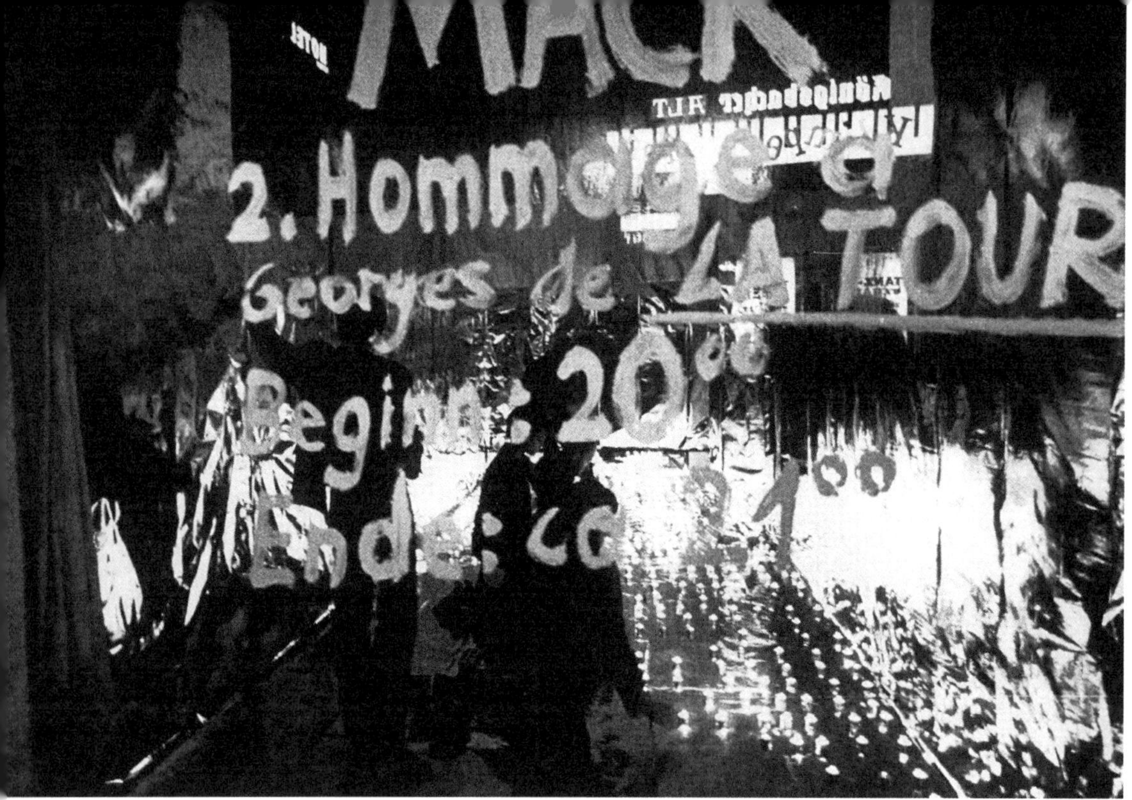

View of the installation
2. Hommage à Georges de La Tour through the window
of Galerie Schmela, Düsseldorf
1965

2. Hommage à Georges de La Tour
1965

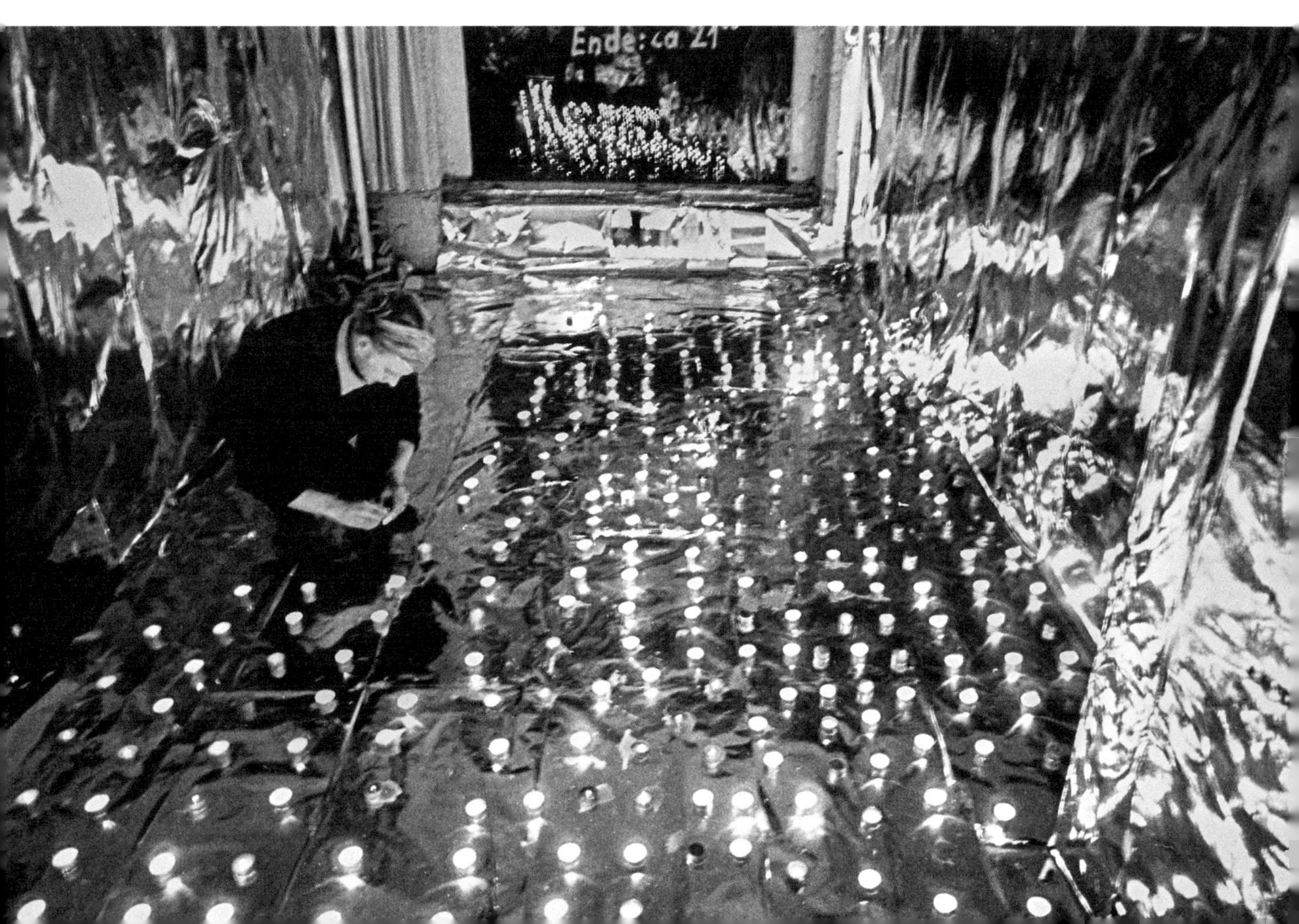

But we were also prepared to make sacrifices in an existential sense. While other people were out dancing, we were working in the studio.

(FEBRUARY 2024) «

»

For the opening of my exhibition in West Berlin in 1960, I built a table sixty centimetres high and exactly two square metres in size, that is, two metres long and one metre wide. There were 100 candles on it, small candles, no bigger than a pencil. They were strictly serialised. It was a lot of work. Then I took a wooden slat and put little candles on it too, the same distance apart. There were no gas lighters in those days; you had to use a match. And you couldn't light one candle at a time, it was too complicated. So, thanks to my patent, you could always light a whole row of candles on the table at the same time using the wooden slat with the small candles. So then the 100 candles were lit. And there were two girls, dressed in snow-white. They were holding a neatly folded white bed sheet. Of course, only I knew it was a bed sheet. Then all the candles were lit, creating an enormous heat, all the other lights were off. It was spectacular. Then the two girls took the sheet, which was completely damp, but the visitors to the exhibition couldn't see that. Then I said: 'five, four, three, two, one, ZERO.' At that moment, they dropped the cloth – and all 100 candles went out. It was really spectacular. It was about creating an afterimage in the eyes that lasted for a long time, similar to the phosphorus room that has now been recreated at the ZKM.[73]

(NOVEMBER 2023) «

What is postmodernism? The term remains controversial and difficult to define. Jean-François Lyotard gave it a philosophical definition in 1979.[74] He saw it as the end of the grand narratives, the belief in the historical models of Marxism and the Western idea of progress, within the framework of which modern art of the twentieth century had developed as a coherent body of thought. Lyotard's analysis was based on the new eclecticism of the self-proclaimed 'postmodern architecture' of the 1970s[75] and anticipated the eclecticism in the visual arts from 1980 onwards. However, the term 'postmodernism' also applies particularly to ZERO around 1960, without ZERO having anything to do with the mixing of historical stylistic references that was later sometimes regarded as genuinely postmodern. Apart from ZERO and Pop Art, which also took unexpected paths, there was no other artistic departure from the dogmas of modern art of the first six decades of the twentieth century – despite the strict canon of forms that ZERO developed in its own way.[76] Is this not the enduring significance of ZERO?

The ZERO founders from Düsseldorf received their first institutional recognition with the exhibition *Junge deutsche Maler* (Young German Painters), held at the Kasseler Kunstverein in 1959, 'in conjunction with *II. documenta* '59 Kassel'.[77] ZERO had thus arrived at the holy grail of international art: the documenta, which had been organised for the first time four years earlier as a world exhibition of modern art. As with the first documenta in 1955 and the third and fourth editions, its founder, Arnold Bode, had to contend with the conservative documenta council headed by Werner Haftmann.[78] Bode therefore showed this accompanying exhibition at the Kunstverein, for which artists[79] had been nominated by art critics. Otto Piene was represented with three ZERO pictures, including *La force pure* (The Pure Force),[80] and Heinz Mack with four works, all untitled, including three *Light Reliefs on Aluminium (Box)*. To be able to participate in the second documenta at the age of twenty-eight: not bad. Mack and Piene were obviously recognised as having the strength to carry on. But they also had ZERO in their quiver.

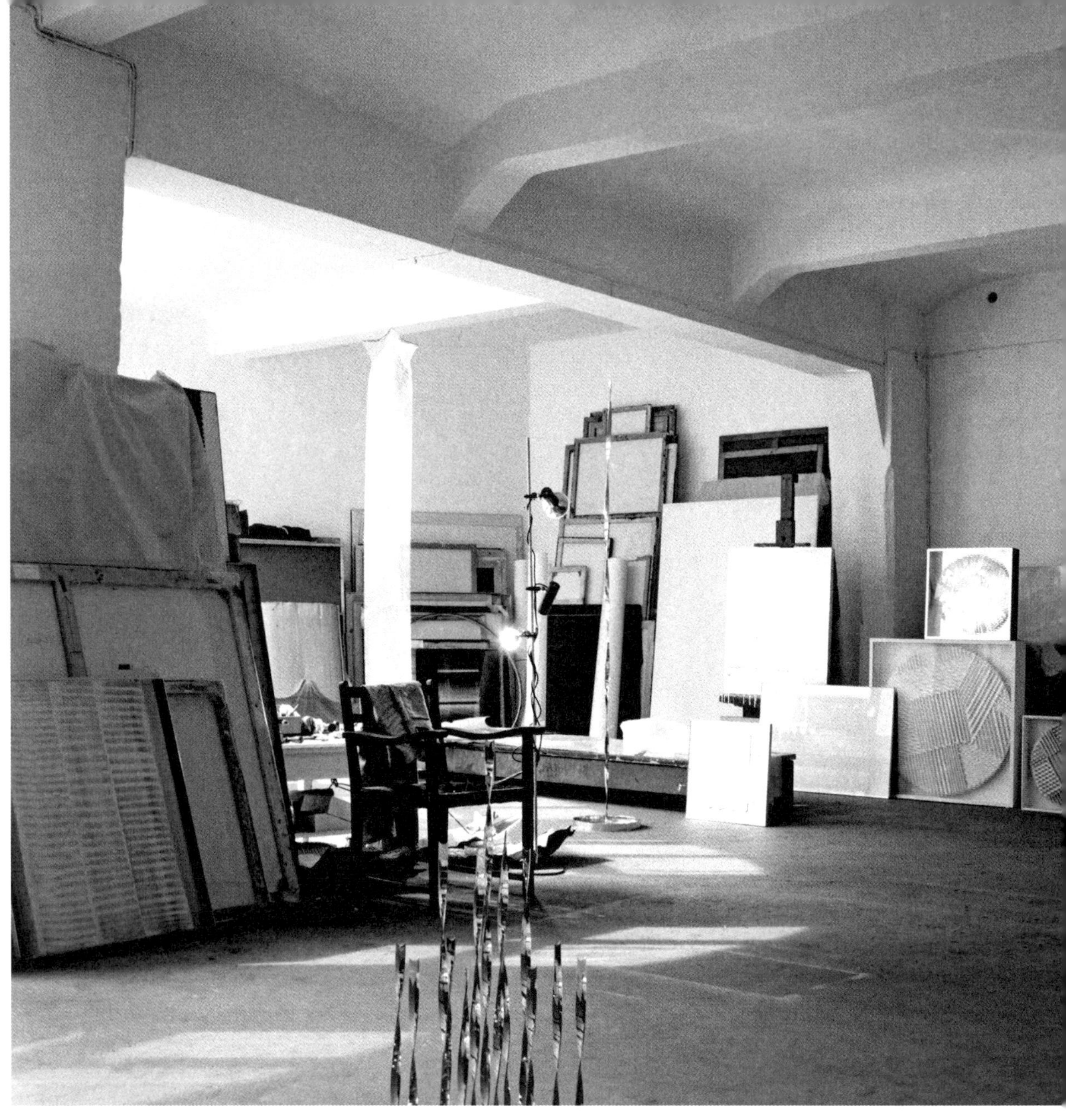

View of Heinz Mack's studio
at Hüttenstraße 104, Düsseldorf,
1965, then the studio building
shared by Otto Piene,
Günther Uecker and Heinz Mack

Heinz Mack, Günther Uecker, and Alfred Schmela with light steles and light reliefs by Mack in the Grugahalle, Essen, on the occasion of the exhibition of the Deutscher Künstlerbund
1966

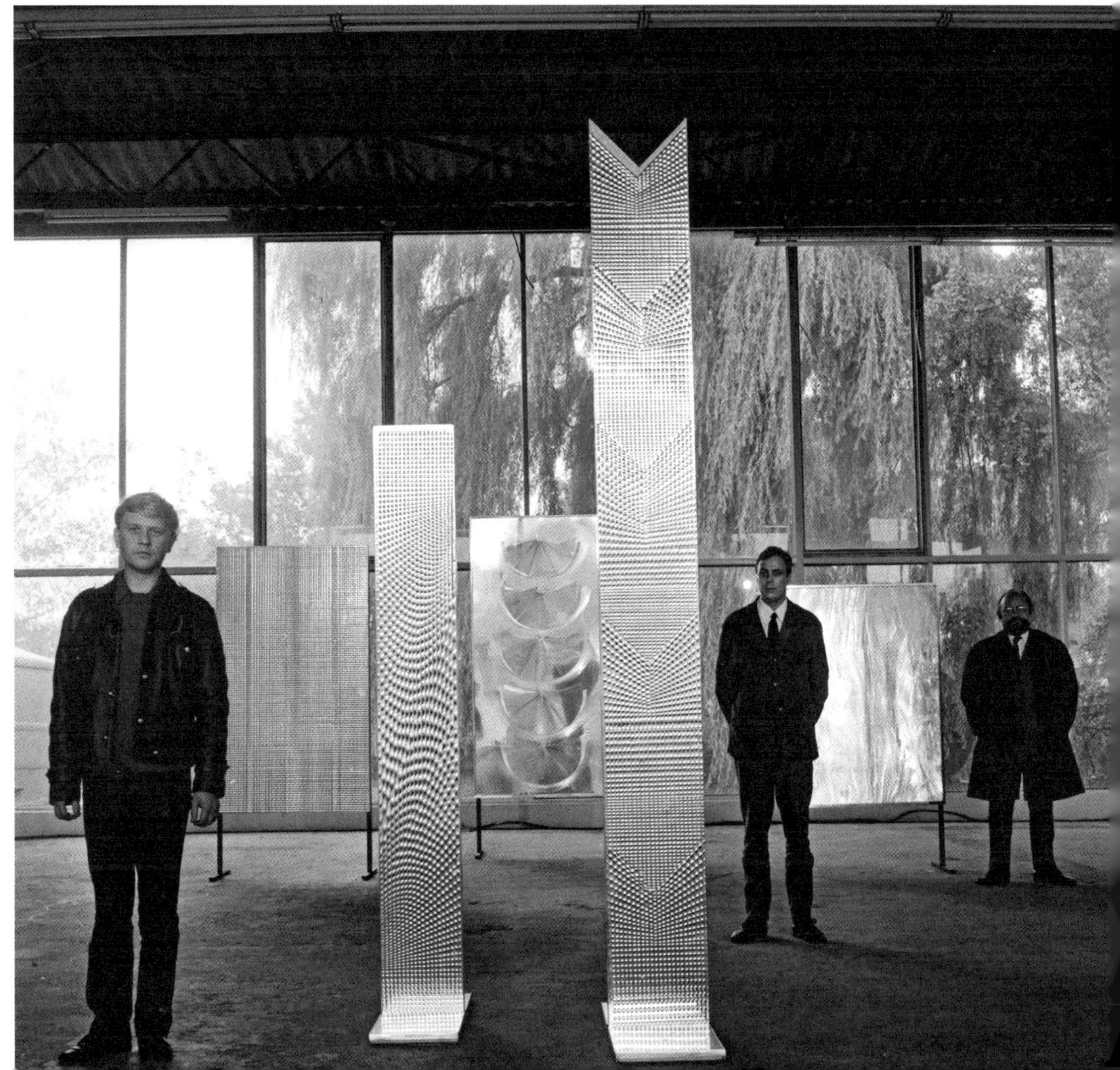

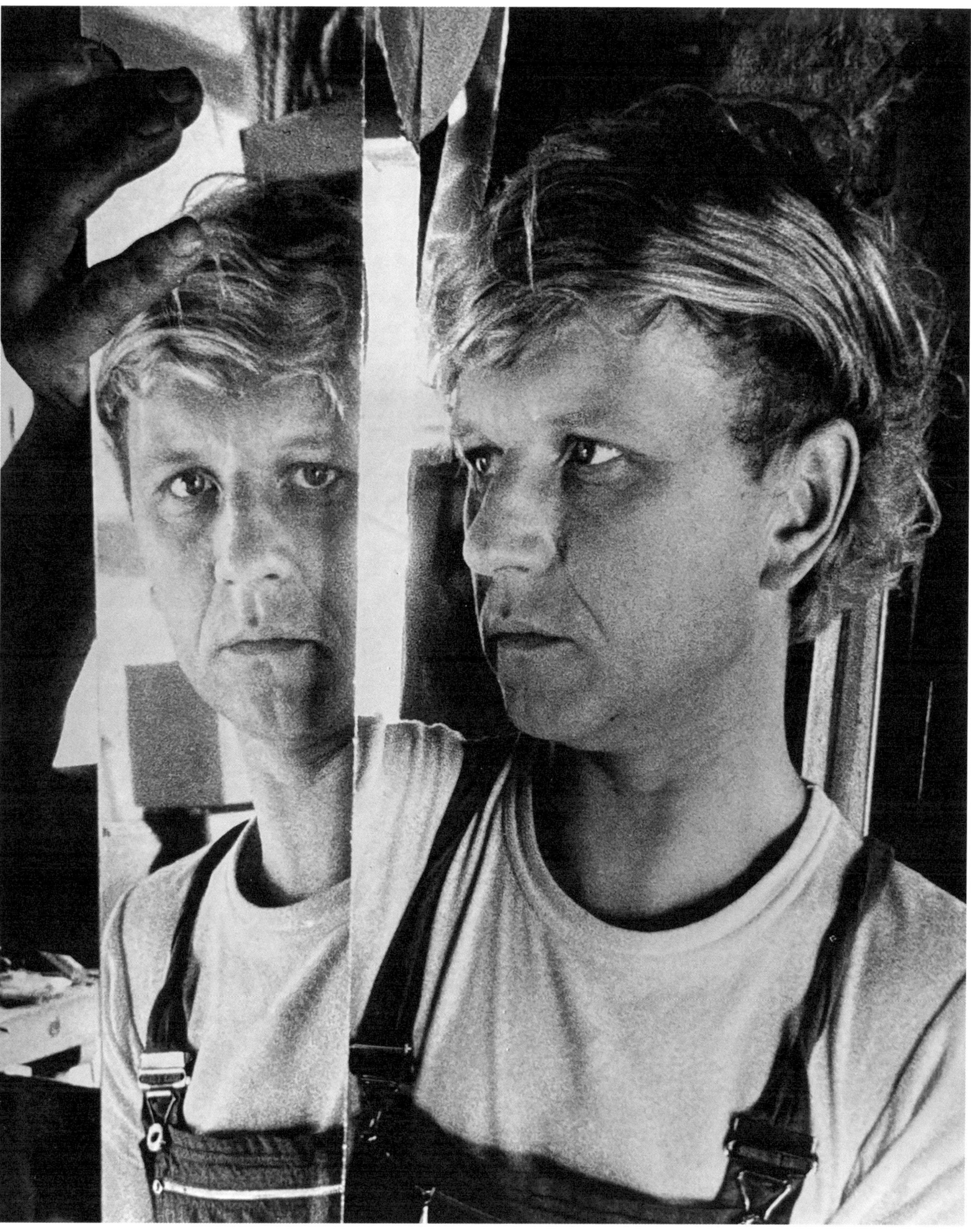

ION · DEMONSTRATION
ERO
XPOSITION

THE ZERO GENERATION

Heinz Mack in front of
Galerie Schmela, Düsseldorf
1961

July 1961: Galerie Schmela in Düsseldorf's old town is boarded up with wooden slats as if it were a building site. On the boarding is written with a broad brush in white and black paint: *ZERO – EDITION · DEMONSTRATION · EXPOSITION* (fig. p. 86). There is nothing more to be seen.

However, there are holes in the wooden slats. Through these one can see the double pages of the third issue of the eponymous magazine on the walls of the enclosed space.[81] *ZERO 3* was launched with an evening event on 5 July 1961 (fig. p. 93). It was no longer the thin, largely self-produced magazine of the first issue in 1958 (p. 65), but a stately publication of over three hundred pages. Professionally printed, it featured thirty-two artists[82] whose work was now grouped under the name 'ZERO', each with a double-page spread. The small Düsseldorf group had become a broader movement. The participating artists from eleven countries each paid for the printing of their double-page spread themselves,[83] so that the now three Düsseldorf ZERO artists were able to produce the largest self-organised anthology of new art from around 1960.[84]

» A comment on the early exhibitions: I would like to point out that Otto Piene and Heinz Mack were solely responsible for the organisation and partly also for the financing (Uecker was only marginally involved). We handled the relevant correspondence, and without having the money for insurance, we also bore the responsibility. We also produced catalogues and publications. No gallery, no museum, no Kunstverein, no patron supported us in this work!

('KURZE AUFLISTUNG DER INTERNATIONALEN ZERO-AUSSTELLUNGEN', UNDATED, MACK ARCHIVE) «

ZERO was now a Western European network that soon extended beyond the continent, developing simultaneously with Neo-Dada in New York, the precursor of Pop Art, with Robert Rauschenberg and Jasper Johns and the Happening artists, and with Nouveau Réalisme in Paris. *ZERO 3* was also an extra-institutional exhibition in the form of a book or magazine, as the Surrealists had occasionally done before with their new publishing practices. Artists from West Germany, Belgium, France, Italy, and the Netherlands, among others, were represented.[85] ZERO was the flag of a young art movement that made do with very simple signs, with white instead of bright colours, which had to do with reduction, with the abandonment of conventional pictorial processes, and with a new approach to technical materials. The spectrum of participants ranged from Piero Manzoni to Yves Klein, from Enrico Castellani to Jean Tinguely, from Jan Schoonhoven to Henk Peeters. Today, these names have a world standing, but at the time they were known only to the well-informed. With the exception of Schoonhoven and Lucio Fontana,[86] they were all born around 1930, so they were around thirty years old and belonged to the same generation. By now, almost all of them knew each other.

The events of 5 July 1961 were not limited to the presentation of the magazine in the boarded-up gallery. The first *ZERO Demonstration* also took place in the surrounding streets. In front of a large audience, Günther Uecker painted part of the cobblestones in front of the gallery white as a *ZERO Zone*. A large, helium-filled balloon hovered above the heads of the crowd as an ephemeral sculpture in

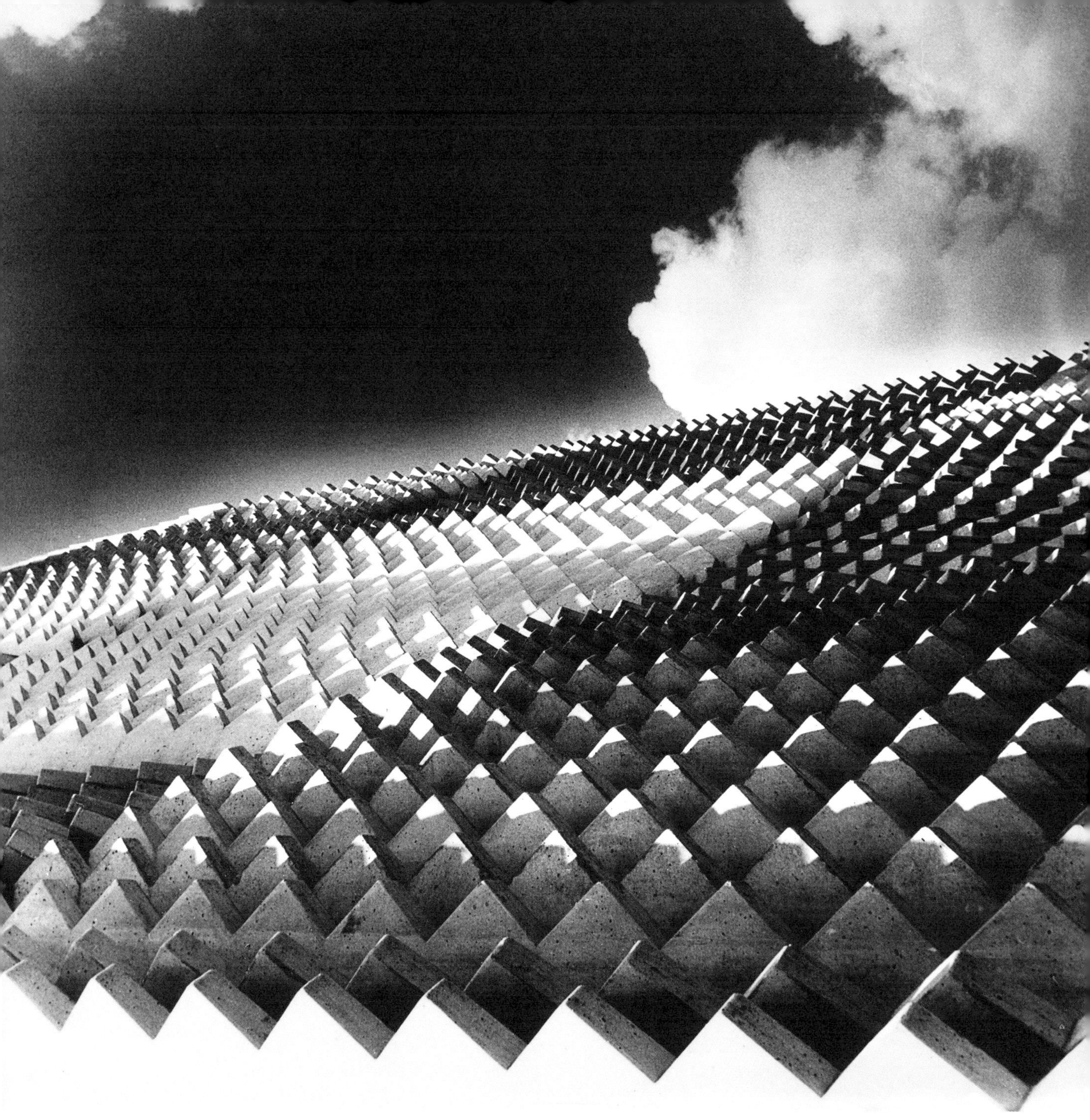

Sahara Reliefs
(detail)
Mathildenhofschule, Leverkusen
1960/61
from: *ZERO 3*

ROT

JEAN TINGUELY SEPT 59 TEXTE PRONONCE AU COURS DE LA SOIRREE I. C. A. LONDON

VAN HOEYDONK

POHL

ARNULF RAINER

TRUTH BECOMES REALITY

YVES KLEIN

ZERO

de monnair ou un jeton a été introduit dans l'ouverture 29 du dispositif 28, par la manœuvre du bouton 30 du rhéostat 27 on peut régler la vitesse du moteur 26. Celui-ci provoque les rotations des arbres 18, 24 et 34.
La rotation de l'arbre vilebrequin 18 provoque

Exposition

YVES KLEIN DAS WAHRE WIRD REALITÄT

LE VRAI DEVIENT REALITE

YVES LE MONOCHROME 1960

voyageur qui arpente les
-e humain, si nous voyons
ciels d'Amérique sont des
gnés. Leurs millénaires se
n'est-il pas le plus grand,
parce qu'il apprend l'éter-
son esprit pour élever son
er complètement l'espace

Edition KAGE

ZUR REALISATION DES OPTISCHEN KONZERTS

UECKER AUBERTIN

ESQUISSE DE LA SITUATION PICTURALE DU ROUGE DANS UN CONCEPT SPATIAL

DORAZIO

Die Expedition unserer Imaginationen entfernt sich
cIten Gewohnheiten, deren archaische Oxydation
der Künstler wird die Funktionäre und Konsumenten

SITUATION PICTURALE

ZERO

RAPHAEL JESUS SOTO

L'ESSENCE PICTURALE SENSIBLE OU MONOCHROMIE

POMODORO

SOTO

Demonstration

REALISME DES ACCUMULATIONS ARMAN

ADRIAN

TINGUELY

BURY

SPOERRI

THE GARDEN PARTY BY J. W. KLUVER

RAINER

BREVET D'INVENTION

HOLWECK

P. V. n° 798.710 N° 1.237.934
Classification internationale : B 43 h — B 44 d

MOLDOW

STATION 1
LES STELES DE LUMIERE
1er lieu: un groupe de 10 st
2e lieu: une stèle unique et

TOTALITY IN THE ART OF TODAY
TOTALITE DANS L'ART D'AUJOURD'HUI
ENRICO CASTELLANI ENRICO CASTELLANI
TOTALITA' NELL'ARTE D'OGGI

CHEMINS VERS LE PARADIS

PIENE

WAYS TO PA

PROGETTI IMMEDIATI
PROJETS IMMEDIATS PIERO MANZONI

Oui, je me souhaite un monde plus vaste.
Devrai-je me souhaiter un monde plus étroit?

SCHOONHOVEN

MAVIGNIER

LE PROJET DU SAHARA

MACK

THE SAHARA PROJECT DAS SAHARA-PROJEKT

Proklamation

ARMAN

LO SAVIO

RAPHAEL JESUS SOTO VIBRATION

JERRIS AUTOTHEATER DANIEL SPOERRI ZU DEN FALLENBILDERN A PROPOS DES TABLEAUX-PIEGES

FONTANA

SALENTIN

MANZONI

PEETERS

! Movement is static! Movement is static
, the only unchangeable. The only cer-
hat is why movement is static. So-called
and permanent things, ideas, works and
ts are snapshots of a movement whose
nly an instant in the great movement.
hing. Static means transformation. Let us
tic! Be movement! Believe in movement's
. Change! Do not pin-point anything!
anges. Believe in movement's static quali-

Das Schweigen ... es, genau es, i
Das Schweigen, dies wunderbare Schw
wahrhaft glücklich zu sein – sei es auc
meßlich lange dauert.
Das Schweigen besiegen, es durchstoße
einatmen – um niemals wieder zu frier
Gegenüber der Sensibilität des Univer
In meiner Kindheit schrieb ich meinen
tastischen imaginären Reise, ausgestr
denn sie versuchen, Löcher in mein bis

CASTELLANI

KLEINT

YVES KLEIN

ZERO

.... l'imperceptible moment ....

LES MONUMENTS DE LA LUMIERE

Poster for
ZERO – EDITION · DEMONSTRATION · EXPOSITION,
Düsseldorf
1961

which extras dressed in ZERO garb blew soap bubbles into the sky (fig. p. 93).

What Mack, Piene, and Uecker called the *ZERO Demonstration* bore all the hallmarks of a Happening, a new art form that had emerged in New York in 1958 around Allan Kaprow, Dick Higgins, and Jim Dine. Happenings introduced the active role of the audience, chance as an organising principle, and the fusion of art and life. Jean-Jacques Lebel from Paris organised the first Happenings in Europe in 1960. In this sequence, the *ZERO Demonstration* of 1961 was the first Happening in Germany.[87] The few surviving photographs of the event capture the atmosphere of a folk festival. ZERO had an immediate impact on society, beyond art institutions. It now stood for a new form of art that intervened in life and proposed to change it in a playful way.

The magazine *ZERO 3* also had a great influence beyond this. Such a publication is passed on in a way that its producers cannot assess or control. A few years before the first attempts to define Minimalism art in New York, a collective programme of a necessary reduction of form and signs to the origin of artistic action, to make a mark or not, emerged here. A few years later, minimal and conceptual art also developed from this line of tradition.

»

We didn't complain about being criticised. We weren't sad about it. We were just in a good mood and very willing to be creative. To do something together. We spurred each other on, motivated each other. It was also a competition. There was a certain solidarity and a shared feeling that we finally had to take a step forward, we had to make discoveries, we had to experiment.

« (SEPTEMBER 2023)

»

My interest in Fontana's art was matched by Fontana's interest in my own. An indication of the mutual respect [is] the fact that the only work of mine that could be sold at Galerie Iris Clert in Paris in 1959 found its owner in Fontana.

Shortly afterwards, Fontana had his first solo exhibition in Paris, just as I had. I was quite surprised when he proudly presented his new acquisition to me in Milan shortly afterwards. It was the first work of mine to come to Italy. So you can see that it is the artists who are the first to see what art is, at a time when nothing is certain. When everything is an adventure that the artist has to go through alone.

('DAS KALEIDOSKOP MEINER ERINNERUNGEN', 1995)[91] «

A generation that perceives itself as such is created by experiences that connect. We have seen that Heinz Mack was involved in entrusting Yves Klein, whom he had met almost by chance in Paris in 1955, with the inaugural exhibition of Galerie Schmela in Düsseldorf in 1957 (p. 62). In April 1959, Klein proposed Heinz Mack for a solo exhibition at his gallery, that of Iris Clert in Rue des Beaux-Arts in Paris,[88] and wrote an inspired text for the invitation card.[89] In 1961, Mack asked the Frenchman to be editor-in-chief of *ZERO 3*, whereupon Yves Klein designed the layout and stipulated that the last page of his own text be partially torn out or burned in each copy. As a result, his contribution ended differently in each copy, and each copy became unique, with Yves Klein's breath emanating from it, so to speak.[90] Otto Piene subsequently used Klein's torn out pages for his own sketches for many years.

In March 1959, Klein, Piene, Mack and his first wife, Margret, travelled in Mack's VW Beetle from Düsseldorf to Antwerp for an exhibition at the Hessenhuis.[92] A conversation ensued in which each of the three artists tried to formulate the greatest vision for their own work. Mack described his *Sahara Project*, which he had been working on since 1958. Klein and Piene commented affirmatively.[93] The *Sahara Project* was published in *ZERO 3* in 1961 (fig. p. 89), documenting it as a precursor to the American Land Art of the late 1960s.

»

Azimuth and ZERO were equally determined to transcend existing borders wherever they appeared. And Manzoni[94] was equally fascinated by the possibility of transcending borders, in fact he almost imagined the possibility of travelling between the European art centres as a kind of foreign minister or ambassador of the art world. But without a mandate or a budget. Much of the correspondence between Manzoni and myself[95] was about money, which neither of us had. Manzoni was probably the best-informed artist between London, Paris, Düsseldorf and Milan in terms of artistic encounters, fertilisations, pregnancies and labour pains, and the resulting happy events, wherever and however these events saw the light of day.

('DAS KALEIDOSKOP MEINER ERINNERUNGEN', 1995)[96] «

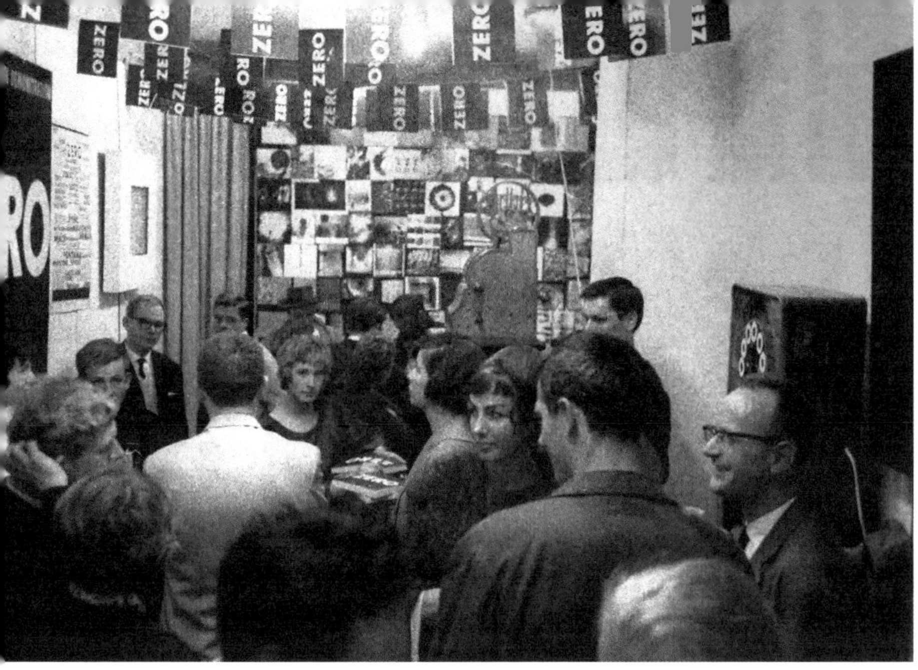

View into Galerie Schmela during
***ZERO – EDITION · DEMONSTRATION · EXPOSITION*,**
Düsseldorf
1961

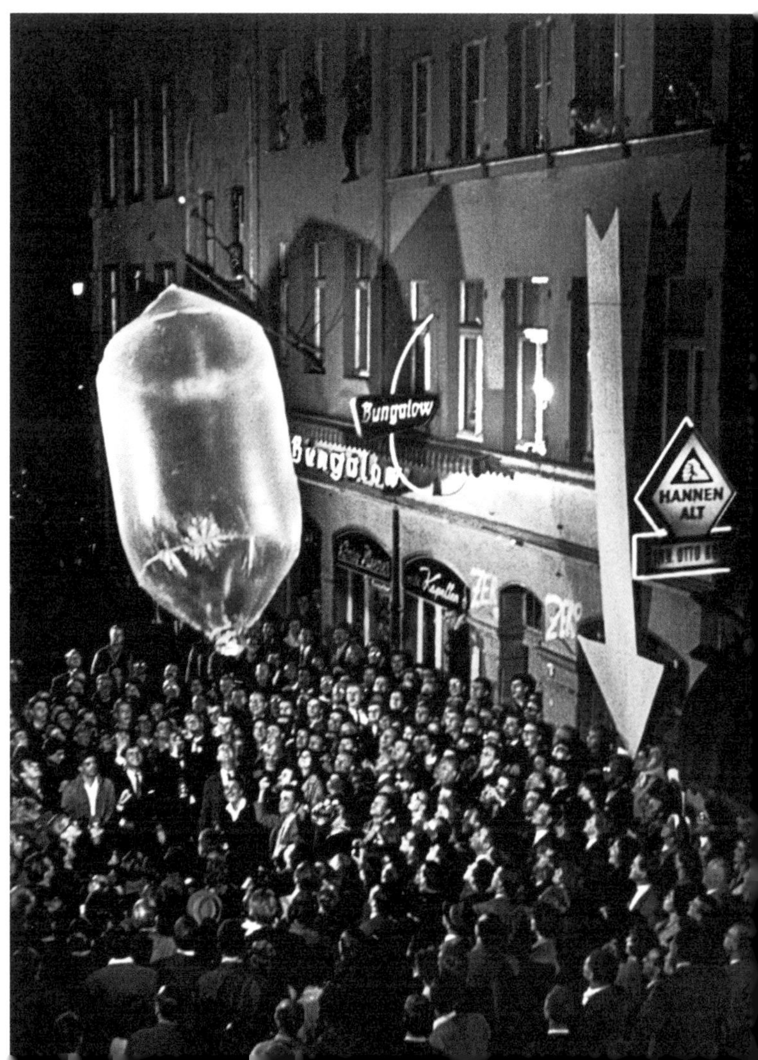

Helium-filled balloon above
Galerie Schmela during
***ZERO – EDITION · DEMONSTRATION · EXPOSITION*,**
Düsseldorf
1961

»

An exciting time. We all got on well back then, and we also all referred to each other and passionately defended each other and assured each other of our friendship, with the external conditions always remaining the same. These were: the scorn and laughter of the audience and the critics, and the constant struggle for existence of the penniless artist.

('DAS KALEIDOSKOP MEINER ERINNERUNGEN', 1995)[98] «

Heinz Mack and Otto Piene realised early on that they needed international connections if they were to establish a *raison d'être* in the German and Rhenish art scenes. In Milan, the magazine *Azimuth* made its presence felt with a gallery of the same name (except for the 'h' at the end), which functioned just like the later artist-run galleries, and in the Netherlands the group *NUL*, which had been in the making since 1960. Together with Paris, this created a spider's web, the gaps of which were soon filled in and which extended as far as Scandinavia. This is reminiscent of the strategies of Surrealism, except that ZERO was organised in a strictly decentralised way. Whenever some artists took an initiative somewhere, they invited others to join in. The membership of ZERO was informal and constantly changing. In the first eight years following the publication of the first issue of the eponymous magazine in the spring of 1958, there were around fifty ZERO exhibitions, including in 'Rotterdam, Amsterdam, Eindhoven, The Hague, Antwerp, Brussels, Ghent, Stockholm, Copenhagen, London, Zurich, Basel, Bern, Vienna, Paris, Venice, Milan, Rome, Bolzano, Barcelona, Madrid, New York, Philadelphia, Washington, Warsaw, Zagreb', as Heinz Mack later noted.[97]

»

There was also a great desire in society to have some fun after so much war. Dancing became important. The desire to travel abroad also gradually emerged. The word 'tourism' wasn't on everyone's lips yet, but there were the first signs of tourism, not mass tourism yet, but it was already an issue. So there was a spirit of optimism at the time, and we responded to it.

(OCTOBER 2023) «

However, in contrast to CoBrA from 1948 onwards, which coincided with New York replacing Paris as *the* cultural metropolis, it was also the first artists' group in half a century that was no longer closely oriented towards Paris.[99] At the same time, with the ZERO movement, Heinz Mack, Otto Piene, and Günther Uecker made Düsseldorf a centre of the international art scene again for the first time since the nineteenth-century Düsseldorf School of Painting, which has continued through several generations to the present day, with Mack and Uecker continuing to make an active contribution as international artists.[100]

As we have seen, the European ZERO movement included artists of the same generation, born between 1925 (Jean Tinguely) and 1938 (Rotraut). If one considers the broad impact of ZERO – for example with the *ZERO Demonstration* of 1961, the *ZERO Festival* on the Rhine meadows in 1962 for the successful television film by Gerd Winkler, the high profile of ZERO art in the media, and the gesture of ZERO art to open the door to a new era – one can ask whether ZERO was and is not much more, namely a generational phenomenon also in sociological terms, a 'ZERO Generation'.

In mid-May 1962, Heinz Mack drove his Volvo through Düsseldorf. He had mounted a roof gallery on the car, from which about seventy helium-filled balloons of various colours floated. When the car was moving and not at an intersection, where traffic was usually controlled by policemen, the balloons waved randomly. It is hard to imagine a more conspicuous vehicle. The artist had borrowed a speaking trumpet from the fire brigade – a metal funnel, not yet an electric megaphone – and from the open side door he invited passers-by to come to the banks of the Rhine at dusk, where a festival and a spectacle involving the general public would take place, the likes of which no one had ever seen before: 'It's called ZERO', he shouted, 'a ZERO demonstration'.

»

Perhaps there really is a ZERO Generation. I have often experienced that people around my age who have nothing to do with art tell me much later that ZERO was important to them.

« (SEPTEMBER 2023)

The action on the Rhine meadows in Düsseldorf took place on 17 May 1962. It was recorded for Gerd Winkler's film about ZERO: *0 x 0 = Kunst. Künstler ohne Farbe und Pinsel* (0 x 0 = Art. Artists Without Paint and Brushes). It was broadcast on WDR on 27 June of that year. One should bear in mind the media landscape of the time: television was *the* new medium; it brought the moving image into private homes. Few families owned a television. People from several households got together to watch television. In free Europe, only the WDR in Cologne – thanks to the German economic miracle – had the financial means to make and broadcast such films about art. So they were quickly picked up and broadcast throughout the German-speaking world.

In the surviving photographs – especially those taken by Reiner Ruthenbeck (fig. pp. 96 f.), who later studied under Joseph Beuys at the Düsseldorf Academy of Art and became a gifted conceptual artist – it is clear that the audience was young, around the age of the Düsseldorf ZERO protagonists, and that the event spoke directly from their hearts. With the simplest of material means, the new life experiences that this generation had recently had in their environment, and which the older generations in the deep conservatism of the post-war decades were sceptical of or even disbelieved in, were translated into new forms of artistic expression that had a direct effect on them. Light, air, wind, water, movement, emptiness, speed, immateriality, rhythm, and chance created a new framework of perception and suddenly translated this emerging world into a visual language that was an incredible relief for this generation after the stressful post-war years. This was their own world, which they felt would be the experience of a generation.

As an artistic movement, ZERO thus represented a generation. A few years earlier, there had been a famous precursor: with the publication of *Howl* (1956) by Allen Ginsberg and *On the Road* (1957) by Jack Kerouac, the term 'Beat Generation' had suddenly emerged.[101] Writing completely freely, against all rules, without thinking, and therefore allowing the form to emerge – as in Mack's ZERO paintings and light reliefs – became a generational characteristic of artists from a wide range of fields, including the songs of Bob Dylan and Joan Baez, the lyrics of the Rolling Stones, the Beatles, whose name was

»

In September 1957, Konrad Adenauer won the biggest election victory of all time. His election posters bore the slogan 'No Experiments!' in bold letters. I crossed out the word 'No' on as many posters as I could in Düsseldorf, so that only 'Experiments!' remained until the police arrived. It was typical that we tried to react publicly. Then it was in the newspaper: scandal, an artist has painted over posters. That's not proper. Someone had misbehaved. So that was all still part of the ZERO spirit.

« (SEPTEMBER 2023)

20-metre-long relief chain by Heinz Mack at the ***ZERO Festival*** on the Rhine meadows, Düsseldorf
1962

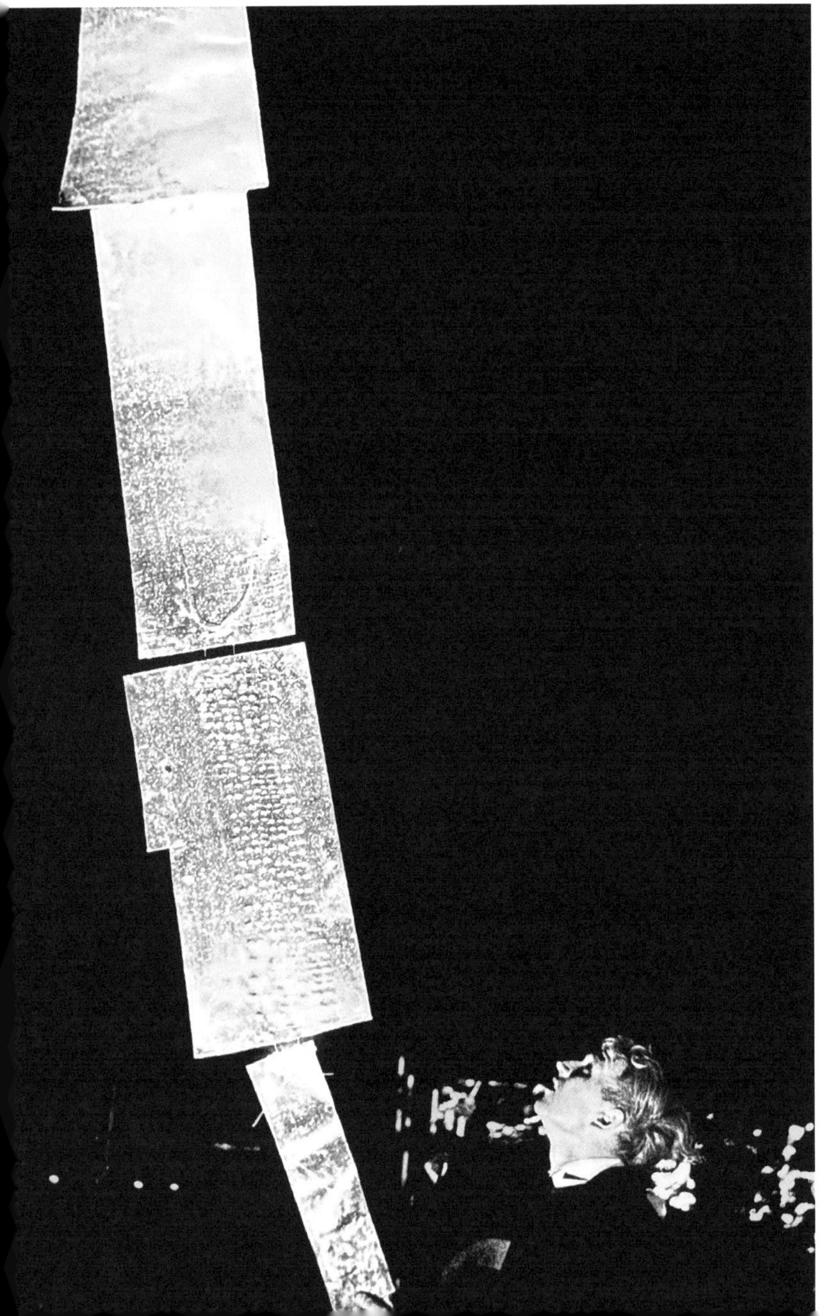

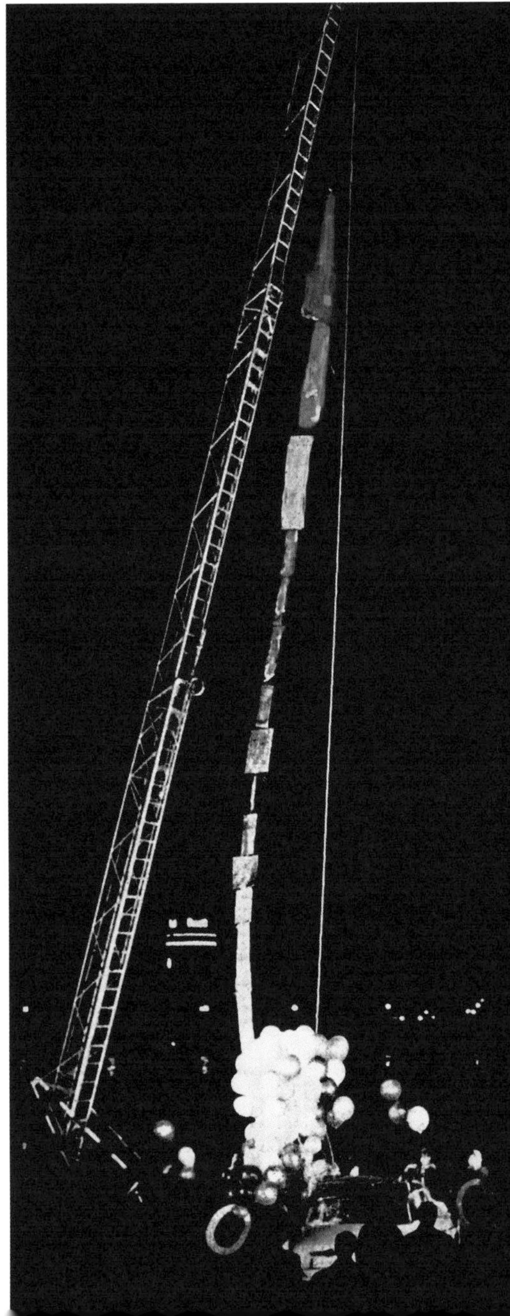

Plantation of aluminium flags
by Heinz Mack at the
ZERO Festival on the Rhine
meadows, Düsseldorf
1962

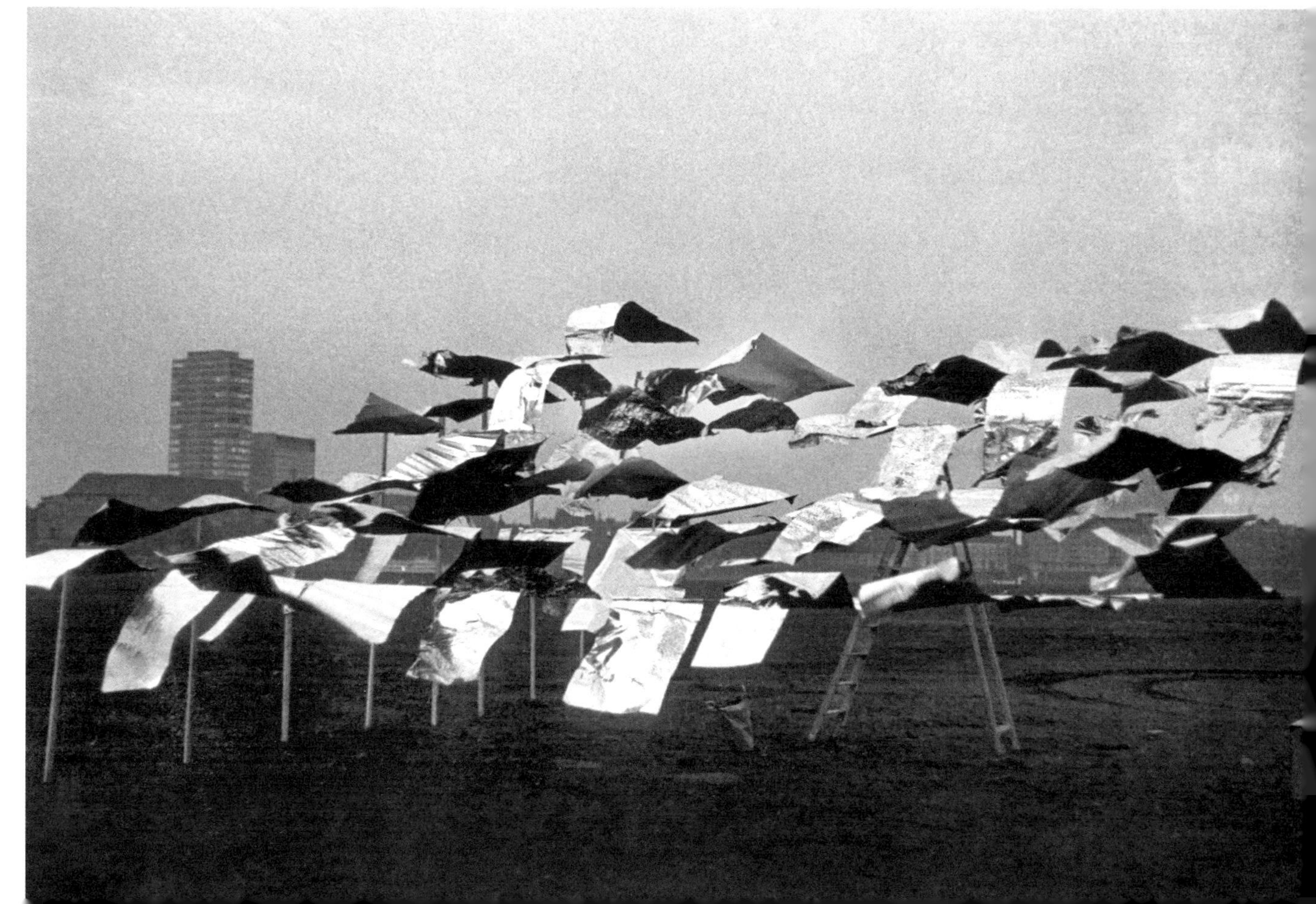

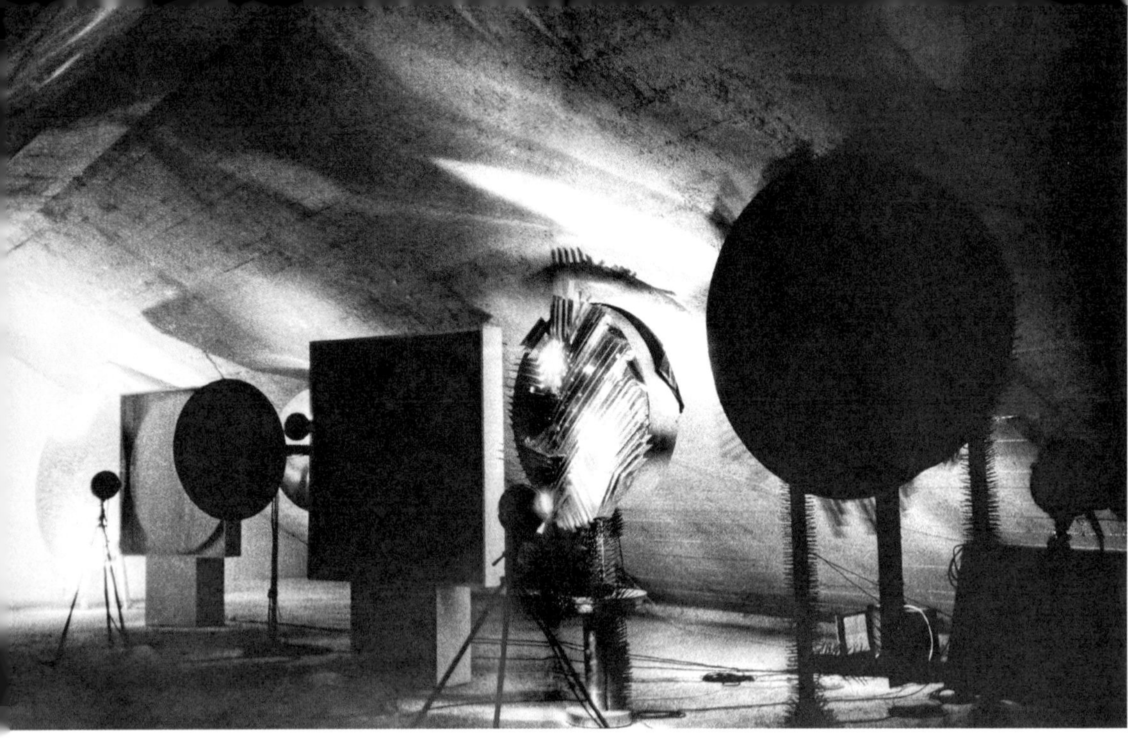

Heinz Mack, Otto Piene
and Günther Uecker
Light Room
(Hommage à Fontana),
at ***documenta III***
Kassel
1964

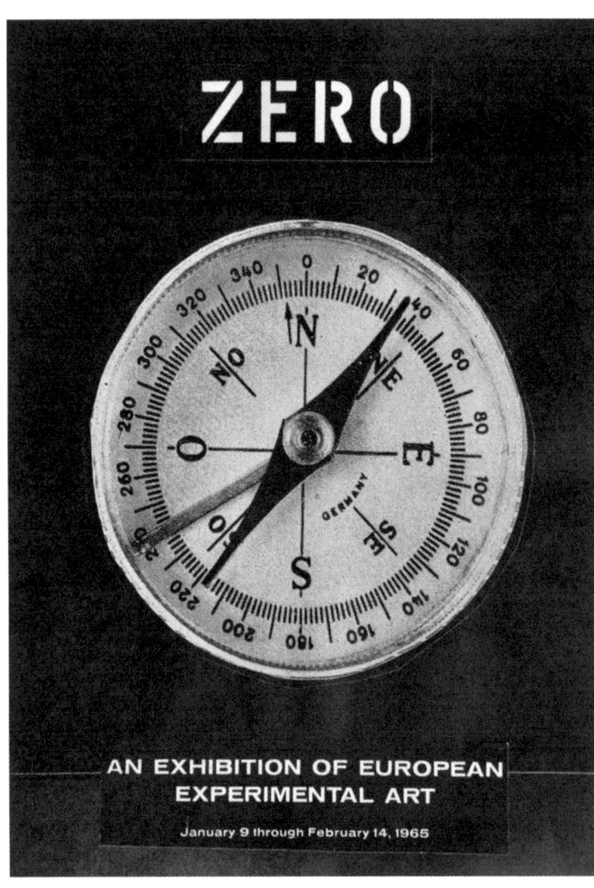

Original design by Heinz Mack
for a poster for the exhibition
Group ZERO at the
Washington Gallery of
Modern Art,
Washington, D.C.
1965

Die Wüste lebt!

.....die Welt von Fontana
ist eine Welt der Leere.
die Phaenomenologie der Leere
ist eine Umschreibung der Wüste.
Fontana ist wie ich ein Bewohner
der Leere. Nur in der Wüste
haben unsere Imaginationen
jene Freiheit der Bewegung,
welche ich die Freiheit des
Künstlers nenne.
Unsere moderne Kultur war
bislang eine Kultur der Großstadt.
Aber die Zeit der Futuristen
ist Vergangenheit, denn unsere
zukünftige Liebe breitet sich
endlos im Raum der Wüste
und im Weltall aus.
terra incognito aeterna est
Viva la concetto spaciale
Ich begrüße meinen Nach-
barn in der Wüste – ich
grüße Fontana!

1961

mack

Düsseldorf, mack

'The Desert Lives!',
poem by Heinz Mack
as an homage to
Lucio Fontana
1961

»

My exhibition at Galleria Azimut[105] [in Milan] also had a fashion challenge during the opening, probably conceived and staged by Manzoni. A dozen young ladies and a few companions had come along for filming, all of whom had to look at my works wearing extravagant futuristic clothes and sunglasses; the latter so as not to be 'dazzled' by the intensity of the artificial and artistic light reflected by my reliefs and rotors.

('DAS KALEIDOSKOP MEINER ERINNERUNGEN', 1995)[106] «

»

The so-called '68 generation, which followed after ZERO, emerged as a political movement primarily through students. The unrest that arose among the '68ers would not have been entirely conceivable without ZERO. In a way, as others have also recognised and ventilated, ZERO was a stimulus for the generation that followed to finally take to the barricades in public and make demands in surprising forms of action. Underneath it all, this probably had something to do with ZERO.

(SEPTEMBER 2023) «

emblematic of the Beat Generation, underground film in New York and California, Happening and Fluxus art in the United States and Western Europe and Viennese Actionism.

In the visual arts, the ZERO Generation is the equivalent of the Beat Generation in literature and music. This can be seen in the magazine *ZERO 3*, where the decision to radically reduce formal means, taken by Heinz Mack and Otto Piene in 1957–58 and later by Günther Uecker, proved to be the programme of an entire generation, with partner groups in Amsterdam, Antwerp, Ghent, Paris, Bern, Milan, Vienna, Copenhagen, London, and Zagreb.

ZERO caught on just as quickly as Pop Art from 1962 onwards. However, no gallerist was ever given an international monopoly on the distribution of ZERO art like Leo Castelli in New York and the gallery network he subsequently established for Pop. The international ZERO movement was organised by the participating artists themselves. It was an idealistic and artistic connection and only marginally a market phenomenon. At the time, any salaried employee could afford the prices. At the heart of this generational alliance was the idea of reinventing art in the face of a radically changing world.

The artists around ZERO rejected Beat, Fluxus, and Happening for their anarchistic, sometimes cynical and, above all, form-dissolving orientation, which led to the 'anti-form' of the 1960s and 1970s.[102] Unlike the Beat Generation, ZERO did not see itself as a counterculture – although it did protest against, for example, German reconstruction architecture.[103] However, with their works, their direct use of light, movement, fire, water, and the hitherto unimaginable forms made possible by new technological materials, as well as their anticipation of the future, these artists quickly became trailblazers, embodying the generational feeling of many of their contemporaries, including those who otherwise had little contact with art.[104]

The phenomenon of the ZERO Generation also includes the influence of ZERO art in fashion, advertising, and everyday life. Volumes could be written on the subject. For example, the metallic clothing collection of the fashion designer Paco Rabanne, a friend of Denise René – Mack's Parisian gallerist from 1961 – with its mirrored dresses, wearable reliefs, and dynamic metallic structures, went viral in the world's media from February 1966.

A highlight in the international history of ZERO was the exhibition *Nul* at the Stedelijk Museum in Amsterdam in March 1962, whose director Willem Sandberg, himself an artist and post-Dadaist poet,[107] brought together everything that had been brewing at the time. Without this exhibition in what was then the most important museum of modern and contemporary art in Europe, ZERO might not have had any lasting impact. Sandberg's successor, Edy de Wilde, followed up in the spring of 1965 with *Nul 1965*. The avant-garde associations Gruppo T from Italy and Gutai from Japan were now also represented, while only Mack, Piene, and Uecker were still represented by ZERO.[108]

As early as the summer of 1964, at *documenta III* in Kassel, the *Light Room* by Mack, Piene, and Uecker had the character of a visionary Gesamtkunstwerk (fig. p. 93). Arnold Bode, the founder of the documenta, wanted to add a younger touch to the conservative selection made by the documenta council and at the last minute invited the three ZERO artists to show their works in the attic of the Fridericianum, the main building of the large-scale exhibition. They first had to clear the rubble from the war-damaged rooms. But their staging of motorised and static light reliefs and ZERO pictures in artificial light was then a highly dynamic environment. In contrast to the largely conventional forms of work at *documenta III*, panel painting and sculpture were abandoned here in favour of new artistic dimensions. Word had spread among the artists that Lucio Fontana had been juried out.[110] Heinz Mack then set up a slide projector in the *Light Room*,[111] which projected a black-and-white photographic image of one of Fontana's slit paintings onto the wall. 'So Fontana was present after all, and in a very immaterial way.'[112] It was the only photographic work at this documenta.

»
While Fontana was still alive, around 1963, Piene, Uecker and I thought about organising a banquet in his honour, just as Picasso had honoured the customs officer Henri Rousseau. We came up with all sorts of ideas. Piene, Uecker and I spent at least a whole night fantasising about how to stage the banquet. We were not unaware that Fontana had a very special sense of grand gestures and stage performances, always combined with an inner sincerity without any vanity. Fontana should have the honour and be asked to slit the tablecloth with a single cut.
« ('DAS KALEIDOSKOP MEINER ERINNERUNGEN', 1995)[109]

Increasingly, however, ZERO proved to be a corset that required a great deal of organisation. With the exhibition *Weiss auf Weiss* (White on White), organised in 1966 at the Kunsthalle Bern by its director Harald Szeemann and the ZERO artist Christian Megert, and subsequently shown by Werner Hofmann at the Museum des 20. Jahrhunderts in Vienna under the title *Kinetika*, the contours of the group dissolved. Other concepts came to the fore. By 1964, Mack and Piene had already travelled to the United States, to other shores.

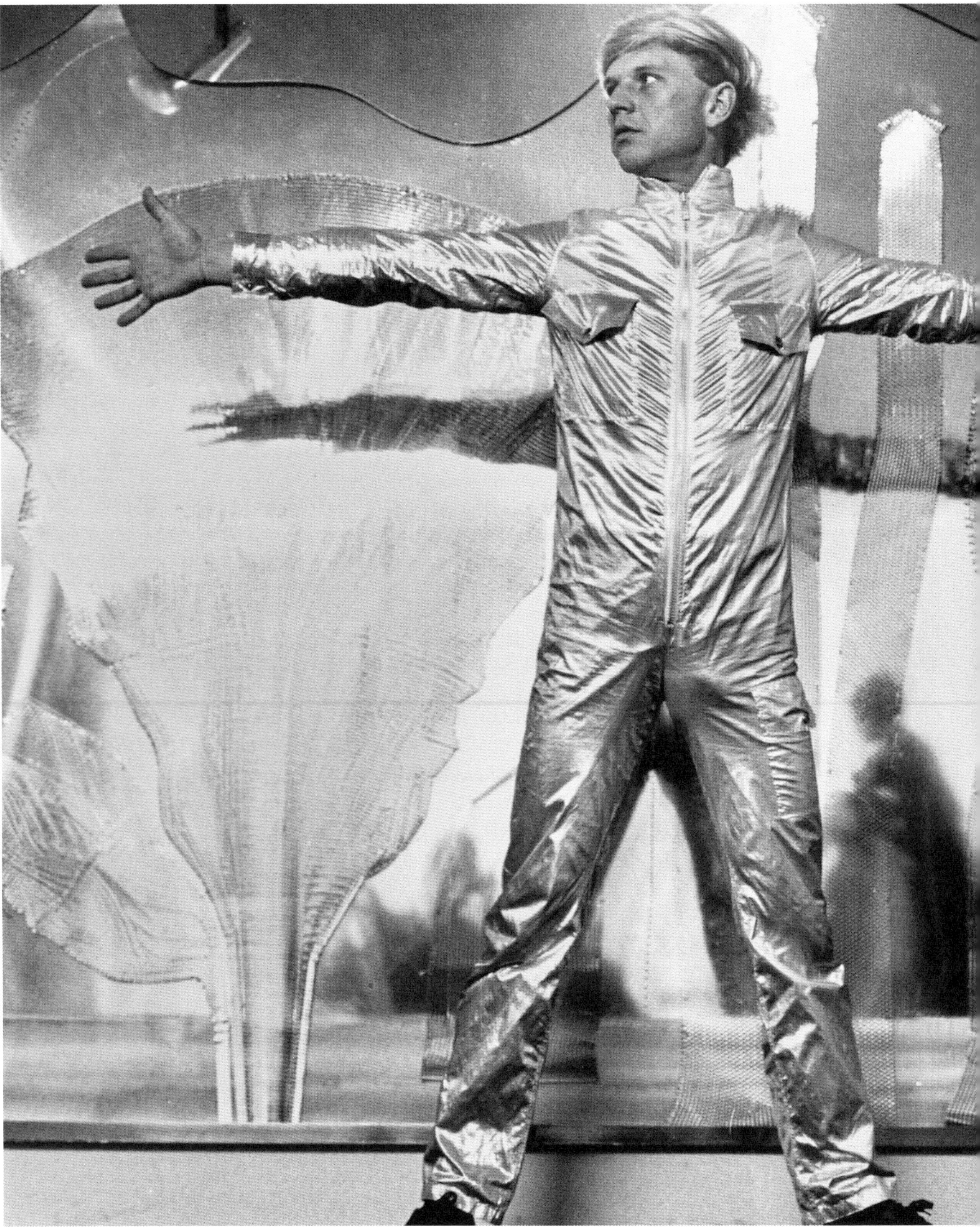

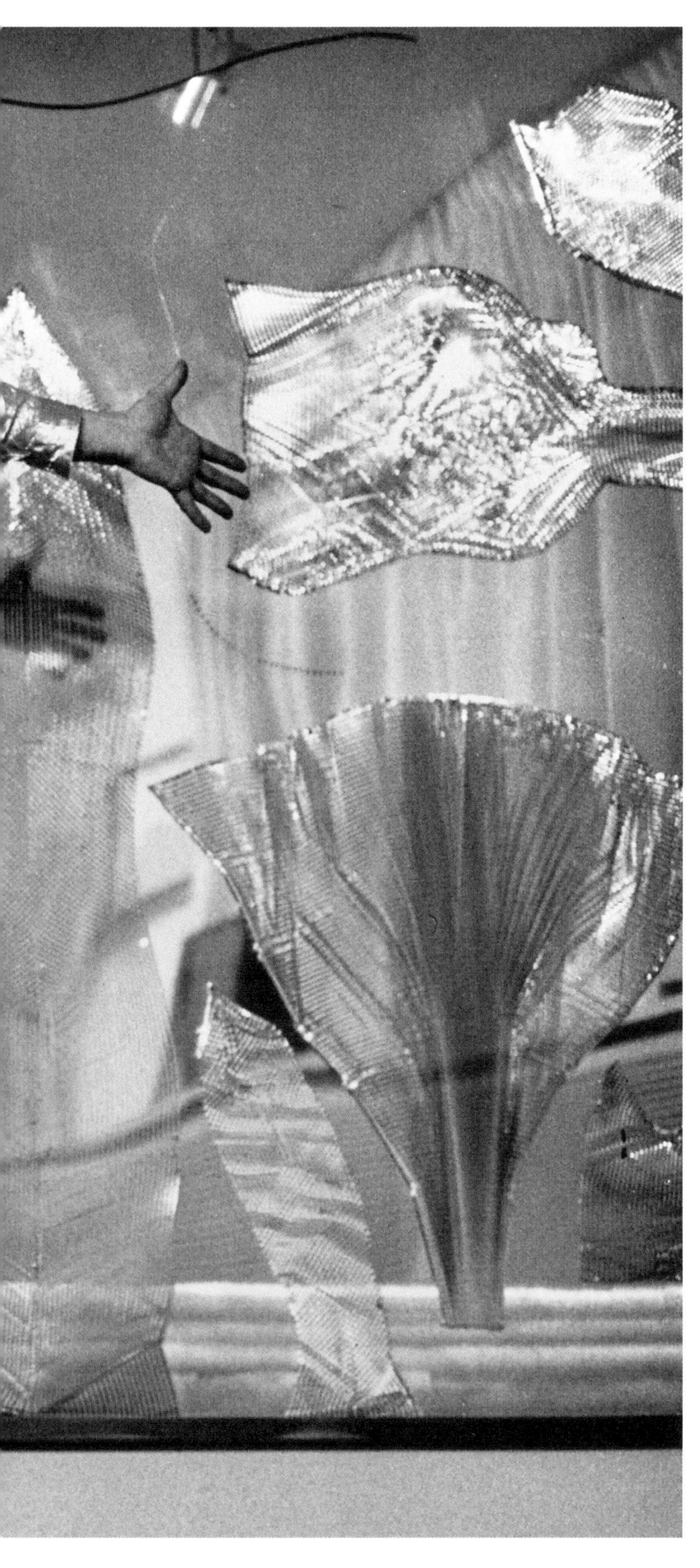

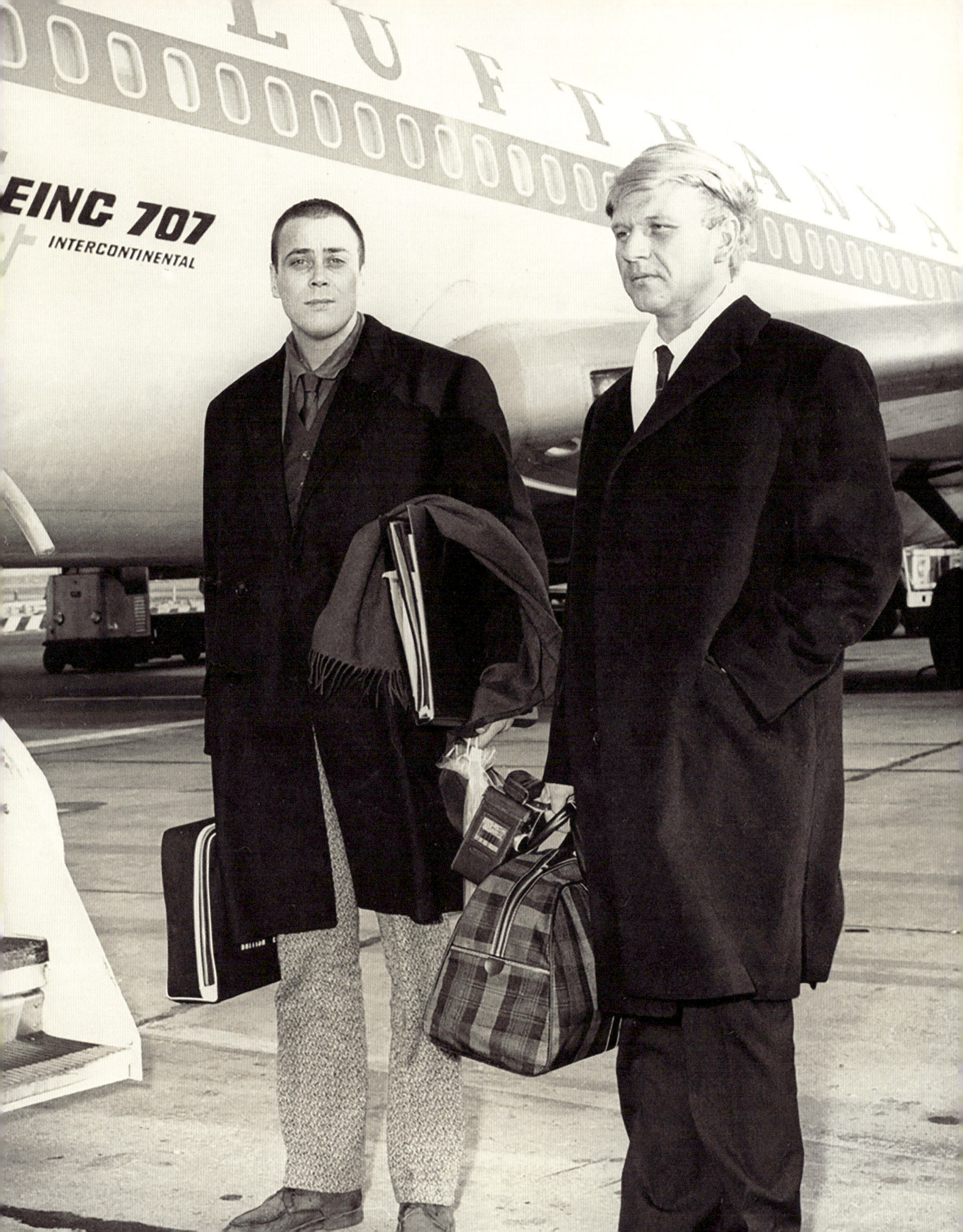
EINC 707
INTERCONTINENTAL

NEW YORK

Günther Uecker and Heinz Mack
at the airport in New York
1964

«

When I was in New York in 1963, I was searching for new materials, hoping they would give birth to ideas. I received a tip from Nam June Paik, who told me to look at one of these appliance wholesale stores on the Bowery where I could find something for very little money. What I chanced upon there was an aluminum honeycomb material that is patented and produced by a company in California – a material I had never encountered before in Germany. It was malleable, and by stretching it I realized that its structure was quite similar to structures in nature. [...] I later learned that the stable and light material I found on the Bowery was also used to fabricate airplanes, rockets, and military vessels.

(JULYAN ELIAS BRONNER, '500 WORDS BY HEINZ MACK', 2014)[113] «

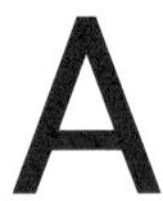utumn 1963: Heinz Mack meets Nam June Paik on the street in New York. Both artists had recently arrived in the city. They know each other from Cologne, where Paik, a highly talented music student who had fled South Korea at the start of the Korean War, had come to Mack's attention through the WDR Studio for Electronic Music and at the Düsseldorf Academy of Art as a dialogue partner of K. O. Götz.[114] Mack takes Paik's advice to heart and comes across a new material in a shop in Canal Street, now a highly fashionable area: honeycomb nets made of aluminium, which were to take his art beyond the concept of ZERO in Düsseldorf.

Why had the artist come to New York? Among the international exhibitions of the ZERO artists Heinz Mack, Otto Piene, and Günther Uecker was one at Howard Wise Gallery in New York from 12 November to 5 December 1964 (fig. pp. 112, 115)[115]. Mack and Uecker spent three weeks in New York in the autumn of 1963 to prepare for the exhibition. They both stayed at the Chelsea Hotel (see: fig. pp. 108 f.), the legendary, cheap artists' hostel on 23rd Street. Larry Rivers, an important painter on the fringes of Pop Art, was one of their neighbours. So they were right at the heart of the scene.

Mack and Uecker returned to Düsseldorf before Christmas 1963. However, Mack, at this time a secondary school teacher, married and the father of two daughters, made one of the most important decisions of his life: he wanted to go to New York as an artist as soon as possible, at least for a while. So he resigned as a teacher, in the middle of the German economic miracle and despite his good salary. The civil servant who received his resignation with astonishment told him that he could return to teaching at any time if things did not work out in New York.[116] But to commit himself solely to a life as an independent artist was a definitive decision.

On 12 November 1964, Howard Wise opened the exhibition *Zero* in his Manhattan gallery, featuring nail objects by Uecker, smoke paintings and sculptures by Piene and light reliefs, light steles, rotors, and a light screen by Mack. The exhibition was well received by the art critic John Canaday in *The New York Times* (fig. p. 114).[117] Mack's works were made in New York. Donald Judd, who had founded Minimalism around this time, wrote in his review of the exhibition in *Arts Magazine*: 'In general the work is unusual and unlike anything here. It is probably the best in Europe, if you include all the related artists, such as Klein and Castellani. [...] Mack is the most original of the three, all, incidentally, in their thirties.'[118]

»

In New York, all the critics, all the press, all the gallerists, all the museum directors, all of them, as it were, only showed American art. And then, of course, it was a sensation for me and for Otto Piene and Günther Uecker that Howard Wise was prepared to organise an exhibition with us. The fact that Denise René, who had connections in New York and later opened a second gallery there, had exhibited my work in Paris also played a role.

« (JANUARY 2022)

Being in New York in 1964 proved to be a special situation. Robert Rauschenberg was awarded the Grand Prize for Painting at the Venice Biennale that year, which was interpreted as New York replacing Paris as the world capital of modern art.[119] Here, the fields were less demarcated than in Europe; people talked to each other differently. Around this time, Pop Art came to Europe from New York like a bolt from the blue. It was quickly followed by Minimalism and conceptual art, also from New York. In 1965, The Museum of Modern Art ennobled Op Art and kinetic art with the exhibition *The Responsive Eye*. Young galleries such as Rudolf Zwirner's newly opened gallery in Cologne, that of Ileana Sonnabend, the former wife of Leo Castelli, in Paris and, a little later, Konrad Fischer's gallery in Düsseldorf, disseminated American art in Europe. The New York galleries were quicker to take the initiative and were more internationally active than those in Paris. All this took place in a much smaller network than today; back then, every voice was heard.

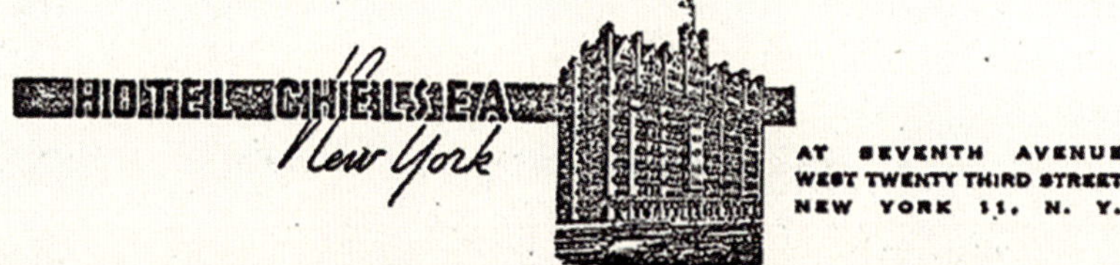
HOTEL CHELSEA New York

AT SEVENTH AVENUE
WEST TWENTY THIRD STREET
NEW YORK 11, N. Y.

TELEPHONE CHELSEA 3-3700
CABLE ADDRESS • HOCHELSEA • NEW YORK

Wenn man in 12000 mtr. Höhe
fliegt u. dann noch einmal
hinauf in den Himmel sieht
– wird es schwarz.

Da ich meine Gedanken
so leicht im Licht u. im
Himmel verliere habe ich
für mich entschieden
eine gewisse Grenze zu
respektieren.

Damit möchte ich sagen
daß ich meine Ideen jetzt
kritischer betrachte, daß ich
weil mehr meine Aufmerksamkeit solchen
Ideen zuwenden werde, die
versprechen sichtbar gemacht
werden zu können.

LARGE and SOUND-PROOF ROOMS

Handwritten note by Heinz Mack on Hotel Chelsea stationery, New York
November 1964

Ich glaube also immer mehr an das, was man *sehen* kann!

Ja, man muß es so gut sehen können, daß das Denken und Fantasieren wieder aufhört.

Wunschlos sehen =
= " glücklich sein.

Oder:
für mich ist das Licht selbst (d.h. alles, was im Licht erscheint) geheimnisvoller als alles, was dunkel ist.

mack

(New-York, Nov. 1964)

»

Howard Wise gave me an advance of $1,000 a month right from the start and said: 'We'll settle up later.' That was his very first decision when he invited me to New York. He'd already told me that by post – I still think that's great. Even the gallerist Alfred Schmela in Düsseldorf was impressed that someone would give money without having seen the finished paintings.

(JANUARY 2022) «

»

My studio in New York was a loft, a single room, 4.5 metres wide and 30 metres long. It was like a long corridor. There were only windows at the ends, very large windows. There were big fans hanging from the ceiling. That was also the heating. So I always had abstract music playing above me. It was a very restless neighbourhood. There was always an unbelievable amount of noise, fights, there was shooting, some of the cars in the streets were completely rusted or burned, lying around in ruins. It was a crazy area, wonderful material for films. When I was freezing in the cold winters, I would put on my black suit, which I must have worn when I was in the eighth grade, and with that black suit and bow tie I would go into the lobbies of the best hotels in New York, sit down in a comfortable armchair and read the newspapers there. I always loved being in a world-famous hotel because it had the best international press.

(JANUARY 2022) «

Heinz Mack returned to New York in early 1964. He first stayed at the Chelsea Hotel again. After a month, he found a studio in the East Village, then a poor neighbourhood in Lower Manhattan. The space, at 410 East 10th Street, was much larger than the studios usually found in Europe. Commercial space in the East Village was cheap to rent.[120] The vastness of the North American continent could be felt here in this way. The artist lived and worked here during his New York years (fig. p. 119).

His Triumph sports car, which he had shipped across the Atlantic, was probably the smallest car in Manhattan for years. Mack racked up a lot of parking tickets, but because the car was registered in Germany, he never had to pay. He pinned them in a thick bundle to the wall of his studio. From time to time, he would spend a week in Düsseldorf with his family.

In New York, Mack now had a new environment in terms of materials, tasks, and encounters. There was a regular exchange with Nam June Paik. Christo and Jeanne-Claude were now also living in the city. Conversations with two living legends of Abstract Expressionism, Ad Reinhardt and Barnett Newman, left a deep impression.

Ad Reinhardt, one of the most radical painters of the first generation of Abstract Expressionists, was a feared polemicist. His thesis of 'the picture after the last picture',[121] an apodictic assertion within Abstract Expressionism, posed a challenge to Mack, a trained philosopher. He would later realise it in his own way in the *Chromatic Constellations*, his polychrome paintings since 1991. It was in New York that Mack realised how much this idea, which can also be found in the work of Mark Rothko and Barnett Newman, had to do with a Jewish pictorial tradition that was hardly to be found in contemporary art in Germany at the time. With the exception of Barnett Newman, however, he had no contact with the other protagonists of Abstract Expressionism.

»

I came into contact with Christo very often and visited his studio several times. We knew each other from Paris, through Yves Klein and his circle of Nouveaux Réalistes and Pierre Restany. Christo was already thinking in terms of landscape. I went to Yayoi Kusama's studio twice, and we saw each other regularly at openings. Once she cooked a meal for me that I will never forget. Ad Reinhardt was almost twenty years older than me and a very difficult but interesting person to talk to, incredibly controversial in his behaviour. But he was also very brilliant. He was somehow interested in me, not because of my art, although he knew what I was doing. He saw my exhibition in London at McRoberts & Tunnard in 1964 and the one at Howard Wise in New York. He always wanted to know what was going on in Europe, and maybe that's why he was interested in me as a person to talk to.

« (JANUARY 2022)

»

It was different with Barnett Newman than with Ad Reinhardt. He was almost like a father to me, he had a fatherly manner and also something of a grandad, very friendly. Like Reinhardt, his main interest was: What was going on in Europe, what was being done there? Including the questions: What was it like with Yves Klein? What was it like with ZERO? He was very interested in all that. Also what Germany was like now, after the murder of the Jews.[122] What I would like to mention is that he invited me to his home – a private invitation. The food he served was kosher, and he made the best pasta in Manhattan. I'll say it again, it's not topical for you, but it is for my generation: he was Jewish, and of course I grew up in the Nazi era, and for a man like that to invite me privately to his home to eat pasta with me and his wife was anything but a matter of course. You always have to say that, because there was still a lot of resentment at the time, even in New York.

« (JANUARY 2022)

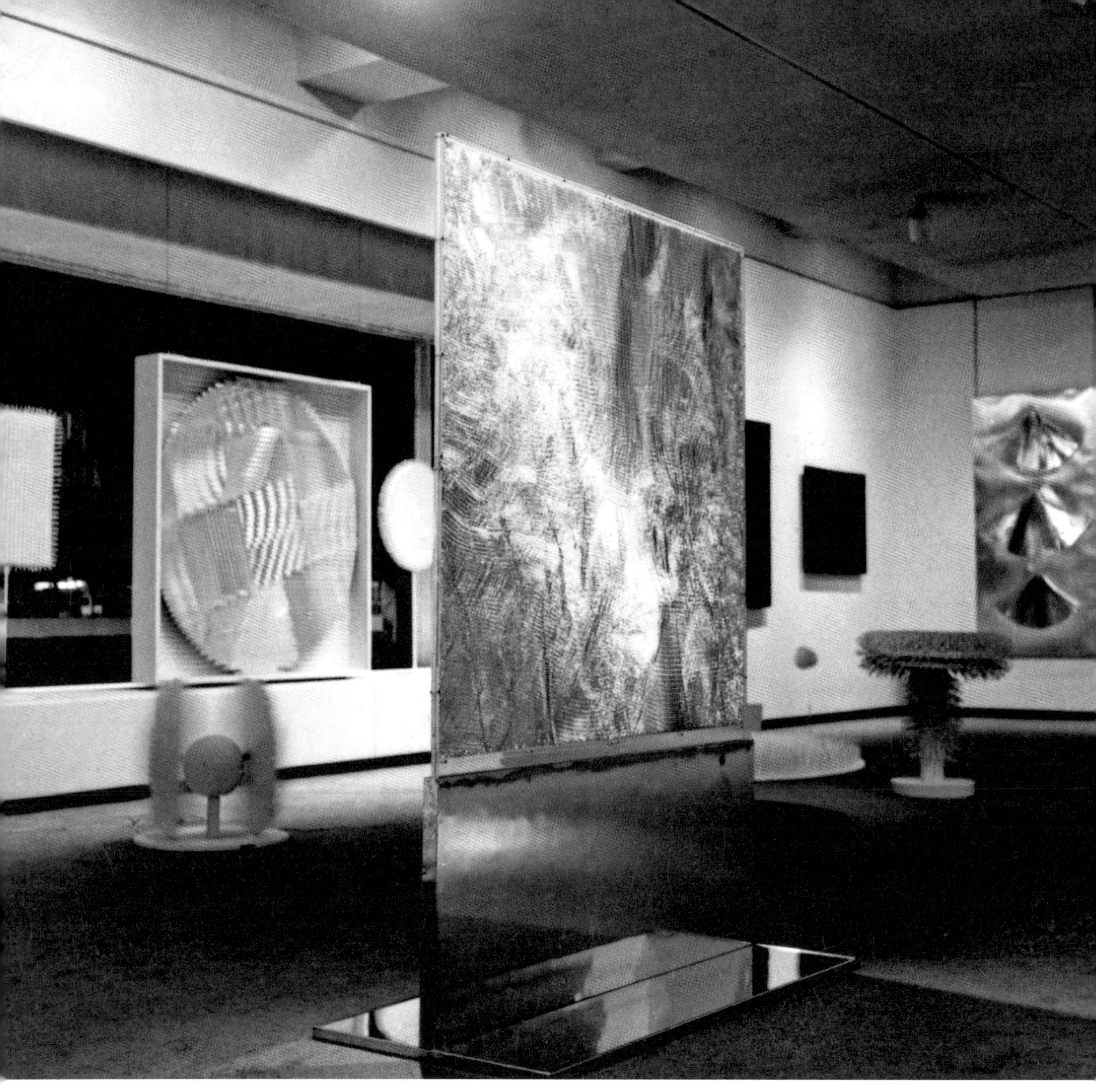

Installation view
Group ZERO,
Howard Wise Gallery,
New York
1964

Was it a coincidence that Barnett Newman, the second radical artist-theorist of the first generation of Abstract Expressionists, was interested in Heinz Mack? Like Ad Reinhardt, Newman did not follow the gestural line of early Abstract Expressionism but created reduced painterly designs in the wake of Piet Mondrian and 'Russian' Constructivism. In his theoretical writings, Newman updated the concept of the sublime from the eighteenth-century philosophical discussions of Edmund Burke and Immanuel Kant for contemporary art. At the same time, he propagated a nominalism of the image – the image is sufficient in itself as an image – that had a broad impact on the New York art scene of the 1960s, from Jasper Johns to Donald Judd and Andy Warhol, and was incorporated into Minimalism and conceptual art. This goes far beyond the original ZERO ideas of 1958–60. Mack's work in New York and after, with the Plexiglas and honeycomb steles, wing-shaped aluminium reliefs and purist rotors, was influenced by these ideas.[123]

»

In 1966, I was also able to produce the first stainless steel sculptures in New York. They became three steles. I called them the *Three Graces*. Barnett Newman came to the workshop where they were made, out of curiosity. I had told him I was going to make steles there. Howard Wise sold the *Three Graces*. They are now in a large sculpture park in Wisconsin.[124] Shortly after that, Barnett Newman made his first iron sculpture, also a stele, but standing on a tip. I doubt there was really no influence. We talked about whether he should leave the welding seams, and I persuaded him to do that.

« (JANUARY 2022)

The Sculptor Nowadays Is the Favorite Son

By JOHN CANADAY

THE 20th century plays favorites. Having birthed abstract art, it has now put the abstract painter on the ropes while revealing a whole category of new punches to the abstract sculptor. For every painter who succumbs to "the exhaustion all around us," there is a sculptor who finds new vigor.

Abstract painting (we are rich in metaphors today) was an incubator baby that thrived on a diet of special injections and expensive stimulants, but is currently living in an iron lung thanks to the around-the-clock ministrations of relatives and friends. It is a rather pretty patient, but the artificiality of its existence must be recognized. There is no reason why it should not hold court under these odd circumstances, as it continues to do, but there is no point in our pretending, as we are expected to do, that it can offer anything more than an even exchange, at best, for the nursing we give it.

Art should return more than even measure; it should reveal and intensify forms of experience common to the artist and the rest of us. The test of a work of art is not the amount of wordage we can expend in convincing ourselves that it is any good, but the extent to which it can hold us, sometimes in spite of all the wordage we might expend in arguing that it shouldn't hold us at all.

The point is made succinctly at the Howard Wise Gallery in an exhibition of work by three members of Group Zero, a well publicized, amorphous cluster of variegated talents, fertile in manifestos, riding high on that treacherous spot, the crest of the avant-garde wave. The paintings by Otto Piene, although they have the fillip of being executed in "oil and smoke on canvas," have nothing more to offer than some more spots of color that can be defended only in words, being defenseless in themselves except as illustrations of experimental esthetics. Illustration of principles is not the same thing as creative expression, and these paintings are subsidiary to the ideas they demonstrate. The ideas have not produced works of art possessed of a life of their own.

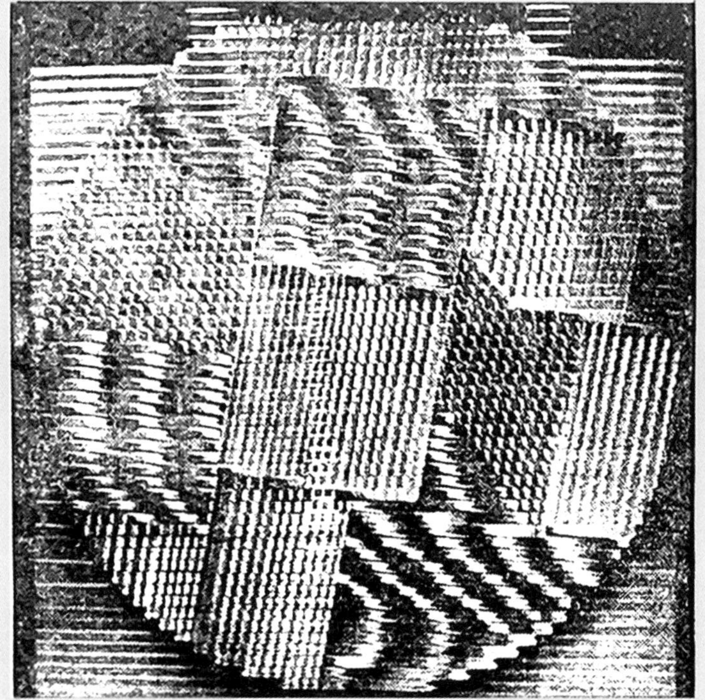

The New York Times (Falk)

Heinz Mack's "White Light-Dynamo"
"... Zero means a zone of silence"

The sculpture in the exhibition by Gunther Uecker and Heinz Mack is another matter. Mr. Uecker works with nails driven into wood, everything painted white. Mr. Mack's materials are aluminum, glass, wood, chromed brass, Plexiglass, mirrors — and water. Plus animating motors.

These materials, adaptable to the silliest kind of gadgetry, have been used to produce objects of visual beauty and great fascination. Mr. Uecker's nails, driven at calculated angles in varying densities, are the three-dimensional elements of compositions that can be called sculptural, but they also cast shadows that are, in effect, a form of painting in light.

Theory Aside

Mr. Mack's scintillant materials fuse form and light in mutual dependence and mutual exhilaration. In "White Light - Dynamo," illustrated here, a disc turns behind a fluted glass pane to produce light patterns that shift and flow with the variety of streamwater running across rocks, but with the imposed order of art. No theorizing is needed to back up the impact of these inventions. The theorizing is there (exhaustively, in published tracts) but the work of art supersedes it. Here theory produces art (or has been derived from the production, who knows?) and, having served its function, may be cast off like the husk of a seed when the plant is rooted.

This has happened to abstract sculpture while abstract painting has remained parasitic for various reasons, and the strongest reason might be that sculpture can never be purely abstract. A nail is a nail, a pane of glass is a pane of glass. Their corporeal substance imposes a reality not comparable to the nominal physical reality of a paint film. Abstract painters recognize this fact every time they build their paint into sculptural thickness—pushing it, punching it and digging back into it. They recognize the same need by their increasing use of collage, which gives them something tangible to work with in a field where intangibles have failed to supplant the satisfactions involved in the imitation of textures in techniques that used to be the painter's delight and preoccupation as a demonstration of skills no longer valued.

New Form

What we are getting is an art form that hybridizes painting and sculpture, a form approached from both directions but sharing more the nature of sculpture than of painting. The world today supplies the material, both ideological and as matter, for this art. New industrial products liberate new sculptural forms, and the scientific industrial world suggests them in machine parts, engineering elements and laboratory instruments. Somehow these forms have served the painter only as patterns for reduction, while the sculptor finds them the genesis of invention. And although the sculptors in this exhibition make the point with extreme directness, the same combination of reality and transformation — drawn from the environment peculiar to our civilization — nourishes the bulk of abstract sculpture today.

These remarks are made without regard to the aims of Group Zero although they deal with three of the group's leaders. Actually, the attachments of the group, whose name indicates "a zone of silence and of pure possibilities for a new beginning" include some of the noisiest artists who seem to me to be most in need of cleaning up, with more joining every day. If this is a bandwagon, we may look forward to its transformation into a sinking ship from sheer overweight, but I would place a bet that Mr. Uecker and Mr. Mack will manage to stay afloat.

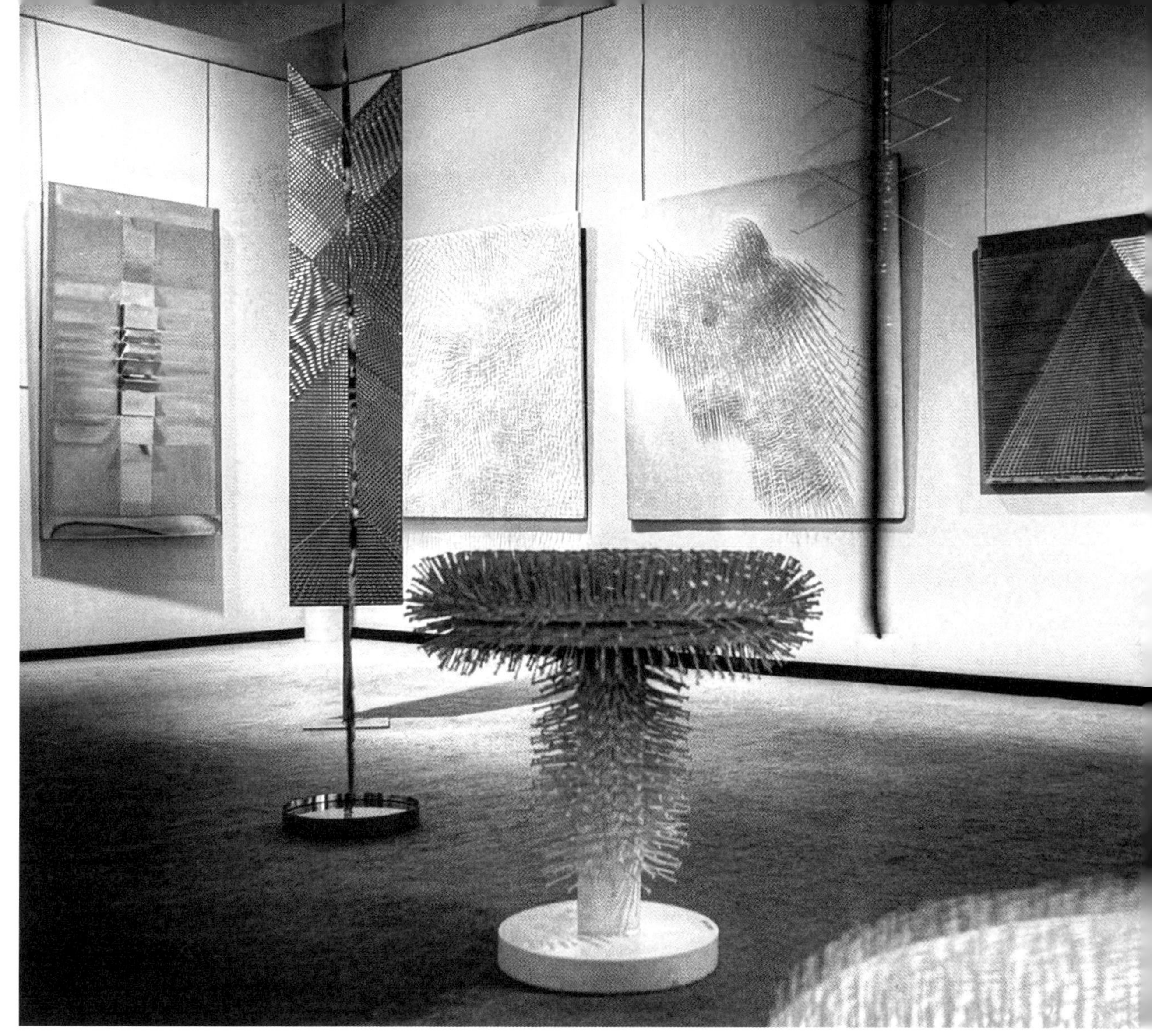

Installation view
Group ZERO,
Howard Wise Gallery,
New York
1964

←
Review of the ZERO exhibition by John Canaday in *The New York Times*
22 November 1964

The artist always returned to his family in Düsseldorf for Christmas, and in 1965 they also spent a holiday together in the Tyrolean mountains.[125] The artist's first wife, Margret Mack, née Rudeloff, kept in touch with galleries and museum people in Europe and handled the relevant correspondence. In April 1965, Mack travelled briefly to Europe for exhibitions of the three Düsseldorf ZERO artists at the Stedelijk Museum in Amsterdam and the Kestner-Gesellschaft in Hannover. In 1965 and 1966, he also had solo exhibitions at Galerie Schmela in Düsseldorf, through which the work he had created in New York became known in the Rhineland.

» *It's really touching that you talk so much about us over there so often and keep the interest alive until Alfred's arrival in the autumn. We think you're right to stay with Howard Wise for the time being;[126] you can keep an eye on the rest and decide later.*

(MONIKA SCHMELA, LETTER TO HEINZ MACK IN NEW YORK, 10 JUNE 1965, MACK ARCHIVE) «

During these years, Heinz Mack also acted as an intermediary between Galerie Schmela in Düsseldorf, the home of ZERO, and Leo Castelli Gallery in New York, the world's leading gallery of the 1960s and 1970s. Born in Trieste in the Austro-Hungarian Empire in 1907, the highly educated Leo Castelli established the first worldwide gallery network, from his gallery in posh 77th Street, between the Frick Collection and The Metropolitan Museum of Art.[127] In this context, Mack organised a meeting between Castelli and Alfred Schmela during the latter's stay in New York in the autumn of 1965, after which Castelli visited Schmela in Düsseldorf. The export of the latest New York art to Europe continued from the end of the 1960s with Minimalism and conceptual art through Konrad Fischer, whose talent as a gallerist Schmela had been the first to recognise. The fact that it also went in the opposite direction is shown, among other things, by the fact that the first canvas by Blinky Palermo, a student of Joseph Beuys at the Düsseldorf Academy of Art, was sold to a collector in New York through the mediation of Heinz Mack.[128]

» I drove to [the gallerist] Castelli several times – I don't know how often, but quite regularly. It was always a long trip uptown. You have to imagine, I came from 10th Street, which was a poor neighbourhood at the time, and Castelli was on 77th Street, the best neighbourhood. It was quite a long drive in my car. Castelli was Jewish, and he was an incredibly charming, very likeable and very intelligent man, he loved wit and good language.

(JANUARY 2022) «

Mack's role in New York is still little known. For his part, it gave him new inspiration for his own art. He bought a large Robert Rauschenberg silkscreen from Leo Castelli, which he still owns, and a Roy Lichtenstein serigraph, which was lost when his car was shipped back to Amsterdam, along with most of his New York archive. Both prints were expensive by his standards. Their acquisition testifies to a range of interests that extends far beyond the ZERO context and encompasses very different notions of art. Mack also bought a large conceptual work by Robert Smithson, a Land Art sketch,[129] from Leo Castelli.

The Venezuelan artist Marisol Escobar, who worked under the name Marisol and was a year older than Mack, had met Mack at the ZERO exhibition in London in 1964.[130] Shortly afterwards, she stood in front of him at Galerie Ileana Sonnabend in Paris and said: 'I knew we would meet again.' They were a couple for the rest of Mack's time in New York (fig. p. 122). 'Marisol was the first true love of my life', he says today.[131] In this early period of Pop Art, before it was codified, she was the female art star of the city, taciturn and mysteriously beautiful. She and Mack were an artist couple, both fascinated by each other and each other's work, although there was no connection between their work and, despite living together, no mutual influence. Marisol remained an important artist to Mack even after their separation. Their work and careers continued to develop on an equal footing, and they remained in constant contact. Mack's private library at Huppertzhof still contains several photographic portraits of Marisol.

»

There were two or three conversations with Andy Warhol that were quite controversial, and I didn't hesitate to stand up to him. I'll never forget one conversation in particular. I was invited to a party with Marisol, and one of the other guests was Ernest Hemingway's widow – an incredibly charming little old lady. I chatted with her and Andy Warhol joined us. The conversation went on between the three of us, and then Warhol made incredibly ironic, almost sadistic comments about people's opinions of television and the media and questioned literature. It went so far that I felt he was insulting Mrs Hemingway in some way. That's when I became very clear and spoke plainly in my own way. But he didn't hold it against me, because I saw him many times later, and it was always 'hello hello'; that's just the way he was.

« (JANUARY 2022)

»

In a luxury hotel there was a club in the basement where the best company, the high society, danced. I was invited there once with Marisol. It was a very special night because Mrs [Jacqueline] Kennedy herself was also dancing there. She knew Marisol and approached her. It was a fun evening, and I actually danced with Mrs Kennedy once. After midnight, we were waiting for a taxi on the big platform in front of the hotel. There was a man standing next to me making a lot of noise and insisting that if a taxi came, he would of course be the first to get in. He was dressed like a dandy, incredibly theatrical in his appearance. That was Mr Dalí. These are things you never forget, of course.

(JANUARY 2022) «

»

Marisol used real clothes for her life-size figures. One day, one of the dresses looked particularly beautiful. It was an incredibly beautiful dress, from Saudi Arabia or something. So I asked: 'Where did you get this dress?' It turned out that Mrs Kennedy had been given it by [Gamal Abdel] Nasser, the Egyptian president, on a state visit. Of course, she didn't want to wear it because it looked too Arabic, so she gave it to Marisol, who then used it as material for a sculptural work using Mrs Kennedy as a model. Three women sit side by side on a sofa, one has a self-cast of Marisol's head, the third being Jackie Kennedy. Next to her is a child modelled in a barrel. This has been interpreted as follows: high society has no sense of children; they live in isolation and so on.

(JANUARY 2022) «

»

Thanks in part to Marisol, I was twice invited to David Rockefeller's house for dinner. After one of these dinners, he personally escorted me to the front door, bid me a very polite farewell and said: 'I am glad to hear that you were born in 1931. Good night, Mr Mack!' I understood this remark very well. As a German a few years older than myself, I would not have been invited. That was part of our reality at that time.

(JANUARY 2022) «

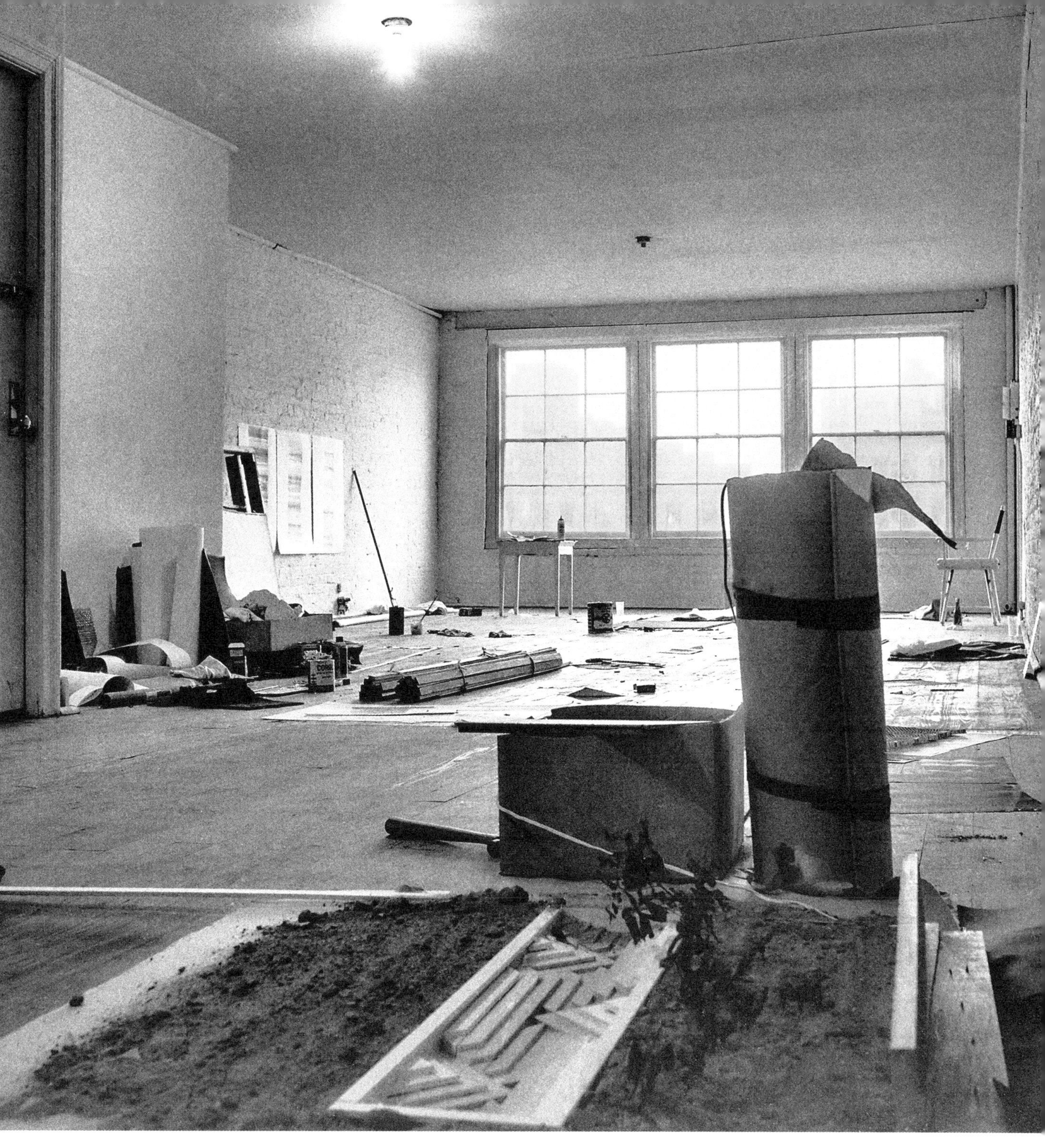

Heinz Mack's studio at
410 East 10th Street
in the East Village,
Lower Manhattan
1964

Heinz Mack's works from the New York period are characterised by an astonishing expansion of the material spectrum. It was the decade of the first Moon landing by the United States and the advent of computer technology and digital processes. Mack used new materials such as honeycomb, aluminium, and Plexiglas both alone and in various combinations. They are both light-reflecting and translucent, seemingly immaterial and in virtual or actual motion. These are all materials that could only be found in the United States at the time. With these materials, he created the light steles, the first works with large Fresnel lenses made of light plastic, most of the rotors and numerous kinetic objects.

Two aspects stand out. On the one hand, there is a change in the relationship between weight and effect. Honeycomb is light as a feather, even when used on large surfaces. It allows an interplay of transparency and reflection, especially when combined with the physically heavy but seemingly weightless Plexiglas. The 'traditional' materials of the ZERO years in Europe, for example, only allowed the use of light as an indirect design element, as had been the case in painting for centuries, rather than working with light itself as a material. This led to a qualitative leap in New York.

» When you fly at an altitude of 12,000 metres and then look up at the sky again – it turns black. Because my thoughts are so easily lost in the light and the sky, I have decided to respect a certain limit for myself. What I mean by that is that I will now look at my ideas more critically, that I will pay far more attention to ideas that promise to be made visible. So I believe more and more in what can be seen! Yes, you have to be able to see it so well that you stop thinking and fantasising. Seeing without desire = being happy [without desire]. Or, for me, the light itself (and everything that appears in the light) is more mysterious than anything that is dark. Mack.

(NOTE ON CHELSEA HOTEL STATIONERY NEW YORK, NOVEMBER 1964, MACK ARCHIVE) «

On the other hand, the free artistic use of these materials actually led to immateriality. It was also a leitmotif for the ZERO artists in Europe. However, the conventional materials there only allowed its suggestion, not its direct realisation. Yves Klein's conclusion in 1959 was the realisation of *Zones de Sensibilité Picturale Immatérielle* as an intellectual, conceptual process. In contrast, Mack's works from the New York years achieve immateriality as a visual experience. That was new.

At the same time, the artist had already spent a dozen years creating art at a high level and had acquired a profound knowledge of materials. Discovering a material like honeycomb – designed for aircraft construction, but now decommissioned and available for a pittance – is one thing. Discovering its artistic use or productive misuse is another. Heinz Mack stretched the material in width with his own body, while it was designed for maximum rigidity in depth. This transformation is an important sculptural act. We remember the years of study in Ewald Mataré's workshop and his handling of material (p. 55). But now Mack had literally arrived in a new technical age that had not even been imagined twelve years earlier.

From 5 to 30 April 1966, Howard Wise Gallery hosted the solo exhibition *Heinz Mack. Lights of Silver*.[132] *Forest of Light* was the title of an ensemble of twenty transparent relief steles made of honeycomb, aluminium, and Fresnel lenses, set in custom-made, towering Plexiglas cubes. Grace Glueck, a critic for *The New York Times*, recognised in this forest of steles an homage to the skyscraper landscape and the unique light of Manhattan.[133] The formal language showed Mack's interest in 'Russian' and Dutch Constructivism. At the same time, it was very new, because there was a play of light of absolute purity that dealt with transparencies and, as a metaphor for technology, was something that had never been seen before, that stayed in the mind.

»

This is my most difficult exhibition; it takes all my energy and self-control. Howard Wise is very good to me; I'm undoubtedly the No. 1 horse in the stable. The gallery now has the best reputation; everything changes quickly in New York. My nerves have been shot three times because I'm afraid of the enormous amount of work; I have to think about every screw and at the same time about the big concept. If the devil would help me, I'd give my soul – that's the situation. Some of the work has turned out to be crazy good, but everything is going a bit slower than I thought it would. I completely changed the concept at the last minute, that is, I discarded older works. I hardly see anyone because I'm almost always alone. Wednesday was the Guggenheim, a very festive opening; there's nothing like it in Europe. My drawings are hanging well and I'm just as big in the catalogue. The director thinks a lot of me, says my work has a certain world stature; whether that can be achieved is still written in the stars. I was only in the museum for a quarter of an hour, then back to the studio. Sometimes I'm the loneliest person in the world because of my work. [...] At Marisol's I saw a magazine from Japan; two of my works are illustrated. Write to Tokyo, see correspondence. I no longer feel at ease with Otto [Piene]; here, too, he is not at all the person he would like to be. Extremely cold here, high gas bills, snow again. [...] But you may know that I am fighting a lonely battle, the worst of my life; after this I don't want to know anything more about exhibitions, for at least two years, regardless of whether everything goes well this time or not. New York and art are a tough place, but it's all or nothing. I'm really spasmodically ambitious, or it's an eternal restlessness in me.

« (JANUARY 2022)

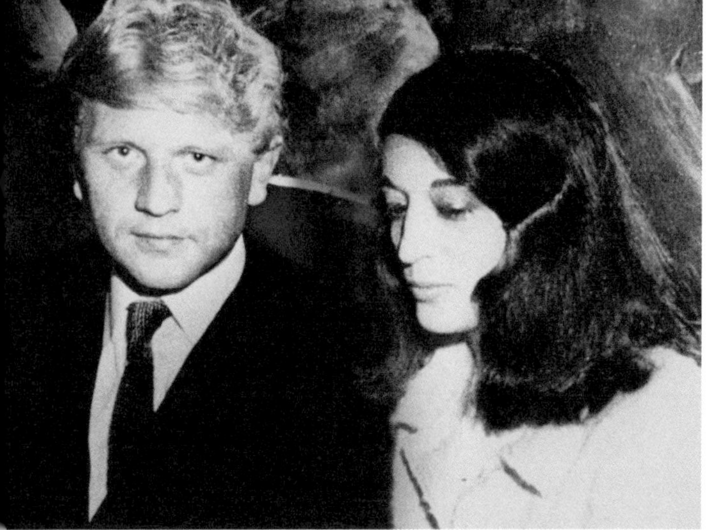

Marisol and Mack in New York
c. 1966

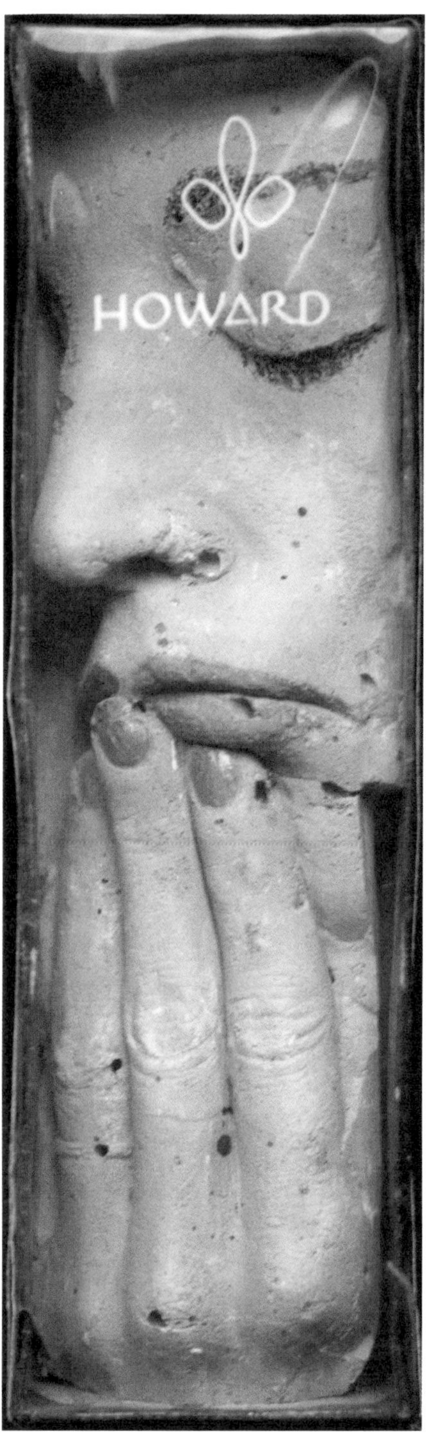

Marisol
Untitled (Self-Portrait)
c. 1965

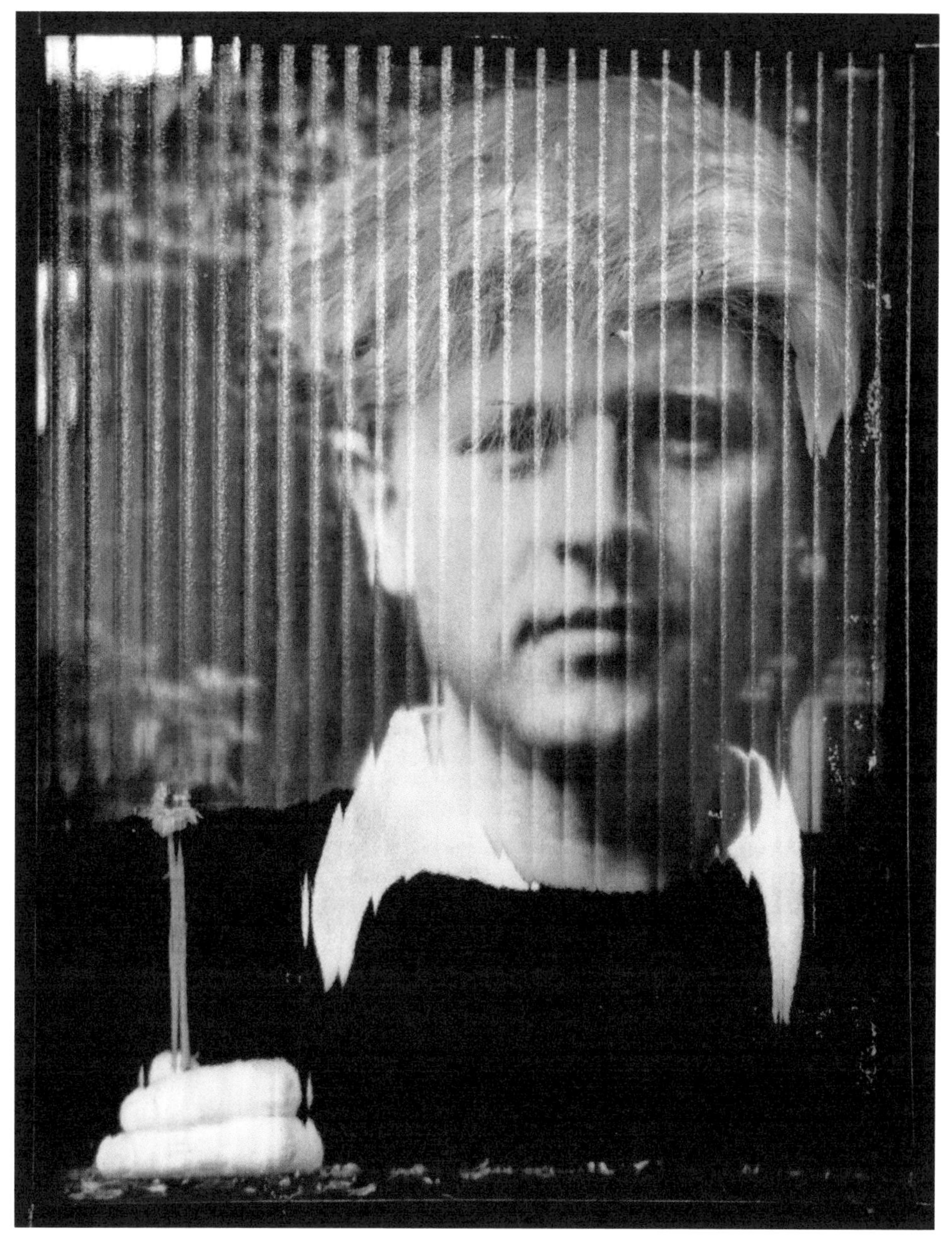

Marisol
Portrait Heinz Mack
c. 1965

»

My exhibition with Howard Wise in 1966 was a success, even though, or perhaps precisely because, the works I showed were largely unknown in New York. Leading museums acquired my work, including the MoMA, the Albright Knox Collection and the Rockefeller Foundation in New York, as well as the Hirshhorn Museum in Washington, D.C.

(JANUARY 2022) «

»

George Rickey had a large studio in a kind of country house in Connecticut, very far from New York City. He invited me over several times for the weekend, and then – if only because of the length of the trip – he made me feel like I was his guest. I was given a bed to sleep in. When I was at his house with Marisol, I said I'd need the nicest bed, of course, and he did as I requested; it was very nice. He gave me his own bed. Other artists were often invited to his house. He had a workshop in the garden where he worked. He let me use the workshop for a few hours. I made a relief there and gave it to him, and then he gave me one of his own works in return, so it was a very nice atmosphere. He was interested in my work, although he was born in 1907 and could almost have been my father. So he was a different generation, although he was very youthful in his whole demeanour. Later, he also visited me privately in Düsseldorf and we once spent a whole day talking intensively on walks. He also wrote a nice text about it.[137] So he really was a very alert contemporary and a very generous host.

(JANUARY 2022) «

Howard Wise's representation of Heinz Mack since 1964 led to the acquisition of his works by American collections, almost all of which are now in museums,[134] commissions for, among others, the headquarters of Murchison Brothers in Dallas,[135] who were among the richest people in the world, and invitations to show his work in group exhibitions at important institutions. The latter included an invitation from the curator Lawrence Alloway to the Solomon R. Guggenheim Museum, in whose exhibition *European Drawings* Mack was represented with two works in 1966 and which subsequently toured museums in the United States for a year and a half. At The Museum of Modern Art, the artist had shown the aluminium relief *Door of Paradise* (1964) the previous year in the exhibition *The Responsive Eye*, an internationally influential survey of current trends in non-figurative painting curated by William C. Seitz.[136] There were few better museum people for contemporary art. Peter Selz, another long-time MoMA curator, had recently become director of the University Art Museum in Berkeley, California's premier museum, and gave Mack a prominent position in *Kinetic Sculpture*, the first museum exhibition of this genre in the United States, which opened in March 1966.

The question arose as to whether Mack wanted to stay in New York permanently, and if so, how? A lasting friendship had developed with the kinetic artist George Rickey.[138] In Connecticut, where Rickey lived, Mack discovered a wooded landscape that reminded him of his childhood and youth in Hesse. It presented itself as an alternative to his permanent residence in Manhattan. Also in Connecticut, in July 1965, Heinz Mack and Marisol visited Hans Richter, a pioneer of the artist film, former Dadaist and Dada historian. Legendary figures like him made it possible to clearly feel the spirit of the early modern art movements in Europe in the 1920s and 1930s, which had been torn apart by dictatorship and war. Mack remained on friendly terms with Hans Richter until his death in 1976. There is a kinship between the black-and-white aesthetics of Richter's artist films and Mack's light works of the 1960s, despite their very different media bases.

Without his years in New York, Heinz Mack's oeuvre would look very different. With the exception of Hans Haacke, no other German artist of the time was so involved in the New York scene.[140] This wealth of experience opened up artistic references for Mack's work that have not yet been sufficiently explored. During his New York years, Mack also learned to navigate the increasingly international art world.

The dialogue with Minimalism, which emerged in New York in 1964–65 and whose main protagonists belonged to Mack's generation, and conceptual art goes even deeper. Mack's steles and his *Forest of Light*, a major work to this day, are in dialogue with the early sculptures of Barnett Newman, which they helped to initiate, but at the same time they have a connection with Minimalism. They are 'specific objects' in the sense of Donald Judd's Minimalism, in that their apparent regularity means that they have no hidden surface, as all sculptures in the European tradition do, according to Judd. At the same time, they intelligently circumvent the rejection of the 'European' verticality of sculpture on the part of New York Minimalism. All this opened up perspectives that Heinz Mack would develop in his later work, far removed from the intellectual and artistic structure

»

In 1966, I was interested in buying a house in Connecticut through a real estate agent because I was really considering staying in New York for a while. Howard Wise said, if I remember correctly: 'Anyway if you're really involved with this idea, I will be ready to buy this house and you can do your work there and you will pay the rent.' He was really a very cooperative man. I looked at two or three properties there and was always very impressed by the size of the plots. The land there was comparatively cheap, unlike the houses. In the end, I couldn't make up my mind because I wouldn't have had the financial means. There were other reasons as well. After two years in New York, I gradually realised that I couldn't find a piece of soil anywhere, a piece of earth, that everything was just concrete and plastic. Subconsciously, of course, something wasn't working for me because I had spent a large part of my youth in the countryside. And somewhere I realised that something was wrong here, something was missing. When I was in Connecticut, it felt a bit like home. Then I realised that nature was still there too. In the end, I gave up on the idea of staying in New York. That would have meant getting divorced in Düsseldorf, marrying Marisol and so on.[139]

« (JANUARY 2022)

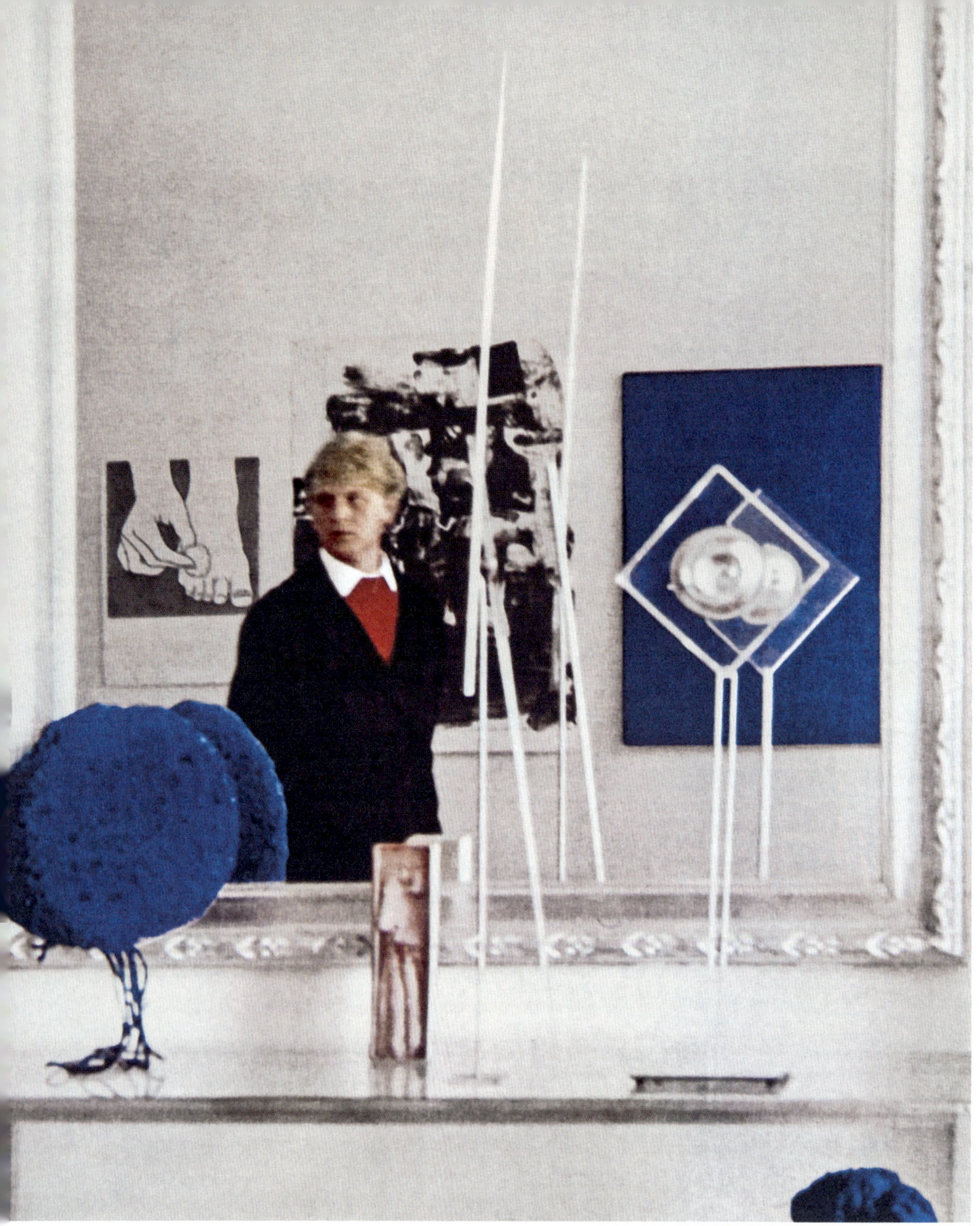

Heinz Mack in his apartment
at Kaiser-Friedrich-Ring 16,
Düsseldorf, 1966, with works
by Yves Klein, Roy Lichtenstein,
Robert Rauschenberg, George
Rickey, Marisol, and Uli Pohl

Forest of Light
in the exhibition
Lights of Silver by Heinz Mack,
Howard Wise Gallery,
New York
1966

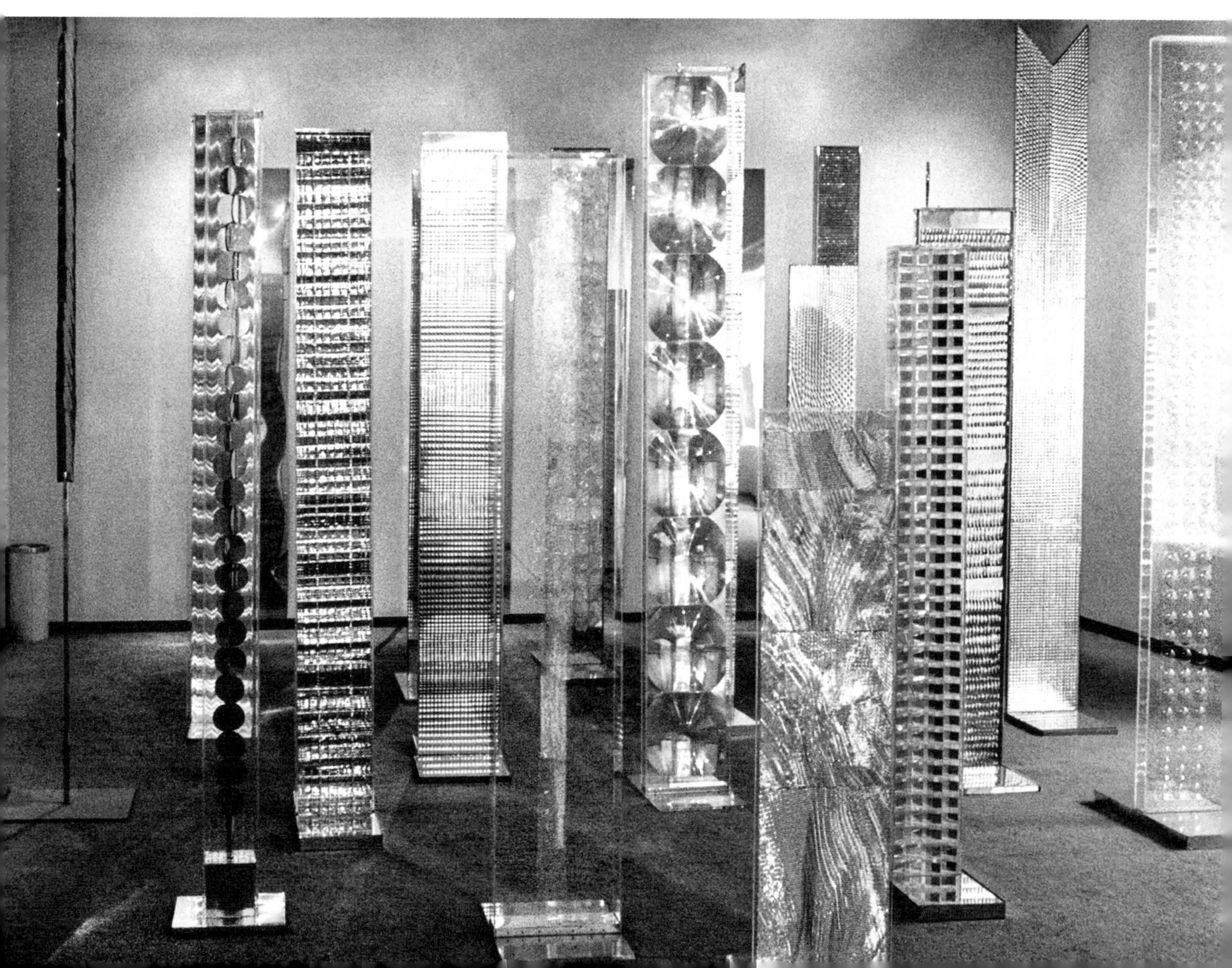

of ZERO Düsseldorf and ZERO international. Back in Europe, the artist had no choice but to try to make a break with ZERO,[141] if only to avoid being tied to it and to expand his further work.

» America was a complete liberation for me in those years. It was only for family reasons that I returned to Europe. I have no idea what would have become of me if I had stayed there. «

('HEINZ MACK. AM ANFANG WAR BACH', CONVERSATION WITH HEINZ-NORBERT JOCKS, 2009)[142]

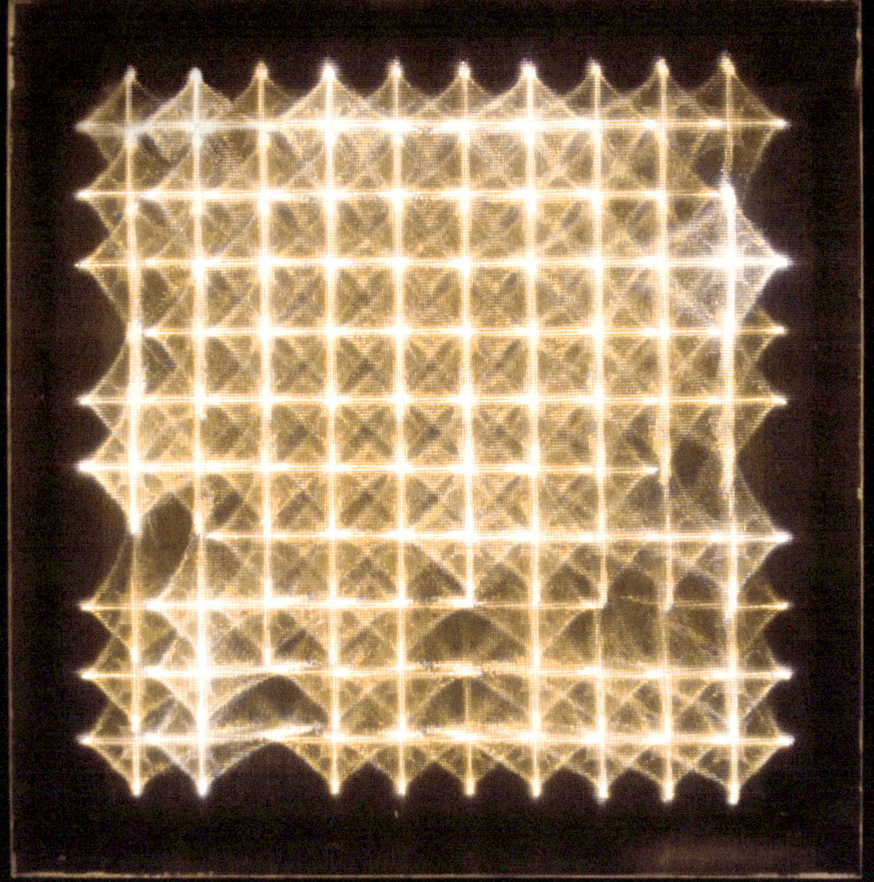

KINETIC

Electric Field
(Light-Time-Space)
1969/70

October 1967: The Museum des 20. Jahrhunderts in Vienna has frosted glass walls all around, yet it is flooded with light on this sunny autumn day. Our art teacher leads us into the building in our first year of secondary school. The room is a discovery, but none of us understands the paintings. Suddenly, a few of us, then more and more, and finally almost the whole class, are standing in front of a large aluminium cabinet with a grooved glass surface – like the kitchen doors of the time – on the front, through which we can see something rotating inside, a large circular surface, slowly and evenly counterclockwise, through which we can recognise – how, we all wondered – overlapping light structures that are new and unpredictable every second. We have the impression that we will never be able to understand this apparatus, even though it is probably quite simple. We have never seen anything like it, and it speaks directly to our time. So there is at least one interesting thing in the '20er Haus', as the first museum of modern art in Austria, which has just celebrated its fifth anniversary, is known in Viennese parlance.[143]

» My uncle was a clockmaker. There were many clocks in his workshop, and I used to watch him repairing them, with all the rotating parts. I later incorporated this into my rotors. After the war, there were still many clocks with a pendulum going back and forth. My first objects were pendulum objects. Jean Tinguely said it was all great, but I had to try it with motors. So I did my first experiments with motors.

(FEBRUARY 2023) «

Our art teacher was Hans Kaliwoda, an important young artist in Austria. He saw that his pupils were fascinated by this apparatus in which something was turning and creating light structures. So he explained to the class that the artist who had made it was Heinz Mack, a German, quite well known. He had founded an artists' group called 'ZERO' and what we were seeing was 'kinetic art'. Kinetic comes from the Greek word for movement. It is art that actually moves and does not simply simulate something in painted pictures. It is completely new, the newest of the new, so to speak. In physics lessons, we learned that kinetic energy is energy in motion. Some of the class still remember that visit to the museum. Hans Kaliwoda also made kinetic art, but without motors, more what was then called Op Art.[144]

The rotor in the Museum des 20. Jahrhunderts, now in the collection of the Museum moderner Kunst Stiftung Ludwig Wien (mumok), is entitled *Sun of the Sea No. 5* (fig. p. 133). It was a very recent work, dating from 1967, after the artist's return from New York. The materials are aluminium, Plexiglas, wood, and a motor. Height and width: 137 centimetres, depth: 17 centimetres, weight: 92 kilograms. Werner Hofmann, the museum's founding director and an eminent art historian[145] who soon became a long-term companion, friend, and supporter of Heinz Mack,[146] acquired the rotor from the *Kinetika* exhibition he curated as the first museum purchase of a rotor by Heinz Mack.

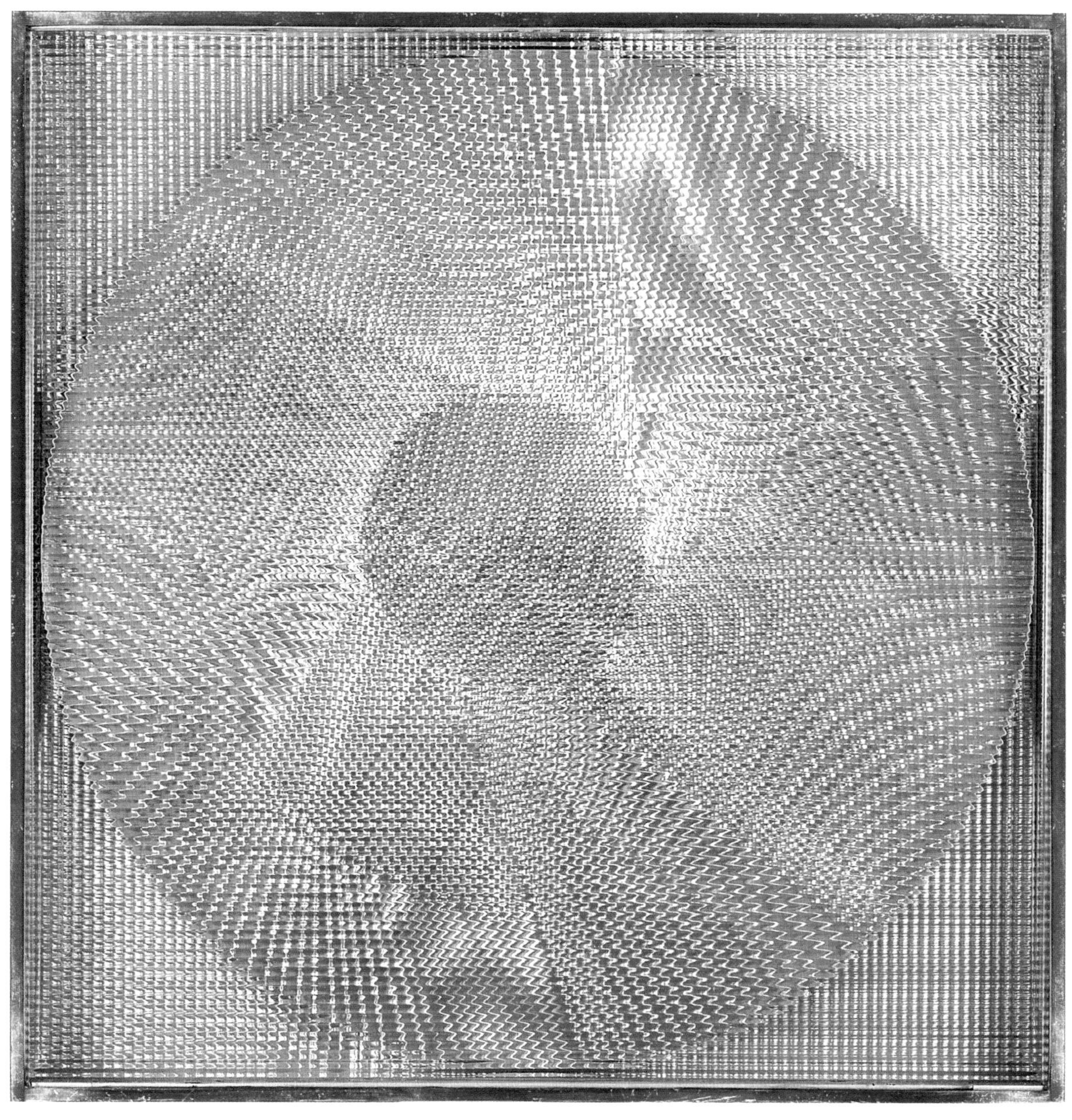

Sun of the Sea No. 5
1967

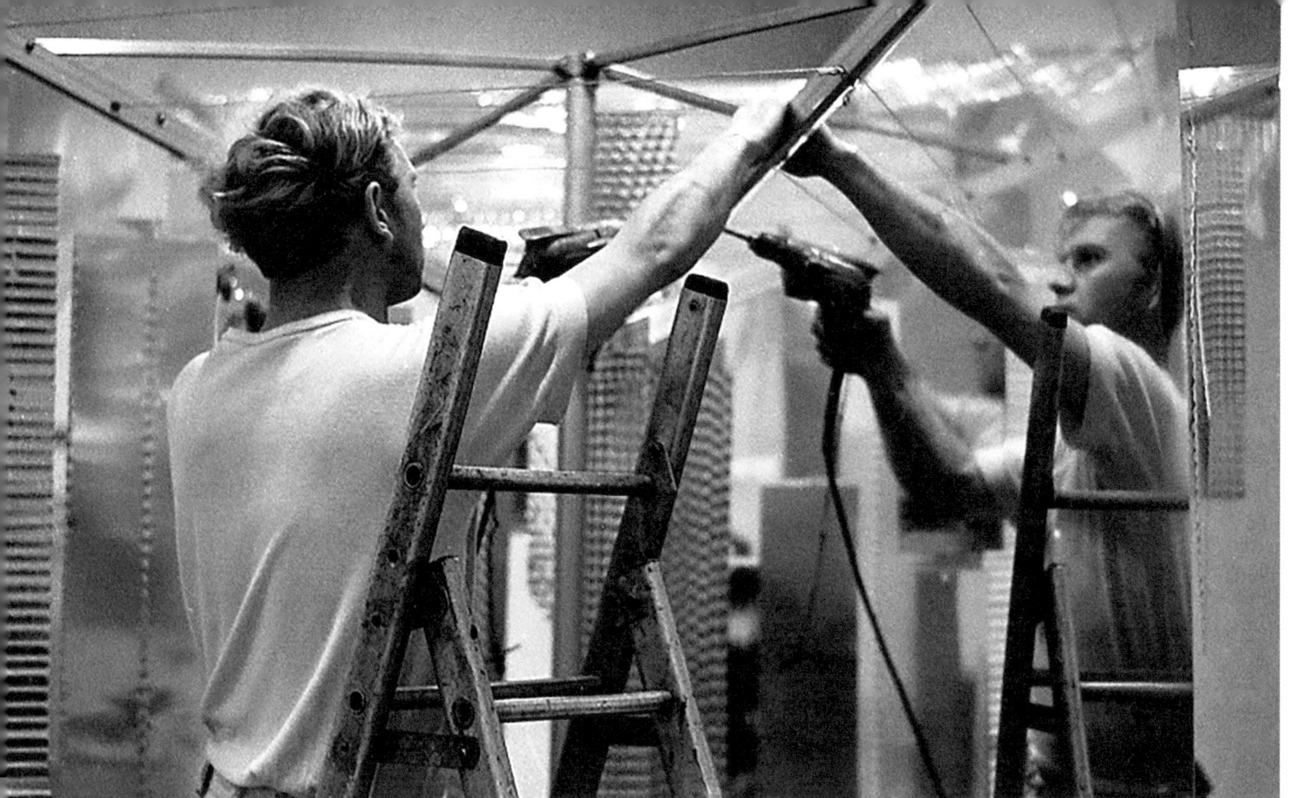

Light Carousel
1962

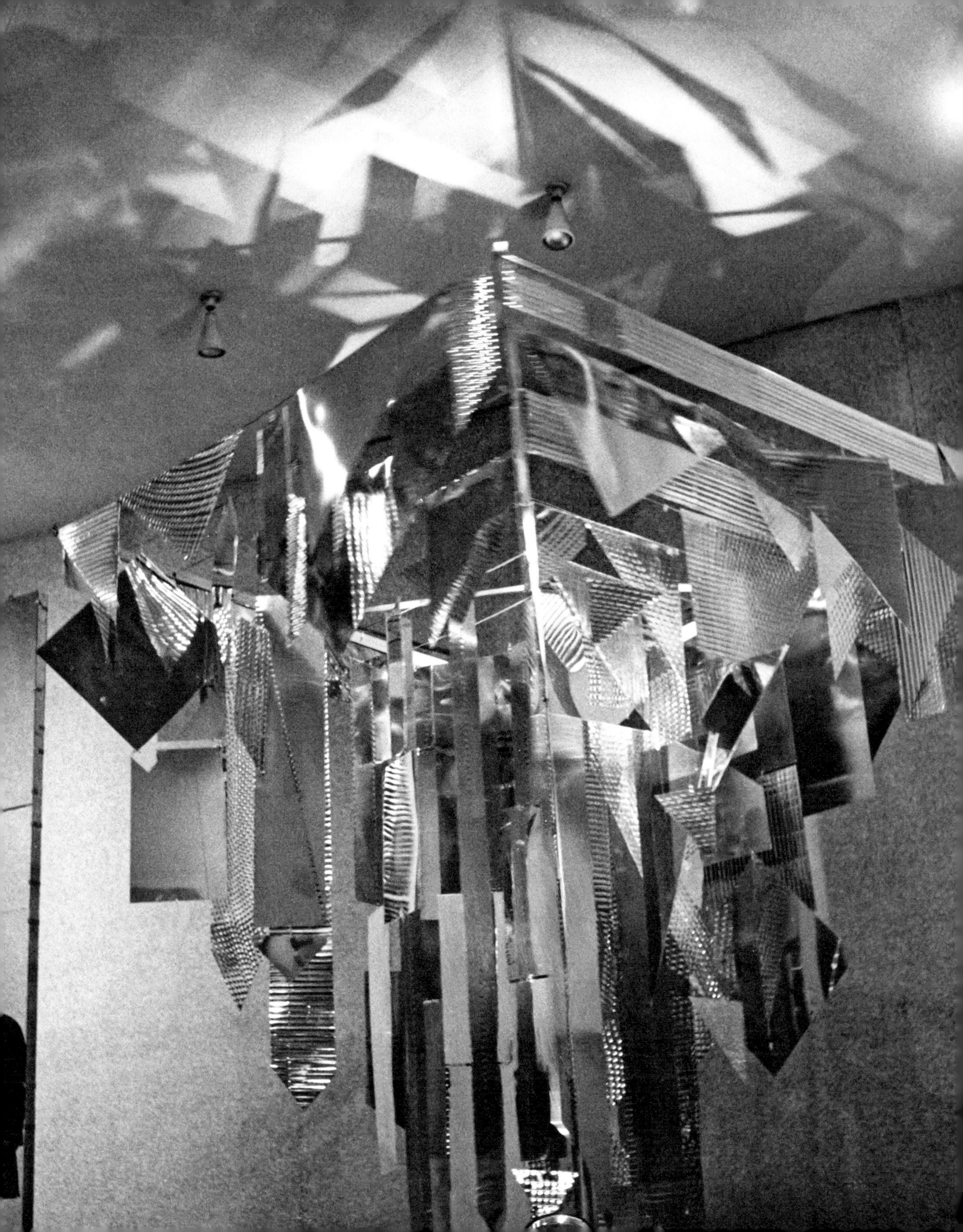

The works shown in *Kinetika* had previously been exhibited at the Kunsthalle Bern under the title *Weiss auf Weiss* (White on White) – *Sun of the Sea No. 5* was only added in Vienna. The director of the Kunsthalle at the time, Harald Szeemann, rose to become the most important exhibition organiser of the second half of the twentieth century.[147] After stops at the Palais des Beaux-Arts in Brussels and the Staatliche Kunsthalle Baden-Baden, the exhibition – before travelling to Vienna – was shown under the title *Licht und Bewegung. Kinetische Kunst* (Light and Movement. Kinetic Art) in February 1966 at the Kunstverein für die Rheinlande und Westfalen in Düsseldorf, which was housed in the same building as the then new Kunsthalle Düsseldorf on Grabbeplatz. On the cover of the catalogue is a honeycomb wing by Heinz Mack, *Light Fan of an Angel* from 1965, from his time in New York. In the Düsseldorf catalogue, Frank Popper, the leading expert on kinetic art at the time[148] and an art critic in Paris, wrote: 'The artistic possibilities of the dynamic structure of light have hardly been better appreciated than by the ZERO group. In 1959, Heinz Mack wrote: "Pure movement does not recognise the relativity of boundaries and mass; without direction and without actuality, it remains with itself. This is its vibration, its breath, its freedom, its vitality, its metaphysics [...] in my light reliefs, in which the light itself becomes the medium instead of the colours, movement brings a new, immaterial colour and tonality to the vibration of the light, whose untouchable and completely non-objective appearance indicates a possible reality, whose emanation and secret beauty we already love."' Popper speaks of the 'common theme of movement [...] as a prelude to the conquest of new aesthetic regions'.[149]

» When I say that I participate in the world around me, I am explicitly saying that I love movement; in our century it has taken on a significance unimagined since the invention of the wheel. (All this has to be seen in a wider context – the art-historical episode of kinetics is only part of it).

(TYPESCRIPT, 1960S)[150] «

The kinetic art of the 1960s had a fascinating immediacy. Heinz Mack's kinetic works still radiate this today. At the same time, this phenomenon of art in motion emerged in his early years with a highly developed historical consciousness. The exhibition *Le Mouvement* had already taken place in 1955 at Galerie Denise René in Paris, in which Pontus Hultén had played a major role.[151] The exhibition *Kinetische Kunst* (Kinetic Art) at the Kunstgewerbemuseum in Zurich in 1960 was groundbreaking. The organisers, Hans Fischli[152] and Willy Rotzler,[153] established a lineage that included Yaacov Agam, Josef Albers, Marcel Duchamp, Heinz Mack, Man Ray, Dieter Roth, Jesús Rafael Soto, Jean Tinguely, and Victor Vasarely. The list can be found almost unchanged in George Rickey's reference text 'The Morphology of Movement. A Study of Kinetic Art' (1965), for which the order of the illustrations is as follows: Duchamp (*Bicycle-Wheel*, 1913), Tatlin, Moholy-Nagy (*Light-Space Modulator*, 1924),

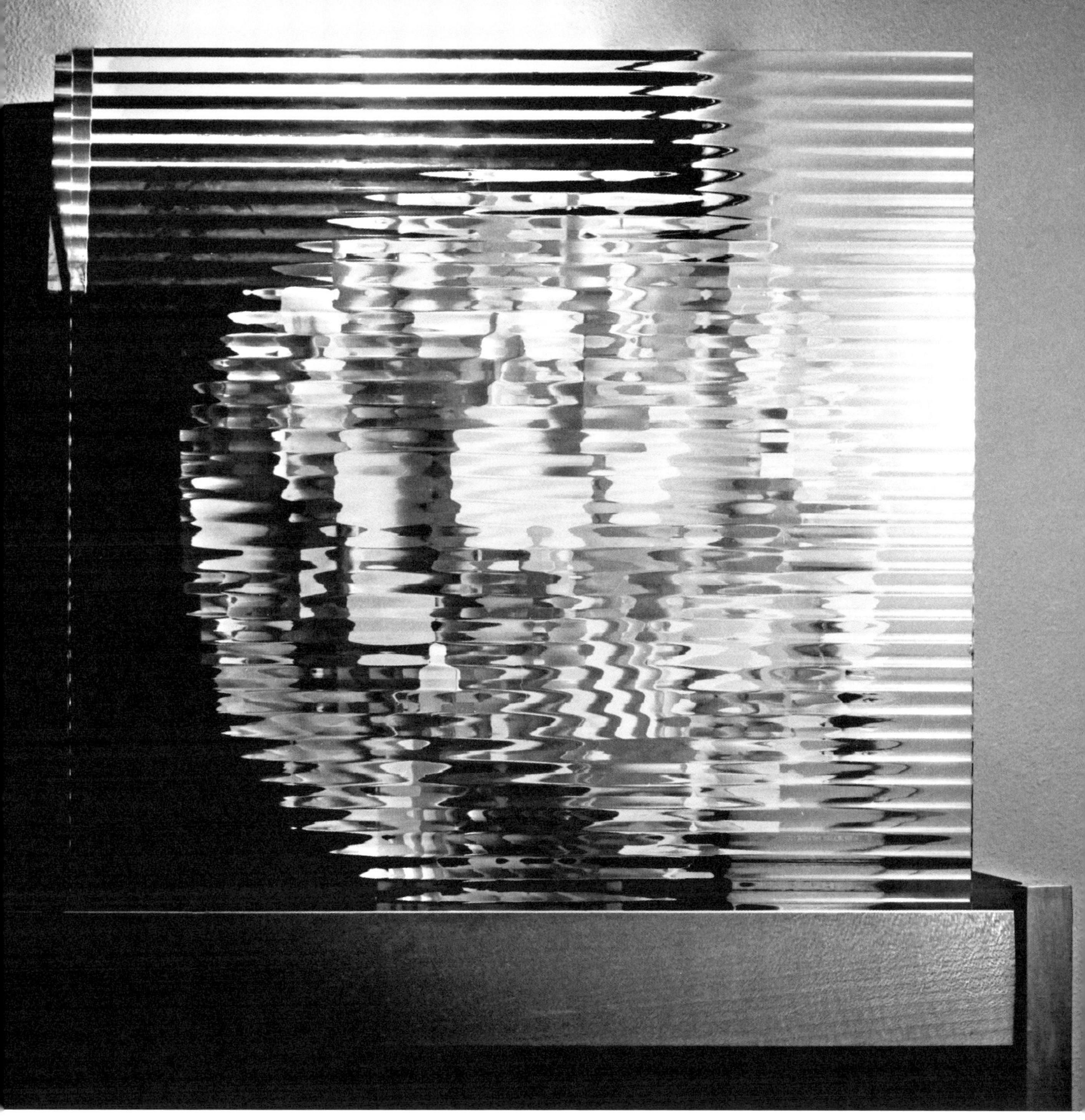

Heinz Mack's first rotor:
Paper Flower Rotor
1958

»

I grew up in humble circumstances and didn't have any toys. But someone made me a little wooden top. It was a real experience. Later, when I was about twenty-five years old, I saw a record player for the first time. Of course, I experimented with it, drew structures or made them out of sheet metal and put them on the turntable, which resulted in a rotation, and held filters over it, such as glasses and glass structures. These experiments were very primitive. But they had a tremendous effect. That's how my rotors came about, because of the experiments with that record player and the glass discs that created an optical distortion. Only much later did I learn that another artist had done something very similar, namely Marcel Duchamp with his Rotoreliefs from 1935 onwards.[156]

(FEBRUARY 2023) «

»

Kinetic [art] was animated by a certain enthusiasm. I, too, was enthusiastic about it. We really wanted to design something that would be a great enrichment for the progress of the world. Again, I accompanied this with philosophy, because what Schiller said about play is very relevant in this case. Schiller realised early on that when children play, they are completely with themselves and follow their inner inclinations. The instinct to play has an important artistic dimension. Artists should sometimes aspire to the unmediated spontaneity of a child.

(FEBRUARY 2023) «

Calder, Mack (*Light Dynamo*, 1960) and Vasarely.[154] Similarly, in the exhibition *Directions in Kinetic Sculpture* curated by Peter Selz at the University Art Museum in Berkeley from March 1966, Mack was at the forefront early on,[155] and these were the years in which Marcel Duchamp, shortly before his death in October 1968, rose to become one of the most important reference artists of the twentieth century.

Heinz Mack's historical inspiration also includes László Moholy-Nagy's *Light-Space Modulator*, the original realisation of which was begun by the Bauhaus teacher in 1922. The original is lost. The first replica dates from 1968[157] and shares with Mack's rotors the slowness of movement generated by an electric drive and the complex interplay of flat and perforated metal surfaces that cast an infinite, abstract ballet of shadows on the walls of the semi-dark exhibition space. Mack's main idea behind the rotors is to hide the movement of the circular elements behind a grooved glass pane, transforming Moholy-Nagy's conceptual transparency into a non-representational, almost magical process in which the light acts in a closed spatial body rather than as a shadow in the surrounding space.

In kinetic art and the intellectual boom of the 1950s and 1960s, the term 'play' was widely discussed.[158] As early as 1795, Friedrich Schiller wrote in the fifteenth letter of 'On the Aesthetic Education of Man': 'For, to declare it once for all, Man plays only when he is in the full sense of the word a man, and *he is only wholly Man when he is playing*. […] This proposition […] will, I promise you, support the whole fabric of aesthetic art, and the still more difficult art of living.'[159] This way of thinking plays an essential role in Mack's entire oeuvre. In his kinetic art, however, it is fundamental and radiates from there to his subsequent work.

From this time on, Heinz Mack also criticised artistic topicality, which became an essential motif in his later artistic work. Was it not completely naïve to suddenly regard real movement as a new territory of art, just as it had become customary in the heyday of kinetic art to celebrate it as a newly conquered instrument of art? The interactive character of kinetic art also led to popular exhibition formats, culminating in participatory exhibitions in museums after 1968, when bouncy castles suddenly appeared in museums, which were regarded as the most advanced and democratic art.[160] 'Don't rush into things' was one of Werner Hofmann's favourite phrases.

In this context, Mack's philosophical thinking came to the fore once again. Movement inseparable from light is much more than 'art and fun' and much more art than optical effect. On the one hand, Mack was a reference in the initially triumphant movement of kinetic art. On the other hand, he kept his distance from the kinetic mainstream. His kinetic works – which he continues to create today, because light, which is at the heart of his artistic work, and movement, whether optical or real, are inseparable – are among the most enduring in the field of kinetic art. Two retrospectives, at the Museum Abteiberg in Mönchengladbach in 2011 and at the ZKM | Center for Art and Media Karlsruhe in 2023–24,[161] have made this clear.

Heinz Mack's special position in the field of kinetic art is particularly evident in his rotors. The first ones date from 1958 (fig. p. 137). In Paris that year, Yves Klein and Jean Tinguely showed Mack an experimental joint work in front of Tinguely's studio, next to the former studio of Constantin Brancusi:[162] they had screwed a circular disc with an ultramarine blue monochrome by Klein onto the pin of an electric motor, causing the painting to rotate faster than the eye could follow.[163] Here, as with Paik in New York (p. 106), the artists sensed that the other was doing something that would inspire them.

»

In 1958, Yves Klein and Jean Tinguely experimented with scrap metal. Tinguely mounted a disc on a fast-rotating electric motor, and Klein painted the disc monochrome blue. They asked me my opinion. I said: 'I'm mostly impressed. What I'm seeing here is a virtual space, like a propeller of an aircraft.' Yves Klein: 'He really got it.' They were pleased with this comment. You really had the feeling that a virtual gas cloud of blue atmosphere was floating above this blue disc, it was completely immaterial, a purely virtual volume. That was a very important key experience. After that, I made my first kinetic object.

« (FEBRUARY 2023)

Most of Heinz Mack's rotors date from the years 1965–67 (fig. p. 133). They were genuinely completely new art objects, in which the homogeneous pictorial form rotates without losing its non-representational character and without becoming literary in the least, while the form is a very simple, unadorned body – a riddle that the viewer is unable to solve. The virtual image is constantly changing in unpredictable ways in a constant light-time continuum in which everything is slow, infinite vibration travelling on a low wavelength. Since everything takes place without colour, it remains pure light.

Exhibition visitors sometimes ask how these rotors work. An aluminium light relief mounted on a circular wooden disc is set in slow, steady motion by a small electric motor via a rubber connecting tube and a much larger wooden disc.

»

[And] what is the relationship between the rhythm of my heart and the intervals of light of a rotor in motion?

« ('FRAGEN UND ANTWORTEN', 1986, MACK ARCHIVE)

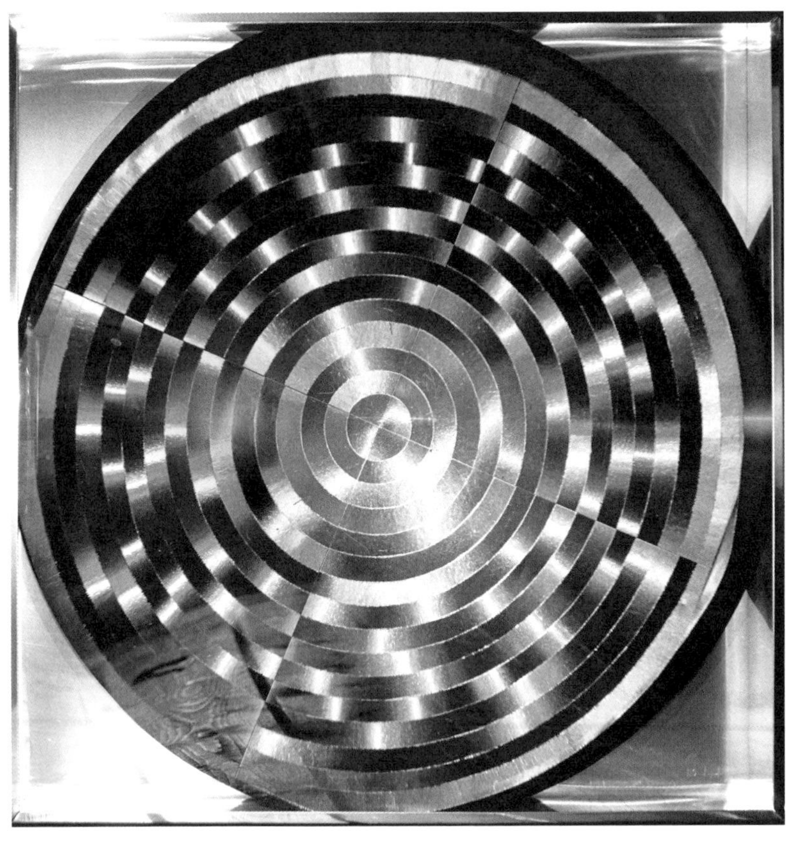

Changing Light
2004

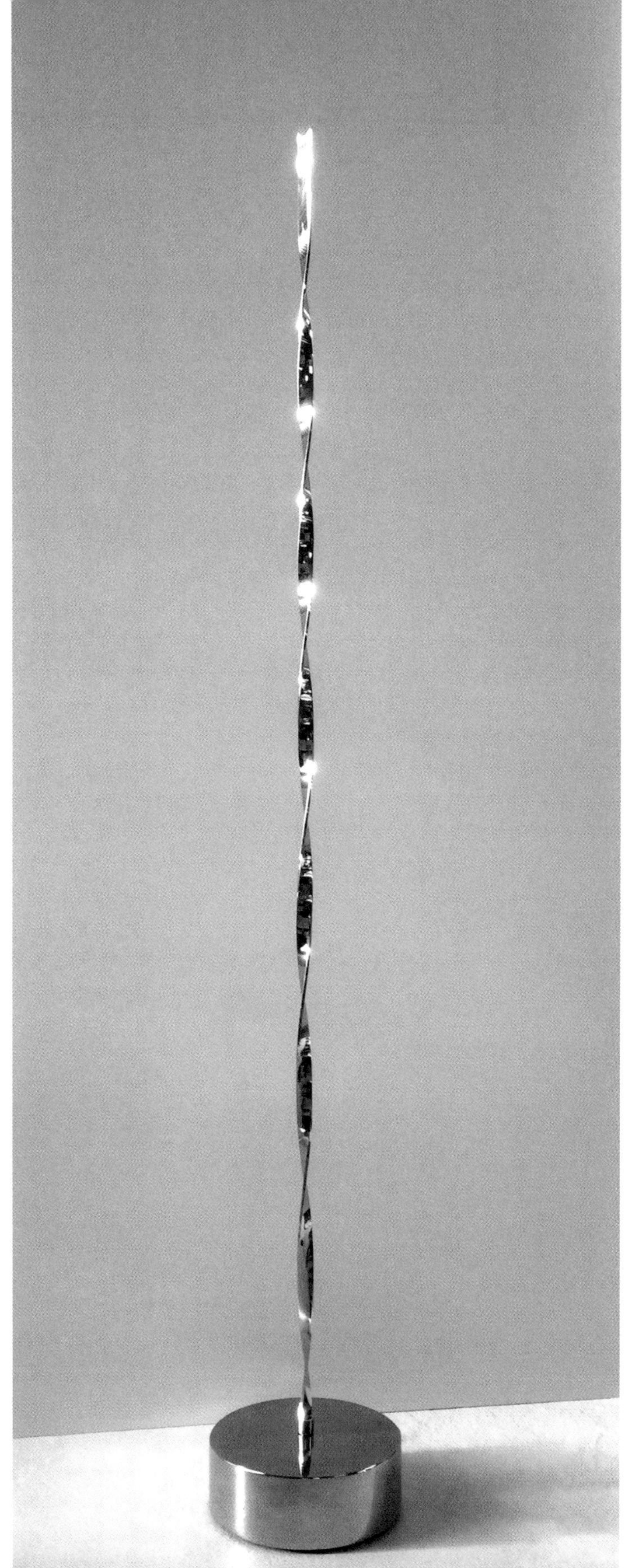

Light Line
1961

Light – Movement – Space
light environment
Great Industrial Exhibition,
Berlin (West)
1970

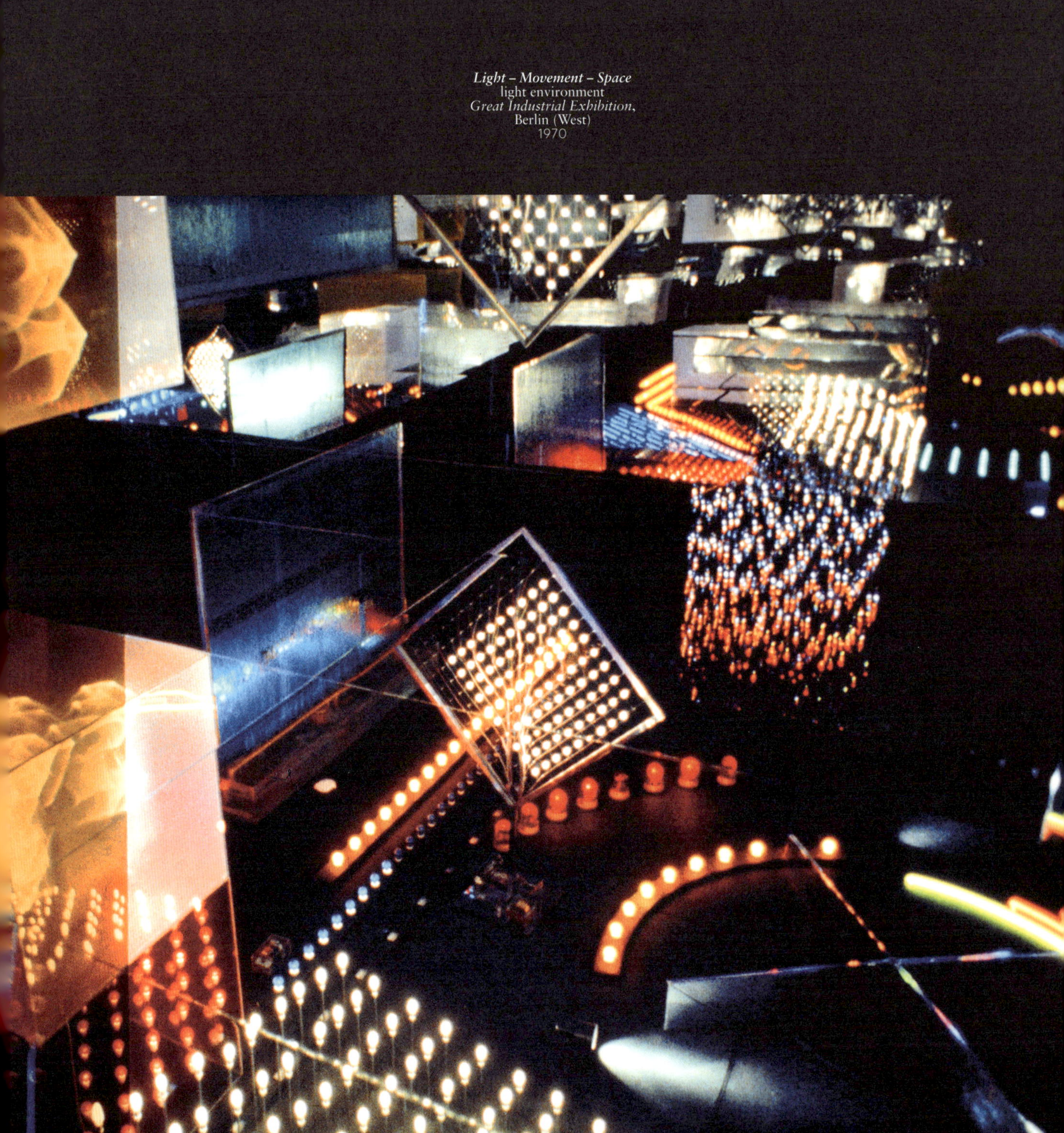

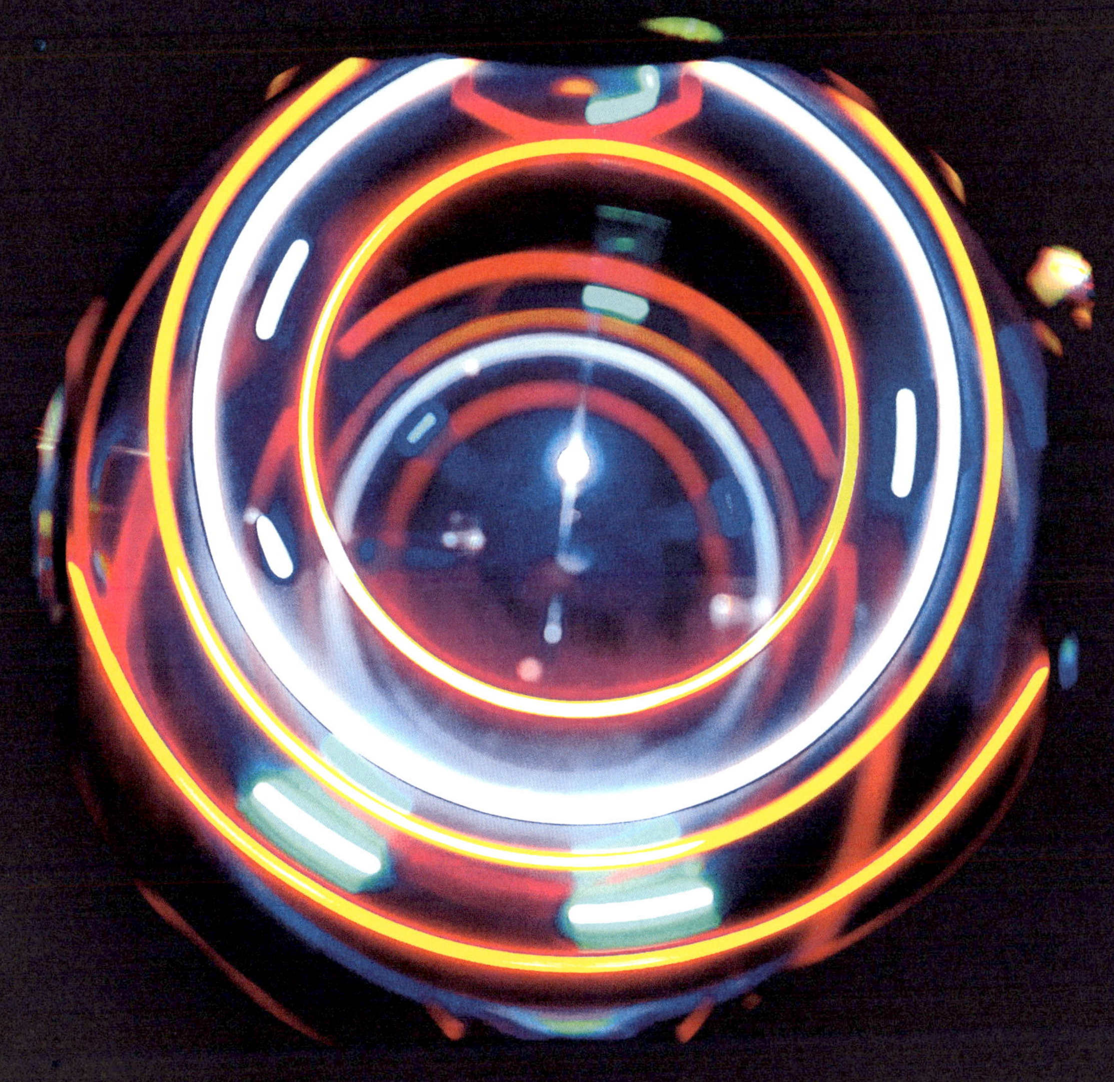

Light Fan
2009

»

I then also had an exhibition in New York with Denise René, my gallerist from Paris. In 1971, she opened her New York gallery on 7th Street, not far from Howard Wise Gallery, the first branch of a European gallery in triumphant New York. She invited me to have a solo exhibition there. After Howard Wise had shown only steles in 1966 (fig. p. 127), I came up with the idea that Denise should show only rotors – and she agreed. There were five or six large rotors of mine.

(FEBRUARY 2023) «

Everything is homemade. The square wooden box containing the machine is topped with a grooved glass or Plexiglas disc. The structure is technically very simple, but the effect is highly complex.[164]

Standing in front of a Mack rotor is a new perceptual experience. The catalogue *Mack. Un rotorelief* for the exhibition at Galerie Denise René in Paris in 1967 contains – without text, as a pure sequence of images – overall and detail shots of a single rotor by Heinz Mack. The image is completely dissolved and different at every moment. Light and non-light become more and more contrasting as the ambient light diminishes, until perception merges into an incomprehensible but structured continuum in which the vibration of light has arrived at itself. Heinz Mack's kinetic concept of the work is always about the cancellation of a real or optical movement into a virtual one, which, as an immaterial manifestation, is a phenomenon of thought and no longer of mechanics.

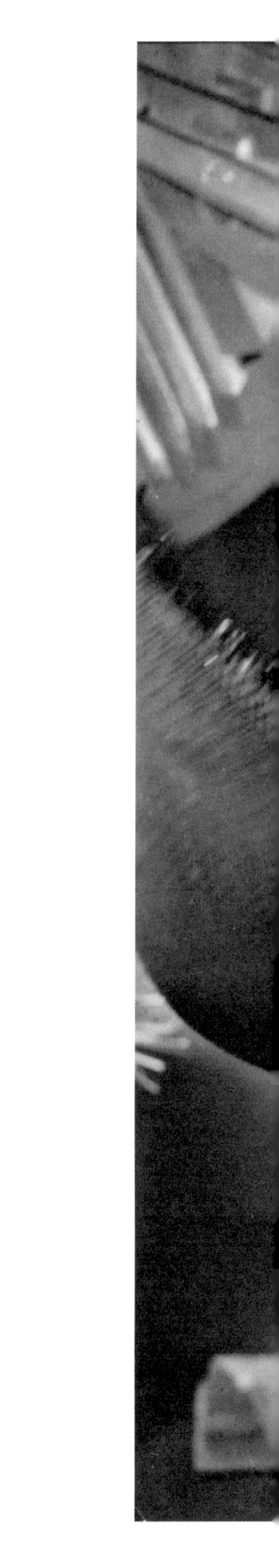

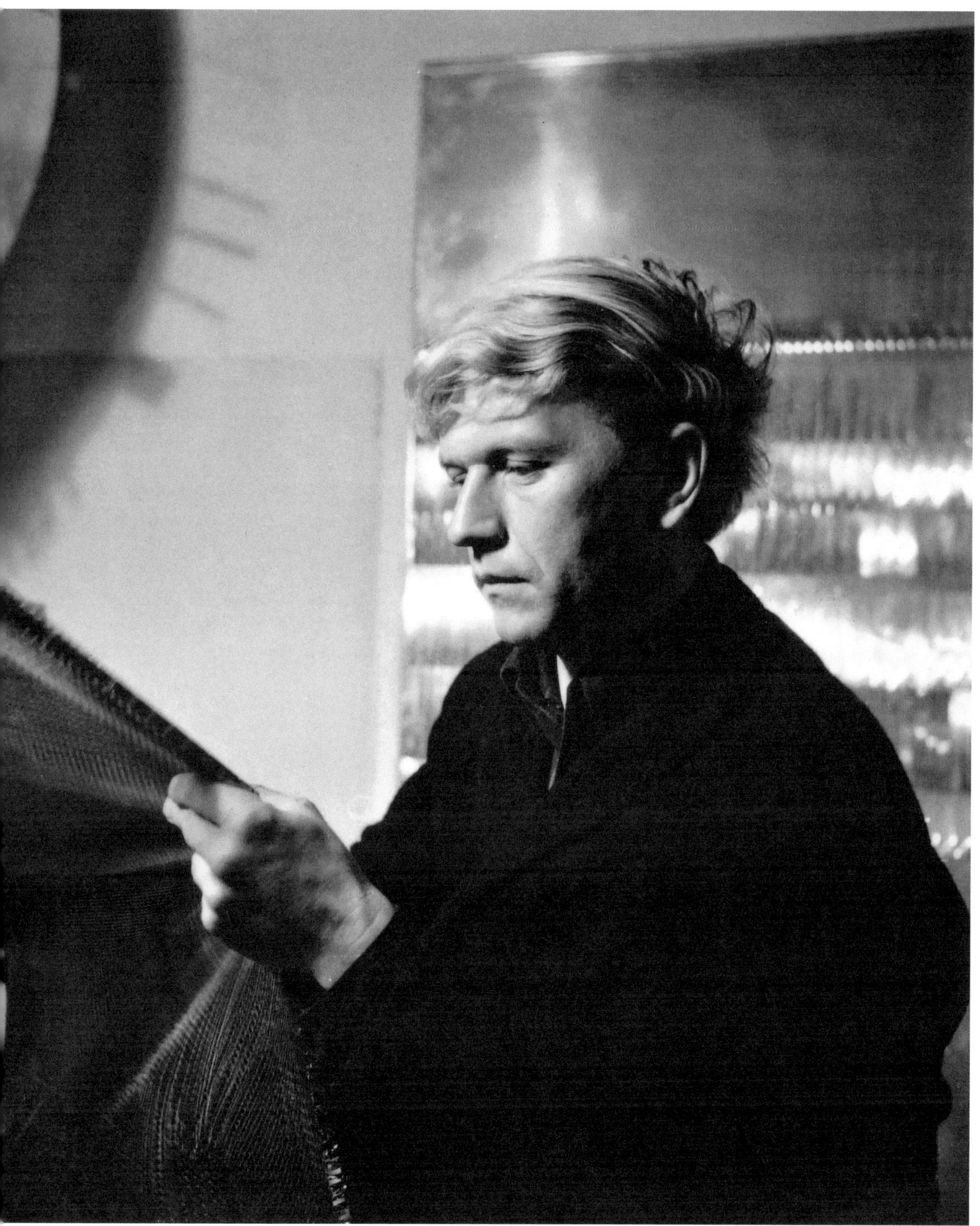

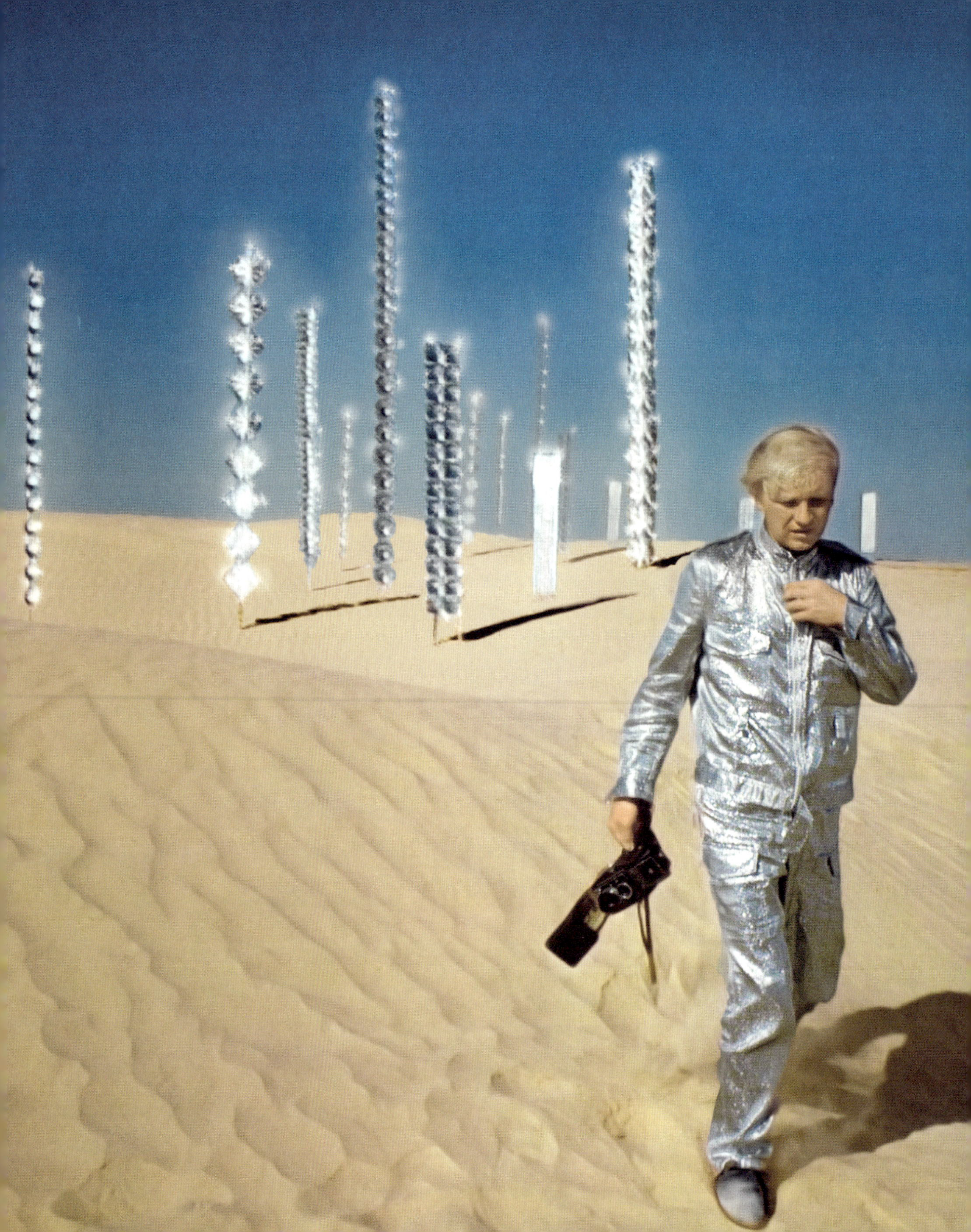

TIME SLICE 1969

Heinz Mack during the shooting of the film *Tele-Mack* in the Grand Erg Oriental, east of the Kebili oasis, Tunisia
1968

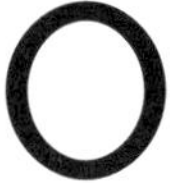n 26 May 1969, Heinz Mack is a guest on the WDR radio programme 'Kulturelles Wort' (Cultural Word). The interview presents the artist in a decisive phase of his life, his career, and his artistic concept. ZERO is a historical fact and lies in the past. The art market and museums have begun to take an interest in his work. But this also raises questions for him: Was that all from an artistic point of view? Am I now just going to repeat everything, like many artists in this situation? Will I settle down comfortably, with a professorship for financial security and a work that is recognisable like a trademark? Or are there new horizons? Do they possibly transcend the previous framework of art even further than ZERO proposed? Could the social role of art be reconsidered, even beyond the zeitgeist of the late 1960s in which it is central?

In 1969, Heinz Mack is thirty-eight years old. The interview is a kind of taking stock of his career to date. He redefines the perspectives of his own work for the next phase of his career. Today, more than fifty-five years later, he continues to act with great consistency within this newly defined framework. At that time, he had realised that his original artistic idea still had a completely different potential dimension. As in the early years of ZERO, his work has since grown out of this dynamic. His subsequent turn to artistic projects in public space, whether temporary or permanent, was courageous.

Hanno Reuther asked the questions on the radio programme. Excerpts from the interview are reproduced here:

»

Mr Mack, the question of the social commitment of artists is once again very much in the limelight today.

> I'm not a political person, and when I have the opportunity to talk to politicians of any stature, I always try to bring up artistic issues as soon as possible. That doesn't mean I'm not interested in the news of the day, but I don't see a direct connection between artistic endeavour on the one hand and political, social and societal endeavour on the other. But there are undoubtedly indirect connections, and I am sure that artists, even if they are only a minority in a sociological sense, [...] that we [artists] – precisely because

we are free in what we do and are in no way obliged to react immediately to political circumstances – perhaps have some chance of indirectly influencing what is apparently not expected in a direct sense every day: namely art as an expression of human freedom.

Looking back on more than ten years of the ZERO movement, we are still fascinated, even in retrospect, by this utopian impulse, this optimistic drive towards a better, healthier world. Behind this call to action is something like a gently positive attitude towards the world as it is. But how is it? Full of constraints and regulations. Does anything about this ZERO credo of yesteryear seem to you to be in need of revision today?

Again, my answer is yes and no. Of course, we invested a level of enthusiasm at the time that I wouldn't be able to muster to the same extent today. I may have become more critical as a result of certain experiences, but I would still consider my commitment to have integrity, and I would still claim it for myself today. This does not necessarily mean that I now negate the world or that I find it wonderful and accept it fully. The world is certainly in need of correction, it always will be, and artists have something of an artistic moral duty to maintain that vigilant awareness, that attention. You also have to bear in mind that we were in a time when there were very destructive tendencies in art. The post-war period had by no means been overcome, vanquished, and much of what was happening at that time, for example in the fine arts, Tachism, was a very destructive and disruptive tendency. And at that time, we very consciously and almost polemically defended ourselves against this attitude and argued for a better world to live in, not [meaning] the most beautiful of all worlds, the most beautiful of all times, but with this aspiration to use the enormous possibilities that our century offers for the better and to use these enormous energies for things that make life more beautiful. And this is meant literally, in the classical sense of Plato, that the beautiful is also the good – so, as you can see, it is not only an aesthetic claim, but also a moral one.

Mr Mack, people who emphasise the social function of art today can be found mainly among our militant students, among the groups of so-called anti-authoritarians. These people would probably call you a capitalist – you are a wealthy artist; you have made your breakthrough after many years of hard work. How would you respond to this accusation, which could certainly be levelled at you, or perhaps has already been levelled at you?

I'm not a capitalist, and my tax returns are clear evidence of that. On the other hand, I am not afraid to ask my price for my work, in which I invest not only expensive materials but also a lot of energy – just as other artists of distinction do and have done. There is a simple reason for this: when I make a work, I first make it exclusively for myself. Then I hand it over, I agree to sell it, so that there's room in my studio for new work – and not just in my studio, but also in my mind, so that I can prepare myself for new work. I don't have a collection of my own work. I charge a high price so that these works, which I am nevertheless very attached to and which mean a lot to me, don't end up on a scrap heap after a few days. The high price is something like an insurance policy. And if I put that into perspective and compare it to a Porsche or any other object that commands a similar price, I can say in favour of the value of my work that a Porsche will be worth much less in five years' time, whereas I hope my work will retain its value. So that's what I have to say about capitalism. On the other hand, I ask myself, and I would reproach my students, my critics: Why can't the artist have money? It would be traditional nonsense to expect an artist today to live like van Gogh. The fact that a van Gogh had to live like van Gogh is a tragedy. I, for my part, have also had my tragedies, but at the moment when a public, whatever it may be – be it museums, galleries or private collectors or institutions or the state itself – [...] when such institutions and collectors are interested in my work, I cannot forbid them to acquire my works.

Let's go one step further. Occasionally, from the desks of contemporary artists, rather bitter appeals are made to their esteemed colleagues to subvert the art world by refraining from tying artistic ideas to an object that, as a materialised object, serves only as an occasion for beautiful emotion for a select few, perhaps financially strong collectors. Do you think there might be something to this theory of refusal?

> Yes, I kind of adhere to that too, and in the last ten years I have also done some things that you can't hang on the wall, that you can't put in a museum. And I have said very clearly and emphatically that I am against museums, even though my works hang on the walls of forty museums around the world. In other words: I make things that can be hung on the wall, and I make things that can't be hung on the wall. For example, almost ten years ago I developed a project, the so-called *Sahara Project*, which, apart from its purely artistic relevance, was a kind of polemic against the culture industry, in that I proposed moving art to an area that was free of fingerprints, free of the occupations of the culture industry. I have just finished a film (fig. pp. 156 f.)[165] – a film, in which I only show things that exist exclusively in the film itself, on a television set, things that do not exist at all outside the medium of television, that are not for sale, that are only intended to reach a mass audience so that they can engage with these new phenomena that I'm presenting, but which are not, as you assumed, reserved for an elite audience.

Your *Sahara Project*, which has finally been realised – an old ZERO project, if I remember correctly – also removes the marketable, the saleable object from the art industry, apart from the fact that this film from the desert sets a completely new date within the conventional system of mediating art.

> Yes, after having harboured the desire to bring my works to the desert for about ten years, the unexpected opportunity arose last autumn to realise this wish for the first time. This does not mean that the whole *Sahara Project* as such

has been realised – it is far too complex for that – but it does prove that it is not a utopia, but that it is in principle entirely feasible. And the form in which this realisation has taken place is television, [with which] I try to reach this mass audience and present [them] with something that, as I said earlier, cannot really be hung on the wall, that cannot be sold, but that can be communicated as art, that presents itself to a completely open society and even works with this somewhat sensitive and cautious tactic of presenting art in such a way that the question of whether it is art or not does not even arise, but the fascination should be so great that this classic stumbling block falls by the wayside for the time being.

What do you think museums should look like in the future? Do we still need museums at all – what do you think?

Yes, well, the crucial thing is that I also question museums, and I did so at a time when it was perhaps not fashionable to do so. When we organised our exhibitions in the streets in 1961, [...] they were demonstrations that [we were] quite sure at the time could not be realised in a museum. The museum undoubtedly has fantastic merits, at least historically – no doubt about it. On the other hand, the museum today is undoubtedly in crisis. Even the most modern museum a priori runs the risk of being restorative, of preserving only that which is actually preserved in this way outside of society. And society – and in this respect I do think socially – has a right to be confronted with what artists are manifesting today. And this right is most likely to be made accessible if artists are given the opportunity to realise their works within an urban structure, a landscape structure, in the open air, so to speak, so that they are accessible to everyone, whether intentionally or not. So that all people have the opportunity to engage with these objects, as it were by chance, in passing, without this somewhat intrusive claim to cultural exchange, to intellectual dialogue, but rather in a natural and self-evident way, just as beautiful natural phenomena in this world still fascinate the ordinary public. In my opinion, man-made works in nature could also surprise people and invite them to an encounter. The population, the individual person, the individual citizen should, so to speak, be encouraged by what the artist has done to find the courage to expect things – I don't want to say demand things – to expect things that really mean something, like a better life.

And would you say that the real social effect – modestly speaking – that the real social effect of art production could lie in this effect?

Only in this way, only in this way...

«

→
Stills from the film ***Tele-Mack***
Tunisia, 1968/69
first broadcast on WDR
2 May 1969

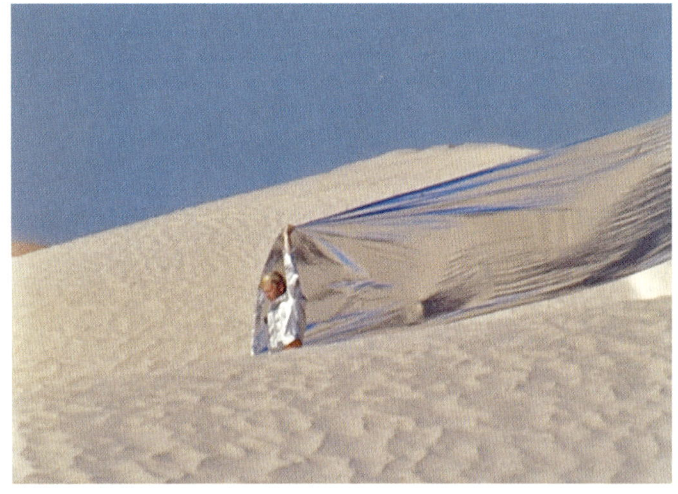
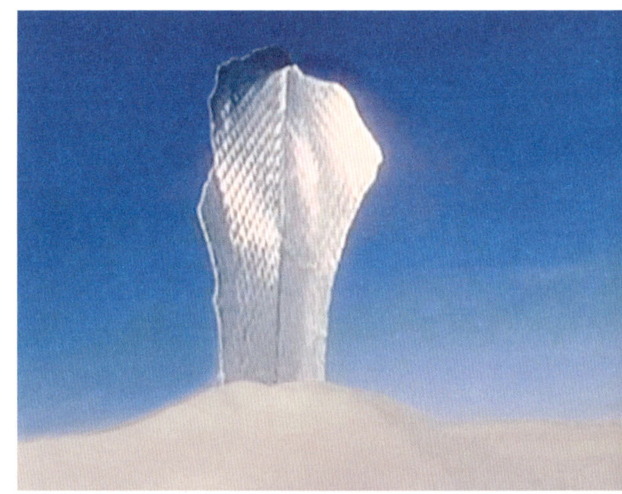
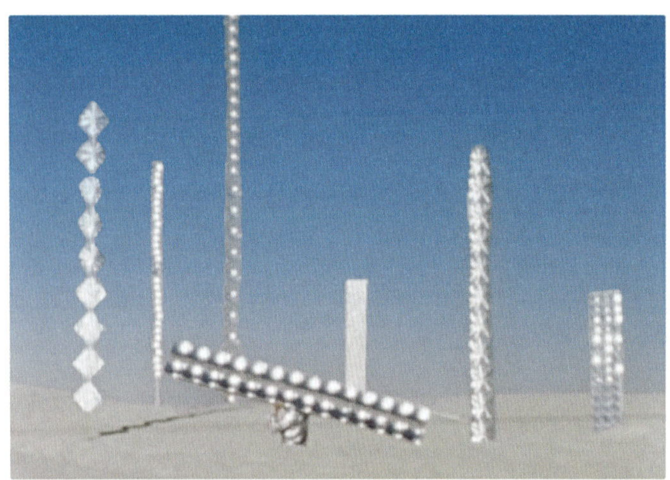
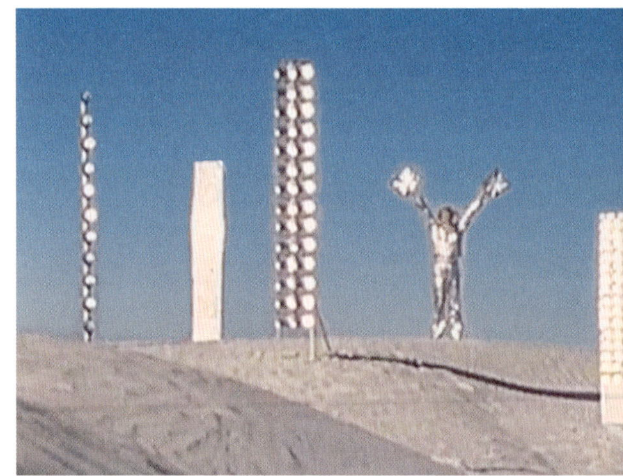
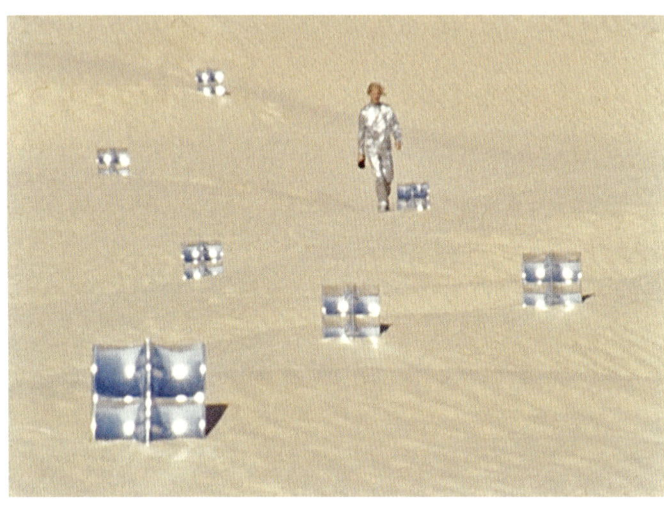
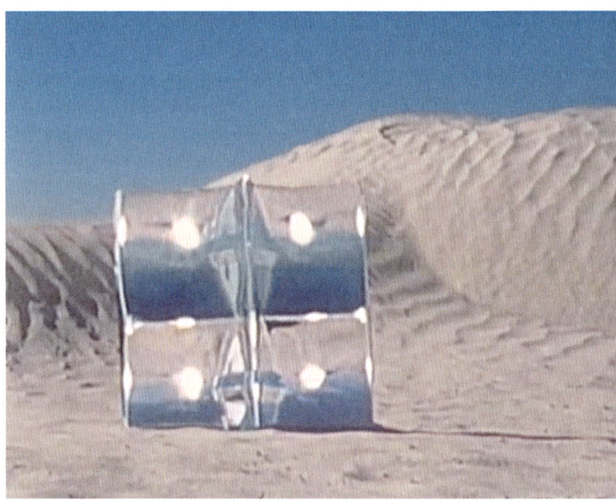

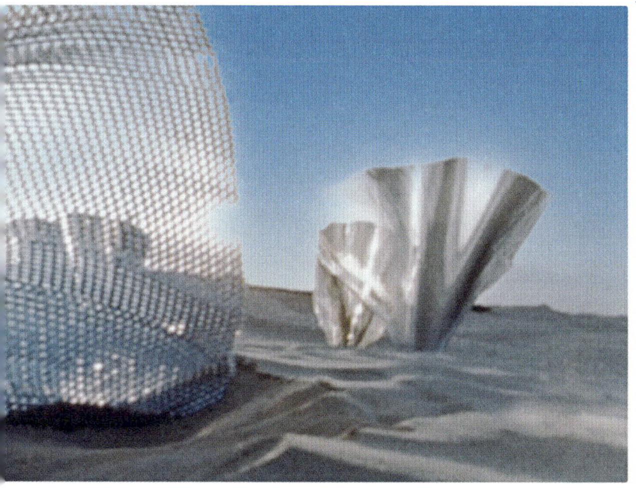
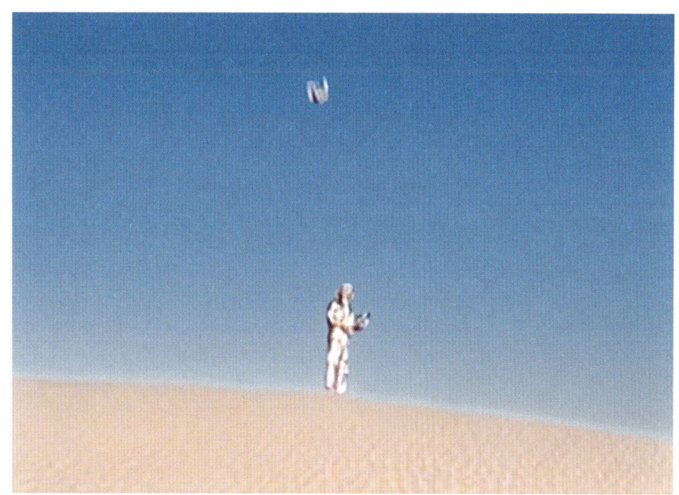
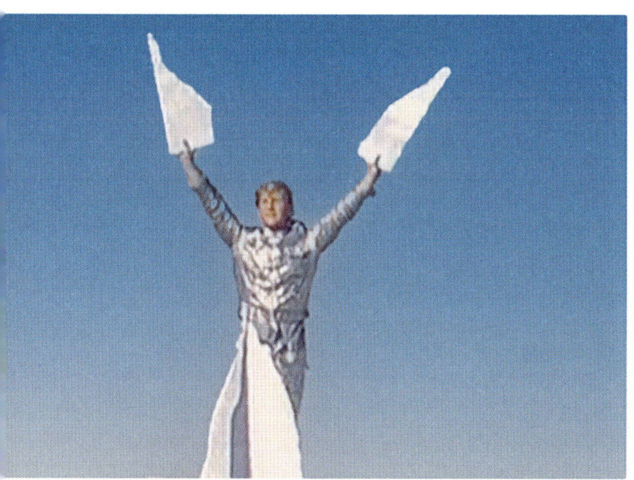
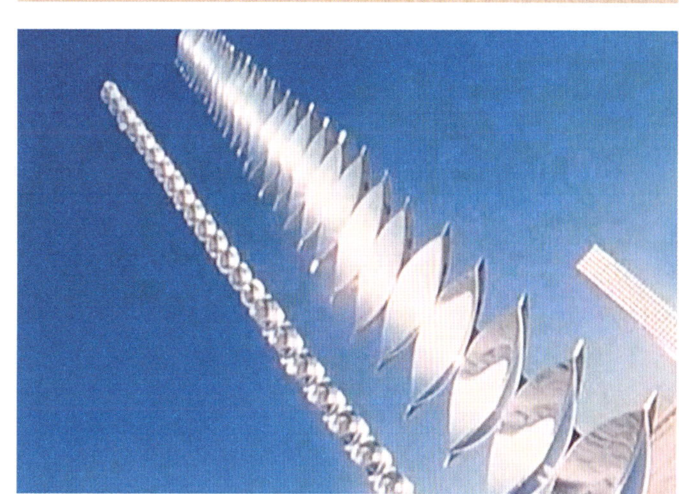
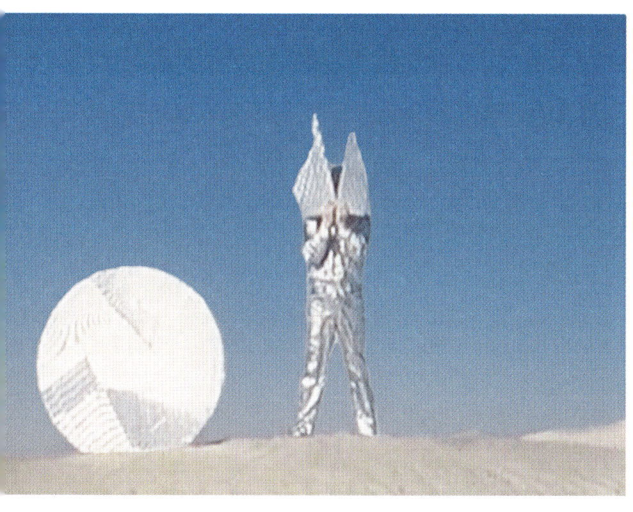
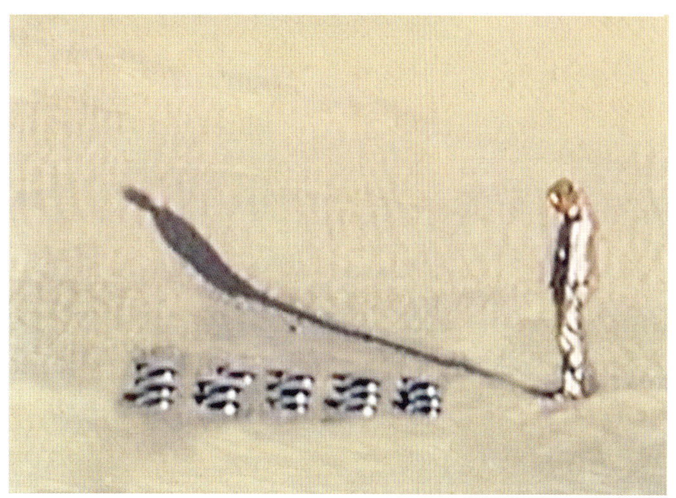

TIME SLICE, 1969

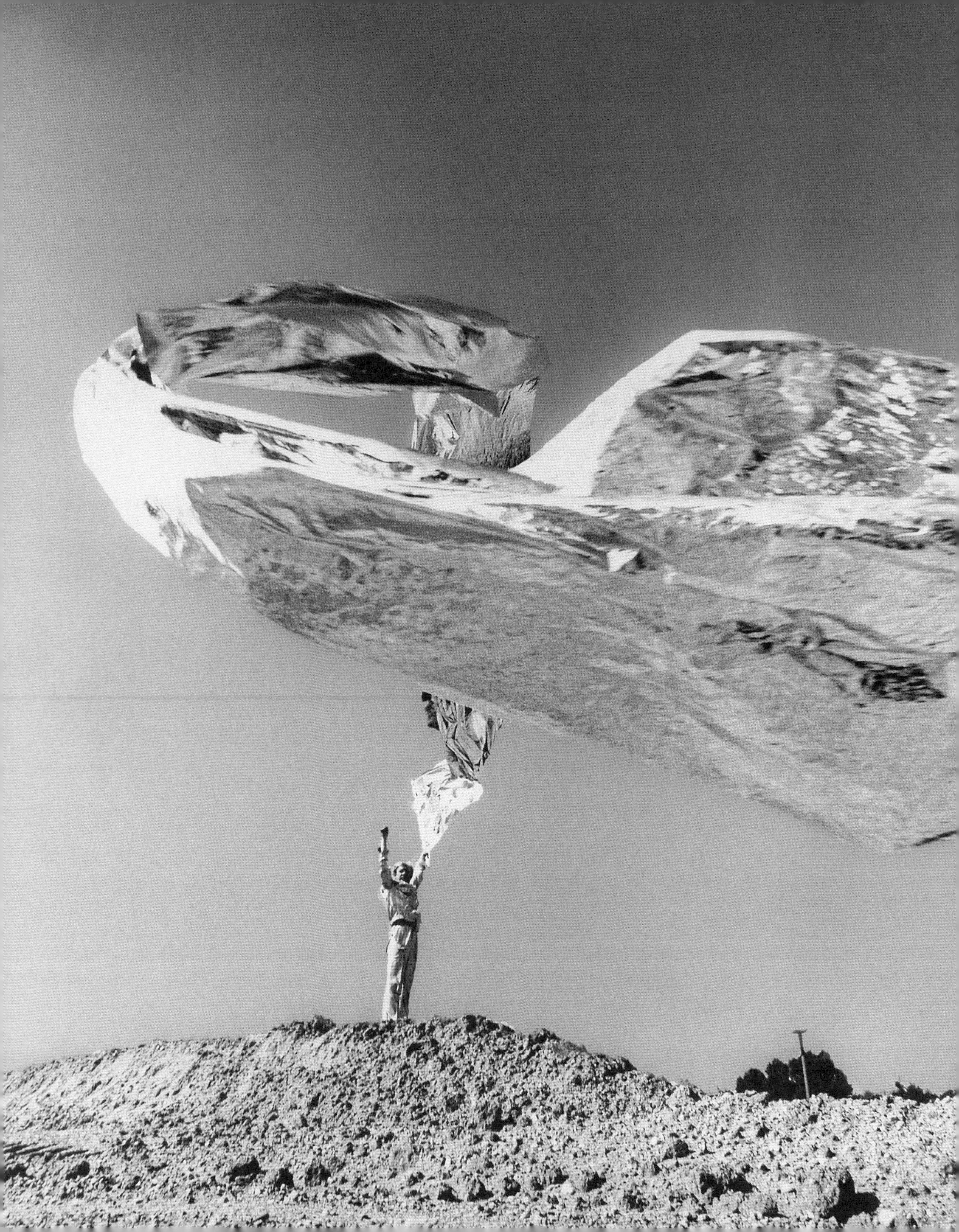

NEW SPACES

Heinz Mack with a silver flag
in a quarry, West Germany
c. 1970/71

Munich, August–September 1972: A vast park has been created for the Olympic Summer Games, housing the main stadiums and sports facilities as well as green and water areas. Unlike conventional parks, it has no clearly visible internal boundaries and thus breathes something of a new, indefinable space. The largest single area is taken up by an artificial lake whose outer edges form concave and convex curves. The various squares and promenades around this water bring together the visitors to the various sports venues, so that, due to the huge crowds at the first Olympic Games to be held in Germany since those in Berlin in 1936, at the time of National Socialism, there is almost always a large number of people strolling and socialising here, even after dark.

At regular intervals, the surface of the water begins to move in one place. A broad, shapeless column of water rises from the lake at a height of eight metres (fig. pp. 162 f.). It is transformed by the wind into a cloud that floats above the Olympic Lake with many internal reflections, illuminated by the sunlight or by 112 underwater spotlights. It is a poetic event that visualises the elements of water, air, and light and their interaction. After about a minute, the cloud of water begins to slowly dissipate, only to rise again half an hour later. The phenomenon is triggered by a computer programme. Occasionally, the process is multiplied several times. A second computer programme is then used to create the impression that an air vortex is lifting the *Water Cloud*. The fountain then reaches a height of 36 metres. At night, this version is illuminated from the air by twenty-four additional floodlights on the site. Every minute, 74,000 litres of water are spun through the air. All of this, this ephemeral sculpture of water, light, and air, takes place on the Olympic Lake, on a highly visible, 30 by 14 metre (420 square metre) section of the Olympic site.

Heinz Mack's *Water Cloud* of 1972 became an artistic symbol of these Munich Games, which were brutally interrupted a few days before the closing ceremony by the Palestinian hostage-taking and murder of Israeli athletes.

For the artist, his participation set several key markers for his subsequent work. The interaction with a mass audience, who had come for the largest sporting event in the world, not for an art event, led to a direct impact of his art in the urban, natural, and social space beyond the museum walls, as he had already formulated in his radio talk on WDR in 1969 (pp. 150–155). At the same time there was a change of scale. Mack had worked in real space, in its dimensions, and in a form appropriate to it. The sculpture consists of pure elements: water, air, and light. It thus makes do without conventional artistic materials. Moreover, it is just as ephemeral as the appearance of these materials to our eyes, which means that transience is also inscribed in its artistic form. At the same time, it is potentially infinitely repeatable.[166] A new temporality emerges. The sculpture exists only in real time, not in the 'frozen' time of conventional sculpture, although real time had already been introduced in the artist's kinetic works. This is because each rotor rotates in real time and is a constantly changing phenomenon of light (fig. p. 133). But when you pull the plug after the museum closes, it stands there lifeless. Here, however, in the Olympic Lake, real time and real space become the dimension of the work.

Many of the features mentioned above can be found in Mack's work from the late 1960s onwards, when the artist underwent a radical change in his work and reinvented himself as an artist beyond ZERO, taking the ZERO experience in a new direction. With the *Water Cloud* in Munich's Olympic Park, something also emerges that characterises Mack's subsequent sculptural interventions in public space, as well as his projects in the Sahara (previously) and the Arctic (fig. p. 294 f.): it is the treatment of an arbitrary, irrelevant, contourless space. We saw at the beginning of this chapter that the Olympic Park is an early example of how the ideological intention of creating an 'open', non-exclusionary space gave rise to a non-space, a post-urban space that has neither coordinates nor contours. Mack indirectly addressed this type of space and the challenge it posed to artistic work early on, namely in his *Sahara Project*, formulated in 1958 and published in the magazine *ZERO 3* in 1961.[167] This form of open space without definable dimensions and coordinates had been a utopia for the artist ever since he first travelled through the North African deserts in his VW Beetle in 1955 and discovered the infinite, coordinate-less, and direct space of the sand and stone desert. In 1968, a WDR film portrait of Heinz Mack unexpectedly made the first realisation of the *Sahara Project* in the Tunisian desert possible. The result was the film *Tele-Mack*, which caused a sensation when it was first broadcast on West German television in May 1969, and which remains a pioneering achievement to this day, also in terms of media art and the use of a mass medium as a direct medium of art.[168] Heinz Mack, all alone in the sandy desert under indescribable light, experimenting with light sculptures (fig. p. 156 f.), wearing a silver suit like the US astronauts on the Moon a good six months later, gradually broadcast on television throughout the entire Western Hemisphere, shifted the coordinates of art and made art interesting, especially for a younger generation that knew little about it. But *Tele-Mack* was also an opportunity for other artists, both in the new way of dealing with a deterritorialised space and in the combination of ephemeral works in the landscape and film as a new medium of visual art. Robert Smithson did something similar a few years later with the documentary films about his pioneering works of early earth art, later called Land Art, which emerged from the New York art scene of the time.[169]

For fifty years, the question has been asked whether Mack was a forerunner of Land Art or vice versa and whether the two are not comparable. The question can be answered quite simply by comparing *Tele-Mack* and Mack's work in the Tunisian desert with American Land Art. In Heinz Mack's work, there was a maximum deterritorialisation of space and sculpture, while Land Art carried out a maximum reterritorialisation[170] and land occupation in undefined places, desert-like areas in the Midwest

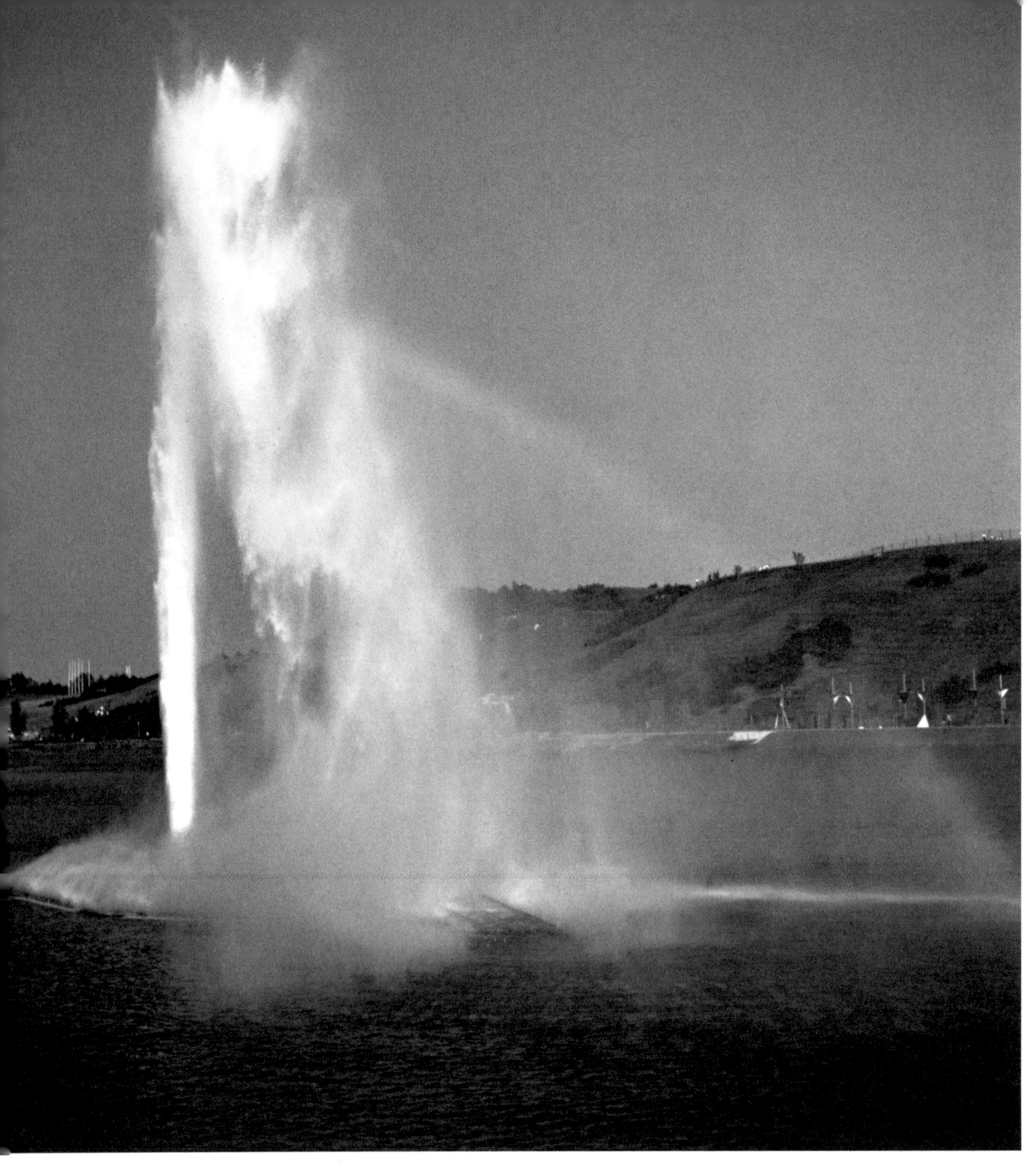

Water Cloud
Olympic Park, Munich
1972

Water Cloud
Olympic Park, Munich
1972

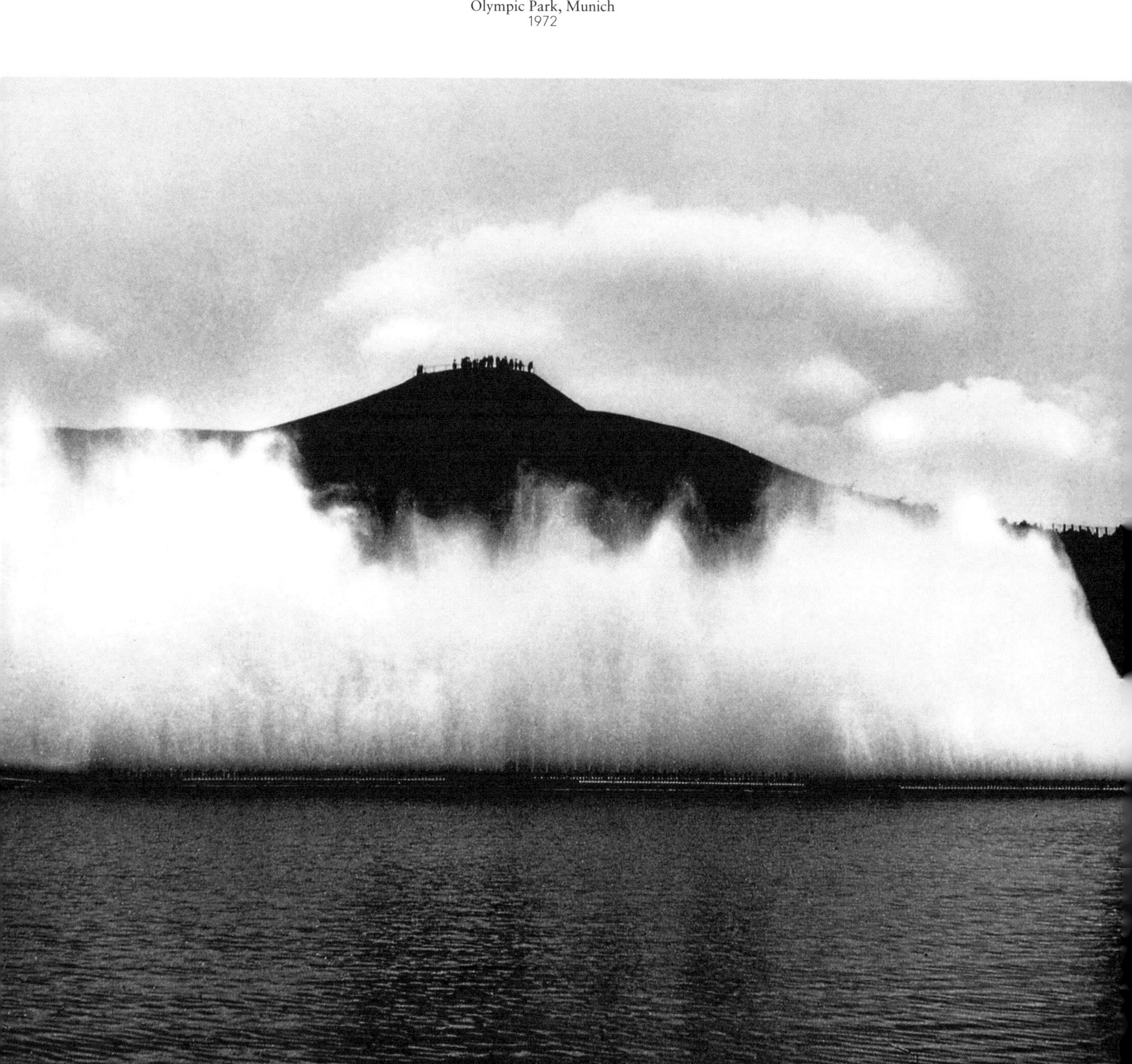

and the South of the United States. Mack acted alone in the desert in front of the WDR camera, and he left it unchanged. The protagonists of American Land Art, already supported by sponsors and the new financing model of the Dia Art Foundation, realised their Land Art works with gigantic bulldozers that transformed some of the vacant areas they had chosen into oversized landscape sculptures. Some of these works can still be seen today – they were never returned to the desert.

In 1968, *Tele-Mack* was filmed in the Tunisian desert.[171] In 1972, on the Olympic site in Munich, Mack's work encountered a comparable form of outdoor space – without definable dimensions or recognisable coordinates – that anticipated the dissolution of urbanism into arbitrary spaces[172] in the urban planning of the last fifty years. It was within this framework that Mack had to think about his sculpture for the Olympic Summer Games in Munich. He conceived it as a temporary, infinitely repeatable sculpture that seems to come out of nowhere but suddenly bundles the entire space of this unmanageable site. When the second, intensifying computer programme[173] was switched on, causing a vortex of air to pull the horizontal *Water Cloud* up to a height of thirty-six metres, this immaterial, ever-changing, ephemeral form of the *Water Cloud* communicated particularly impressively with the spectacular vertical struts of the neighbouring buildings by Günter Behnisch and Frei Otto, two world-class architects.

I might also mention in passing that I was by far the youngest member to be appointed to the West Berlin Academy of Arts. There was also an exhibition there that was very important to me,[174] which the person in charge of exhibitions at the academy passed on to the Musée d'art moderne de la Ville de Paris, where it was accompanied by an important catalogue.[175] The Academy of Arts was very prestigious. There were writers, philosophers of language, musicians and composers – a lasting friendship developed with György Ligeti – art historians such as Werner Hofmann, film people, architects and so on. But there was never any real communication between the disciplines. Günter Grass once gave a big speech against technology.

A solo exhibition with the title *mack. Objekte – Aktionen – Projekte*, which is characteristic of the new phase of his work, began in 1972 at the Academy of Arts in West Berlin and was subsequently shown at the Städtische Kunsthalle Düsseldorf (fig. p. 171), the Musée d'art moderne de la Ville de Paris, and the Stedelijk Van Abbemuseum in Eindhoven. Four of the most important institutions for new art in Europe at the time were thus brought together in collaboration. In the catalogue for the Paris exhibition, the kineticist George Rickey describes the artist as follows: 'His portrait: intelligence, confidence, a consistent tendency towards the dramatic, a style conquered dangerously early, charm, serenity, the energy of an iconoclast, a *Bilderstürmer*. This is also the portrait that Marisol made of Mack: a blond head with a serious but mischievous face behind grooved glass (fig. p. 123). Paradoxically, he lives on a fifteenth-century farmstead in the peaceful countryside of Mönchengladbach. That said, there is a Jaguar parked at the gate.'[176]

I felt attacked, stood up and said: 'Dear Günter Grass, as far as I know you, you are full of contradictions. If tomorrow your life is in danger because of a traffic accident and you end up in hospital, I am sure you will be very interested in the functioning of technology. If not, then I'd like to say goodbye to you now.' It was something like that. Twenty years later, in 1992, after reunification, when the East and West academies in Berlin were about to merge, as if the East members had not all been dignitaries of the totalitarian regime, I resigned from the Academy of Arts, along with Georg Baselitz and a total of twenty-five other members.

« (OCTOBER 2022)

»

I was often criticised and taunted for my sports cars, starting with the Aston Martin, the James Bond car. There were only two of them in Germany. However, I never bought them at a high price, but rather in some cases from entrepreneurs from the Ruhr area, who were embarrassed by them, or from the red-light districts of Duisburg and Cologne. For an artist, who is by nature independent and free, such things are neither embarrassing nor suspicious. An automobile is a perfect kinetic object.

« (DECEMBER 2022)

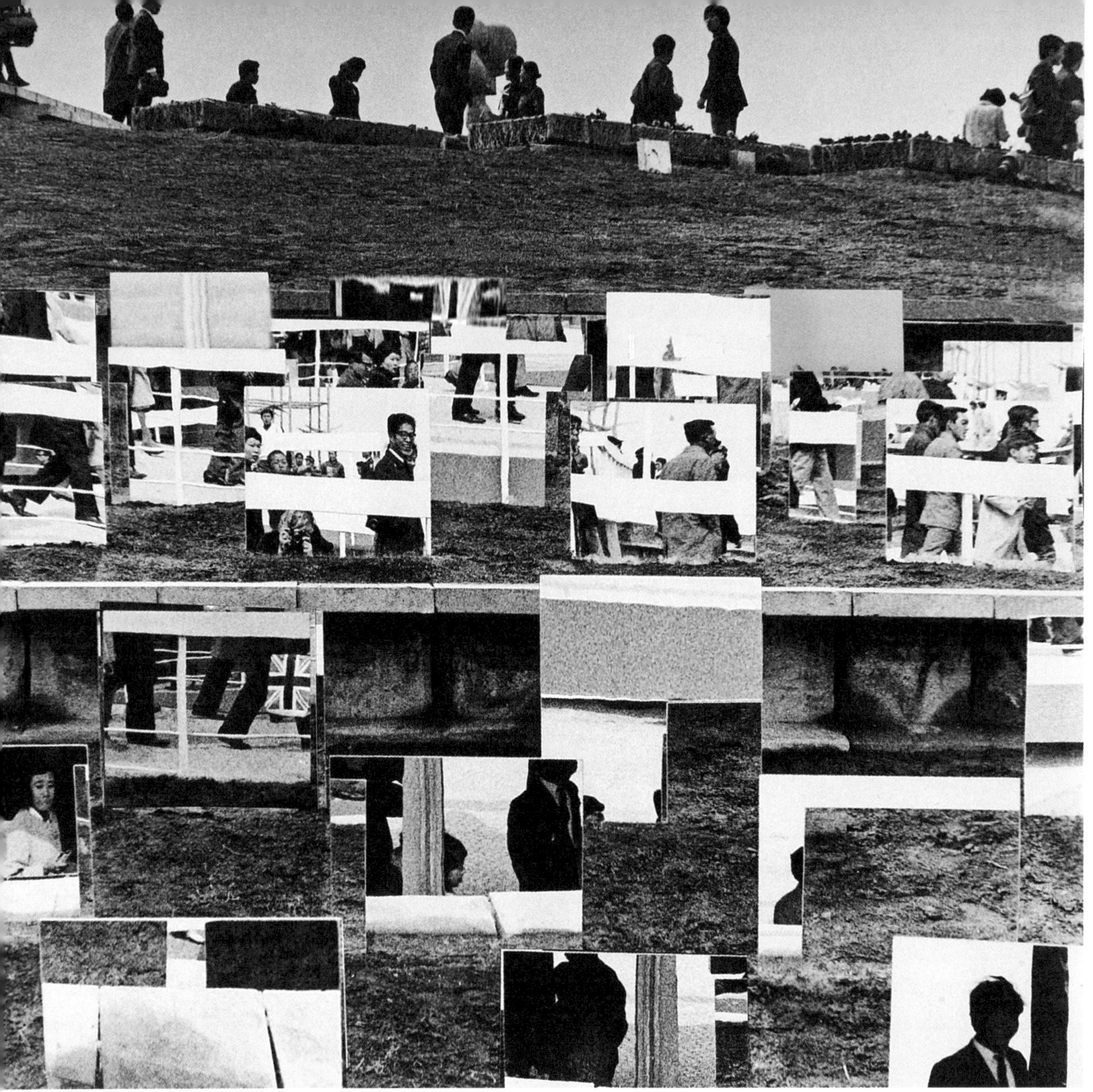

Design of the entrance spiral to
the German Pavilion at the Japan
World Exposition in Osaka
1970

Venice in the summer of 1970: Heinz Mack represents the Federal Republic of Germany at the Biennale, the world's most important cyclical art exhibition alongside the documenta in Kassel.[177] At the invitation of Dieter Honisch, then curator at the Museum Folkwang in Essen, he shares the German Pavilion with Thomas Lenk, Georg Karl Pfahler, and Günther Uecker, with Pfahler and Uecker intervening in the exterior space on the façade. In the apse-like curve of the main room, Heinz Mack presents a forest of steles (fig. pp. 168–169), which takes up the formal principle of the first forest of steles at Howard Wise Gallery in New York four years earlier (fig. p. 127) but is very different in nature. The group of sculptures in Venice is site-specific, oriented to the height of the space, with all twenty-three steles rising along a translucent cube of light that cancels the frontality of the 1966 New York configuration. The Venice ensemble is non-monumental in the best sense of the word. It is not ostentatious and does not occupy space. Rather, it dissolves the architectural space into various rhythms. At the centre is a transparent, cubic light column ten metres high. To the left and right of it, slender wooden steles structured as bas-reliefs and repeatedly folded, flat metal steles orchestrate the polyphony of this ensemble in materials that dissolve Mack's basic theme of structure into rhythms that the viewer composes for him or herself.

The conceptual artist Helmut Schweizer, fifteen years younger than Mack, still remembers his visit to the Venice Biennale with fellow students Lothar Baumgarten and Anselm Kiefer. Standing in front of the forest of steles, they said: 'The ZERO people really initiated the opening that we are benefiting from.'[178]

However, Mack's forest of steles in the German Pavilion was not only site- and space-specific.[180] He also stripped the architecture of some of its monumentality and historical references, transforming the central hall into a neutral, 'inconsequential' space, from which the ensemble of sculptures drew a particular energy and concentration. We have already seen a similar process and concept of space in the *Water Cloud* in Munich in 1972. In Venice, this reference had its own special character: Adolf Hitler had commissioned the redesign of the German Pavilion in 1934 after his visit to the exhibition at the time, played a key role in shaping the architecture and opened it for the 1938 Biennale. Paradoxically, as Venice was not bombed during the Second World War, it is the best-preserved example of Nazi architecture. In 1970, Mack and Uecker – the latter covering one of the four Nazi-era pillars at the entrance to the building with a surface of oversized nails – initiated the long series of

»

I was walking down the main street in Essen; I can't remember why. And by chance a man came up to me and said: 'Hello. You're Heinz Mack, aren't you?' I said: 'Yes, I'm Heinz Mack', and he said: 'I'm Dieter Honisch.' There was a café nearby, so we had a coffee together. That day I had read in the newspaper that they were looking for a new general director for the Neue Nationalgalerie in West Berlin, and I said to Honisch that he could also apply. He made a face at me as if I had been talking to a brick wall. It turned out that he had applied, and he became the director of the Neue Nationalgalerie. A wonderful correspondence soon developed between him and me, which was also very personal.

« (JUNE 2023)

»

I am 'grateful' (if I may say so) to a society that does not tell me what to do and how to do it, with small, unreal suggestions, with more or less fantastic ideas, whose character is to be an expression of freedom, which is always also the freedom of others to accept or reject my works.

« (IN: DIETER HONISCH, 'GESPRÄCH MIT HEINZ MACK', 1977)[179]

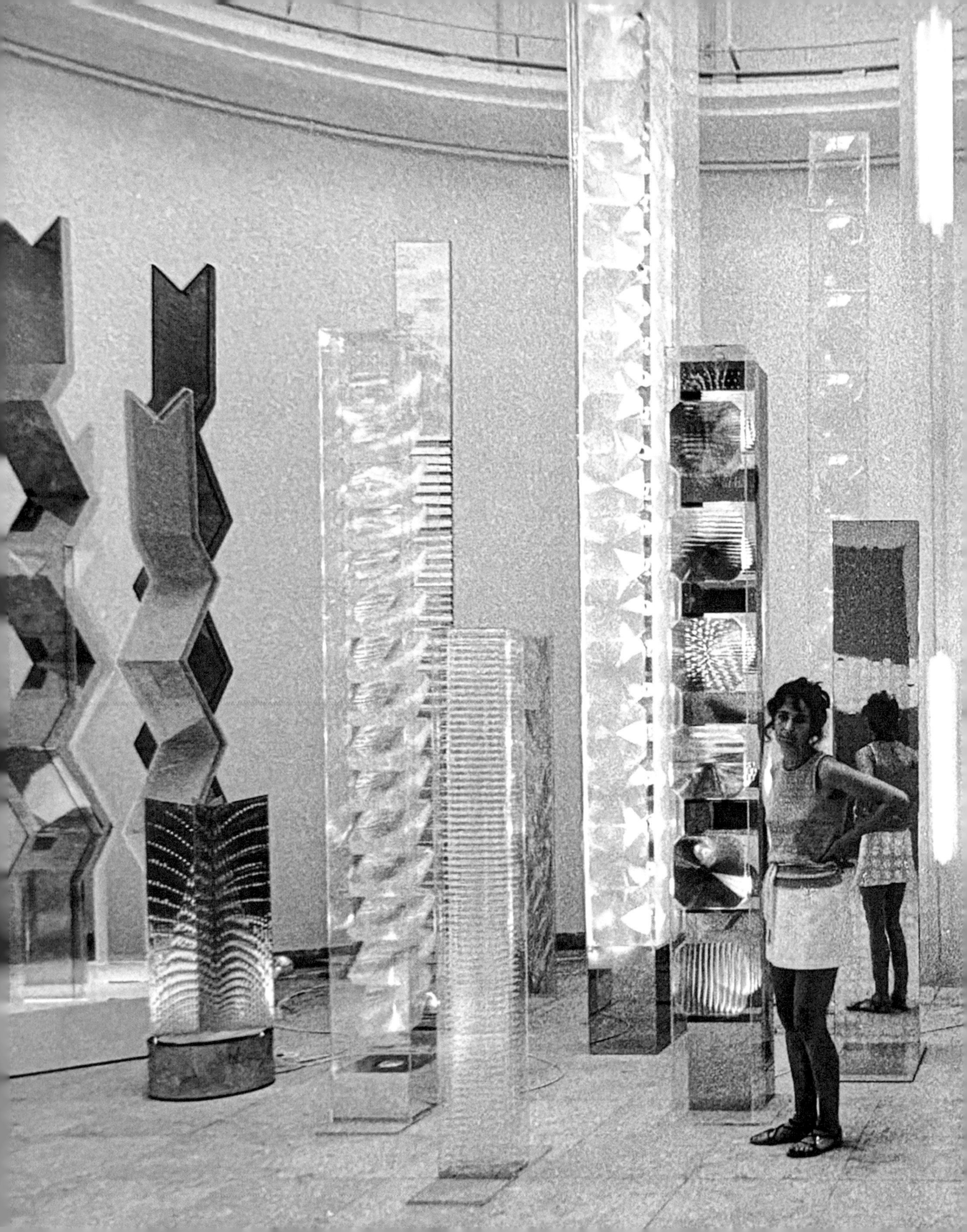

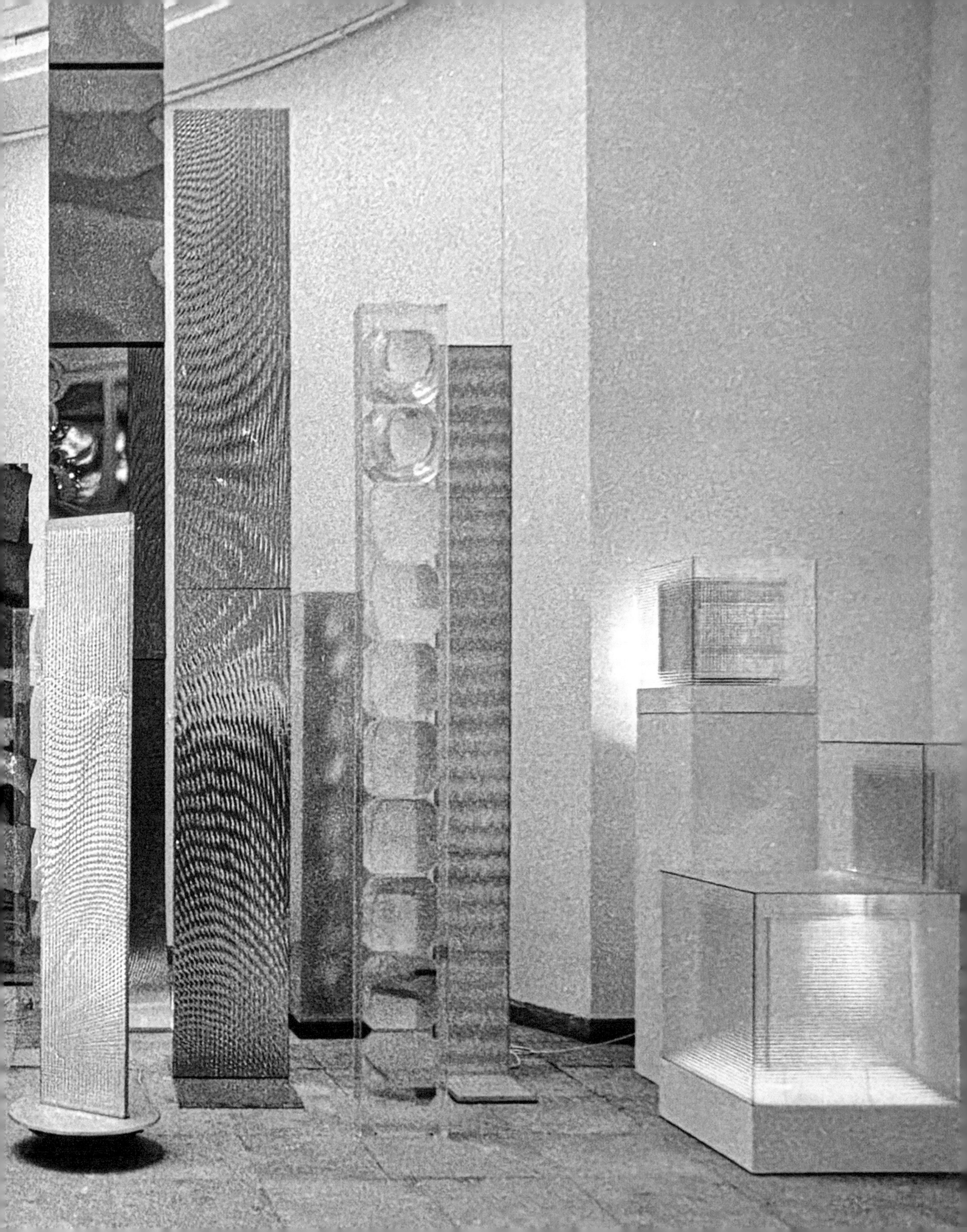

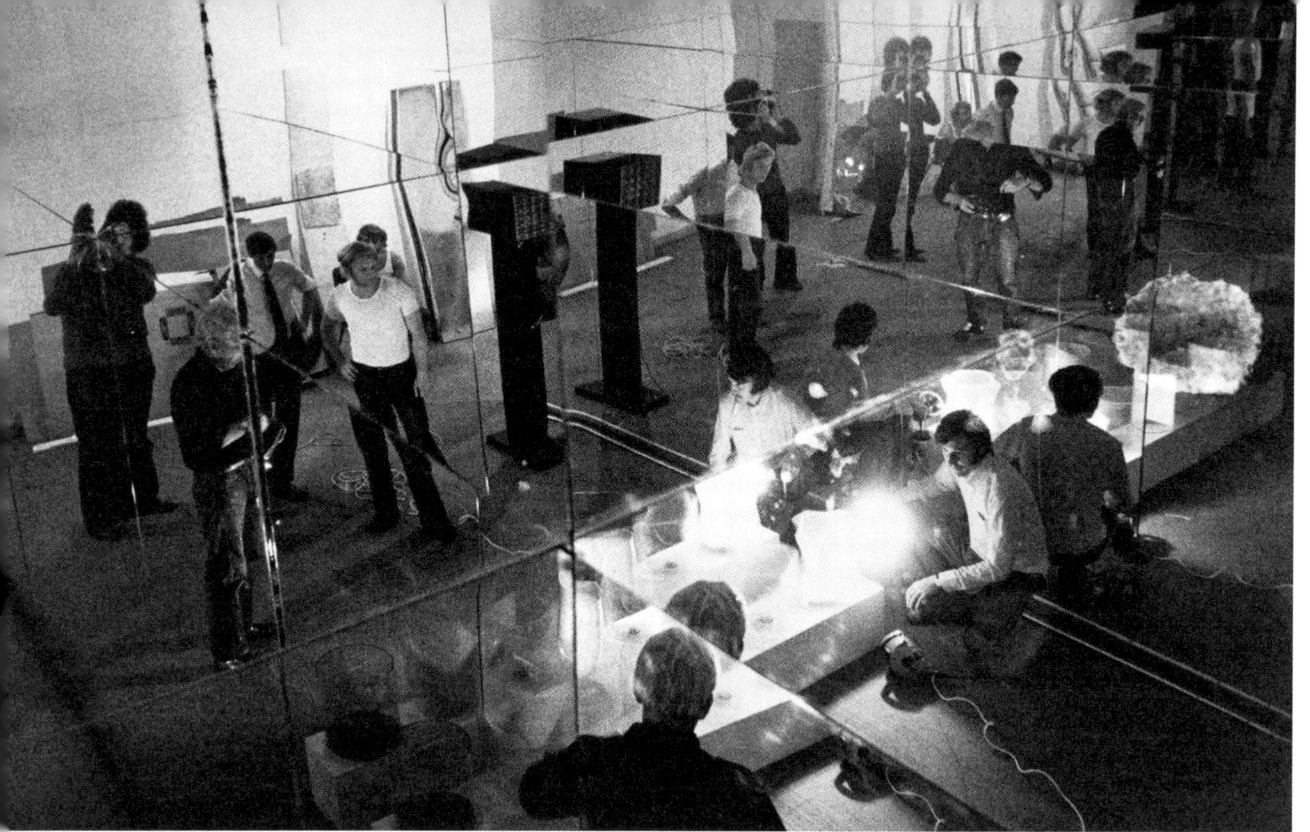

Mirror cabinet in the exhibition
mack. Objekte – Aktionen – Projekte,
Städtische Kunsthalle Düsseldorf
1972

←
Cubes and light steles by Heinz Mack
in the German Pavilion at the 35th
Venice Biennale
1970

Installation view
mack. Objekte – Aktionen – Projekte,
Academy of Arts, Berlin (West)
1972

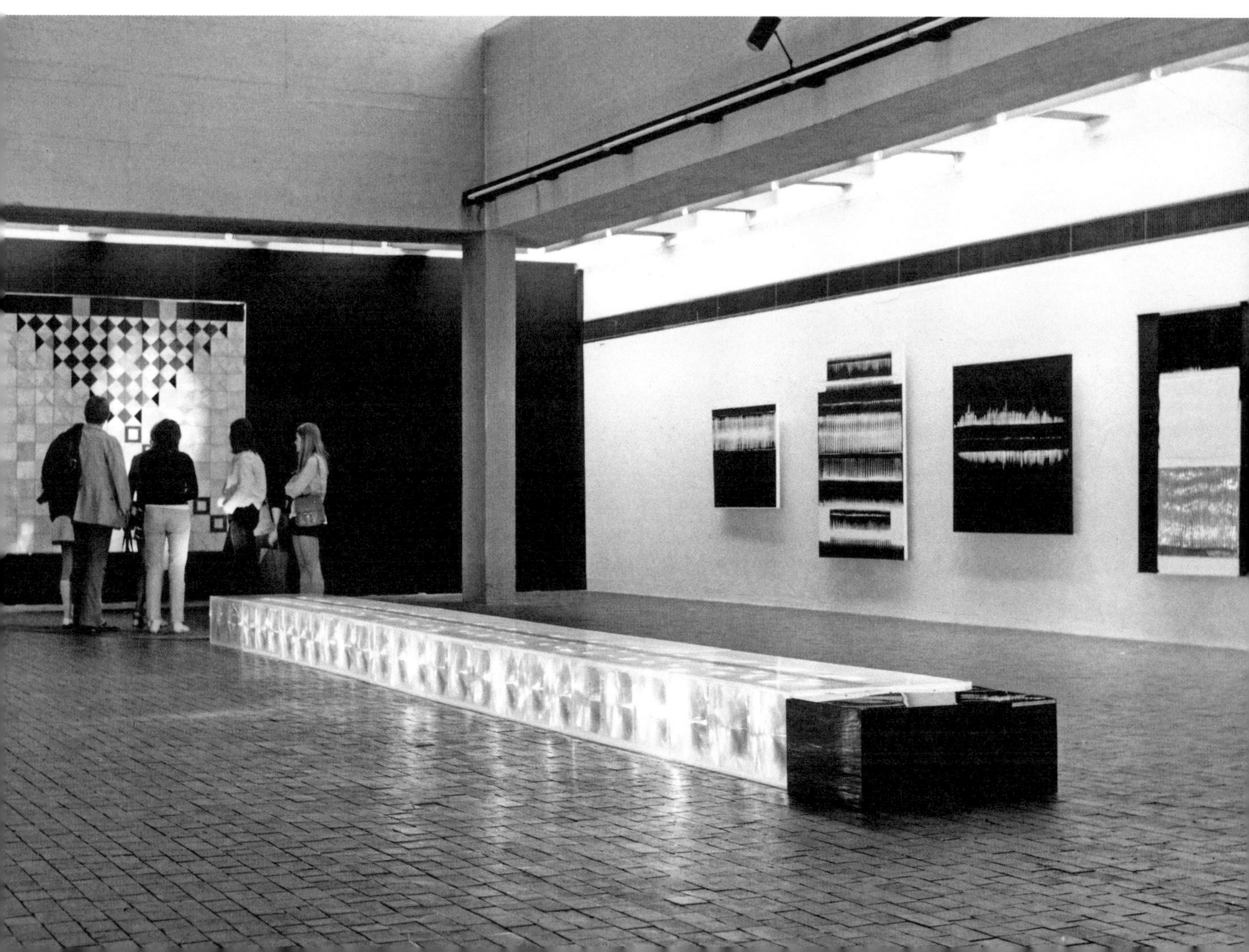

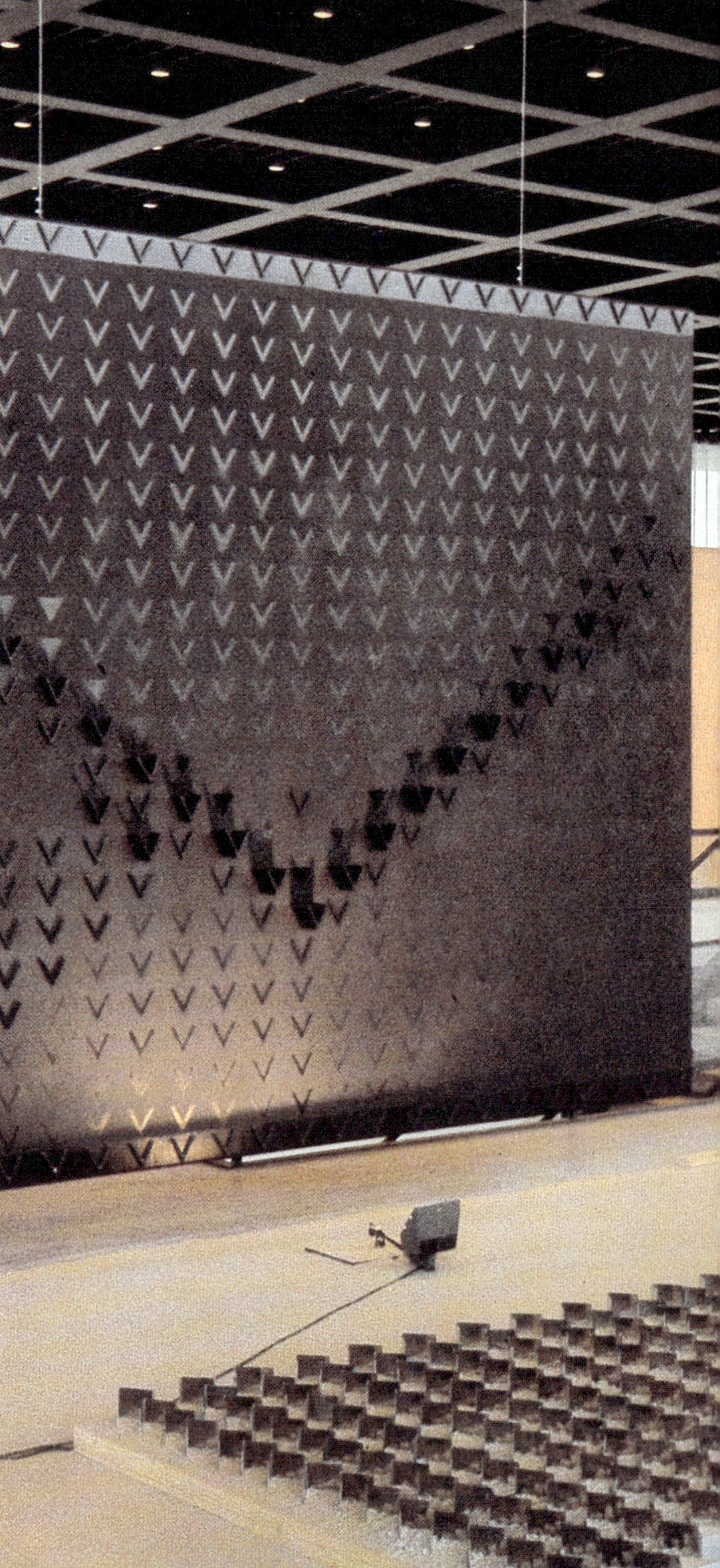

The Seasons of the Desert
1974/76
in the exhibition
Kunstübermittlungsformen,
Neue Nationalgalerie, Berlin (West)
1977

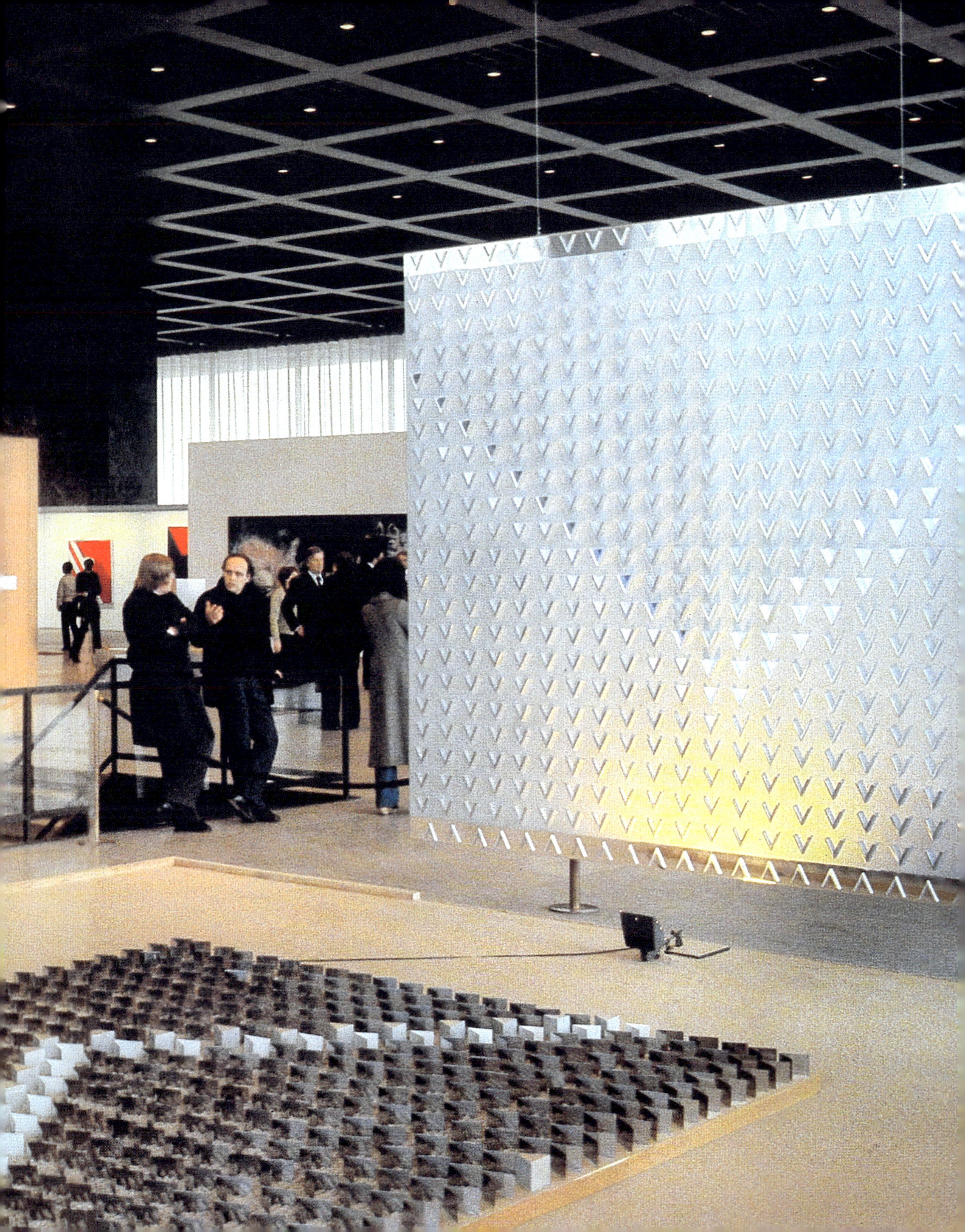

»

In 1970, at the Japan World Exposition in Osaka, Germany allowed itself the luxury of creating its own pavilion for music. I provided the concave inner surface of this cell construction with a light structure, creating a starry sky whose light functioned in perfect synchrony with Stockhausen's music. With the technical means available at the time, this was a real no-go. In principle, the only way to synchronise the light spectacle with the music was to use magnetic tape. We were still a long way from the digital possibilities of today. That was a very important story.

(OCTOBER 2022) «

German Biennale contributions that have since critically examined the building, culminating in the destruction of the Hitlerian marble floor by Hans Haacke, Mack's artist colleague from New York (p. 125), at the 1993 Biennale and which has been repeated rather unoriginally by German Biennale contributions to this day.

For the Japan World Exposition in Osaka in the summer of 1970, the artist created his first site-specific, architecture-related, and interdisciplinary light installation for a major international event with a mass audience. The Expo '70 was the first to be held in Asia. It saw itself as a window to the future – Japan had the best new technologies – and at the same time as the inaugural event of an ecological perspective against the backdrop of the first warnings of climate catastrophe. The German Pavilion was located underground beneath a meadow. Heinz Mack designed a spiral that led the public down into it, with 500 mirrored glass panels, each one square metre in size, transforming the surrounding landscape into 'real natural space montages'[181] (fig. p. 166), which at the same time represented an examination of the relationship to nature in Japanese culture. For the underground music dome, Karlheinz Stockhausen, Mack's friend and a major composer of new music, produced specially conceived electronic music that was synchronised with a lighting system that Mack had developed with the Structural Research Centre in Würzburg. Contacts with Japanese researchers and Jiro Yoshihara of Gutai, a group of artists in Japan comparable to ZERO and rediscovered internationally from the 1990s onwards, even before ZERO, led to Mack's appointment as professor of fine arts at the Osaka Academy in 1970, a post he resigned after only a year because a research institute he had been promised was never approved.[182]

Looking at the major works of these years, it is clear that Heinz Mack took a radical turn after his time in New York and the dissolution of ZERO. He opened up a new register that had to do with active interventions in public space and its unpredictable audience. In particular, he was confronted with open spaces without boundaries or contours, for which he found highly innovative artistic solutions. They are aesthetically independent, developing their own formal language and an unmistakable approach to the work. This is also true of the twelve-metre-high *Stele for the Sky* (fig. p. 176) with two light program phases, which was erected in front of the Osaka Art Museum during the Expo '70, then in front of the Neue Nationalgalerie in West Berlin during a group exhibition and later in Düsseldorf's Horten Park. The same can be said of the fourteen-metre-high light column erected in Hamburg's Planten un Blomen park in 1973 and to *Falling and Rising Meteor* from 1984, two ten-metre-high kinetic steles in front of and behind the façade of the Philips headquarters in

Eindhoven.[183] The kinetic light programme of 2003 on the upper third of Jean Nouvel's *Cologne Tower* (2001) is also part of this series of works, the concept of which is rooted in the *Sahara Project*, whereby these interventions in public space have an inherent dimension that is critical of urban development.

Here we see the first characteristic of the 'second Mack', which is to work with real space like hardly any other artist in those decades.[184] An important example of this is the ensemble on Jürgen-Ponto-Platz in Frankfurt am Main, completed in 1981, which also transforms a postmodern arbitrary space into a sculptural space and endows it with a poetic commemorative function.[185]

The second characteristic of the 'second Mack' is the theoretical exploration of his work, which replaced the extensive manifesto production of the ZERO period. Published in rapid succession between 1967 and 1975 were *Mackazin*, an experimental collage of Mack's ZERO works and their references to Futurist design; *Heinz Mack. Eine Monographie* by Margit Staber, the first comprehensive art historical analysis of Mack's work and one of the first publications of the newly founded Institute for Modern Art in Nuremberg; *Mack. Kunst in der Wüste* (Art in the Desert) with an introduction by the important sign theoretician Max Bense; *mack. Objekte – Aktionen – Projekte*, a catalogue raisonné produced by the Academy of Arts in West Berlin; *Mack. Handzeichnungen* (Drawings) by Friedrich B. Heckmanns; *Mack. Imaginationen. 1953–1973* by Kurt Weidemann; and the Mack monograph by Karin Thomas, one of the most prominent authors of the time, in the prestigious series *Monographien zur rheinisch-westfälischen Kunst der Gegenwart* (Monographs on Contemporary Art in North Rhine-Westphalia).[186] The culmination of these publications came a few years later, in 1986, with the catalogue raisonné *Mack. Skulpturen. 1953–1986* by Dieter Honisch, the long-standing director of the Neue Nationalgalerie in (West) Berlin, who had already been artistically responsible for Mack's contribution to the German Pavilion at the 1970 Venice Biennale. The artist found an important and enduring dialogue partner in him, as well as in the eminent museum experts Werner Hofmann and Wieland Schmied and the art historian Anette Kuhn.

To return to Heinz Mack's work in real space: comparatively isolated in the West German art scene of the 1970s, he created a new form of art that was very different from that of Joseph Beuys, but at about the same time dealt directly with society as the basis of artistic work. None of the other Düsseldorf ZERO artists did the same. Some things may have already been laid down in the context of ZERO, but the decision to draw out this new register of artistic endeavour had nothing to do with ZERO. It was no longer about thinking in new

»

In the late 1970s, I gave a lecture at the Academy of Fine Arts Stuttgart on the topic: 'What will the world look like in the year 2000?', then also at a large artists' congress in West Berlin in the so-called Europahalle.[187] The video artist Ulrike Rosenbach, wearing an Arafat cap, ran up to me through the crowded hall, snatched my manuscript and shouted into the microphone: 'What is your social relevance?' The point was: Mack, this luxury artist, doesn't give a damn about society. I answered briefly and then said: 'Why don't you ask my tax consultant?' Today, when I read what I dreamed up for the year 2000, some of it has remained utopian, and some of it has developed in ways that were not foreseeable at the time. The future was a big topic

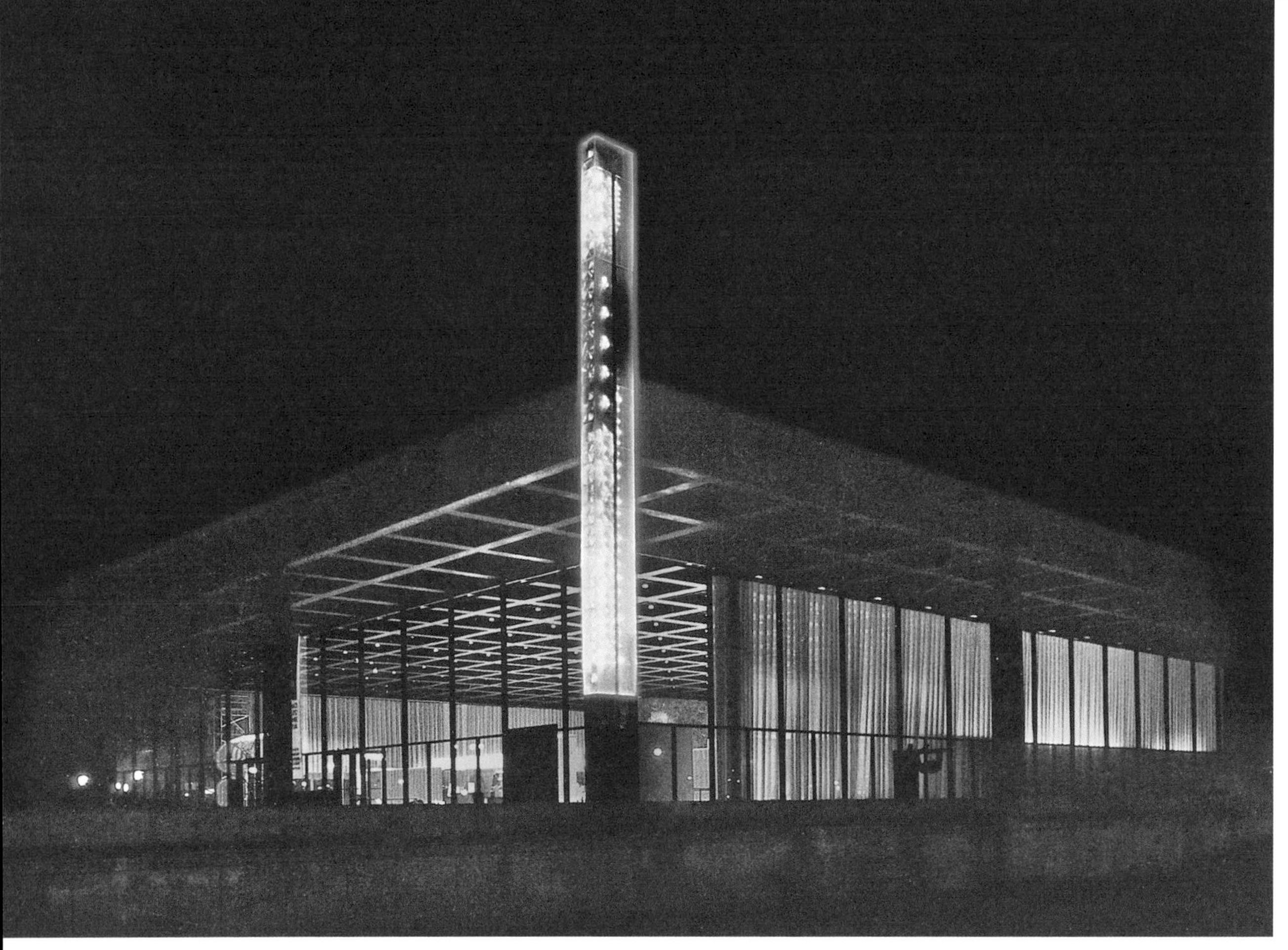

Stele for the Sky
1970
in front of the Neue Nationalgalerie,
Berlin (West)

The Sign of Peace
1974 – 1979

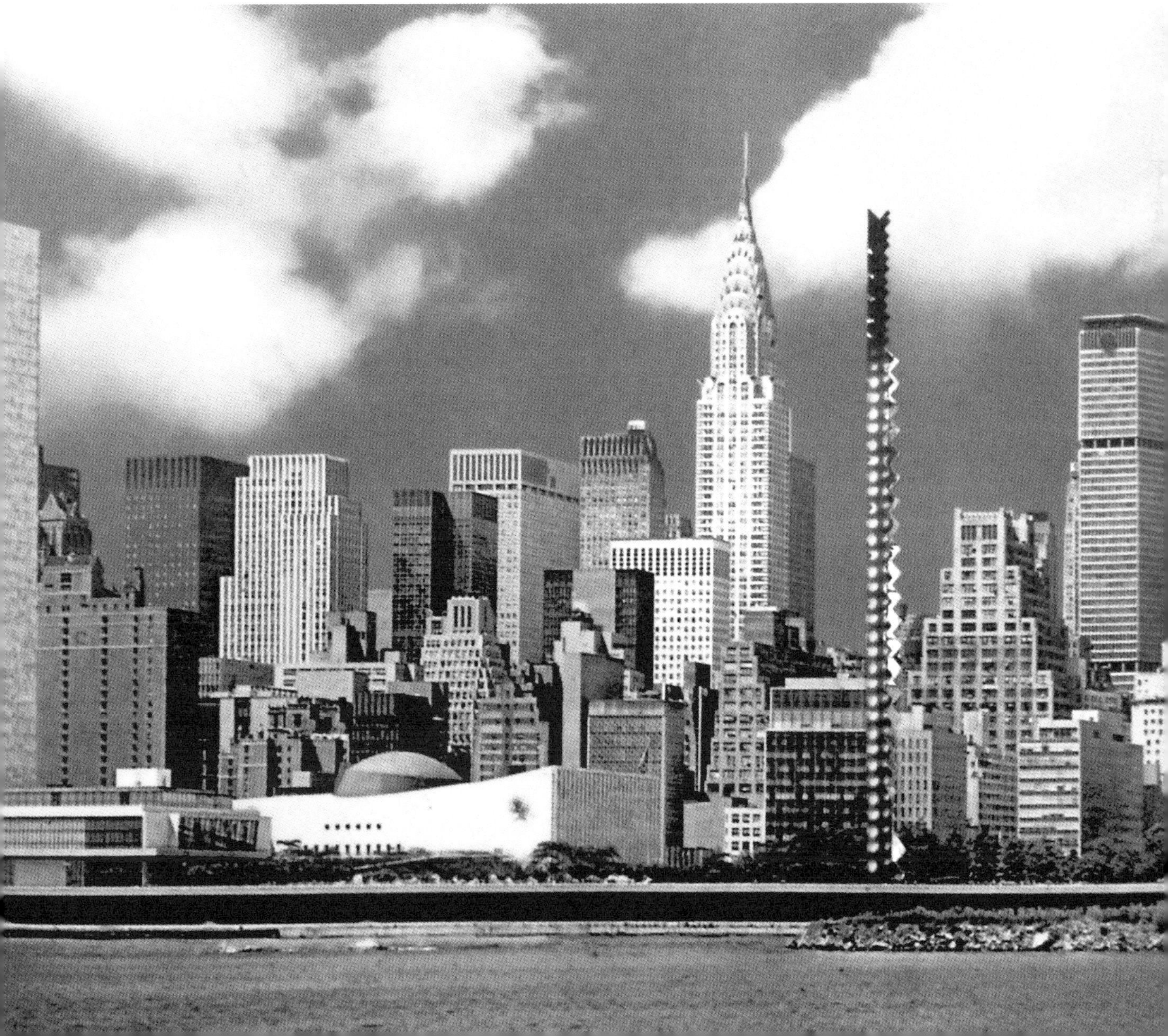

back then – but not on the 'official' side. Robert Jungk was the only German-language futurologist. Prof. Dr Horst Ehmke had previously been responsible for cultural issues and development in the Bonn government under Chancellor Willy Brandt. We were relatively good friends at the time, and he said: 'Futurology is a foreign word to us.' Imagine that!

(OCTOBER 2022) «

images. It was very radically about an art that concerned the whole of society, worldwide and without national borders and, unlike Beuys, without ideology.

There is a surprising reference to this in Jacques Lassaigne's preface to the catalogue of the 1973 exhibition at the Musée d'art moderne de la Ville de Paris. The author, then director of the museum, had been director of the 1965 Biennale de Paris, held in the same building: 'Eight years ago, Heinz Mack had already made a brilliant appearance at the 4th Biennale de Paris, where he represented new German art with kinetic works in aluminium and presented a joint work with his friends Piene and Uecker, *Le Moulin lumineux* (The Light Mill). This had already taken place in this building, where we are delighted to be able to organise the artist's first retrospective. [...] Mack is a man of today, that is to say, always looking forward, inventing new materials, discovering their logic and possibilities, seeing art as an action (one is not far from an apostolate attitude) that could well take hold of people in order to change them or make them aware of themselves.'[188]

This calls into question the common, still largely unspoken assumption of continuity in Heinz Mack's work, which emanates from ZERO. In artistic developments, continuity is often a retrospective (art-)historical construction. As was already evident in the 1969 WDR interview (pp. 150–155), Mack opted for discontinuity, for a change in the framework for which he conceived his art, and for a direct approach to real space.

The failure of the *Sign of Peace* project in the park in front of the UN headquarters in New York was a great disappointment to the artist (fig. p. 177). Proposed by the West German government in 1974 – the Federal Republic of Germany, like the German Democratic Republic, had become a full member of the United Nations a few months earlier as a result of the West German government's so-called Ostpolitik and the temporary political détente in the GDR – Heinz Mack's light stele was to be seventy-six metres high. It would have been an unparalleled light-kinetic sculpture in front of the glass façade of the UN building. Negotiations at the highest level, between Foreign Minister Hans-Dietrich Genscher and Chancellor Helmut Schmidt with UN Secretary-General Kurt Waldheim, dragged on until 1979. Several times it seemed that everything had been finalised. In the end, however, the decision was negative.

You have to be able to deal with that kind of disappointment when you work in a public space where the artwork is no longer protected by the art world. In this case, the public space was essentially a diplomatic and global political space. The artist was well aware of this, because in the 1980s he broadened his creative spectrum without abandoning the theme of real open space that he had addressed in his work in the 1970s.

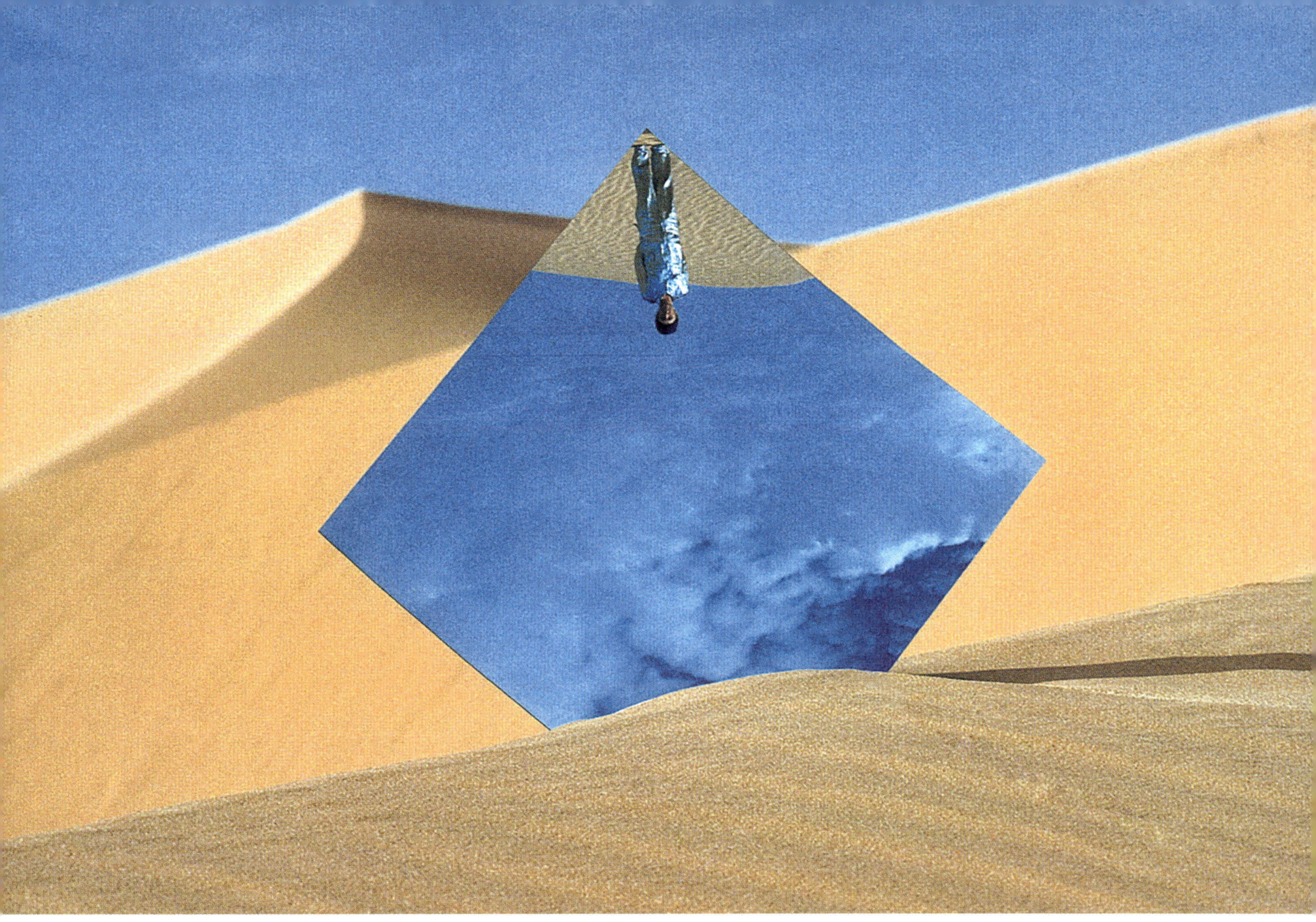

Upside Down
Grand Erg Occidental,
Algeria
1976

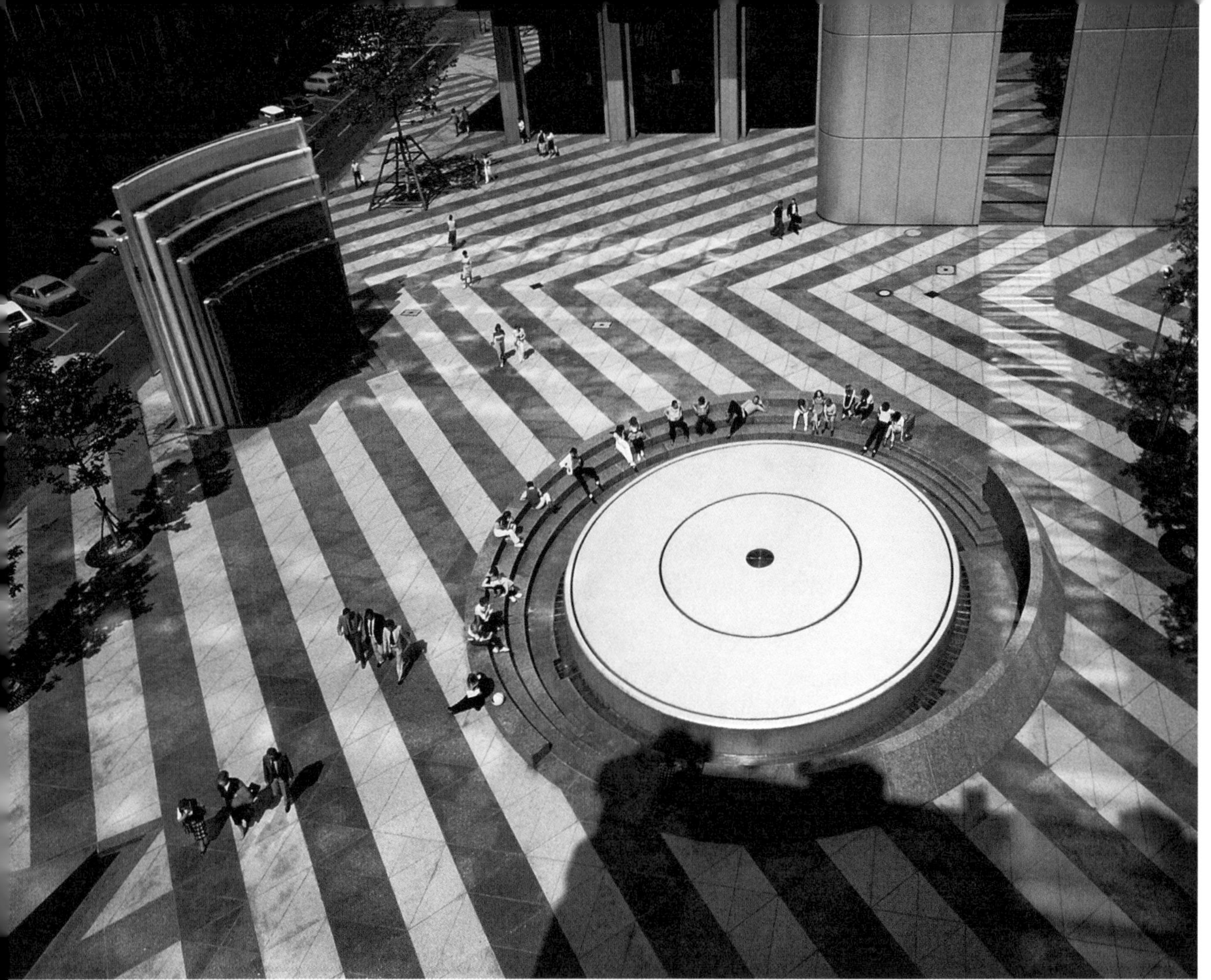

Overall design of
Jürgen-Ponto-Platz,
Frankfurt am Main
1976–1981

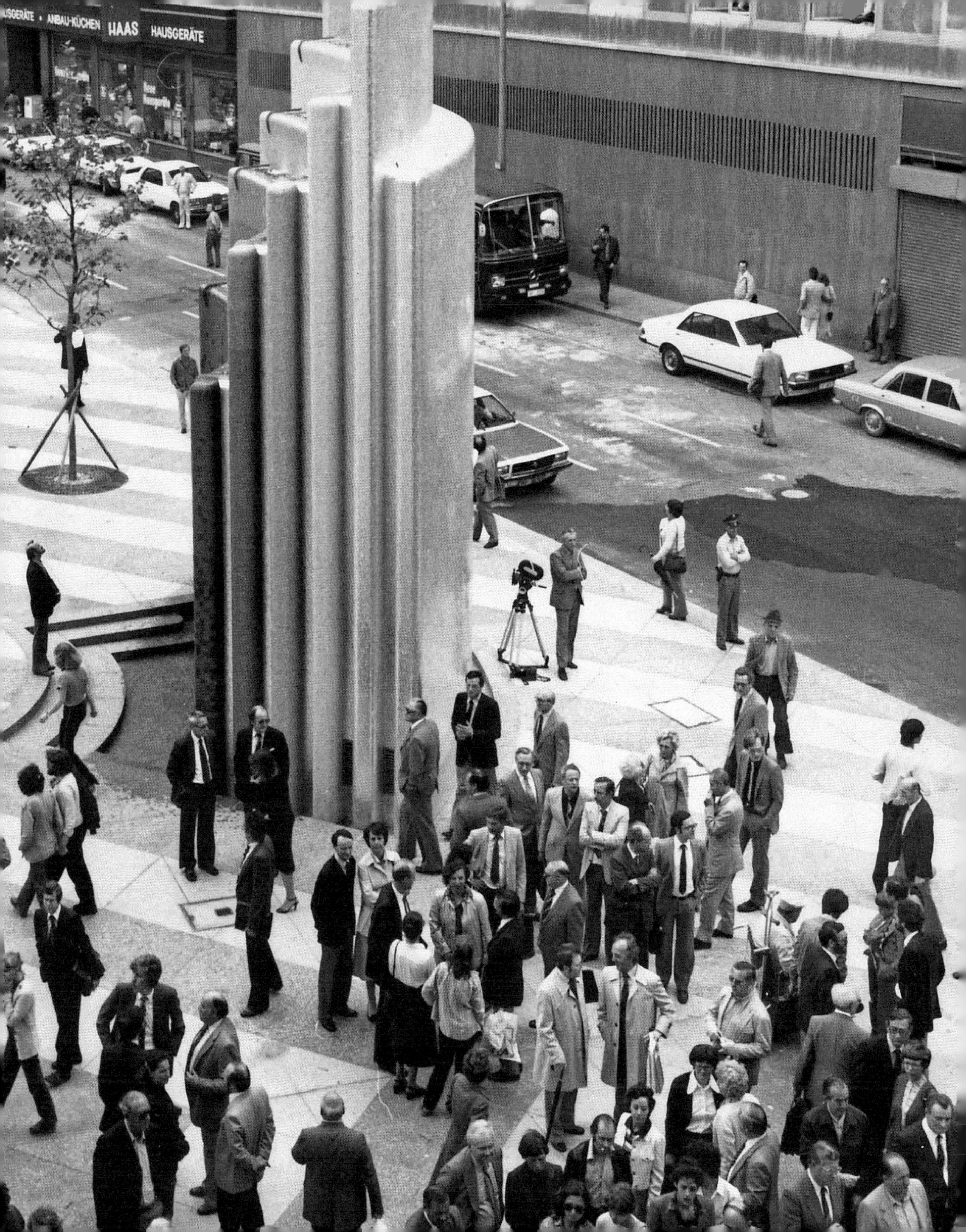
ANBAU-KÜCHEN
HAAS
HAUSGERÄTE

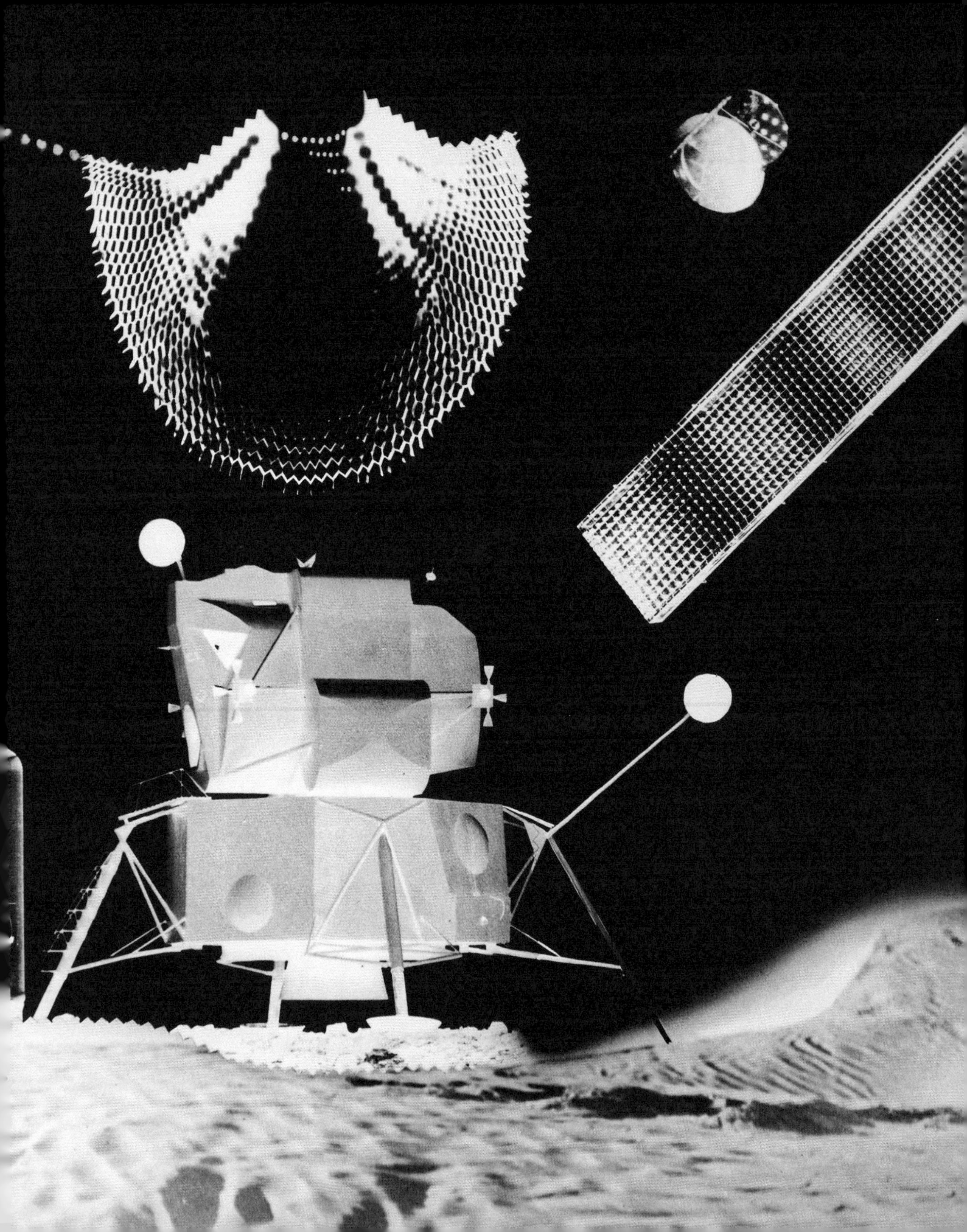

THE TWELVE TOPOI OF HEINZ MACK

Moon Project with Light Wing and Light Grid
1963–1973

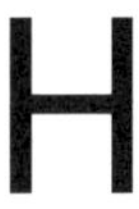einz Mack's artistic oeuvre is a prime example of 'cyclical creation'. This refers to an oeuvre that revolves around a number of ideas, concepts, and notions and that progresses in circular movements rather than in successive stages of development. How can this be reconciled with the breaks and productive discontinuities we have observed in Heinz Mack's oeuvre? The artist has reinvented himself several times: in Paris in 1950, in 1957–58 with the creation of ZERO, from 1959 onwards with the *Sahara Project* to 1976 with the *Expedition Into Artificial Gardens*, from around 1970 with the move towards projects in public space and, as we shall see, with the expansion of the spectrum with the *Chromatic Constellations* from 1991 onwards and the ceramic works from 1997 onwards. He has the rare ability to reinitialise himself on a regular basis, each time in a way that was previously unforeseeable in his work. Usually, however, he does this by building on earlier things or by playing through several recurring thoughts.

»

My work does not show a linear temporal development; rather, everything goes round in circles (in this respect I am closer to Far Eastern philosophy than to the linear thinking of the West).

(HANDWRITTEN NOTE, UNDATED, MACK ARCHIVE) «

If you delve into Heinz Mack's archive at the Huppertzhof, into the Leitz binders with their disorderly files of texts and notes from all periods, which he actually only uses for himself, occasionally leafing through them or looking for a specific note, for example for a sculptural work he is currently working on, you quickly get the impression that his entire oeuvre revolves around a few ideas, almost just a few sentences, which constantly recur in his thinking, in his artistic work and in his statements. You could call them 'the twelve topoi' of Heinz Mack, his twelve basic ideas, whereby the Greek term '*tópos*' goes further, as it also assigns a place to the thought. These twelve topoi form the artist's intellectual grammar.

At the end of a day's work in Mack's archive at the Huppertzhof, I say to him: 'I'm halfway through. There are so many things I've never seen before. So many things that you can't find anywhere or that were published a long time ago but have long since been forgotten. Could it be that your work revolves around certain topoi? First of all, it's a cyclical, circular oeuvre.' Heinz Mack: 'Yes, that's true.' – 'And it revolves around about twelve topoi, a term that unites theme and place. I could list these topoi almost off the top of my head.' After a short pause, Mack says: 'I hadn't thought of it like that. It's a good idea. Twelve topoi: that's not a small number. It's actually quite considerable. No less than twelve.'

»

My work is not a one-way street like that of many of my colleagues who always do the same thing. Think of Castellani with his cloths draped over structures. My work is like traffic chaos, a spaghetti web of streets, like in Los Angeles.

(SEPTEMBER 2023) «

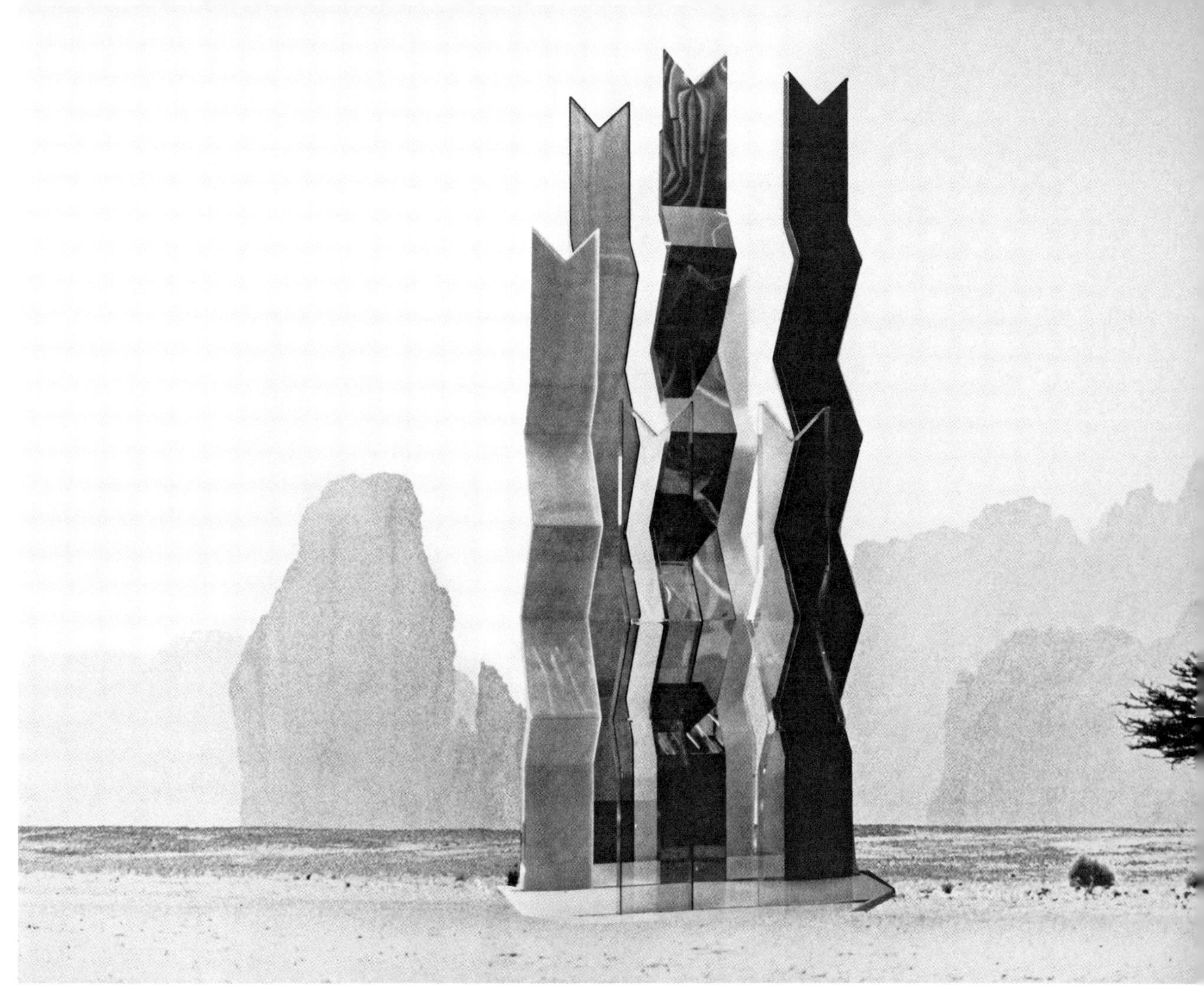

The Rhythm of Africa
1968–1970

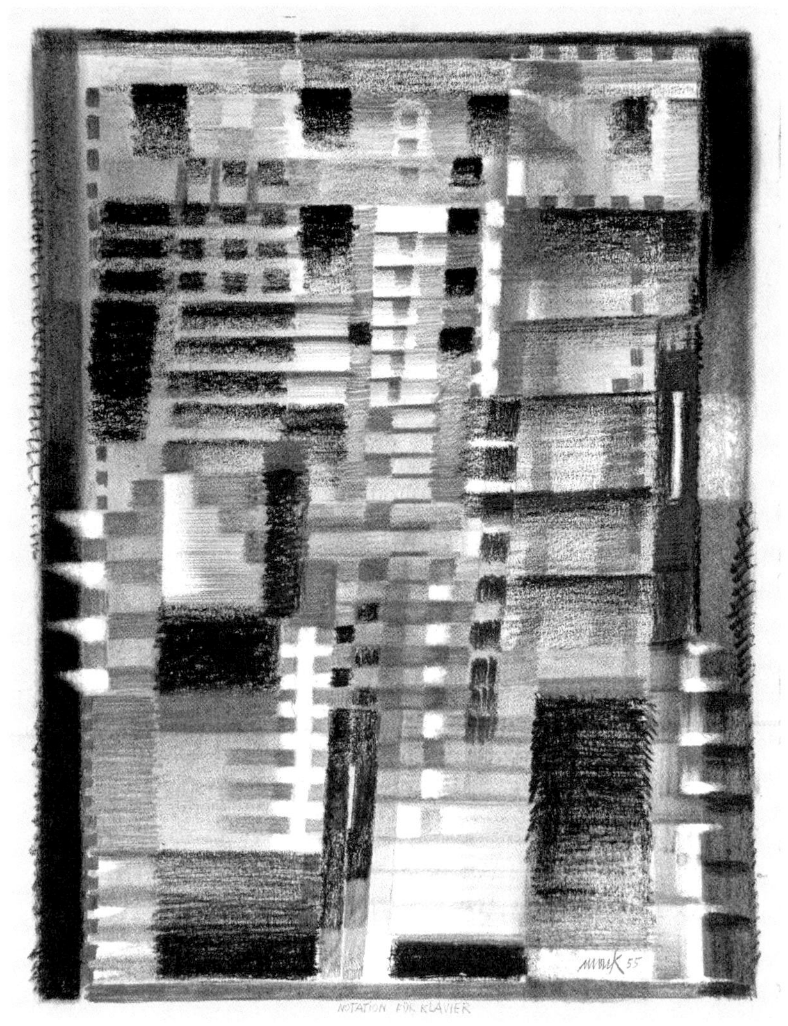

Notation for Piano
1955

View into the residential building at the Huppertzhof, Mönchengladbach
c. 1970
with light steles and Heinz Mack at the piano

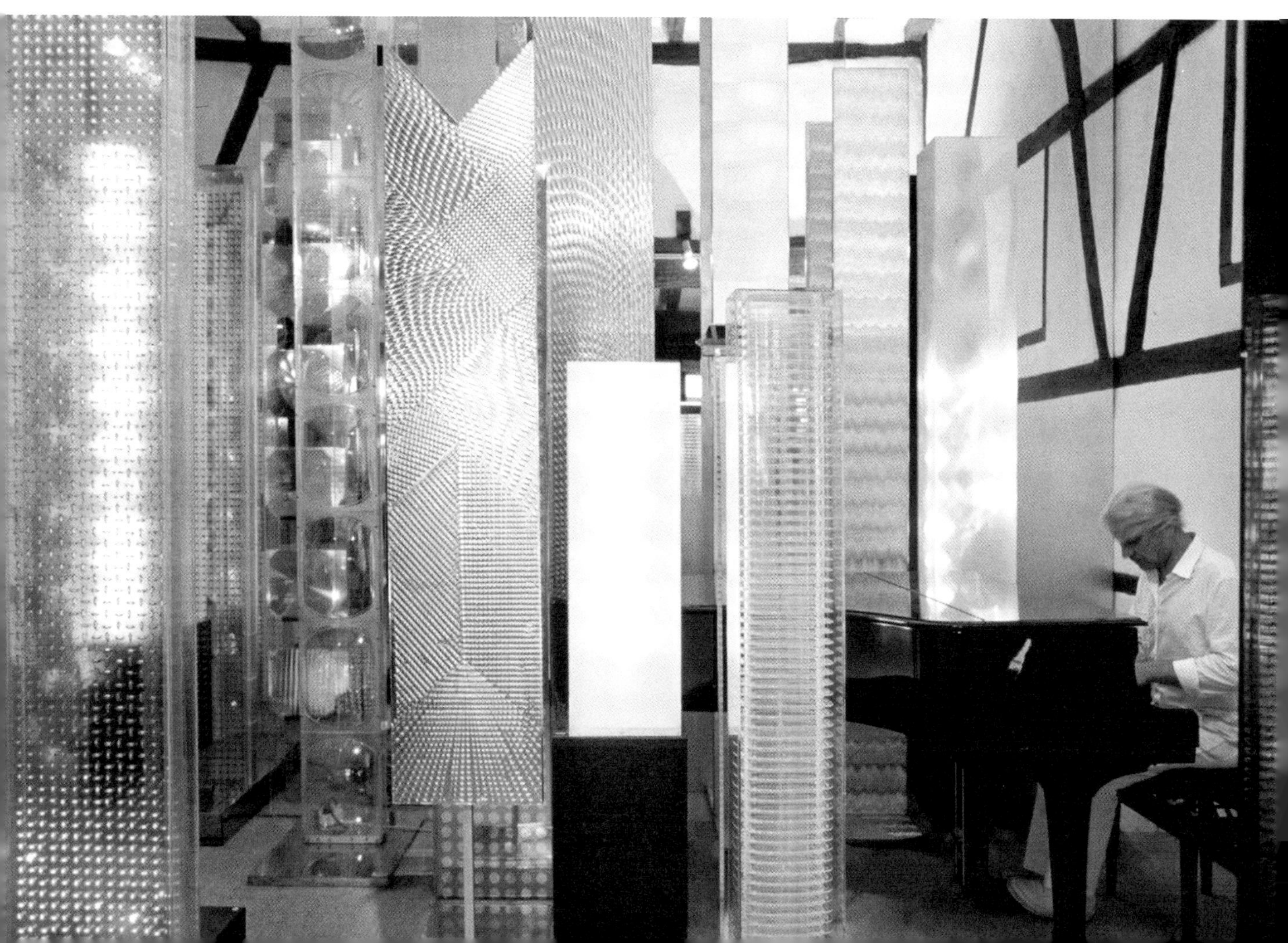

1 Bernard of Clairvaux and Space

'God is height, width and depth.' This statement by Bernard of Clairvaux has been a leitmotif for Heinz Mack from the very beginning. Although he stresses that he is not religious and has no religious feelings, he adds that he fully agrees with this statement by the French Cistercian from the Middle Ages. The concept of space that he formulated is completely abstract. It does not revolve around a collection of optical data such as the central perspective of the Renaissance – which is still in our cameras – nor does it explain space and time in metaphysical terms. In a certain sense, what Werner Hofmann, a friend and companion of the artist, describes in his standard work *Grundlagen der modernen Kunst* (Foundations of Modern Art, 1966) for the classical modernism of the twentieth century as a return to medieval art and aesthetic thought is taking place: reduction to the essential, abandonment of central perspective, and oscillation between the poles of 'great abstraction' and 'great realism' (Wassily Kandinsky).[189]

» Almost 1,000 years ago, St Bernard of Clairvaux answered the question of what God is by saying: 'Height, width and depth.'

(LETTER TO DIETER HONISCH, JUNE 1986, MACK ARCHIVE). «

Visual thinking in the sense of Clairvaux's statement, as found in Heinz Mack's work, goes beyond the conceptual world of classical modernism. It is concerned with an abstract concept of space that is not determined by forms and proportions nor by the objects that are in it. This abstract space is a priori in the sense of Immanuel Kant. At the same time, such an understanding of space is not limited to an abstract thought but is a lived fact for the artist. Dealing with it becomes an inexhaustible field of activity that is not about representation, but about capturing, reflecting, and organising forces. In this way, light reliefs and rotors, Fresnel lenses and steles as well as the *Chromatic Constellations* come into being as if by themselves.

» Light not only illuminates, delineates, accentuates and models three-dimensional objects; it not only makes the three dimensions of bodies visible, but is itself a dimension of perception. If time is called the fourth dimension, then I would like to call light the fifth dimension – or, to be more precise, light is the very first condition under which I can perceive height, width, depth and extension in time.

(TYPESCRIPT, UNDATED, MACK ARCHIVE) «

'God is height, width and depth.' This statement speaks of a nominalistic view of the world. This also characterises the work of Heinz Mack. Nominalism is an important trend in philosophy, especially since the Middle Ages. It guards against any mysticism of light. Nominalism can be described as a radical scepticism of language, or with Gertrude Stein's famous verse 'Rose is a rose is a rose is a rose' from the 1913 poem 'Sacred Emily'. Accordingly, Mack has a pronounced aversion to Expressionist art, which seems to him a hollow

» Light is a medium in which the object becomes resistance. My works are therefore objects of light, instruments of light. These sculptures derive their sensuality from light, which 'blinds' our analytical, critical thinking. The ability of light to give objects a varied, lively appearance, as

gesture, as well as to any form of romanticism, although he himself, with his accessible nature, may sometimes appear to be a romantic character. A nominalist view does not exclude a poetic approach to the world and to the making of art. This is expressed in the theme of angels, which one would not expect from Mack, as well as in the artist's statements that, like Henri Matisse, he believes in God during his artistic work, but no longer after its completion.

nature shows, not only finds its equivalent in art; it is also a prerequisite for the objects filled with light to become the expression of a spiritual energy.

« ('DAS LICHT AUF DER OBERFLÄCHE', 1994)[190]

»

I believe in angels; I believe in spiritual energies that conceptual thinking cannot reach. That's why I see Leonardo as an outstanding artist, because he was an engineer who painted angels.

« (TYPESCRIPT, BEFORE 1986)[191]

»

When Matisse was painting the chapel in Vence, Picasso was a member of the Communist Party and asked the old Matisse: 'How did you come to create a chapel for the Roman Catholic Church?' In this context, Matisse was asked if he believed in God. He said: 'When I'm working: yes, but when I put down my brush, no longer.' I feel the same way.

« (SEPTEMBER 2022)

2

»

The corpses burned by the lava in Pompeii – do they call Giacometti's sculptures into question?

« (HANDWRITTEN NOTE, UNDATED, MACK ARCHIVE)

3 Materials

Materials and the concept of materials are a recurring theme in Heinz Mack's work. 'I'm trying out a new material here. It's granite from Austria. It reacts very differently. Great grain. It is a structure in itself.'[192] On the one hand, this means – and this has been expressed programmatically since around 1970[193] – playing with and having played through almost all the materials of the visual arts: sandstone, marble, granite, iron, steel, glass, mirror glass, ceramics, aluminium, Plexiglas/acrylic glass, oil paint, acrylic paint, pastels, paper, photography, film and printmaking in all their techniques. Mack's oeuvre can also be read as an encyclopaedia of the artistic materials of the second half of the twentieth century. This is the artist's intention, and it is quite extraordinary. Then there are the stained-glass windows and other forms of work in public and religious spaces, such as in the three artist chapels in Neuss, Mettmann, and Kaiserslautern,[194] by this thoroughly non-religious artist, as well as the temporary works in the desert and the Arctic, with sand, light, water, and ice. For Mack, the utopian goal of a universal practice of materials is essential to a responsible approach to art in the present.

» If my work in the studio comes 'easily', it is because I have a rationally incomprehensible 'knowledge' of the material. I make my work, at least the decisive part of it, with my own hands. It is part of my experience that, in a sense, I simply do what the material wants, even if I have to overcome its resistance. So at best, I am only the tool of an idea if the form or structure that grows towards me corresponds to my feelings.

(MAY 2022) «

Today, material aesthetics is a specialised branch of art history, alongside the history of style, iconology, and the history of images. Among other things, it examines the material history of art. Heinz Mack was never particularly interested in this, although material aesthetics would find a wealth of research approaches in his work. More important for his approach to materials is the reference to the philosophical materialism of the eighteenth century. Mack often refers to Gottfried Wilhelm Leibniz, who invented the first mechanical calculator and created the concept of the monad. One can also think of Denis Diderot, who, in the materialist branch of the Enlightenment, surmised a new relationship to nature and described the immanence of art beyond any transcendence in its treatment of matter. In Mack's work, the material theme is a sign of the immanence of this work and its radically anti-metaphysical character.

» I have never been a conceptual artist. The sensual qualities of works of art are essential to me. I also have an erotic, sensual relationship with art.

(CONVERSATION WITH FÉLICIE D'ESTIENNE D'ORVES AND OLIVIER SCHEFER, HUPPERTZHOF, MÖNCHENGLADBACH, JULY 2024) «

»

The oldest work of art in the world, we now know thanks to radiocarbon dating, is a piece of pottery from 30,000 BC. Imagine that! 30,000 BC! Not long after that, in 25,000 BC, the first bronze casts appeared. Both ceramics and bronze are ancient techniques, and both last forever. Ceramics found in Anatolia date from between 1,500 and 2,000 BC and look as if they were made yesterday. That's quite a phenomenon. In Germany, ceramics have been labelled as arts and crafts, in other words, as negligible. If someone works with ceramics, it's decoration at best. This is in stark contrast to the Mediterranean region, where ceramics are the most natural thing in the world. It starts with the Moorish Spaniards, very early on during the Oriental occupation of Spain, and then continues throughout the Levant, via Morocco, Tunisia, Algeria, Libya and so on, all the way to the furthest Asian countries, all the way to China. Ceramics play an important role everywhere. It is the main art form throughout the Persian region. Then there is the fact that Picasso devoted about five years of his working life to ceramics, creating over 1,500 pieces. Miró devoted three years almost exclusively to ceramics because he was suddenly self-critical about his own painting as a result of his involvement with the Surrealists, to whom he did not really feel he belonged. Fontana made a lot of ceramic works. I now have a few hundred pieces.

« (MAY 2022)

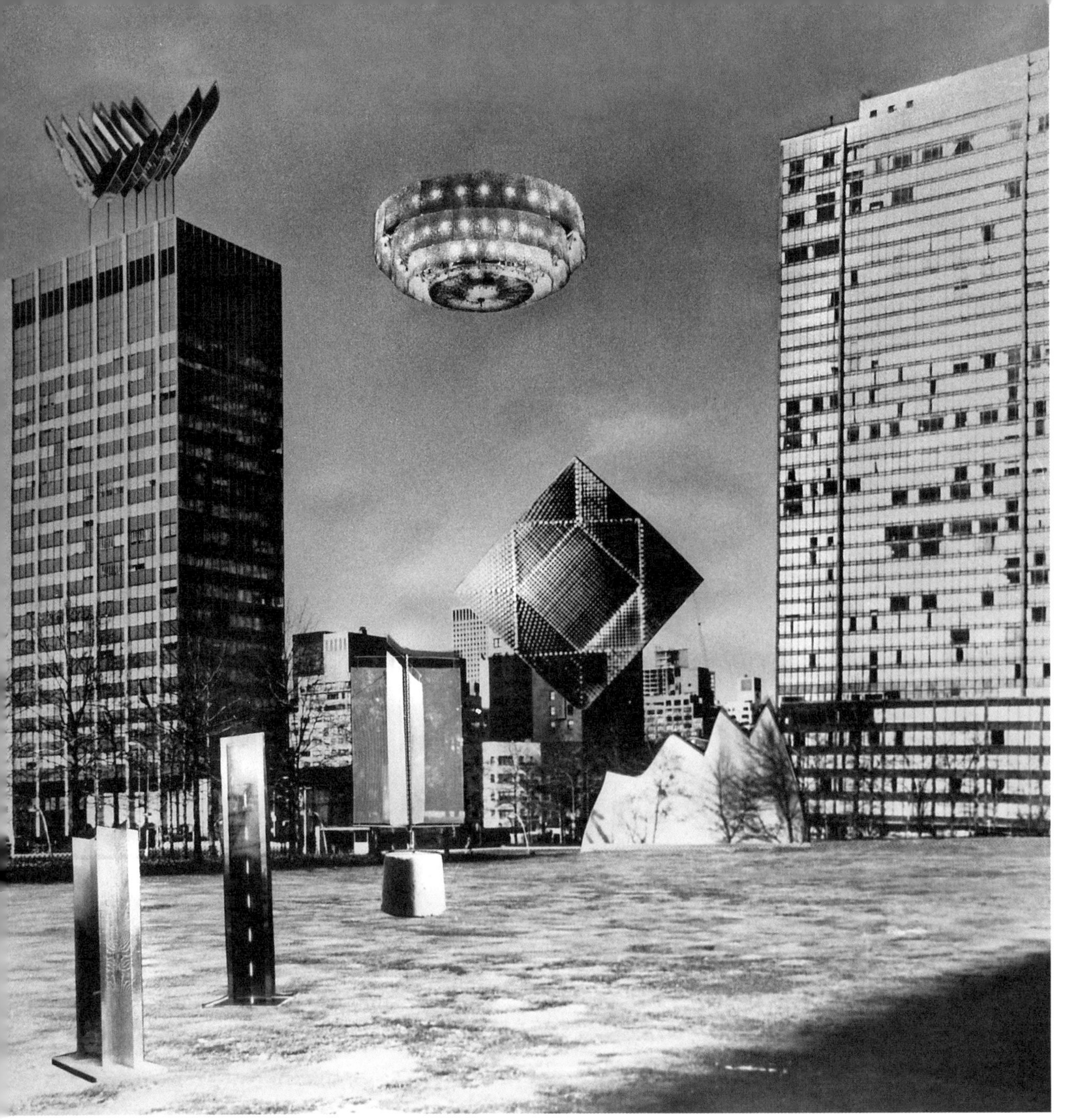

The Unexpected Encounter
(Project for the City of New York)
1963–1973

→
Handwritten note by Heinz Mack
undated

Die Realität ist stärker als die Utopie. – aber ohne sie hat Realität keine Freiheit, keine Zukunft, keinen Raum, keine Perspektive.

Realität ist Utopie
Utopie ist Realität

Träume von einer besseren Welt sind eine condition humaine

Ideen und Projekte, welche die Chance, realisiert zu werden, nur bedingt enthalten, sind für mich eine unverzichtbare Option auf die Zukunft.

Utopien sind eine Art Zukunftsplanung.

4 The Secret Relationship with Music

Mack thinks of visual art in musical terms. We have already seen the biographical connections: piano lessons from the age of seven, early training as a pianist, playing the piano at a high level on a daily basis to this day, a strong interest in new music as well as in the laws and formal worlds of older classical music, acquaintance and sometimes collaboration with high-ranking composers and music theorists such as Karlheinz Stockhausen, Nam June Paik, and György Ligeti. The artist shares this constellation with the philosopher Vladimir Jankélévitch. When asked about his relationship to music, the latter explained: 'I practise it like a professional musician. But it has never been my profession. That's probably why I have such a relaxed relationship with it. I often think about it subconsciously.'[195]

» When I enrolled at the Düsseldorf Academy of Art in 1950, my application documents were so non-objective and abstract that they were more reminiscent of my piano sheet music.

('NOTIZEN ÜBER MODERNE MUSIK', DECEMBER 2022, MACK ARCHIVE) «

More important than the question of the artist's musical interests is the question of the musicality of his work. Most of Heinz Mack's works are musical in their repertoire of forms and intrinsic structure. They often consist of rhythms, intervals, chromaticism, tones (as pure colour tones or as light/dark, high/low, reflection/non-reflection), sequences and series as well as all conceivable interferences and superimpositions of these forms, which then produce melodic effects. A fundamental musicality runs through his entire oeuvre, from the young artist's early notational drawings to the *Forest of Light* in New York in 1966 (fig. p. 127), which also produces a melody, to the painterly oeuvre of the *Chromatic Constellations* since 1991 (fig. pp. 265–285), in which the melody plays a subliminal but indispensable role in each painting.[197] For the two films about his work (*Tele-Mack*, 1968/69, and *Lichtkunst*, 1990), the artist chose the compositions for the musical accompaniment. Mack's is one of the few works of visual art that could be analysed using exclusively musicological concepts and methods. A corresponding research project has yet to be undertaken.

» I was particularly interested in musicians and composers of my own generation, such as Stockhausen and Ligeti – I felt a personal connection with the latter and dedicated a large painting to him. There were also the Americans Terry Riley, Steve Reich, and Philip Glass, as well as John Cage, who had anticipated many things a generation earlier. He was the first to add noise or its total absence, silence, to sounds. He disrupted the symmetry of rhythms and was the first to use the principle of the aleatoric in a surprising way. These composers adopted the 'anticipation of dissonance' that had begun with Schoenberg's atonality.[196] In addition, Schoenberg emancipated timbre after Debussy, in short: the concept of timbre now replaced tones.

('NOTIZEN ÜBER MODERNE MUSIK', DECEMBER 2022, MACK ARCHIVE) «

This peculiarity in the artist's work is not in itself good or bad, but it is one of its characteristics. Towards the end of his studies, Heinz Mack had decided to reject everything figurative and representational in his own pictorial work and to proceed exclusively non-representationally. A short time later, he created the ZERO paintings (fig. pp. 63, 70), which answered the question of non-representationalism in a virtuosic and unmistakably independent way. In many artistic processes of the time, one can see how difficult it was for artists to move from representationalism to non-representationalism. Mack circumvented the problem from his musical, per se non-representational experience. The overwhelming freshness of his ZERO paintings is also striking – even today. It comes as well from music, from painterly musical progressions. It was here that the twenty-five-year-old found the methodology that immediately gave his non-representational art a solid foundation: rhythms, intervals, tones, sequences, serial structures, and all sorts of interferences and superimpositions. The fact that this set of methods was practically at hand when Mack began to practise an exclusively non-representational visual art based on musical thinking explains the singularity and lightness of his oeuvre at the time and later.

In turn, the musical paths of this conception have much to do with the latest developments in music at the time, with the succession of the Schoenberg school and serial music, with pre- and post-structuralist music. The pianist Heinz Mack's favourite pieces are Maurice Ravel's *Boléro* and preludes and fugues from Johann Sebastian Bach's *Well-Tempered Clavier*. He plays them with virtuosity, not melodically, but unconsciously and above all structurally. Mack's artistic work is laid out or almost contained in his own daily piano interpretations of such music.[198]

»

'Quietness of disquiet' – 'disquiet of quietness', as musical movement, as heart rhythm.

« (HANDWRITTEN NOTE, UNDATED, MACK ARCHIVE)

»

Later, [Steve] Reich's original minimalism became more complex and eventful, replacing tonal monotony with chromatic timbres. I see this as an artistic neighbour to my painting of *Chromatic Constellations*.

« ('NOTIZEN ÜBER MODERNE MUSIK', DECEMBER 2022, MACK ARCHIVE)

5 The Daily Practice of Philosophy

Philosophy is the strength of this artist in his visual thinking. Philosophy is never left out of a conversation, for which one should be well prepared. Then it is a pleasure, because the result is a professional discussion on a high level, which is not about Mack's own visual work, as is usually the case with artists. Philosophy has an intrinsic value here.

» As a student of philosophy, I was also able to recognise what Plato had to say about astronomy. For him, history did not develop in a linear way, but [in] the circular course of the celestial bodies, and these also move eternally and infinitely in a circular form. I later realised that my artistic work has not developed in a linear way either but also corresponds to a circular process in which I often return to things that lie far in the past. «

(CONVERSATION WITH FÉLICIE D'ESTIENNE D'ORVES AND OLIVIER SCHEFER, HUPPERTZHOF, MÖNCHENGLADBACH, JULY 2024)

When Heinz Mack talks about light, the main theme of his art, or when he thinks about light in his studio and works with it as a material, the essential traditions of thinking about light from Plotinus to the present day are evident.[199] The debate between Johann Wolfgang von Goethe and Isaac Newton on the theory of light and colour plays a role in every painting and every sculpture. Direct engagement with the elements, a credo since the ZERO work, is based on conceptual precision and a philosophical tradition that comes from ancient Egypt and Greece, where one cannot afford to be an imprecise dialogue partner.[200] At the same time, Heinz Mack is relaxed: 'I just wanted to test you, and I don't want to be alone in this.'

» It is part of the metaphysics of vision and light that the eye is like the sun, otherwise it could not see the sun. This insight was not made by Goethe in Weimar, but by Plotinus in Greece some 2,000 years ago. It is therefore no coincidence that I seek the proximity of the Mediterranean because I am happy in its light. «

(1994)[201]

6 Utopia

In 1998, Wieland Schmied wrote: 'Heinz Mack – for me, the name is synonymous with utopia. […] Nothing seems impossible to Heinz Mack, at least in the field of art. Heinz Mack's work is animated by an enormous enthusiasm. He radiates boundless optimism. "I need big ideas, and I believe that if I were given the task of planning a new universe, I would be crazy enough to do it." This confession is 250 years old and comes from Piranesi – if I did not know its author, I would not hesitate to attribute it to Heinz Mack. Just as I would trust him to try again with the Tower of Babel. It would probably be a tower of light that he would tackle, more infinite than Brancusi's *Endless Column*, a vibrating light stele that connects Heaven and Earth. […] Everything Heinz Mack does is conceived as a utopia, is designed to achieve the impossible. Everything in his work is conceived on a grand scale and demands realisation on a gigantic scale – the more monumental the better, says Mack. "I have always explained", he states in a ZERO text from 1988, "albeit often in vain, that a large number of my works have the character and significance of models and projects and that only a monumental realisation in public space would make their true meaning visible. My sculptures should be exposed to this public, in cities as well as in open, wide landscapes, monumentality not as an expression of pathos and hubris, but as a striking and vital shaping of our environment." In this sense, a colourful picture in Heinz Mack's work is at the same time a design for a garden stretching for kilometres, a mirror object is a model for a city of light in the desert. As I said, the name Mack is synonymous with utopia.'[203]

»

This brings me back to the subject of utopia. Wieland Schmied wrote about my work in his book *Utopie und Wirklichkeit* (Utopia and Reality): 'With Heinz Mack, utopia has failed, but at a very high level.'[202]

« (OCTOBER 2023)

»

Reality is stronger than utopia – but without it, reality has no freedom, no future, no space, no perspective. / Reality is utopia / Utopia is reality / Dreams of a better world are a condition humain / For me, ideas and projects that have only a limited chance of being realised are an indispensable option for the future. Utopias are a way of planning for the future.

« (HANDWRITTEN NOTE, UNDATED, MACK ARCHIVE)

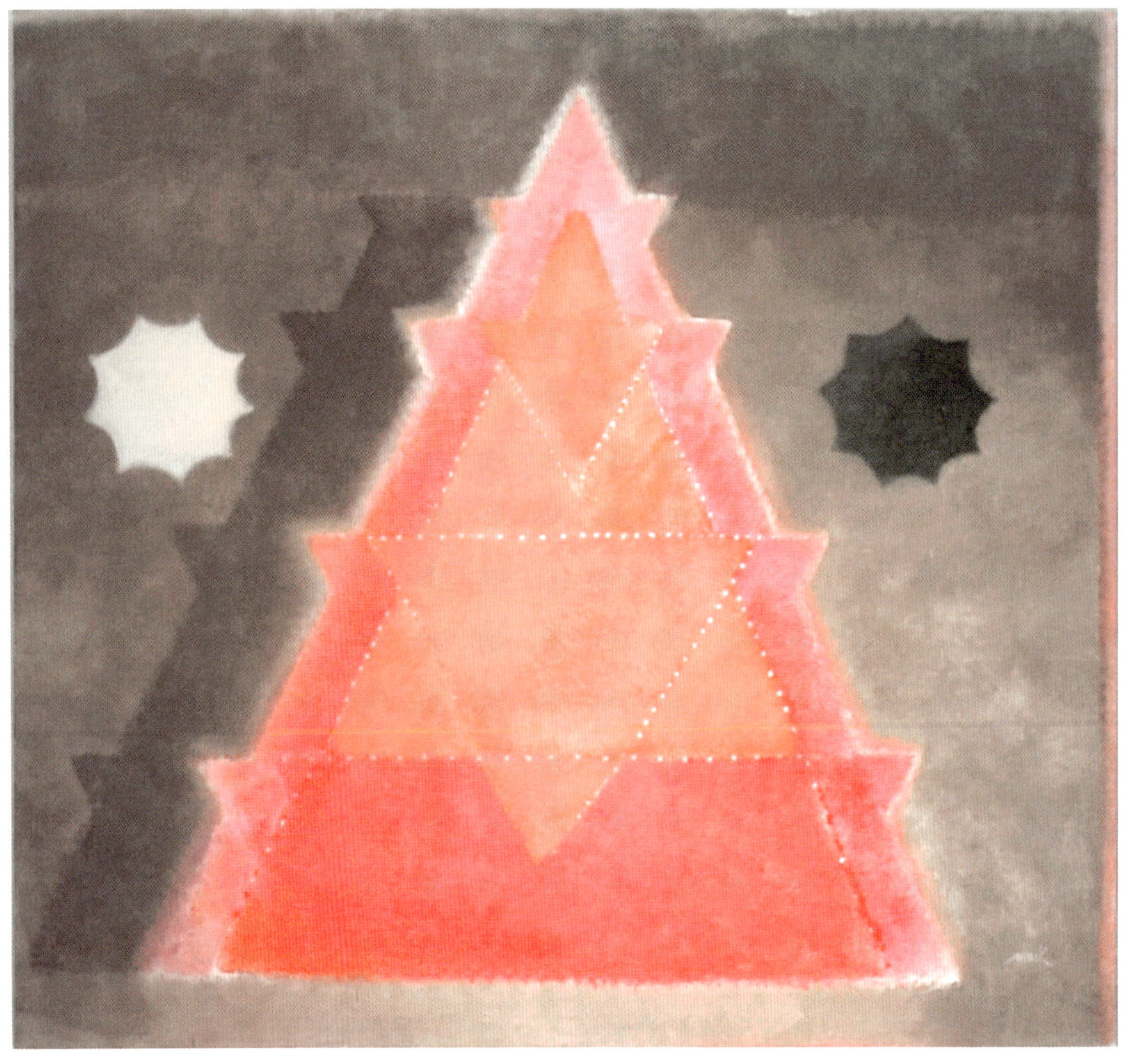

The Pink Pyramid
(Chromatic Constellation)
2006

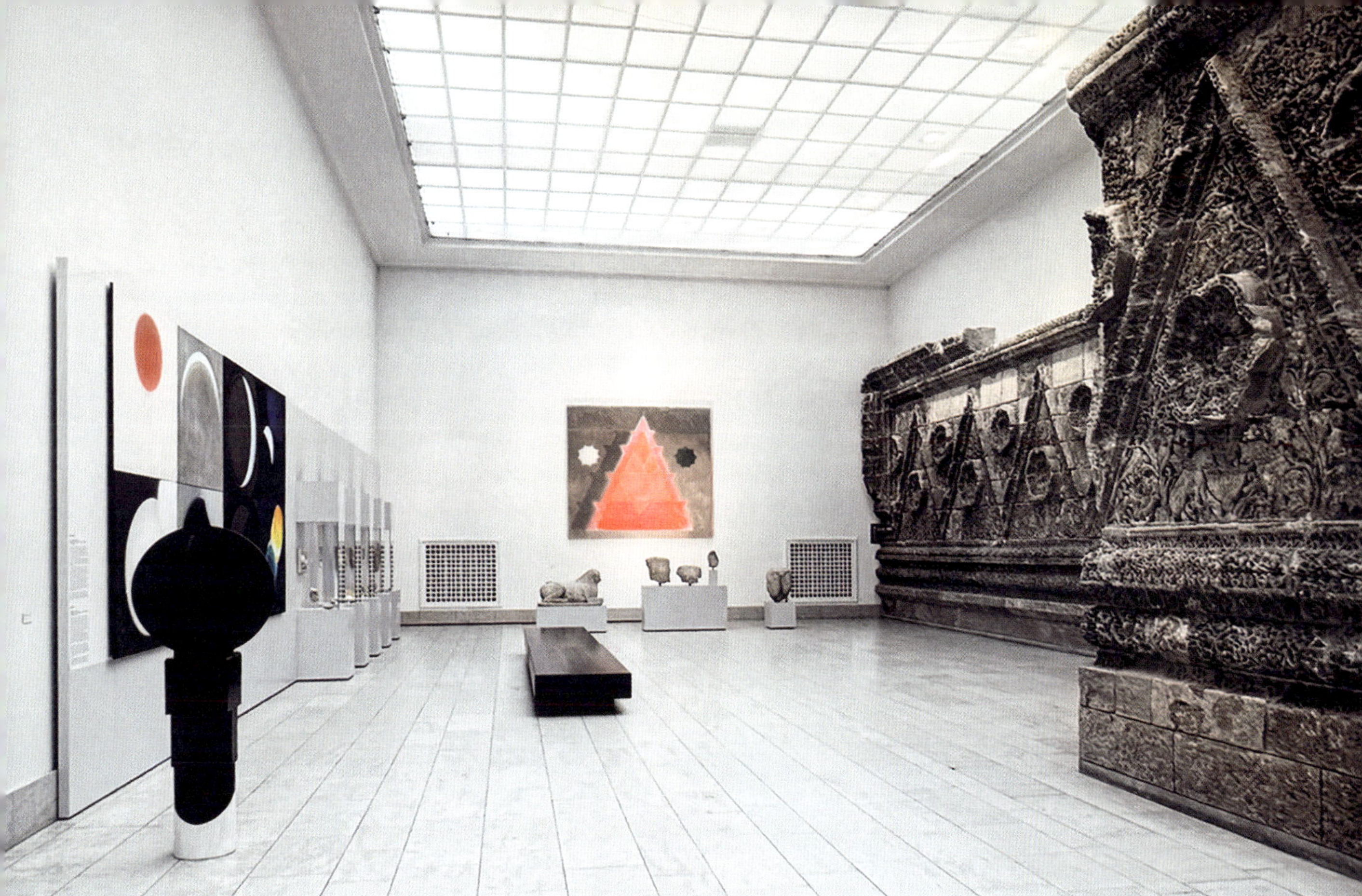

Installation view
Mack – Transit zwischen Okzident und Orient
Museum für Islamische Kunst in the Pergamonmuseum, Berlin
2006

7 'Russian Constructivism'

The reference to 'Russian Constructivism' is a recurring theme in Heinz Mack's work. This refers to an extraordinary generation of painters, sculptors, filmmakers, musicians, dancers, poets, and linguists – including many women – quite a few of whom came from Ukraine, who were active in Tsarist Russia, Munich, Rome, Paris, and Berlin from around 1910 and who, in intensive dialogue with each other and with Western artists, developed particularly concise formal languages and visions of modern art at the beginning of the twentieth century. Important protagonists include Anna Akhmatova, Alexander Archipenko, Alexander Blok, Mikhail Bulgakov, Marc Chagall, Velimir Khlebnikov, Sonia Delaunay, Ilya Ehrenburg, Sergei Eisenstein, Pavel Filonov, Naum Gabo, Natalya Goncharova, Roman Jakobson, Wassily Kandinsky, Gustav Kluzis, Mikhail Larionov, Jacques Lipchitz, El Lissitzky, Vladimir Mayakovsky, Kazimir Malevich, Osip Mandelstam, Konstantin Melnikov, Vladimir Nabokov, Boris Pasternak, Anton Pevsner, Lyubov Popova, Alexander Rodchenko, Olga Rozanova, Dmitri Shostakovich, Varvara Stepanova, Igor Stravinsky, Vladimir Tatlin, Elsa Triolet, Marie Vassilieff, Alexander Volkov, Osip Tsadkine, and Marina Tsvetaeva. Many of this probably strongest artistic generation from the same region of origin in the twentieth century, who were unable to escape permanently to the West, paid for their artistic work with their lives during the first two decades of Leninist and Stalinist rule in the Soviet Union.

» Before I came into contact with Russian painting, I was more familiar with Russian music. I was most interested in learning about Stravinsky, but as an eighth-grader I also had the opportunity to listen to the string orchestras of [Dmitri] Shostakovich, who was under the control of the Russian security service and only managed to escape his guards during a visit to New York and immediately fled to a record shop to listen to Stravinsky's music. I also became interested in the Groupe des Six very early on, because their music was still unknown in Germany after the war. Leonard Bernstein's family came from [today's Ukraine], the [family of] the sisters Nadia and Lili Boulanger [was] Russian-French [...].[207] Tragically, Lili Boulanger was only twenty-four years old and had just been awarded the famous Rome Prize – the first time a woman had been honoured with this prize (but her father had already won it). «

(LETTER TO THE AUTHOR, AUGUST 2024, PRIVATE ARCHIVE)

Suppressed in the Soviet Union, the movement was represented outside the country by only a few original works of art.[204] This art became widely known in 1979 through the major exhibition *Paris – Moscou* at the Centre Georges Pompidou in Paris, which had opened two years earlier (the show was curated by the museum's founding director Pontus Hultén).[205] The Constructivist paintings of Lyubov Popova and Olga Rozanova in particular still have an existential effect on Heinz Mack today. In the 1910s, they created paintings with abstract surfaces and signs that – in the tradition of icons and in parallel with Malevich's *Black Square on a White Ground* of 1915[206] – were energetically charged and made the abstract painting of Western Europe of the same period seem like harmless little games. When this art became widely known after 1979 – much of the abstract painting of the post-war period had already been forgotten – it had a powerful influence on the art of the following decades.

Heinz Mack's relationship to 'Russian Constructivism' goes beyond mere artistic inspiration. It is an art that was largely created away from the art market and a wider public, and that had been threatened and endangered ever since the October Revolution of 1917 and therefore arose out of pure artistic necessity. These paintings breathe the unconditionality of their creation, regardless of whether anyone would see them or not, whether anyone would consider them good or not. For Heinz Mack, the highly emotional relationship to this art is a kind of corrective to the zeitgeist, in whatever form it may take.

The artist's relationship with 'Russian Constructivism' goes back to the beginnings of his own work. In the mid-1950s, word spread that important paintings by Kazimir Malevich had miraculously survived Stalinism, National Socialism, and the Second World War and were located in West Berlin. Heinz Mack and other artists tried to persuade Paul Wember, who had opened Haus Lange in Krefeld in 1954 as the first exhibition space for contemporary art in a West German museum, to purchase the works. Willem Sandberg beat him to it and acquired the works for the Stedelijk Museum in Amsterdam, where they remain a centrepiece of the collection to this day. Mack then travelled with several artists from Düsseldorf to Amsterdam to view the paintings. It was during these years that the idea of ZERO began to take shape.[209]

»

I often ask myself: [...] Did Matisse know the works of Wassily Kandinsky or Malevich and vice versa? What did Picasso even know about Mondrian or Malevich? Was Yves Klein aware that Rodchenko had already painted three monochrome pictures in 1921, and that Władysław Strzemiński had also created a few small monochrome works in the early 1930s, of which Malevich was obviously completely unaware, although they had met in Warsaw? Furthermore, I also wonder, was Rothko aware of Olga Rozanova's painting, which quasi unconsciously anticipated his own painting?

« (2003)[208]

8 Goethe as a Guide

In the spring of 2018, the Goethe Museum in Düsseldorf organised the multifaceted exhibition *Taten des Lichts. Mack & Goethe* (Deeds of Light: Mack & Goethe).[210] It juxtaposed instruments, drawings, and texts by Johann Wolfgang von Goethe with sculptures, kinetic works, paintings, and drawings by Heinz Mack, demonstrating how closely Mack's work is interwoven with Goethe's colour theory, morphology, and world view. For example, the painterly concept of the *Chromatic Constellations*, already anticipated in a pastel on paper from his time in New York, derives directly from Goethe's experiments with light and colour, without the artistic independence of Mack's work suffering as a result. On the contrary: the direct reference to Goethe's colour spectrum positively isolates it in contemporary painting and gives it a basis that has nothing to do with the general development of painting in recent decades.

Mack's decisive encounter with Goethe took place at the Krefeld secondary school in the years after 1945, when the war-wounded German and philosophy teacher Dr Hülsmann repeatedly proclaimed that the only way out of the intellectual and human crisis was to adhere to Goethe. The pupil's drawings already show his preoccupation with Goethe's morphology. This has not changed to this day. 'Colours are the deeds of light, deeds and sorrows.'[211] Goethe's sentence from the foreword to the *Theory of Colours*, always flows into Mack's sculptures. Johann Wolfgang von Goethe remains the *vade mecum* of this artistic existence.

»

You know how interested I am in the phenomenon of appearance, which continues to pose fascinating puzzles for me. And I do this in the spirit of Goethe: 'Look for nothing – nothing at all – behind the phenomena; they themselves are the lesson.' In short, I too always start from pure observation, and I follow theories only hesitantly and intellectually, even in my work! Goethe: 'When views disappear from the world, objects are often lost; in a higher sense, one can say that the view is the object.' Surely the 'view' must mean the 'insight' that occurs in pure (sensory) perception. That is extremely bold! A maxim that could stand above my work! This is also in line with his remark: 'Thinking is more interesting than knowing, but not more interesting than seeing!' [...] I believe that the biblically old Goethe recognised colours as the purest wonder of nature, and that pure light was for him a kind of proof of God. [...] In this sense, I see Goethe as an advocate of my interests. His insistence on the contemplation of phenomena is an encouragement to me, because it is only in pure contemplation that something happens that transcends all physics – and thus reaches a metaphysical dimension. [...] In short, as an artist I am interested in forms and colours, and I cannot help but pay homage to Goethe, the author of the 'Morphology of Forms' and the Theory of Colours.

(LETTER TO ANETTE KUHN, APRIL 1995, MACK ARCHIVE) «

9 Judaism

Heinz Mack came into contact with Judaism during his years in New York. While the Auschwitz trials in West Germany in 1963, just three years after the Eichmann trial in Jerusalem, brought the Nazi genocide of the Jews to public attention for the first time, in New York Mack was able to perceive the unique cultural and artistic competence of Judaism as a matter of course. Howard Wise, ultimately his most important gallerist, was Jewish, as was the gallerist Leo Castelli, the globally active king of Pop Art. Mack's conversations with Barnett Newman (p. 111) revolved around the anxious question of how things could go on in Germany after all that had happened. And David Rockefeller told the young German that without his 'late birth' he would not have been welcome in his home (p. 118).

Since then, Heinz Mack's relationship with Judaism has been a matter of personal commitment. Only Konrad Klapheck, who studied at the Düsseldorf Academy of Art a few years after Mack, shared this commitment to such an extent.[212] It is not directly reflected in Mack's work, but it speaks of the attitude that pervades it and characterises his personality. It has to do with a sense of duty, but it goes beyond that. One is reminded of the words of Hans Hartung, born in Leipzig and exiled under the Nazis, who in 1942 refused to go into exile in the United States and expressed his wish to return to the French Foreign Legion in Algeria, to which he had previously belonged. In response to the astonishment of the US diplomat in Lisbon, Hartung said: 'A German must do his duty.'[213] Heinz Mack was awarded the Moses Mendelssohn Medal in 2017 for his commitment to Judaism in Germany, expressed, for example, in his *Memorial to Anne Frank* (1980–1986, Rabbiner-Neumark-Weg, Duisburg).

»

As far as I know, more or less all the notable gallerists in New York in the mid-1960s were Jewish. All the important museum directors, as far as I can remember, were Jewish. And all the important collectors that I remember were Jewish. It's quite striking that high culture was best looked after by Jews. That's something you have to say as a huge compliment to these people – and Howard Wise was also Jewish. When Denise René opened a gallery in New York, it also played a role that she was Jewish. It was not easy for a German to be there not many years after the end of the war. I have the greatest respect for the fact that Jews have played such an enormous, extremely important role in cultural history. That goes for all of modern art, for the whole century, it's just phenomenal. It also applies to the natural sciences and the humanities. So what would Germany be without this incredible spiritual, intellectual capital? That's why I always read the weekly newspaper *Jüdische Allgemeine* as well as the *Frankfurter Allgemeine Zeitung*. In 1972, my then wife Michi and I accepted a personal invitation from the Jewish Museum to New York, where we stayed for ten days at the posh Regency Hotel. Every day there was a new bouquet of flowers in our room: 'With compliments of the Jewish Museum'. For the first time in New York, I felt honoured, so unexpectedly.

« (JUNE 2023)

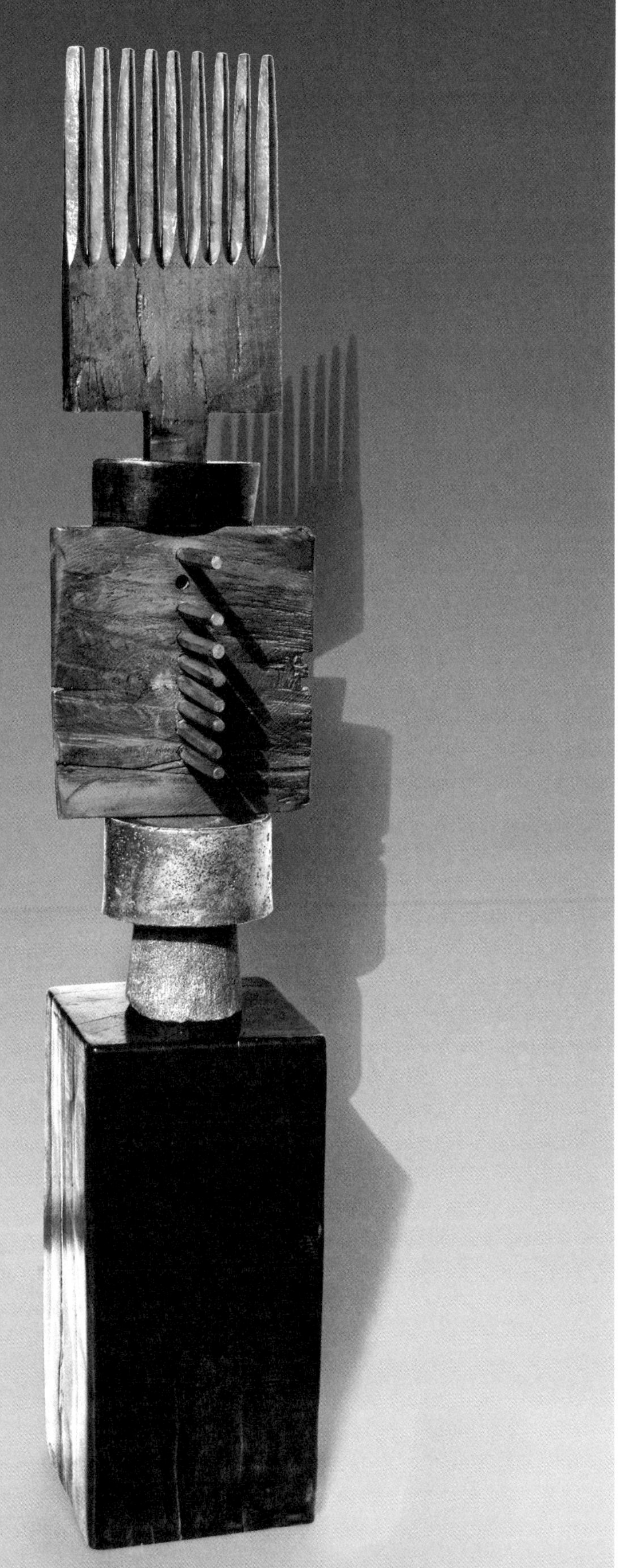

The Hand
1954

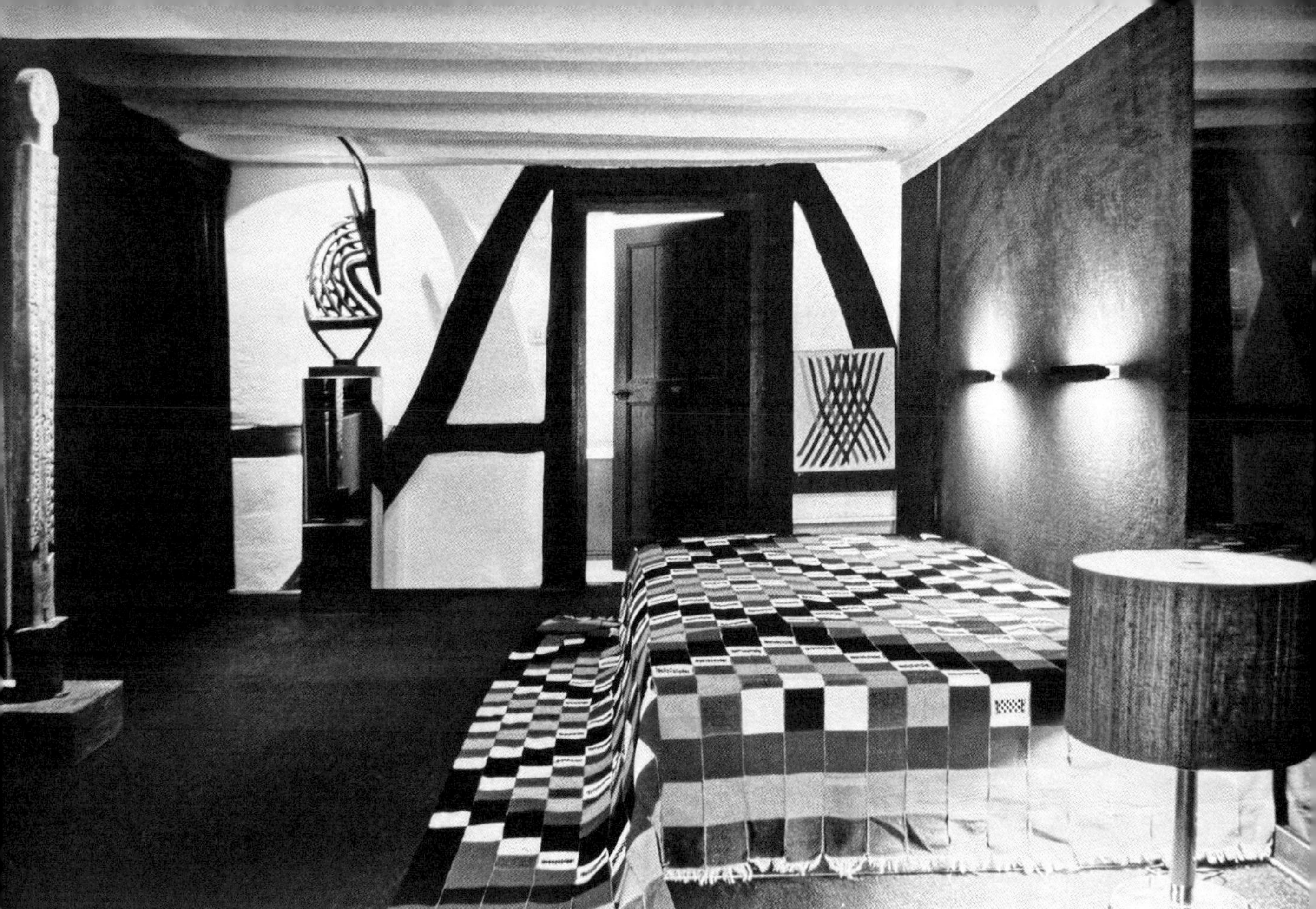

View of the artist's living quarters at the Huppertzhof, Mönchengladbach, 1970s with two African sculptures and a painting by Piero Dorazio

10 Orient and Occident

Probably the best retrospective of Heinz Mack's work to date took place in 2016 at the Sakıp Sabancı Museum in Istanbul.[215] Norman Rosenthal, one of the most influential curators of the last fifty years and, together with Nazan Ölçer, the curator of this exhibition, had previously organised a retrospective of ZERO art at the same museum.[216] On this occasion, Mack's work *The Sky Over Nine Columns* was installed directly on the Bosphorus. He had shown it for the first time in Venice in 2014. This sculpture is probably the work in which the artist most intensively embodied his relationship with the Orient. The nine steles, with monochrome Venetian mosaics made in Dubai using the latest digital technology from Murano, had an unforgettable impact in the lagoon city, which for centuries had served as a gateway between the Orient and the Occident, right on the waterfront opposite St Mark's Square. Mack has repeatedly stated that he dreams of realising his works in an immeasurably large urban or landscape space – this was achieved in Venice in 2014, with a site-specific concept and in front of an audience of millions and global media covering the Architecture Biennale taking place there at the same time.[217]

» For more than half a century, I have repeatedly encountered Oriental culture, the influence of which I could not and did not want to escape. Alongside this creative transfer of ideas, however, I have also encountered affinities of choice and visual affinities that have surprised me, that is to say, that have seemed accidental. That's what fascinates me. In the Orient and the Far East, there is a completely non-objective, non-figurative art, in which ornamental structures define a two-dimensional space and thus develop an independent aesthetic.

(2006)[214] «

The 2016 retrospective in Istanbul was organised 'in reverse'. Beginning with new works by the artist, it returned to ZERO art and even earlier sculptures, while also focusing on the work's close relationship to oriental art traditions. From the play of pure coloured surfaces, their structural arrangement, the approach to ornament and its renewal to the methodology of repetition and barely perceptible difference, artistic processes unfolded that Heinz Mack draws from the arts of the Orient.

» In his 1951 book *The Rebel*, Albert Camus concludes his reflections with a chapter on the 'Mediterranean mind'. He writes: 'The profound conflict of this century is [...] rather between German dreams and Mediterranean traditions.'[218]

(OCTOBER 2023) «

For the artist, this theme also began early, with Johann Wolfgang von Goethe's 1819 collection of poems *West-Eastern Diwan*, which in the original edition began with an Arabic text on the frontispiece: 'The Eastern Diwan by a Western author.' Goethe turned to the Orient in detailed studies, partly as an alternative to the emerging German nationalism. Parallel to the first *Chromatic Constellations*, Heinz Mack created a suite of over 140 sheets in pastel colours and black ink on the Diwan, not as illustrations, but as a kind of declaration of love by a contemporary artist to Goethe's late poetry. It was published as an artist's book in 1999.[219]

Since his first trip to Morocco in 1955 and the *Sahara Project* (fig. pp. 156 f.), his interest in African artistic traditions, especially North African cultures, has been equally intense, for example with sub-Saharan forms such as the concrete reliefs and water walls at the hospital in Djourbel, Senegal, from 1966, through the building up of a high-calibre collection of African sculpture, numerous journeys and most recently an exhibition at the Museum of African Art in Dakar at the invitation of its director Malick Ndiaye.[220]

In two museum exhibitions, Heinz Mack attempted a pictorial 'transit between Occident and Orient'. The exhibition at the Tehran Museum of Contemporary Art[222] in 2001 took place during a more liberal phase of the Iranian regime and attracted a considerable number of visitors. The same was true of Mack's exhibition at the Pergamon Museum in Berlin five years later.[223] Both exhibitions were held in venues that are hardly in the focus of contemporary art events. As a result, they received little attention from the art world. This could change in retrospect if the current discourse on post-colonialism discovers the pioneering role of Heinz Mack's work in his ongoing dialogue with the Global South.

»

Mr Vömel was a small man, very well-groomed, very noble, almost aristocratic, always perfectly dressed, dark blue suit, white shirt, tie, very polite, a very nice man. He had a gallery in Königsallee in Düsseldorf, on the 3rd floor.[221] You had to ring the bell. He would open the door himself and say: 'Well, Mr Mack, come in.' Once he had an exhibition of African art. It was all sensational. I didn't even know African art existed at the time. Nobody had ever talked about it. There were only African objects, including a throne embroidered with thousands of beads, incredibly precious, a real throne for a king. It was also there that I first saw Kandinsky's coloured woodcuts.

« (MAY 2023)

11

»

We artists want our work to be understood by other people. But when I see the passion, patience and energy with which we are prepared to devote our entire existence to art, regardless of the rest of our lives – and when I see how much indifference and incomprehension or casual interest the public shows towards these works, then the existential effort seems to me more than absurd or grotesque.

« (JUNE 2023)

12 The Question of Beauty

Heinz Mack brings up the question of beauty in almost every conversation. Ever since he studied philosophy, it has seemed to him to be the inescapable finality of art. In the same breath, he explains how isolated he feels, since the concept of beauty has not been part of the artistic vocabulary for more than a century, and its use leads to the greatest misunderstandings, especially through the common confusion of beauty and kitsch. In Mack's artistic work, however, there is no 'quiet' beauty, but rather a *fougue*, albeit often concealed, something stirring, lively, with expressive intensities without being expressionist. His unwavering adherence to beauty, against God and the world, so to speak, also plays the role of a source of energy in the artist's personal economy, and an area in which he must exercise and practise his sense of humour in order not to end up in a dead end.

»

Another concept is beauty, which, as we all know, has been suppressed as completely dubious and obsolete, but which I still claim, making me the target of countless criticisms, including vilification. In this context, Karl Heinz Bohrer has been an important partner for me, for whom the concept of 'beauty' is centred on 'radiance'.[224] The [...] 'apparition', which is already a theme with Valéry,[225] was later taken up by Adorno, namely as an epiphany.[226] In short, this character of apparition, combined with the highest presence, is for me not just a phenomenon, but the actual essentia of a work of art. This means that all scientific logic should no longer have any meaning. It goes hand in hand with imagination and fascination, which fill the viewer to such an extent that his or her rational thinking and seeing is freed from the question: 'Is this art or is it not art?'

(LETTER TO HARTMUT BÖHME, 5 DECEMBER 2022, MACK ARCHIVE) «

The art historian Werner Hofmann has repeatedly explored the dimension of beauty in the work of Heinz Mack. In 1998, Wieland Schmied edited *Utopie und Wirklichkeit im Werk von Heinz Mack* (Utopia and Reality in the Work of Heinz Mack), prominently published by DuMont in Cologne, with texts by important current and former museum professionals. Werner Hofmann contributed an essay on the concept of beauty in the artist's work.[228] In it, he explains that none of the numerous methods of deconstructing beauty that have emerged in modern and contemporary art in the twentieth century are applied in this work.

»

Werner Hofmann recognised: 'Mack, you always make such beautiful things.' He also wrote a text for me in which he virtually celebrates me for this richness. He uses the word 'splendour' to characterise me.[227] At the same time, he makes a comment to the contrary, giving me a little kick in the arse: 'The fact that we live in a world that is completely torn apart, that is full of contradictions – strangely enough, this does not appear at all in your work. We should really have a conversation about that.'

(JULY 2023) «

Eight years later, in March 2006, Hofmann sent the artist a birthday card. In it, he mentions a book of his own that he sent with it, his reissued *magnum opus* from 1960, *Das irdische Paradies. Kunst im 19. Jahrhundert* (The Earthly Paradise: Art in the Nineteenth Century), written when the author was thirty-one years old. In it, he rehabilitates the art of the long-despised nineteenth century in a way that has nothing to do with the re-recognition of nineteenth-century salon art as presented in the Musée d'Orsay, which opened in Paris in 1986 and against which Hofmann railed.[229] In his birthday card, Hofmann writes of the dialectic of every artistic development, in which all art moves and in which beauty always responds to an anti-aesthetic, the great buzzword of the 1960s. This was followed by an exchange of letters (preserved in Heinz Mack's private archive) that is instructive with regard to the artist's ongoing theme of 'beauty'.

Beauty in 'opposition' and as a 'weapon' has been a topos of the artist since around 1960. Since the 1970s, this theme has also been a source of his artistic humour. It has often been asked[230] whether the special power of the best German art since 1960 does not derive from its confrontation with an urban environment that, since the years of reconstruction, has been more aesthetically inadequate than anywhere else, with the same pedestrian zones in small and large towns all over the country and a lot of meaningless architecture. For someone like Heinz Mack, who is also at home in Spain and knows Italy and the Orient, this is a daily slap in the face.

In 1998, Werner Hofmann analysed Mack's proposals from the 1970s to 'mirror away' the ugliness of cities in a way that can also be read as a characterisation of the artist: 'The mirror is used for this, which has always been an instrument of transformation, making the world of appearances more visible and robbing it of its clarity. At the same time, the mirror radiates a questioning and mesmerising power. Mack refers to this when he counters the planned "disorientation that prevails in the megacities of this century" with an "unplanned, poetic disorientation of a conceivably unreal appearance"', "in which all the buildings are completely mirrored or at least dissected in a quasi-cubist or kaleidoscopic manner by mirrors as tall as houses placed opposite the buildings". Once again, empirical reality is recognised for its provisional nature, but instead of turning away from it to postulate a new, better reality in the utopian nowhere – a New Jerusalem – this quick-change artist places his imagination in the middle of the urban chaos, transforming it into an optical labyrinth with mirror weapons – another Don Quixote who, instead of fighting windmills, allies himself *with them*.'[232]

»

Dear Heinz Mack,
This book (from 1960) is not only about your great theme, but also about its counter-worlds, in short: about the 'crazy reality' that drives you. Our very best wishes for the 8th of March 2006 & far beyond! *Werner & Jacqueline*

Dear Werner and Jacqueline,
How do I behave in a world where chaos is the order of the day? I am in opposition to the world we live in. Beauty is my weapon.

«

(CORRESPONDENCE BETWEEN WERNER AND JACQUELINE HOFMANN AND HEINZ MACK, MARCH 2006, MACK ARCHIVE)

»

One [...] aspect is the possible 'blinding' or 'overlaying' of the ugliness of the entire urban conglomerate by fragmenting the city kaleidoscopically through various crystalline mirror facets, which would then give rise to completely new abstract forms of appearance.

«

('DIE VERSPIEGELTE STADT', PROJECT FROM 1978)[231]

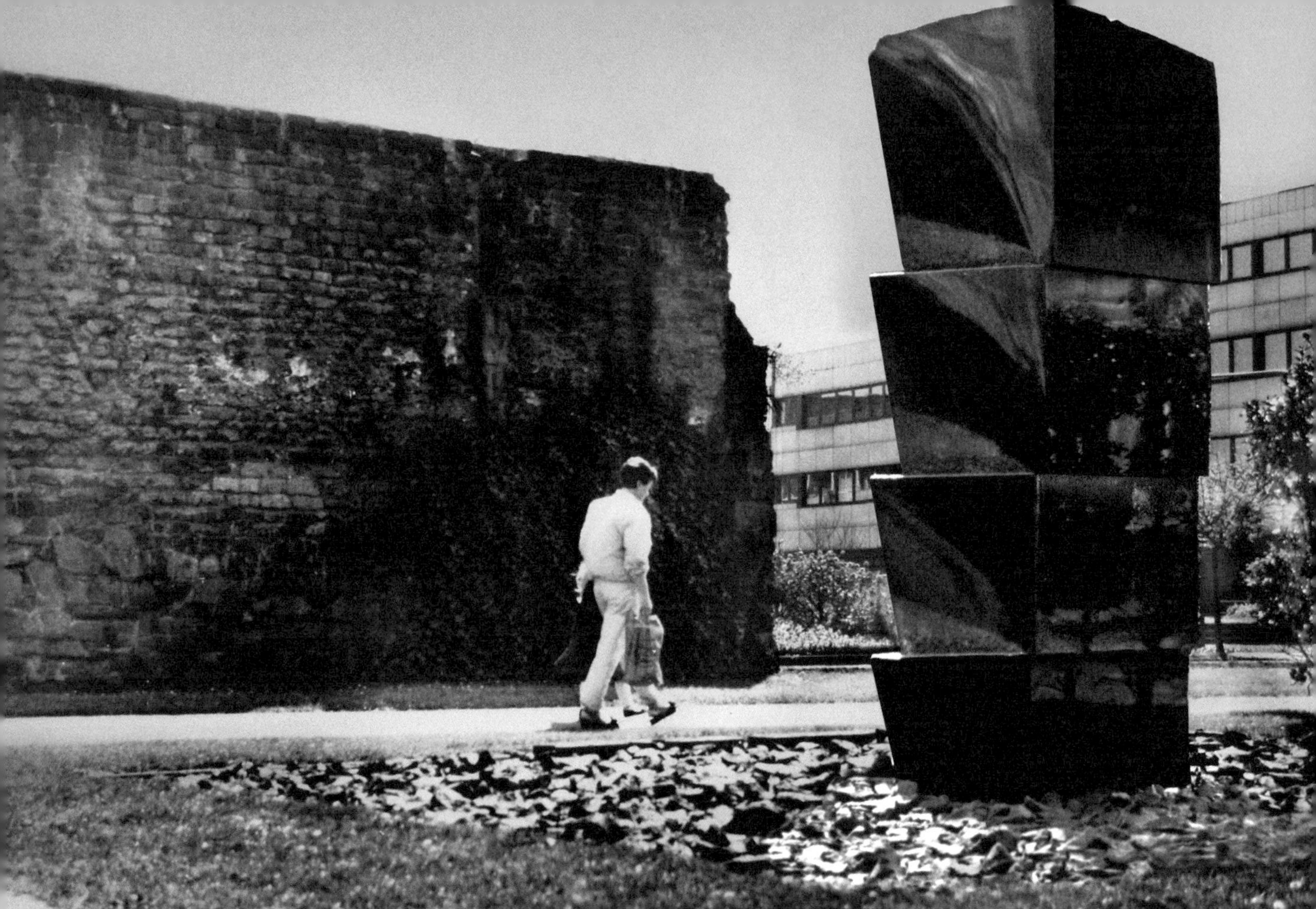

Memorial to Anne Frank
Rabbiner-Neumark-Weg, Duisburg
1980 – 1986

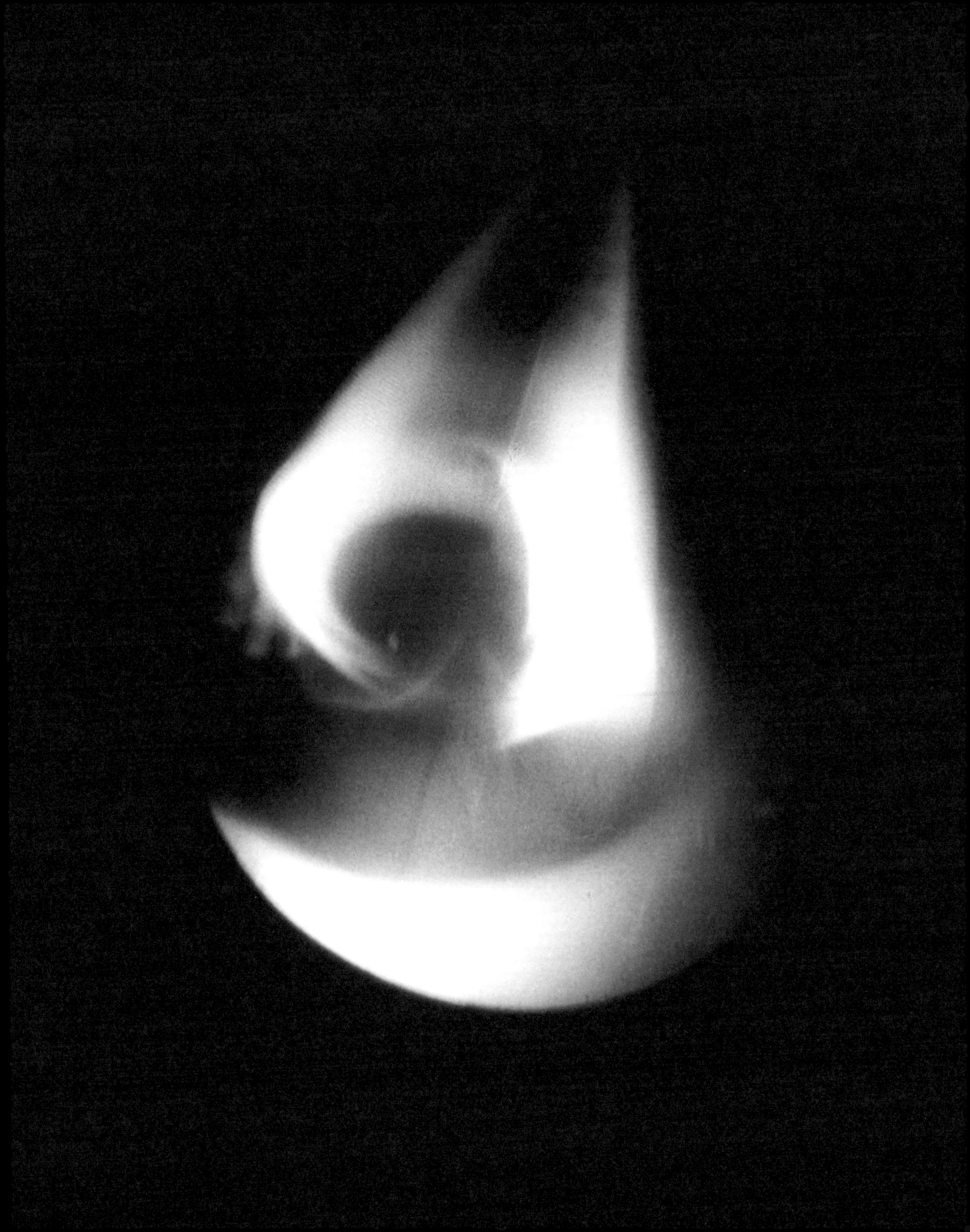

HEINZ MACK AND PHOTOGRAPHY

Light Cone
from the *Silver Light* suite
1958/73

During one of our meetings in April 2023, Heinz Mack stands in front of his studio at the Huppertzhof and photographs his stone, steel, and mirror sculptures with a Leica viewfinder camera. 'I was given this a few days ago, for my ninety-second birthday. I'm familiarising myself with it.' We can't believe our eyes. Leica and viewfinder cameras are an important part of the history of photography. Mack learned to take pictures with them very early on, even before he was a teenager. Now he takes a few more shots with the new camera in his private sculpture garden before sitting down for another interview for this book. The Leica Q2 he is holding is the best of the best of today's digital cameras. With it, colour and grey tones, the play of light and non-light in photography can be taken further than ever before. This digital camera in the old Leica body is as light and easy to handle as any Leica M. He seems to like it. The *way* Mack holds such a camera in his hands speaks volumes. Professional photographers recognise each other by this and by their chosen model. So this is obviously someone who is deeply involved in photography, but not at all known for it. Will we get to see his photographs? Why does he take them?

Photography is a kind of blind spot in Heinz Mack's work. It is seldom seen outside the artist's work environment, but it is the foundation of his entire visual thinking, underpinning the visual solutions in the most diverse media, materials, and areas of expression and providing the coherent context of the overall ensemble, which is a miracle in view of the diversity of its materials, media, themes, and approaches. 'Heinz Mack and photography' – there are hardly any exhibitions or literature on this subject. Yet it is a central theme of his artistic oeuvre and thus a treasure yet to be discovered.

There have only been two exhibitions of Heinz Mack's photographic work to date. Both were comparatively modest in scale. In 2006, on the occasion of the artist's seventy-fifth birthday, the Städtisches Museum Abteiberg in Mönchengladbach showed *Silver Light*, a series of 'seventy-five projections on photographic paper', which Mack himself had named, produced, and compiled (fig. p. 212).[233] *Silver Light* is the first surprise when viewing the photographic oeuvre. The photographs date from 1944 to 2006, covering almost all his creative periods. They reveal an extraordinary sensitivity and experience in dealing with the photographic image and a multifaceted approach to photography. Working simultaneously in a wide range of media, over the decades Mack has translated technical innovations into black-and-white photography without negating its inner laws or becoming arbitrarily experimental. Here we find a sparkling wealth of inventions on the problems of light and the analogue photographic image, as well as on photographic control and the photographic rethinking of his own work.

» I hate photography, this so-called photographic art in art exhibitions. «
(APRIL 2023)

A second exhibition of Heinz Mack's autonomous photographic works was organised by Mario-Andreas von Lüttichau, curator at the Folkwang Museum in Essen, also in 2006 at the Stadtsparkasse Essen with colour Diasec prints that the artist had made over a long period of his own sculptural works and various light phenomena (fig. p. 225).[234] Mack began making colour photographs in the mid-1960s, during his time in New York, when Kodak introduced affordable slide film. They continue to permeate his work to this day, although the artist is decidedly reticent about the results. There are several hundred photographs on slide film that he has selected as fully valid works, many of which have been developed, listed in the catalogue raisonné, and properly stored.

The photographs are not an ensemble of works within Heinz Mack's oeuvre that was conceived as such from the outset, but they do hold it together. This begins with his very first artistic works, which he made as a boy in Lollar, Hesse, in 1943–44 (fig. p. 289). An uncle who worked for the nearby Leitz company had access to film and processing materials that were otherwise largely denied to the population during the war years. Mack's first works are sensitive black-and-white photographs of structures, of felled trees and their circular patterns on the cut surfaces, of stacked tree trunks and stele-like accumulations of wood. It is possible to see in them the foreshadowing of later pictorial ideas.[235] In any case, in the very complicated situation of the late Nazi era, the young Heinz Mack learned to see and think in images through photography, far removed from the oppressive ideology.

Photography opens up a little-known dimension in the work of Heinz Mack. His photographic activity has never ceased. However, it has not yet become an explicit approach to his work. When Mack was a schoolboy and then a student, there was hardly any photography in exhibitions and museums. The exhibition *The Family of Man* at The Museum of Modern Art in New York in 1955, which subsequently went on a world tour, was limited to reportage photography. The Surrealists produced photographic art in the modern sense but were unable to show it beyond private exhibitions. It was not until the fifth edition of the documenta in Kassel in 1972, curated by Harald Szeemann, that photographs were shown as fully-fledged works of art. Even Yves Klein himself did not exhibit his now famous photographs of *Anthropometries* and experiments with flamethrowers and naked women at the Gaz de France test centre in 1961–62. This was only done posthumously by his wife and artistic partner Rotraut, after 1970, when photography was recognised as a fully valid artistic medium. The fact that Heinz Mack photographs intensively on the one hand but is sceptical about the term 'photographic art' on the other is related to this background.

It is also misleading to interpret the ZERO movement in Düsseldorf from 1957–58 onwards, and then throughout Western Europe, too much on the basis of the photographic images that document it and, not least, make it so present today. There were gifted young artists who took highly sensitive photographs, most notably Reiner Ruthenbeck, then a student of Joseph Beuys and later one of the most important

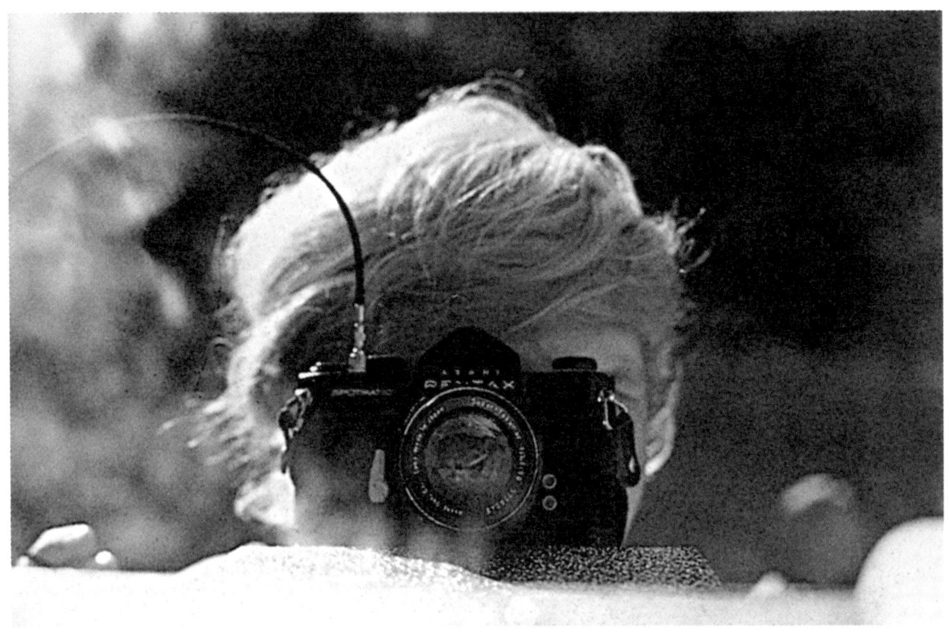

Self-Portrait
1992

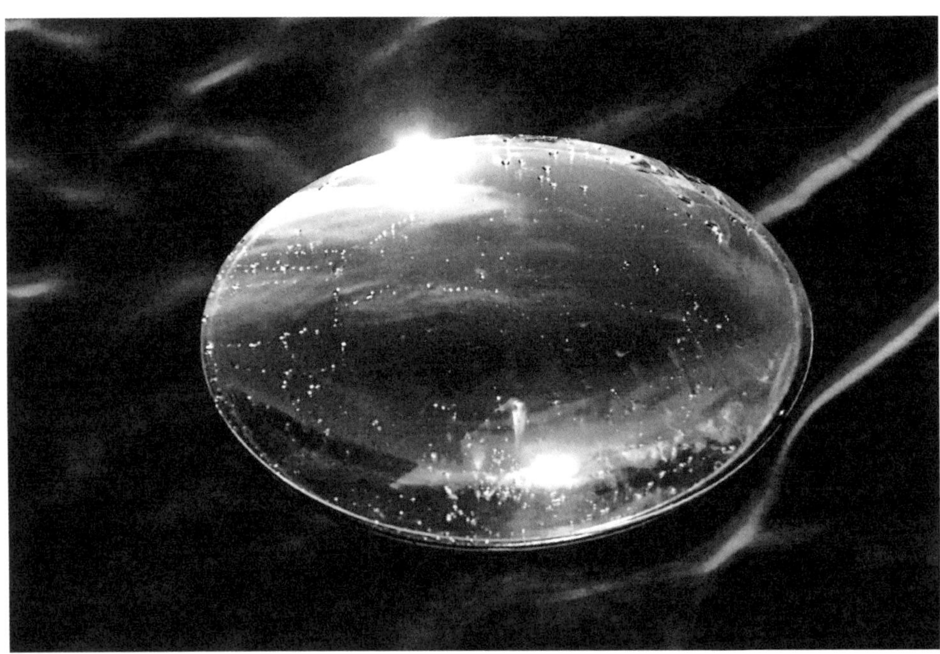

Project for a Floating Island in the Sea
1968

conceptual artists in Germany. His photographic aesthetic has strongly influenced our image of the ZERO festivals today (fig. pp. 96 f.). Photography, however, did not play a role as an artistic medium among the ZERO artists. Yet today it is fundamental to the life of ZERO. The ZERO years up to 1966 were about surprising sculptural works, magazines, exhibitions, and festivals that took place live, like the Happenings in New York, and were fortunately also photographed.

For ZERO, then, photography was documentation and, in the case of Heinz Mack, inspiration beneath the surface. This was first revealed in the *Light Room* by Heinz Mack, Otto Piene, and Günther Uecker in the attic of the Fridericianum in Kassel as part of *documenta III* in the summer of 1964 (fig. p. 92), where a painting by Lucio Fontana, who had been juried out of the exhibition at the instigation of Werner Haftmann,[236] was projected onto the wall by Heinz Mack as a slide projection, that is, as a photograph, in homage to the much older artist and mentor of the avant-garde. Above all, however, Mack's photograph of this *Light Room* is a masterful, inspired shot, with a slightly longer exposure time that captures the movement and play of light: a congenial translation of this major ZERO work into the photographic medium, and at the same time a leap from photographic documentation to an autonomous means of artistic expression. This is also confirmed by the dust jacket of Heiner Stachelhaus's seminal book *ZERO*, published in 1993, which states: 'Cover design Heinz Mack'.[237] The photograph of the *Light Room* from 1964 is printed on the front of the dust jacket as a positive and on the back as a negative, which in turn results in an artistic work. The photograph anticipates the first realisation of Mack's *Sahara Project* in the Tunisian desert in 1968 in connection with the film *Tele-Mack*, whereby photography and film became an artistic medium per se (fig. pp. 156 f.). This brings us to Mack's work after the dissolution of the ZERO group. There are also autonomous photographic works in dialogue with a desert-like landscape, such as *Marking of the Earth*, made in 1960 in Hubbelrath near Düsseldorf on a field that Mack had covered with light-coloured fertiliser lime (fig. p. 218), an anticipation of Land Art and the later works of Gina Pane in France.

Mack was therefore always committed to photography. He documented his visit to his father's grave in the prisoner of war cemetery near Bordeaux in 1948 with a photograph (fig. p. 42). There is also a self-portrait of his first visit to the Sahara in the summer of 1955, when he was a teacher and used his holidays to travel to Paris and Morocco, showing him with his VW Beetle. In the same year, he met Yves Klein in Paris, with whom he used a slide projector to project slides he had brought with him from Düsseldorf onto the surrounding rooftops.[238] Around this time, Heinz Mack was still struggling with Art Informel painting, which he tried out entirely in black. The nocturnal slide projections already hinted at the idea of ZERO. It seems obvious that many of Heinz Mack's pictorial ideas came from photography.

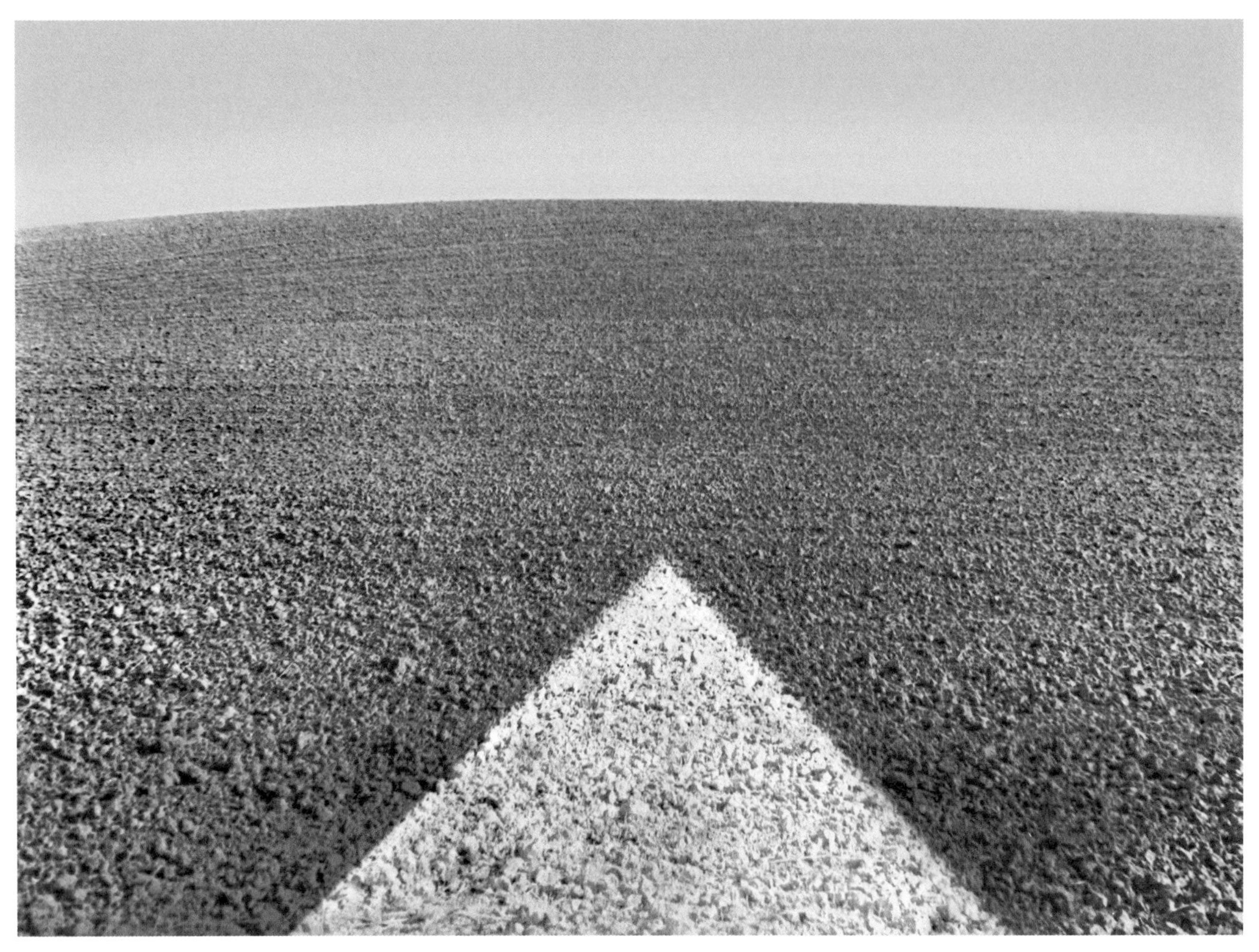

Marking of the Earth
Hubbelrath near Düsseldorf
1960

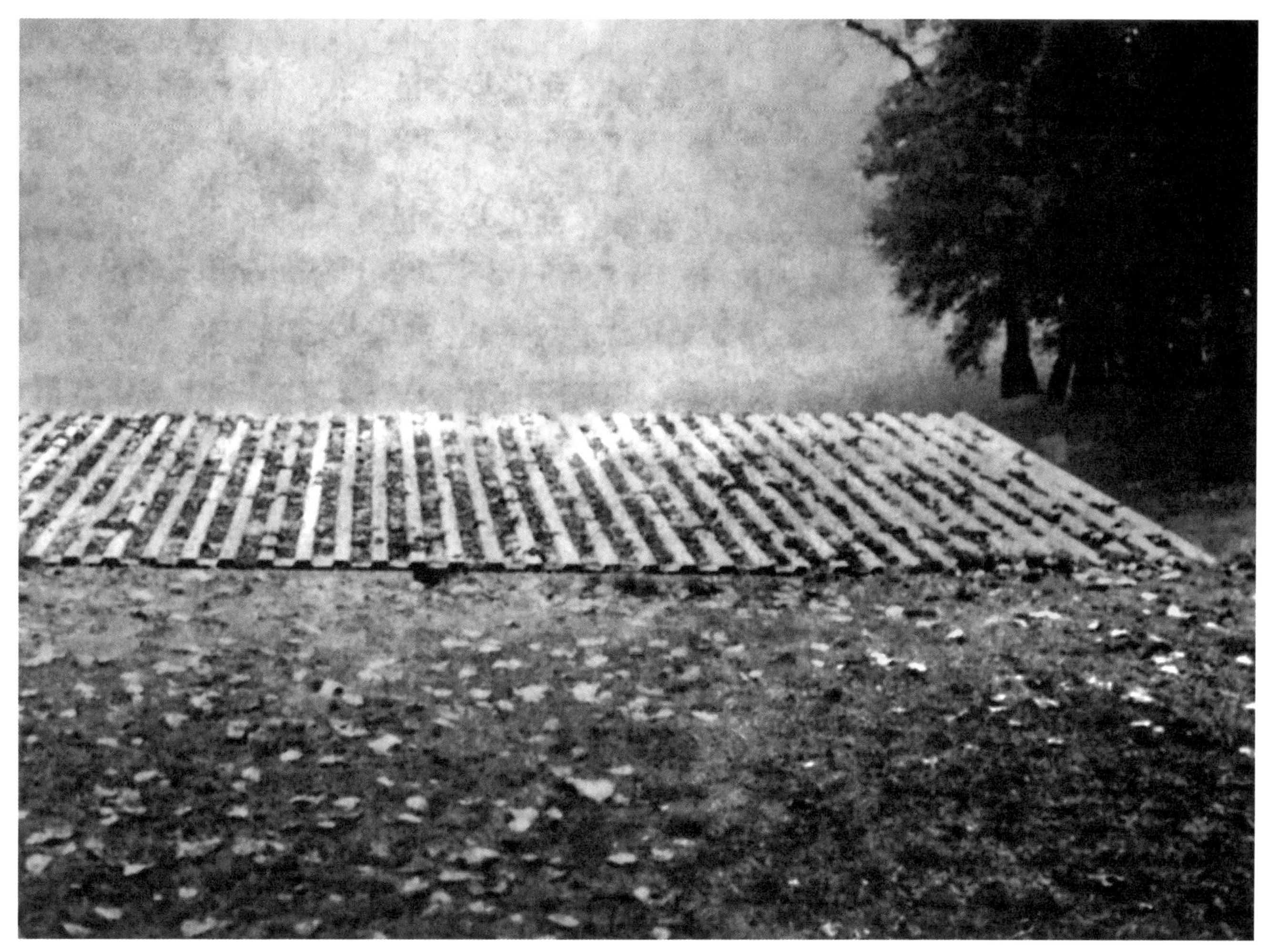

Land Art Project
Hubbelrath near Düsseldorf
1960

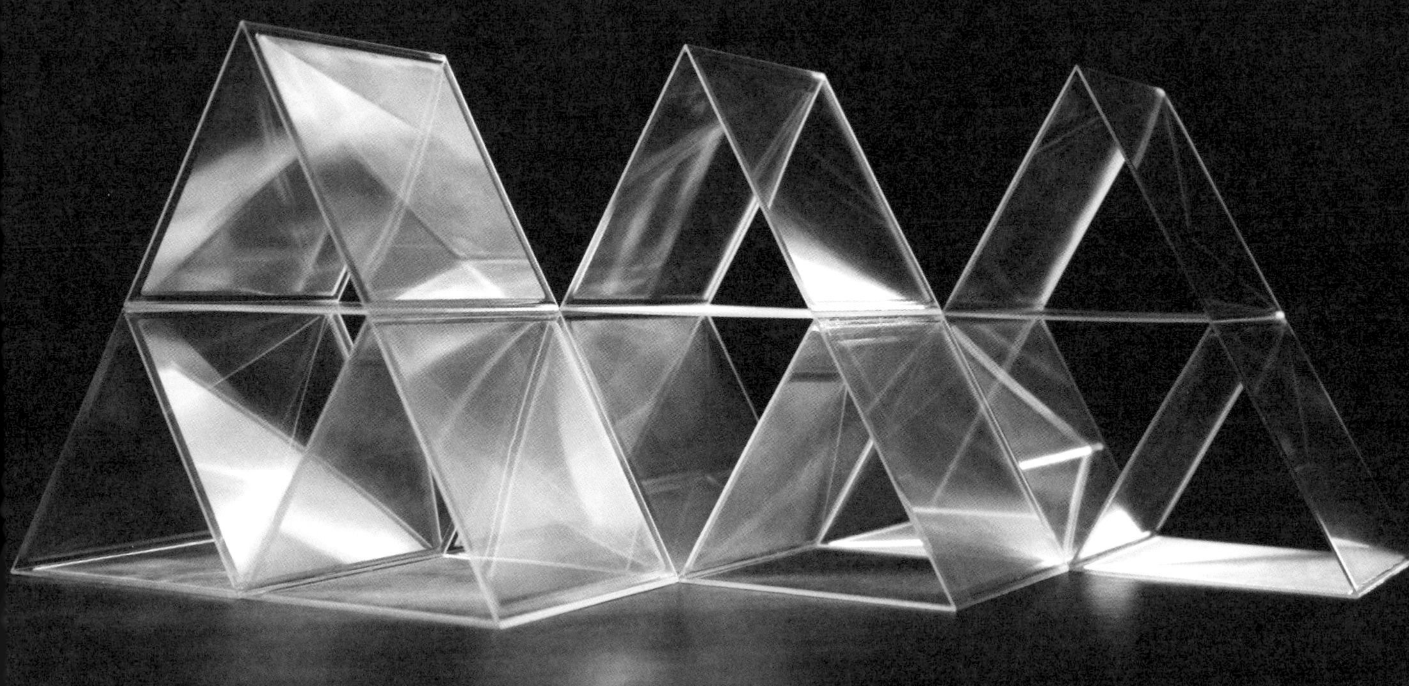

Light Experiments with
Glass Prisms
2020

→
Untitled
2010

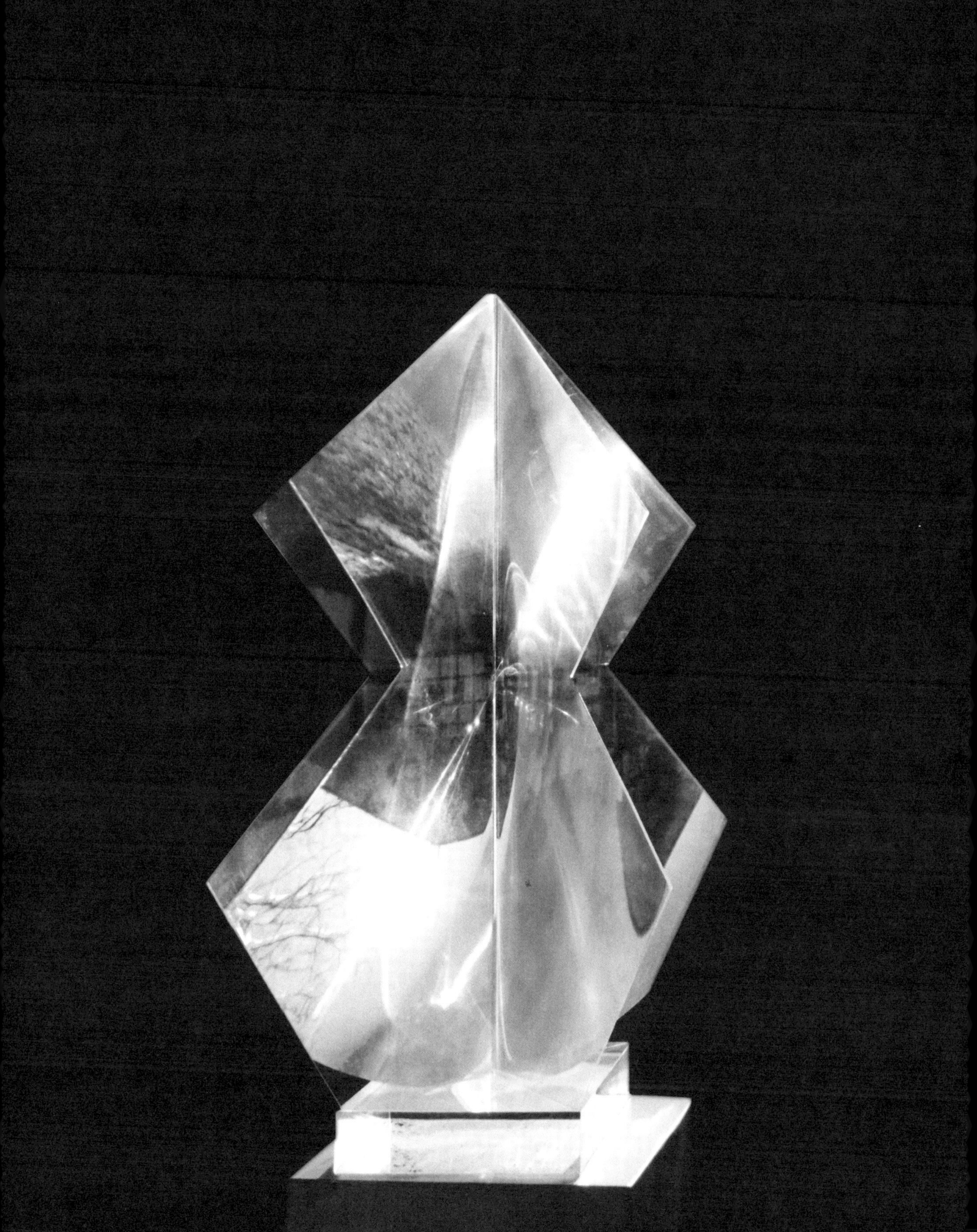

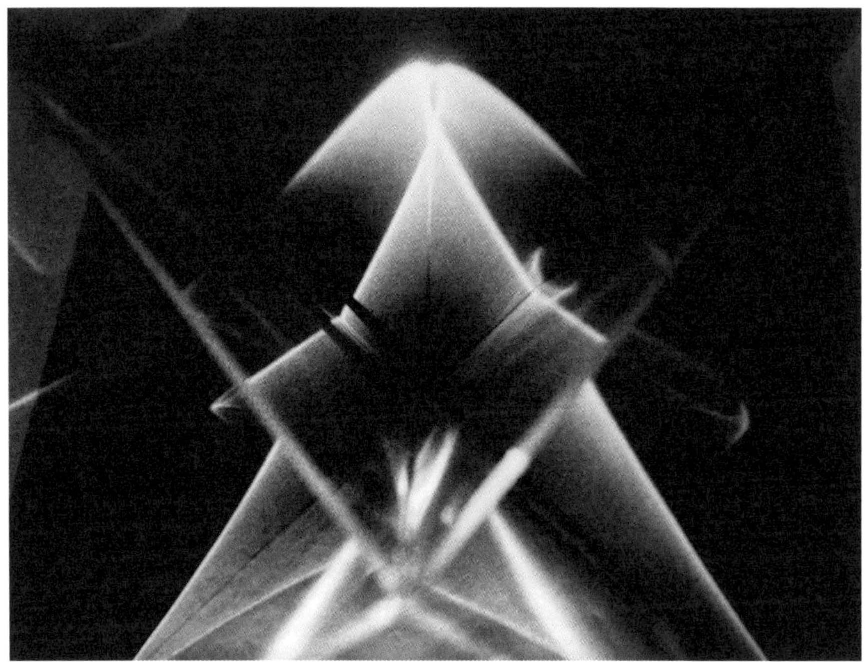

Photo Experiment
undated

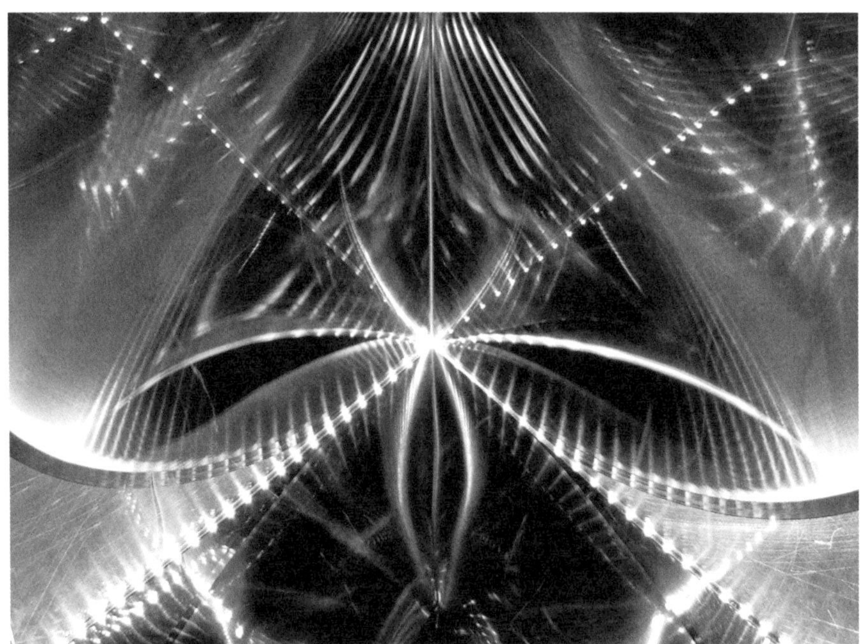

Untitled
2016

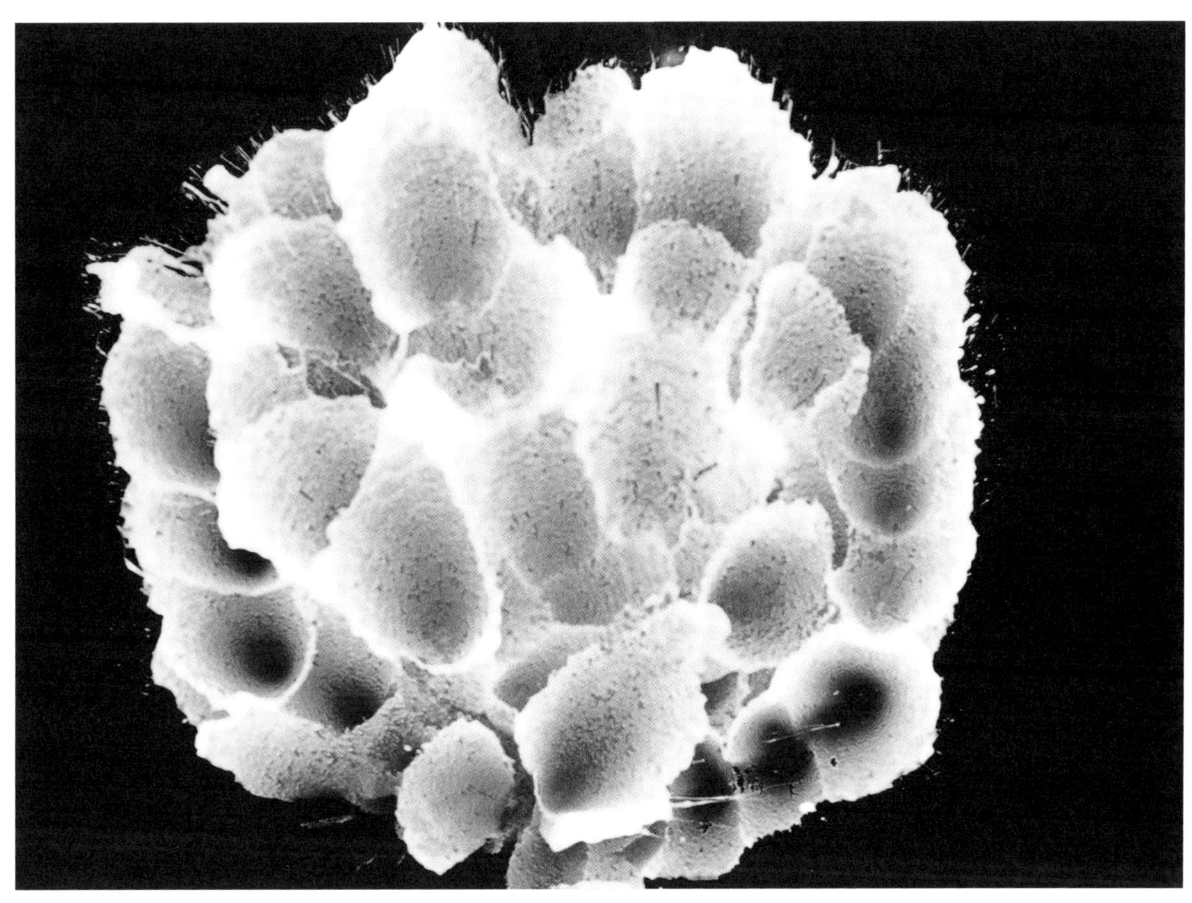

Untitled
2023

→
Radiance (Light Experiment)
2004/06

This is still part of his daily studio routine. Heinz Mack leaves his studio every day to go to the smallest building of the Huppertzhof, which serves as his office and where he has a personal room that he calls his 'safe'. No one else has access to it. This is where he keeps the small, toy-sized maquettes for his most important works. There are also several drawers containing hundreds of his own photographs and slides as well as scientific photographs, mostly cut out of the *Frankfurter Allgemeine Zeitung*. Mack consults both sets of photographs when working on sculptures and paintings, all of which – like photographs – form structures and light drawings. Nothing is taken over directly but is viewed freely and associatively.

In this context, an interesting photo and video work was created in 2010–11 for the artist's retrospective at the Bundeskunsthalle in Bonn. In preparation for the exhibition, Mack contacted the Jülich Research Centre (FZJ). After a day-long visit to its various departments for nuclear physics, botany, biology, supercomputers, etc., the scientists realised that there was an inner relationship between the photographic, microscopic, and other images they were working with and Mack's pictorial structures. On their own initiative, they then created a filmic sequence of photographs,[239] for which they had selected scientific photographs reminiscent of Mack's work that they deal with on a daily basis in their own basic research – these could be seen in the exhibition. Both types of images switched from left to right and vice versa without warning, so that the viewer could not tell which was a photograph of Mack's work and which was a photograph of current scientific research.

Heinz Mack repeatedly photographs his own models for art in public spaces under different lighting conditions and rethinks them on the basis of the photographic results. He also photographs variations for sculptures and changes the works based on the photographs. To this day, on his study trips to distant places and cultures, he devotes himself to landscape photography on the same level. These pictures are also studies for the further development of spatiality in his pictorial work.

Most importantly, Heinz Mack has photographed most of his sculptural works since 1957. The published images of his works are always the artist's own photographs. While working on the first catalogue raisonné of his sculptures, published in 1986, the art historian Dieter Honisch told Mack that he photographed his own sculptures with a photographic eye 'as only Brancusi had done before'.[240]

In fact, he was inspired by Constantin Brancusi's photographs of his own sculptures, which Mack had seen in the artist's untouched Paris studio in 1958, which Jean Tinguely showed him a few months after the artist's death.[241] Since the early 1920s, Brancusi had been pursuing three things: the stele, the unity of sculpture and pedestal, and photographing all this himself. Heinz Mack is basically following his example.

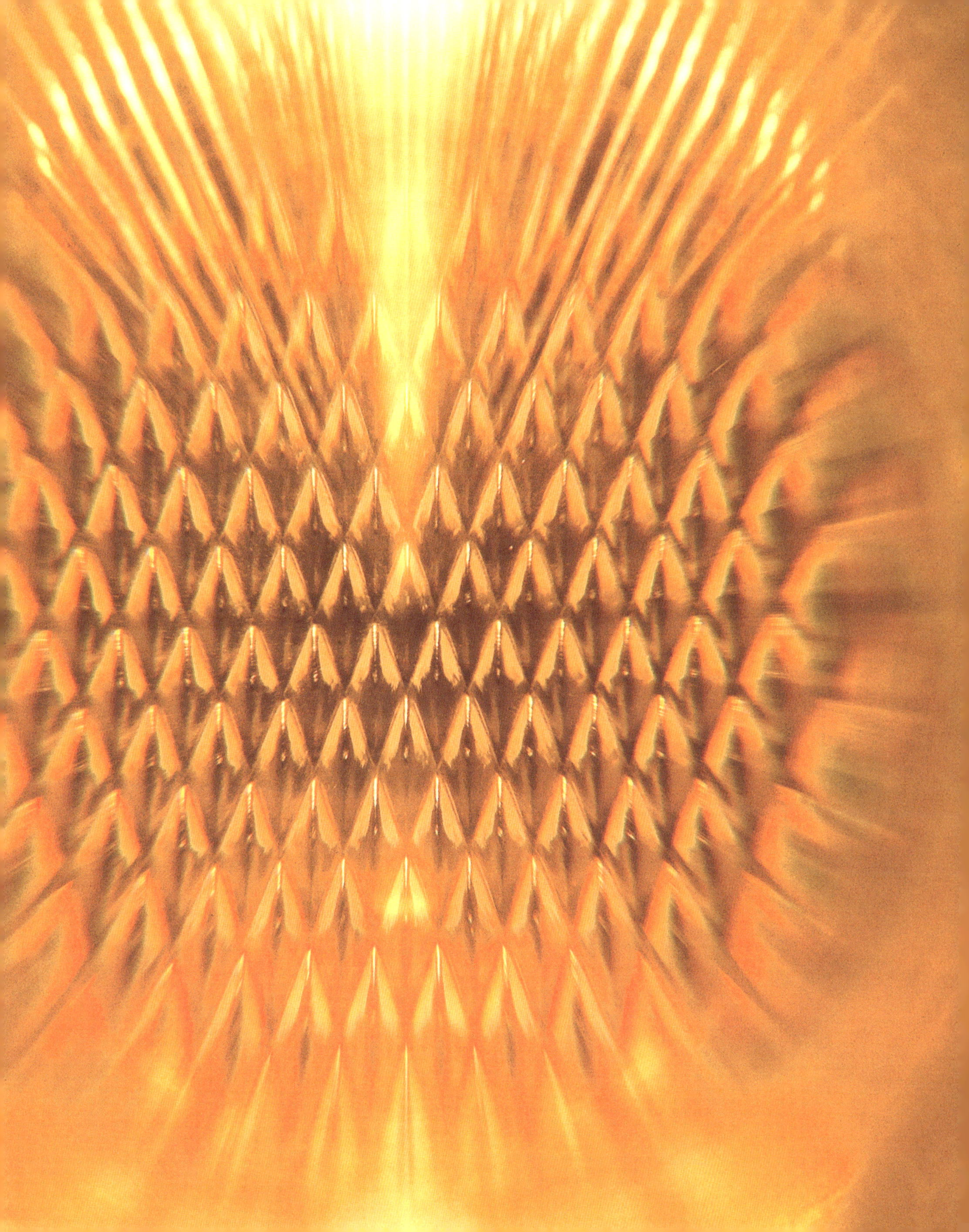

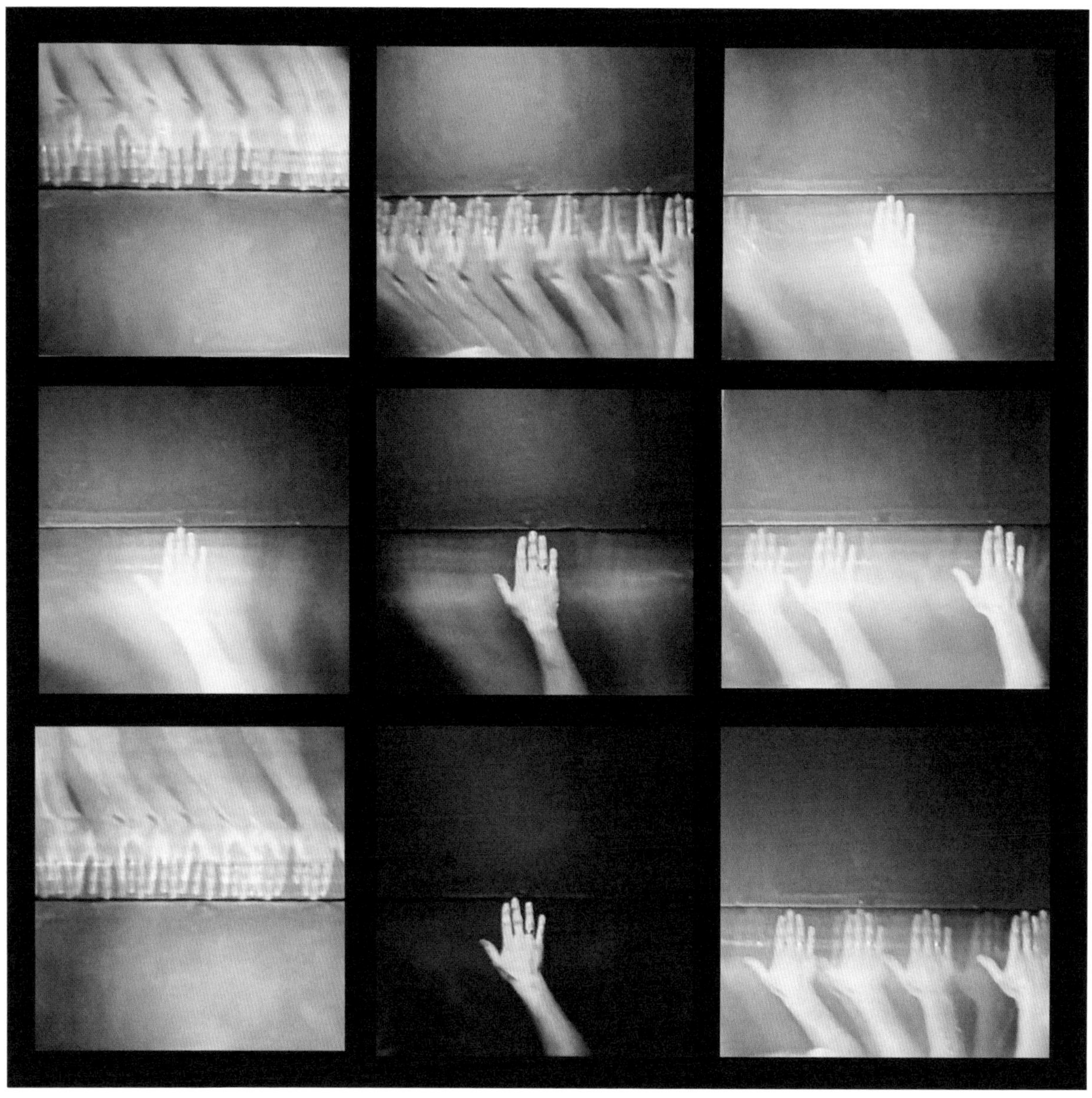

Photo Experiment with the Artist's Hand
c. 1961

For Heinz Mack, photography – directly linked to all other artistic media – is therefore a universe that holds his work together beneath the surface and is worth discovering. Here, too, the formal language of signs is reduced to concise forms in order to allow only light, rhythm, and dynamic structures to speak and to arrive directly at the elements that constitute his entire artistic intention.

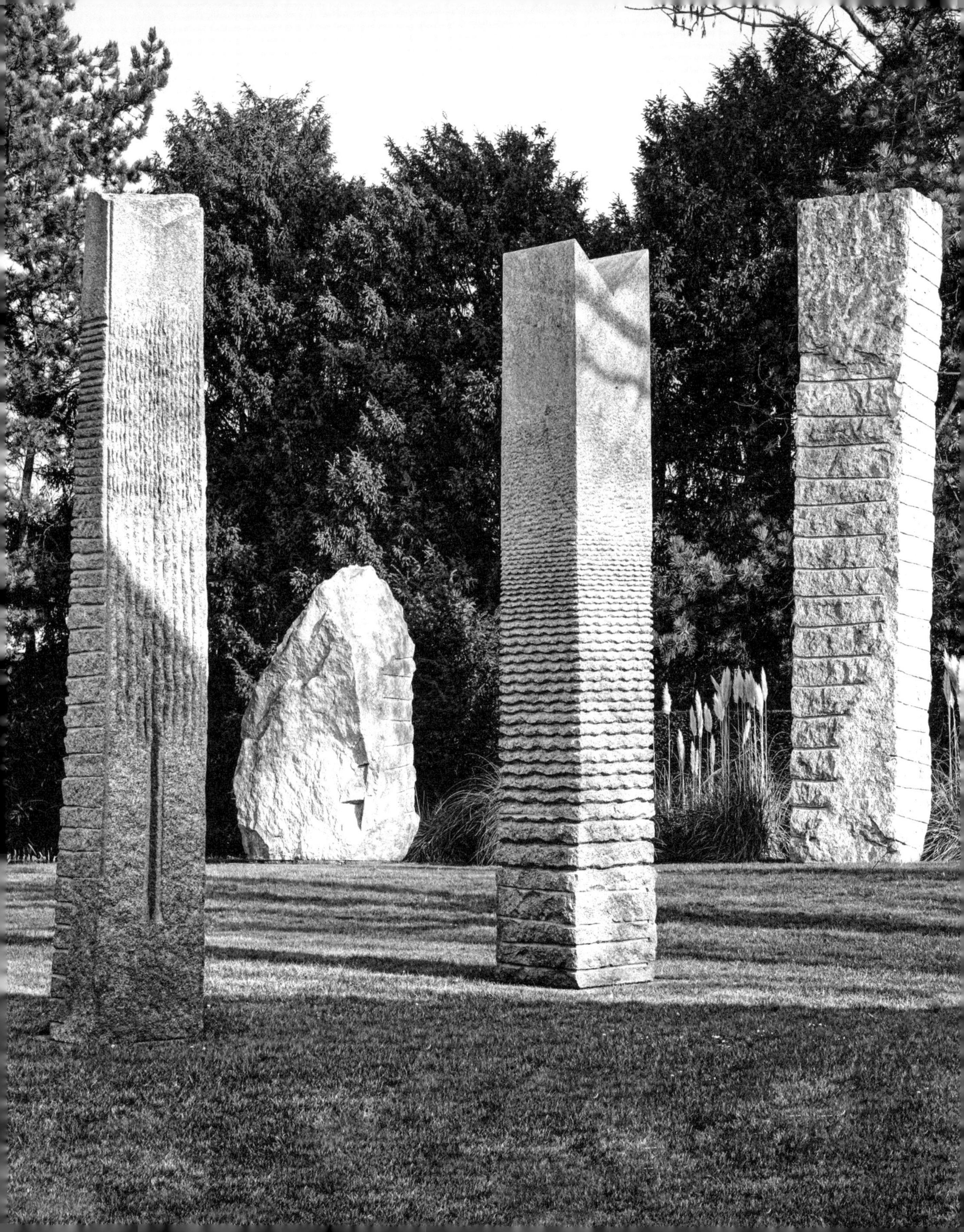

WHO STILL MAKES STONE SCULPTURES ANYMORE?

Monolith Ensemble
1979

Tony Cragg and Heinz Mack are two of the most important sculptors working today. They only met in 2020. This is surprising because Cragg, now Britain's most important living sculptor, had already moved to Wuppertal, near Düsseldorf and Mönchengladbach, in 1977. He was active for many years at the Düsseldorf Academy of Art, including a stint as rector from 2009 to 2013. He was also teaching there in 1984, when Norbert Kricke – an eminent sculptor and long-standing rector of the academy – visited Mack at the Huppertzhof to persuade him to make himself available for a professorship and the post of rector. After some consideration, Mack declined the offer, preferring to make art in complete freedom. Nevertheless, Mack and Cragg never crossed paths, either then or after Cragg founded the Waldfrieden Sculpture Park in Wuppertal in 2008. Today, this sculpture park is one of the most beautiful places for contemporary art in a region that is richer than any other in terms of institutions of international standing dedicated to contemporary art.

In 2020, Heinz Mack heard from the collector Thomas Lange, CEO of the Nationalbank in Essen, that one of his sculptures was on display in the Villa Waldfrieden in Tony Cragg's sculpture park. Cragg had bought it on the spur of the moment from an art dealer (fig. p. 231). This puzzled Mack because artists usually contact each other and say: 'I like your work. Shall we exchange?' The fact that Cragg had purchased and exhibited one of his sculptures on his own initiative touched Mack as an unexpected sign of appreciation from a famous colleague of a later generation.

Mack then contacted Cragg, and a visit by the British artist to the Huppertzhof was arranged. Cragg is well versed in the current and historical art scene, thinks far ahead and is outspoken. After entering the studio premises, he paused in amazement. Faced with the ensemble of monumental steles in the centre of the Huppertzhof (fig. p. 228), he exclaimed: 'Who still makes stone sculpture anymore?'

This statement was meant to be appreciative, and Heinz Mack understood it as such. For centuries since the Renaissance, stone had been the most highly regarded material in the hierarchy of European sculpture. It lost this role in the twentieth century, when modern sculpture incorporated materials not previously used in art and developed new forms of work. Stone sculpture was thus relegated to a niche.[242] With his own expansion of sculpture and the concept of sculpture, Heinz Mack has been at the forefront of this development since the ZERO years, with his rotors, aluminium honeycomb works, and kinetic sculptures. He continues all these strands of expanded sculpture to this day. This is probably what Tony Cragg had in mind when he entered the Huppertzhof. But it is precisely here that stone sculpture is honoured in a way that is seldom seen today. This is indeed astonishing.

The first meeting between the two artists was cordial, with an expression of appreciation for each other's work and the mutual timidity that arises when two monuments sit opposite each other. Tony Cragg, eighteen years younger than Heinz

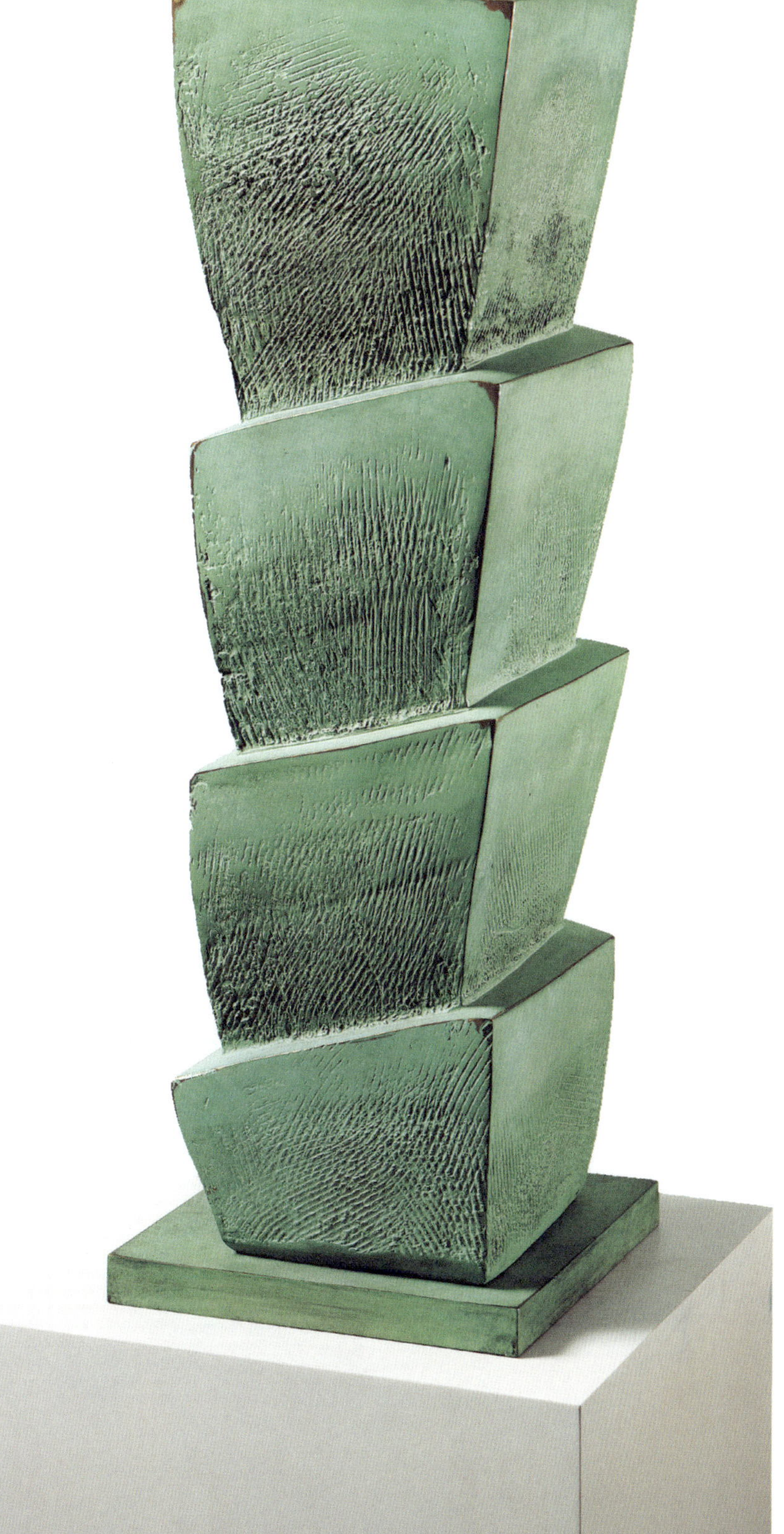

Rhythm and Growth
1998

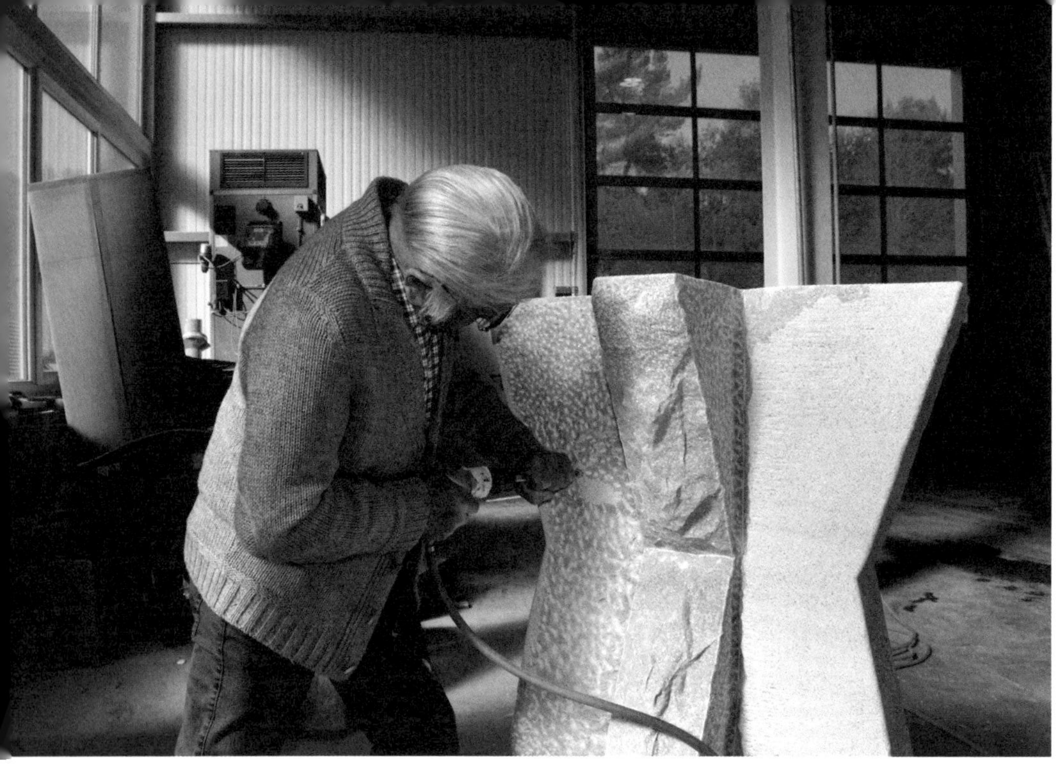

The artist at work
on the sculpture
Untitled
2010

Carrara quarry
early 2000s

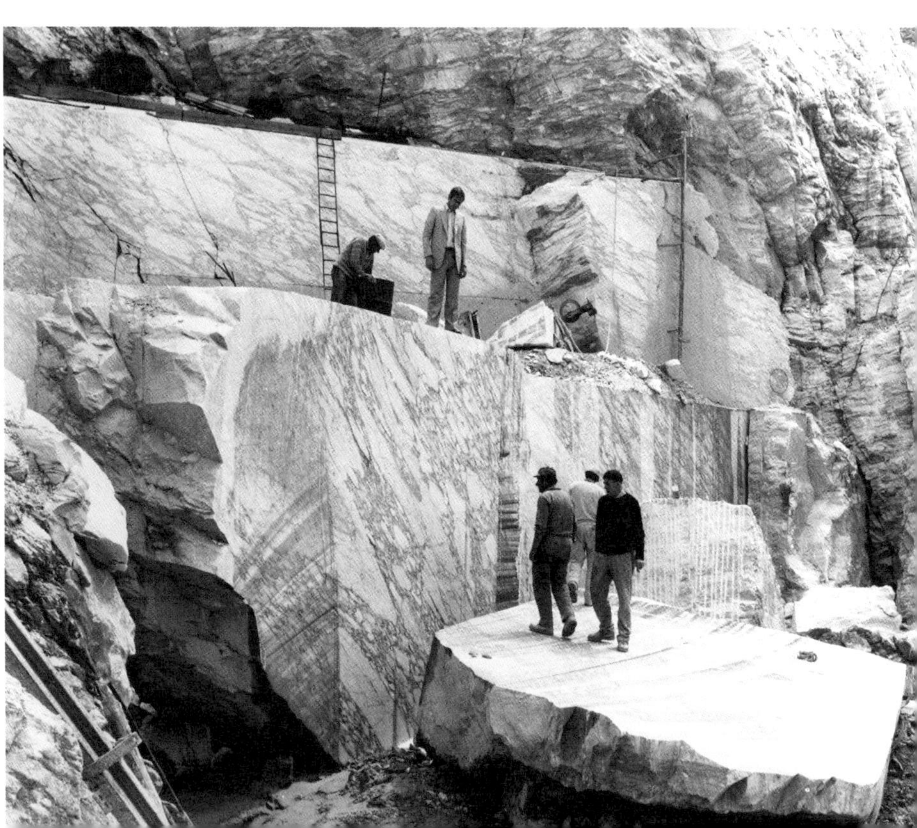

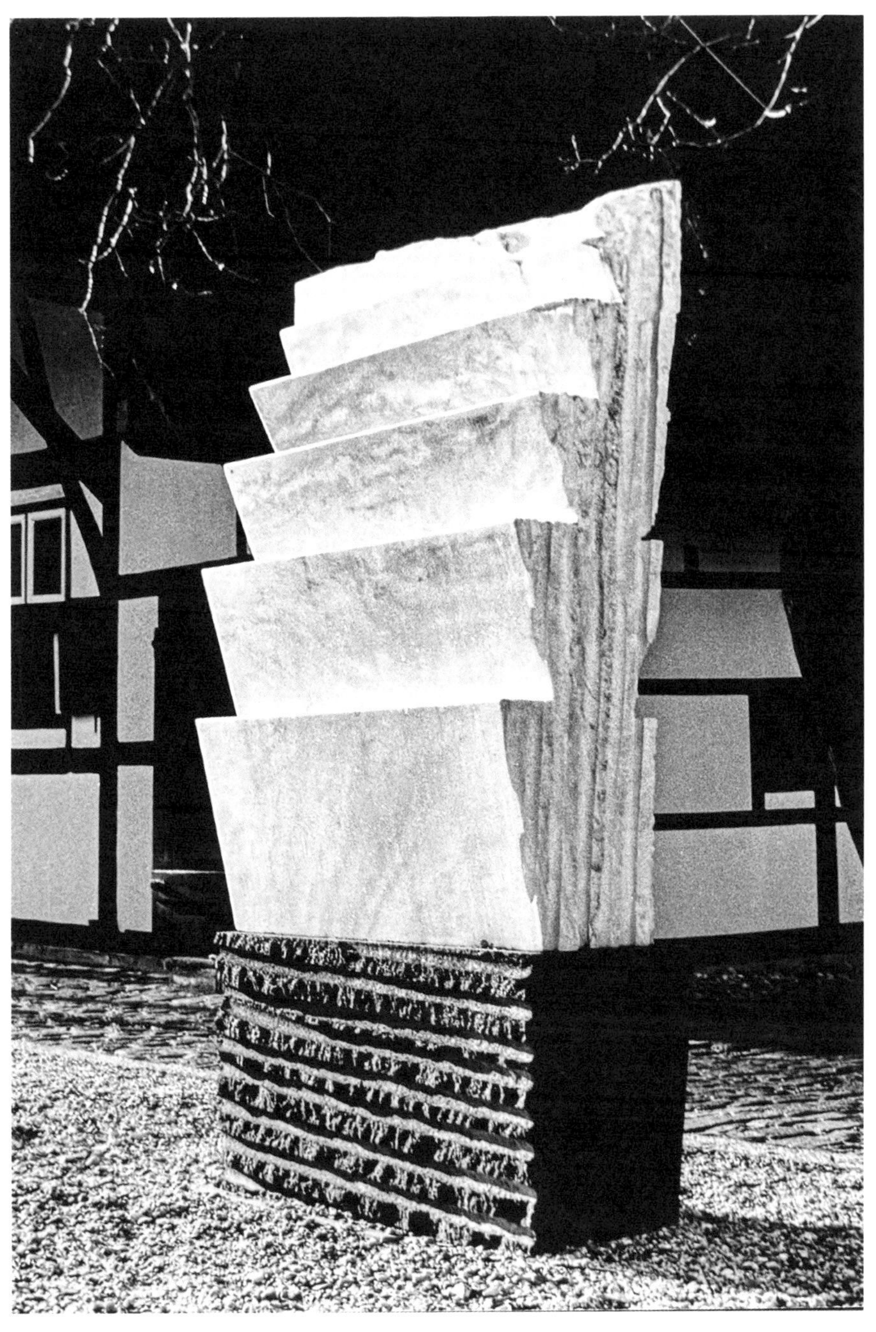

Steps of Shadow and Light
1985

»

With the irrevocable demand that I make on myself to avoid the figurative-sculptural temptations, I was obliged from the beginning to renounce my own sensuality, which would have yielded to those very temptations. This was not so easy, and perhaps the steles in the desert remain a final formulation of a manifestation of the human being, standing upright – with dignity – in boundless space: the stele as a final reduction and compression of space, time and light, and at the same time the stele as the backbone and upright posture of the body per se.

(DECEMBER 2021) «

Mack, winner of the Turner Prize and appointed Commander of the British Empire by Queen Elizabeth II, and Heinz Mack both come from humble backgrounds, were educated and trained in the 1950s and 1960s, and have made highly individual ascents to world fame through sculptural statements developed from within, for which they both had to endure years of disparaging judgement from the art world, a tide which turned in relation to both of them in the 2000s. At times, one is so impressed by the other that no real dialogue develops. Such first encounters are often disappointing.

But Tony Cragg has a knack for making quick, clear decisions: 'Mr Mack, your stone sculptures must be exhibited. I suggest the Waldfrieden Sculpture Park. The summer exhibition. We have six months left.' This was during the COVID-19 pandemic, when artists were largely cut off from the outside world, from exhibitions, audiences, and art fairs.

The exhibition *Heinz Mack. Sculptures* was held at the Waldfrieden Sculpture Park in Wuppertal from 4 July 2021 to 2 January 2022.[243] It was the first exhibition dedicated to the artist's stone sculptures. In the fully glazed hall of the Sculpture Park, aluminium and acrylic glass steles were juxtaposed with wooden sculptures, the visual proximity to the trees of the Sculpture Park adding to the intensity of the works. The smaller hall, at the lower end of the site, featured an ensemble of transparent reliefs and freestanding works in which Mack reinterpreted and reworked aluminium structures and panels a few years ago. At the centre of the exhibition, however, in the third hall with a beautiful view over Wuppertal, were stone sculptures by Heinz Mack. Even the layout of the exhibition was astonishing. A heavy haulage company had to be hired to install the stone sculptures. Works weighing up to 17.5 tonnes were moved into place with precision to the centimetre. This work resembled a dance with heavy loads. One could sense what it means to make stone sculptures today and the special potential they hold.

»

It's been a long time since I've seen a colleague so uninhibitedly committed to a work because he's simply fascinated by it. It really is a phenomenon.

(APRIL 2021) «

Heinz Mack began working with stone sculpture in the mid-1970s, originally in connection with his projects for public spaces. He soon discovered a previously unforeseen effect for his three-dimensional work. Each stone weighs several tonnes, which excludes it from conventional forms of exhibition. Furthermore, unlike wood, metal, and plastic, the internal structure of a stone is not homogeneous and predictable. This means that a stone can sometimes break unexpectedly due to internal stresses. This happened when a stone stele was erected in front of the glazed hall at the Waldfrieden Sculpture Park and, despite the most careful handling of the work, a piece of it suddenly broke off at the top. 'Everything is different with stone', explained the restorer.

» Sculpting is far from easy. Everything costs an incredible amount of money and does not sell at all. What I'm left with are enormous storage costs. It's a crazy world, but a very real one. When works are finally shown in public, it's almost a miracle. I'm hardly exaggerating. « (APRIL 2021)

The artistic effect is also surprising. The ensemble of four black stone sculptures, which was exhibited in the outdoor space next to the upper hall of the Sculpture Park (fig. p. 236), created light effects of a special kind that cannot be achieved with paint on canvas, aluminium, steel, or plastic. At times the stones simply absorbed the sunlight, however strong, and at others they gave off a rhythmic shimmer that changed with the clouds and the time of day. The stones, with their physical weight, formed an absolute setting. But the reflections of light emanating from them dematerialised them, so to speak. One continued to move within Mack's oeuvre, within his formal language.

» Although it may seem that I have dedicated my work exclusively to light, I must explain that although I cannot imagine a sculpture that can live without light, at best light can only ever have the function of immaterialising, dematerialising the material of a sculpture, so that the appearance of the art is enhanced to the point of unreality, which can no longer be explained. « (1994)[244]

Heinz Mack has rethought stone sculpture on the basis of his principles of form. These lead to sculptural approaches to stone that traditional, established stone sculptors would reject from the outset or not consider legitimate and purposeful, starting with the fact that the artist does not carve a sculpture out of the stone, but leaves it in the form in which it came from the quarry. This contradicts the view of both old and new stone sculpture, according to which a figure must be carved out of a block of stone. Surprisingly, however, the stone remains in its cubature as a specific object, resulting in an internal dialogue with Donald Judd and the Minimalism created in New York in the 1960s that continues uninterrupted to this day. The towering granite steles are specific objects in that the viewer is never unaware of the 'back' because he or she recognises that, unlike in the European tradition of sculpture, it certainly cannot be different from the 'front'. Nevertheless, Judd would never have made sculptures in stone: 'Impossible! Much too European!', as Heinz Mack postulates.[245] This gives him an interesting saddle position.

Heinz Mack expands the stone into a sculpture by working its surfaces. He accentuates them either flat or grooved (fig. p. 236). In the first case, this results in seemingly organic, irregular surfaces in which the substance of the respective stone expresses itself and absorbs sunlight and ambient light in different lighting conditions. Alternatively, the surfaces can be polished until the stone takes on a reflective quality. Grooved, horizontal, or vertical structures transform surfaces into reliefs. A stone sculpture whose volume is untouched, and which works only through its lateral surfaces, through their structuring, stands out in the history of sculpture.

» When I work on a sculpture or a relief, I make sure that it expresses no more than a single idea, even though the relationships between the parts may be very complex and multi-layered. « (MAY 2021)

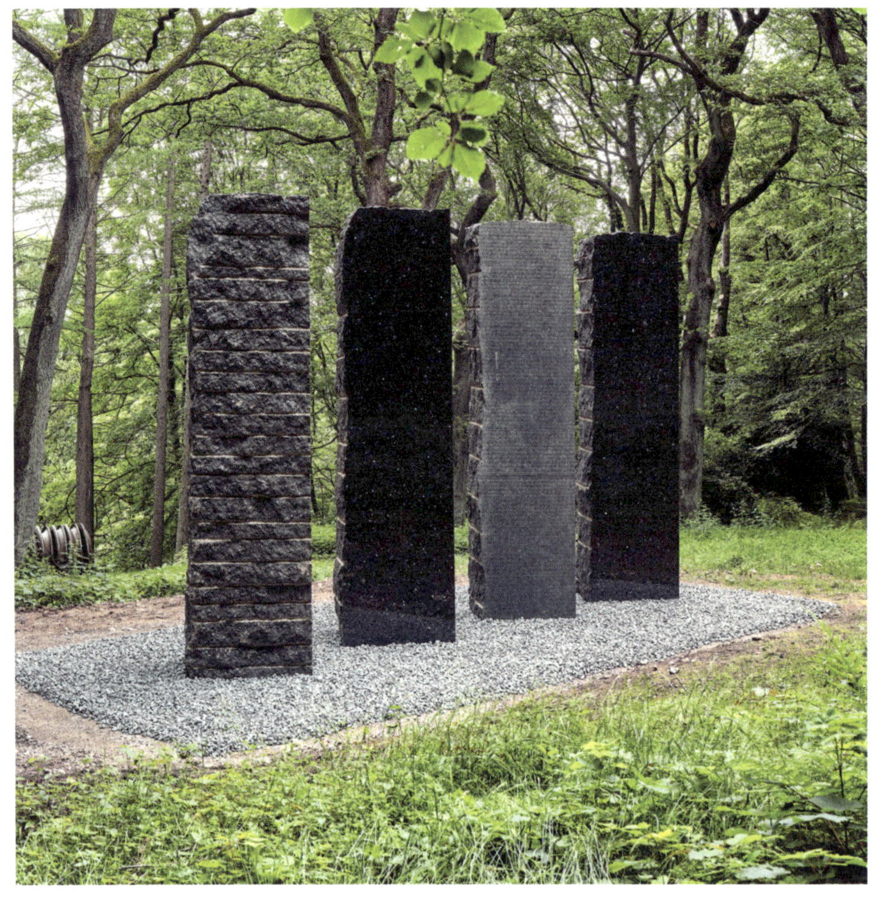

Four Stone Steles, 1995,
in the exhibition
Heinz Mack. Skulpturen
in the Waldfrieden
Sculpture Park, Wuppertal
2021

Ensemble of basalt and granite
sculptures in the exhibition
Heinz Mack. Skulpturen
in the Waldfrieden
Sculpture Park, Wuppertal
2021

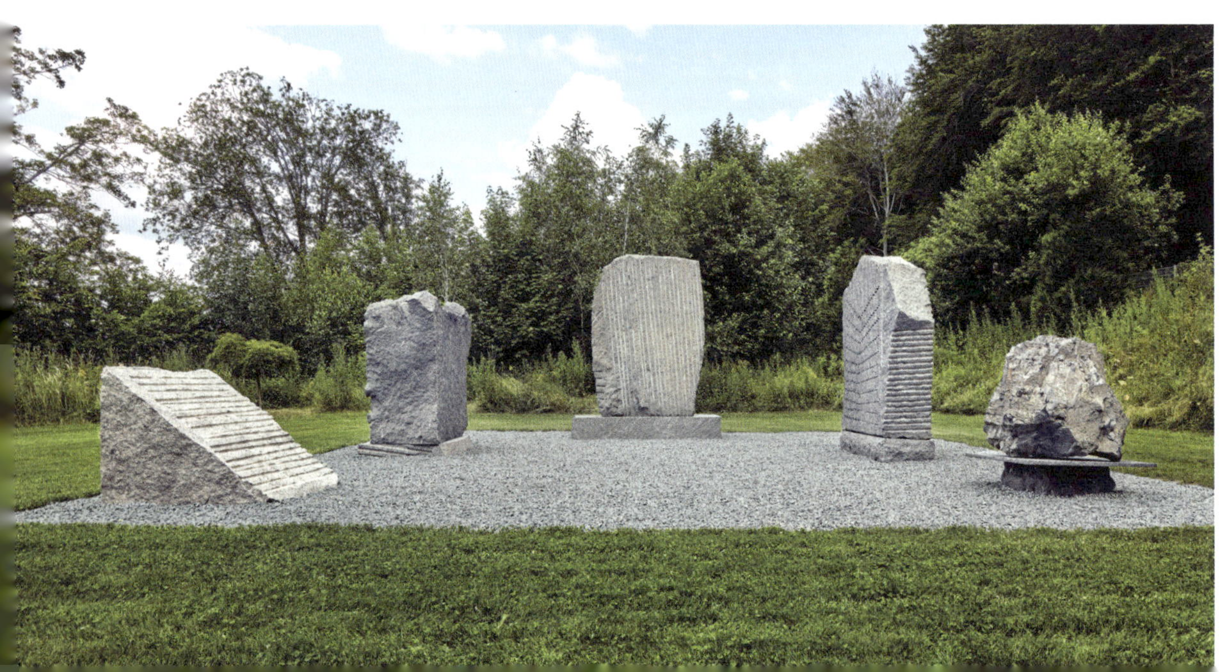

When working with stone, Mack is also concerned with the direct handling of light and rhythm through dynamic structures. It is not the stone that is the object, but its resistance to light. Relief or smooth surface, homogeneous materiality or material combinations characterise the sculptural work in stone. Next to the small building at the Huppertzhof is a test ensemble, a kind of open-air laboratory (fig. p. 240–241). It consists among other things of two dozen sculptures in stone or materials combined with stone, ranging in height from one to two and a half metres. In this relatively small format, the sculptures are tested over months and years to see what would be sculpturally viable in larger dimensions in public space. There is pure marble from Carrara or Austria, worked so that some of the external surfaces are mirrored, with the internal grain of the stone creating a natural dynamic structure. There are also blocks of marble with inlays of rusted steel that rise up, allowing the materials to interact. Glass, stainless steel plates, granite, marble, sandstone, and polished aluminium, each with a different internal structure, appear in various combinations in these test sculptures.[247] Here, nothing has been finalised yet. But this part of the work is obviously very dynamic and capable of development.

» My sculptures are new objects in space, reflectors of light and instruments of movement. Time is visible in their rhythmic structures. I do not make 'objects' because I do not participate in the objectification of our world. « (TYPESCRIPT, BEFORE 1986)[246]

» My new works in granite or marble are resistances to light and at the same time defenders of shadow. They can be as much an expression of energy as the works in metal, whose shiny skin reflects the light. « ('DAS LICHT AUF DER OBERFLÄCHE', 1994)[248]

The basic form of all these sculptures is the stele. Alongside the surface structure and the combination of materials, this is the third essential characteristic of Heinz Mack's large sculptures. The stele is an unusual form that does not exist in the centuries-long history of European sculpture, at least not as an independent form. In Mack's oeuvre, it is rooted in the light steles of the ZERO period and the New York years. The fact that the *Forest of Light* (fig. p. 127), made of aluminium and Plexiglas, would 'transform' into stone could not have been foreseen in 1966. References to this use of the stele form can be found in non-European sculptural traditions, such as the ancient Egyptian obelisks and the later Greek steles, as well as the upright monumental stones – for example at Stonehenge – which can be understood as the primordial gesture of sculpture in human history. However, the experience of the desert was certainly decisive: during Mack's expeditions in 1968, 1976, and 1997, the stele proved to be the ideal form to withstand a space without coordinates and its light (fig. p. 148). This also testifies to the continuity of Mack's oeuvre, which is characterised by numerous discontinuities.

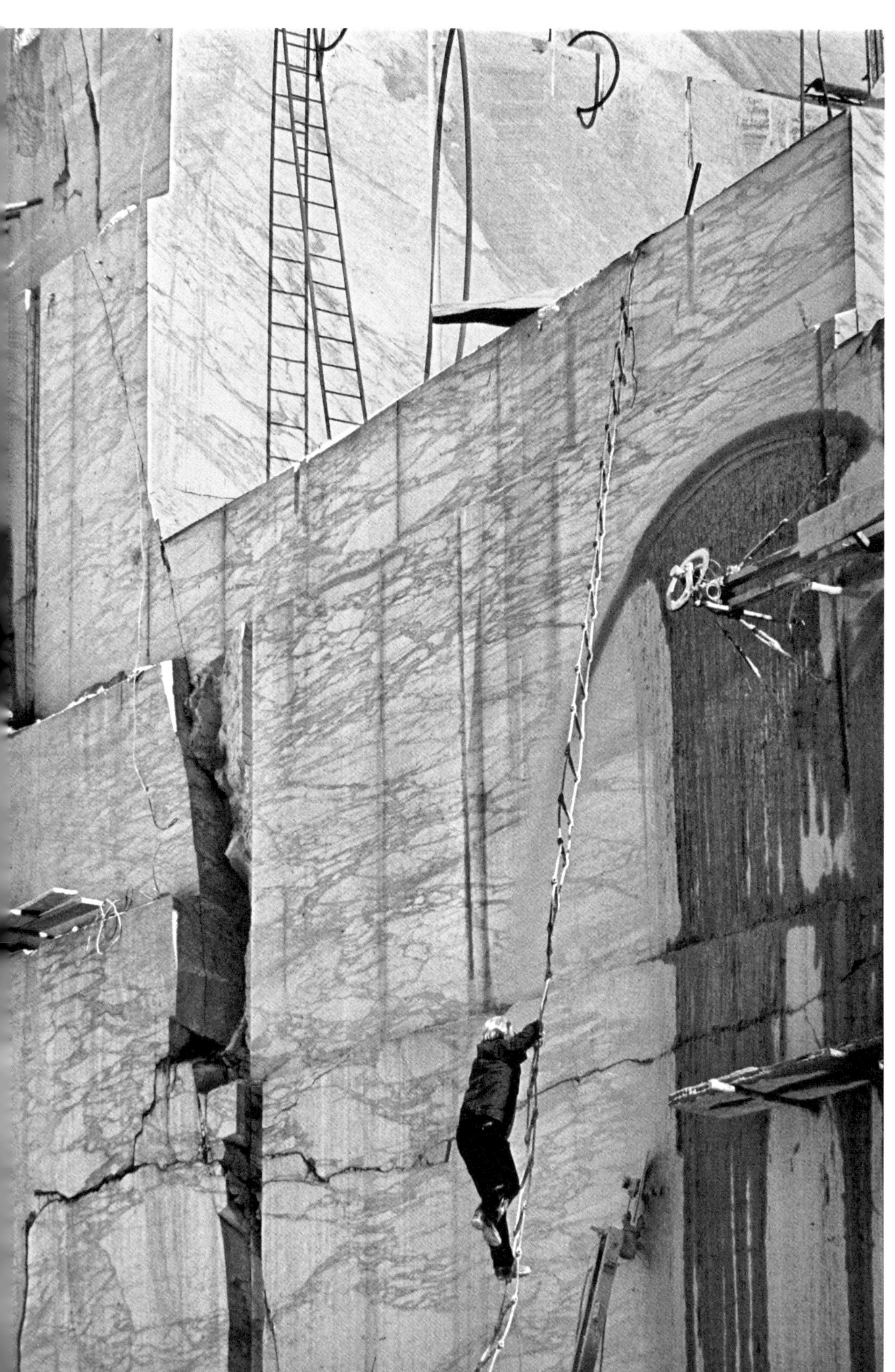

The artist on a swinging ladder
in the Carrara quarries
1983

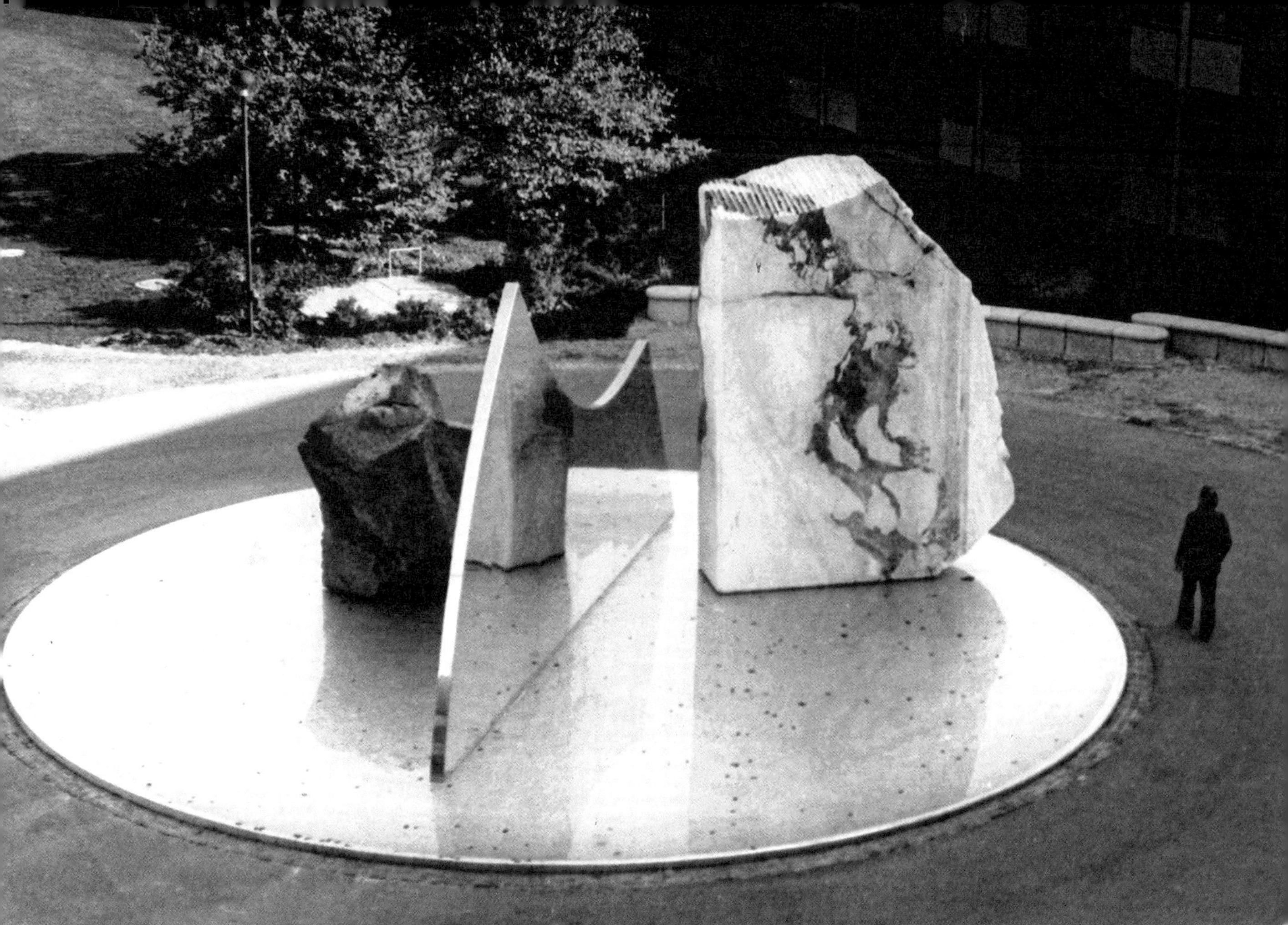

The Love of Stones
1983/84

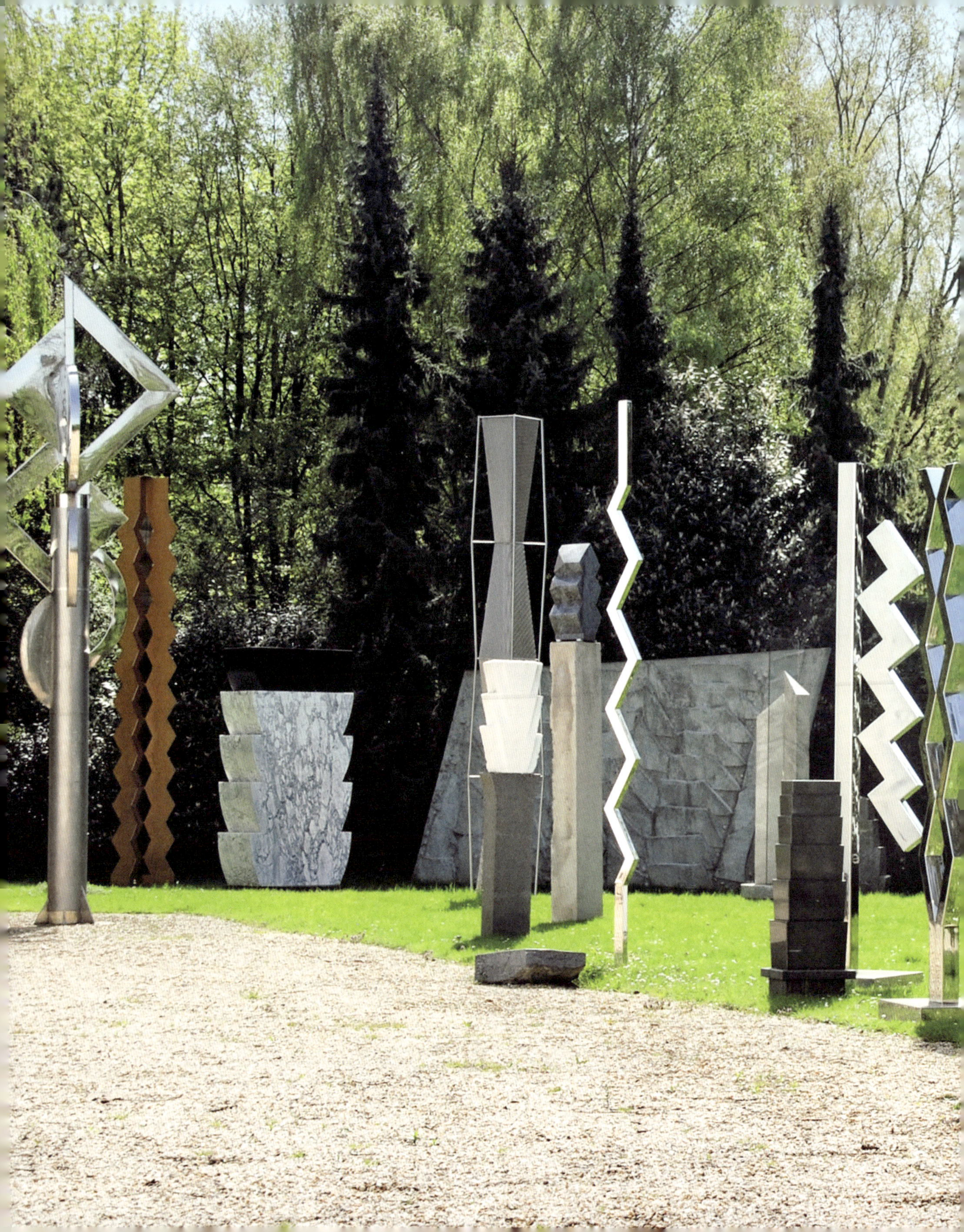

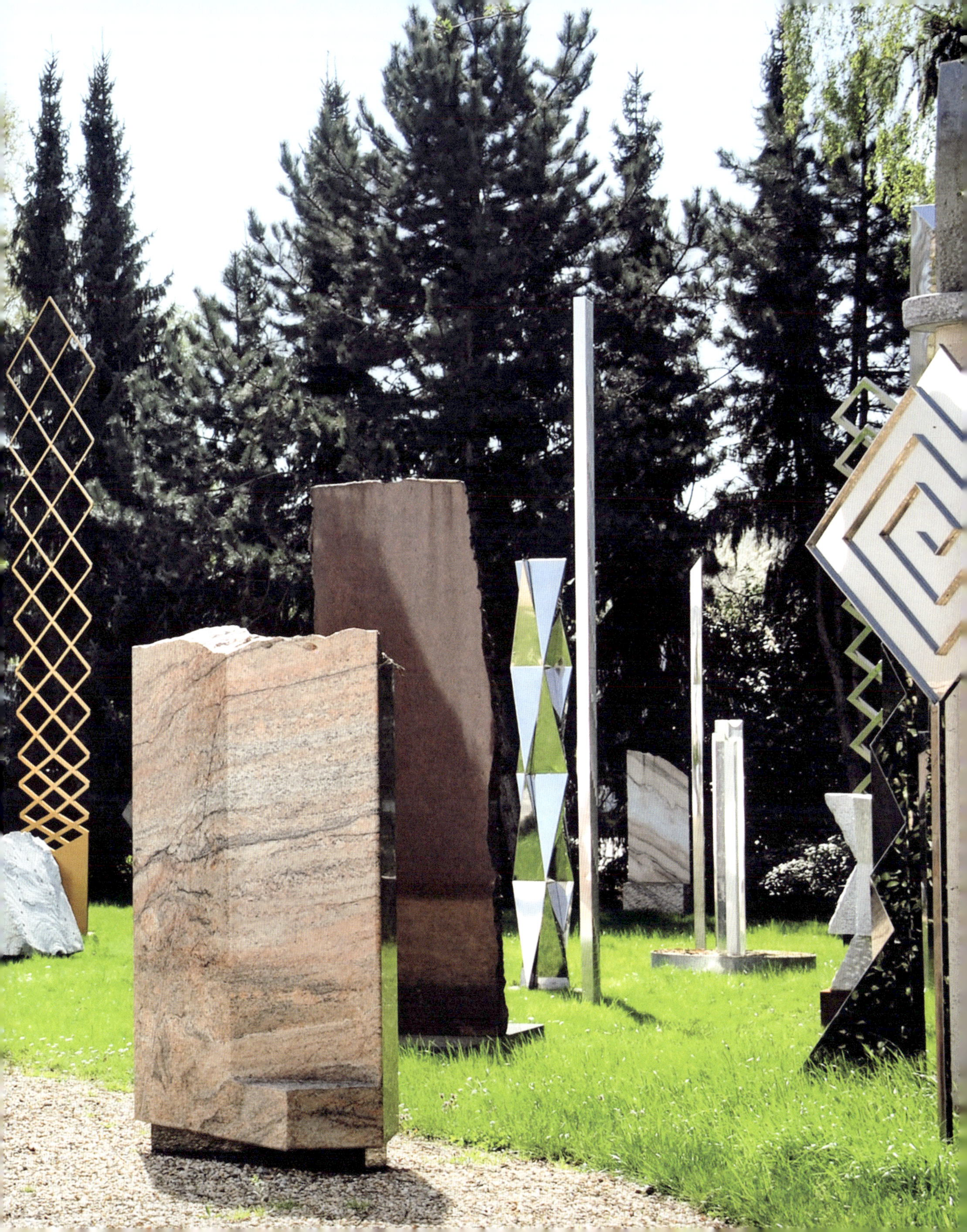

Sculpture, working on sculptures, conceptualising them and the hands-on approach to their final realisation are essential to Heinz Mack. This explains the immediate rapport at the first meeting with Tony Cragg. The only difference is that for the last four decades many of Heinz Mack's sculptures have been made of stone, i.e. volcanic or sedimentary material from the Earth.

All the surfaces of a stunning sculpture that stands – for domestic use, so to speak – near the fishpond at the Huppertzhof (fig. p. 243), are made of polished steel and mirrored glass. The lower half is a square cube. The upper half repeats the same volume with equally reflective rods in a free spatial drawing that could, in a sense, be an homage to Norbert Kricke. The whole thus presents itself as a low, two-part stele. Day after day, the cube of the lower part reflects the immediate surroundings: the lawn and the pond with the Japanese fish that register every human presence. The dialogue between light and sculptural volume continues here in a completely reflective work. Like many of the artist's sculptures, this one is radical. In another context of light and environment, it would be dead. Here, however, it is phenomenal because it has been positioned so that it is always in the light.

» I am a painter on the one hand and a sculptor on the other. I cannot separate the two. And I finance the sculpture, which is difficult to sell, with the painting.

(MAY 2023) «

←
View of the artist's sculpture garden in Mönchengladbach
2021

→
Spatial Grid
1977/78
(based on a design from 1964)

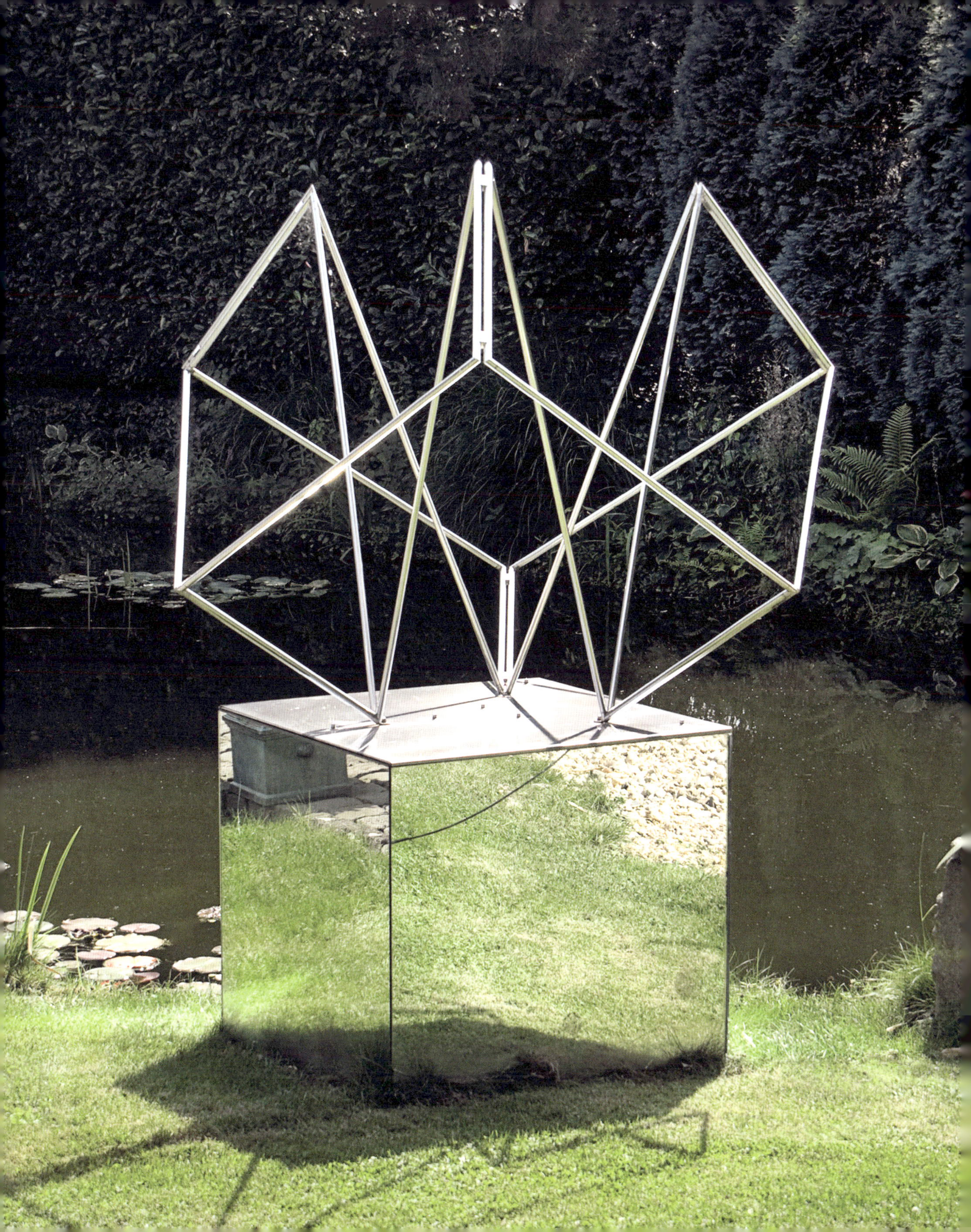

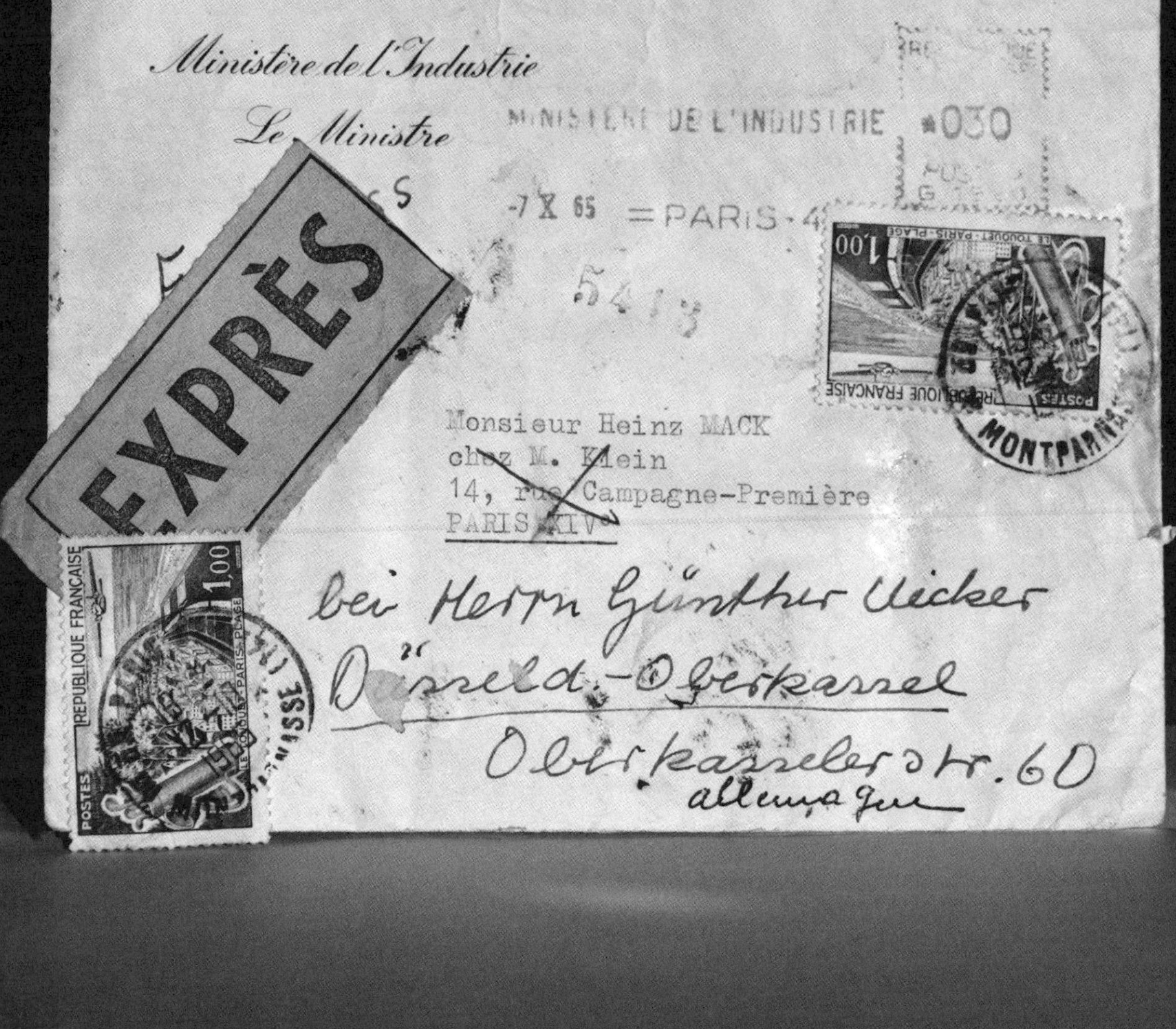
Ministère de l'Industrie
Le Ministre
MINISTERE DE L'INDUSTRIE
030
-7 X 65
PARIS
EXPRÈS
1,00
LE TOUQUET - PARIS - PLAGE
POSTES
REPUBLIQUE FRANÇAISE
MONTPARNASSE
Monsieur Heinz MACK
chez M. Klein
14, rue Campagne-Première
PARIS XIV
bei Herrn Günther Uecker
Düsseld.-Oberkassel
Oberkasselerstr. 60
allemagne

THE IMAGINARY MUSEUM

Envelope for a letter, probably from Pierre Restany, from the office of the French Minister of Industry to Heinz Mack, initially addressed to the flat of the (deceased) Yves Klein in Paris, then to Günther Uecker in Düsseldorf
7 October 1965

André Malraux was one of the most influential figures of the decades around the middle of the twentieth century. He was a world-famous novelist, an organiser of the anti-fascist movement of European artists against Hitler's Germany, a fighter in the Spanish Civil War on the Republican side, a leading figure in the French Resistance, a general in the French army during the victory over Nazi Germany, one of Charles de Gaulle's closest confidants in the politically turbulent post-war period and, under his presidency from 1959, the first French minister exclusively for culture and, as Ministre d'État, the number two in the government. His speeches as Minister of Culture – including at the first state funerals for visual artists[249] – have gone down in literary history. Meeting Malraux must have been an unforgettable experience. A novelist with the charisma of Ernest Hemingway and James Joyce, he was also one of Pablo Picasso's closest interlocutors.

»

In 1965, I was awarded a prize at the Biennale de Paris. The curator of the German contribution was the Art Informel painter Thomas Grochowiak. Mr Malraux, the Minister of Culture, shook my hand. It was a cash prize, several thousand French francs. You had to spend the money in France. That was impractical. I said to Mr Malraux, in English, that it was a pity our countries didn't have a common currency. It would simplify a lot of things. He agreed and, speaking unflinchingly in French, moved on to the next prize-winner.

(NOVEMBER 2021) «

Malraux was a colourful character. After only nine months in his ministerial post, he organised the first Paris Biennale in 1959, only the third biennale at the time alongside the Venice Biennale, founded in 1898, and the São Paulo Biennale, which had been held since 1952. This Biennale de Paris was explicitly a 'Biennale des Jeunes', an exhibition for young artists selected for each country by independent art critics. The German selection for 1965 included Heinz Mack, who was awarded the Biennale Prize. Katharina Sieverding also took part, at the time still a student in Theo Otto's stage design class at the Düsseldorf Academy of Art and a successful freelance set designer, before switching to Joseph Beuys's class and, based on new forms of the image,[250] becoming a conceptual artist, related to André Malraux. She remembers the evening when, after Heinz Mack had been awarded the prize, the artist Rotraut received a small group in her apartment in Rue Campagne-Première, where she had lived with Yves Klein. Being allowed to go there as a twenty-four-year-old made a big impression on Sieverding. It was one of those moments when you realise what an international artistic career is and how to go about it.[251]

André Malraux's lasting significance in the art world, however, is based on a book that he published in its first version in 1947 and expanded into a multi-volume series around 1950, in which he presented 'world art' as such for the first time, using – for technical reasons – exclusively black-and-white photographs. *Le Musée imaginaire* from 1947 has been translated as *Das imaginäre Museum* since the first German edition was published in 1949.[252] This is literally correct, but it narrows down the resonant French spectrum of meaning of *l'imaginaire*, which includes 'pictorial imagination'.[253]

In his preface, Malraux writes: 'Today, every student has access to colour reproductions of the most important works of art. They also discover many second-rate sculptures as well as archaic art, Indian, Chinese, Japanese and pre-Columbian sculpture from their respective heyday, some Byzantine art, Roman frescoes, African art and folk art. For comparison, how many statues were reproduced in 1850? Today's art books have found their most concise field in sculpture, which black-and-white illustrations reproduce more faithfully than paintings. In the past, people only knew the Louvre (and a few smaller collections). Visits to museums were poorly remembered. By contrast, we have access to precise images of far more important works than the largest museum imaginable could display. And the precision of the images helps our memory where it fails, especially in the details and in the big picture. An imaginary museum has been created that will take the incomplete confrontation with art that takes place in real museums into entirely new realms. In response to the challenge posed by museums, the visual arts have invented the printing press for themselves.'[254]

In his conclusion, André Malraux refers to the revolution unleashed by Johann Gutenberg's invention of the printing press in the fifteenth century, an epochal event. The mechanical reproduction[255] and publication of all available works of art thanks to new photographic techniques and offset printing would fundamentally change artistic production, Malraux argued in 1947.[256]

» I tried to learn something as quickly as possible and get an overview of what was happening in the world. That ended again, I guess at the end of the 1950s, with Malraux. «

(NOVEMBER 2021)

» I will not continue or repeat such attempts to paint in direct dialogue with other works, as exciting and challenging as they were for me. I am aware that these pictures, painted after Matisse and Gauguin (fig. pp. 248 f., 252 f.), have not produced any fundamental innovations. You could say that I have re-orchestrated and transformed a classical musical composition. «

(DECEMBER 2022)

Heinz Mack has been exploring the concept of the imaginary museum intensively over the past few years. It began with two paintings (fig. pp. 249, 253) that were created during the COVID-19 pandemic in 2021–22, in direct confrontation with paintings by Paul Gauguin and Henri Matisse that had impressed him early on. They mark the beginning of the freedom of colour that has characterised his work ever since.

The artist then went on to examine in detail works that he considered to be references in the history of painting, resulting in an innovative chapter in the monograph *Painting* from 2023.[257] In the context of the retrospective of his kinetic and ZERO works at the ZKM | Center for Art and Media Karlsruhe in the same year, he began to extend this reflection on works that were or are important to him in terms of his entire oeuvre, resulting in his *Compendium*[258] (fig. pp. 258–261), which in its development can be compared to the *Mackazin* of 1967.[259]

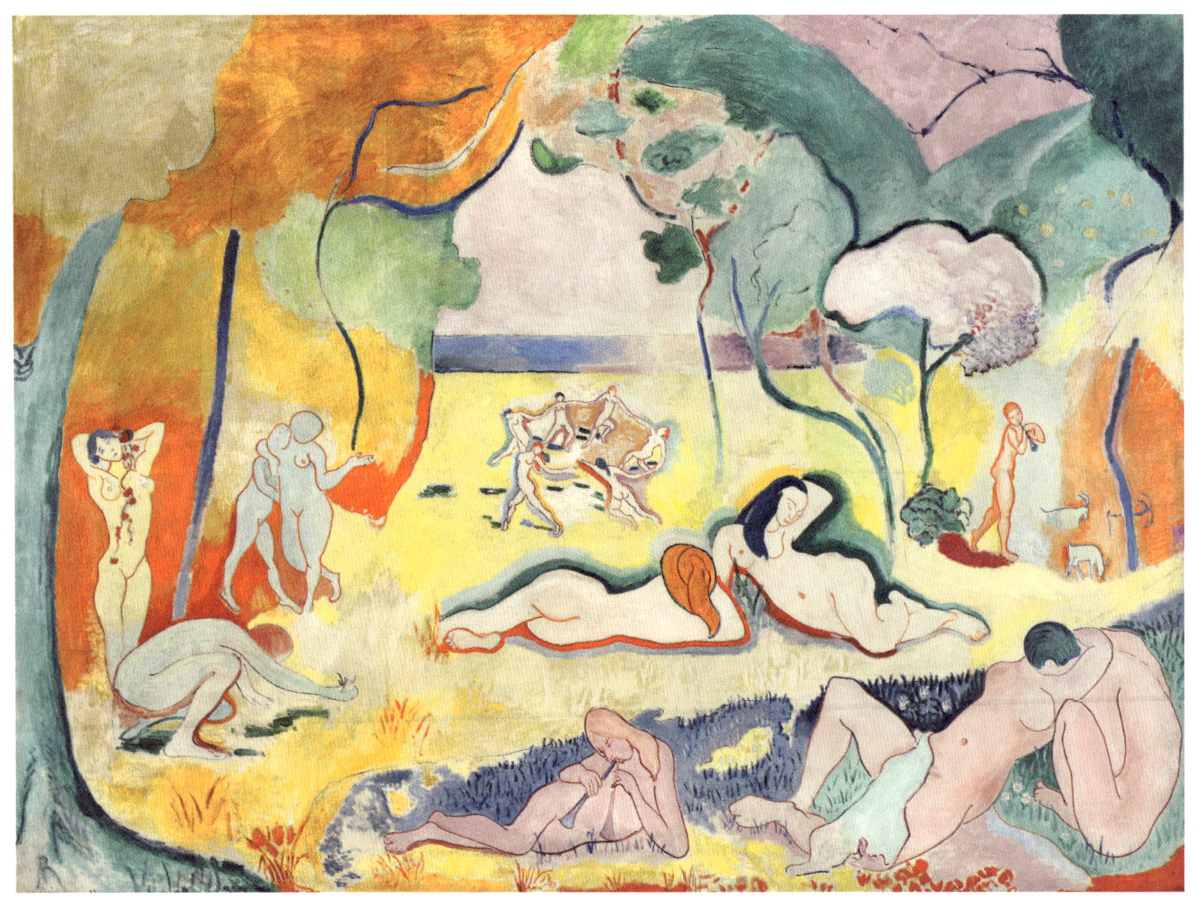

Henri Matisse
Le Bonheur de vivre
(*The Joy of Life*)
1905/06

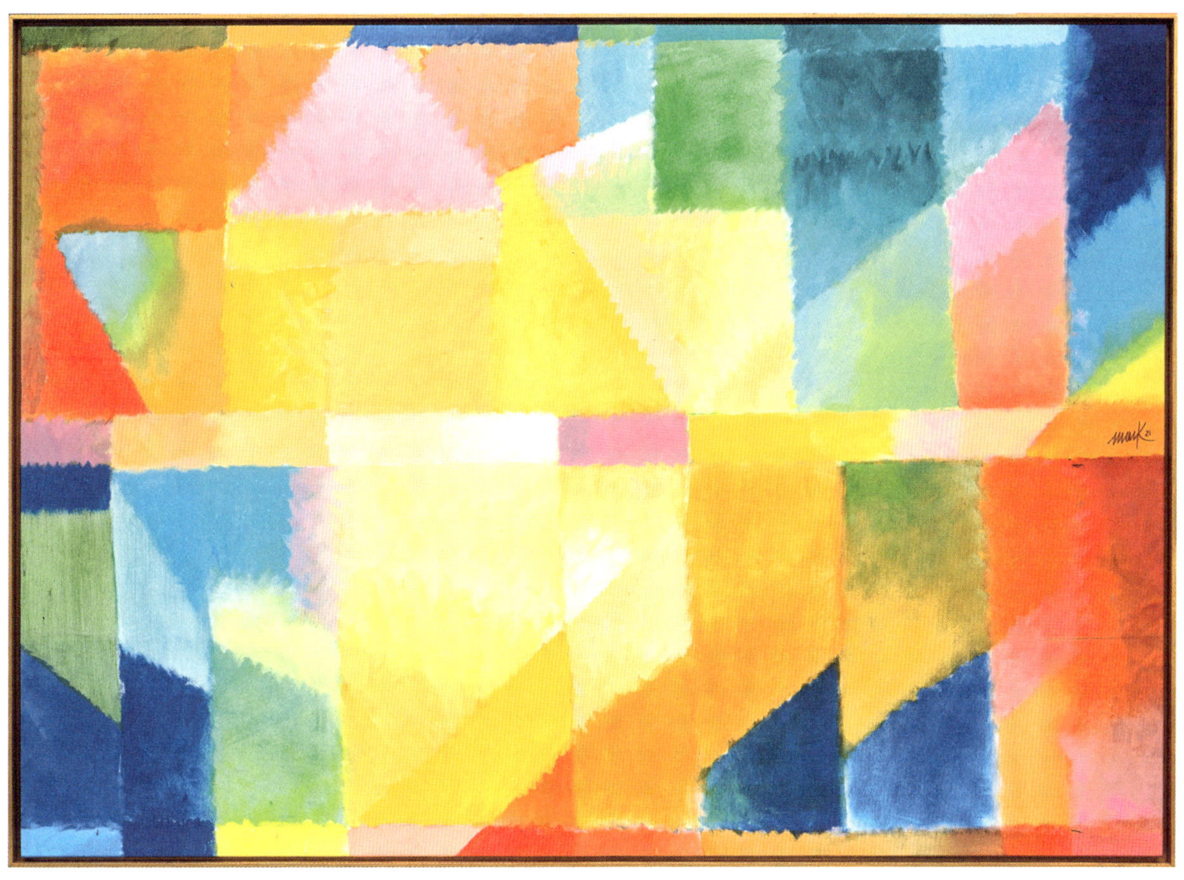

Untitled
(Chromatic Constellation)
2021

»

This anthology, this compendium that I have created, means a lot to me. All this material is still being completed. We are by no means at the end. It would be exciting if later on interested parties or art historians would compare things I have done with things others have done and see that these elective affinities have emerged unconsciously, by chance, and that they are made visible. There's a chapter that we carefully put together, Sophia Sotke and I (fig. pp. 258–261). There are drawings that I made that are reminiscent of the diagrams that the atomic physicists in Jülich see under the microscope. We try to maintain this contact with science. This brings us back to the old claim from the Renaissance. So the old story is still relevant today, that art and science have a relationship. And that brings us back to the topic of structure, because these scientists all think structurally.

(FEBRUARY 2024) «

Malraux was less interested in what the imaginary museums of individual artists would look like than in the phenomenon itself. In particular, he believed that there was now a first generation capable of creating an imaginary museum of works of art from different parts of the world and all periods of human history through illustrations in books, and thus of rethinking art.

For this first generation of the imaginary museum, the unexpected situation, the wealth of associations and the equivalence that Malraux presented in his book must have been breathtaking. It was a generation that experienced at a young age how great parts of human history that had never before been photographed were brought into consciousness: Troy, Egyptian royal tombs, the Majas and other non-European peoples, the remaining Indigenous peoples, cave paintings. André Malraux was also thinking of this generation because, for the first time, they were able to use photography as a matter of course and thus potentially had the entire art of mankind at their disposal in pictorial form. His great merit lies in his visionary description of how this would change everything for artistic production.

Heinz Mack's awareness of belonging to this first generation of the imaginary museum, which was able to deal with the pictorial co-presence of art from the entire history of mankind through its photographic reproduction, predates the invention of ZERO in 1957–58. ZERO itself is therefore not least a child of the imaginary museum.[260] At that time, it was no longer necessary to visit the Musée du Louvre in Paris or the British Museum in London, the only comprehensive museums of human art in Western Europe at the time. André Malraux's illustrated books from the 1950s, each five hundred pages long, deal with different aspects of world art, present them simultaneously, and manage almost without linguistic commentary. From 1954, when optimism returned after the hard post-war years, major comprehensive art history exhibitions on all eras were organised by the Council of Europe. The imaginary museum was thus present on several occasions.

How is the imaginary museum reflected in ZERO? Archaising references of various kinds, relief forms, memories of fire cults and sun worship, the independent, pictorially sparse ornamentation that is charged in a new way in ZERO art, were not present in the strictly European repertoire of forms of previous generations of artists.[261] Here, all this was co-present for the first time. ZERO, or at least its aspects beyond the utopia of a technological age, is inconceivable without the 'imaginary museum'.

ZERO is also interesting for contemporary artists because the works created at that time are a conglomerate of the latest and the oldest art. ZERO was about the art of the future. To a considerable extent, however, it was reinvented from several millennia-old forms. Was this easier around 1960, when the 'imaginary museum' was still young, than it is today, when we have access to images of all kinds in the age of a virtual, potentially all-encompassing archive? In any case, Heinz Mack's oeuvre spans a period that began with the 'imaginary museum' as a new idea and a new reality, right up to the present day, seventy years later, with the co-presence of supposedly all the images that have ever been created.

For Heinz Mack, the awareness of an imaginary museum beyond ZERO is fundamental to his work. One concept familiar to the artist from his philosophical studies has not yet been discussed: dialectics. From the 1960s to the 1980s, many people could no longer hear this word because it was used like a mantra in Marxism-Leninism and neo-Marxism. Yet dialectics – thesis, antithesis, and their resolution – plays a central role in Heinz Mack's artistic thinking and in his approach to the entire history of art. Much of his work is conceived and constructed dialectically.

Heinz Mack became an artist of the imaginary museum above all in his 'second oeuvre', which began in the late 1960s, after the dissolution of ZERO. The *Compendium* he has compiled since 2023 is only at first glance comparable to Gerhard Richter's *Atlas*, which was prominently exhibited at *documenta X* in Kassel in 1997. Richter's work is an ensemble of potential or concrete source images for his own works, whereas Mack's *Compendium* consists of comparative images and elective affinities. These come from the fields of technology and science or reflect works of art from all times and cultures.

Heinz Mack's imaginary museum is characterised by the fact that it does not consist of book knowledge, although his library is well stocked for this purpose, but of memories of art monuments that he himself has seen on all continents, especially outside the European cultural sphere. We saw at the beginning of this volume that there is no day off or holiday for Heinz Mack. Nor does he go on tourist or pleasure trips. Every now and then he sets off on a long journey for study purposes, and he is well prepared. Recent trips have taken him to little-explored regions of Central Asia and sub-Saharan Africa. Mack's imaginary museum is based on what he sees on site, on real objects, and not, or only marginally, on photographic images, as presented in Malraux's analyses and series of books from 1947 onwards. These inspired Mack to take an almost encyclopaedic look at non-European, ancient, and prehistoric art in order to place his own artistic work on a much broader cultural basis than had previously been conceivable.

» I am neither the first nor the last person to ascribe an important role to the triangle. I am very keen to think in larger art historical dimensions, so as not to get caught up in the events of the day. So I am a passionate advocate of looking at art in terms of art historical comparisons. They are so incredibly important. «

(DECEMBER 2022)

Although the artist never uses the term, there is an educational ideal behind it. Anyone who has been influenced by Johann Wolfgang von Goethe, Friedrich Schiller, and Wilhelm and Alexander von Humboldt to such an extent cannot avoid this in his

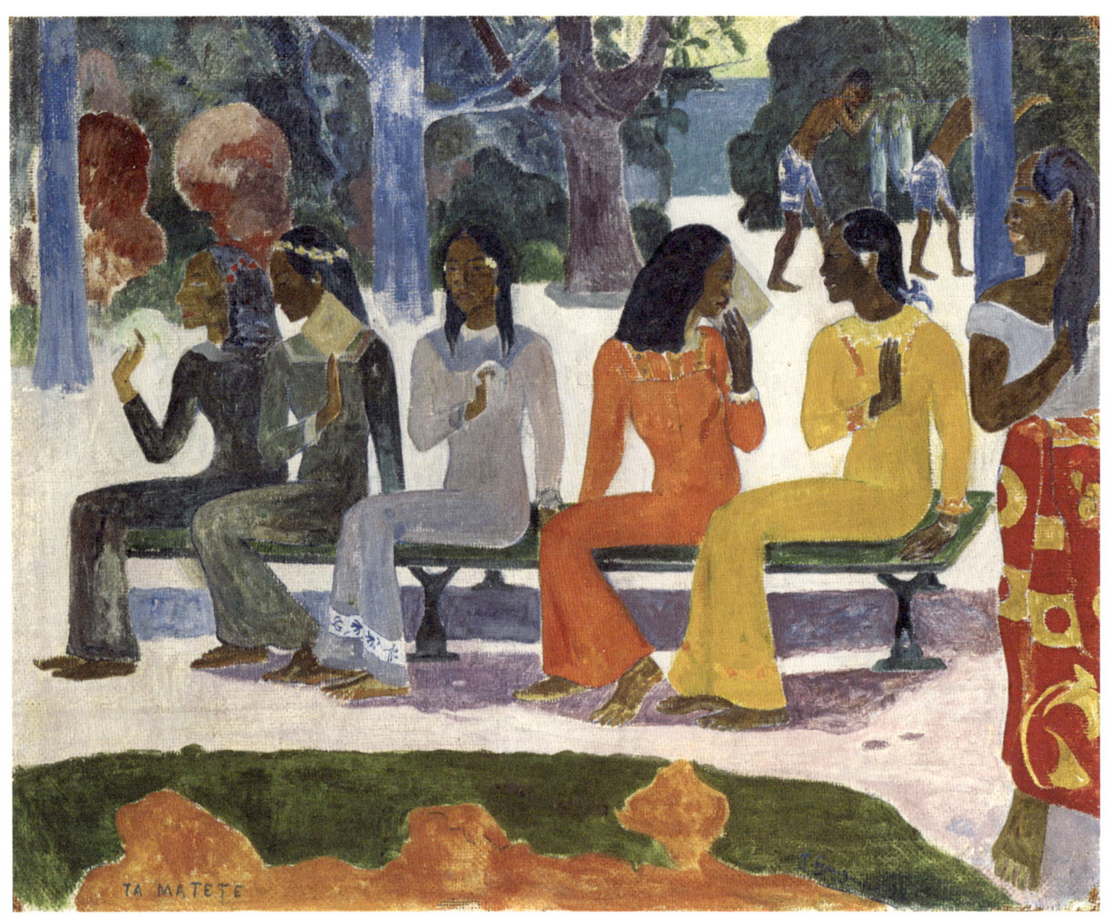

Paul Gauguin
***Ta matete* (*Le Marché*)**
1892

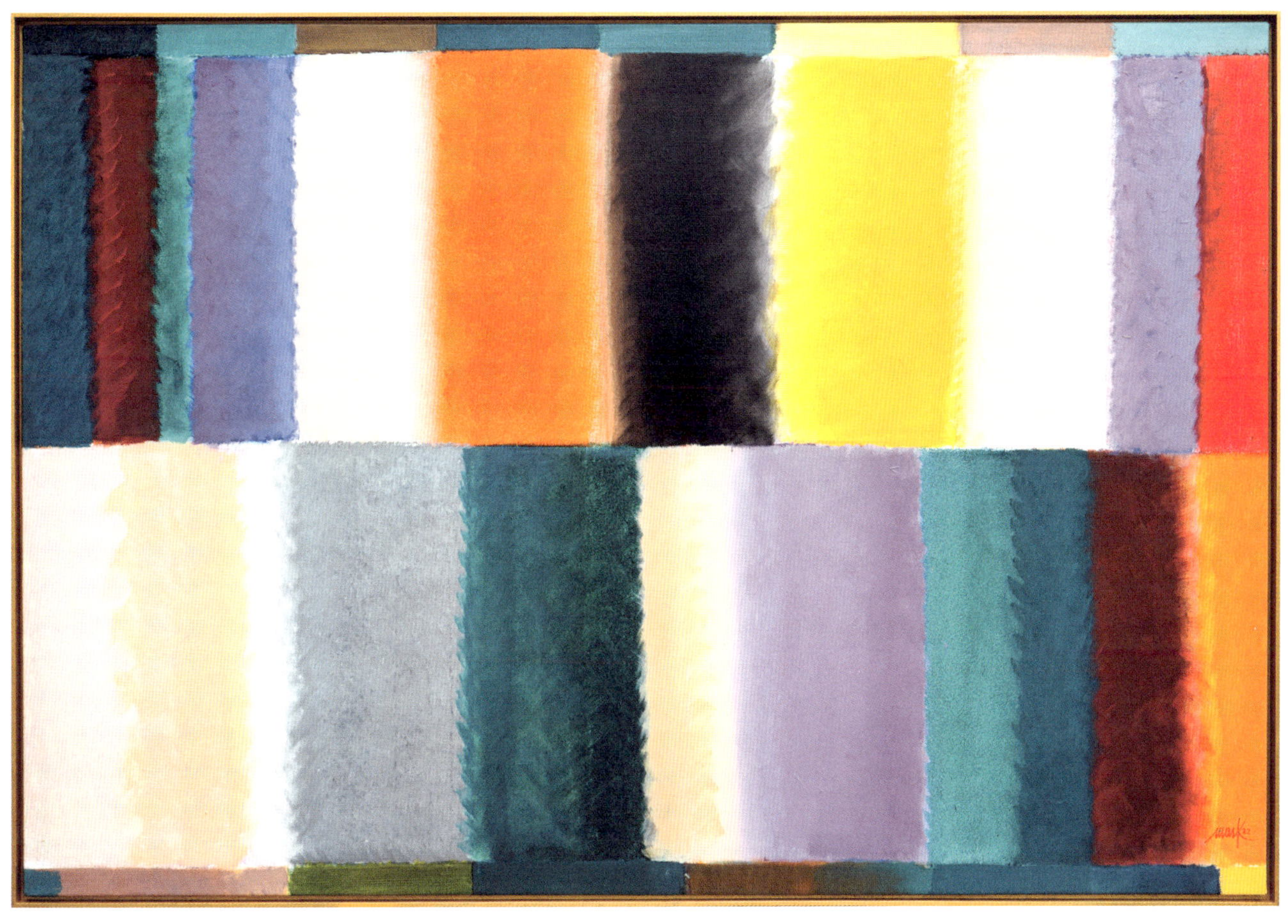

After Gauguin – Ta matete
(Chromatic Constellation)
2022

»

For me, Brancusi's *Endless Column* has always been a point of reference. So these are all things that I have seen personally, on site, all the things in China, India, Indonesia, and Burma. Then there's Africa. Of course, all of that has found its way into my work somewhere, in terms of rhythm, sequencing, different principles of sequencing, and that has a lot to do with my sculptures as well.

(SEPTEMBER 2021) «

own life. Over the decades, Heinz Mack has acquired an education in the sense of the German intellectual tradition of the nineteenth century that is rare in our time. It is, however, much more oriented towards the art of all humanity and science than was usual two hundred years ago, when it was largely limited to Greek and Roman antiquity and their successors. This is linked to a second concept, which the artist also does not express in relation to himself, but which is present in his mind: humanism. This has had bad press in the last fifty years or so, but it results from the practised and, so to speak, globalised ideal of education as a lived attitude. In a third respect, it corresponds to the ideal of universality. The fact that Heinz Mack uses all the materials of sculpture, including glass and ceramics, which north of the Alps are often derided as second-rate forms of applied art, has not always been understood, but is explained by the universality that is essential to his artistic approach.

From today's perspective, Malraux's 'imaginary museum' is conceived in a postcolonial way:[262] with the emancipation and equal treatment of all arts, artistic forms of expression, peoples and times, and this for their own intrinsic value, always at the respective highest artistic level. The idea behind this is that folklore and the spirit of the times do not transcend the present day in any culture – rather, transcending time is the eminent task of art. From Malraux, Heinz Mack also learned to 'think in the three hundred centuries of art', as Pierre Soulages used to say.[263]

Mack's interest in knowledge, which underlies his approach to the imaginary museum, is also evident in two extraordinary collections of non-European artefacts that the artist has assembled, some of which are present in his living and working environment. One consists of kilim carpets, the other of African sculptures.[264] In both cases, the selected objects are arranged in rows so that, although the works come from very different civilisational and cultural contexts, they are related to the formal language that the artist called 'dynamic structure' in 1958 (cf. p. 65). Together with his own sculptures, paintings, and objects, this results in an ongoing intercultural dialogue, traces of which can be found throughout his oeuvre.

»

In the Occident, we are arrogant about things and have long taken it for granted that art should imitate. In Europe, we had completely forgotten that the whole of the Orient is entirely non-objective. Around 1910, Europe finally caught up, and the first completely non-objective pictures were painted here. At that time, nobody thought or talked about the fact that it already existed all over the world. For a long time, art history was incredibly

wo Kommen wir her
wo Kommen wir her
wo Kommen wir her

wo sind wir
wo sind wir
wo sind wir

wohin gehen wir
wohin gehen wir
wohin gehen wir

Where Do We Come From?
Where Are We?
Where Are We Going?
1960

narrow-minded. The Eurocentric perspective on art history or the West-centric perspective has been criticised for some time now, and there are many publications on the artistic appropriation of African and Oceanic art. In early abstract art, the Orient was very much taken up. Jackson Pollock, in turn, would have been inconceivable without Native American art, to which he made extreme references and which he collected with passion. But at that time, around 1955, it wasn't an issue. It was not talked about. The 'new Americans' were the stars and the heroes.

(MAY 2023) «

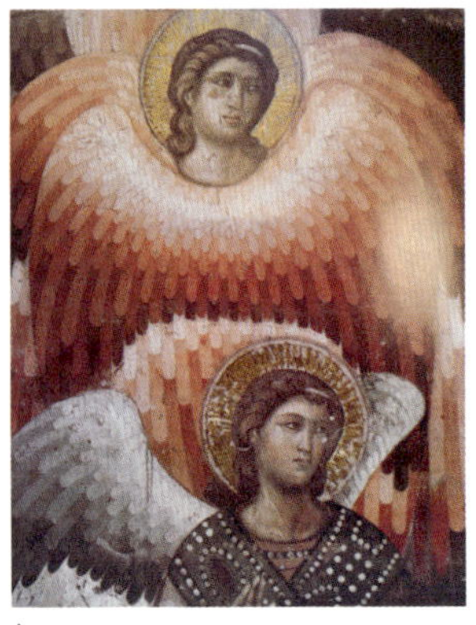

A

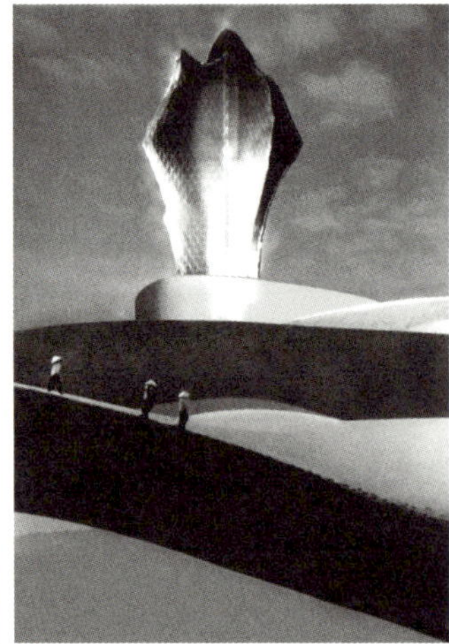

B

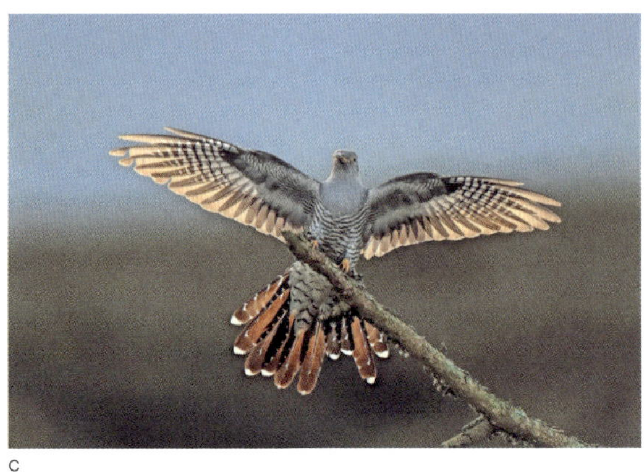

C

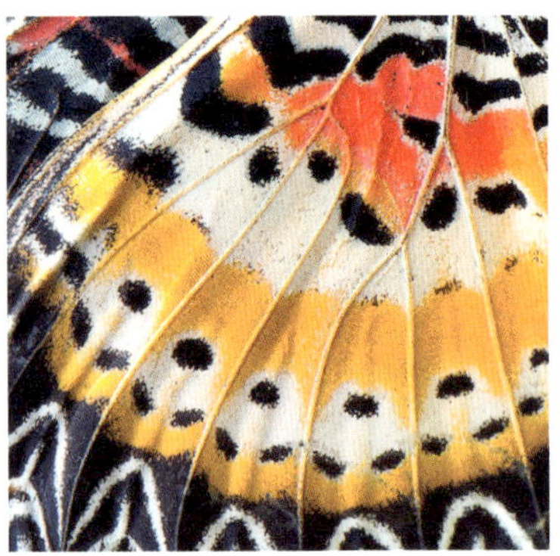

D

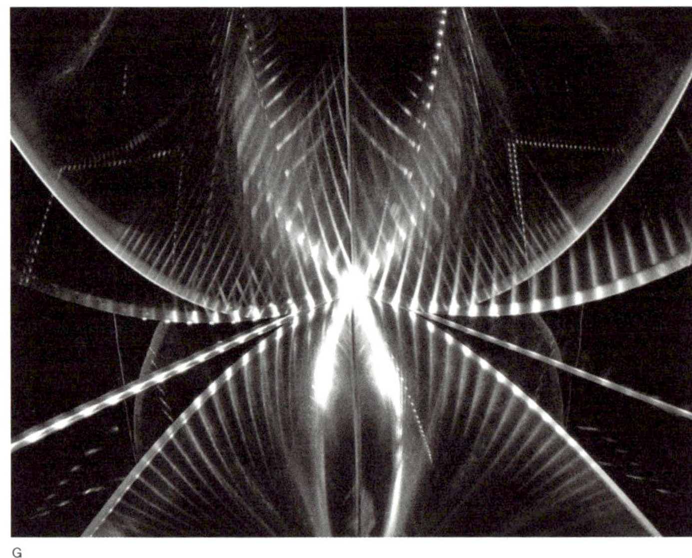

G

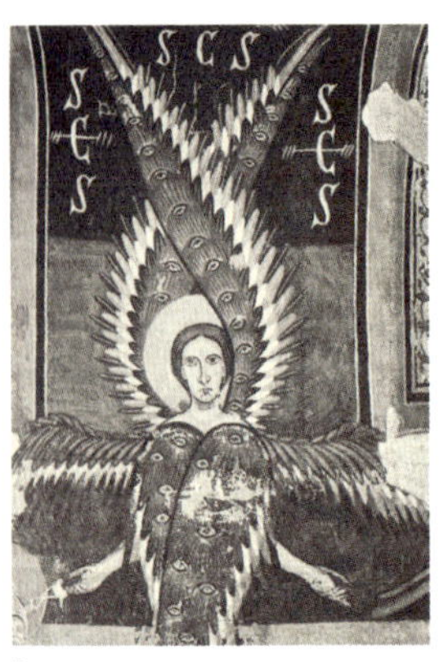

E

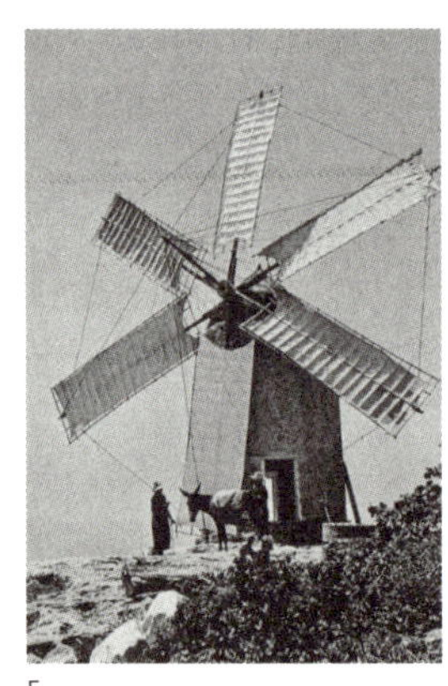

F

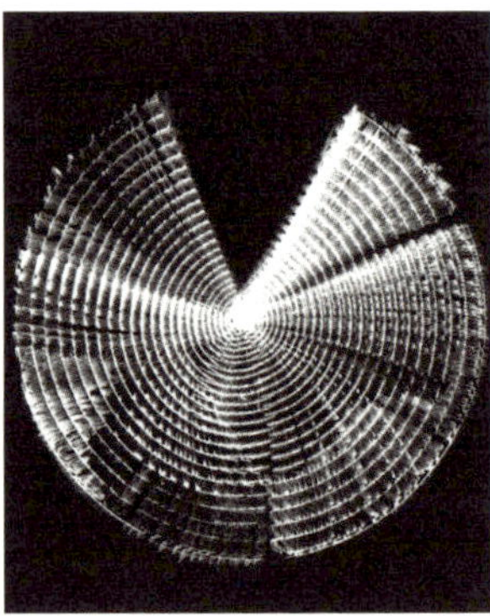

H

Extract from Heinz Mack's *Compendium*

A Pietro Cavallini, *Jesus Christ with Angels from the Last Judgement* (detail), Santa Cecilia in Trastevere, Rome, c. 1289/93
B Heinz Mack, *Night and Light Sculpture in the Desert*, c. 1970
C Cuckoo
D Close-up of the wing of a monarch butterfly
E *Seraphim fresco*, 13th century, Sant Climent de Taüll, Catalonia
F Windmill on Formentera, Balearic Islands
G Heinz Mack, *Untitled (Photo Experiment)*, 2016
H Heinz Mack, *Drawing of a Wing*, c. 1970
I Heinz Mack, *Light Wings in the Sky*, c. 1970
J Large futuristic passenger aeroplane with combined wing shapes
K Jacques Rougerie, *Model of the city of Mériens*, 2015
L Naum Gabo, *Linear Construction No. 2*, 1970/71
M Kinetic energy weapon of the US Army for the Homing Overlay Experiment, 1980s
N Heinz Mack, *Photo Experiment with Acrylic Glass Object*, undated

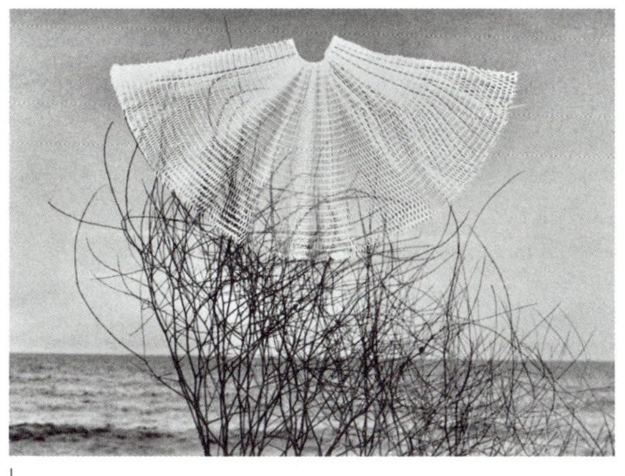
I

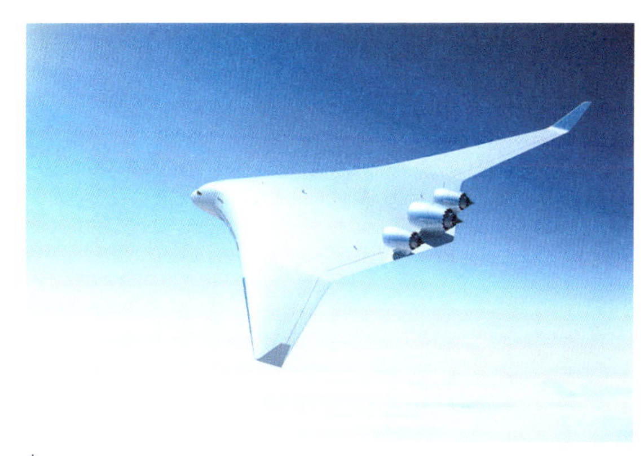
J

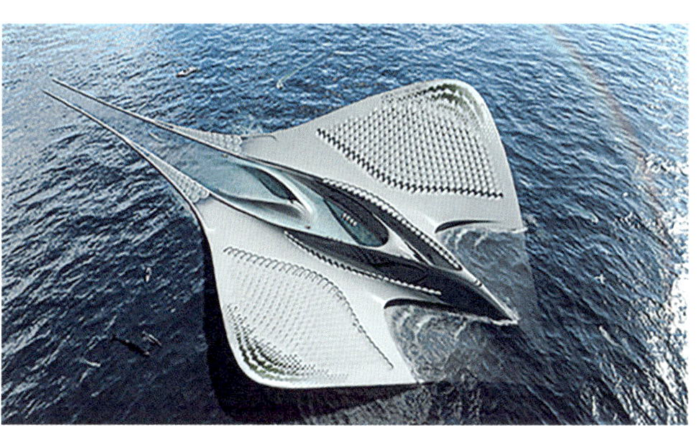
K

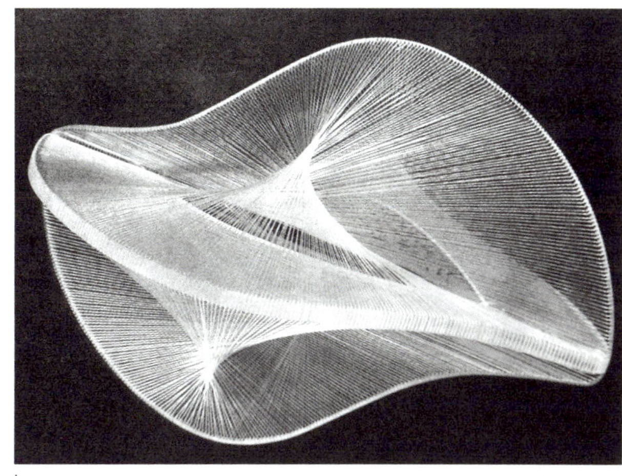
L

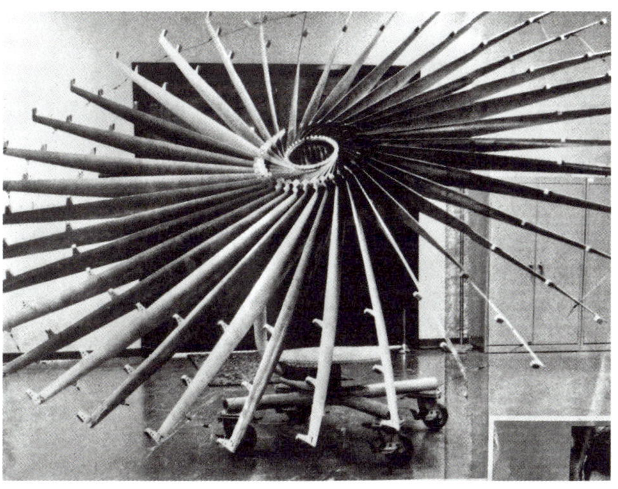
M

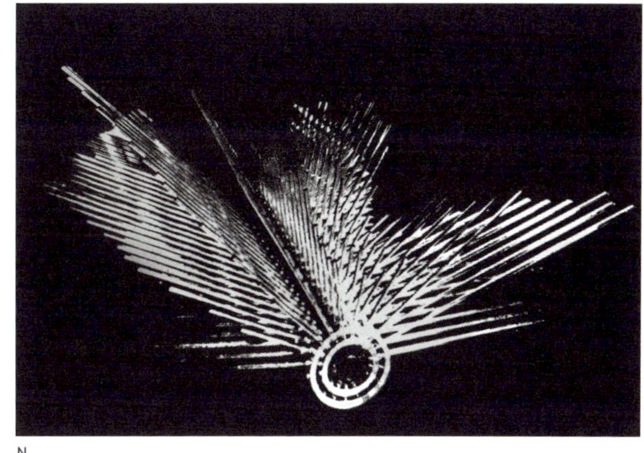
N

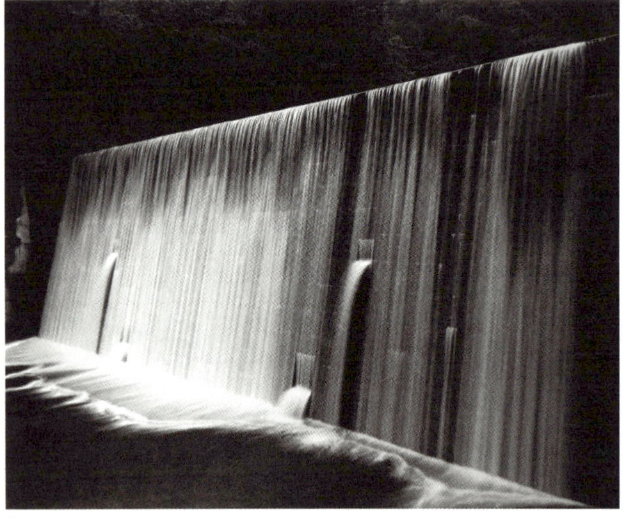

O

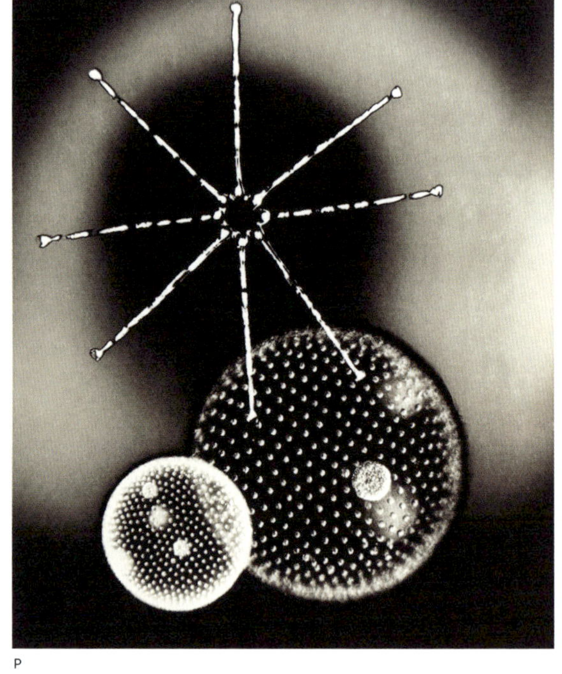

P

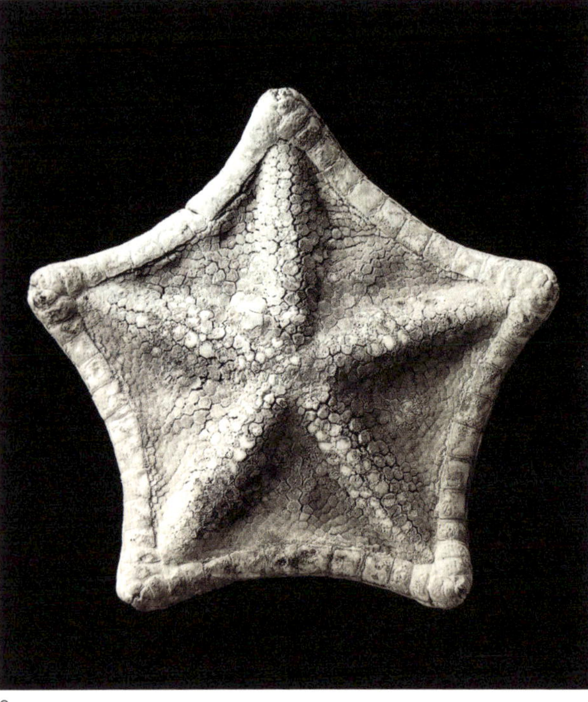

Q

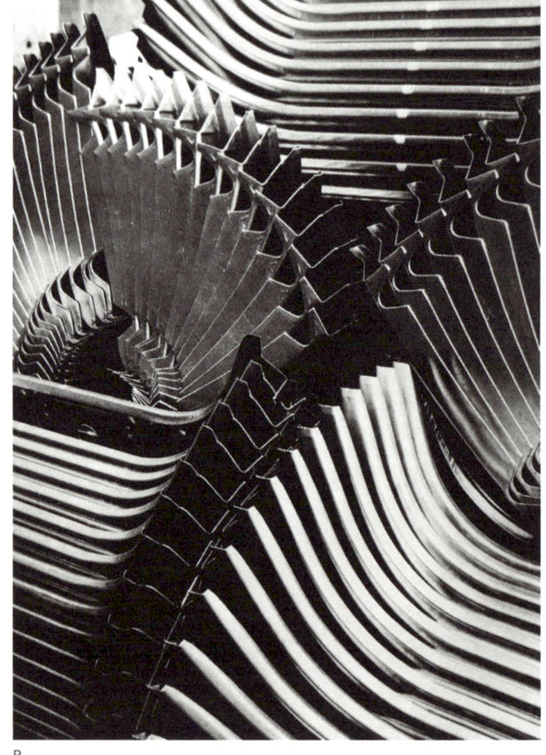

R

O *Kuroiso City*, 1989
P Plankton, 1950
Q Cushion starfish
R Volkswagen sheet metal, 1953
S 'Paper boat'
T Porcelain snail
U Cycas revoluta
V Shadow tornado
W Pullman railcar
X Pearl boat

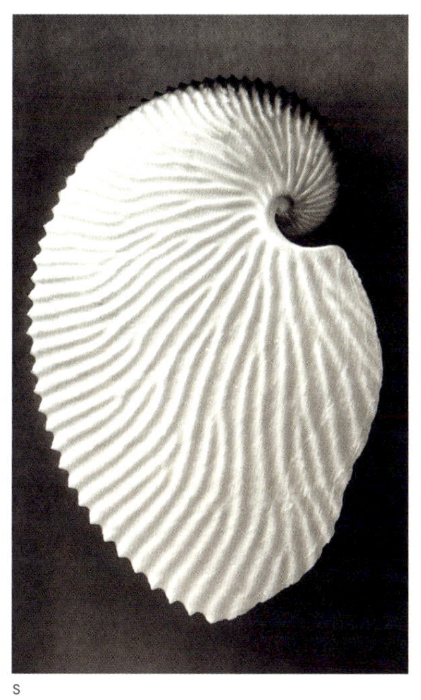
S

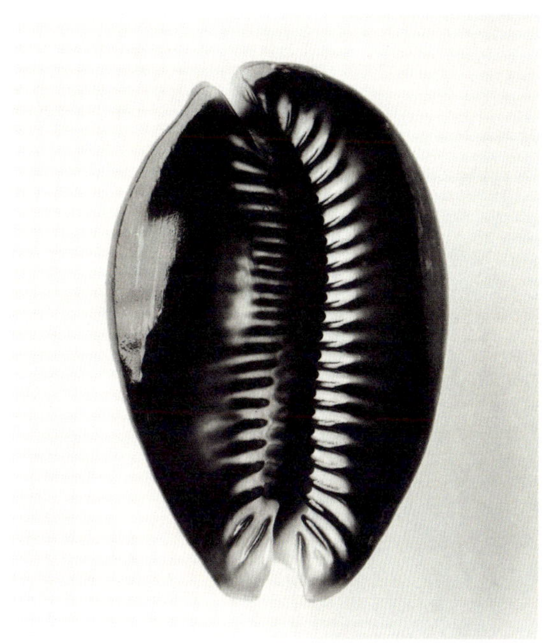
T

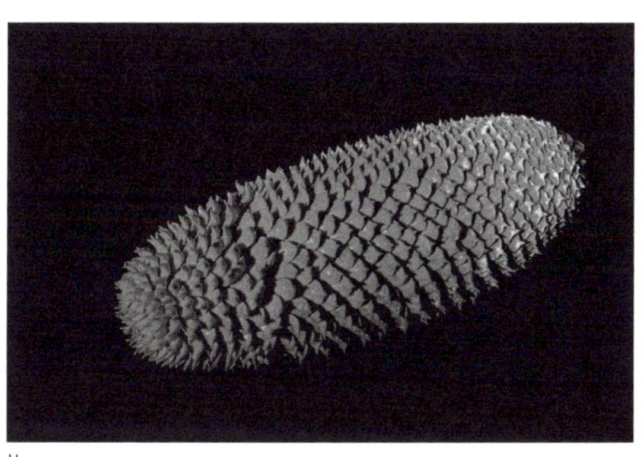
U

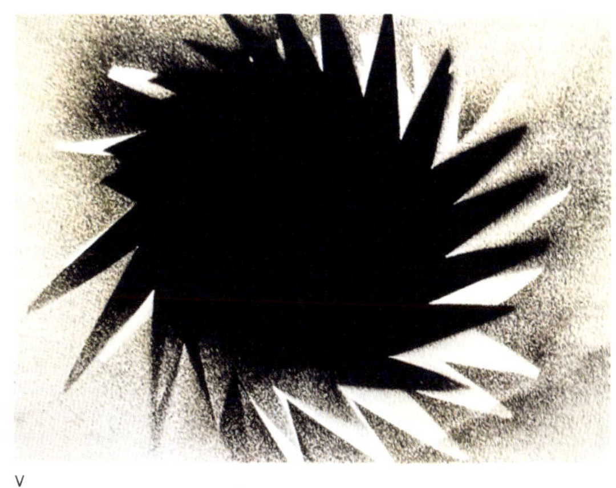
V

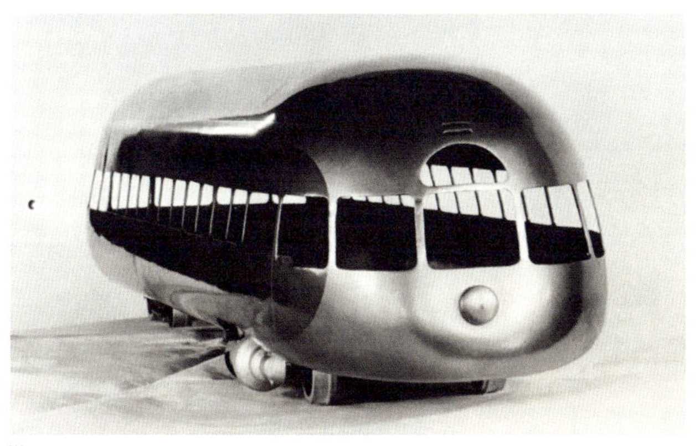
W

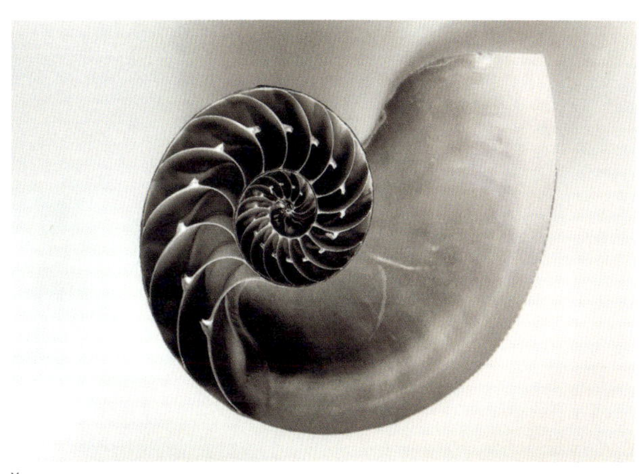
X

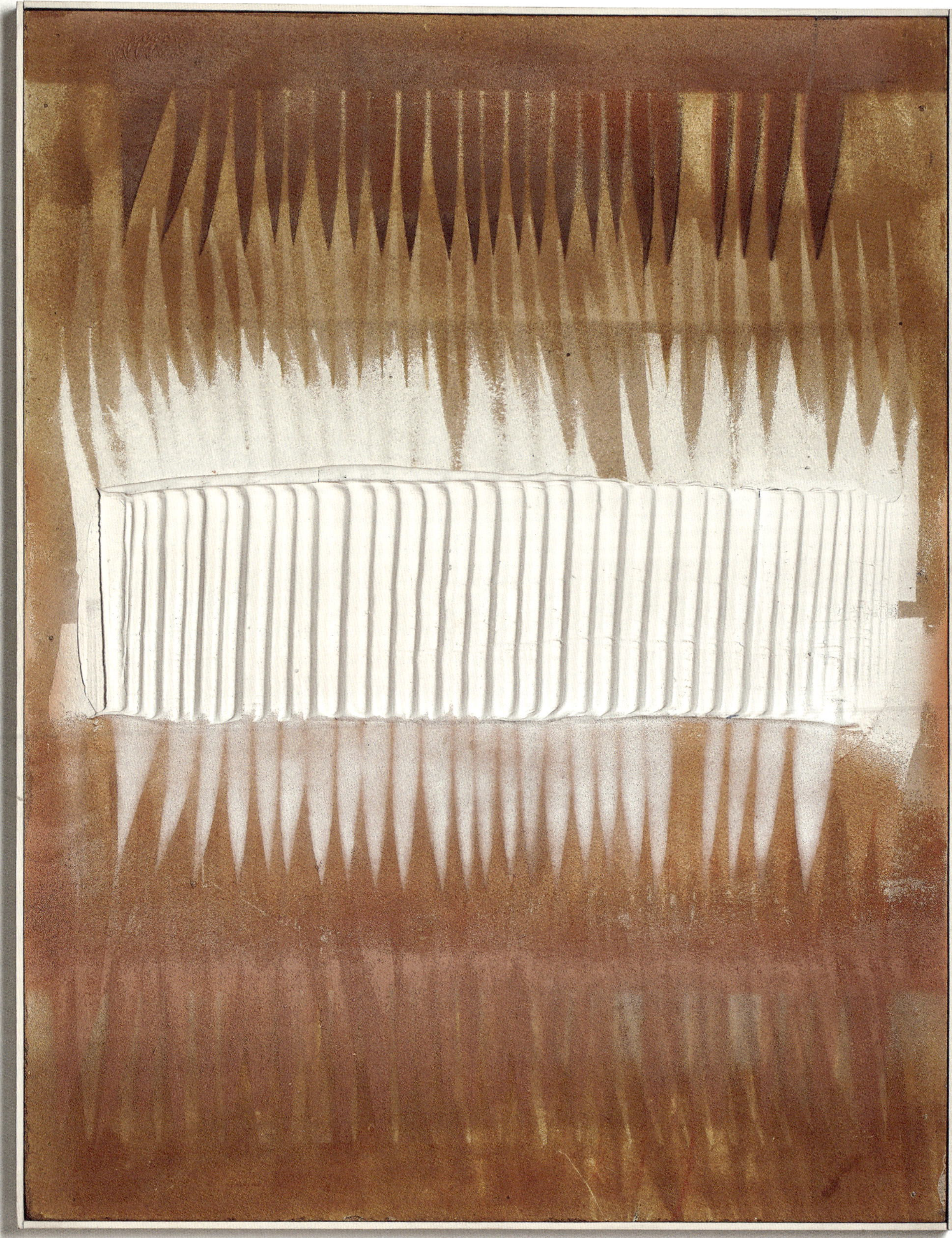

PICTURES AFTER THE LAST PICTURE

The last ***Dynamic Structure***
in the style of the ZERO period:
Untitled
1968

»
The happiness that colours give me cannot be replaced by any other.

(LETTER TO VEIT LOERS, JANUARY 2017)[265] «

The picture is simple (fig. p. 265).[266] The eye immediately recognises the principle, the structure, the colour scale, the dialogue of light and colour on the surface, the rhythmic sequence of chromatic tones, and the structural regularity with almost equally large monochrome fields and few colour tones on the canvas. Through its simplicity – which is profoundly devised – the work speaks directly to the senses and, at the same time, has a spiritual dimension that the viewer also perceives immediately.

The fact that the picture is simple is one of its great qualities. This characteristic applies to Heinz Mack's entire oeuvre of polychromatic painting. The corresponding phase of his artistic work began in 1991, in the artist's sixtieth year – a biographically unique development. The question is: Does the one have to do with the other – the simplicity in the complexity with the innovative pictorial design?

Let us take a closer look at the work *Ibiza Colours* from 2015. Our gaze first falls on a vertical surface at the top left that, like all the other fields of colour in the painting, is monochrome, in this case in a light pink tone that has been applied so transparently that the light from the white background penetrates through. Immediately to the right of this is a narrower, likewise vertical, now orange-red and less translucent field of colour. Altogether, the work was created as an ensemble, much like a musical score, from left to right and from top to bottom. The orange-red field is followed, optically progressing from left to right in the painting, by a blue zone of paint, applied somewhat more thickly than the second, which is followed by a whitish-yellow surface that jumps out of the ensemble like a light effect. The orange next to it contrasts with a sap green monochrome field, bordered by a broad, still vertical turquoise area. The first colour sequence of the painting concludes with a blue that differs from the previous blue tone and thus with a changed relationship of the colour to the pictorial light that penetrates from the white canvas.

In the above, we have only described the top third of the painting, which is divided into horizontal bands of colour. Recapitulating our first impression, questions arise: Does it all fit together somehow? Is it permissible to place colours and hues in this way in unexpected, sometimes harmonising, sometimes highly conflictual adjacencies? Can a painted picture be composed in this way at all, beyond the numerous innovations in twentieth-century modern painting from which this artist emerged and of which he is very conscious?

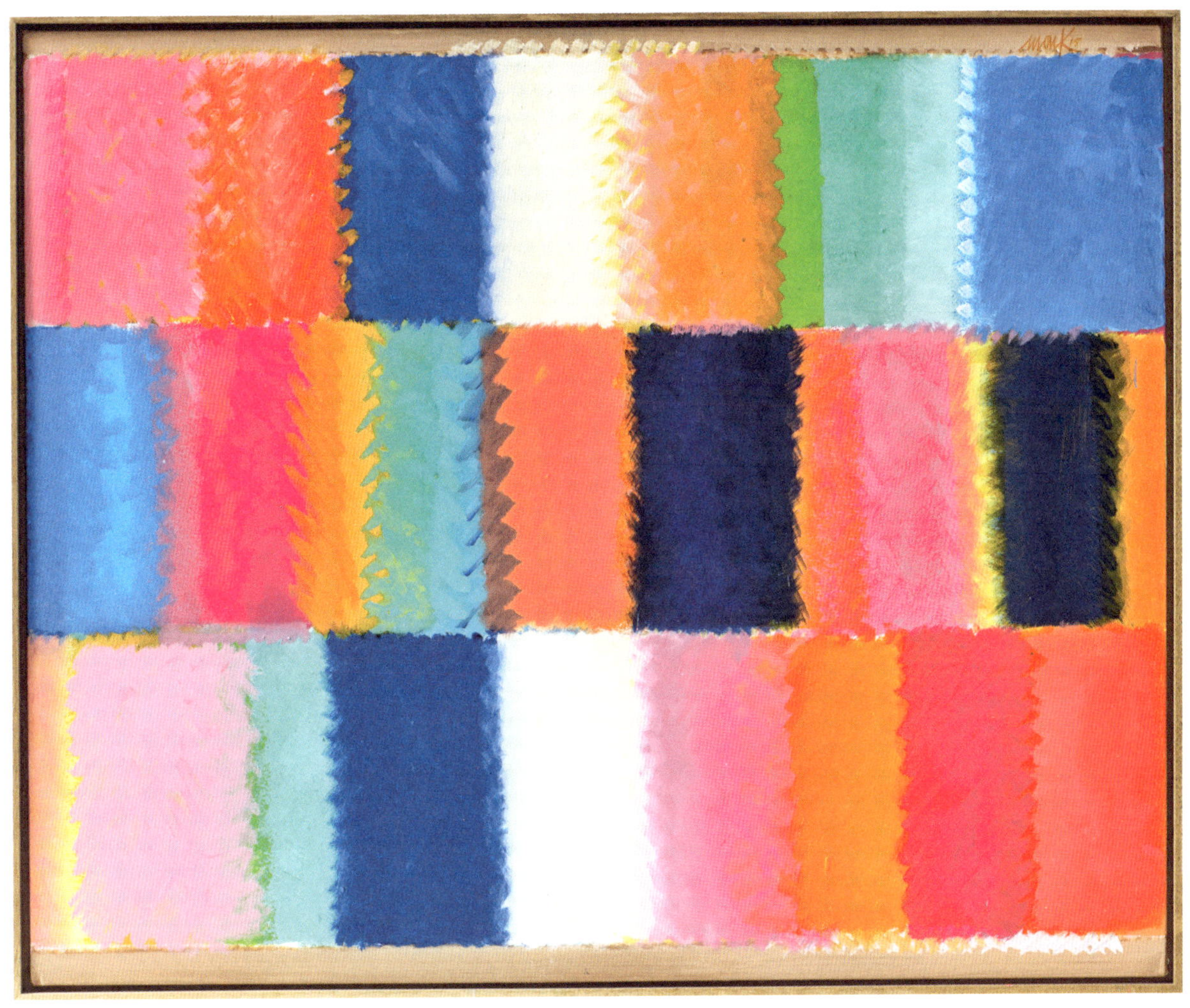

Ibiza Colours
(Chromatic Constellation)
2015

»

My *Chromatic Constellations* present the colours as light and the light as colour; they have no shadows! Why two colours love each other, and two others do not remains a mystery. If a third colour is added, two incompatible colours can suddenly become friends. If other colours appear on the picture surface – colours of different intensity and density, one louder, the other quieter – a kind of family is created. For me, their familial relationships are a property of the *Chromatic Constellations*. This is determined by a spectral relationship of order that must be sought and found time and again in order to lead to harmony.

('THE PRIMACY OF COLOUR', 2023)[267] «

The answer is: yes, it fits together. The painting proves this by appearing to us as a thoroughly harmonious ensemble, despite the fact that the chromatic adjacencies of the monochrome fields are far from harmonious in detail. This essential 'artifice' – an old-fashioned art-historical expression that denotes a new solution to problems that lie in the air but remain unspoken – leads Mack to find in his *Chromatic Constellations* a new pictorial form for painting as a whole, an independent pictorial design and pictorial idea.

In each *Chromatic Constellation* – flat pictorial spaces composed of monochrome fields – their chromatic adjacencies and contrasts produce a different rhythm. The colour fields are arranged differently from picture to picture. They are predominantly transparent, with the white ground shining through. Occasionally, however, the colour is so saturated that the surface design of the monochrome fields reflects the surrounding light so that it invokes the colour in the respective area. Accordingly, in all cases, an intense dialogue between colour and light is created, which is only found in this form in Heinz Mack's *Chromatic Constellations*.

In the translucently composed paintings, this dialogue lends the colour an unusual lightness. It is dematerialised. Suddenly, the conceptual art of the first hour, of the years around 1965, finds itself manifested in a new, unpredictable way – and this in painting, which at that time, when Mack lived in New York, represented the anti-medium par excellence for conceptual art. By dematerialising the art object and the pictorial media, early conceptual art sought to establish for the viewer a direct connection between seeing and thinking. This is also the case with Mack's *Chromatic Constellations*, in that the pictorial light dematerialises the colour, which, in this form and especially on canvas, is – as far as I know – only to be found here, despite the diversity of painting of the twentieth and early twenty-first centuries.

Another consequence of this pictorial invention is that light and its role in this type of painting remain independent, that light is never subordinated to colour, as is otherwise the case in the painting tradition up to the present day, with only a few exceptions. When painting makes it possible to make light directly visible, as in the *Chromatic Constellations*, the perception of time also arises in parallel. In these works, time is modulated differently from picture to picture.

The individual fields do not have linear boundaries. Most of them are irregularly jagged at the edges. And their arrangement on the canvas does not follow a rigid geometry, but rather a felt geometry or a memory of it, a replication of geometry. This leads to an open pictorial design.

In each work, the colour sequences and structures are reinvented. Paintings that are poetically harmonious in chromatic terms alternate with disharmonious and particularly tense works in which the colour sequences seem to 'crash' at several points but are 'rescued' by an unexpected following hue and develop their intensity in this unstable balance. None of this is predetermined but is rather improvised by the artist directly on the canvas. This way of working is reminiscent of sequences of colour tones or melodies and clusters, the method of creation of which is similar to improvisation in piano playing, the first art that Mack learned and practised at a high level as a youth, until an accident made a professional career impossible (p. 50). Today, the artist still plays his concert grand piano daily, in a structural conception of highly sophisticated music.

With regard to the paintings, dynamic ensembles are thus created which produce a free play of colour and light, as well as chords of monochrome fields, which can also consist of the variation of a single basic colour but regularly allow the 'emancipation of dissonance' in the spirit of Arnold Schoenberg.[268]

The *Chromatic Constellations* are conceived in purely painterly terms. They do not transpose sculptural problems and procedures into the two-dimensional medium. The autonomous concurrency of both fields – sculpture, from which Mack defined his artistic intentions from the beginning, and painting, which he took up again in 1991 with the *Chromatic Constellations*, long after the ZERO paintings – characterises this oeuvre. Beyond this, there are a number of echoes between the *Chromatic Constellations* and the earlier or contemporaneous sculptural work, for example in that stele-like forms appear as picture-filling signs or post-ornamental patterns and repetitions of non-representational forms that are in dialogue with the art of the Orient, which once again distinguishes this pictorial thinking (cf. pp. 206 f.).

It was a courageous step to take up painting again at the beginning of the 1990s, when the medium was considered 'written off' and historically outdated. It is equally courageous to pursue it in this form today, since painting is 'fashionable' again, albeit often as a means of communicating the new ideological trends of our century. In contrast, Heinz Mack's paintings are autonomous, reduced to the play of light and colour, thus embodying non-representational painting, evident in their manifestation, very complex in their pictorial structure, and independent in terms of their iconography.

It is characteristic of this extensive series of works that they are always 'pictures after the last picture'. What does this mean? The artist began his oeuvre in the early 1950s with drawings and wooden sculptures, which, in this phase, generally consisted of staggered surfaces (fig. p. 204), which makes for an interesting comparison with the *Chromatic Constellations*. In the following years, Mack's sculptural activity was accompanied by equally intensive painting. In this field, the development at that time ran from Tachist works via monochrome black paintings, which subjectively represented a dead end for the artist, to the first ZERO works from 1957–58 onwards,[269] in which the repetitive rhythmic progression of a single colour on the picture surface results in a simultaneous rhythmic form, which liberated tradition-based painting – similar to other essential artists of the twentieth century – from a great deal of ballast. During this period, Mack's ZERO painting was already part of a comprehensive project, namely ZERO art, which he had conceived together with Otto Piene in 1957–58 in order to place the creation of art in all media and fields of expression on a new basis, which – put simply – came from the future and not the past.

»

I first became interested in the primary colours red, yellow and blue in the late 1950s; and so at the beginning of the ZERO period I also made blue, yellow and red paintings in my studio, but their monochromaticity was to be enlivened by frequency-like rhythms and colourful rows of facets. I then decided on my own – just like Piene – to do without colour, and we felt vindicated when we soon learned that Castellani and Manzoni had made the same decision at virtually the same time and had committed themselves to achromaticism. I still don't know when Fontana created his first painting without colour, describing white as the sum of all colours. His 'Manifesto blanco', first published in 1946, was not published in Germany until more than a decade later.

(LETTER TO VEIT LOERS, DECEMBER 2016)[270] «

Around 1964, in connection with the imminent dissolution of ZERO, ZERO painting came to an end. Accordingly, there are indeed 'last pictures' in Mack's artistic biography due to a (provisional) conclusion of painting on canvas,[271] which partly explains the dynamics of his oeuvre as a whole. On the one hand, the ZERO art project consisted of working directly with the elements as sculptural material – with fire, light, smoke, water, sand, earth, and sky, as well as with movement, and this in real space, against any principle of pictorial representation.[272] On the other hand, this was accompanied by the use of industrial materials, some of which were new or had previously remained outside the realm of art, such as aluminium, Plexiglas, glass, mirrors, electric motors, and electric light. As a result, panel painting became obsolete and an obstructive genre in the development of sculptural work. 'Departure from the picture' is one term for this moment, which can be found not only in the art of ZERO, but also in Happening and Fluxus, as well as in Minimalism and conceptual art.[273] In Heinz Mack's oeuvre, these new approaches to work cumulate in New York in 1966 with the steles made of aluminium and Plexiglas (fig. p. 127), in the contemporaneous rotors (fig. p. 133) and, in 1968, with the first realisation of the *Sahara Project* (fig. pp. 156 f.) in Tunisia, which had already been formulated in 1959. Art was put on a new footing.

For several decades thereafter, Mack's visual thinking moved beyond the realm of painting and the traditional tools of the painter's trade – paint, brush, and canvas. It developed in a space that was often described with the catchphrase 'expanded concept of art', not least of all as environments for public spaces. In this particular chapter of recent art history, Mack's oeuvre represents a weighty statement with a pioneering function and a wealth of formal inventions and elaborations of form of historical significance. The liberation that made this possible developed from the gradual fading out of the ZERO phase, beginning in the years in New York, and the decision to conclude

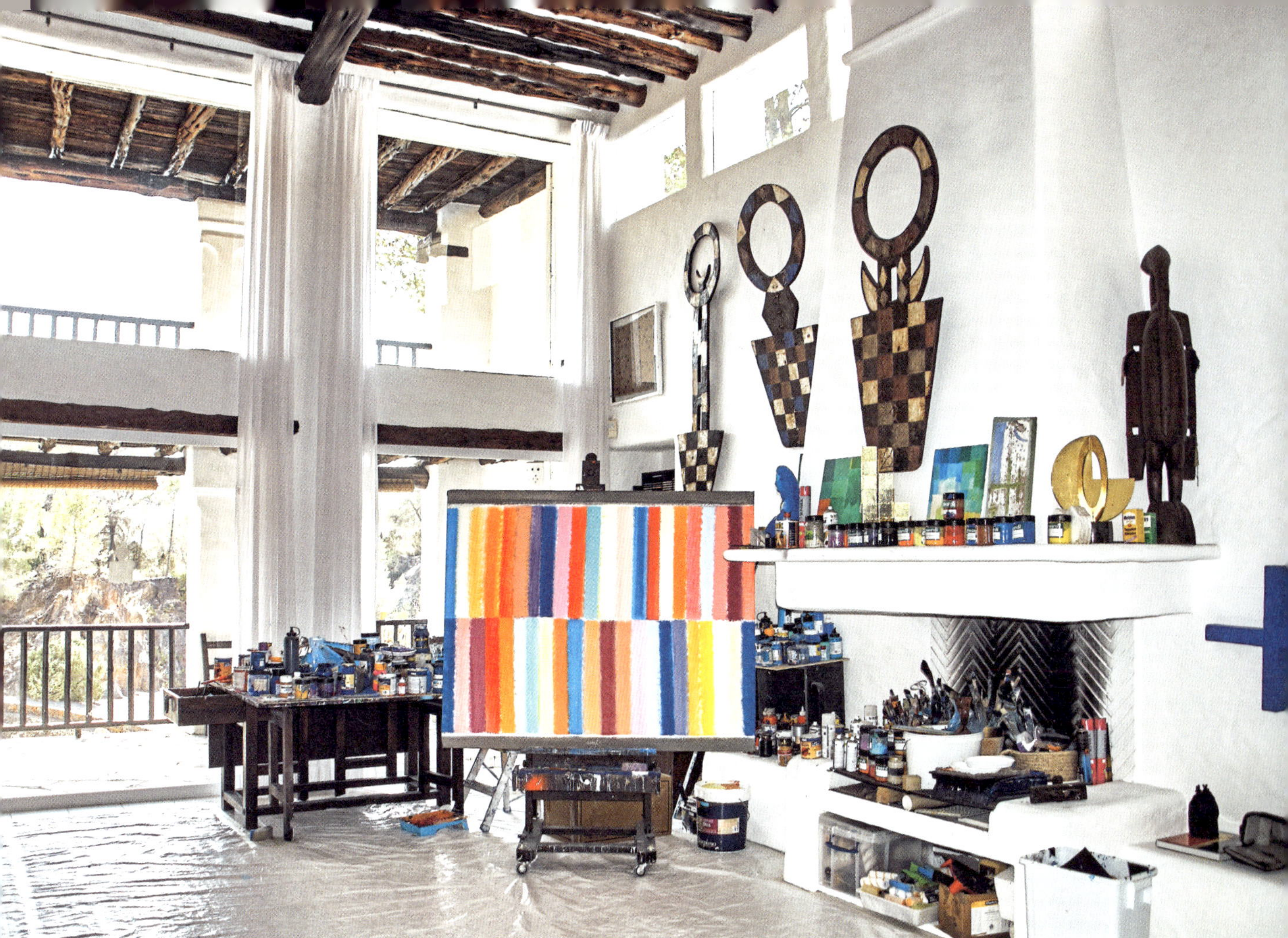

View of the artist's Spanish studio,
Can Micali, Ibiza
2015

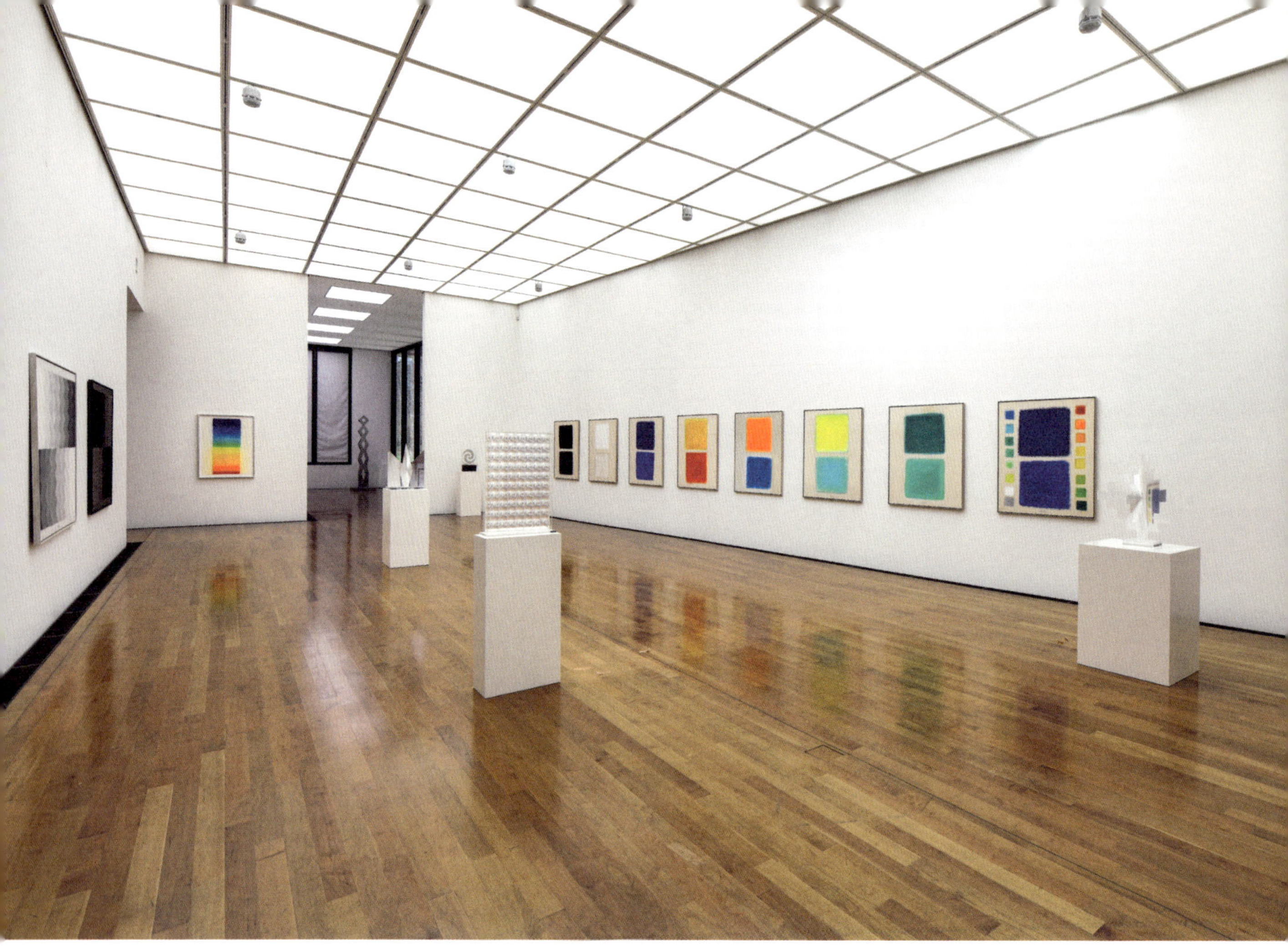

Installation view
Heinz Mack. Werke im Licht,
Museum Ritter, Waldenbuch
2021

painting on canvas. With Heinz Mack, 'the last picture' thus exists as a conscious artistic decision – one that he has never retracted as such.

The *Chromatic Constellations* stand alongside the work of a direct handling of the elements, especially light, which continues to this day, and are in dialogue with these works, which come from ZERO art, and not least derive their lightness and experimental character from this. Above all, however, they are an important group of works in the painting of the last decades. As 'pictures after the last picture', they are particularly freely conceived and composed. This makes their innovative, unbound technical structure possible, the fusion of light and colour without subordination and, above all, a reinvention of the image and structure from one canvas to the next, from one pastel on paper to the next. A detailed study of the relationships within the *Chromatic Constellations* and their course of development is still to be undertaken. However, as they are all, each in their own right, literally a first picture 'after the last picture' – a specific feature of Heinz Mack's oeuvre – they seem to be without preconditions. Each picture represents a new beginning.

»
All I need for my painting now is canvas, paints, brush – nothing else. I've given up my painting technique which I developed during the ZERO period. I don't need the special technique any more. My painting technique is very simple now; my colour forms are very simple; in general I try to keep everything as simple as possible so that I can focus entirely on the painting. An important difference between my paintings of yesterday and today can be seen in the fact that I used to paint almost exclusively ascetically white and black grid paintings (fig. p. 70), but now my passion is strongly coloured, large-scale painting, filled with light.
« ('STRONG COLOURS – SIMPLE FORMS', 2011)[274]

This is why the ensemble of *Chromatic Constellations* is so diverse. There are the monochrome paintings (fig. p. 198), which consist merely of variations of a single colour tone and unfold a telluric energy that makes one wonder where it comes from. There are the colourless, black-and-white or almost black-and-white works, and those in white on white, occasionally with light brown tones, in which one senses a great reflexivity. These pictures develop a physical weight despite or as a result of the colour that has been removed – a weight that is purely optical, for the pictures are as light as a feather. They enter into a subtle dialogue with Mack's stone sculpture from the last four decades, which was most recently honoured by his artist colleague Tony Cragg with a major exhibition in the Waldfrieden Sculpture Park in Wuppertal (fig. p. 236). And there are also quite free works within this group, consisting of geometric lines seemingly arranged on the picture surface without any particular order, and which carry within them sections of chromatic colour (fig. p. 274).

If one were to seek art historical comparisons to these linear *Chromatic Constellations*, one would think of Piet Mondrian's *Broadway Boogie-Woogie* (1942–43),[275] a work from the New York exile of the style-defining non-representational painter of the first half of the twentieth century. In Mack's pictorial wit and his so clearly different solution to a distantly related pictorial idea, one sees how independent this oeuvre actually is, how much it is based on a newly conceived relationship of colour and light, and how distanced and at the same time close these works are to the visual habits of our media-based, digital present.

»

In the 'beginning of the beginning' of the ZERO period, Mondrian's Boogie-Woogie paintings were still a kind of final reduction of Constructivism and its inherent meaning of composition; at the same time, however, these paintings were a departure into the new zone of the structural, the open grid. The primary colours they contained seemed to be ordered by chance.

(LETTER TO VEIT LOERS, DECEMBER 2016)[276] «

Each painter sums up the history of painting in his or her own way: This statement by Gilles Deleuze from 1981 makes it possible to describe art history from the artists' point of view.[277] Each artistic oeuvre unfolds its own line of tradition, not in a planned way, but one that is always highly interesting in terms of art history. In the case of the *Chromatic Constellations*, two paintings from recent years mentioned earlier provide the first evidence of this. They are variations on the works of Paul Gauguin and Henri Matisse respectively (fig. pp. 248 f., 252 f.). When we contemplate them, it is possible to sense how Heinz Mack engages in a dialogue with the history of painting and how he develops his *Chromatic Constellations* in the process. '*Aérien*' is the name given in French to the particular constellation of colour and light achieved by Gauguin in his last paintings, as well as by Matisse, inspired by them, in his early 'Fauve' works around 1906 and thirty-five years later in his last works during the German occupation in Nice. There is no adequate equivalent in English. The French adjective '*aérien*' means airy, light, and weightless, floating away into the air, all at the same time, which also applies to Mack's *Chromatic Constellations*.

»

I was fascinated by Paul Gauguin's work *Ta matete (Le Marché)* from 1892 (fig. p. 252), a smaller, medium-format painting that I had admired – even loved – in the form of a postcard when I was a schoolboy and was only able to view in the original much later. I took a closer look at paintings by Henri Matisse and Gauguin and – unintentionally – let myself be inspired by them. Such attempts are admittedly conceivably problematic and in a certain sense downright dangerous. I virtually seduced myself and had to expect to fail here. Of course, it cannot be said here that I see myself in an artistic tradition that now goes back more than a hundred years. Why such attempts? Here, it is obviously the colours in their dynamic and painterly constellation that have stimulated me like an orchestral

An important theme for Mack is his inspiration from the history of art and culture (cf. fig. pp. 258–261). Like good literature, philosophy, art history, and art criticism, good art always arises from an imaginary dialogue with what has already been created. From this, one can sense what the 'dark total idea'[279] of one's own, yet to be realised creation could be. In his latest catalogue raisonné of the *Chromatic Constellations*, the artist has formulated his own summary of the history of painting.[280] Few artists have dared to do this in a comparable form, for it is a double risk, both to themselves and to the recipients. With regard to the former, there is the idea that such introspection could paralyse the creative intelligence and form a labyrinth of references from which one can no longer escape as an artist. Even greater is the courage with regard to the public: Does one not automatically incur reproaches for such comparisons with one's own works? In this case, such prejudices are wrong in many ways. Heinz Mack is – despite the fact that his public image occasionally suggests the opposite – a highly modest person and artist who, perhaps because of his degree in philosophy and his broad and profound education, is fully aware of the limits, the inadequacy, and ultimately the – inevitable – failure of the absolute demand on one's own work, which one must however face if one wants to turn one's artistic activ-

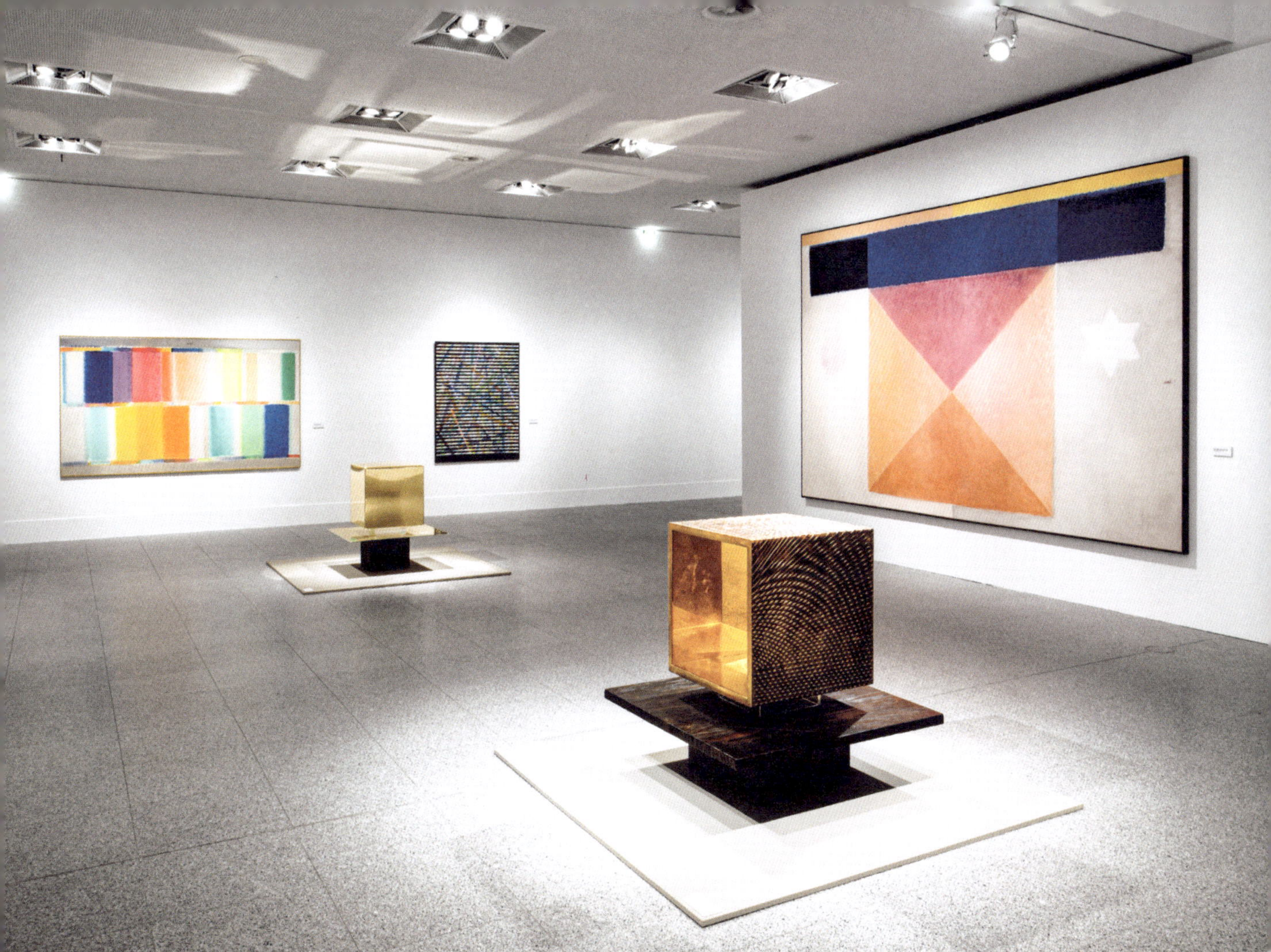

Installation view
Heinz Mack:
Light – Space – Colour
Bundeskunsthalle, Bonn
2011

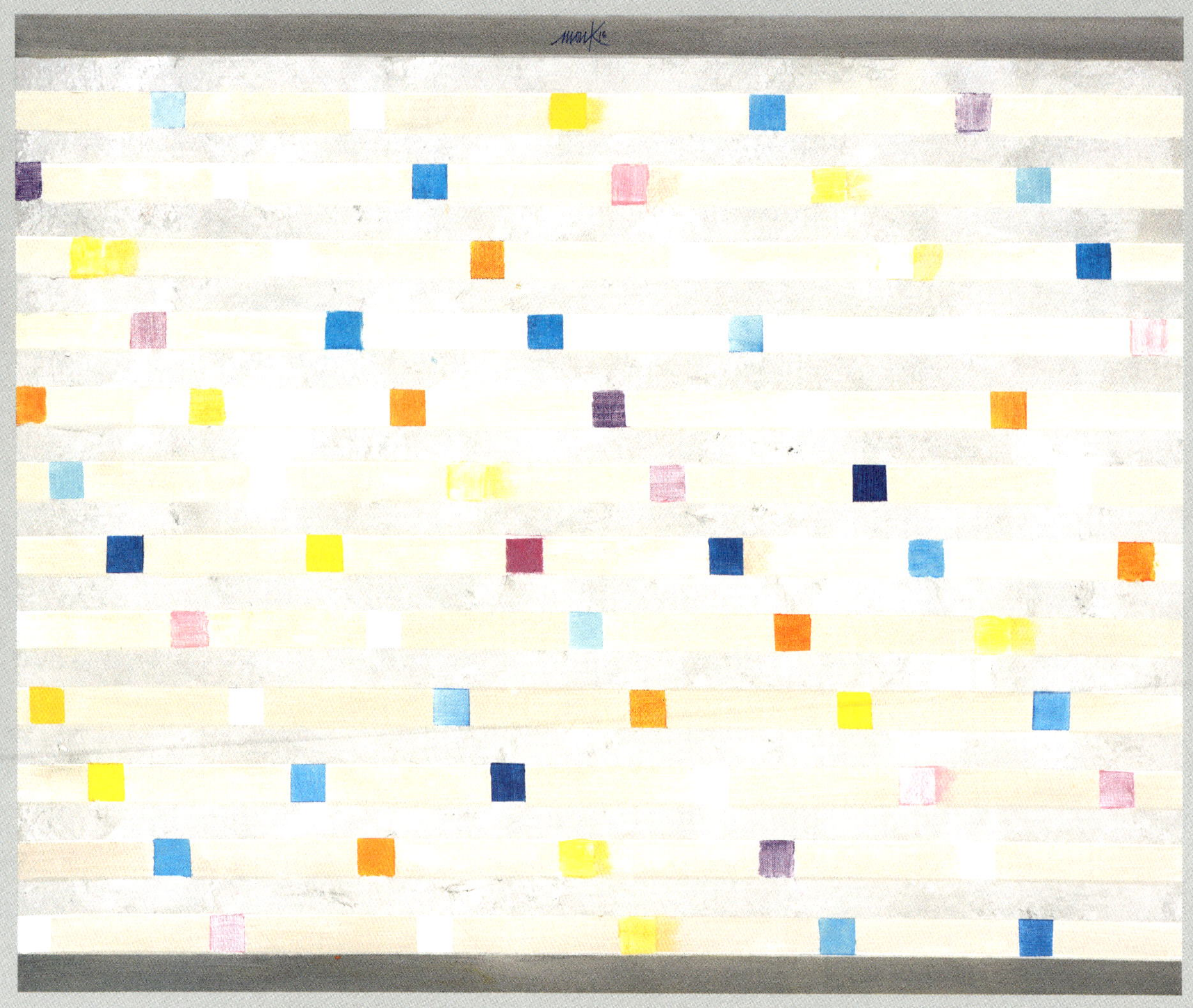

Untitled
(Chromatic Constellation)
2016

ity into something sustainably effective. Those artists whom he mentions in reverence and modesty as imaginary dialogue partners were likewise aware of this. 'Russian Constructivism', which has accompanied Mack's work since the 1950s, plays a major role in his private notes, from the Suprematism of Kazimir Malevich to the dynamism of the women artists he admired, Lyubov Popova and Varvara Stepanova (cf. p. 200 f.). During Heinz Mack's stay in New York, these were complemented – and quite uniquely so in the contemporary art of the last sixty years – by Barnett Newman and Ad Reinhardt with dialogues about the anti-expressionist approach in the fading Abstract Expressionism and the questions of monochromaticity and time. Barnett Newman wanted to know from Heinz Mack how things could continue in Europe after Art Informel and the École de Paris. Another question was whether, with Yves Klein's monochrome paintings, European panel painting had come to an end.[281]

sound. You could say that, in each case, I have orchestrated and transformed a classical composition in a new way. These paintings of mine are 'outsiders', so to speak, within my oeuvre, which I do not want to deny.

« (2023)[278]

»

Finally, we were fascinated by Yves Klein's ultramarine monochrome, a kind of reduction of all the reductions of polychromy that had dominated Western painting since the Renaissance. Rodchenko's anticipation of pure monochrome in 1921 was unknown to us at the time, and probably to Yves Klein as well. [...] As for the dominant part of a triad in Yves Klein's work, the ultramarine, in Rodchenko's three monochrome panel paintings of 1921 it looks like a triad with equal primary colours – no colour dominates, and I therefore do not perceive it as a sacred expression or dogma. You cannot paint consistently monochrome colour panels, or black or white squares in Malevich's work, for the rest of your life – these three artists of world importance in art history probably suspected this or even knew it. Does art history know of another, older anticipation? In fact, I was fascinated by my early discovery and realisation that the Christian paintings of the Annunciation at the beginning of the Renaissance were basically in purple, ultramarine (lapis lazuli) and gold, in which not alchemy but the

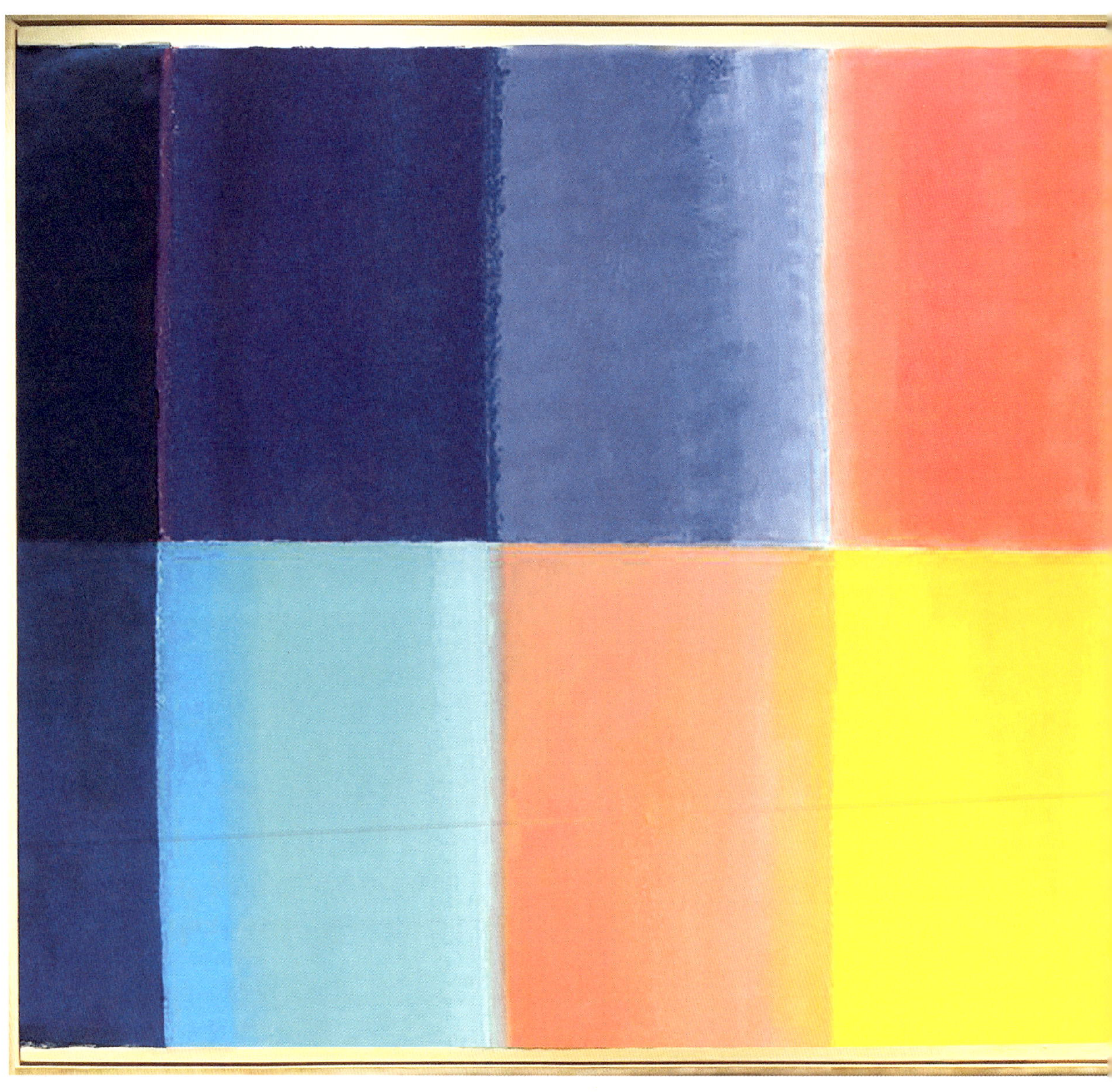

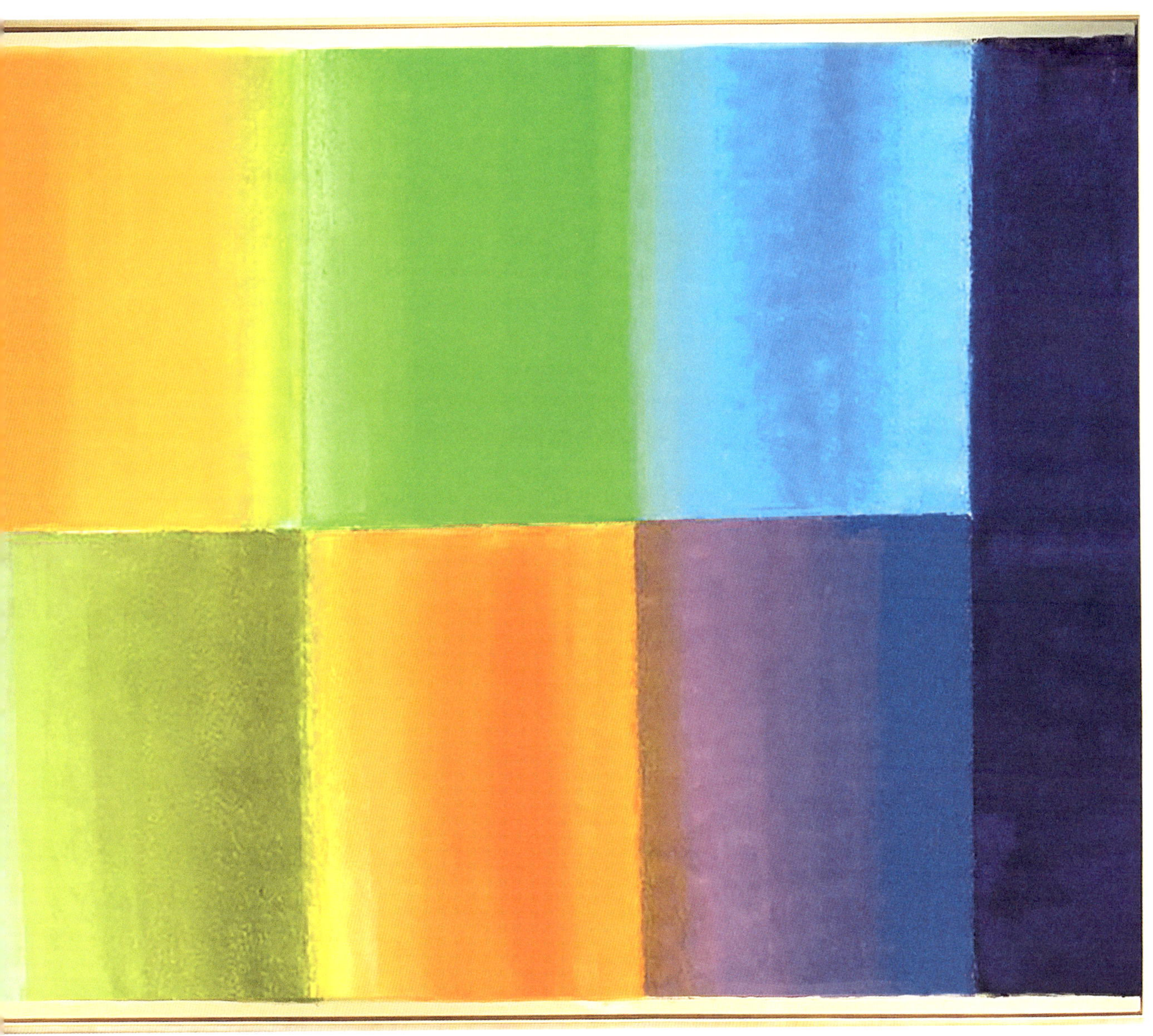

Large Chromatic
(Chromatic Constellation)
2023

spiritual interests of a metaphysics of light in the Christian epiphany prevailed. Think of Simone Martini's wonderful Annunciation in the Uffizi or Fra Angelico's painting in Arezzo, and Yves Klein's triad is put into perspective!

(LETTER TO VEIT LOERS, DECEMBER 2016)[282] «

»

The questions that inadvertently accompany me when I paint are more numerous than the answers I try to give myself. It starts with the fact that completely unexpected ideas contain a kind of driving energy and evoke the question of whether a discovery might be in the offing. So the adventure of painting also begins with the question of whether something new is to be expected or whether my artistic discovery has already been made by others.

(LETTER TO VEIT LOERS, JANUARY 2017)[283] «

»

Sometimes I paint a hundred of the clearest possible colours additively in succession, and even here I strive for a colourful overall tone. The juxtaposition and interaction of the colours is determined by a spectral relationship of order that must arise intuitively – without this, chaos would prevail. Order must always be sought and found anew. Colour theories are only crutches: Who will walk with them, let alone dance or float? I find it

Heinz Mack's visual thinking is highly structural in nature. All *Chromatic Constellations* are structures, structural images, inherently open structures. This is their underlying working principle. Mack's interest in works from the history of painting is also based on this – they can form points of orientation and corrective elements in the working process, but they are almost never starting points for pictorial ideas, as was the case in the postmodern painting of the 1980s. If one thinks away the narrative, a major work by the Renaissance artist Piero della Francesca, for example, is a structural image that can serve as a good conversation partner today. '*Principio d'arte*' is what the Italian conceptual artist Michelangelo Pistoletto calls this: the visual arts thrive on the fact that the baton is constantly passed on, across generations. This also applies to budding artists from various generations, as can be seen from the fact that, at the Düsseldorf Academy of Art where Mack once studied, he is now considered a living legend – more than he himself realises.

→
Garden for Starflowers (Chromatic Constellation)
2000
in the exhibition
Heinz Mack – Elective Affinities
at the Tehran Museum
of Contemporary Art
2001

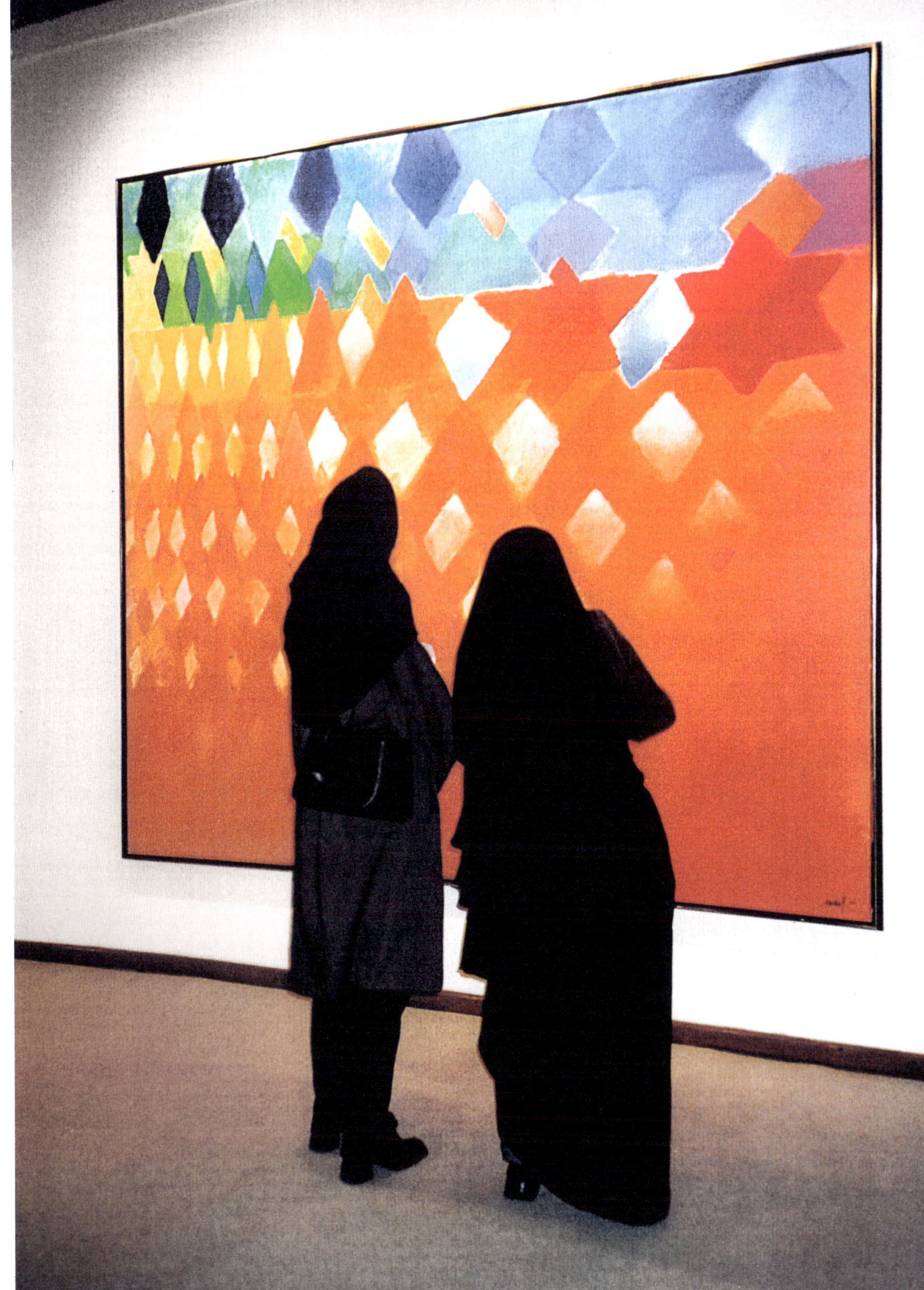

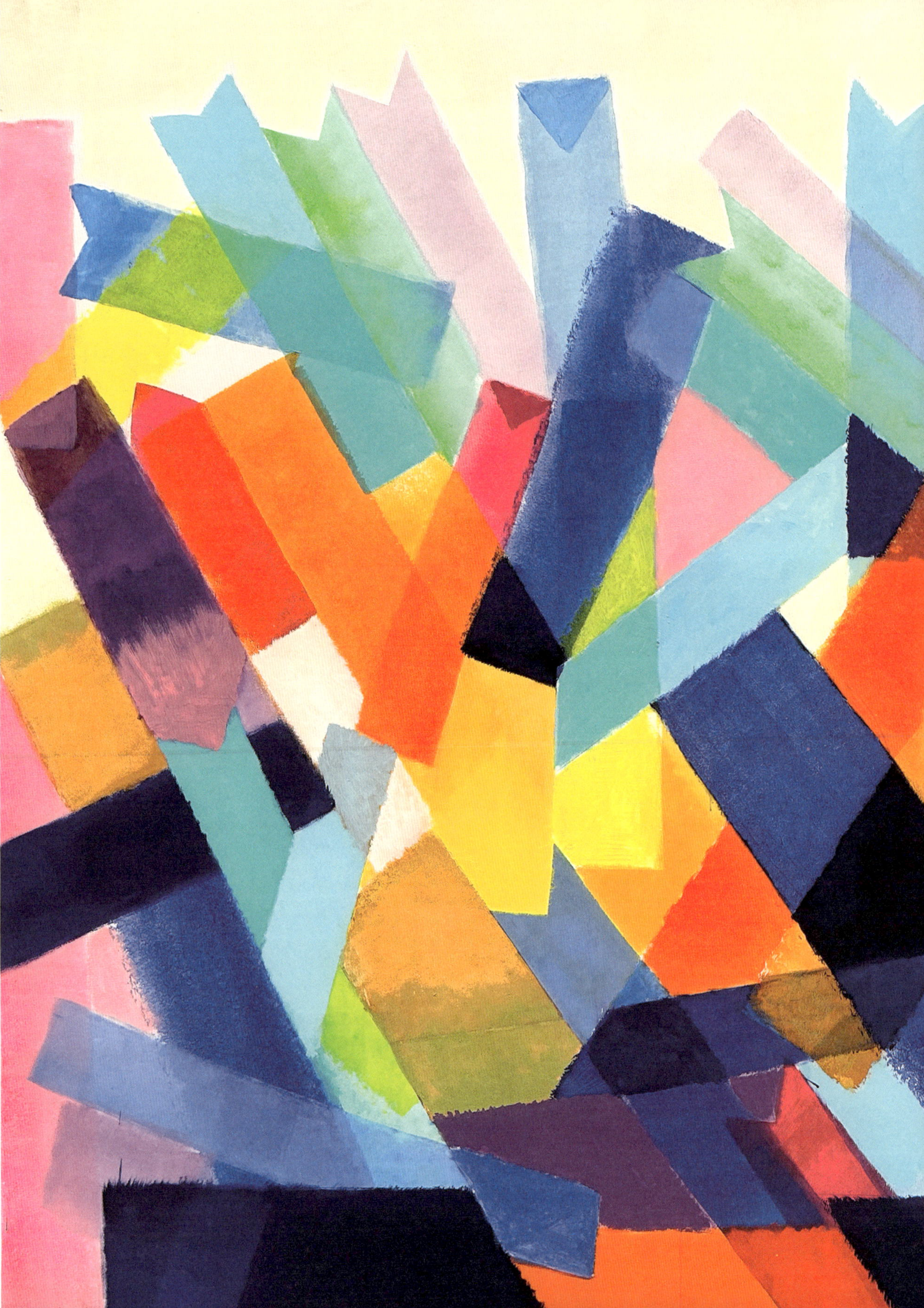

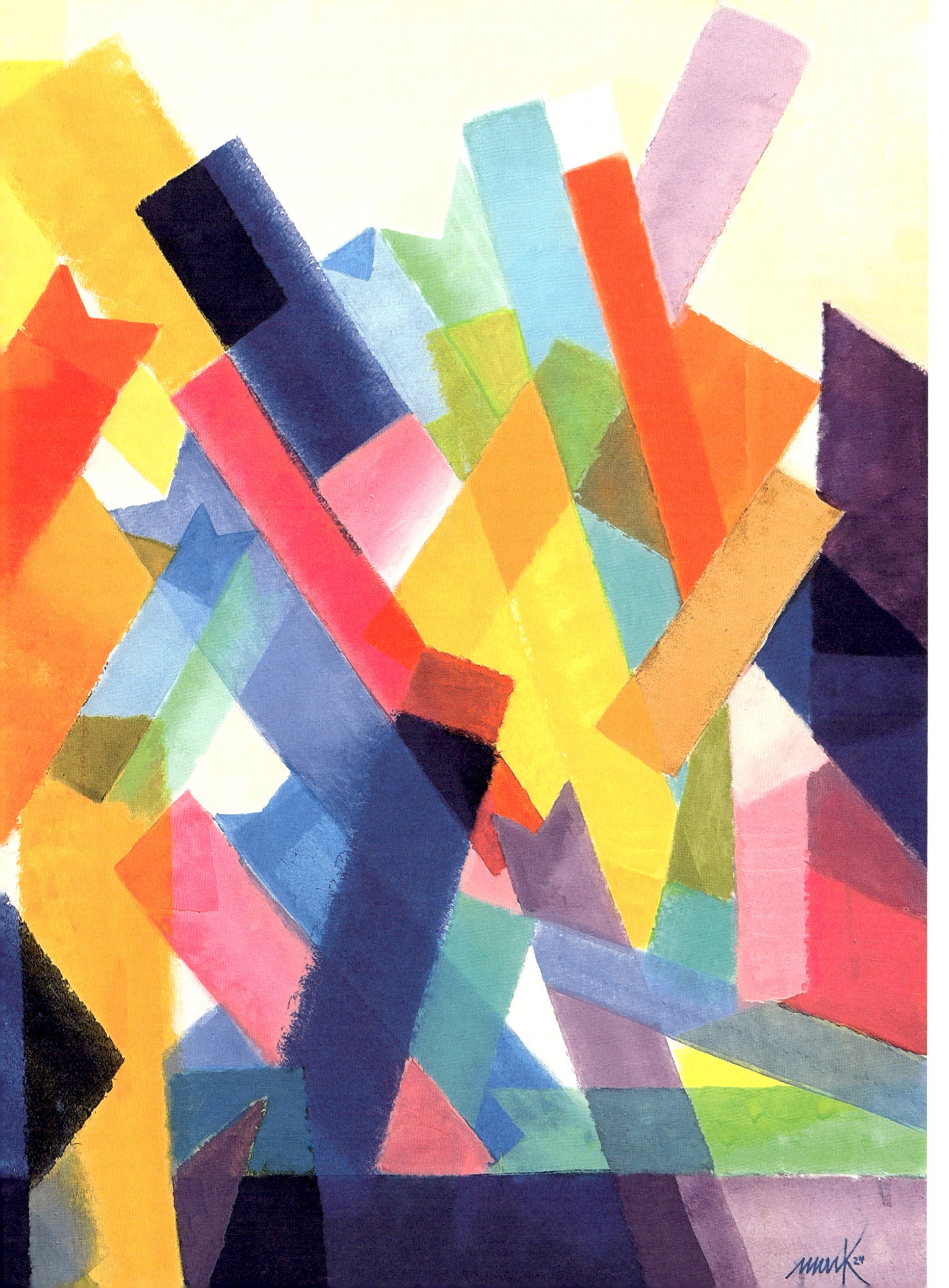

remarkable that young people seem to have no problem at all with such an abundance of colours. I wonder what Goethe would have thought if he had seen a painting with a hundred colours.

(LETTER TO VEIT LOERS, JANUARY 2017)[284] «

The special colour mood and palette that characterise the *Chromatic Constellations* has an identifiable origin in the colour theory of Johann Wolfgang von Goethe, as well as in his colour wheel. Both were developed around 1800, at the height of the European Enlightenment. Goethe opposed the scientistic theory of light and colour formulated by Isaac Newton in the seventeenth and early eighteenth centuries with a concept based on a holistic observation of nature. Goethe's colour wheel, in contrast to that of Newton, includes white and black as fully valid and equal colours and thinks differently from the British scientist about light and non-light, as well as about the occurrence of colour phenomena. Goethe's theory of colour remains controversial to this day; however, it has been widely recognised among artists since the second half of the nineteenth century. It is the basis of modern painting.

What makes Heinz Mack's *Chromatic Constellations* unique within recent and current art production is the fact that, here, the experimental treatment of Goethe's conception of colours, as well as of light and non-light, is elevated to the partial basis of a new form of painting.[285] As already explained, we are still dealing here with 'pictures after the last picture', which opens up the possibility of rethinking painting.[286] The principle behind these pictures is to work exclusively with a colour wheel, or rather to make it the basis of the pictorial form – whereby it is Goethe's colour wheel: one that was created two centuries ago to help artists reproduce representational motifs, objects, and light moods in which it disappears or, in Georg Wilhelm Friedrich Hegel's dialectical sense, 'dissolves', that is to say, preserves on the one hand and dissolves on the other, thus becoming chromatic material itself.[287] This is unique in this form and decidedly innovative. 'Pictures after the last picture' can also be created behind or beyond painting or the way in which paintings have been conceived up to now.

Heinz Mack is familiar with Goethe's conception of colours. He deals with Goethe's colour wheel in a similar way to a composer such as Arnold Schoenberg, who developed his 'method of composition with twelve tones'[288] into one of the richest, most precise and lasting works of the twentieth century,[289] since the limitation of its combinatorics opens up almost infinite possibilities. Mack, too, always proceeds economically with the compositional material of his paintings and always plays through only a few tones. The exclusive use of Goethe's colour wheel and the thinking behind it as the starting point and material for the *Chromatic Constellations*, each of which emerges as a continuous, coloured train of thought, is found nowhere else in contemporary painting. The strictness of the self-imposed specification and the sensitive handling of the subsequent chromatic improvisation produce a broad spectrum of results and a pictorial mode that is unique to Heinz Mack. This also applies to the ostensibly

←
Summer Party
(Chromatic Constellation)
2024

'colourless' paintings that feature only white and black. In these, the lyrical keynote of the polychromatic pictures tips over into something dramatic, something bottomless as it were.

Seen from today's perspective, the *Chromatic Constellations* are also digital images. They can be read without exception digitally, because – for three decades, long before the emergence of our digital society – they have been built up from the structure 1-0-1-0-1-0 etc. In this way, they anticipate and accompany our digital world of the present but also form critical alternatives to the mass production of homogenised images that characterises it. The positive creation of legends around Heinz Mack and his work among younger generations has a great deal to do with the digital dimension of the *Chromatic Constellations*.

Ultimately, these works can be explained by a longing for images. It is often forgotten that all good art emerges from this. In Heinz Mack's case, this means proposing an alternative approach to the main trends in painting of recent decades and the present, in which light and colour enter into a dance of their own. Throughout his oeuvre, light acts as a liberation from imposed forms and a release of art into areas where art deals directly with the elements. To rethink this on canvas, so to speak, elevates ZERO beyond itself. How can light and colour enter into the most intimate dialogue possible on the surface? This is the subject of Heinz Mack's second painterly oeuvre since 1991.

»

Karl Kraus: 'Science is spectral analysis, art is light synthesis' – a puzzling, not exactly logical formulation. However, I know that if the physics of light prevails in art, then art loses. So: if the colours are sometimes unfriendly to me, I continue to paint with the risk of failing or winning. This is also an impulse, inspired by the hope that it will be the last to die and that the bad colours will turn into good colours. Goethe's 'sensual and moral effect of colour' is perhaps best understood by translating it as sensations and their relationship to the intellect, to the spirit.

« (LETTER TO VEIT LOERS, JANUARY 2017)[290]

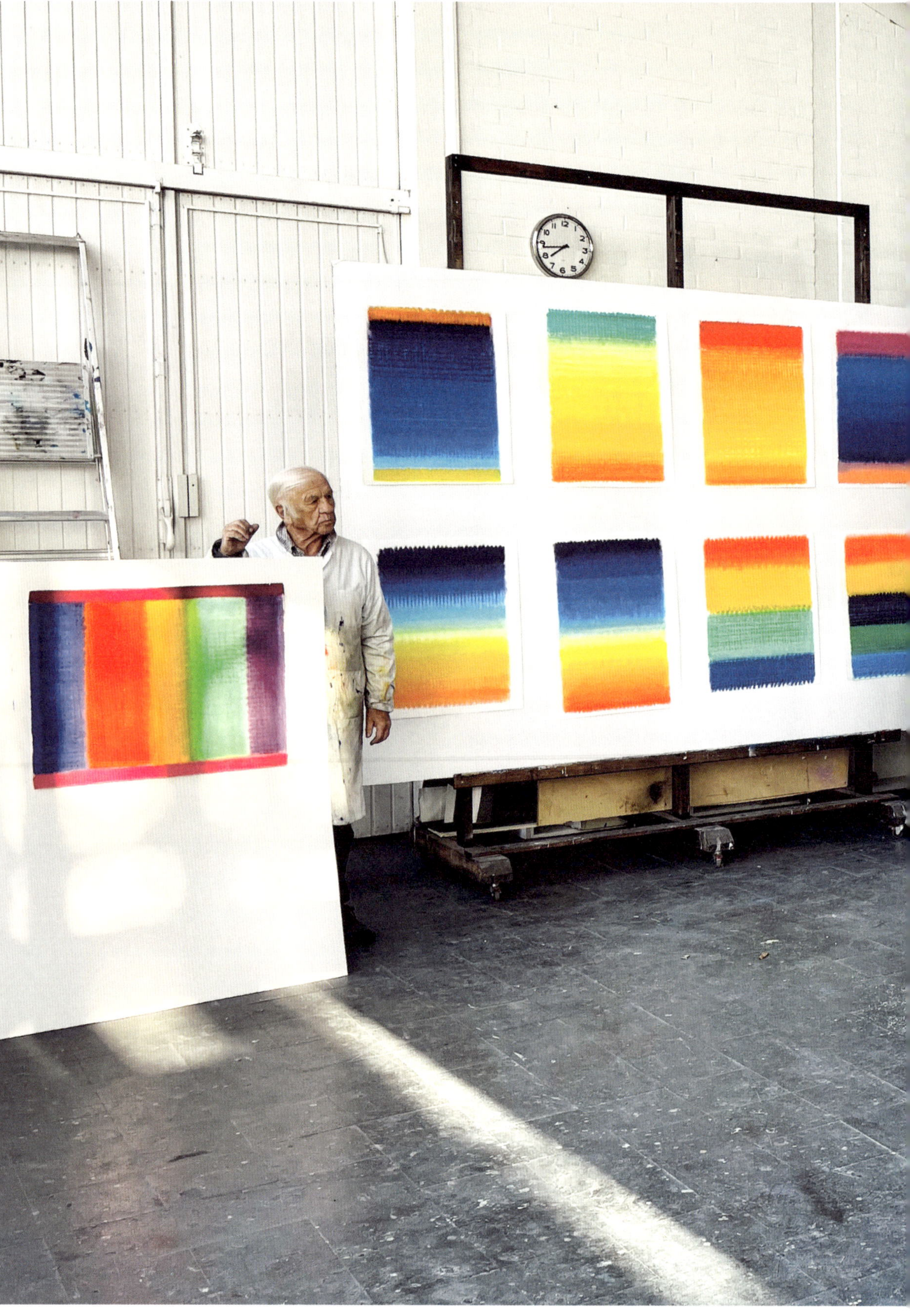

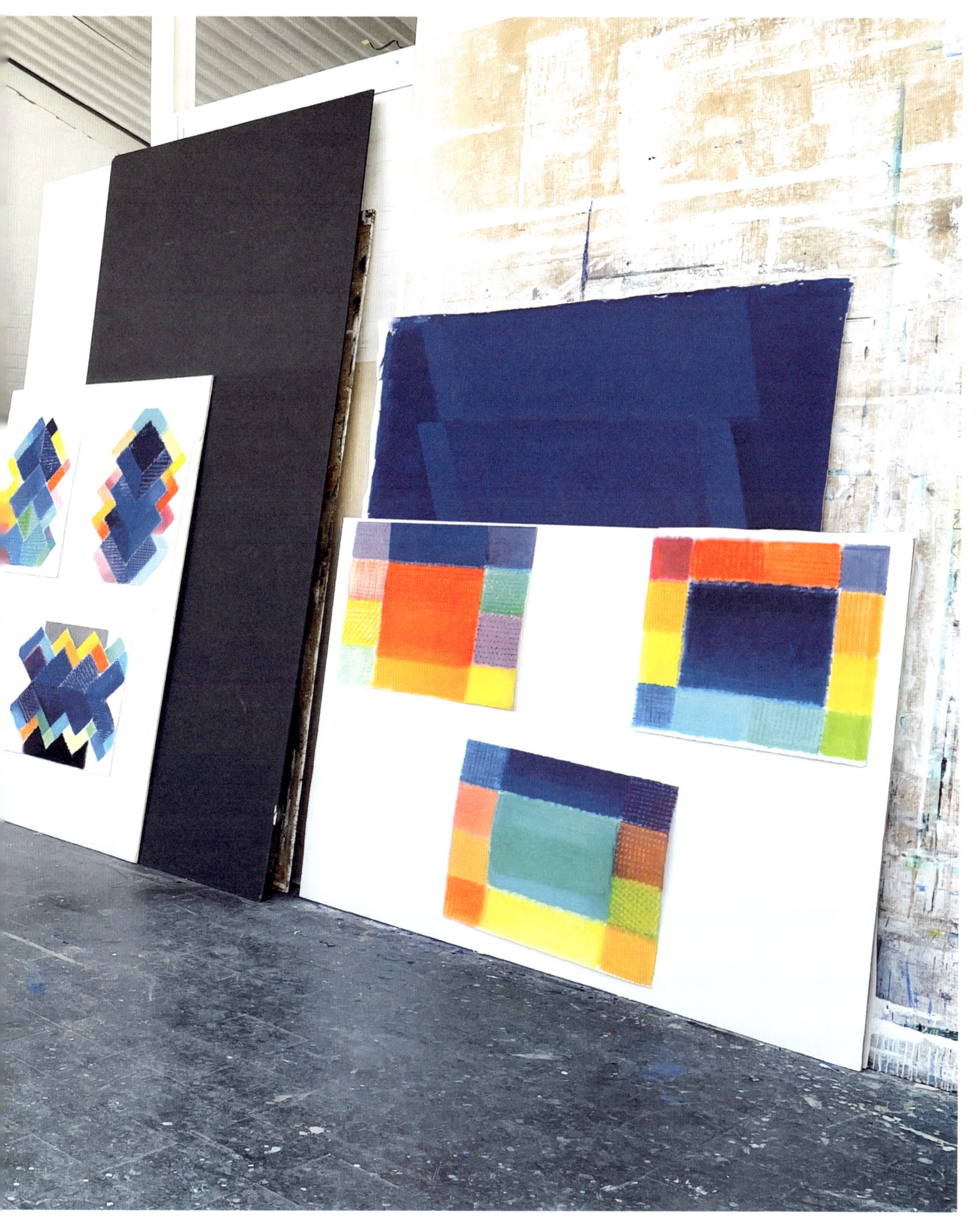

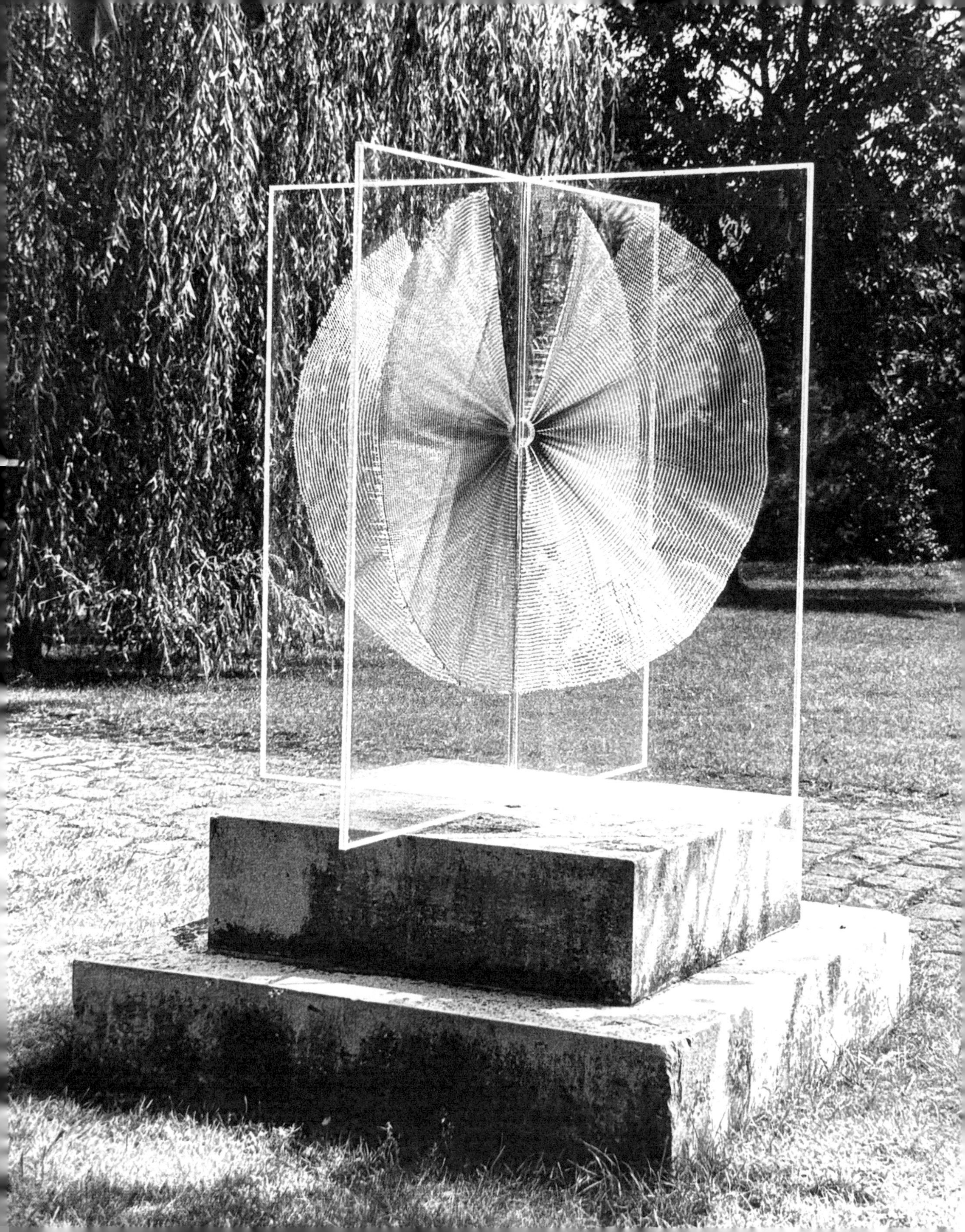

NATURE

Wing Sculpture
1980

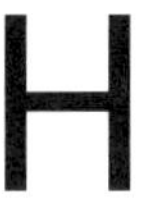einz Mack's work contains many other dimensions. This may come as a surprise given the clear, simple formal language he has maintained for decades and could be misunderstood as a simple field of meaning. On the contrary, the work is extraordinarily multi-layered and multi-sensory. Each level of meaning opens up to another, previously unimaginable level, which leads to the next and so on. This almost infinite chain of meaning is characteristic of Mack's work.

One of these unexpected aspects is the underlying concept of nature.[291] This is surprising at first glance, as the artist is generally associated more with technology and the technical side of civilisation. However, his understanding of nature is omnipresent in the artistic process. It has three main levels.

»

It is incredibly important for all children to play. We made do with the circumstances. When we were allowed to go out into nature, I was always outside. There was a landscape with woods and fields all around, so I could do whatever I wanted. My classmates were all there too, we were always out and about. When it rained, well, it was just... I don't remember what I did then.

(DECEMBER 2023) «

»

Nature refers not only to my homes and workplaces in Mönchengladbach and Ibiza, with their closeness to nature and artificial gardens.[293] It also refers to the fact that I started experimenting with water, fire, the elements, earth, air, foam and so on very early on, in the early 1950s, while I was still at the art academy, until around 1960–62. So that was my elementary relationship with nature.

(DECEMBER 2023) «

The first level concerns his childhood and youth. Heinz Mack spent most of these years in Lollar, Hesse, in a largely unspoilt natural environment. His first creative works date from this period, such as the carefully shot black-and-white photographs of wooden structures created when logs are cut with a circular saw or when cut branches are stacked conically to dry (fig. p. 289). Incidentally, the photographs also document a way of dealing with nature that was destroyed for decades, if not forever, by the industrialisation of agriculture and forestry from the 1950s onwards.

Once you start looking for nature in Heinz Mack's work, you will find it at every turn. His most relevant works in this respect were created during his years as a student in the class of Ewald Mataré at the Düsseldorf Academy of Art. They are three-dimensional collages made of wood in which one can sense both his familiarity with organic material and his sense of structure, created in the 1950s from the study of Johann Wolfgang von Goethe's morphology and its graphic realisation through the observation of nature. His experiments with a priori non-artistic elements of nature, such as water, fire, etc., which seemed to the art world of the time like pipe dreams,[292] also began during his years at the academy. Without them, however, the ZERO concept in 1957–58 would have had no further foundation.

The artist commented on this childhood influence while on the grounds of the Huppertzhof, which opens onto a large field that had been harvested the day before one of our conversations, so that the corn stalks were still lying around in more or less geometric structures, and the view was once again unobstructed: 'Fortunately, this field has not yet been rezoned as building land. I grew up surrounded by nature, and I couldn't work without this presence.'[294] Later that day, when the artist was back in his glazed studio, once again in front of a canvas, a deer leapt calmly across the adjacent

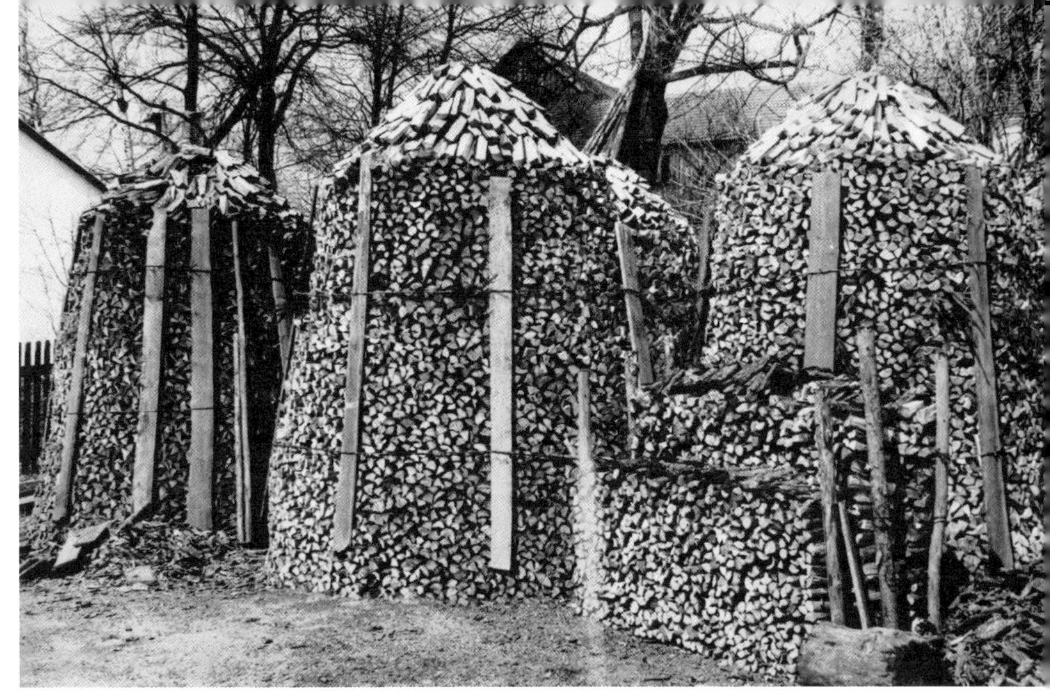

Stacked Firewood
nature photograph from Lollar
mid-1940s

Bull's-eye Wood
nature photo from Lollar
mid-1940s

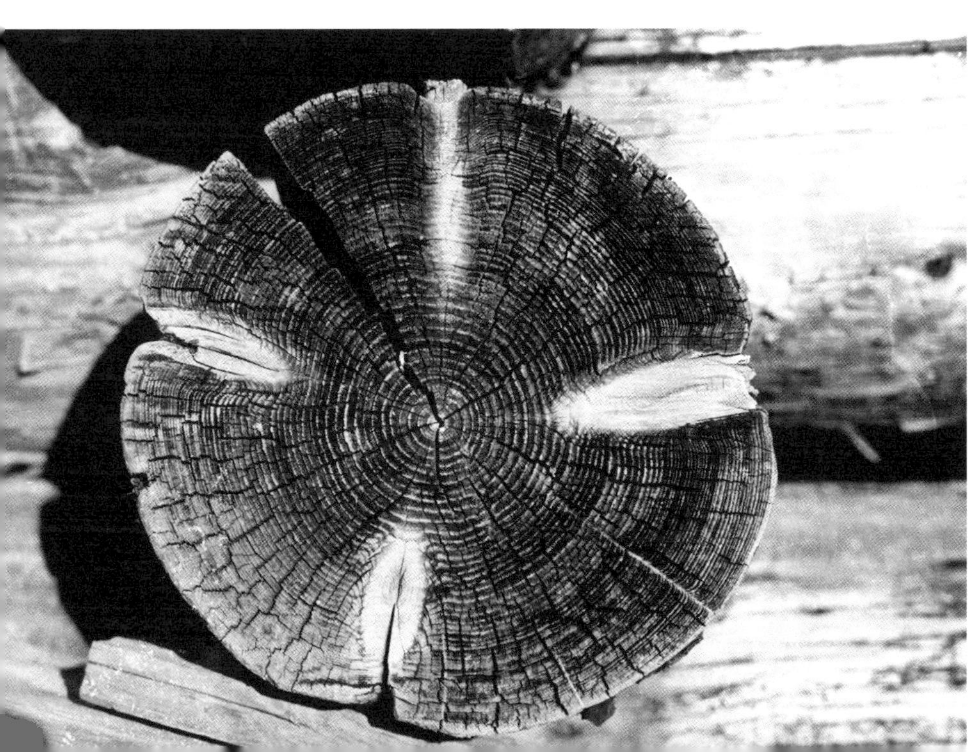

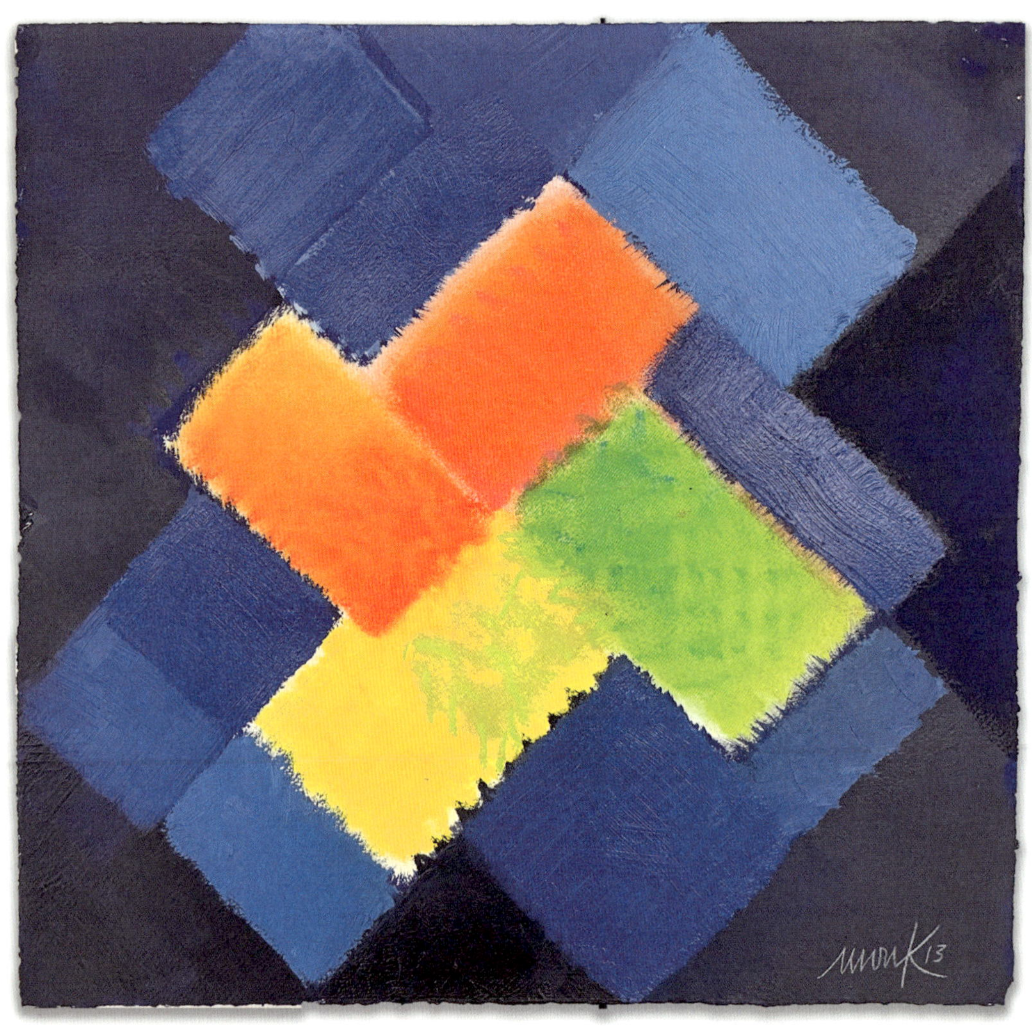

Untitled
2013

field. From time to time, herons can be seen rising from the network of plants around the fishpond where they nest.

The second aspect of Heinz Mack's understanding of nature comes from philosophy. In the current discourse on ecology, there is a widespread idea that Western philosophy since the sixteenth or seventeenth century has understood nature as 'anti-nature' and is responsible for the industrialisation that increasingly endangers the survival of our planet. This is absurd. European philosophy over the last five centuries has been one of the richest in natural philosophical thought since philosophy was established as a school of free thought in ancient Greece, and continues unabated to the present day.[295]

A few years ago, Heinz Mack was deeply impressed by his exchange with the philosopher Gernot Böhme and his brother, the cultural scientist Hartmut Böhme, who developed an aesthetics of nature based on the early ecological movements of the 1970s and discovered the artist's work in the mid-1990s.[297] The correspondence with Gernot and Hartmut Böhme as well as texts by both on Mack's work, in particular on the occasion of the 2018 exhibition *Taten des Lichts. Mack & Goethe* (Deeds of Light: Mack & Goethe) at the Goethe Museum in Düsseldorf, can serve as a starting point for exploring Mack's contemporary reflections on nature.[298] In 2023, Hartmut Böhme wrote to the artist: 'You know better than anyone that one cannot do whatever one wants with light, but that one must not only accept its physicality as a condition for the possibility of light art, but also appreciate it. Then the limitation imposed by materiality can even become the inner core of the working process. When what is actually light about light emerges, or when the Earth can be experienced as the Earth, then the glowing core of the creative process is reached with the highest degree of respect for the given.'[299]

'Nature' is therefore a very reflective theme in Heinz Mack's work. It is not a naïve or romantic understanding of nature. Let us take a random work from the last few decades: an untitled painting on handmade paper from 2013 (fig. p. 290) is primed with a deep blue hue, on which irregular rectangles in different shades of blue stand out but at the same time enclose four rectangles painted with pastel chalk, again freely designed, which are set in the Goethean colour spectrum (cf. pp. 202, 282) of yellow, orange, red, and green and create an intense inner vibration. The painting is like a power station. It can withstand all light conditions. It is as strong in the dark as it is in daylight. Above all, it harmonises very well with a natural environment. Is there not a grammar of colourful natural conditions at work here? Put simply, it is a structure of abstractly

»

I was educated at a science-oriented secondary school. One of my main subjects was Weizsäcker, who published his lectures on the history of nature three years after the end of the war. This little booklet was our reading material, so we came into contact with Carl Friedrich von Weizsäcker, the philosopher and scientist, at a very early age. I still have the booklet, printed in 1948, just before I left school.[296]

« (DECEMBER 2023)

»

My philosophy studies and part of my time at secondary school were very open to physical problems. Much of it is artistically relevant. Leibniz's monad, for example. Closer to our time, with Nicolai Hartmann and in quantum physics, there is the concept of the indeterminacy relation. It plays an important role in art. Art is probably the only domain in which there is the freedom that something is not planned in advance, cannot be planned in advance. Heisenberg was of course important to read and analyse.[300]

« (DECEMBER 2023)

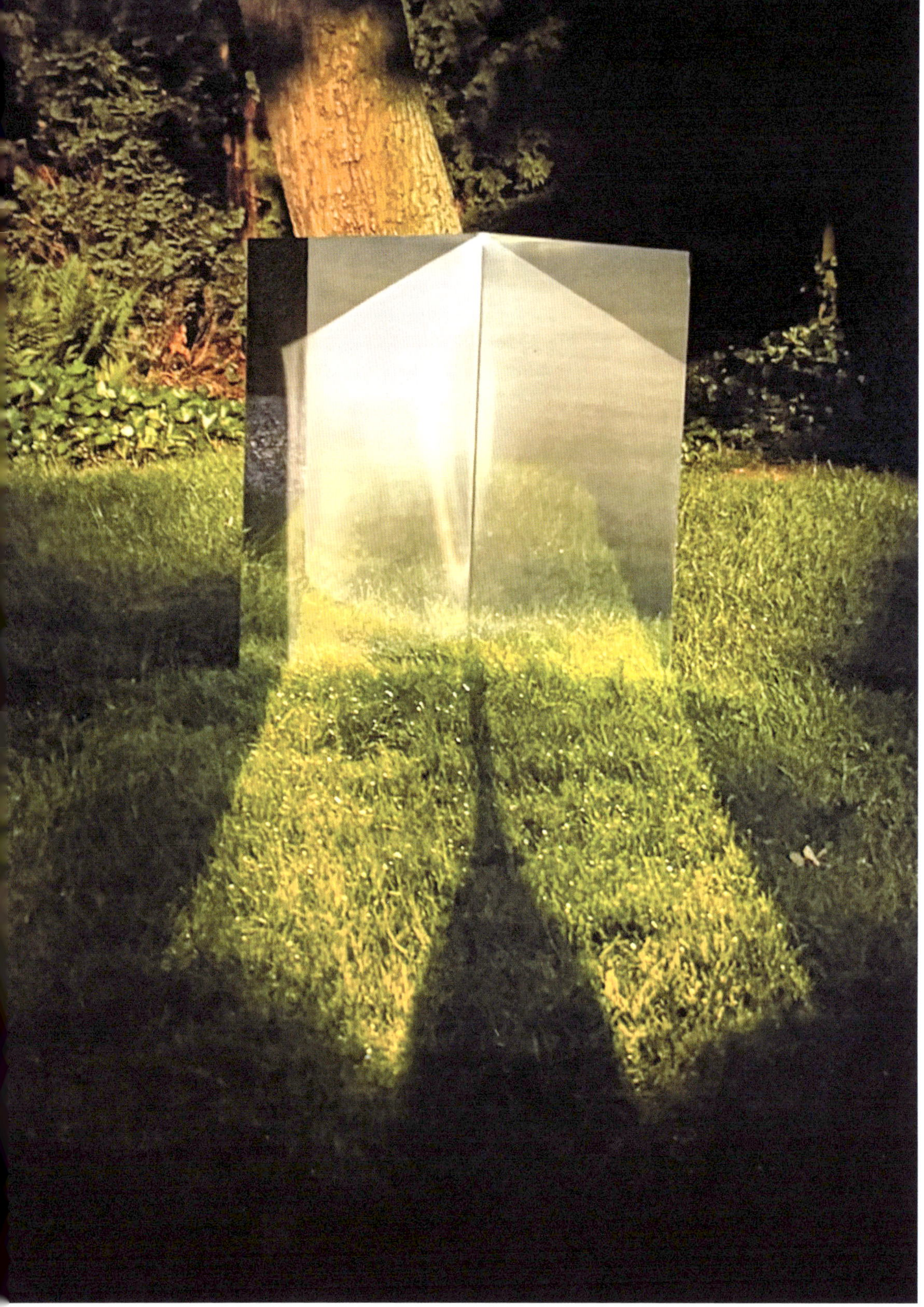

Mirror Experiments (Project in the Artist's Garden)
1997

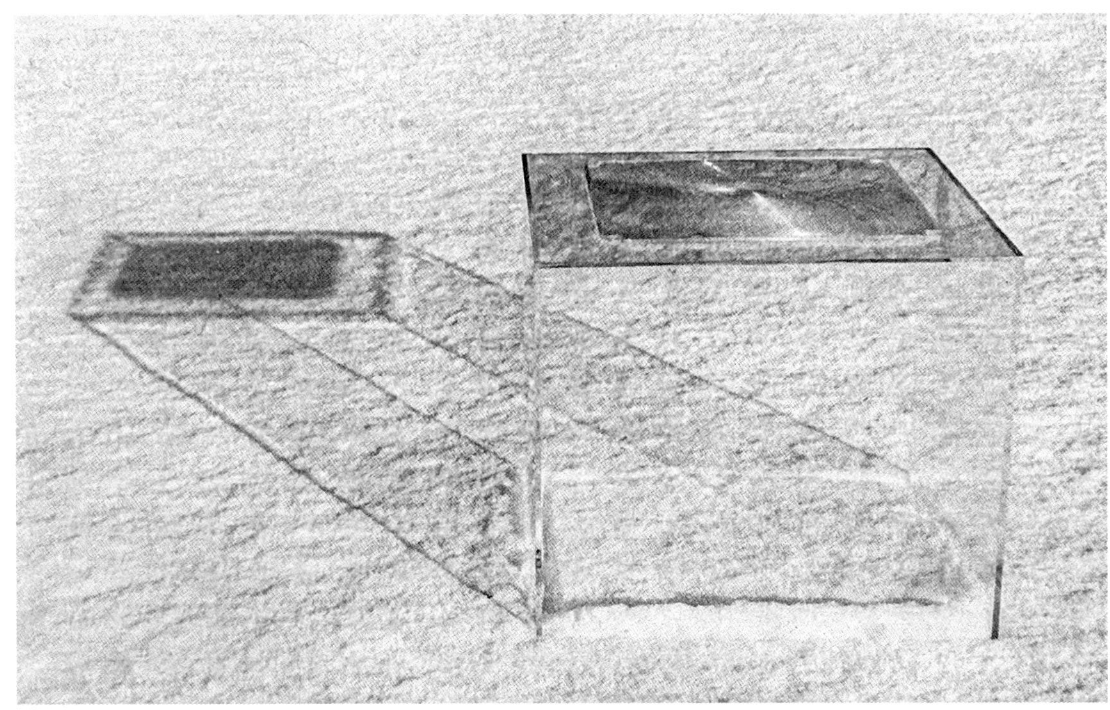

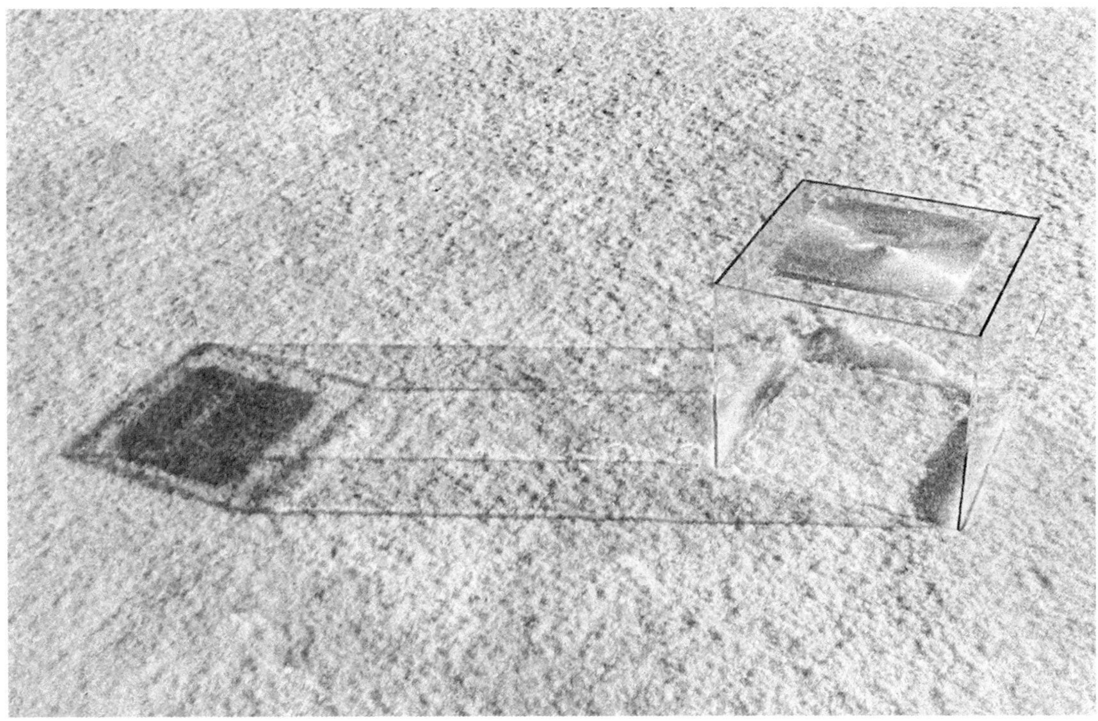

The Shadow of Nothing –
Glass Cube in the Snow
1980

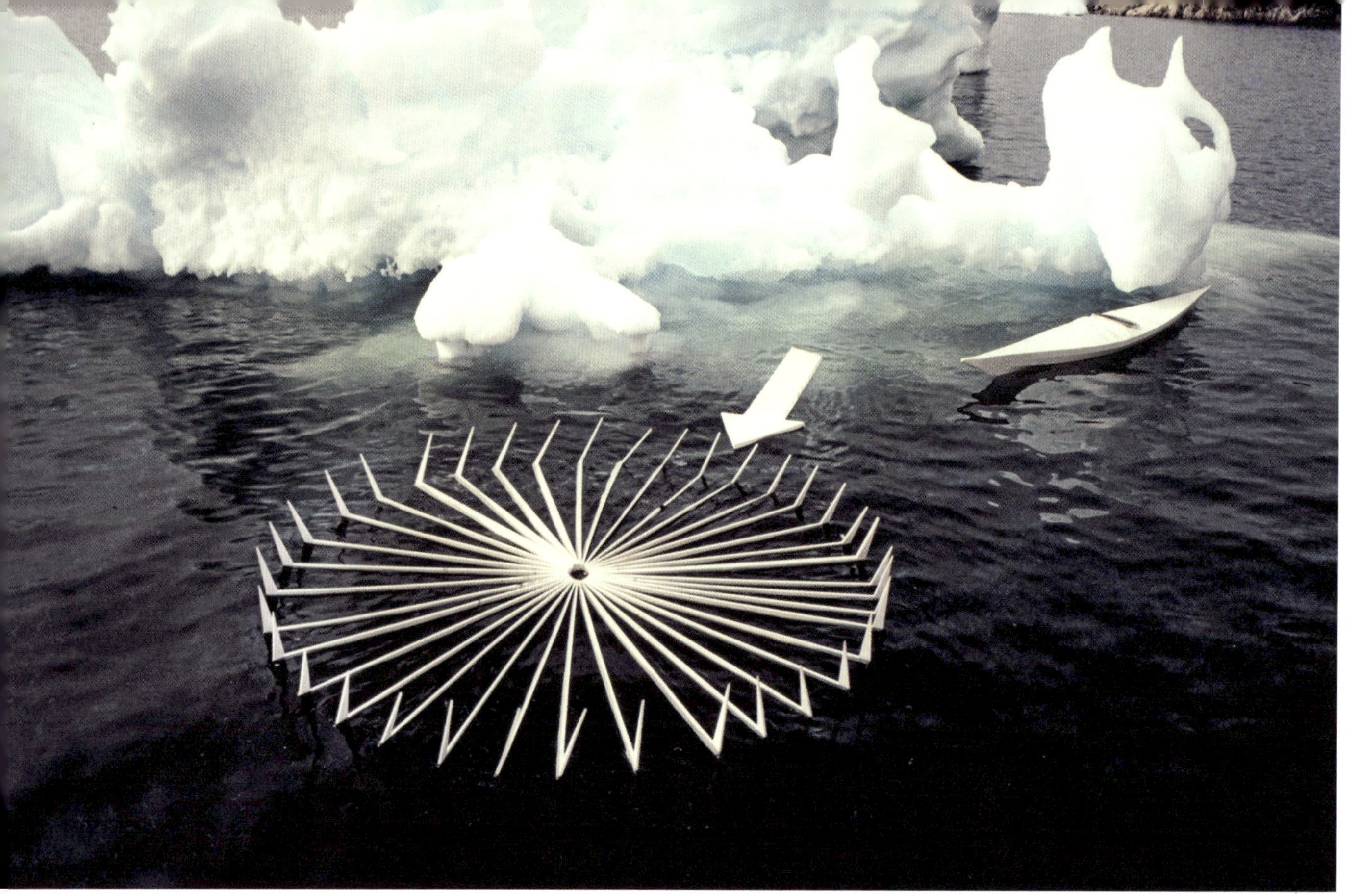

Water Lily in the Arctic
Disko Bay, Greenland
1976

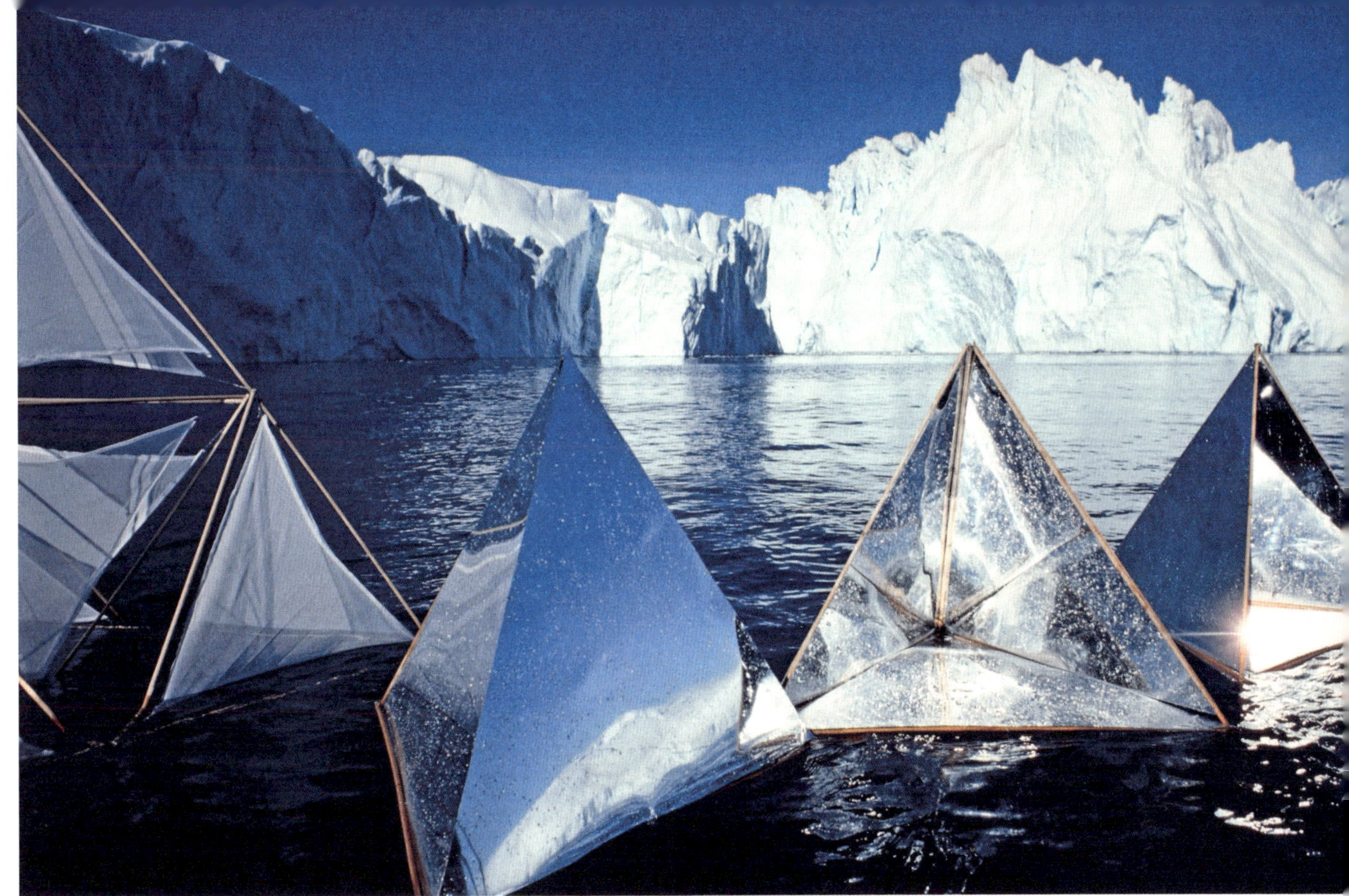

Light Prisms in the Arctic (Model for a Floating Research Station),
Disko Bay, Greenland
1976

→
Fire in the Desert – Light Experiment
Sahara
1974

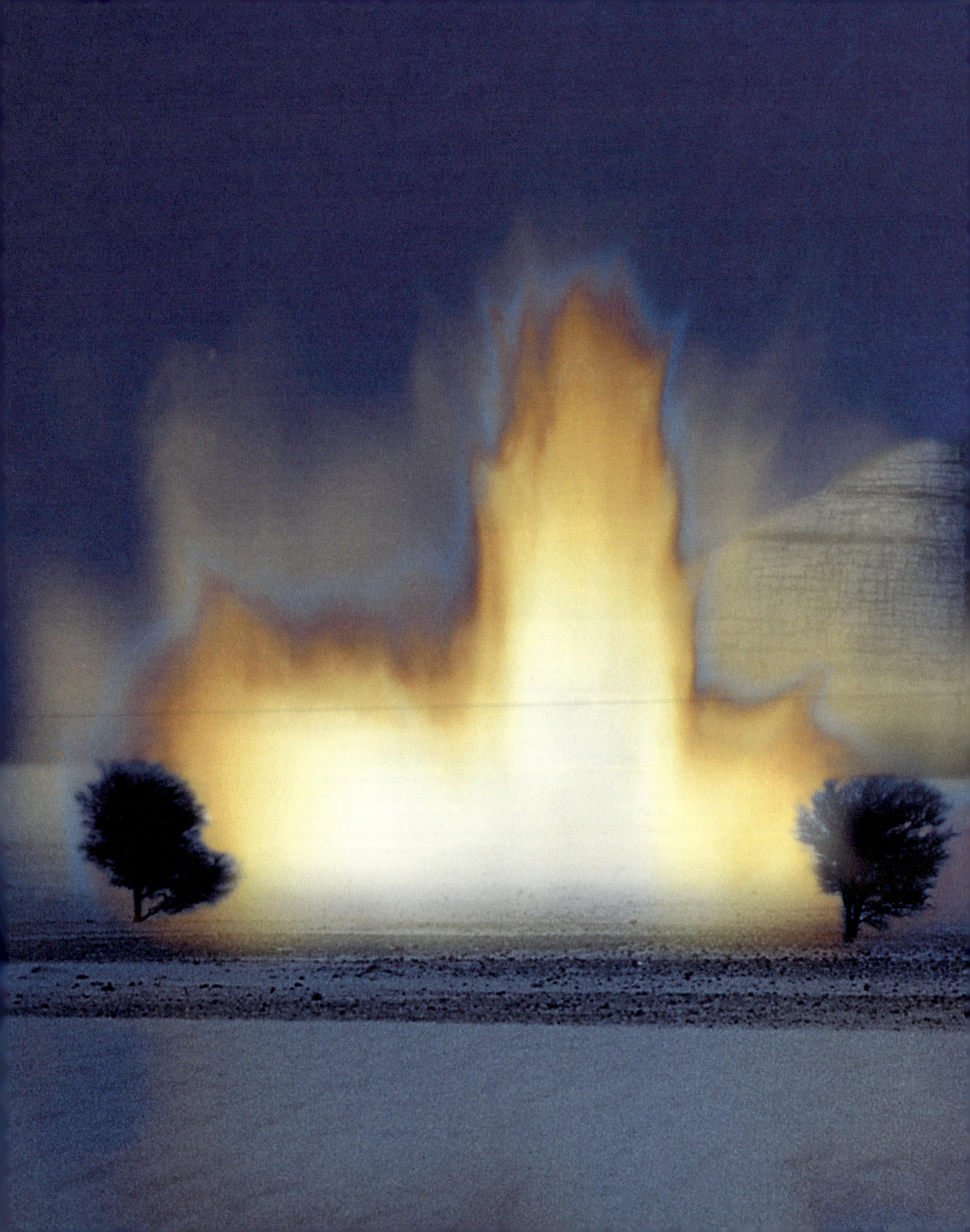

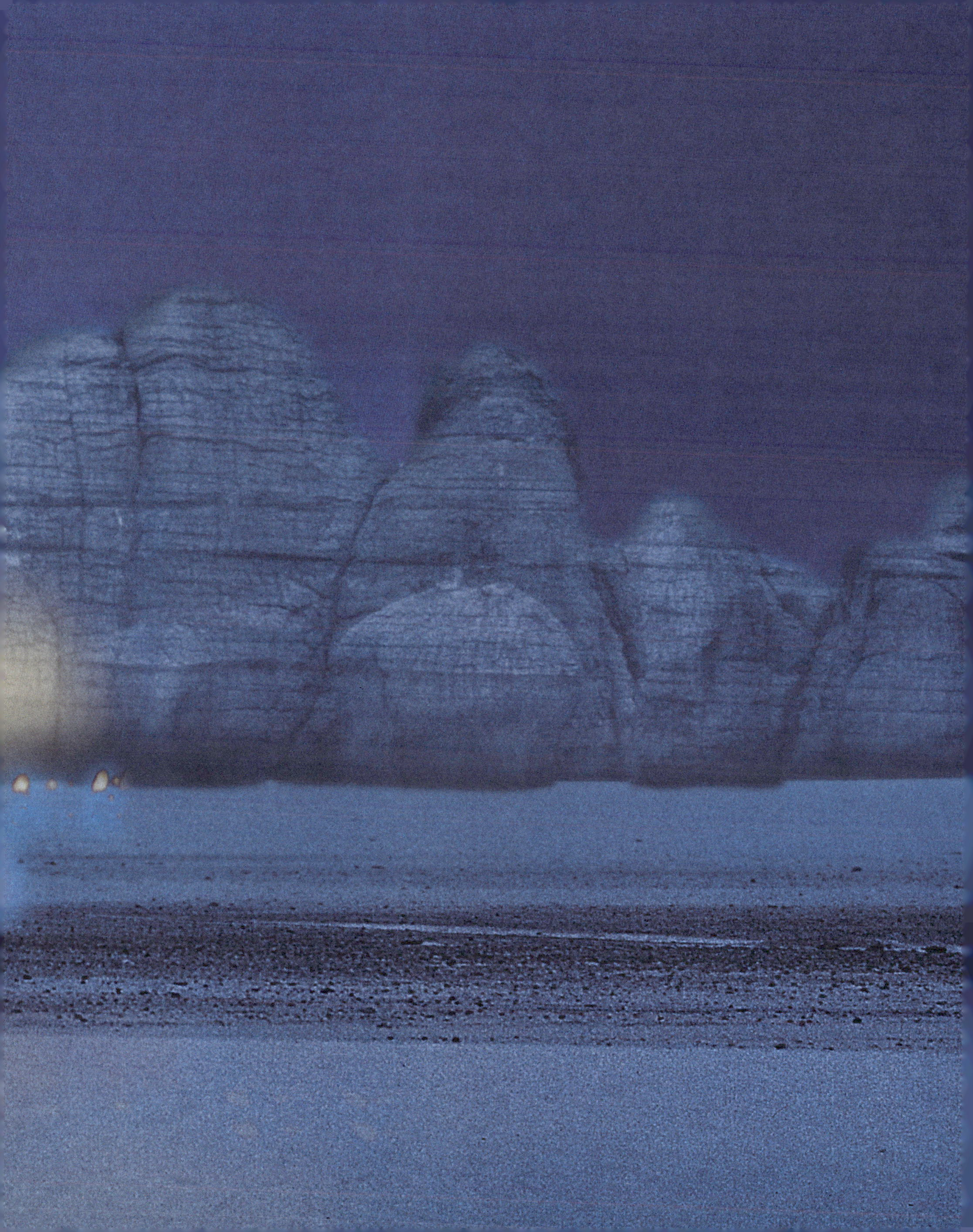

»

In classical European art, fire, water, air and earth were represented mimetically, imitated. The Old Masters painted everything in such a way that you could visualise it exactly: this is water, this is fire and so on. But the art of the ancient Syrians already shows that they used these things – earth, water, fire, air – as material to make things that speak of them symbolically. You see, this is something quite unique. They were practically using these elements of nature as material for a design.

(DECEMBER 2023) «

conceived fields. In any case, we are infinitely far from 'technical civilisation'.

The third aspect of Heinz Mack's understanding of nature concerns the confrontation with the elements. As a contemporary artist, it is also an almost Sisyphean task to deal for decades directly with light, something that the ancient Egyptians and Greeks had already failed at, at least in our eyes, and to deal as directly as possible with the Earth, water, and the sun.[301]

The artist draws a wealth of experience from this exploration, since the desire to experiment with light, water, fire, or air in order to create a work of art is linked to practical and theoretical experimentation with these very elements – and has been for seven decades. Mack's wealth of experience in this form is unique in contemporary art. This also partly explains the astonishing parallels with the model of current physics, according to which matter and the atmosphere are in constant vibration. Only at absolute zero, minus 273.15 degrees Celsius, do the particles come to a standstill. Only there does the vibration stop. This has much to do with Mack's oeuvre, in which vibrations, oscillations, and wavelengths of various kinds create signs and forms.

This wealth of experience in turn underlies the ability to react spontaneously and at the same time coherently and innovatively to the possibilities of dealing with extreme landscapes, as Heinz Mack did in the first realisation of the *Sahara Project* in the Tunisian desert in 1968 and again in the Sahara and the Arctic in the second realisation in 1976 (fig. pp. 294–297). There, the improvisational character of the artistic settings, in which Mack had to react directly to environmental conditions that he had never before perceived, represented one of the great qualities of the works in its ecological coherence with the unknown milieu. Not unlike *The Sky Over Nine Columns* in Venice in 2014 (fig. pp. 310–311), it was the combination of the urgent realisation of the conceived work and the unusual, almost unlimited location in direct communication with the sunlight. Such settings can only be created on the basis of a wealth of experience gained from countless experiments in art and nature.

»

[I have] visited nature reserves because they are large spaces in which an unrivalled light breathes – after all, my objects live almost exclusively from light and in space. So I wanted to find out how space and light affect them and whether these small objects have a chance to assert and articulate themselves in the infinite expanse and all-encompassing brightness. In a way, I work like a researcher who later publishes the optical results of his work.

(IN: DIETER HONISCH, 'GESPRÄCH MIT HEINZ MACK', 1977)[302] «

Observing and experimenting with nature on a daily basis is an inner necessity for Heinz Mack. It is similar to the need for observation and experimentation described by Johann Wolfgang von Goethe, an essential orientation for Mack since his final years at secondary school, even before he took the step into the visual arts. The artist would not mention this reference to his own life situation – but

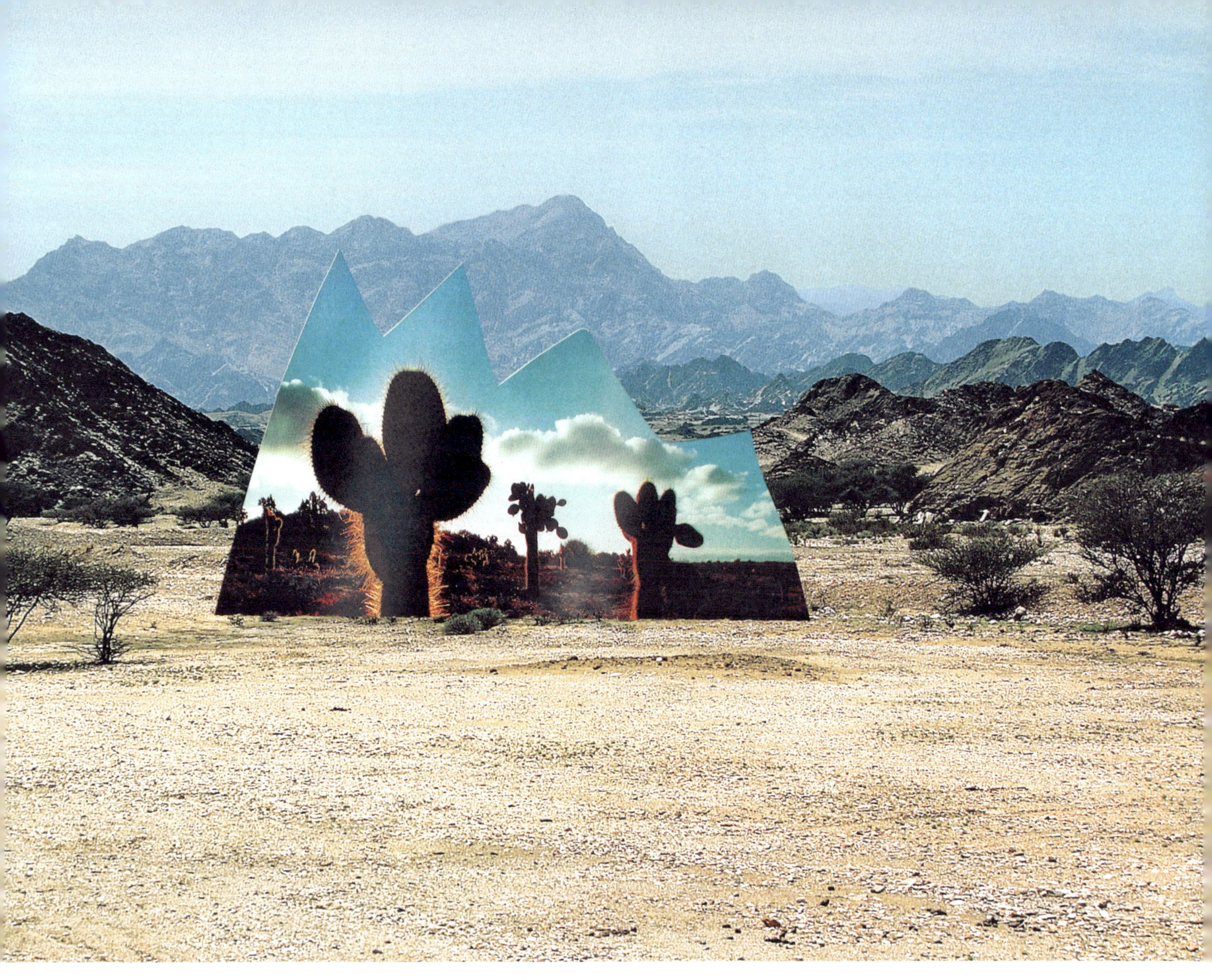

Large Mirror
(In Honour of Alexander von Humboldt)
1999

»

I placed glass cubes on a snow surface, and it was really exciting.

(JUNE 2022) «

it is present, also in the absolute seriousness of this activity. The observation of nature had led Goethe to consider his theory of colours and *The Metamorphosis of Plants* (1790/1817) more important than his literary work.[303] Heinz Mack would never accept this for his own oeuvre. The idea seemed absurd to him, so we did not discuss it. In his view, Mack has no 'other' work apart from his visual art. Despite his intensive involvement with philosophy and music, no 'second' or 'third' strand of work has emerged from this.

However, this does not exempt him from the regular theoretical examination of his relationship with nature. 'Unlike Monet, I don't go into the garden to paint. What I see in my sculpture park (fig. pp. 13, 17) is not a motif, not an inspiration for my work as a painter and sculptor. Interestingly, the dominant colour, green, which is rich in its nuances, is rarely used in abstract art and almost never in concrete art, probably because of its organic properties', Mack writes of his relationship with nature. 'It is far more the atmosphere that stimulates me. Since the park is large and there are many different principles of organisation, the impressions and sensual perceptions also change. Just as the time of day and the seasons are constantly changing, so are the light, the temperature, and the wind. All this is real and corresponds to the daily weather reports, but it also has an aesthetic appeal. The ephemeral phenomena of nature awaken and brighten throughout the day, reaching their maximum brightness at the height of the day, when all colours virtually "bleach out", losing their contrasting effect and appearing more as light and less as colour.'[304] This reveals a relationship with nature that is as far removed from current dystopias as it is from Neo-Romanticism.

»

Today, in addition to the theory of evolution, we must be allowed to clearly recognise and express the fact that nature acts completely randomly, that it is not goal-oriented, not teleologically directed, that it shows no continuity in its developments, and that – what I find particularly interesting – chance plays a major role, the aleatory motif, which, of course, also plays a recurring role in my work.

(DECEMBER 2023) «

One day, after lunch, Heinz Mack suddenly says to himself: 'You've made something that's become too orderly; it needs a bit of disorder'[305] – and goes back to his glazed studio.

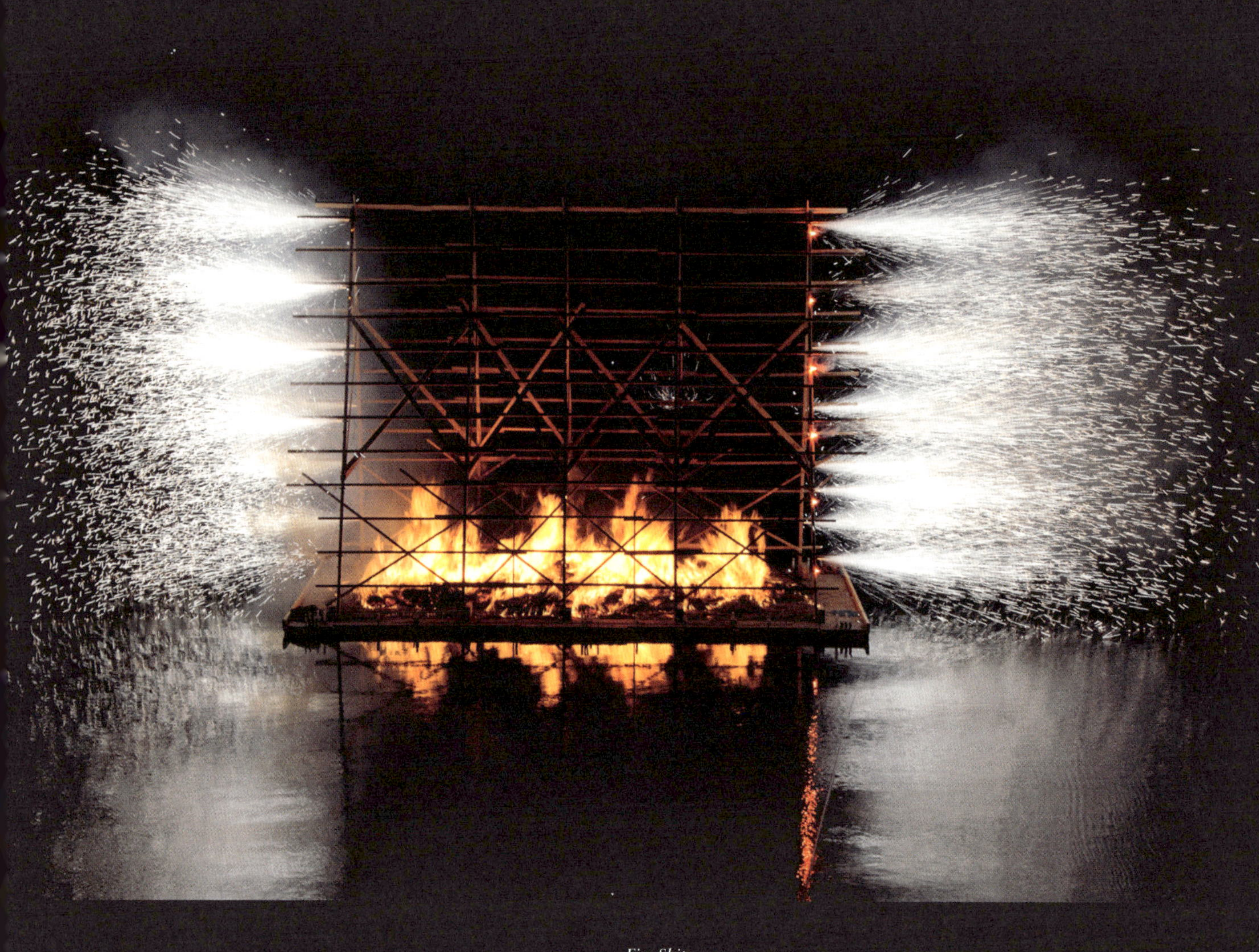

Fire Ship
Düsseldorf media harbour
2010

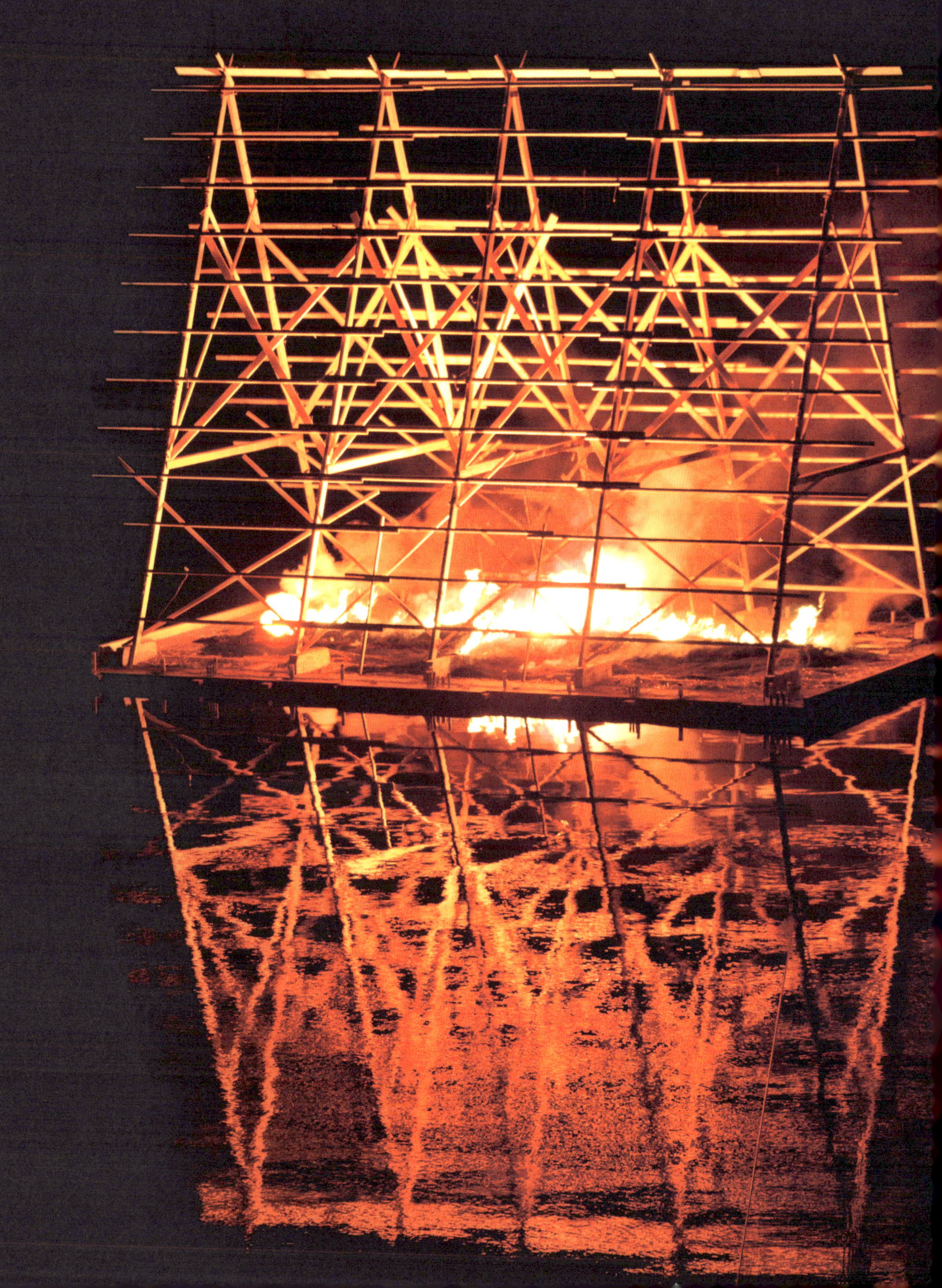

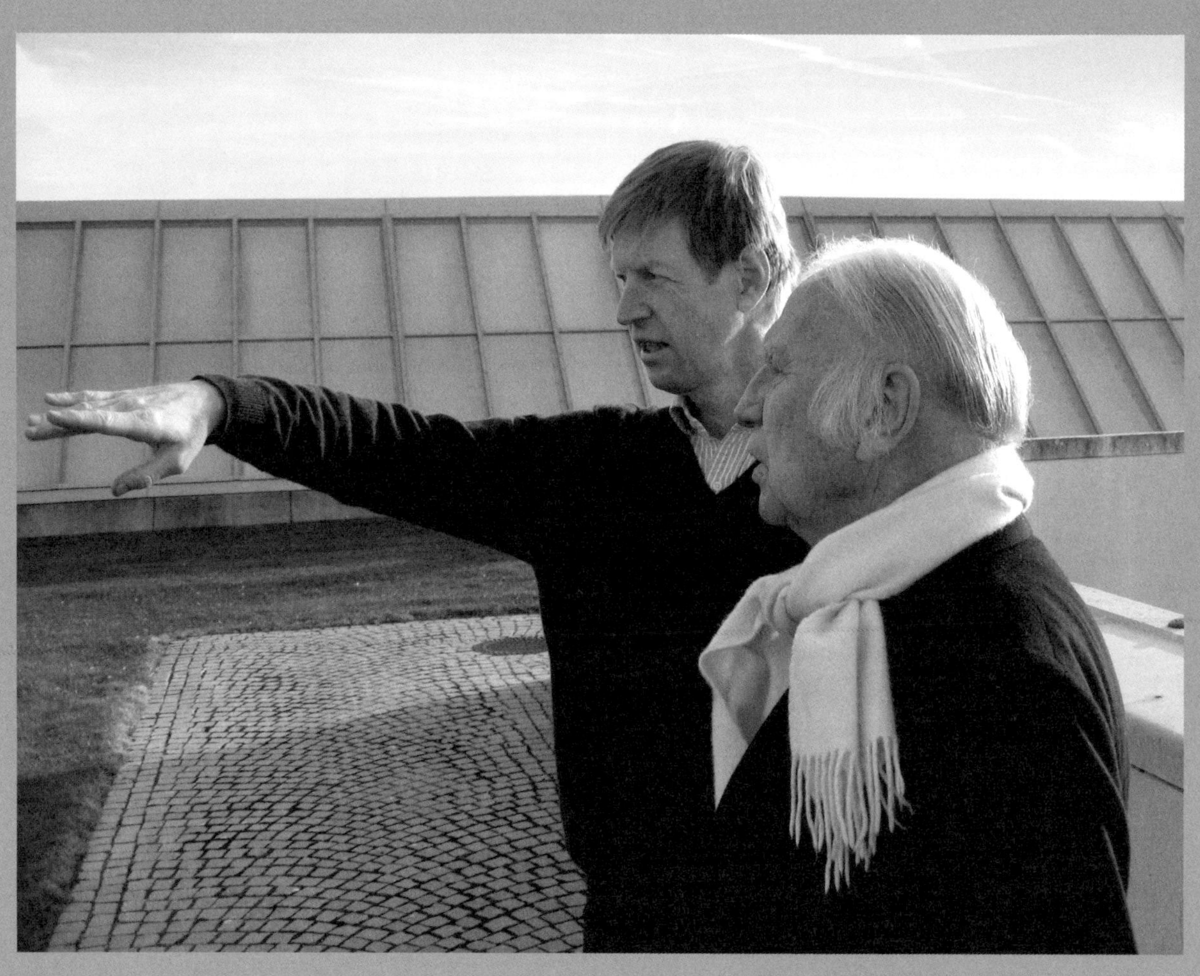

TAKING STOCK 2025

Robert Fleck and Heinz Mack on the rooftop of the Bundeskunsthalle, Bonn
2011

January 2025: Heinz Mack is relaxed. Over the past two decades, the situation for his artistic work has changed dramatically. Its future seems secure. This is the greatest relief for any artist, as Mack tells us today in conversation at the Hupertzhof. At the same time, one does not change with age – Heinz Mack now gets up and goes to his studio. Every day is still a working day for him. When he is told that Jacques Villeglé, a companion of Yves Klein's who was five years older than Mack, decided at the age of 90 to make one last series of works and one very last exhibition, and then was overjoyed to have left the making of art behind him,[306] Mack simply shakes his head.

» There are things I spontaneously realised or prophesied that did not come to pass in the ZERO years but are very topical today: the lamella plantations in the desert, the mirror plantations in the desert, several square kilometres in size, the huge mirror houses in Saudi Arabia. History has taken a very different turn. Back then, the term 'solar cell' was largely unknown; and for the general public, solar technology had nothing whatsoever to do with energy generation – if it did, it was for purely artistic reasons. Today it is a global issue, highly topical, ecological, to save the planet. I read somewhere that there is a space being designed, 50 by 50 by 50 metres, in which there will be nothing but absolutely pure air. This is very topical and was already conceivable with ZERO. That's why the research on ZERO is so important, and why the ZERO foundation is so important. What is also important to me is that ZERO was never an ideology. It was an experiment.

(JANUARY 2024) «

The cycle that brought ZERO back into the public eye began in 2006, when the first ZERO retrospective in several decades was organised under Director General Jean-Hubert Martin at the Museum Kunstpalast in Düsseldorf, the former municipal art museum.[307] Two years later, at the suggestion of Mattijs Visser, the ZERO foundation was established in Düsseldorf, with works by and archive holdings of the three Düsseldorf ZERO artists Heinz Mack, Otto Piene, and Günther Uecker, and a thirty-year funding commitment from the city. Since then, the possibilities for research and exhibitions have been placed on a new footing.

Parallel to this, in 2006, the Lenz Schönberg Collection presented the exhibition *ZERO. Künstler einer europäischen Bewegung* (ZERO. Artists of a European Movement) at the Museum der Moderne Salzburg.[308] Three years later, it published a comprehensive two-volume catalogue of its holdings;[309] and on 2 February 2010, it sold forty-nine works at the *Epoch ZERO* auction at Sotheby's in London, which attracted considerable attention and fetched remarkable prices. The German art magazine *monopol* commented: 'This [...] finally establishes the Zero group on the international market.'[310]

It was around this time that we met. In January 2009, I was unexpectedly appointed director of the Bundeskunsthalle in Bonn. On the table was a list of four exhibitions that Christoph Vitali, the interim director, had planned but not yet finalised. We organised the exhibition on Amedeo Modigliani, which was a great success. I cancelled the other three for various reasons, including one on Heinz Mack. Of course, I knew who Mack was and what ZERO was, but I wanted to make the Bundeskunsthalle in Bonn a major centre for contemporary art from Germany, which was gaining international recognition. I had already achieved something similar as director of the Deichtorhallen in Hamburg with Michel Majerus, Hans Haacke, Georg Baselitz, Stephan Balkenhol, and Katharina Fritsch. For Bonn, Rosemarie Trockel and Thomas Schütte were at the top of the list and said yes. The aim was to keep up with the major exhibition venues such as the Centre Georges Pompidou in Paris and the Solomon R. Guggenheim Museum in New York, and at the same time to offer the high-calibre German art scene the forum for which the Bundeskunsthalle was founded.

Heinz Mack responded to my cancellation of his exhibition with a strongly worded letter: he would never, ever accept this decision. I also heard that he had activated all his contacts to have the cancellation withdrawn. During a stay in Hamburg, the art historian Werner Hofmann, a great role model for my generation, contacted me by telephone. It was immediately clear that he had thought carefully about what he wanted to say, in his Viennese manner: 'I don't want to tell you what to do. I know exactly what it's like when you take over an institution. You have to conceive and realise a series of exhibitions that will endure for years and play a leading role internationally. But I am also telling you this as a friend: think carefully about your decision regarding Heinz Mack. If you choose well, you can put on a very good exhibition. And I know him, we're friends, and I'm telling you that you can of course uphold the cancellation, that's your right. But then you'll never get rid of him. That's the way he is. He'll never let it go, not even after years. So think about it.'

Two weeks later I travelled to the Huppertzhof on the outskirts of Mönchengladbach for my first meeting with Heinz Mack – together with a trusted colleague, Rainald Schumacher, on the assumption that the artist would read me the riot act and that I would need a bodyguard, so to speak. But Mack stood in the doorway of the main building and said: 'This is the first time we've met. I suggest we behave like people who are meeting for the first time and forget that there was anything before.' That showed grandeur. He added that he himself had organised more than three hundred exhibitions in his life. The one at the Bundeskunsthalle, he said, was something I had to conceive together with the team there.

A few weeks later, however, he came to Bonn for a working meeting with a finished model of his exhibition. All aspects of his work were mixed up. After he left, we – Nathalie Hoyos, Henriette Pleiger and I – sat down as a team to think about how to deal with this. My impression was that Heinz Mack's work needed to be differentiated, not mixed up. We cut up his model and reassembled it according to the different aspects of the work. We took this model to the next meeting, again at the Huppertzhof. Heinz Mack stood speechlessly over the model for several minutes. At first sight he could not believe what we had done. The tension in the room was palpable. This

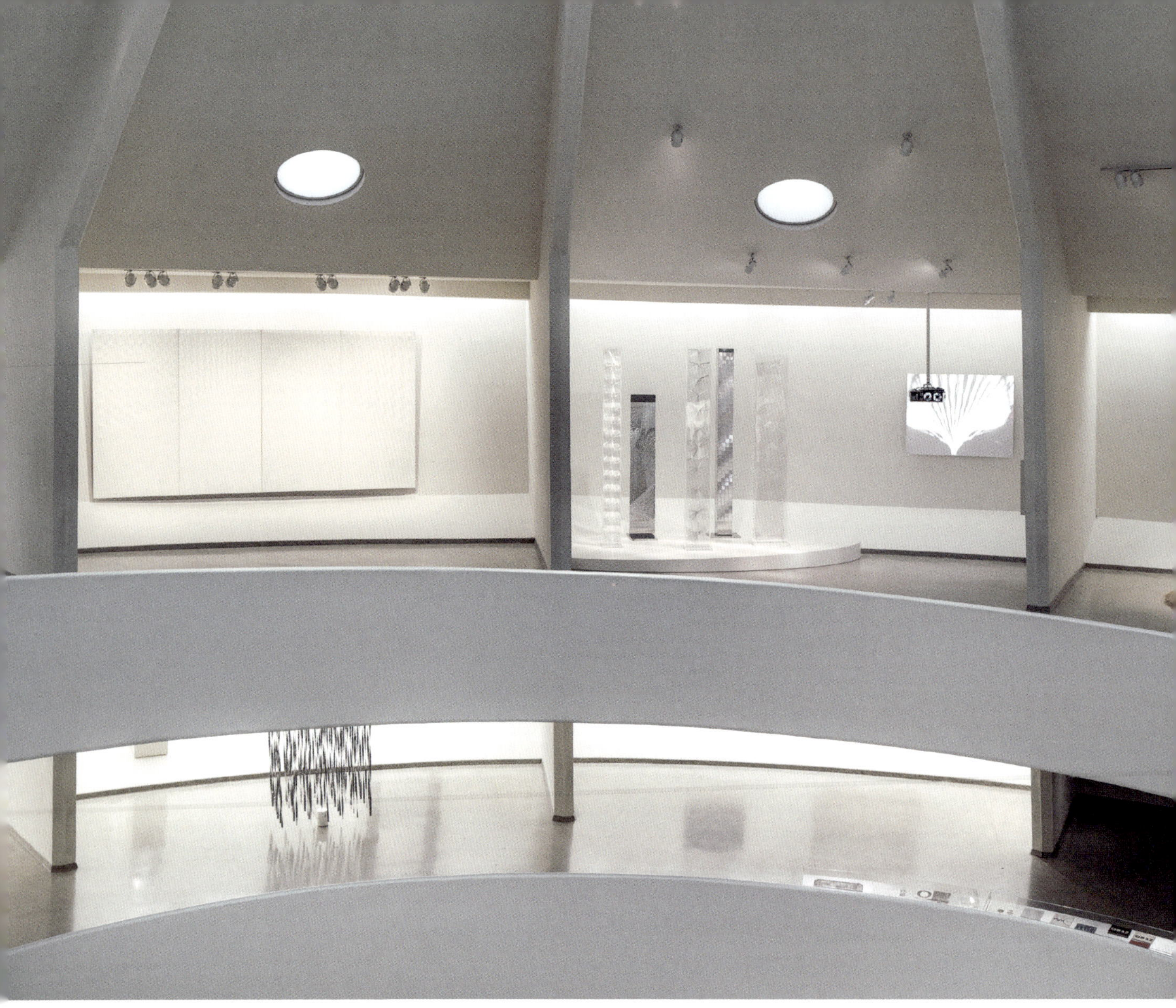

Installation view
***ZERO. Countdown to Tomorrow*,**
Solomon R. Guggenheim Museum,
New York
2014

was the big exhibition for his eightieth birthday. Was he going to suddenly exclaim angrily, 'You can't treat me like this!', or was he going to cry? Those seemed to be the alternatives. After about ten minutes, he said calmly: 'It's better this way.' That, too, showed grandeur.

In autumn 2010, at an international museum congress, when asked what I would be showing next at the Bundeskunsthalle, I replied: 'Heinz Mack'. The response baffled me: 'You're doing that because it's fashionable now.'[311] For the catalogue of the Bonn exhibition, two stars of the international art scene, Daniel Birnbaum and Hans Ulrich Obrist, interviewed Heinz Mack.[312] In the spring of 2011, a team from the Solomon R. Guggenheim Museum in New York, including the curator Valerie Hillings, spent several days at the Bundeskunsthalle for the well-attended exhibition *Heinz Mack. Light – Space – Colour*. It was clear that the New Yorkers were working on an exhibition about ZERO. In 2013, Heike van den Valentyn, curator of the 2006 ZERO retrospective in Düsseldorf, organised a ZERO exhibition tour in Brazil,[313] which, like the whole of Latin America, was experiencing a museum boom.

In October 2014, after three years of preparation, the Guggenheim Museum opened *ZERO. Countdown to Tomorrow*, the largest retrospective of ZERO art to date.[314] On the initiative of the Guggenheim and the ZERO foundation, it was subsequently shown at the Martin-Gropius-Bau in Berlin and the Stedelijk Museum in Amsterdam. ZERO was finally canonised. Parallel to this, Heinz Mack had high-profile gallery exhibitions in New York, London, Hong Kong, and Paris on a scale not seen for decades.

Artists have to be very careful in such situations. On the one hand, they have always dreamed of such attention one day, preferably in their lifetime. On the other, we know from experience that such a phase does not last forever. Around 2010, ZERO art experienced a revival like no other art movement of the post-war decades.[315] However, the ZERO exhibition at the Sakıp Sabancı Museum in Istanbul in 2015 remains the last ZERO show in a major museum to date.[316] For Heinz Mack himself, the exhibition cycle has been more stable, with retrospectives at the Museum Frieder Burda in Baden-Baden in 2015, the Sakıp-Sabancı Museum in Istanbul in 2016, the Düsseldorf Kunstpalast and the Skulpturenpark Waldfrieden in Wuppertal in 2021, and the ZKM | Center for Art and Media Karlsruhe in 2023,[317] as well as a continuing international gallery circuit.

In such phases, it is particularly urgent to keep up with the sudden rise to international standing of one's own older work. At first glance, this seems almost impossible. However, there is nothing worse for an artist than to be told that their current work is a poor copy of a work from more than fifty years ago that is now considered to have lasting art historical significance. Many protagonists in the ZERO circle have had this painful experience.

→
The Sky Over Nine Columns
Venice
2014

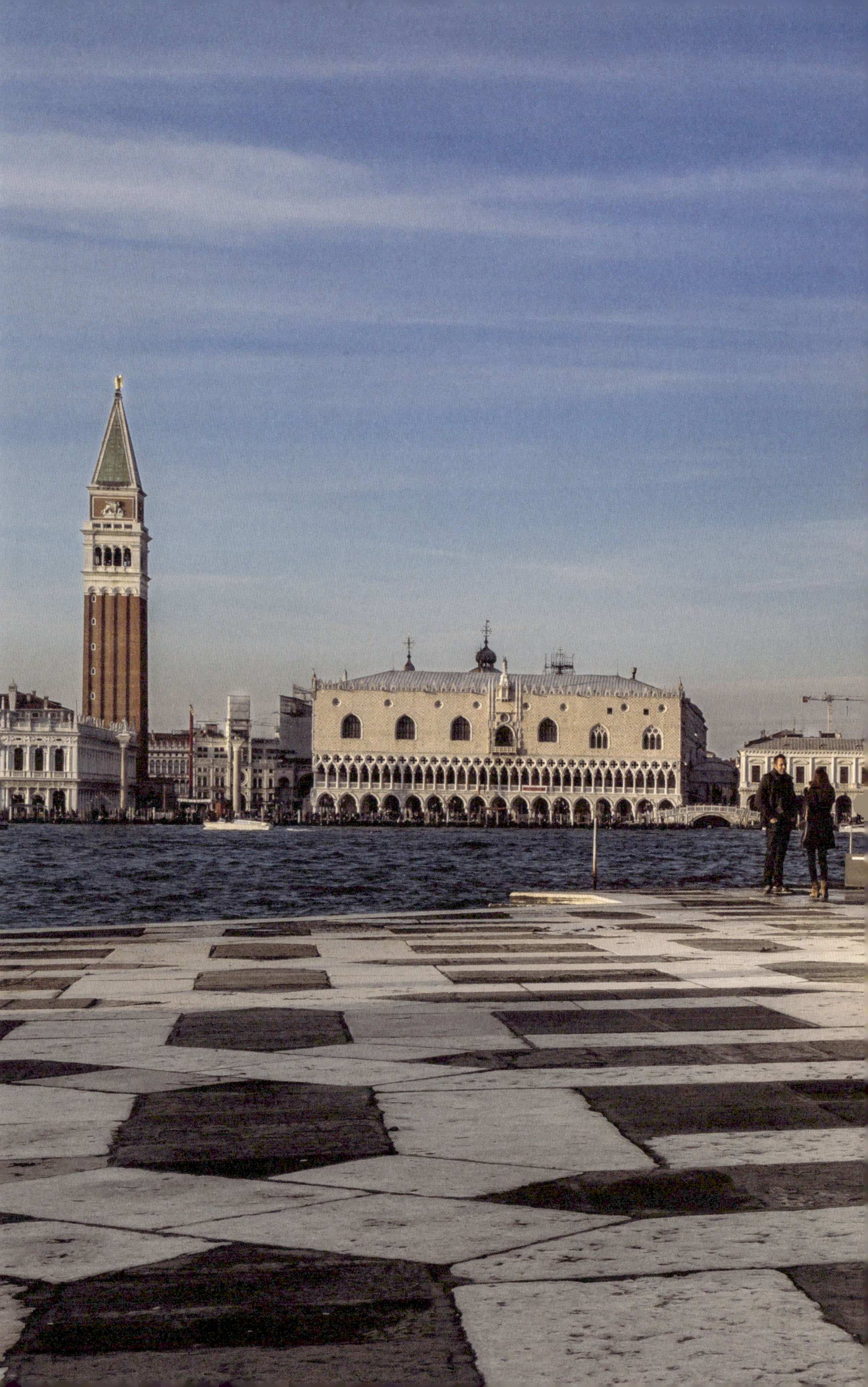

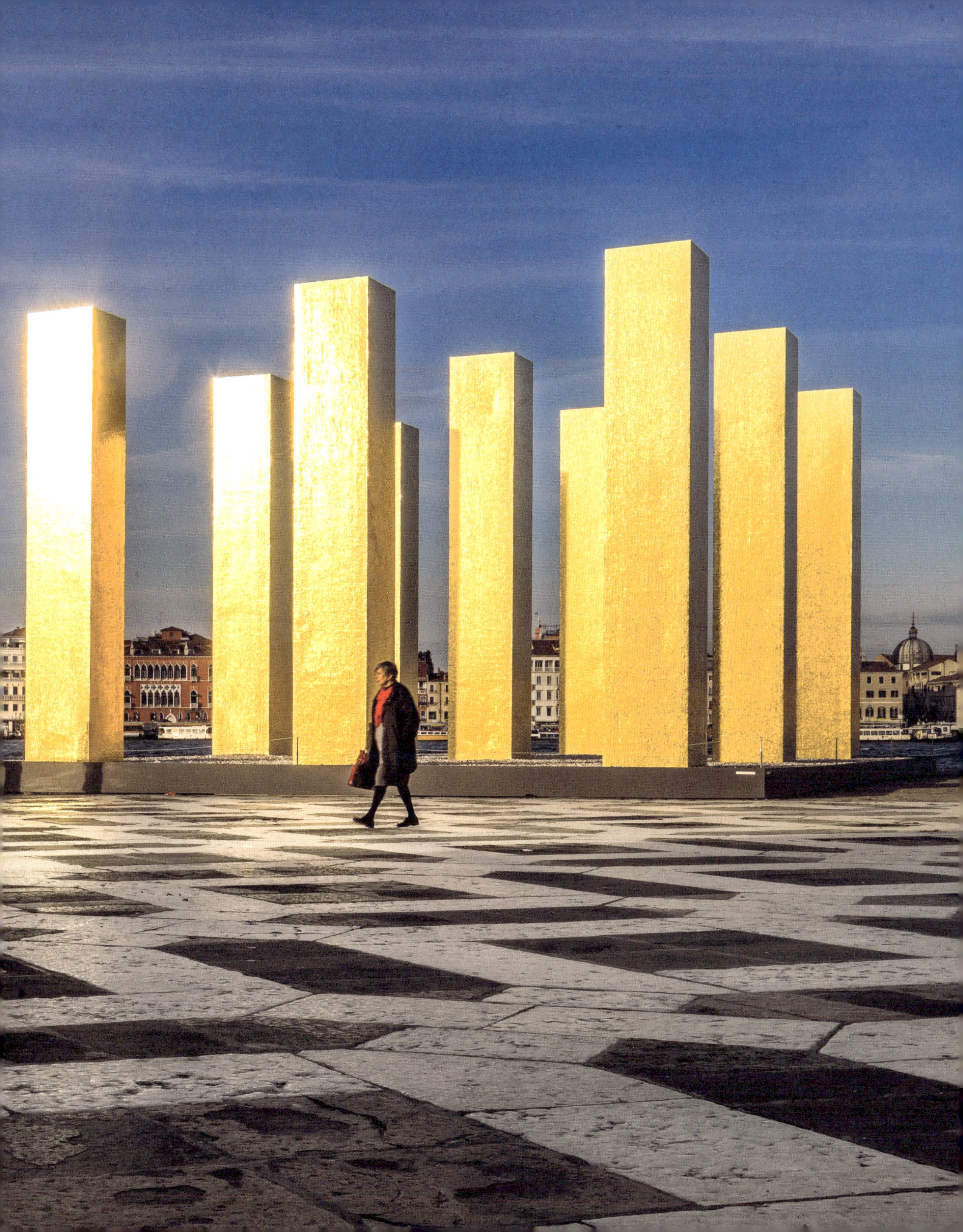

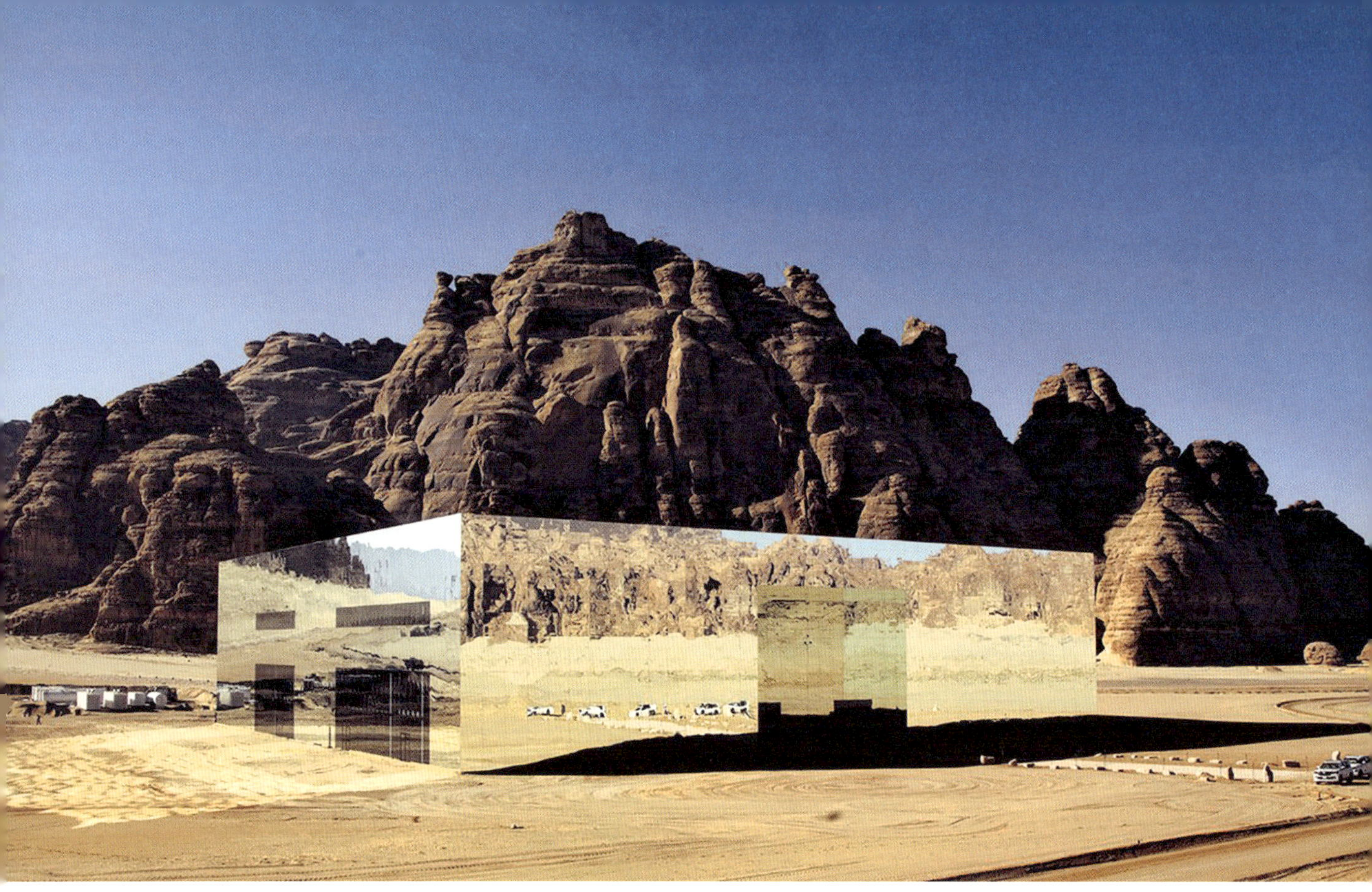

Maraya Concert Hall,
Al-Ula, Saudi Arabia
2019

Topology of Space
Grand Erg Occidental, Algeria
1976

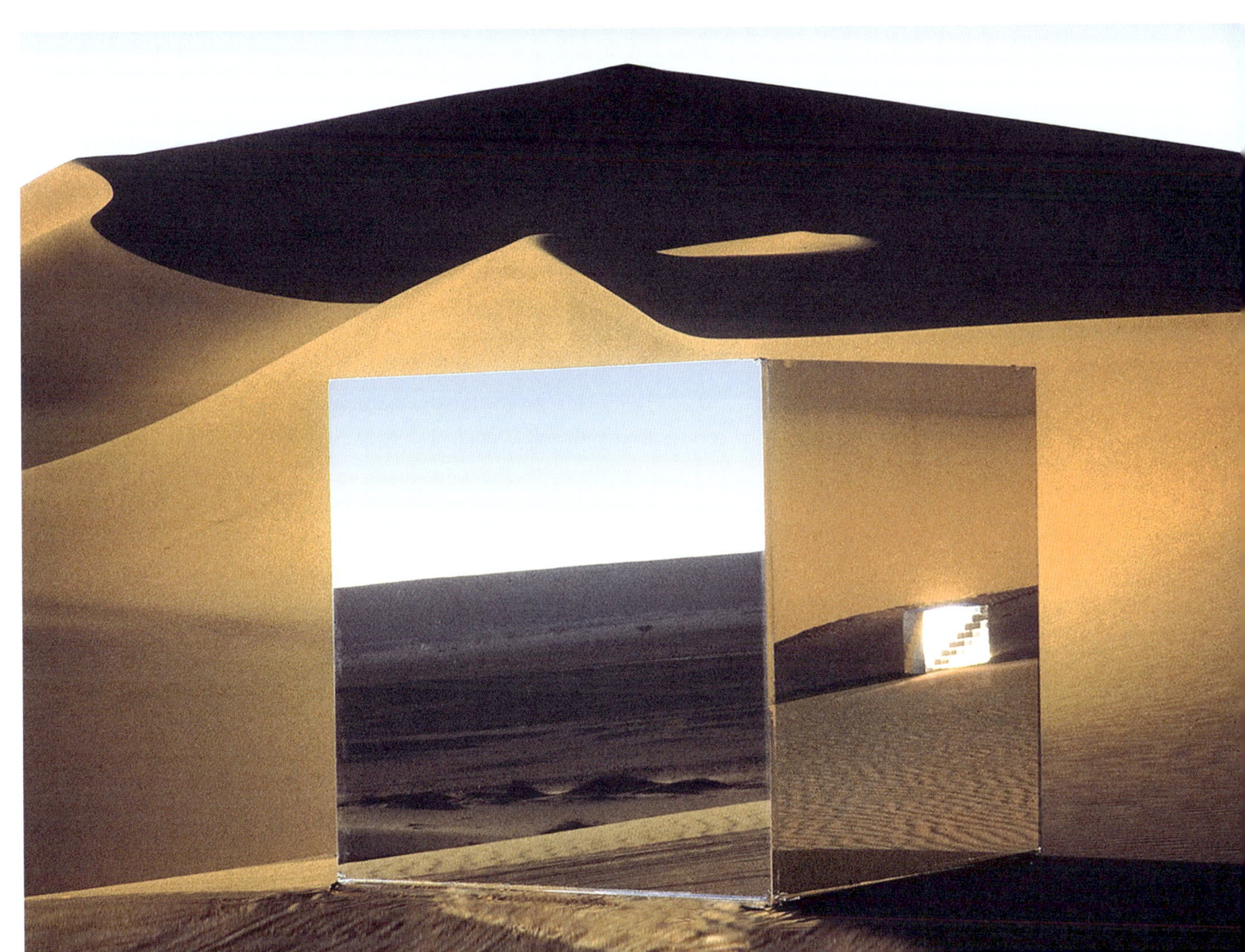

In June 2014, even before the ZERO exhibition at the Guggenheim, the exact opposite happened with Mack's *The Sky Over Nine Columns* in Venice (fig. pp. 310–311). This sculptural installation in the open space between the lagoon and Andrea Palladio's Church of San Giorgio Maggiore, which ran parallel to the Architecture Biennale, was a compelling and internationally acclaimed demonstration that the artist's current work could at least match, if not surpass, the rise of his older work to international prominence. From the perspective of 2025, this was a decisive moment, perhaps *the* decisive moment, for the recognition of Heinz Mack's entire oeuvre.[318]

Concrete experiences are very important in the artistic process. For the opening of the exhibition in Venice, I stayed at the Fondazione Cini in a simple room, probably a former monastery cell, on the island with the Palladio church, in front of which the *Nine Columns* now stood. The experience of spending the night with only five other people on an island in the middle of Venice is overwhelming. Around midnight I went back to the steles, partly to take photographs, and this time they looked different. In the residual light of the city at night, they suddenly cast a black light back on the illuminated St Mark's Square. In the days that followed, and throughout the six months of the exhibition, the *Nine Columns* appeared both as colourless light- swallowers and as objects that brought the sun directly into the lagoon city, changing their effect every second. Heinz Mack had essentially concentrated the entire utopia of his work into a single project.

The hotel where Ute, Valeria, and Heinz Mack were staying was on the Giudecca, just one vaporetto stop away. The next morning, the artist was waiting for me at the hotel entrance. He seemed happy, and not just about the opening and the worldwide press coverage. As he told me on the way to the breakfast table, his daughter Valeria had told him that morning that she had decided to give up her own career as a designer and look after his work alongside Mack's wife Ute, her mother. So the future was secure in that respect too.

The strand of work that followed this event continues to this day. It has several levels. Firstly, the artist has been incredibly busy ever since. To this day, 'diligence' in relation to art is often ridiculed. This is linked to the myth of the artist who produces everything out of inspiration.[319] But this cliché does not reflect reality. Working through – as Heinz Mack has been doing for the past ten years – everything that has not yet been worked through, including his early work and the eight years of ZERO, is not an idle undertaking. As a result, he has produced a similar number of precisely dated works as an artist would normally produce in a lifetime. The process is fascinating. The artist proceeds calmly and deliberately, with great perseverance.

»

In a conversation with one of my employees, the question came up as to how many works I had made in my life so far. I would probably be given figures that would shake me to the core. In all areas, everything has to be multiplied by a factor of 100. It's such an unbelievable abundance that I should actually say: 'Stop now, you've done enough.' It's a really strange moment. I don't know how to evaluate it. To put it ironically: Was anyone more industrious than me?

(JANUARY 2024) «

Parallel to this, a large part of Heinz Mack's oeuvre has been scholarly processed. Two art historians, Sophia Sotke[320] and Bettina Weiand, work in the Mack Studio, whose database of texts and images is now exemplary. Catalogues raisonnés are indispensable, especially in the case of an extensive and wide-ranging oeuvre. In addition to a detailed technical description of each work and an art historical assessment, they list all the exhibitions in which the work has been shown, as well as its provenance, from the artist's studio to the present day. In this way, forgeries are excluded or immediately identifiable, and the art market has certainty with regard to the oeuvre. This, in turn, is crucial to the high prices at which Heinz Mack's ZERO paintings have been trading since the ZERO revival of the 2010s. The 2017 catalogue raisonné of the ZERO paintings[321] is just one of two dozen scholarly publications that have appeared within a decade on all aspects of the artist's oeuvre. With the third volume of the catalogue raisonné of sculptures – the first volume of which was published in 1986 in collaboration with Dieter Honisch – covering the years 2003 to 2020 and including an essay by Beat Wyss, the sculptural oeuvre to date has also been fully catalogued.[322] This also applies to the prints.[323] The quality of the list of authors is equally impressive.[324]

In late April 2014, we were sitting at Heinz Mack's table in the first room of the small house at the Huppertzhof, which is used as an office and archive. 'Mr Mack', I said, 'I'm sure you've heard that Wieland Schmied has passed away.' – 'Yes.' Silence. 'So the last of those who worked with me has died.' Long silence, then suddenly, turning to me: 'Do *you* want to continue?' I had never heard anything like that from an artist before. A quiet conversation developed about what was still missing. 'As far as gallery shows are concerned, there is everything you can imagine. That's not a priority. What's missing is a theoretically elaborated monograph and international museum exhibitions to definitively secure the position of the work.' The monograph turned out to be the easiest undertaking.[325] International museum exhibitions, however, are hotly contested. The solo exhibitions in Baden-Baden in 2015, Istanbul in 2016, Düsseldorf and Wuppertal in 2021, and Karlsruhe in 2023 were organised outside this context but perfectly fulfil the goal set in 2014.

In his current creative phase, Heinz Mack has been producing highly autonomous work since 2010. We have already seen this in his paintings, with the radically dissonant hues in the *Chromatic Constellations* since 2020 (fig. pp. 276–277). It is also evident in the glazed studio at the Huppertzhof (fig. pp. 320–321). Mack uses the sunlit, vertical working surface for new, sometimes very large-format canvases, mostly composed in pastel, which is surprising for such formats. On the other side of the room, where the sun is in your face, there are about twenty optical experiments with polished aluminium bodies, glass prisms, a frosted glass surface in front of a white body fragment, series of glasses, stones, and so on. They are directly exposed to

→
Untitled
(Chromatic Constellation)
2024

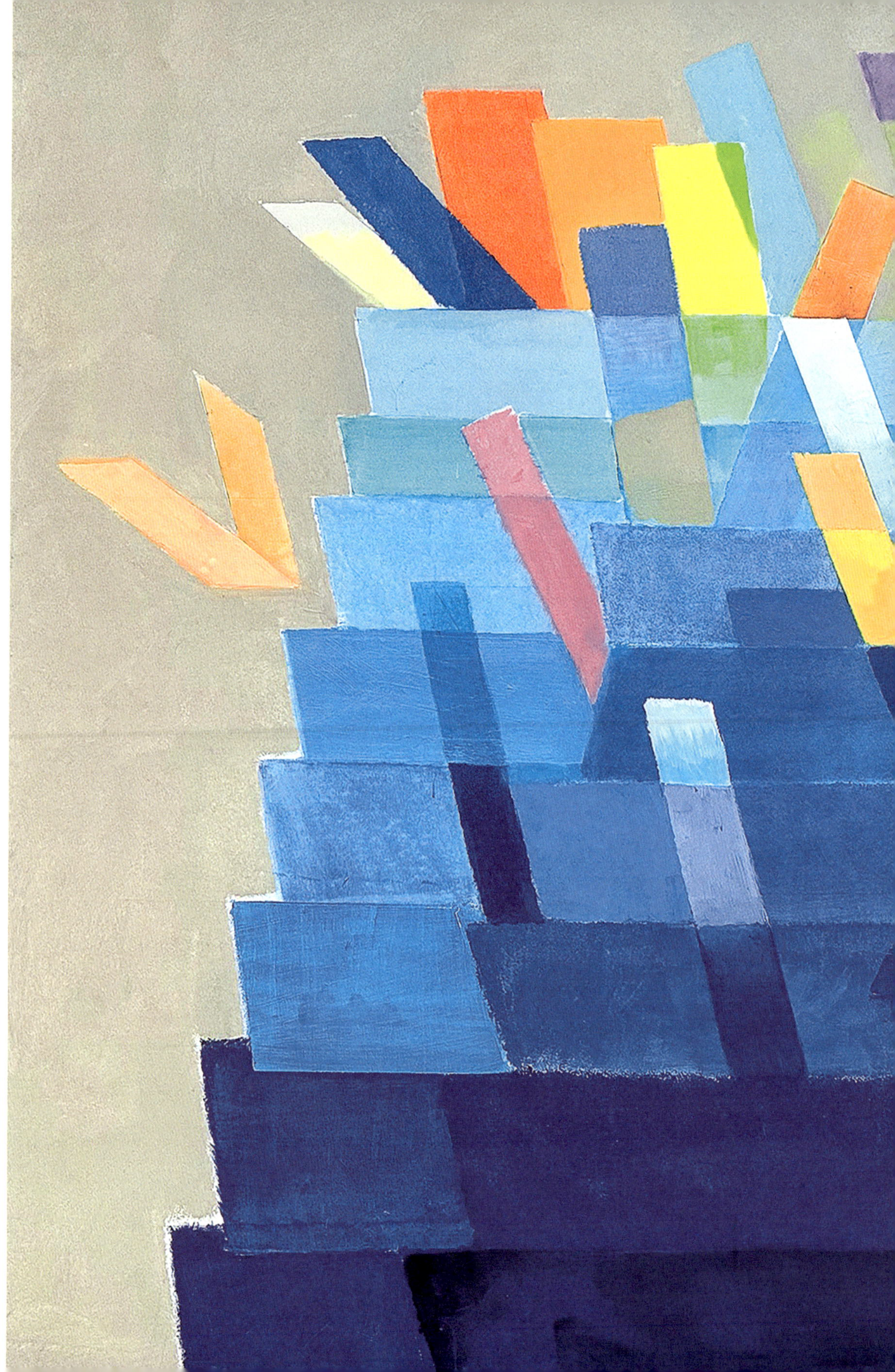

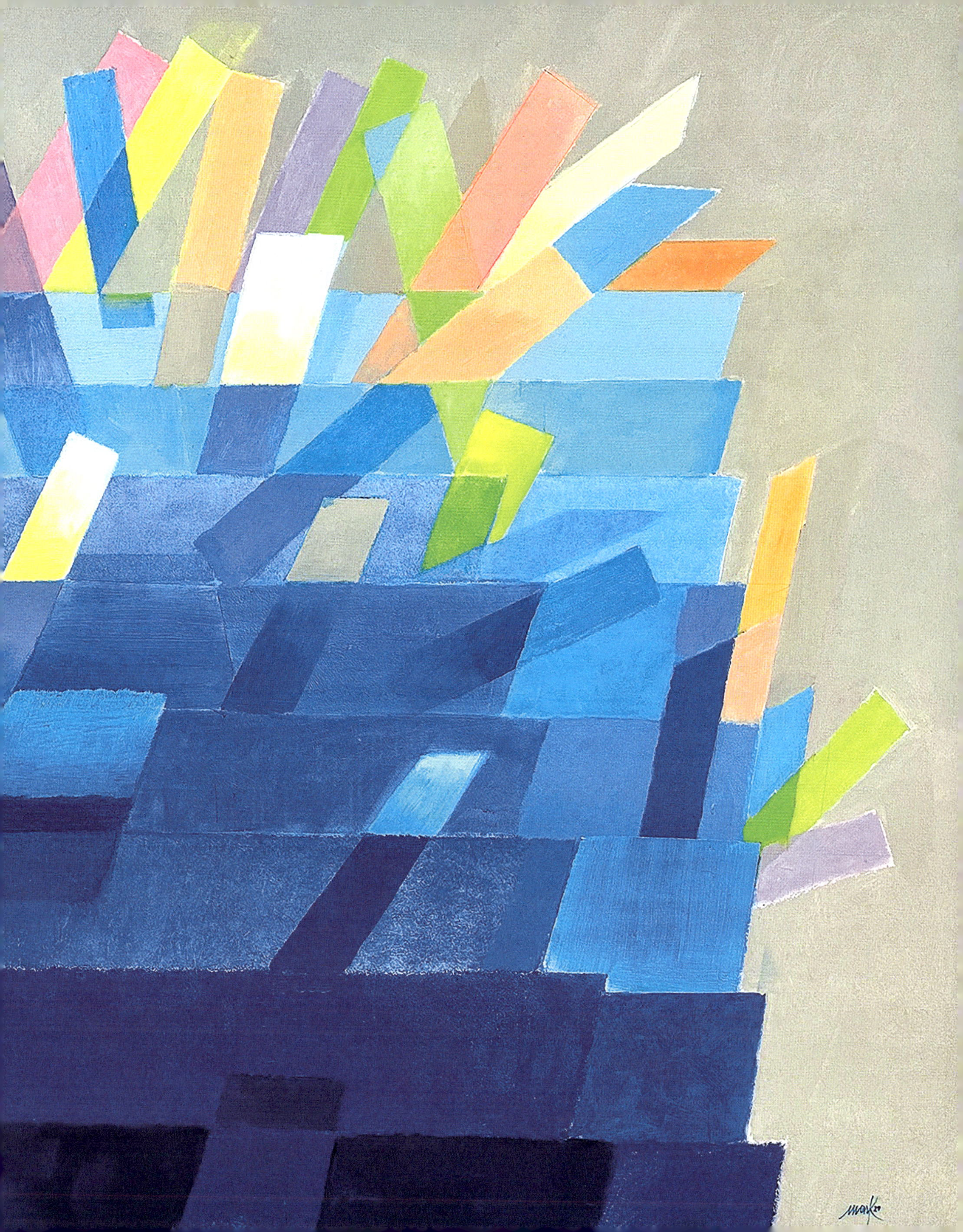

the afternoon sun. The studio is therefore still primarily a laboratory. Equally experimental is Heinz Mack's contact with scientists at the Jülich Research Centre, which began in 2010.[326]

This extreme autonomy is not only evident in the artist's work since 2010, but also in our regular encounters. At the beginning of this period, on the occasion of his exhibition at the Bundeskunsthalle in 2011, he had a great deal under control and also sought this certainty in order to assert his work in public. In 2025, his attitude is different: 'I'm going to show you something in the studio. You would never have suspected it, knowing the development of my work. It's an experiment. Perhaps the beginning of something.'

There has also been an important change in the reception of the work. In 2012, students at the Düsseldorf Academy of Art knew the name Heinz Mack. But two years later, the lecture theatre was packed for a talk with the artist as part of a lecture series.[327] This was also the case in 2015, when Heinz Mack and Otto Piene[328] were awarded honorary membership in the academy's auditorium. The students' relationship to Heinz Mack's work has changed dramatically in recent years. Whenever I mention his name, I now hear again and again: 'What? You know Heinz Mack personally?' As if looking for proof, one student added: 'When did you last see him?' – 'Last Friday.' – 'What?' He couldn't believe it.

This new relationship between younger generations of artists and Heinz Mack's work points to two things: there are stars, legends, and symbols. Stars are names you have to know if you want to find your way in the current art scene. Legends are names that we know are very important, even if we do not know exactly why. Symbols stand above both, embodying an entire era or more. This is also what distinguishes works of art in the long term. Heinz Mack is a living legend, at least for younger generations of artists.

This is accompanied by a change in the general view of the work, which may be decisive for the future. The art market still makes a strict distinction between works from the ZERO years and those made since. For younger generations of artists, however, this distinction is irrelevant. There are so many recognisable bridges and continuities between the current and the earlier work that they are the focus. The digital principle throughout the artist's work is important for the reception of younger generations. We are reminded of the beginnings of ZERO art, with paintings and reliefs (pp. 60–83). They consist of a constant sequence of light and non-light, signs and non-signs. It is this principle of form that runs through all of Mack's work to this day. It is not technically executed, but rather done by hand, resulting in an extensive digital oeuvre. New generations of artists have been familiar with the digital image since childhood. Mack's work speaks directly to their digital gaze. It is a reference and a vast encyclopaedia of how a digital image can be read and developed further.

Based on this, the entire oeuvre can be seen in a new light. It is a work that allows us to understand digital imagery,[329] regardless of whether it was created in connection with ZERO or after.

One result of the events outlined here was the establishment of the Mack Foundation in the summer of 2024. It is one of the few foundations in a German-speaking country to be established during an artist's lifetime. It has been secured for decades by the state of North Rhine-Westphalia and the city of Mönchengladbach and also has a presence in New York. Today, the Mack Studio resembles a family business, with Mack's wife Ute, daughter Valeria, and son-in-law Marc. The Mack Foundation has a legally and financially well-positioned board of directors and an advisory board. The foundation's assets include several hundred important works by the artist. They are available for exhibitions and permanent loans to museums. Real estate is available in the form of the large tripartite studio with adjoining sculpture park, which was built in 1985 a few hundred metres from the Huppertzhof in an industrial estate (fig. p. 17) and itself appears as an architectural work in the list of sculptures.[330] There are also funds to finance research work. The Mack Foundation now acts as a central point of contact for enquiries and collaborations of all kinds. The city of Mönchengladbach, which is represented on the foundation's advisory board, has passed a council resolution to stabilise the Huppertzhof as an artistic biotope for decades to come. Against such a background, artists can work freely and unencumbered.

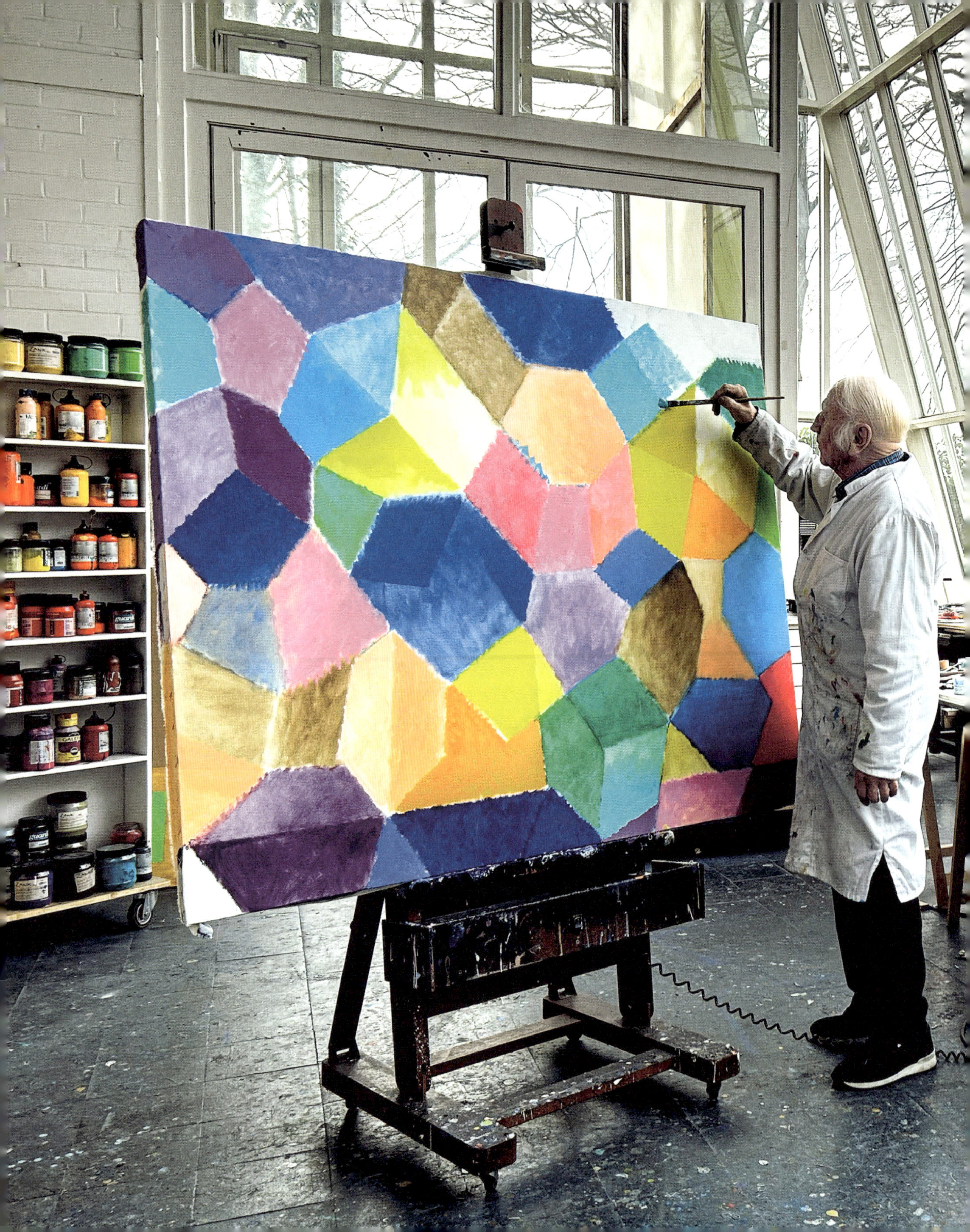

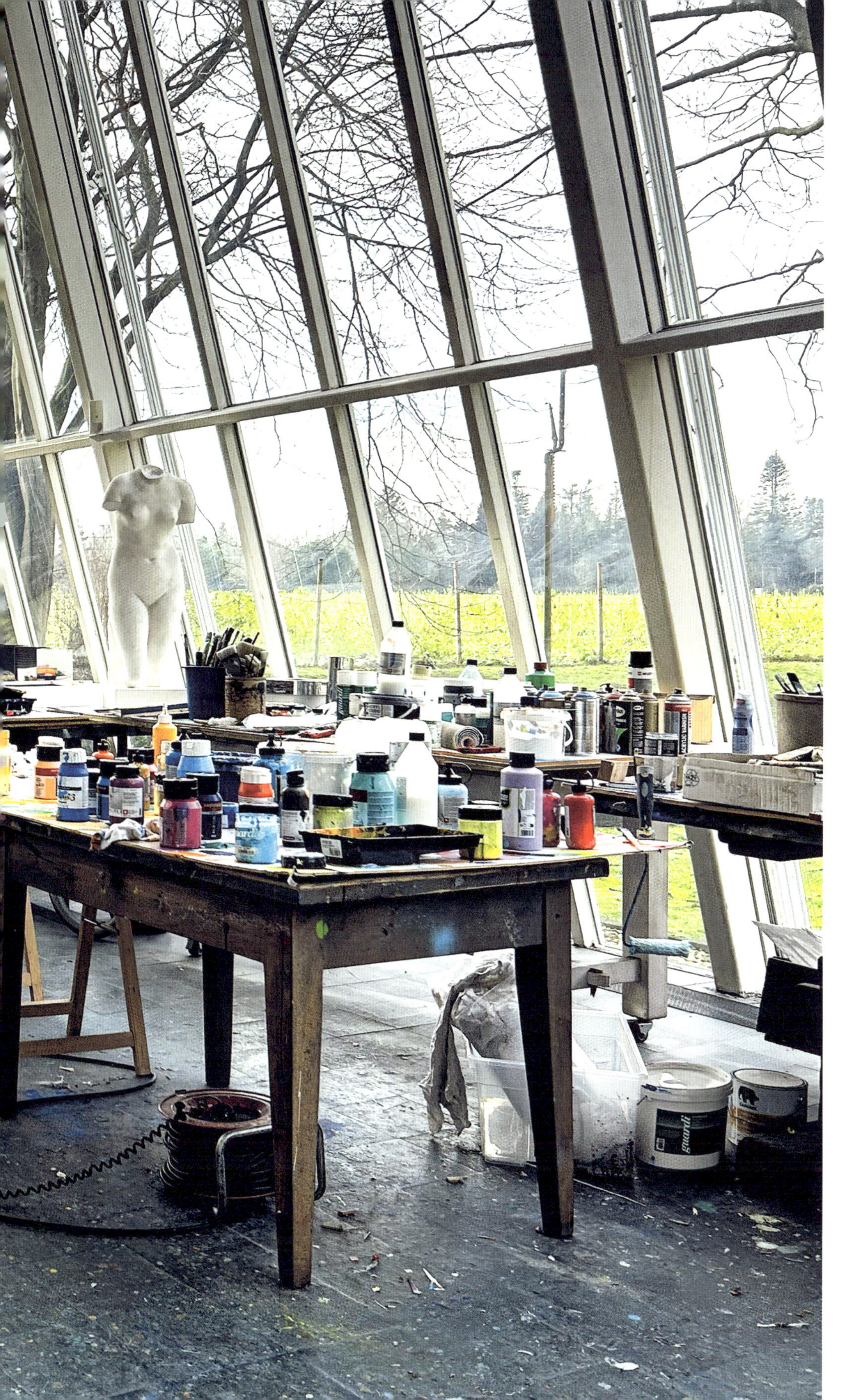

Notes

1 Beat Wyss, 'Die Kunst des Scheinens', in: idem, *Mack. Skulpturen 2003–2020* (Munich: Hirmer, 2021), pp. 10–19.

2 Conversation with Heinz Mack, Huppertzhof, Mönchengladbach, January 2022 [translated].

3 Wieland Schmied (ed.), *Utopie und Wirklichkeit im Werk von Heinz Mack* (Cologne: DuMont, 1998).

4 'It is the dreams that go beyond any realisation that, measured against these dreams, imply the failure of his undertakings. But then Heinz Mack's failure would be nothing more than an unmistakable sign of his greatness, and in his case, as so often in human history, greatness and failure are closely intertwined.' Wieland Schmied, 'Arbeit am Projekt der Moderne. Über Heinz Mack und den Mythos vom Künstler als Konstrukteur neuer Welten', in: ibid., here p. 13 [translated].

5 Conversation with Heinz Mack, Huppertzhof, Mönchengladbach, December 2022 [translated].

6 Mack Archive, Huppertzhof, Mönchengladbach [translated]. The note to himself meant that the number of the arrondissement in Paris was important in order to find his way around or to be able to ask for directions.

7 Mack Archive, Huppertzhof, Mönchengladbach [translated].

8 Conversation with Heinz Mack, Huppertzhof, Mönchengladbach, November 2022 [translated].

9 See: Laszlo Glozer, 'Eine andere Kunst. Paris nach der Befreiung', in: idem, *Westkunst. Zeitgenössische Kunst seit 1939*, exh. cat. Museen der Stadt Köln (Cologne: DuMont, 1981), pp. 127–171.

10 See, for example: Heinz Mack, 'ZERO und Existentialismus', in: *ZERO-Zeit. Mack und seine Künstlerfreunde*, exh. cat. Beck & Eggeling, Düsseldorf 2014, pp. 34–36.

11 Mack read Lévi-Strauss's main work *Tristes Tropiques* (1955, translated into English by John Russell as *A World on the Wane*) after the publication of the German translation by Suzanne Heintz (1960). He still refers to the book today.

12 In the years after 1945, Surrealism in Paris was a shadow of its former self compared to its revolutionary power in the inter-war period, and in the German-speaking countries hardly any of the many artists who took an interest in Surrealism after the Second World War went beyond being epigones. There were exceptions such as K. O. Götz, Friedensreich Hundertwasser, Maria Lassnig, and Arnulf Rainer.

13 The famous final sentence of Nadja is: 'La beauté sera *CONVULSIVE* ou ne sera pas' (Beauty will be CONVULSIVE or will not be at all). 'Convulsive' also means 'full of tension'. In retrospect, there are many echoes between Breton's story with Nadja and the relationship between the Venezuelan artist Marisol and Heinz Mack in Paris and New York in the 1960s.

14 Without the concept of the 'avant-garde', which has fallen out of use since the 1980s, it is impossible to understand modernism from around 1905: especially Constructivism from 1910 onwards, Dada from 1916, and Surrealism from around 1918, as well as the post-war art and the 'neo-avant-gardes' of the 1960s, including ZERO. The avant-garde was about the constant attempt to break new ground in art. The term comes from military jargon and means 'vanguard' or 'advance guard'. All innovative artistic movements from 1905 to 1980, including in Latin American modernism and in various forms in the socialist hemisphere, saw themselves as the vanguard of society. From 1980 onwards, this intellectual constellation of art imploded with the integration of free art into the financial capitalism of the present. Heinz Mack comes from a completely different place than the contemporary art industry. He comes from a world in which even a picture by Henri Matisse cost only two months' salary of a senior employee, in which art had little monetary value and could therefore be seen as the avant-garde of society.

15 During these years, Paul Éluard published several texts in which he formulated his idea of 'pure light' (lumière totale) as the indispensable horizon of painting and the visual arts in general. One of the chapters is entitled 'Il n'y a pas de lumière abstraite' (There Is No Abstract Light). Paul Éluard, 'Lumière et morale' [1953], in: idem, *Anthologie des écrits sur l'art* (Paris: Gallimard, 1978), pp. 516ff.

16 After completing his studies at the Düsseldorf Academy of Art and the University of Cologne, Heinz Mack became a secondary school teacher in 1956 at the age of twenty-five. He had recently bought a VW Beetle, the least expensive car available at the time. In the autumn of 1955, he travelled back to Paris, where he met the young Yves Klein, who was not yet famous, among a group of his contemporaries at the already legendary Brasserie La Coupole in Montparnasse. The two hit it off, and Klein took Mack on a tour of the cabarets in the red-light district of Pigalle in Montmartre, where Klein knew his way around. His later *Anthropometries*, which Mack still rejects as misogynistic, are based on his perceptions of this neighbourhood. They agreed not to touch the dancers. Mack still vividly remembers the performance of an African dancer that went beyond all European dance traditions. Klein, the son of a well-known artist couple, had only started making art himself a year earlier after years in judo and the art trade. He was now experimenting with monochrome painting. He invited Mack to stay with him in Rue Campagne Première so that he would not have to spend what little money he had on a hotel room. Mack slept in his bed, while Klein himself slept on the floor in the kitchen. Mack had brought slides of his own work, which they projected from a skylight onto the

surrounding rooftops of Paris at night. In 1957, together with Norbert Kricke, Mack advised the painter Alfred Schmela, who was about to open a small but ambitious gallery in Hunsrückstraße in Düsseldorf's old town, to show Yves Klein in a solo exhibition instead of Antoni Tàpies – who had seemed snooty to Mack when he met him in Paris. This exhibition became an unparalleled catalyst in the Rhineland. See: Robert Fleck, *Yves Klein. L'Aventure allemande* (Paris: Manuella éditions, 2018).

17 See: *ZERO und Nouveau Réalisme. Die Befragung der Wirklichkeit*, exh. cat. Stiftung Ahlers Pro Arte/Kestner Pro Arte, Hannover 2016.

18 Under the presidency of Charles de Gaulle, Malraux was appointed the first French Minister of Cultural Affairs.

19 Afterwards, Rotraut, an important artist, Yves Klein's widow and Günther Uecker's sister, invited Mack and other German participants to her flat, which she had left unchanged after the death of Yves Klein. Katharina Sieverding, then a student of stage design at the Düsseldorf Academy of Art, was left with a lasting impression. See Robert Fleck, conversations with Katharina Sieverding, Düsseldorf, since 2014 [translated].

20 Heinz Mack passed the state examination in art education at the Düsseldorf Academy of Art in 1953 and in philosophy at the University of Cologne in 1956. The university in Düsseldorf, today's Heinrich Heine University, was not founded until 1965.

21 The artist had several traumatic experiences during the war: a piece of shrapnel went in next to his knee and he still has the scar. Once, on the ten-kilometre walk home from school, an officer gave him a lift in an open car that was attacked by a low-flying aircraft. The car overturned and the driver was killed.

22 After changing schools several times during and after the war, Heinz Mack finally attended a science-oriented secondary school in Krefeld. His was the first post-war class to graduate.

23 Mack Archive, Huppertzhof, Mönchengladbach.

24 Less than eighty students were enrolled at the Düsseldorf Academy of Art in the post-war period. Those studying to become teachers, like Heinz Mack, had to draw nudes in the morning five days a week.

25 See: Uwe Fleckner, 'Heinz Mack und die "Stunde Null" der deutschen Kunstgeschichte', in: *Heinz Mack. Review and Outlook – A Special Selection*, exh. cat. Samuelis Baumgarte Galerie, Berlin, Bielefeld and Singapore 2016, pp. 2–8.

26 In 1967, the psychoanalysts Alexander and Margarete Mitscherlich – Margarete was one of the first women authors to receive widespread recognition in the German-speaking humanities – caused a sensation with their empirical study Die Unfähigkeit zu trauern (The Inability to Mourn), which examined the strategies of repression and denial used by former supporters of Adolf Hitler. Heinz Mack read the study soon after its publication and was very impressed by it. The main material used for the study was the Nuremberg Doctors' Trial of 1947 – the first version of the text also dates from this period. See: Alexander and Margarete Mitscherlich, *Die Unfähigkeit zu trauern. Grundlagen kollektiven Verhaltens* [1967] (Munich: Piper, 1977).

27 Conversation with Heinz Mack, Huppertzhof, Mönchengladbach, February 2023.

28 In 1953, more than ten years before the advent of the mass university, university studies were a rarity. All students were in close contact with their professors and assistants.

29 See: Daniel Birnbaum and Hans Ulrich Obrist, 'Das Einfache ist das Komplexe. Gespräch mit Heinz Mack', in: *Heinz Mack. Licht, Raum, Farbe / Light, Space, Colour*, ed. Robert Fleck and Nathalie Hoyos, exh. cat. Kunst- und Ausstellungshalle der Bundesrepublik Deutschland, Bonn (Cologne: Snoeck, 2011), pp. 10–29.

30 Heidegger was very much in vogue in German post-war art: 'An der Städelschule in Frankfurt schwor man auf ihn', conversation with Franz Erhard Walther, Düsseldorf, October 2016 [translated]. Cf.: Martin Heidegger, *Die Kunst und der Raum* [on the occasion of the opening of an exhibition of works by Eduardo Chillida, 1969], LP (St. Gallen: Galerie der Erker/Erker-Verlag, 1969–89).

31 See: Michel Foucault, *Phénoménologie et psychologie, 1953–54* [Coll. Hautes Études] (Paris: EHESS/Gallimard/Seuil, 2021); idem, Le Discours philosophique, 1966 (Paris: EHESS/Gallimard/Seuil, 2023), pp. 141, 203f.

32 See: Otto Friedrich Bollnow, *Existenzphilosophie* (Stuttgart: Kohlhammer, 1949); Max Bense, *Was ist Existenzphilosophie?* [Berckers Kleine Volksbibliothek] (Kevelaer: Butzon & Bercker, 1949). Max Bense went on to become the leading German sign theorist, playing a key role in ZERO from 1957–58 onwards and in the *Sahara Project* a decade later. 'A humanistic individualism is clearly recognisable in existential philosophy, supported by a high degree of liberalism'; Heinz Mack, letter to the author, Mönchengladbach, 22 December 2023, private archive [translated]. See: Mack 2014 (see note 10).

33 'I was also particularly interested in Camus's T*he Rebel* (1951). This was preceded by my reading of Jaspers, which began in my final year at secondary school, thanks to an excellent philosophy teacher. Here is the basic insight: spirit and freedom are unmediated, direct characteristics of man, quasi-immanent'; Heinz Mack, letter to the author, Mönchengladbach, 22 December 2023, private archive [translated].

34 Jean-Paul Sartre's essay *Reflections on the Jewish Question* (1946) was published in German as early as 1948, translated by Hedi Wurzian.

35 Between 1950 and 1952, Paul Schneider-Esleben, sixteen years older than Mack, created one of the finest modernist buildings of the post-war period: the glass Haniel Garage in Düsseldorf-Grafenberg, now the BMW Sales Centre. His Mannesmann Tower (1954–58) on the banks of the Rhine in Düsseldorf was the first high-rise building in Europe. And his new St Rocco's Church, one of the most radical church buildings after the Second World War, was also completed in Düsseldorf in 1953, the year of the industrial trade fair. This interesting personal environment during Mack's student days has received too little attention to date.

36 In Cologne there was already Hein Stünke's resolutely West-oriented gallery Der Spiegel, which, like Galerie Rudolf Springer in West Berlin, had a direct continuity with the years before 1945; see: Robert Fleck, 'Diaspora', in: *Berlin – Berlin*, ed. Miriam Wiesel, exh. cat. 1. Berlin-Biennale (Ostfildern: Cantz, 1998), pp. 93–96, 129f.

37 Mack Archive, Huppertzhof, Mönchengladbach [translated].

38 Conversations with Heinz Mack, Huppertzhof, Mönchengladbach, 2017–19 [translated].

39 See: Fleck 2018 (see note 16).

40 For more details, see: ibid.

41 Schmela eventually sold every painting by Klein that the artist gave him, including later works from his estate, at the high prices that Klein had already set in 1957; conversation with Rotraut Klein-Moquay, Paris, 2016.

42 See: Karl-Heinz Hering, Vom Kaisertrotz zum Grabbeplatz, in: Marie-Luise Otten (ed.), *Von Dada bis Beuys. 30 Jahre Kunstverein für die Rheinlande und Westfalen mit Karl-Heinz Hering* (Ratingen: Schwarzbach Presse, 1998), pp. 49, 125. Later, the ZERO movement was also shown comparatively rarely in Düsseldorf institutions, until the 2006 retrospective under Jean-Hubert Martin at the Museum Kunstpalast.

43 See: Marie-Luise Otten (ed.), *Auf dem Weg zur Avantgarde. Künstler der Gruppe 53*, exh. cat. Museum der Stadt Ratingen (Heidelberg: Edition Braus im Wachter-Verlag, 2003).

44 Willi Baumeister, *Das Unbekannte in der Kunst* [1947] (Cologne: DuMont, 1960) – this was one of the defining books of post-war German art.

45 For more on Klaus Jürgen-Fischer, see pp. 50f in the present volume.

46 It is worth noting that Max Bense spoke in Mack and Piene's studio, not at the art academy. There was not yet a university in Düsseldorf.

47 Among the women artists were Hanne Brenken, Hal Busse, and Herta Junghans-Grulich.

48 These included Yves Klein, Günther Uecker, Konrad Klapheck, Gotthard Grauber, Gerhard Hoehme, Georges Mathieu, and Rupprecht Geiger. Klaus Jürgen-Fischer gave an introduction.

49 I use the historical term 'Plexiglas', which is also a brand name, because 'acrylic glass' did not yet exist in the 1950s and 1960s.

50 See: *ZERO. Countdown to Tomorrow, 1950s–60s*, exh. cat. Solomon R. Guggenheim Museum, New York 2014; *ZERO. Countdown to the Future*, ed. Mattijs Visser and Thekla Zell, exh. cat. Sakıp Sabancı Müzesi, Istanbul 2015.

51 Heinz Mack, 'The New Dynamic Structure', in: idem and Otto Piene (eds.), *ZERO* [ZERO 1] (Düsseldorf: Otto Piene, 1958), pp. 15f., reprinted in: Robert Fleck (ed.), *Heinz Mack. ZERO-Malerei / Painting. Catalogue raisonné 1956–1968*, prepared by Andrea Knop and Bettina Weiand (Munich: Hirmer, 2017), vol. 1, pp. 33–35. This text is extremely stringent. Just under two years earlier, in 1956, Heinz Mack had passed his state examination in philosophy at the University of Cologne, one year before Otto Piene.

52 See: Jürgen Claus, *Kunst heute* [rowohlts neue enzyklopädie] (Reinbek: Rowohlt, 1965), p. 85.

53 Mack 1958 (see note 51).

54 Heinz Mack, 'Struktur', July 2010, typescript, Mack Archive, Huppertzhof, Mönchengladbach [translated].

55 Mack 1958 (see note 51).

56 Ibid.

57 In the original recording of the launch of *Explorer 1*, one can clearly hear that the speaker continues counting after 'ZERO!': 'Plus one, plus two' and so on. The journey went into the future. Cf. the exhibition title of the major ZERO retrospective at the Solomon R. Guggenheim Museum in New York in 2014: *ZERO. Countdown to Tomorrow.* Zero is the basis of arithmetic and, indirectly, of modern mathematics. It was known to the Mayans, who used it at least half a millennium before Indian scholars. From the latter, Arab scholars passed it on to Europe, see Claude Lévi-Strauss, *Race et histoire* [1952], Paris: Gallimard, 2024, p. 40, trans. by Robert Fleck (German translation first by Traugott König as *Rasse und Geschichte*, Frankfurt am Main: Suhrkamp, 1972).

58 *Just what is it that makes today's homes so different, so appealing?*, 1956, Kunsthalle Tübingen.

59 During his years in New York from 1964 to 1966, Heinz Mack collected works by Pop Art artists such as Roy Lichtenstein and Andy Warhol. The latter fundamentally rejected what he saw as Richard Hamilton's cynical attitude – not unlike that of Marcel Duchamp, who first became famous around this time and with whom Hamilton worked closely – which Mack would also encounter in the Fluxus movement a few years later. Conversation with Heinz Mack, Huppertzhof, Mönchengladbach, May 2023 [translated].

60 This is structurally related to the purely black paintings of Pierre Soulages, which the French Abstract Expressionist painter created from 1979 onwards, i.e. much later, with a completely different artistic intention and concept. See: Robert Fleck and Hans Ulrich Obrist, *Pierre Soulages* (Paris: Manuella éditions, 2017).

61 Dieter Honisch, 'Essay', in: idem, *Mack. Skulpturen, 1953–1976. Werkverzeichnis* (Düsseldorf and Vienna: Econ, 1986), pp. 8–27.

62 Theoretically founded by Wilhelm Worringer in his dissertation *Abstraktion und Einfühlung* (Munich: Piper, 1908), whose *Problematik der Gegenwartskunst* (Munich: Piper, 1948) had served as an early orientation for Heinz Mack.

63 Key authors of post-structuralism, such as Gilles Deleuze, Michel Foucault, and Jean-François Lyotard, sharply rejected this label in relation to their own work.

64 Conversation with Heinz Mack, Bonn, 2011 [translated].

65 The exhibition was mediated by the art critic Rochus Kowallek from Frankfurt am main. See: Robert Fleck, *Avantgarde in Wien. Die Geschichte der Galerie nächst St. Stephan, 1952 bis 1982. Kunst und Kunstbetrieb in Österreich* (Vienna and Munich: Löcker, 1982), pp. 203–205.

66 Karl Ruhrberg was the founding director of the Städtische Kunsthalle Düsseldorf from 1965 on and the second director of the Museum Ludwig in Cologne from 1978 on. Together with Wieland Schmied, he became the designated co-artistic director of *documenta 6* in 1972, but both stepped down in 1974.

67 See: Theodor W. Adorno, *Aesthetic Theory* [1970], ed. Gretel Adorno and Rolf Tiedemann, trans. Christian Lenhardt (London and Boston: Routledge and Kegan Paul, 1984).

68 Roland Barthes, *Am Nullpunkt der Literatur. Objektive Literatur. Zwei Essays*, trans. Helmut Scheffel (Hamburg: Claassen, 1959). Translated into English as: *Writing Degree Zero*, trans. Annette Lavers and Colin Smith (London: Jonathan Cape, 1967). Heinz Mack says he does not know the book; conversation with Heinz Mack, Huppertzhof, Mönchengladbach, February 2023 [translated].

69 Through Cologne, music and the WDR, Heinz Mack also came into contact with Karlheinz Stockhausen, the world's most prominent German composer of the 1960s and 1970s, and Nam June Paik. The first realisation of the *Sahara Project* with the 1968 film *Tele-Mack* also came about through the WDR.

70 Light, whether artificial or natural, also has different qualities for Mack; see: Heinz Mack, 'Licht ist nicht Licht', 1966, typescript, Mack Archive, Huppertzhof, Mönchengladbach.

71 The term 'Nouveau Réalisme' (New Realism) came from Restany. Klein was initially against it. Conversations with Pierre Restany, Paris, and others, from 1980, with Raymond Hains, Paris, from 1994, and with Rotraut Klein-Moquay, Paris, since 2015.

72 Conversations with Heinz Mack, Huppertzhof, Mönchengladbach, since 2021. See also: Karl-Heinz Hering, Vom Kaisertrotz zum Grabbeplatz, in: Heiner Stachelhaus, *ZERO. Mack – Piene – Uecker* (Düsseldorf et al.: Econ, 1993), pp. 15ff.

73 *Hommage à Georges de La Tour*, 1960/2023, reconstructed in collaboration with the ZKM | Center for Art and Media Karlsruhe, now in its collection.

74 Jean-François Lyotard, *The Postmodern Condition: A Report on Knowledge*, trans. Geoff Bennington and Brian Massumi (Minneapolis: University of Minnesota Press, 1984).

75 See: Robert Venturi et al., *Learning from Las Vegas* (Cambridge, MA: MIT Press, 1972).

76 Minimalism and conceptual art remained far more connected to the beliefs of classical modernism and Abstract Expressionism, which explains the freshness of ZERO for younger generations of artists compared to the dominant neo-conceptual art of our present day.

77 'Junge deutsche Maler. Eine bedeutsame Ausstellung im Kasseler Kunstverein', in: *Kasseler Post*, no. 172, 29 July 1959, p. 4, ZERO foundation, Düsseldorf, shelf no. mkp.ZERO.1.II.121 [translated].

78 Robert Fleck, Conversations with Kasper König, Berlin, 1992, and Alfred Nemeczek, Hamburg, 1997.

79 Compared to II. *documenta*, which took place at the same time, the percentage of women artists was much higher.

80 *La force pure III*, 1959, Centre Georges Pompidou, Paris.

81 See the reprint of all three *ZERO* issues and further material in: Dirk Pörschmann and Mattijs Visser (eds.), 4 3 2 1 ZERO (Düsseldorf: Richter|Fey, 2012).

82 This time, no women artists were represented.

83 Only the French artists, including Jean Tinguely and Yves Klein, did not pay, despite Mack's repeated requests. Conversation with Heinz Mack, Huppertzhof, Mönchengladbach, September 2021 [translated]. This may be explained by the currency restrictions in France at the time of the currency reform of 1960, or also by the Algerian War of those years; see the exhibition Pierre Bourdieu: *Der Algerienkrieg und die Fotografie*, curated by Robert Fleck for the Deichtorhallen, Haus der Photographie, Hamburg, 2016 (no catalogue was produced).

84 Public funding for such artistic publications was still a decade away.

85 Other artists came from Austria, Switzerland, Monaco, Brazil, Venezuela, and the United States.

86 Heinz Mack had seen the first canvas painting with pierced holes by Lucio Fontana at the 1954 Venice Biennale. He reported on it in Germany: for him, it was either the end of painting or the beginning of a new art. See: Heinz Mack, 'Das Kaleidoskop meiner Erinnerungen', in: *Zero Italien. Azimut/Azimuth 1959/60 – und heute*, ed. Renate Damsch-Wiehager, exh. cat. Galerie der Stadt Esslingen, Villa Merkel (Ostfildern: Cantz, 1995), pp. 178–180.

87 See: *Happening & Fluxus*, exh. cat. Kölnischer Kunstverein, Cologne (Cologne: Verlag der Buchhandlung Walther König, 1971). The Fluxus festivals in Wiesbaden and Düsseldorf and the first actions by the Viennese Actionists did not take place until 1962.

88 In the years that followed, Iris Clert had a white painting by Heinz Mack hanging above her bed, which she never paid for. Conversation with Heinz Mack, Huppertzhof, Mönchengladbach, May 2022 [translated].

89 See the illustration of one of the invitation cards and the transcription of the text by Yves Klein in: Robert Fleck and Antonia Lehmann-Tolkmitt, Heinz *Mack. A Twenty-First-Century Artist.* Monograph, trans. Gérard A. Goodrow (Munich: Hirmer, 2019), p. 24. A silver light relief is printed on the invitation card. The cards were sent in black envelopes to enhance the visual effect when the envelope was opened.

90 Archives Yves Klein, Paris; ZERO foundation, Düsseldorf; Mack Foundation, Mönchengladbach.

91 Mack 1995 (see note 86), p. 179 [translated].

92 The exhibition, which became known under the title of the catalogue, *Vision in Motion – Motion in Vision*, is considered a landmark in the history of the ZERO movement, as 'it was the first time that artists from different parts of the world, who had hardly known each other before, if at all, exhibited together and whose works showed an astonishing convergence of artistic intentions'. Heinz Mack and Otto Piene, 'Dynamo', in: *Nota*, no. 4, 1960, unpaginated [translated].

93 Heinz Mack, biographical notes, undated, ZERO foundation, Düsseldorf, shelf number mkp.ZERO2VI.

94 Piero Manzoni had co-founded the magazine *Azimuth* in Milan.

95 Now in the holdings of the ZERO foundation, Düsseldorf, Vorlass (promised bequest) Heinz Mack, shelf number mkp.ZERO.VL Mack (1).

96 Mack 1995 (see note 86), p. 179 [translated].

97 Heinz Mack, 'Kurze Auflistung der internationalen ZERO-Ausstellungen', undated, Mack Archive, Huppertzhof, Mönchengladbach.

98 Mack 1995 (see note 86), p. 180 [translated].

99 See: Serge Guilbaut, *How New York Stole the Idea of Modern Art. Abstract Expressionism, Freedom, and the Cold War* [1983], trans. Arthur Goldhammer (Chicago: The University of Chicago Press, 1985).

100 Otto Piene died in 2014, shortly after the opening of his retrospective at the Neue Nationalgalerie in Berlin and just before the opening of the ZERO retrospective at the Solomon R. Guggenheim Museum in New York, which greatly affected the other two protagonists at the time.

101 See: Jack Kerouac, 'The Origins of the Beat Generation', in: *Playboy*, vol. VI, no. 6, June 1959, pp. 31–33, 42, 79.

102 See: '"Fluxus hatte meines Erachtens keine ausreichende intellektuelle und auch keine wirkliche moralische Dimension". Interview mit Heinz Mack', in: Klaus Gereon Beuckers and Christine Korte-Beuckers, for any instrument. *Die Anfänge der Aktionskunst in den 1950er/60er Jahren im Rheinland* (Munich: edition text+kritik, 2021), pp. 9–46.

103 Conversation with Heinz Mack, Huppertzhof, Mönchengladbach, December 2023 [translated].

104 Politically, the 1960s were marked by an overwhelming neo-conservatism, with the governments of Ludwig Erhard and Kurt Georg Kiesinger in West Germany and Josef Klaus in Austria attempting to build on the years 1933–45, the presidency of General Charles de Gaulle in France and US President Lyndon B. Johnson. One example of this is the only covert neo-racist theory of Konrad Lorenz, bestselling author at the time and winner of the 1973 Nobel Prize for Medicine. In contrast, ZERO virtually opened a window: let there be light and air and free space.

105 In 1960, Heinz Mack took part in the exhibition *La nuova concessione artistica* at Galleria Azimut, and in the same year he had a one-man show there, at the opening of which Lucio Fontana read a text he had written on Mack's work. At the same time, Mack wrote an important letter in favour of Fontana at the suggestion of Udo Kultermann, director of the Museum Morsbroich in Leverkusen, who was a committed advocate of the new art and who paid for this commitment by being dismissed and emigrating to New York, where he wrote an important art theoretical text; cf. Heinz Mack, letter to Udo Kultermann, January 1962, ZERO foundation, Düsseldorf, shelf number mkp.ZERO.1.I.1396.

106 Mack 1995 (see note 86), p. 178 [translated].

107 He often wrote letters to the artists in barely comprehensible poetic form; see the examples in the Fondation Hans Hartung et Anna-Eva Bergman, Antibes. It was a far cry from the bureaucratised museum business of the present day. Sandberg was extremely cultured and, as a Jew, had survived a dictatorship and a world war. In West Germany, it would have been unthinkable for a long time to have a Jewish director of a major art museum.

108 Heinz Mack's monumental *Light Carousel*, like other works, was irreparably damaged during the dismantling of the exhibition.

109 Mack 1995 (see note 86), p. 178 [translated].

110 Werner Haftmann had told the documenta council that if 'this charlatan Fontana' remained on the list of artists, he would resign from the committee, which the *documenta* could not afford, given that he was by far the most respected art critic in Germany at the time; conversation with Kasper König, Berlin, May 1992. Kasper König was a trainee or assistant to Arnold Bode at this documenta, which Alfred Nemeczek also remembered well; conversation with Alfred Nemeczek, Hamburg, April 1997. Nemeczek was the press officer for *documenta III* and later co-founder of the magazine *art*.

111 Mack, Piene and Uecker titled the work *Light Room* (Hommage à Fontana).

112 Mack 1995 (see note 86), p. 179 [translated].

113 Julyan Elias Bronner, 'Heinz Mack talks about his New York exhibitions', in: *Artforum*, 5 December 2014, URL: https://www.artforum.com/columns/heinz-mack-talks-about-his-new-york-exhibitions-222366/ [last accessed 27 December 2024].

114 Paik had borrowed Götz's rare original editions of the early Dada publications. At his first solo exhibition at Galerie Parnass in Wuppertal, he cited Götz as the inspiration for the idea of the electronic image; see: Robert Fleck, *K. O. Götz, West, Hundertwasser* (Cologne: Snoeck, 2017), pp. 21, 30. Paik went on to become a pioneer of video art. He was Professor of Video Art at the Düsseldorf Academy of Art from 1979 to 1996.

115 In the summer of 1964, McRoberts & Tunnard Gallery in London had organised an exhibition of these three ZERO artists. Charles Tunnard had approached the collector and gallerist Howard Wise in New York about the ZERO artists; see: https://www.aaa.si.edu/collections/howard-wise-gallery-records-9357/series-3, Box 6, Folder 94 [last accessed 27 December 2024].

116 Conversation with Heinz Mack, Huppertzhof, Mönchengladbach, January 2022 [translated].

117 John Canaday, 'The Sculptor Nowadays Is the Favorite Son', in: *The New York Times*, 22 November 1964, p. X19.

118 Donald Judd, 'In the Galleries. Mack, Piene, Uecker', in: *Arts Magazine*, vol. 39. no. 4, January 1965, p. 55; reprinted in: idem, *Complete Writings, 1959–1975*, ed. Kasper König (New York and Halifax: New York University

Press and Press of the Nova Scotia College of Art and Design, 1975), p. 157.

119 See: Robert Fleck, *Die Biennale von Venedig. Eine Geschichte des 20. Jahrhunderts* [Fundus-Bücher, no. 177] (Hamburg: Philo Fine Arts, 2009).

120 In Paris, the abolition of rent controls by the de Gaulle government had begun to drive artists out of the city and into the banlieues, while in SoHo it was still possible to secure very favourable long-term leases until the late 1970s.

121 See: *Das Bild nach dem letzten Bild / The Picture After the Last Picture*, ed. Peter Weibel and Jean-Christophe Ammann, exh. cat. Galerie Metropol, Vienna (Cologne: Verlag der Buchhandlung Walther König, 1991), pp. 150–155.

122 The term 'Holocaust' for the Nazi genocide of the Jews only came into use in West Germany after 1978, following the broadcast of the US television series of the same name.

123 Reinhardt died in 1967, Newman in 1970.

124 In the Lyden Sculpture Garden, Milwaukee.

125 Wieland Schmied, letter to Heinz Mack, Hannover, 10 January 1966, Mack Archive, Huppertzhof, Mönchengladbach.

126 This refers to the gallerists Alfred Schmela in Düsseldorf and Howard Wise in New York.

127 See: Annie Cohen-Solal, *Leo and His Circle. The Life of Leo Castelli* (New York: Knopf, 2010).

128 Conversation with Heinz Mack, Huppertzhof, Mönchengladbach, January 2022 [translated].

129 The term 'Land Art' only emerged a few years later.

130 See: *Group Zero. Mack, Piene, Uecker*, exh. cat. McRoberts & Tunnard Gallery, London 1964.

131 Conversation with Heinz Mack, Huppertzhof, Mönchengladbach, January 2022 [translated].

132 See: https://www.aaa.si.edu/collections/howard-wise-gallery-records-9357/series-3, Box 7, Folder 11 [last accessed 28 December 2024]. Otto Piene had an exhibition with Howard Wise in November 1965; this was followed by a show dedicated to Günther Uecker in November 1966.

133 Grace Glueck, 'Art Note. A Hanging Museum', in: *The New York Times*, 17 April 1966, Arts & Leisure, p. 134.

134 This was researched in detail by Stephanie Weber in 2010–11 for the exhibition at the Bundeskunsthalle, cf. exh. cat. Bonn 2011 (see note 29), p. 7; the corresponding documents can be found in the Mack Archive, Huppertzhof, Mönchengladbach.

135 *Large Veil of Light*, 1964, formerly Jon Murchison Collection, Dallas, Texas; see: Honisch 1986 (see note 61), p. 505. The work was sold to another private collection in the United States in the 2000s. Mack Archive, Huppertzhof, Mönchengladbach.

136 In the catalogue, Howard Wise Gallery, New York is listed as the lender, which shows how well anchored the artist was locally; see: *The Responsive Eye*, exh. cat. The Museum of Modern Art, New York 1965, p. 47. The trip from his studio flat to The Museum of Modern Art and the Guggenheim Museum was long, but within walking distance. The work is now in the collection of the Kunstpalast, Düsseldorf.

137 See: George Rickey, 'Heinz Mack. Recollections', undated, typescript, Mack Archive, Huppertzhof, Mönchengladbach. Mack also placed Rickey with Galerie Schmela in Düsseldorf; see: George Rickey, letter to Heinz Mack in New York, 11 February 1965, Mack Archive, Huppertzhof, Mönchengladbach.

138 They knew each other from the exhibition *Bewogen – beweging* at the Stedelijk Museum in Amsterdam in 1961 and the ZERO room at *documenta III* in Kassel in the summer of 1964. Rickey recalled: 'I saw Mack setting up his sculptures for the ZERO exhibition at Howard Wise's gallery in New York in 1964, and I remember Howard Wise's bewilderment, oblivious to Mack's determined energy.' [translated]. The first visit to Rickey in Connecticut, with Marisol and Uecker, obviously took place in connection with that 1964 exhibition; George Rickey, 'J'ai rencontré Heinz Mack' [1972], in: *Heinz Mack*, exh. cat. Musée d'art moderne de la Ville de Paris 1973, unpaginated.

139 Marisol then came to Düsseldorf to persuade him to return to New York, which led to the break-up of their relationship and, a little later, of Mack's first marriage.

140 'Hans Haacke was a dialogue partner for me in New York, although we didn't really understand each other, so we were polite and talked to each other. He was very interested and was also the first person to see my exhibition at Howard Wise, and he saw at it several times'; conversation with Heinz Mack, Huppertzhof, Mönchengladbach, January 2022 [translated]. Hans Haacke had solo exhibitions with Howard Wise, in January 1966 the show *Wind and Water* and again in January 1968.

141 The tensions between Mack and Piene, including the reserved attitude of Galerie Schmela towards the latter, with whose first family Monika Schmela always kept in contact, came to a head during these years; see the documents in the Mack Archive, Huppertzhof, Mönchengladbach.

142 Anna Lenz and Ulrike Bleicker-Honisch (eds.), *Das Ohr am Tatort. Heinz-Norbert Jocks im Gespräch mit Gotthard Graubner, Heinz Mack, Roman Opalka, Otto Piene und Günther* Uecker (Ostfildern: Hatje Cantz, 2009), p. 56 [translated].

143 Now the Belvedere 21.

144 A brief note on the intellectual atmosphere at the time: in the same school year, Hans Kaliwoda was dismissed without notice by the headmaster in front of our eyes when he had us make collages from West German weeklies he had brought with him. One of the pupils found a naked breast in one of them and included it in his collage. The teacher did not censor it – and had to leave the school immediately. Before 1968 and its aftermath, the post-war period had been one of oppressive paternalism.

145 See: Werner Hofmann, *Grundlagen der modernen Kunst. Eine Einführung in ihre symbolischen Formen* (Stuttgart: Kröner, 1966). Werner Hofmann, three years older than Mack and trained at The Museum of Modern Art in New York, created one of the best exhibition programmes of the 1960s as founding director of the Museum des 20. Jahrhunderts in Vienna. Later, as longstanding director of the Hamburger Kunsthalle, he laid the foundations for a new understanding of the nineteenth century and thus of modernism as a whole with the exhibition series *Kunst um 1800* (Art Around 1800).

146 Hofmann remained in close contact with Mack. He also established direct contact between the artist and me in 2009; see: Robert Fleck, conversations with Werner Hofmann, Hamburg, 2010–13, autograph transcription, c. 450 pages, in the Werner Hofmann Estate, Germanisches Nationalmuseum, Nuremberg. The joint book project came to an end with Werner Hofmann's death in March 2013.

147 *Weiss auf Weiss* was organised in collaboration with the artist Christian Megert, who had himself participated in several ZERO exhibitions, ran a gallery in Bern that formed the Swiss base of ZERO, and has been closely associated with Mack since the beginning of his professorship at the Düsseldorf Academy of Art in 1976. With his mirror works, Christian Megert is an important representative of non-motorised kinetic art; see: *Christian Megert*, ed. Robert Fleck, exh. cat. Akademie-Galerie – Die Neue Sammlung, Düsseldorf Academy of Art 2017.

148 See: Frank Popper, Die kinetische Kunst. *Licht und Bewegung. Umweltkunst und Aktio*n (Cologne: DuMont, 1975); Hans-Jürgen Buderer, *Kinetische Kunst. Konzeptionen von Bewegung und Raum* (Worms: Wernersche Verlagsgesellschaft, 1992).

149 Frank Popper, 'Einführing', in: *Licht und Bewegung. Kinetische Kunst*, exh. cat. Kunstverein für die Rheinlande und Westfalen, Düsseldorf 1966, pp. 3–8. Mack was represented in the exhibition with three works from 1965, two rotors and the honeycomb wing, all from the New York period.

150 Heinz Mack, early typescript, undated, p. [105], Mack Archive, Huppertzhof, Mönchengladbach [translated].

151 Like Harald Szeemann, an artist not an

art historian, Pontus Hultén became the most important museum founder of the second half of the twentieth century, with the Moderna Museet in Stockholm, the Centre Pompidou in Paris, the MOCA in Los Angeles, the Palazzo Grassi in Venice, the Bundeskunsthalle in Bonn and the Museum Tinguely in Basel. In 1968, he curated the seminal exhibition Art in the Machine Age at The Museum of Modern Art in New York.

152 Hans Fischli was the father of Peter Fischli from the Swiss artist duo Peter Fischli/David Weiss.

153 See: Willy Rotzler, Objektkunst. *Von Duchamp bis Kienholz* (Cologne: DuMont, 1972).

154 Text and illustrations in: Gyorgy Kepes (ed.), *Wesen und Kunst der Bewegung* [sehen + werten. Untersuchungen über heutige wissenschaftliche und künstlerische Leistungen und deren Integration in der modernen Welt, vol. 3] (Brussels: La Connaissance, 1969), pp. 81–115.

155 Almost at the same time, Heinz Mack had a solo exhibition at the Moderna Museet in Stockholm under its founding director Pontus Hultén, which Wieland Schmied, director of the Kestner-Gesellschaft in Hannover, at the time the most important exhibition venue for contemporary art in the Federal Republic of Germany, opened at the artist's request; Wieland Schmied, letter to Heinz Mack, Hannover, 10 January 1966, Mack Archive, Huppertzhof, Mönchengladbach.

156 In 1935, Marcel Duchamp created optical graphics with his Rotorreliefs, which he presented on record players and which became a visual impression that the eye and brain could no longer fully comprehend. With these innovative works, which he had patented and presented not in an exhibition but at the Concours Lepine inventors' fair in Paris, he brought the new sensory impressions of film into the visual arts, anticipating almost one-to-one the kinetic art of the 1960s. All this only became more widely known in 1958, when the Philadelphia Museum of Art opened a permanent retrospective of his most important works, organised by Duchamp himself. Heinz Heinz Mack saw it in 1964 when he gave a lecture on his *Sahara Project* on the occasion of the ZERO exhibition in Philadelphia, organised by Otto Piene. Duchamp was very much present in New York and Paris in the 1960s. He lived until 1968, André Breton, the founder and leader of the Surrealists, until 1966, so there was an unimaginable personal continuity in relation to the great innovations of modern art from around 1910 to 1930.

157 See: *The Machine as Seen at the End of the Mechanical Age*, exh. cat. The Museum of Modern Art, New York, et al. (Greenwich, Connecticut: New York Graphic Society, 1968).

158 See: Johan Huizinga, *Homo Ludens: A Study of the Play-Element of Culture* [1938] (London: Routledge & Kegan Paul, 1949).

159 Friedrich Schiller, On the Aesthetic Education of Man [1795], trans. Reginald Snell (Mineola, New York: Dover Publications, 2004), p. 80 [emphasis original].

160 I refer, for example, to the first exhibition by Haus-Rucker-Co with a minimal art bouncy castle at the Museum des 20. Jahrhunderts in Vienna in 1972, after the Viennese art scene had chased Werner Hofmann away to Hamburg. Populism also existed back then, not least around kinetics and interactivity, which attracted a mass audience.

161 *Mack. Kinetik*, exh. cat. Museum Abteiberg, Mönchengladbach (Düsseldorf: Richter, 2011); Mack Reflected. *Expanding the ZERO Code*, ed. Alistair Hudson, exh. cat. ZKM | Center for Art and Media Karlsruhe (Munich: Hirmer, 2024).

162 I use the spelling 'Brancusi' (not: Brâncuși), as the artist called himself during his decades in France (1906–57) and as he also signed the corresponding donation to the French state – following the example of his teacher, Auguste Rodin – before his death, after Romania had rejected the donation of his entire oeuvre. Brancusi's deed of donation is in the Bibliothèque Kandinsky, Centre Georges Pompidou, Paris, while Rodin's is in the Musée Rodin, Paris.

163 Conversation with Heinz Mack, Huppertzhof, Mönchengladbach, February 2023 [translated].

164 The Museum of Modern Art in New York declined to lend the rotor from its collection (*Silver Dynamo*, 1964) for the exhibition *Heinz Mack. Light – Space – Colour* at the Bundeskunsthalle in Bonn in 2011, as damage to even one element, especially the grooved glass pane, would mean a total loss, as these materials no longer exist. Archive of the Kunst- und Ausstellungshalle der Bundesrepublik Deutschland, Bonn.

165 This refers to the 1968/69 film *Tele-Mack* about Mack's *Sahara Project*.

166 The technical system still exists in Munich's Olympic Lake but has not been in operation for years due to cost. Generating the *Water Cloud* consumes 400,000 watts.

167 For more on the *Sahara Project* and all related issues, see: Sophia Sotke, *Mack – Sahara. From ZERO to Land Art. Heinz Mack's Sahara-Project, 1959–1997*, trans. Gérard Goodrow (Munich: Hirmer, 2022).

168 Colour television had only recently been introduced. Its inauguration took place on 25 August 1967 at the *Große Deutsche Funkausstellung* in West Berlin, with Willy Brandt, who had been Lord Mayor of the city until 1966 and went on to become Chancellor of the BRD in 1969.

169 Robert Smithson was killed in a plane crash in 1973 while photographing a work in progress. Sophia Sotke has examined the unspoken dialogue between Mack and his *Sahara Project* with the protagonists of Land Art; see: Sotke 2022 (see note 167).

170 For more on the two terms 'deterritorialisation' and 'reterritorialisation', see the chapter '1227: Treatise on Nomadology—The War Machine', in: Gilles Deleuze and Félix Guattari, A *Thousand Plateaus. Capitalism and Schizophrenia* [1980], trans. Brian Massumi (Minneapolis and London: University of Minnesota Press, 1987), pp. 351–423.

171 'The space that Mack considered for the Sahara Project also becomes a medium of aesthetic states, that is to say, of innovation created from light, which through vibration, concentration, and reflection is given over to a freedom of design of a selection that, beyond Kandinsky, no longer allows us to speak only of the emancipation of colour and form, but also of the emancipation of light. [...] Finally, the objects – the steles, the mirrored walls, the sails, the panes of glass, the sand reliefs – all bearers of aesthetic states that give the endless and equally probable labyrinth of the desert, of space, of light, a singular discontinuity, an interruption, a visual innovation, an improbability of information.' Max Bense, 'Das Sahara-Projekt Heinz Mack', in: idem, *Artistik und Engagement. Präsentation ästhetischer Objekte* (Cologne: Kiepenheuer & Witsch, 1970), p. 153 [translated].

172 I refer to Gilles Deleuze's concept of *espaces quelconques* from his lectures from 1981 to 1983 and to books on film, especially from Italian Neorealismo onwards.

173 At the time, almost no one had any idea what a 'computer' was. The first personal computers were invented ten years later and only became available to the general public ten years after that.

174 *mack. Objekte – Aktionen – Projekte*, exh. cat. Academy of Arts, Berlin (West) 1972 – an important artist's book.

175 The significance of the 1973 exhibition in Paris goes far beyond this assessment. It was the first solo exhibition of a living German artist in a leading French museum since the war (Max Ernst and Hans Hartung, who lived in France, were no longer German citizens). The unusually high-profile patronage for a forty-two-year-old artist by the German Foreign Minister Walter Scheel, the French Foreign Minister Maurice Schumann and Jacques Duhamel, a successor to André Malraux as French Minister of Culture, testifies to an extraordinary understanding of art. It shows that the exhibition contributed to the establishment of the Franco-German leadership duo in the European Community under President Georges Pompidou and Chancellor Willy Brandt. The fact that this was not an exhibition of favouritism on the part of the French, although most of the loans for Mack's exhibition came from the Academy of Arts in West Berlin, can be seen from the fact that the

main curator was André Berne-Joffroy, one of the most important curators of the time, and from the catalogue, which contains the first 'Glossary of Terms and Ideas' by Heinz Mack, translated and compiled from his original German texts, as well as a dozen statements by important French and international artist colleagues; see: exh. cat. Paris 1973 (see note 138).

176 Rickey 1972 (see note 138), unpaginated.

177 See: Fleck 2009 (see note 119): pp. 196–209 (on the German pavilion), p. 205 (on the 1970 Venice Biennale).

178 Conversation with Helmut Schweizer, Düsseldorf, January 2024 [translated]. The Karlsruhe artists' group PUYK around Helmut Schweizer also invited Max Bense as a lecturer in Karlsruhe from 1969, as Mack and Piene had done in Düsseldorf ten years earlier. In the spring of 1970, Schweizer, Baumgarten and others presented their works as PUYK in the entrance area of the exhibition *Jetzt. Kunst in Deutschland* at the Kunsthalle Köln directly opposite a large light relief work by Heinz Mack and were very impressed to be exhibiting next to Mack. For their younger generation, the artist was now an authority.

179 Henri Nannen (ed.), *Expedition in künstliche Gärten* (Hamburg: Gruner + Jahr, 1977), unpaginated [translated].

180 Dieter Honisch, 'Heinz Mack', in: *La Biennale di Venezia. 35. Biennale internazionale d'arte*, exh. cat. Venice 1970, pp. 36f.; Dieter Honisch (ed.), *lenk, mack, pfahler, uecker. XXXV. biennale di venezia padiglione tedesco* (Essen: Museum Folkwang, 1970).

181 Conversation with Heinz Mack, Huppertzhof, Mönchengladbach, June 2023 [translated]; cf. *Mack. ars urbana – Kunst für die Stadt, 1952–2008* (Munich: Hirmer, 2008), pp. 144f., 329f.

182 At that time, Mack and Piene took opposite paths in life. With the exception of a brief interlude in Japan, Mack worked radically independently. Piene, on the other hand, was director of the Center for Advanced Visual Studies founded by Gyorgy Kepes at the Massachusetts Institute of Technology (MIT) in Cambridge until 1994. In 1984, Mack was asked by his sculptor colleague Norbert Kricke, rector of the Düsseldorf Academy of Art from 1972 to 1981, to take up a professorship in Düsseldorf and become rector. After some consideration, Mack declined, feeling that such a position was incompatible with his artistic path.

183 The sculpture in Horten Park in Düsseldorf was irreparably damaged in a storm in 1983, the one in Hamburg was destroyed by vandalism and the one in Eindhoven was dismantled by the company in 2009 without the artist being informed. Art in public space is always vulnerable.

184 See: ars urbana 2008 (see note 181).

185 See: ibid., pp. 240–249, 340.

186 See also: the reprint of *ZERO* [1, 2, 3] (Cologne: DuMont Schauberg, 1973); Heinz Mack, *... daß Silber meine Farbe ist* (Duisburg: Hildebrandt, 1977). It was also during these years that the Sahara experience was translated into graphic collages as editioned objects, i.e. in a democratic medium, which are still very present on the art market today.

187 See: Kunstreport, no. 11, 1978 ('Bundeskunsthalle'); Heinz Mack, 'Kunst 2000', in: *Kunstforum International*, no. 29, May 1978 ('Internationales Künstlergremium, Symposium 1978 in Berlin'), pp. 46–55.

188 Jacques Lassaigne, 'Préface', in: exh. cat. Paris 1973 (see note 138), unpaginated [translated].

189 Hofmann 1966 (see note 145), pp. 86–103; cf. Johan Huizinga, *Herbst des Mittelalters. Studien über Lebens- und Geistesformen des 14. und 15. Jahrhunderts in Frankreich und den Niederlanden* [1919], ed. and trans. Kurt Köster, based on the 1923 translation by Mathilde Wolff-Mönckeberg (Stuttgart: Kröner, 1975).

190 *Heinz Mack, 'Das Licht auf der Oberfläche', in: Mack – Lichtkuns*t, ed. Burkhard Leismann, exh. cat. Kunstmuseum Ahlen (Cologne: Wienand, 1994), p. 217 [translated].

191 From an undated typescript, reprinted in: Honisch 1986 (see note 61), p. 352 [translated].

192 Conversation with Heinz Mack, Huppertzhof, Mönchengladbach, January 2024 [translated].

193 See exh. cat. Berlin (West) 1972 (see note 174).

194 See: Stephan Mann, *Von Matisse bis Mack. Künstlerkapellen im 20. Jahrhundert* (Frankfurt am Main: Peter Lang, 1996).

195 'Vladimir Jankélévitch: un homme libre', France Culture 1996, rebroadcast 12 August 2024, radiofrance.fr [translated].

196 John Cage studied under Arnold Schoenberg in Los Angeles.

197 See: Stephan Geiger, 'Farbe, Klang, Strukturen. Heinz Mack und die Musik', in: *Heinz Mack. Ich sehe die Musik*, exh. cat. Galerie Geiger, Constance 2023, pp. 5–19.

198 There is an album with Mack's piano interpretations (*Playing for Me and You*, 2001), which has not yet been released; Mack Archive, Huppertzhof, Mönchengladbach. In addition, Mack's piano recital at the Academy of Arts in Berlin on 6 June 2015, in which he played jazz improvisations from the 1950s and 1960s, has been released on DVD by carbon & ziegenruecker.

199 See: Birnbaum/Obrist 2011 (see note 30).

200 See: Gernot Böhme and Hartmut Böhme, *Feuer – Wasser – Erde – Luft. Eine Kulturgeschichte der Elemente* (Munich: C. H. Beck, 1996).

201 Exh. cat. Ahlen 1994 (see note 190), p. 137 [translated].

202 Schmied 1998 (see note 3), p. 13 [translated].

203 Ibid., pp. 10f. [translated]. For more on the theme of utopia, see also: Karin Stempel, 'Die Parameter des Utopischen', in: exh. cat. Ahlen 1994 (see note 190), pp. 227–231.

204 One exception was poetry, which was extensively and prominently translated, for example by Elsa Triolet, a poet and companion of Louis Aragon in the powerful French Communist Party.

205 See: *Paris – Moscou, 1900–1930*, exh. cat. Musée national d'art moderne – Centre Georges Pompidou, Paris (Paris: Gallimard, 1979). The exhibition was the result of a diplomatic initiative made possible by the détente brought about by the Helsinki Accords signed at the Conference on Security and Cooperation in Europe (CSCE) in 1975.

206 Today in the Tretyakov Gallery, Moscow.

207 Nadia Boulanger was the teacher of the six composers who formed the Groupe des Six and musically dominated the first post-war period in Paris. Darius Milhaud, whose opera *Bolivar* Heinz Mack saw in Paris in 1950, was a member of the Groupe des Six.

208 Quoted in: Robert Fleck and Heinz Mack, *Mack – Painting*, trans. Gérard Goodrow (Munich: Hirmer, 2023), p. 242.

209 For more on the sale of the Malevich paintings in the 1950s, see: *Kazimir Malevich and the Russian Avant-garde*, exh. cat. Stedelijk Museum Amsterdam; Bundeskunsthalle, Bonn, Bielefeld/Berlin: Kerber, 2014. Yves Klein was also aware of Malevich when he began developing his work in 1955 onwards. The question of whether he was aware of Alexander Rodchenko's three monochromes, first exhibited in Moscow in 1921, when he conceived his own monochrome painting mains unresolved; see: Fleck 2018 (see note 16), p. 98, note 12.

210 See: *Taten des Lichts. Mack & Goethe*, ed. Barbara Steingießer, exh. cat. Goethe-Museum, Düsseldorf (Berlin: Hatje Cantz, 2018).

211 Johann Wolfgang von Goethe, 'Schriften zur Farbenlehre' [1810], in: idem., *Gedenkausgabe der Werke, Briefe und Gespräche*, ed. Ernst Beutler, vol. 17: Naturwissenschaftliche Schriften, part 2 (Zurich: Artemis, [1952]), p. 9 [translated].

212 Konrad Klapheck's father Ludwig taught art history at the art academy, was dismissed by the Nazis after being interrogated by the Gestapo and died shortly afterwards, completely isolated in the Rhineland bourgeoisie after his dismissal. His mother, Anna Klapheck, was the most important art critic in Düsseldorf in the post-war decades; she also taught art history at the art academy. In 1960, Konrad Klapheck married Lilo Lang, a Jewish woman who had survived the Holocaust with her parents in the Netherlands. Their daughter Elisa is a

rabbi in Frankfurt am Main and chairwoman of the General Conference of Rabbis of Germany. Konrad Klapheck began translating Yves Klein's letters and writings from French in 1957 and thus came into contact with Heinz Mack in the ZERO circle, despite their different artistic paths. In 1965, a year before his death, the Surrealist leader André Breton dedicated his last text to Klapheck's painting for the catalogue of his solo exhibition at Galerie Ileana Sonnabend in Paris. The mutual appreciation between Mack and Klapheck lasted for decades.

213 Hans Hartung, 'Bildbeispiele aus den dreißige Jahren', in: *Deutschlandbilder. Art from a Divided Country*, ed. by Eckhart Gillen, cat. 47, Berliner Festwochen/Cologne: DuMont 1997, pp. 78–84.

214 *Mack. Transit zwischen Okzident und Orient. Faszination und Inspiration der islamischen Kultur. Ein Werk-Aspekt, 1950–2006*, ed. Claus-Peter Haase, exh. cat. Pergamonmuseum, Berlin (Cologne: DuMont, 2006), p. 16 [translated].

215 *Mack. Sadece isık ve renk / Just Light and Colour*, exh. cat. Sakıp Sabancı Müzesi, Istanbul 2016. The exhibition was closed after the attempted coup against Recep Tayyip Erdoğan in July 2016. However, Heinz Mack still has a large market in Turkey and the Middle East.

216 See: exh. cat. Istanbul 2015 (see note 50).

217 See: *Mack. The Sky Over Nine Columns*, exh. cat. Venice (Düsseldorf: Beck & Eggeling, 2014).

218 Albert Camus, *The Rebel. An Essay on Man in Revolt* [1951], trans. Anthony Bower (New York: Alfred A. Knopf, 1954), pp. 265f.

219 *Mack. Ein Buch der Bilder zum West-östlichen Divan von Johann Wolfgang v. Goethe* (Mönchengladbach: B. Kühlen, 1999).

220 *Heinz Mack. Mouvement et Lumière / Movement and Light*, exh. cat. Musée Théodore-Monod d'art africain, Dakar (Düsseldorf: Geuer & Geuer Art, 2019); Maria Valeria Mack, *Afrikanische Kunst der Sammlung Mack / African Art from the Mack Collection*, ed. David Zemanek (Munich: Hirmer, 2018).

221 In March 1933, Alex Vömel, who had previously been the managing director of Alfred Flechtheim's gallery in Düsseldorf, took over Flechtheim's premises at Königsallee 34 and set up his own gallery. From 1949 to 1967, it was located at Königsallee 42.

222 Heinz Mack. *Wahlverwandtschaften*, ed. Bernd Finkeldey, exh. cat. Tehran Museum of Contemporary Art; Wilhelm-Hack-Museum, Ludwigshafen (Teheran 2001). The Tehran Museum's collection of contemporary art was assembled at great expense by Empress Farah Pahlavi in the mid-1970s and was one of the finest international collections of its time.

223 On the occasion of this exhibition, *Mack. Transit zwischen Okzident und Orient* (see: exh. cat. Berlin 2006 [see note 214]), the project with the nine golden steles was conceived, which was then realised for the first time in Venice in 2014.

224 See: Karl Heinz Bohrer, *Suddenness: On the Moment of Aesthetic Appearance* [European Perspectives: A Series in Social Thought & Cultural Cticism], trans. Ruth Crowley (New York: Columbia University Press, 1994).

225 Paul Valéry, *Pièces sur l'art* (Paris: Gallimard, 1934).

226 Adorno 1970 (see note 67).

227 Werner Hofmann, 'Licht, Glanz und Pracht', in: Schmied 1998 (see note 3), pp. 136–139 [translated].

228 'In his Sahara Project, he combined the sublime nature of the desert spaces with the immaterial beauty of his steles and mirror objects. A rare event in the art of our century, which generally avoids the triad of light, lustre and splendour'; ibid., p. 139 [translated].

229 Robert Fleck, Conversations with Werner Hofmann, typescript/transcript, Werner Hofmann estate, Germanisches Nationalmuseum, Nuremberg.

230 Robert Fleck, Conversations with Katharina Fritsch, Düsseldorf, since 2008.

231 Heinz Mack, 'Die verspiegelte Stadt sowie Verspiegelte Museen', in: Schmied 1998 (see note 3), p. 259 [translated].

232 Hofmann 1998 (see note 227), p. 137 [translated, emphasis original].

233 See: Heinz Mack, *Silberlicht*. 75 Projektionen auf Fotopapier, exh. cat. Städtisches Museum Abteiberg, Mönchengladbach (Mönchengladbach: B. Kühlen, 2006).

234 See: Heinz Mack, *Lichtbilder*, exh. cat. Sparkasse Essen, 2006. The *Lichtbilder* suite comprises thirty-five motifs in various formats as C-prints using the slide process on 4mm aluminium composite panels.

235 These early photographs were shown for the first time and very convincingly in the retrospective of the artist's work curated by Heike van den Valentyn at the Kunstpalast in Düsseldorf in 2021. The curator recently reported that, based on her research in Mack's studio at the time, she would have liked to include photography as a central thread of the work, but that this still seemed too daring for the artist at the time, as he feared it might distract from his main work; Robert Fleck, conversation with Heike van den Valentyn, Düsseldorf, June 2024. See: *Heinz Mack*, ed. Heike van den Valentyn, exh. cat. Kunstpalast, Düsseldorf (Cologne: Verlag der Buchhandlung Walther und Franz König, 2021).

236 Conversation with Kasper König, Berlin, May 1992.

237 Stachelhaus 1993 (see note 72) [translated].

238 Cf. the projections of black-and-white photographs and video works by Imi Knoebel in Düsseldorf (1968–71), which are a successor to ZERO. Mack's entire oeuvre is full of anticipations of this kind; see: *Vienna Secession 1898–1998: The Century of Artistic Freedom*, ed. Robert Fleck, exh. cat. Wiener Secession, Vienna; Rudolfinum, Prague (Munich and New York: Prestel, 1998), p. 172.

239 *Sehverwandtschaften. Heinz Mack und das Forschungszentrum Jülich*, copy in the Mack Archive, Huppertzhof, Mönchengladbach.

240 Conversation with Heinz Mack, Huppertzhof, Mönchengladbach, April 2023 [translated].

241 Conversation with Heinz Mack, Huppertzhof, Mönchengladbach, December 2021.

242 Since the 1950s, largely initiated by the sculpture school of Fritz Wotruba and his successors, as well as simultaneous efforts in the former Eastern Bloc, symposia for stone sculpture have been held every year during the summer months at various locations. Renowned artists have always taken part. However, they have had virtually no influence on the development of sculpture in recent decades. Heinz Mack never participated in any of these symposia.

243 See: *Mack*, ed. Cragg Foundation, exh. cat. Waldfrieden Sculpture Park, Wuppertal (Berlin: Hatje Cantz, 2021).

244 Exh. cat. Ahlen 1994 (see note 190), p. 137 [translated].

245 Conversation with Heinz Mack, Huppertzhof, Mönchengladbach, February 2022 [translated].

246 From an undated typescript, quoted in: Honisch 1986 (see note 61), p. 44 [translated].

247 The theme of combination was a favourite topic of Mack's art historian friend Werner Hofmann; see: Werner Hofmann, 'Ars combinatoria', in: *Jahrbuch der Hamburger Kunstsammlungen*, vol. 21, 1976, pp. 7–30.

248 Exh. cat. Ahlen 1994 (see note 190), p. 217 [translated].

249 André Malraux was also the initiator of these ceremonies: after the death of Georges Braque in 1963, with a state ceremony at his coffin in the Cour Carrée of the Louvre. In December 2022, Pierre Soulages, Mack's artist colleague and eleven years his senior, whose concept of light in painting had interested him since the 1950s, was bidden farewell with a similar ceremony, which left a deep impression on Mack.

250 Udo Kultermann published an essential ‚exhibition' on this in book form: Udo Kultermann, *Neue Formendes Bildes* (Tübingen: Wasmuth, 1969).

251 Robert Fleck, Conversations with Katharina Sieverding, Düsseldorf, since 2014.

252 André Malraux, *Psychologie der Kunst. Das imaginäre Museum*, trans. Jan Lauts (Baden-Baden: Woldemar Klein, 1949); French original: *Psychologie de l'art: Le Musée imaginaire* (Geneva: Albert Skira, 1947); critical edition: *Écrits sur l'art*, 2 vols. (Paris: Gallimard, Bibliothèque de la Pléiade, 2004). The first English edition, translated by Stuart Gilbert and published by Pantheon Books in New York in 1949, was titled Museum Without Walls.

253 Cf. Jean-Paul Sartre, *The Imaginary: A Phenomenological Psychology of the Imagination* [1940], trans. Jonathan Webber (London and New York: Routledge, 2004).

254 André Malraux, *Le Musée imaginaire* (Paris: Gallimard, 1996), pp. 15f. [translated].

255 In the 1930s in Paris, Malraux met the German émigré Walter Benjamin, who in 1935 published the essay 'The Work of Art in the Age of Mechanical Reproduction'. This text, which became a foundation of artistic thought for decades, was largely forgotten until the late 1960s.

256 Malraux 1996 (see note 253), among others pp. 15f., 28.

257 Heinz Mack, *'Inspiration from Works of Art and Cultural History'*, in: Fleck/Mack 2023 (see note 208), pp. 195–259.

258 Heinz Mack, 'The Compendium,' in: Hudson/ZKM 2024 (see note 161), pp. 280–289.

259 Heinz Mack, *Mackazin. Die Jahre 1957–67* (no place of publication noted, 1967); cf. Heinz Mack, *Mackazin*, vol. 2 (New York: Sperone Westwater, 2011).

260 It would be worth several doctoral theses to shed more light on this.

261 Japonisme and the reception of sub-Saharan art did nothing to fundamentally change this.

262 It emerged at the same time as the decolonisation process began.

263 Robert Fleck, Conversations with Pierre Soulages, Sète and Paris, since 1992. Cf. Fleck/Obrist 2017 (see note 60) [translated].

264 Cf. Mack 2018 (see note 220).

265 Veit Loers, 'Gespräch mit Heinz Mack', in: exh. cat. Düsseldorf 2018 (see note 210), p. 447 [translated].

266 This chapter is a revised version of the text of the same title in: Fleck/Mack 2023 (see note 208), pp. 5–15.

267 Fleck/Mack 2023 (see note 208), p. 23.

268 Arnold Schönberg, *Harmonielehre* (Vienna: Universal-Edition, 1911), p. 19 [translated]; see also: Arnold Schoenberg, 'Opinion or Insight?' [1926], in: *Style and Idea: Selected Writings of Arnold Schoenberg*, ed. Leonard Stein, with translations by Leo Black (New York: St. Martins Press, 1975), pp. 258–264.

269 Several paintings made as early as 1956 are counted among them; see: Fleck 2017 (see note 51), vol. 2, pp. 16f.

270 Exh. cat. Düsseldorf 2018 (see note 210), p. 439 [translated].

271 In 1962, Mack made forty-three ZERO paintings, in 1963 only seventeen and in 1964 just nine. In 1965, not a single ZERO painting was made. A certain echo reveals itself in the five ZERO paintings of 1966, as well as in one each from 1967 and 1968. These are the last to date; see: Fleck 2017 (see note 51), vol. 2, pp. 67–79.

272 See: *Samson D. Sauerbier, Gegen Darstellung. Ästhetische Handlungen und Demonstrationen – Die zur Schau gestellte Wirklichkeit in den zeitgenössischen Künsten* (Cologne: Buchhandlung Walther König, 1978).

273 Laszlo Glozer, 'Ausstieg aus dem Bild. Wiederkehr der Außenwelt', in: exh. cat. Cologne 1981 (see note 9), pp. 234–238. In 1981, Heinz Mack was represented with two works and in several documentary films in Westkunst, the first 'major exhibition' of the Federal Republic of Germany, a groundbreaking survey.

274 Quoted in: Marion Agthe and Ute Mack (eds.), *Mack. Malerei / Painting, 1991–2011* (Mönchengladbach: B. Kühlen, 2011), p. 33.

275 The painting is in the collection of The Museum of Modern Art, New York.

276 Exh. cat. Düsseldorf 2018 (see note 210), p. 437 [translated].

277 Gilles Deleuze, *Sur la peinture. Cours mars – juin 1981*, ed. David Lapoujade (Paris: Les Éditions de Minuit, 2023), pp. 228ff., 301ff. Cf. idem, *Francis Bacon: The Logic of Sensation* [1981], trans. Daniel W. Smith (London and New York: Continuum, 2003).

278 Fleck/Mack 2023 (see note 208), p. 210.

279 Friedrich Schiller, letter to Johann Wolfgang von Goethe, 27 March 1801, in: Fritz Jonas (ed.), *Schillers Briefe* (Stuttgart, Berlin and Leipzig: Deutsche Verlagsanstalt, 1896), vol. 6, p. 262 [translated].

280 See: Mack 2023 (see note 257).

281 Conversations with Heinz Mack, Huppertzhof, Mönchengladbach, 2021 [translated].

282 Exh. cat. Düsseldorf 2018 (see note 210), p. 437 [translated].

283 Ibid., p. 443 [translated].

284 Ibid., pp. 447, 449 [translated].

285 For more on the close relationship between Mack's oeuvre and Goethe, see the catalogue to the highly successful exhibition *Taten des Lichts – Mack & Goethe*, ed. Barbara Steingießer, exh. cat. Goethe-Museum Düsseldorf (Berlin: Hatje Cantz, 2018).

286 The influential curator Norman Rosenthal has the merit of having based a retrospective of Heinz Mack on the *Chromatic Constellations* for the first time in Istanbul in 2016 and of having opened the exhibition with them; see: exh. cat. Mack 2016 (see note 215). The retrospective in Istanbul began with eight *Chromatic Constellations* titled *Colour-Octet (Hommage à Goethe)* from 1998, in which the artist plays through the entire colour spectrum starting with 'black-black' and 'white-white' in dialogues of colour-contrasting, nearly square surfaces (fig. p. 270).

287 One can also see this as a Duchampian readymade.

288 Arnold Schoenberg, 'Composition with Twelve Tones' [1941/48], in: idem, *Style and Idea: Selected Writings of Arnold Schoenberg*, ed. Leonard Stein, with translations by Leo Black (Berkeley and Los Angeles: University of California Press, 1975), pp. 214–249.

289 Heinz Mack plays jazz brilliantly on the piano, with and without any swing, comparable to Schoenberg's structures.

290 Exh. cat. Düsseldorf 2018 (see note 210), p. 443 [translated].

291 See: Johannes Cladders, 'Artefakt und Natur. Versuch einer Annäherung an das Werk von Heinz Mack', in: Schmied 1998 (see note 3), pp. 69–73.

292 Once again, the rule that artists should not publish their experiments and results too early proves to be valid. Otherwise, they will be penalised for it.

293 For more on the garden as an important topos in Heinz Mack's work, see, among others: Karin Thomas, 'Das Paradies auf Erden schon zu Lebzeiten betreten. Gartenkünstlerische Aspekte bei Heinz Mack', in: exh. cat. Berlin 2006 (see note 214), pp. 43–49; Barbara Könches, '*Des Malers Glück im Garten', in: Vom Klang, von der Struktur und von der Farbe. Hommage an Heinz Mack zum 90. Geburtstag*, exh. cat. Galerie Bentler, Bonn 2021, pp. 36–39.

294 Conversation with Heinz Mack, Huppertzhof, Mönchengladbach, June 2024 [translated].

295 See: Robert Fleck, *Kunst und Ökologie* (Vienna and Hamburg: Edition Konturen, 2023).

296 Carl Friedrich von Weizsäcker, *Die Geschichte der Natur. Zwölf Vorlesungen* [transcriptions of lectures held in Göttingen in 1946] (Leipzig, Stuttgart, and Zurich: Hirzel, 1948).

297 See: Gernot Böhme, *Atmosphäre. Essays zur neuen Ästhetik* (Frankfurt am Main: Suhrkamp, 1995); Böhme/Böhme 1996 (see note 200).

298 Gernot Böhme, 'Licht am Werk. Licht-Ästhetik bei Goethe und Mack', in: exh. cat. Düsseldorf 2018 (see note 210), pp. 161–167; Harmut Böhme, 'Bilder und Bildungen des Lichts bei Goethe und Heinz Mack', in: ibid., pp. 175–195; idem, 'Goethe, Ovid und Heinz Mack. Über Formen und Formwandel', in: ibid., pp. 307–327.

299 Letter to Heinz Mack, Hamburg, 14 January 2023, Mack Archive, Huppertzhof, Mönchengladbach [translated].

300 See: Werner Heisenberg, *Wandlungen in den Grundlagen der Naturwissenschaft* (Stuttgart: Hirzel, 1947).

301 Heinz Mack read the German translation of Albert Camus's philosophical essay *The Myth of Sisyphus* – first published in French in 1942 and translated into German by Hans Georg Brenner and Wolfdietrich Rasch in 1950 – early on, at the latest during the creation of ZERO in 1957–58; Conversations with Heinz Mack, Huppertzhof, Mönchengladbach, since 2012.

302 Nannen 1977 (see note 179), unpaginated [translated].

303 See: Hartmut Böhme, 'Goethe, Ovid und Heinz Mack. Über Formen und Formwandel', in: exh. cat. Düsseldorf 2018 (see note 210), pp. 307–327.

304 See: Heinz Mack, 'Mein Verhältnis zur Natur. Ein Arbeitspapier', September 2022, typescript, Mack Archive, Huppertzhof, Mönchengladbach.

305 Conversation with Heinz Mack, Huppertzhof, Mönchengladbach, January 2022 [translated].

306 Robert Fleck, Conversations with Jacques Villeglé, Paris, 1994–2019.

307 *ZERO. Internationale Künstler-Avantgarde der 50er/60er Jahre*, curated by Heike van den Valentyn, exh. cat. Museum Kunstpalast, Düsseldorf; Musée d'art moderne, Saint-Étienne (Ostfildern: Hatje Cantz, 2006).

308 Since 1985, the collection had organised comprehensive ZERO exhibitions at important institutions in Barcelona, Madrid, Munich, Moscow (in 1989!), Bremen, Innsbruck, Warsaw, and Zagreb. In the 1980s, Hubertus Schoeller also organised ZERO exhibitions; see, for example: Gruppe ZERO, exh. cat. Galerie Schoeller, Düsseldorf 1989. And since the early 1990s, Renate Wiehager has taken up the subject as a curator, museum director and author. In addition, the dissertation by Anette Kuhn – *ZERO. Eine Avantgarde der sechziger Jahre* (Frankfurt am Main and Berlin: Propyläen, 1991) – and the book by Heiner Stachelhaus, published in 1993 (see note 72), should also be mentioned.

309 Ulrike Bleicker-Honisch (ed.), in cooperation with Anna and Gerhard Lenz, *The Zero Era. The Lenz Schönberg Collection: Living in Art* (Ostfildern: Hatje Cantz, 2009).

310 'Epoche Zero. Sotheby's versteigert Werke aus der Sammlung Lenz Schönberg', 8 February 2010, www.monopol-magazin.de/sothebys-versteigert-werke-aus-der-sammlung-lenz-schönberg [last accessed 17 January 2024] [translated].

311 Robert Fleck, Conversation with Suzanne Pagé, Shanghai, November 2010 [translated]. Pagé has been the most important museum director in France for decades; at the time, she was the founding director of the Fondation Louis Vuitton in Paris.

312 Birnbaum/Obrist 2011 (see note 29).

313 It took place in 2013–14 at the Museu Oscar Niemeyer, Curitiba, the Fundação Iberê Camargo, Porto Alegre, and the Pinacoteca do Estado de São Paulo.

314 Exh. cat. New York 2014 (see note 50).

315 Pop Art has always remained present through high prices, as have Minimalism and conceptual art, here through early self-theorisation and an equally early establishment as historically significant. Other movements such as Art Informel, Tachism, Happening, and Fluxus, the body art of the 1970s and the Neo-Expressionists in painting of the 1980s are still waiting in vain for a wider rediscovery.

316 One reason for this may have been that the major New York exhibition took place at the Guggenheim, a world-class institution: the subject was thus 'occupied' and therefore of less interest to mid-sized and other major museums in North America and Europe. Interestingly, the Guggenheim was unable to persuade any other world-class museum to co-produce or take over the ZERO exhibition. While nearly 300,000 visitors each saw the ZERO exhibitions at the Guggenheim and the Stedelijk, only 60,000 visited the Martin-Gropius-Bau. However, the Kunstpalast in Düsseldorf is planning a major exhibition to celebrate ZERO's seventieth anniversary in 2028.

317 *Heinz Mack. Licht Schatten*, ed. Helmut Friedel, exh. cat. Museum Frieder Burda, Baden-Baden (Munich: Hirmer, 2015); exh. cat. Istanbul 2016 (see note 215); exh. cat. Düsseldorf 2021 (see note 235); *Mack*, curated by Tony Cragg, exh. cat. *Skulpturenpark* Waldfrieden, Wuppertal (Berlin: Hatje Cantz, 2021); Hudson/ZKM 2024 (see note 161).

318 Also new on this occasion was the situation surrounding the production of the work – made possible by the high prices for works from the ZERO years – with Galerie Beck & Eggeling, Düsseldorf, and Atelier Mack, Mönchengladbach, with the strong support of Count Sigifredo di Canossa in Venice. The nine steles were subsequently purchased by a German entrepreneur and a replica was made, which was exhibited in Istanbul in 2015, then in Valencia and St. Moritz; see: Mack. *The Sky Over Nine Columns*, exh. cat. Fondazione Giorgio Cini, Isola San Giorgio Maggiore (Düsseldorf: Beck & Eggeling, 2014).

319 See: Ernst Kris and Otto Kurz, *Die Legende vom Künstler. Ein geschichtlicher Versuch* [1934] (Frankfurt am Main: Suhrkamp, 1995).

320 Sophia Sotke completed her doctorate on Heinz Mack's *Sahara Project* at the University of Cologne in 2020; see: Sotke 2022 (see note 167).

321 Fleck 2017 (see note 51).

322 Wyss 2021 (see note 1), oeuvre catalogue by Valeria Mack and Sophia Sotke; Ute Mack and Uwe Rüth, *Mack. Skulpturen 1986–2003* (Mönchengladbach: B. Kühlen, 2003); Honisch 1986 (see note 61).

323 Anette Fulda-Kuhn (ed.), *3/100. Druckgraphik und Multiples von Heinz Mack* (Stuttgart: Edition Cantz, 1991); Ute Mack (ed.), *Mack. Druckgraphik und Multiples 1991–2000* (Mönchengladbach: B. Kühlen, 2000); *Mack. Druckgraphik 2001–2011* (Düsseldorf: Geuer & Geuer, 2011); Ute Mack (ed.), *MACK. Druckgraphik 2011–2018* (Düsseldorf: Kunstverlag Till Breckner, 2019).

324 Including, among others, Marion Agthe, Stephanie Bailey, Tayfun Belgin, Eugen Blume, Gernot Böhme, Hartmut Böhme, Daniel Birnbaum, Édouard Derom, Helmut Friedel, Werner Hofmann, Heinz-Norbert Jocks, Joseph D. Kettner, Barbara Könches, Antonia Lehmann-Tolkmitt, Gunda Luyken, Helga Meister, Hans Ulrich Obrist, Matthieu Poirier, Francesca Pola, Norman Rosenthal, Wieland Schmied, Susanne Titz, Corinna Thierolf, Wolfgang Ullrich, Heike van den Valentyn, Jon Wood, and Beat Wyss.

325 I wrote it together with Antonia Lehmann-Tolkmitt, beginning in 2015; see: Fleck/Lehmann-Tolkmitt 2019 (see note 89).

326 See: Sophia Sotke and Matthias Meier-Grüll, 'Light, Energy, Cosmos. Heinz Mack's Sahara Project as a Vision for the Twenty-First Century', in: Hudson/ZKM 2024 (see note 163), pp. 153–165.

327 Robert Fleck, artist talk with Heinz Mack as part of the lecture series 'Das Bild' (The Picture), Düsseldorf Academy of Art, 16 December 2014; see: Ute Eggeling and Michael Beck (eds.), *Heinz Mack. Künstlergespräch* (Düsseldorf: Beck & Eggeling Kunstverlag 2016).

328 Otto Piene received the distinction posthumously; it was presented to his artistic partner and widow, Elisabeth Goldring-Piene; see the exhibition *Otto Piene* in the Akademie-Galerie/Die Neue Sammlung, Düsseldorf Academy of Art, 2017. Günther Uecker had previously been awarded honorary membership. He was a professor at the academy from 1974 to 1995.

329 However, Heinz Mack still does not have a wristwatch, a mobile phone, or a computer.

330 Mack/Rüth 2003 (see note 322), pp. 238f.

List of Illustrations and Image Credits

All works, if not otherwise stated: collection of the artist
All written documents, if not otherwise stated: Mack Archive, Huppertzhof, Mönchengladbach
All photos, if not otherwise stated: © Heinz Mack Archive

PP. 2–3 Heinz Mack in his studio at Hüttenstraße 104, Düsseldorf, 1967

PP. 6–7 The artist's hands while working on a pastel, 2011

A VISIT

P. 8 Entrance area of the Huppertzhof in Mönchengladbach, 2020, with the sculpture *Pillar and Capital*, 1986/87, marble, granite, 355 × 105 × 50 cm

P. 12 The Huppertzhof in Mönchengladbach, early 1960s

P. 13 The Huppertzhof in Mönchengladbach, today

P. 14 In 1969 Heinz Mack accepts an invitation from David Rockefeller and jokingly sends a life-size photograph of himself in a dinner jacket mounted on cardboard to him in New York. It is folded so that it can sit at the table with the other guests and listen to the conversations; photo: Alfred Stattler / *Time Magazine*

P. 17 Heinz Mack's large tripartite studio with sculpture park in Mönchengladbach, 1990s

P. 21 View of the artist's studio at the finca Can Micali, Ibiza, 2009

P. 22 Heinz Mack in his glazed studio at the Huppertzhof, Mönchengladbach, 2016; photo: Boris Kralj

P. 23 View into the artist's glazed studio at the Huppertzhof, Mönchengladbach, 2015

PARIS, 1950

P. 24 *Notre-Dame de Paris*, 1950, India ink with reed pen on paper, each 31.5 × 23.5 cm

P. 27 Heinz Mack's student card, State Academy of Art, Düsseldorf, 1950

P. 27 The Düsseldorf Academy of Art in ruins, 1946; photo: Oskar Söhn / Düsseldorf Academy of Art Archive

P. 29 Heinz Mack at Café de Flore, Boulevard Saint-Germain, Paris, 1950

P. 30 The Opéra Garnier, Paris, 1950s; photo: Mary Evans / Classic Stock / C. P. May

P. 33 Henri Matisse, *Nature morte aux Oranges (Still Life with Oranges)*, 1912, oil on canvas, 95 × 84.8 × 2 cm, Musée Picasso, Paris, inv. no. MP2017–21; photo: bpk / RMN – Grand Palais / René-Gabriel Ojéda

P. 34 Poster for Heinz Mack's exhibition at the Musée d'art moderne de la Ville de Paris, 1973

P. 35 Installation view, Musée d'art moderne de la Ville de Paris, 1973; photo: Titus E. Czerski

EARLY PAINTINGS

P. 38 Heinz Mack in his studio at Herzogstraße 44, Düsseldorf, c. 1952

P. 41 *Untitled*, 1950, egg tempera on hardboard, 76 × 104 × 0.5 cm, Mack Foundation

P. 42 Mack at his father's grave near Bordeaux, 1948

P. 44 *Untitled (Female Nude)*, 1954, graphite on paper, dimensions unknown

P. 45 *Self-Portrait*, 1952, graphite on paper, 53 × 35.5 cm

P. 48 *Untitled*, 1953, egg tempera on canvas, 78 × 100 cm, Mack Foundation

P. 49 Handwriting experiments on the way to a signature, c. 1950

P. 53 Installation view *Heinz Mack. Unbekannte Skulpturen,* 1954–1984, Galerie Denise René – Hans Mayer, Düsseldorf, 1984

P. 54 *Monument to the Unknown Political Prisoner (Model),* competition entry, 1st version, 1953, cast iron, cement base, 150 × 25 × 47 cm, Mack Foundation

P. 54 *Monument to the Unknown Political Prisoner (Model),* competition entry, 2nd version, 1953, cast iron, cement base, 150 × 23 × 47 cm, Mack Foundation

P. 56 *Obelisk*, 1952, sundial stele with drinking fountain made of concrete and ceramic shards, height 900 cm, forecourt of the Saalhausen primary school, North Rhine-Westphalia, architect: Paul Schneider-Esleben

P. 57 View of the industrial exhibition *Alle sollen besser leben*, with display elements by Heinz Mack and Otto Piene, Ehrenhof, Düsseldorf, 1953; Otto Piene Archive, ZERO foundation, Düsseldorf

ZERO AND THE BEGINNING OF POSTMODERNISM

P. 60 *The Sky over Samarkand* (detail), 1963, mixed media on canvas, 220 × 180 cm, Private Collection; Premio Marzotto Selezione, 1964

P. 63 *Dynamic Structure White on Yellow*, 1963, synthetic resin on nettle cloth, 130 × 150 cm

P. 66 Invitations to seven of the eight *Evening Exhibitions*, held in the Düsseldorf studios of Heinz Mack and Otto Piene from April 1957 to October 1958

P. 67 Heinz Mack with a *Dynamic Structure* in his studio at Gladbacher Straße 69, Düsseldorf, c. 1958; photo: Charles Wilp

P. 70 *Cardiogram of My Heart, No. 2*, 1962, synthetic resin on nettle cloth, 180 × 140 cm

P. 71 Merchandise Mart, Chicago, 1930s, the world's largest building at the time of its opening; architects: Graham, Anderson, Probst, and White; photo: Mary Evans / Greenville Postcard Collection

P. 74 *Light Relief*, 1959/60, aluminium on hardboard, 48 × 48 cm, Private Collection

P. 74 *Classical Micro-Relief*, 1959, aluminium on hardboard, c. 30 × 40 cm, lost

P. 75 *Untitled*, 1960, graphite on Ingres paper, 70 × 50 cm

P. 75 *Untitled*, 1961, graphite on laid paper, 79 × 54 cm; Mack Foundation

P. 76 Poster for the exhibition of works by Heinz Mack and Otto Piene, Galerie St. Stephan, Vienna, 1961, designed by Heinz Mack

P. 76 Otto Piene and Yves Klein, 1958; photo: Heinz Mack

P. 78 View of the installation *2. Hommage à Georges de La Tour* through the window of Galerie Schmela, Düsseldorf, 1965; photo: Jörg Boström

P. 79 *2. Hommage à Georges de La Tour*, 1965, environment with 200 candles on mirror film, Galerie Schmela, Düsseldorf; photo: Walter Vogel

P. 82 View of Heinz Mack's studio at Hüttenstraße 104, Düsseldorf, 1965, then the studio building shared by Otto Piene, Günther Uecker and Heinz Mack, today seat of the ZERO foundation

P. 83 Heinz Mack, Günther Uecker, and Alfred Schmela with light steles and light reliefs by Mack in the Grugahalle, Essen, on the occasion of the exhibition of the Deutscher Künstlerbund, 1966

P. 85 Portrait of the artist, c. 1966

THE ZERO GENERATION

P. 86 Heinz Mack in front of Galerie Schmela, Düsseldorf, 1961

P. 89 *Sahara-Reliefs* (detail), 1960–61, concrete, height 1,300 cm, Mathildenhofschule (today: Astrid-Lindgren-Schule), Leverkusen, destroyed; from: *ZERO 3*, 1961, unpaginated; photo: H. Erdmann

P. 90 Poster for *ZERO – EDITION · DEMONSTRATION · EXPOSITION*, Düsseldorf, 1961, ZERO foundation, Düsseldorf, shelf no. mkp.ZERO.1.VII.86

P. 93 View into Galerie Schmela during *ZERO – EDITION · DEMONSTRATION · EXPOSITION*, Düsseldorf, 1961; photo: Manfred Tischer, © Estate of Manfred Tischer

P. 93 Helium-filled balloon above Galerie Schmela during *ZERO – EDITION · DEMONSTRATION · EXPOSITION*, Düsseldorf, 1961; photo: Paul Brandenburg

P. 96 20-metre-long relief chain by Heinz Mack at the *ZERO Festival* on the Rhine meadows, Düsseldorf, 1962; photos: Reiner Ruthenbeck

P. 97 *Plantage* of aluminium flags by Heinz Mack at the ZERO Festival on the Rhine meadows, Düsseldorf, 1962; photo: Reiner Ruthenbeck

P. 98 Heinz Mack, Otto Piene and Günther Uecker, *Light Room (Hommage à Fontana)* at *documenta III*, Kassel, 1964; photo: Gitta von Vitany; today Kunstpalast, Düsseldorf, inv. no. mkp.0.1992.4-10

P. 98 Original design by Heinz Mack for a poster for the exhibition *Group ZERO* at the Washington Gallery of Modern Art, Washington, D.C., 1965

P. 99 'The Desert Lives!', poem by Heinz Mack as an homage to Lucio Fontana, 1961

PP. 102–103 Heinz Mack in front of his work *Small Forest* (1966, aluminium, wood, acrylic glass, 204 × 304 × 7 cm, today Kunstpalast, Düsseldorf, donation from Fritz Bagel, inv. no. mkp.0.2019.1) in the exhibition *MACK*, (op)Art Gallery, Esslingen, March 1967; photo: Helmut M. Schmitt-Siegel

NEW YORK

P. 104 Heinz Mack and Günther Uecker at the airport in New York, 1964, ZERO foundation, Düsseldorf, Estate of Heinz Mack ZERO.1.V.173; photo: Lufthansa

PP. 108 f. Handwritten note by Heinz Mack on Hotel Chelsea stationery, New York, November 1964

P. 112 Installation view *Group ZERO*, Howard Wise Gallery, New York, 1964

P. 114 John Canaday, 'The Sculptor Nowadays Is the Favorite Son', review of the ZERO exhibition in *The New York Times*, 22 November 1964

P. 115 Installation view *Group ZERO*, Howard Wise Gallery, New York, 1964

P. 119 Heinz Mack's studio at 410 East 10th Street in the East Village, Lower Manhattan, 1964

P. 122 Marisol and Mack in New York, c. 1966

P. 122 Marisol, *Untitled (Self-Portrait)*, c. 1965, plaster relief behind plastic foil, embedded in wooden box (not illustrated), 35 × 30 × 4 cm

P. 123 Marisol, *Portrait Heinz Mack*, c. 1965, collage under corrugated glass, 35.5 × 28 × 5.5 cm

P. 126 Heinz Mack in his apartment at Kaiser-Friedrich-Ring 16, Düsseldorf, 1966, with works by Yves Klein, Roy Lichtenstein, Robert Rauschenberg, George Rickey, Marisol, and Uli Pohl

P. 127 *Forest of Light* in the exhibition *Lights of Silver by Heinz Mack*, Howard Wise Gallery, New York, 1966

KINETIC

P. 130 *Electric Field (Light-Time-Space)*, 1969/70, aluminium, wood, festoon lamps, Pyra-Plexiglas, 143 × 143 × 22.5 cm, Private Collection

P. 133 *Sun of the Sea No. 5*, 1967, aluminium, Plexiglas, wood, motor, 137 × 137 × 17 cm, mumok – Museum moderner Kunst Stiftung Ludwig Wien, Vienna, inv. no. B 148/0; photo: © mumok – Museum moderner Kunst Stiftung Ludwig Wien, Vienna

PP. 134 f. *Light Carousel*, 1962, aluminium, Plexiglas, mirror, motor, c. 400 × 400 × 400 cm, exhibited at the Palais des Beaux-Arts, Brussels in 1962 and at the Stedelijk Museum in Amsterdam in 1965, subsequently destroyed by incorrect disassembly and storage; photos: Ad Petersen

P. 137 Heinz Mack's first rotor: *Paper Flower Rotor*, 1958, paper, corrugated glass, motorised, c. 50 × 50 × 20 cm, Private Collection

P. 140 *Changing Light*, 2004, aluminium, stainless steel, glass, wood, motor, 53.5 × 53.5 × 30 cm, Musées de Picardie, Amiens

P. 141 *Light Line*, 1961, chrome-plated brass, stainless steel, motor, height 200 cm, ø 2.5 cm; base: height 10.5 cm, ø 30 cm, Private Collection, Northern Germany

P. 142 *Light – Movement – Space*, light environment, *Great Industrial Exhibtion*, Berlin (West), 1970

P. 143 *Light Fan*, 2009, wood, motor, Fresnel lens, electrical accessories, 53 × 40 × 40 cm, Mack Foundation

PP. 146–147 Heinz Mack in his studio at Hüttenstraße 104, Düsseldorf, 1966; photo: Lieselotte Strehlow

TIME SLICE, 1969

P. 148 Heinz Mack during the shooting of the film *Tele-Mack* in the Grand Erg Oriental, east of the Kebili oasis, Tunisia, 1968; photo: Edwin Braun

P. 156 f. Stills from the film *Tele-Mack*, Tunisia, 1968/69; directors: Hans Emmerling and Heinz Mack, cinematographer: Edwin Braun, digital colour video transferred from 16mm film, sound, 45:40 min., Institut für moderne Kunst, Nuremberg; produced by Telefilm Saar GmbH for Saarländischer Rundfunk and WDR/Westdeutsches Fernsehen; first broadcast on WDR on 2 May 1969

NEW SPACES

P. 158 Heinz Mack with a silver flag in a quarry, West Germany, c. 1970/71; photo: Lothar Wolleh, *Portrait Heinz Mack*, © Lothar Wolleh Estate, Berlin. The idea for the setting came from Lothar Wolleh; the photo was first published in his book *Art Scene Düsseldorf* (Stuttgart: Belser, 1971).

P. 162 f. *Water Cloud*, 1972, water, pump units, 112 underwater floodlights, 24 floodlights, height 8–max. 36 m, surface area 3,000 × 1,400 cm, Olympic Park, Munich; photos: Lothar Wolleh

P. 166 Design of the entrance spiral to the German Pavilion at the Japan World Exposition in Osaka, 1970, 500 double mirrors, each 100 × 100 cm

PP. 168–169 Cubes and light steles by Heinz Mack in the German Pavilion at the 35th Venice Biennale, 1970

P. 170 Mirror cabinet in the exhibition *mack. Objekte – Aktionen – Projekte*, Städtische Kunsthalle Düsseldorf, 1972

P. 171 Installation view *mack. Objekte – Aktionen – Projekte*, Academy of Arts, Berlin (West), 1972

PP. 172–173 *The Seasons of the Desert*, (1974/76, wood, aluminium, steel, canvas, sand, five panels, each 285 × 337 × 6 cm), in the exhibition *Kunstübermittlungsformen. Vom Tafelbild bis zum Happening – Die Medien der bildenden Kunst*, Neue Nationalgalerie, Berlin (West), 1977, Mack Foundation

P. 176 *Stele for the Sky*, 1970, in front of the Neue National galerie, Berlin (West), Plexiglas, aluminium, stainless steel, electrical accessories, two light programme phases, height 1,200 cm, destroyed

P. 177 *The Sign of Peace*, 1974–1979, photomontage for the project of a 70-metre-high light stele in the park of the UN headquarters in New York (not realised)

P. 179 *Upside Down*, Grand Erg Occidental, Algeria, 1976, concave mirror, c. 80 × 80 cm; photo: Thomas Höpker

PP. 180 f. Overall design of Jürgen-Ponto-Platz, Frankfurt am Main, 1976–1981, images from the early 1980s; photos: Robert Häuser

THE TWELVE TOPOI OF HEINZ MACK

P. 182 *Moon Project with Light Wing and Light Grid*, 1963–1973, photocollage, planned dimensions c. 265 × 150 × 70 cm (not realised)

P. 185 *The Rhythm of Africa*, 1968–1970, Plexiglas, stainless steel, aluminium, 460 × 152 × 132 cm, Mack Foundation

P. 186 *Notation for Piano*, 1955, wax crayon, charcoal, graphite on laid paper, 68 × 54.5 cm

P. 187 View into the residential building at the Huppertzhof, Mönchengladbach, c. 1970, with light steles and Heinz Mack at the piano

P. 192 *The Unexpected Encounter (Project for the City of New York)*, 1963–1973, photocollage, 160 × 150 cm

P. 193 Handwritten note by Heinz Mack, undated

P. 198 *The Pink Pyramic (Chromatic Constellation)*, 2006, acrylic on canvas, 288 × 308.5 cm, Private Collection, Munich

P. 199 Installation view *Mack. Transit zwischen Okzident und Orient*, Museum für Islamische Kunst in the Pergamonmuseum, Berlin, 2006; photo: Thomas Bruns

P. 204 *The Hand*, 1954, wood, pigments, 90 × 28 × 25 cm, Mack Foundation

P. 205 View of the artist's living quarters at the Huppertzhof, Mönchengladbach, 1970s, with two African sculptures and a painting by Piero Dorazio (destroyed in a fire in the house in 1984)

P. 210 *Memorial to Anne Frank*, 1980–1986, granite, 257 × 115 × 80 cm, Rabbiner-Neumark-Weg, Duisburg

HEINZ MACK AND PHOTOGRAPHY

P. 212 *Light Cone*, from the *Silver Light* suite, 1958/73, photogram, 40 × 30 cm, Mack Foundation

P. 216 *Self-Portrait*, 1992, photograph

P. 216 *Project for a Floating Island in the Sea*, 1968, Plexiglas model, ø 50 cm

P. 218 *Marking of the Earth*, Hubbelrath near Düsseldorf, 1960, lime on a field, triangle 700 × 700 × 700 cm

P. 219 *Land Art Project*, Hubbelrath near Düsseldorf, 1960, corrugated iron on a field

P. 220 Light experiments with glass prisms, 2020, 28 × 32.5 × 16 cm each

P. 221 *Untitled*, 2010, Fresnel lenses, 64 × 48 × 48 cm, Private Collection, Germany

P. 222 *Photo Experiment*, undated, photogram, 48 × 60 cm

P. 222 *Untitled*, 2016, polarisation of LED light chains, photo experiment

P. 223 *Untitled*, 2023, photo experiment with fluorescent colour on cardboard, 45 × 45 cm

P. 225 *Radiance (Light Experiment)*, 2004/06, C-print/Diasec (4 mm), 180 × 135 cm

P. 226 *Photo Experiment with the Artist's Hand*, c. 1961, photograph taken with a self-timer, 18.5 × 19.5 cm

WHO STILL MAKES STONE SCULPTURES ANYMORE?

P. 228 *Monolith Ensemble*, 1979, Flossenbürg and Dolomite granite, plaster, dimensions of the two sculptures in the foreground: 438 × 76 × 54 and 435 × 78 × 66 cm, Huppertzhof, Mönchengladbach

P. 231 *Rhythm and Growth*, 1998, bronze, green patina, 81 × 28 × 28 cm, cast 4/6, Cragg Foundation / Waldfrieden Sculpture Park, Wuppertal

P. 232 The artist at work on the sculpture *Untitled*, 2010, marble (from Marmara, Turkey), 126 × 85 × 60 cm

P. 232 Carrara quarry, early 2000s

P. 233 *Steps of Shadow and Light*, 1985, marble (from Dionysos), basalt lava (base), 213 × 158 × 60 cm, Private Collection, North Rhine-Westphalia

P. 236 *Four Stone Steles*, 1995, black granite (from Norway), each c. 340 × 60 × 90 cm, in the exhibition *Heinz Mack. Skulpturen* in the Waldfrieden Sculpture Park, Wuppertal, 2021; photo: Michael Richter, © Cragg Foundation

P. 236 Ensemble of basalt and granite sculptures in the exhibition *Heinz Mack. Skulpturen* in the Waldfrieden Sculpture Park, Wuppertal, 2021; photo: Michael Richter, © Cragg Foundation

P. 238 The artist on a swinging ladder in the stone quarries of Carrara, 1983

P. 239 *The Love of Stones*, 1983/84, basalt, marble (from Portugal), stainless steel, silver mosaic (from Venice), height 520 cm, ø 1,250 cm, formerly IBM, Stuttgart, now in the collection of the State of Baden-Württemberg; photo: Albert Schäfer

PP. 240–241 View of the artist's sculpture garden in Mönchengladbach, 2021

P. 243 *Spatial Grid*, 1977/78, stainless steel, max. 120 × 150 cm, mirror glass and stainless-steel base: 82 × 86 × 86 cm, based on a design from 1964: *Model for a Ready-Made in The Museum of Modern Art, New York*

THE IMAGINARY MUSEUM

P. 244 Envelope from the office of the French Minister of Industry to Heinz Mack, initially addressed to the flat of the (deceased) Yves Klein in Paris, then to Günther Uecker in Düsseldorf, 7 October 1965, probably for a letter from Pierre Restany, speechwriter for several ministers, in connection with the awarding of the prize to Heinz Mack by André Malraux at the 4th Paris Biennale.

P. 248 Henri Matisse, *Le Bonheur de vivre (The Joy of Life)*, 1905/06, oil on cavnas, 176.5 × 240.7 cm, The Barnes Foundation, Philadelphia; photo: © Succession H. Matisse / Bridgeman Images

P. 249 *Untitled (Chromatic Constellation)*, 2021, acrylic on canvas, 152.5 × 217 cm

P. 252 Paul Gauguin, *Ta matete (Le Marché)*, 1892, oil on jute, 73.2 × 91.5 cm, Kunstmuseum Basel, gift from Dr. h. c. Robert von Hirsch 1941; photo: © Kunstmuseum Basel / Martin P. Bühler

P. 253 *After Gauguin – Ta matete (Chromatic Constellation)*, 2022, acrylic on canvas, 147.5 × 217.5 cm

P. 255 *Where Do We Come From? Where Are We? Where Are We Going?*, 1960, watercolour on handmade paper, 20 × 30 cm

PP. 258 f. Extract from *Heinz Mack's Compendium*, 2023–24; illustrated in: Alistair Hudson (ed.), *Mack reflected. Expanding the ZERO Code*, exh. cat. ZKM | Center for Art and Media Karlsruhe (Munich: Hirmer, 2024), p. 281

A Pietro Cavallini, *Jesus Christ with Angels from the Last Judgement* (detail), c. 1289/93, Santa Cecilia in Trastevere, Rome
B Heinz Mack, *Night and Light Sculpture in the Desert*, c. 1970
C Cuckoo; photo: Mauritius
D Close-up of the wing of a monarch butterfly; photo: Tiger Stocks / Shutterstock
E *Seraphim fresco*, 13th century, Sant Climent de Taüll, Catalonia
F Windmill on Formentera, Balearic Islands
G Heinz Mack, *Untitled (Photo Experiment)*, 2016
H Heinz Mack, *Drawing of a Wing*, c. 1970
I Heinz Mack, *Light Wings in the Sky*, c. 1970
J Large futuristic passenger aeroplane with combined wing shapes; photo: Michal Krakowiak / Getty Images
K Jacques Rougerie, *Model of the city of Mériens*, 2015; © Jacques Rougerie
L Naum Gabo, *Linear Construction No. 2*, 1970/71, Tate Gallery, London, inv.-no. T01105
M Kinetic energy weapon of the US Army for the Homing Overlay Experiment, 1980s
N Heinz Mack, *Photo Experiment with Acrylic Glass Object*, undated

PP. 260 f. Second part of the *Compendium*, 2025

O *Kuroiso City*, 1989; photo: Shibata
P Plankton, 1950; photo: C. Strüwe
Q Cushion starfish
R Volkswagen sheet metal, 1953
S 'Paper boat'
T Porcelain snail
U *Cycas revoluta*
V Shadow tornado
W Pullman railcar
X Pearl boat

PICTURES AFTER THE LAST PICTURE

P. 262 The last *Dynamic Structure* in the style of the ZERO period: *Untitled*, 1968, synthetic resin on nettle cloth, 76 × 60 cm, E.ON Art Collection, Düsseldorf

P. 265 *Ibiza Colours (Chromatic Constellation)*, 2015, acrylic on canvas, 130 × 160 cm, Private Collection, North Rhine-Westphalia

P. 269 View of the artist's Spanish studio, Can Micali, Ibiza, 2015

P. 270 Installation view *Heinz Mack. Werke im Licht*, Museum Ritter, Waldenbuch, 2021; photo: Franz-Josef Wamhof | © VG Bild-Kunst, Bonn 2025

P. 273 Installation view *Heinz Mack. Light – Space – Colour*, Bundeskunsthalle, Bonn, 2011; photo: David Ertl

P. 274 *Untitled (Chromatic Constellation)*, 2016, acrylic on canvas, 130 × 160 cm

PP. 276 – 277 *Large Chromatic (Chromatic Constellation)*, 2023, acrylic on canvas, 211 × 517 cm

P. 279 *Garden for Starflowers (Chromatic Constellation)*, 2000, acrylic on canvas, 230 × 266 cm, in the exhibition *Heinz Mack. Elective Affinities* at the Tehran Museum of Contemporary Art, 2001

PP. 280 – 281 *Summer Party (Chromatic Constellation)*, 2024, acrylic on canvas, 210 × 310 cm

PP. 284 – 285 Heinz Mack with pastels in his glazed studio at the Huppertzhof, Mönchengladbach, 2022

NATURE

P. 286 *Wing Sculpture*, 1980, aluminium, acrylic glass, granite base, 156 × 106 × 106 cm, formerly IBM, Stuttgart, current whereabouts unknown

P. 289 *Stacked Firewood*, nature photograph from Lollar, mid-1940s, 28.2 × 41.5 cm

P. 289 *Bull's-eye Wood*, nature photo from Lollar, mid-1940s, 27 × 40 cm

P. 290 *Untitled*, 2013, acrylic, pastel chalk on handmade paper, 38 × 39.5 cm, Private Collection, France

P. 292 *Mirror Experiments (Project in the Artist's Garden)*, 1997, stainless steel, polished, c. 100 × 80 cm

P. 293 *The Shadow of Nothing – Glass Cube in the Snow*, 1980, acrylic glass, 90 × 90 × 90 cm

P. 294 *Water Lily in the Arctic*, Disko Bay, Greenland, 1976, movably installed wooden elements that follow the wave motion of the water, ø c. 600 cm; photo: Thomas Höpker

P. 295 *Light Prisms in the Arctic (Model for a Floating Research Station)*, Disko Bay, Greenland, 1976, nylon, fibreglass, stainless steel, height c. 200 cm; photo: Thomas Höpker

PP. 296 – 297 *Fire in the Desert – Light Experiment*, Sahara, 1974, photograph

P. 299 *Large Space Mirror (In Honour of Alexander von Humboldt)*, 1999, digital photomontage, project with electropolished stainless steel near the Cordillera Oriental, Mérida, Venezuela, 1,000 × 1,700 cm (not realised)

PP. 302 f. *Fire Ship*, Düsseldorf media harbour, 2010, pyrotechnics, wooden construction, approx. 1,000 × 1,500 × 700 cm

TAKING STOCK, 2025

P. 304 Robert Fleck and Heinz Mack on the rooftop of the Bundeskunsthalle, Bonn, 2011

P. 308 Installation view *ZERO. Countdown to Tomorrow*, Solomon R. Guggenheim Museum, New York, 2014; photo: David Heald, © Solomon R. Guggenheim Foundation

PP. 310 – 311 *The Sky Over Nine Columns*, 2012/14, tesserae (mosaic stones, each 2 × 2 cm, with 24 carat gold leaf, yellow gold), nine steles, each 7,500 × 1,250 × 1,250 cm, first realised in 2014 by Beck & Eggeling International Fine Art and Sigifredo di Canossa in Venice; photo: Bruno Biancardi

P. 312 Maraya Concert Hall, Al-Ula, Saudi Arabia, 2019; photo: Florian Boje, architecture: Giò Forma Architects, Milan

P. 313 *Topology of Space*, Grand Erg Occidental, Algeria, 1976, mirror cube made of mercury-vapourised plastic, 160 × 160 × 160 cm; photo: Thomas Höpker

PP. 316 – 317 *Untitled (Chromatic Constellation)*, 2024, acrylic on canvas, 210 × 315 cm

PP. 320 – 321 The artist in his glazed studio, Huppertzhof, Mönchengladbach, February 2025

PP. 342 – 343 Light steles by Heinz Mack in the exhibition *Seeing Through Light. Selections from the Solomon R. Guggenheim Museum*, Guggenheim Collection Abu Dhabi, 2014; photo: Petra und Erik Hesmerg Photography

Robert Fleck, born in Vienna in 1957, has been living in France since 1980. After studying History, Geography, Philosophy, and Art History in Vienna, Innsbruck, and Paris, he was, among other things, Director of the Deichtorhallen in Hamburg from 2004 to 2008, Director of the Bundeskunsthalle in Bonn from 2009 to 2012 and Professor of Art and the Public at the Düsseldorf Academy of Art from 2012 to 2025, where he also served as prorector from 2013 to 2023. He has published extensively on Heinz Mack, including the monograph *Heinz Mack. A Twenty-First Century Artist* (2019), co-authored with Antonia Lehmann-Tolkmitt.

Sophia Sotke, born in Düsseldorf in 1987, has been a research assistant in the studio of Prof. Heinz Mack since 2013. She completed her master's degree in History and Art History at the Heinrich Heine University Düsseldorf in 2014. In 2020, she completed her PhD on Heinz Mack's *Sahara Project* in the international context of ZERO and Land Art under Prof. Dr. Günter Herzog at the University of Cologne (published in 2022). In her role at the artist's studio, she co-curates exhibitions, supervises publications and catalogues raisonnés, and gives lectures on Heinz Mack and the ZERO movement at international museums and institutions.

We would like to thank ***Antonia Lehmann-Tolkmitt***, art consultant and chairwoman of the ZERO foundation, Düsseldorf, and ***Florentine Bücker***, artist and student at the Art Academy Düsseldorf, who have supported this publication from the very beginning and who have provided much assistance. In particular, we would like to thank them for their collaboration on the conception of this book and for transcribing the many recorded conversations with the artist.

Founded in 2024, the non-profit Mack Foundation owns numerous works from all of the artist's creative periods. Its mission is to preserve Heinz Mack's multifaceted artistic legacy and to promote knowledge and awareness of his work.

The Mack Foundation also houses the extensive archive of the Huppertzhof in Mönchengladbach, where Mack has lived and worked since the 1960s. It is therefore an important point of contact for cultural institutions, collectors, and academics interested in the art historical significance of the artist's work. In 2008, Mack co-founded the ZERO foundation in Düsseldorf, which is dedicated to all artists of the international ZERO movement. The new foundation will now focus specifically on the work of Mack himself.

In addition, the Mack Foundation aims to support scholarly publications and academic research with a special funding programme for doctoral students.

mackfoundation.com

Colophon

MACK – FACE TO FACE
An Artist's Life

Author
Robert Fleck
in collaboration with Sophia Sotke

Assistance
Antonia Lehmann-Tolkmitt
Florentine Bücker

Editing
Sophia Sotke

Picture Editing
Daria Khvoinytska

Project Management, Hirmer Publishers
Jutta Allekotte

Translation
Gérard A. Goodrow

Copy-editing
Olivia Parkes

Graphic Design and Typesetting
Studio Lanhenke
Dominik Lanhenke

Production
Hannes Halder

Prepress and Repro
Reproline Genceller, Munich

Paper
Salzer Touch White 120 g/m2

Typeface
TT Commons, Sabon

Printing and Binding
Printer Trento S. r. l., Trento

Printed in Italy

Bibliographic information published by the Deutsche Nationalbibliothek:

The Deutsche Nationalbibliothek lists this publication in the Deutsche Nationalbibliografie; detailed bibliographic data is available online at https://www.dnb.de.

ISBN 978-3-7774-4543-4 (English edition)
ISBN 978-3-7774-4542-7 (German edition)

Hirmer Publishers
(Hirmer Verlag GmbH)
Managing Director: Kerstin Ludolph
Bayerstraße 57–59
80335 Munich
Germany

www.hirmerpublishers.com
www.hirmerpublishers.co.uk

Front cover: Heinz Mack with a portrait drawing in his studio at the Düsseldorf Academy of Art, c. 1950; photo: Heinz Mack Archive

Despite careful research, it was not always possible to identify the right holders. Justified claims will, of course, be settled within the framework of the usual agreements.

With the kind support of the Mack Foundation, Mönchengladbach.

MACK FOUNDATION

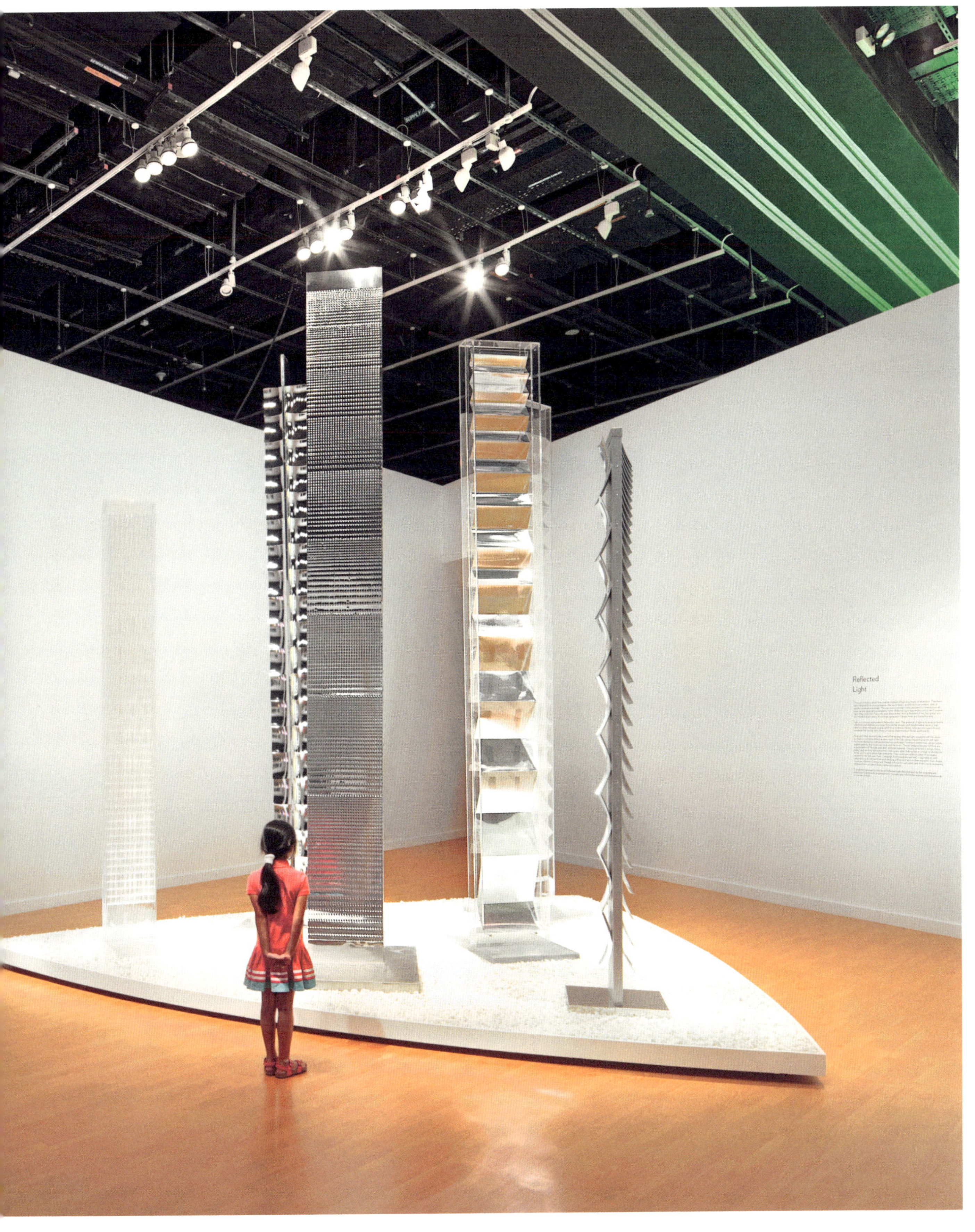
Reflected
Light